LabVIEW Graphical Programming

Practical Applications in Instrumentation and Control

Gary W. Johnson

Second Edition

McGraw-Hill

New York   San Francisco   Washington, D.C.   Auckland   Bogotá
Caracas   Lisbon   London   Madrid   Mexico City   Milan
Montreal   New Delhi   San Juan   Singapore
Sydney   Tokyo   Toronto

Library of Congress Cataloging-in-Publication Data

Johnson Gary W., date.
    LabVIEW graphical programming : practical applications in
instrumentation and control / Gary W. Johnson.—2nd ed.
       p.   cm.
    Includes bibliographical references and index.
    ISBN 0-07-032915-X
    1. LabVIEW. 2. Scientific apparatus and instruments—Computer
simulation. 3. Computer graphics. I. Title.
Q185.J46 1997
006—dc21   1001337987

                                                97-17180
                                                  CIP

McGraw-Hill

A Division of The McGraw·Hill Companies

1 2 3 4 5 6 7 8 9 0 DOC/DOC 9 0 2 1 0 9 8 7

P/N 032957-5

Part of ISBN 0-07-032915-X

*The sponsoring editor for this book was Steve Chapman and the
production supervisor was Claire Stanley. It was set in Century
Schoolbook by North Market Street Graphics.*

Printed and bound by R. R. Donnelley & Sons Company.

McGraw-Hill books are available at special quantity discounts to use as
premiums and sales promotions, or for use in corporate training programs. For more information, please write to Director of Special Sales,
McGraw-Hill, 11 West 19th Street, New York, NY 10011. Or contact your
local bookstore.

 This book is printed on recycled, acid-free paper containing a minimum
of 50% recycled, de-inked fiber.

To my parents, Bill and Shirley

Contents

Foreword

I have known Gary since the dawn of the LabVIEW era. He was one of the early pioneer users of LabVIEW 1 (the Jurassic version), all of whom deserve Purple Hearts for their efforts. For years, Gary has participated in the evolution of LabVIEW by providing valuable feedback on his experiences using it in numerous applications and by offering many thoughtful suggestions and the occasional stinging critique. He has built and rebuilt uncountable VIs, always striving for the most lucid diagram. I can't think of anyone more qualified to write a LabVIEW book.

It is a little more than 10 years since the introduction of LabVIEW 1 triggered the virtual instrumentation revolution and the momentum continues to build. The growth is fueled by the tremendous advances in personal computers and consumer electronics. The typical computer used in instrumentation today is about 30 times better than the machines of the LabVIEW 1 days—in CPU clock rate, RAM size, bus speed, and disk size and speed—yet the cost is the same. This trend will continue beyond 2010 making it quite clear that PC-based instrumentation will dominate the industry.

But virtual instrumentation isn't just about the compelling price/performance advantages of using personal computers; it is a true paradigm shift. The functionality of an instrument is no longer defined by the vendor but by the user. The user can select how the measurement is made, what analysis is to be done, and how the data should be presented, stored in a database, or transmitted over the network to another application. If a new data analysis or presentation algorithm is developed, you can incorporate it into your virtual instrument simply by loading it from a disk or over the network. It should come as no surprise that virtual instrumentation is still the only place you can find powerful new algorithms like JTFA. The development time for traditional instrumentation is far too long, and the cost is too high.

The power and flexibility of virtual instrumentation comes at a price, however. And that's basically the price of this book—buy it and learn it and you'll quickly be able to exploit that power and flexibility. As with any tool, LabVIEW requires some effort to master, but the payoff in increased productivity is huge. The best way to learn how to use Lab-VIEW to automate measurements would be to work with Gary for a month. The second best way is to study what he presents here.

This book isn't simply a "how-to" book, it explains the "why" also, so you learn principles that can be used in all applications. You learn about diagramming in LabVIEW, about sensors, signal conditioning, data acquisition, and about analysis—all the elements of virtual instrumentation and how they integrate to provide unprecedented power and flexibility in measurement systems.

The examples Gary has chosen illustrate solutions to real-world measurement problems, not just toy problems which are trivial to solve with any tool. The examples cover a variety of application areas and I encourage you to study them all because each one illustrates a principle you can use regardless of the field you're in.

An important addition to this edition of the book is the description of the LabVIEW toolkits and some of the third-party add-on packages. These toolkits and add-on packages provide a broad range of higher-level building blocks that make it even easier to assemble measurement applications. Check here before you embark on building something from scratch.

Authors of books about software products typically have a difficult time keeping up with the evolution of the products. With LabVIEW it's a bit easier. While LabVIEW has grown and evolved a great deal over the last 10 years and will continue to do so, the changes are basically implementation improvements delivering on the original vision of LabVIEW 1. The G language remains the same. The G programming principles you learn will continue to apply in future versions of Lab-VIEW. G is inherently parallel and the parallelism has been simulated diligently since the very first version. When multithreading, preemptive scheduling, and real-time priorities are introduced in future versions of LabVIEW, the performance will increase but the G language will still be the same. All the principles you learn here will still apply. You will be able to build virtual instrumentation applications incorporating SMP (symmetrical multiprocessing) machines and embedded systems, and exploit networked resources all without having to learn anything beyond the fundamental concepts of G.

Computers will continue to advance rapidly; data acquisition hardware will continue to increase sample rates, resolution, and bandwidth; LabVIEW will continue to grow and evolve; more add-on packages will be developed; but the good programming techniques, good measurement practices, and good problem-solving methods that Gary describes here will not go out of style. In this sense, his book is timeless. Reading it is one of the highest-leverage investments you can make.

Gary's relaxed writing style makes reading a pleasure—you can't help learn even if you're not really trying. I hope you will enjoy this as much as I did.

Jeff Kodosky
March 1997

Preface

Fourteen years have passed since the inception of LabVIEW. In that time it has become an enabling technology for the world of instrumentation, data acquisition, control, and data analysis. A product of National Instruments Corporation (Austin, Texas), it is built upon a purely graphical, general-purpose programming language, *G*, with extensive libraries of functions, an integral compiler and debugger, and an application builder for stand-alone applications. LabVIEW runs on Apple Macintosh computers, IBM PC compatibles with Microsoft Windows NT/95/3.1, Sun SPARCstations, HP PA-RISC workstations, and Concurrent PowerMAX workstations. Programs are portable among the various platforms. The concept of *virtual instruments* (VIs), pioneered by LabVIEW, permits you to transform a real instrument (such as a voltmeter) into another, software-based instrument (such as a chart recorder), thus increasing the versatility of available hardware. Control panels mimic real panels, right down to the switches and lights. And all programming is done via a block diagram, consisting of icons and wires, that is directly compiled to executable code; there is no underlying procedural language or menu-driven system.

As an instrumentation engineer, I find LabVIEW indispensable—a flexible, timesaving package without all the frustrating aspects of ordinary programming languages. The one thing LabVIEW had been missing all these years was a useful application-oriented book. The manuals are fine, once you know what you want to accomplish. And the classes offered by National Instruments are highly recommended if you are just starting out. But how do you get past that first, blank window? What are the methods for designing an efficient LabVIEW application? And what about interface hardware and real-world signal-conditioning problems? In this book, I describe practical problem-solving techniques that aren't in the manual, nor in the introductory classes—methods you learn only by experience.

Keeping up with the advancement of a modern software application is quite a challenge—especially in a printed volume such as this one.

This second edition is founded on LabVIEW 4.1, but I've worked closely with National Instruments to ensure its longevity through future versions of LabVIEW. You'll find that the principles and techniques discussed in these pages are so fundamental to the work of a LabVIEW user that your ensuing enlightenment will not soon become obsolete.

Chapter 1, "Roots," starts off with an entertaining history of the development of LabVIEW. The rest of the chapter is devoted to basic advice: choosing equipment for a system and sources for help with your LabVIEW-related problems.

The basics of interface hardware, signal conditioning, and analog/digital conversion are discussed in Chap. 2, "Inputs and Outputs." Notably, this chapter contains no LabVIEW programming examples whatsoever. The reason is simple: more than half the "LabVIEW" questions that coworkers ask me turn out to be hardware- and signal-related. Information in this chapter is vital and will be useful no matter what software you may use for measurement and control.

In Chap. 3, "LabVIEW Programming Techniques," we get down to the principles of programming in G. After a discussion of the principles of dataflow programming, we discuss programming structures and data types, and finish off with a look at the subtleties of timing and file I/O. This is by no means a rewrite of the manuals or other introductory books, nor is it a substitute for a course in LabVIEW basics. You are encouraged to consult those sources, as well, in the process of becoming a skilled LabVIEW user.

Chapter 4, "Building an Application," shows you how to design a LabVIEW application. Here, I assume that you are not a formally trained software engineer, but rather a technically skilled person with a job to do (that certainly describes me!). We'll walk through the development of a real application that I wrote, starting with selection of hardware, then prototyping, designing, testing, and documenting the program.

If you connect your computer to any external instruments, you will want to read Chap. 5, "Instrument Drivers." It begins with the basics of communications and I/O hardware (GPIB, serial, and VXI), then covers recommended driver development techniques and programming practices, including the new VISA (virtual instrument standard architecture) methods. Instrument drivers can be fairly challenging to write. Since it's one of my specialties, I hope to pass along a few tricks.

Chapter 6, "Using the DAQ Library," is a practical view of the data acquisition (DAQ) library, which is the set of LabVIEW VIs that support plug-in data acquisition boards manufactured by National Instruments. All aspects of high- and low-speed analog, digital, and counter-timer operations are discussed in detail, with useful applications.

Some topics may seem at first to be presented backward—but for good reasons. In Chap. 7, "Designing a Data Acquisition System," the first topic is data analysis. Why not talk about sampling rates and throughput first? Because the only reason for doing data acquisition is to collect data for analysis. And, if you are out of touch with the data analysis needs, you will probably write the wrong data acquisition program. Other topics in this chapter are sampling speed, throughput optimization, and configuration management. We finish with some real applications that you can use "right out of the box."

The G language is now available in two development platforms: LabVIEW and BridgeVIEW. The latter is a new product, designed for industrial automation but with the flexibility of the G compiler, and is quite familiar to any LabVIEW user. Chapter 8, "Process Control Applications," covers industrial control and all types of measurement and control situations. We'll look at human-machine interfaces, sequential and continuous control, trending, alarm handling, and interfacing to industrial controllers, particularly programmable logic controllers (PLCs).

LabVIEW has a large following in physics research, so I wrote Chap. 9, "Physics Applications." Particular situations and solutions in this chapter are: electromagnetic field and plasma diagnostics, measuring fast pulses with transient recorders, and handling very large data sets. This last topic, in particular, is of interest to almost all users because it discusses techniques for optimizing memory usage. (There are tidbits like this all through the book; by all means, read it cover to cover!)

My favorite chapter is 10, "Data Visualization, Imaging, and Sound," because it shows off some of the data presentation capabilities of Lab-VIEW. Many third-party products and toolkits (such as IMAQ for imaging) are featured. They enable you to acquire video signals, process and display images, make three-dimensional plots, and record and play sound.

ATE (automated test equipment) is a specialized, but popular, Lab-VIEW application area that is discussed in Chap. 11, "ATE Applications." Important topics include test sequencing with a test executive and reporting of results. *Dynamic data exchange* (DDE), an important interprocess communication technique, is also covered.

As far as possible, this book is platform-independent, as is LabVIEW itself. Occasional topics arise where functionality is available only on one or two of the computers. DDE, for example, is available only under Microsoft Windows. The LabVIEW user manual contains a portability guide that you can consult when developing applications that you intend to propagate among various platforms.

**platform/
directory/
file_name.vi**

A **CD-ROM** is included with this book. On it you will find application notes, many useful utility VIs, and several working example applications (such as a simple data acquisition system). Many of the VIs are discussed in detail in the text. To help you locate these VIs, I've placed an icon in the margin with a path name that will lead you to the appropriate files. The CD-ROM format is compatible with all LabVIEW platforms. No file compression, encryption, or installers were used, so you can run everything right off the CD-ROM. A general index to the disk appears in App. A.

Many important resources are available only via the Internet, using a Web browser or an ftp (file transfer protocol) application on your computer. For your convenience, Internet addresses are interspersed in the text. Also, e-mail addresses and home page addresses of important suppliers are included in App. B, "Sources."

While writing this book, I found that user-supplied example VIs were hard to obtain, owing to the fact that so many of us work for government laboratories and places that just don't like to give away their software. Where it was not possible to obtain the actual code, I attempted to reconstruct the important aspects of real applications to give you an idea of how you might solve similar problems. Third-party LabVIEW products, such as driver and analysis packages, are described where appropriate. They satisfy important niche requirements in the user community at reasonable cost, thus expanding the wide applicability of LabVIEW.

If nothing else, I hope that my enthusiasm for LabVIEW rubs off on you.

*Gary W. Johnson
Livermore, California
January 1997
johnsong@llnl.gov*

Acknowledgments

I would like to thank the following persons and organizations who contributed valuable material, advice, and review services to this book:

John Baker (Lawrence Livermore National Laboratory)

Dr. Edmund Baroth (Jet Propulsion Laboratory)

Biopac Systems, Inc.

Tim Brooks (B&B Technologies, Inc.)

Xavier Chabert (ASTER)

Francis Cottet (LISI/ENSMA)

Dr. Paul Daley (Lawrence Livermore National Laboratory)

Lewis Drake (Process Automation Corporation)

Dennis Erickson (Bonneville Power Administration)

Emmanuelle Geveaux (LISI/ENSMA)

Gaurav Goel (New Visions Engineering)

Lynda Gruggett (G Systems)

Scott Hamilton (Pyxis Corporation)

Brad Hedstrom (Advanced Measurements)

Bill Jenkins (Stellar Solutions)

Andrew Johnson (Sundial Engineering)

Corrie Karlsen (Lawrence Livermore National Laboratory)

Kent Lowrance (Sverdrup Technology, Inc.)

Dan McClung (Quantum Control, Inc.)

Stu McFarland (Viewpoint Software Solutions, Inc.)

Anne Menendez (GTFS, Inc.)

Dave Moschella (Ellipsis Products, Inc.)

Mark Newfield (NASA-Ames)

Dr. Edmund Ng (Lawrence Livermore National Laboratory)

Jeff Parker (Metric Systems)

Kevan Perkins (nuLogic, Inc.)

Dr. Dana Redington (Redwolf Enterprises)

Amy Regan (Los Alamos National Laboratory)

Jeff Rowe (Fast-DAQ)

Mark Scrivener (Lawrence Livermore National Laboratory)

Dan Snider (Snider Integration)

George Wells (Jet Propulsion Laboratory)

I would also like to thank the engineers, developers, and managers at National Instruments who supplied vital information without which this book would not be possible, particularly Jeff Kodosky, Meg Kay, Deborah Bryant, Rob Dye, Gregg Fowler, Greg McKaskle, Omid Sojoodi, Kyle Gupton, Trevor Petruk, Tamra Pringle, Steve Rogers, Tim Hayles, Al Becker, Ed Lowenstein, and Brian Sierer. Credit also goes to my wife, Katharine Decker Johnson, technical illustrator *par excellence,* whose patience during this project cannot be overstated.

And finally, thanks to the people who made it all happen: Jack MacCrisken, for proposing the project and then making me "swallow the elephant," Lisa Wells for managing the overall project, and Tamara Taylor for riding herd on the reviewers.

Roots

LabVIEW has certainly made life easier for this engineer. I remember how much work it was in the early 1980s, writing hideously long programs to do what appeared to be simple measurement and control tasks. Scientists and engineers only automated their operations when it was absolutely necessary, and the casual users and operators wouldn't dare to tamper with the software because of its complexity. This computer-based instrumentation business was definitely more work than fun. But everything changed when, in mid-1987, I went to a National Instruments product demonstration. They were showing off a new program that ran on a Macintosh. It was supposed to do something with instrumentation, and that sounded interesting. When I saw what those programmers had done—and what LabVIEW could do—I was stunned! Wiring up *icons* to write a program? *Graphical* controls? Amazing! I had to get ahold of this thing and try it out for myself.

By the end of the year, I had taken the LabVIEW class and started on my first project, a simple data acquisition system. It was like watching the sun rise. There were so many possibilities now with this easy and fun-to-use programming language. I actually started looking for things to do with it around the lab (and believe me, I found them). Such a complete turnaround from the old days. Within a year, LabVIEW became an indispensable tool for my work in instrumentation and control. Now, my laboratories are not just *computerized,* they are *automated.* A computerized experiment or process relies heavily on the human operators—the computer makes things easier by taking some measurements and simple things like that, but it's far from being a hands-off process. An automated experiment, on the other hand, is one where you set up the equipment, press the Start button on the Lab-VIEW screen, and watch while the computer orchestrates a sequence of events, takes measurements, and presents the results. That's how you want your system to work, and that's where LabVIEW can save the day. Let's start out by taking a look at the world of automation.

LabVIEW and Automation

Computers are supposed to make things easier, faster, or more automatic, that is, less work for the human host. LabVIEW is a unique programming system that makes computer automation a breeze for the scientist or engineer working in many areas of laboratory research, industrial control, and data analysis. You have a job to do—someone is probably paying you to make things happen—and LabVIEW can be a real help in getting that job done, provided that you apply it properly. But debates are now raging over this whole business of computers and their influence over our productivity. For instance, an article I read recently reported that we now tend to write longer proposals and reports (and certainly prettier ones) than we used to when only a typewriter was available. The modern word processor makes it easy to be thorough and communicate our ideas effectively. But does this modern approach always result in an improvement in productivity or quality? Sometimes we actually spend *more* time to do the same old thing. We also become slaves to our computers, always fussing over the setup, installing new (necessary?) software upgrades, and generally wasting time.

You must avoid this trap. The key is to analyze your problems and see where LabVIEW and specialized computer hardware can be used to their greatest advantage. Then, make efficient use of existing LabVIEW solutions. As you will see, many laboratory automation problems have already been solved for you and the programs and equipment are readily available. There are no great mysteries here, just some straightforward engineering decisions you have to make regarding the advantages and disadvantages of computer automation. Let's take a pragmatic view of the situation. There are many operations that beg for automation. Among them are:

- Long-term, low-speed operations such as environmental monitoring and control
- High-speed operations such as pulsed power diagnostics where a great deal of data is collected in a short time
- Repetitive operations, such as automated testing and calibration, and experiments that are run many times
- Remote or hazardous operations where it is impractical, impossible, or dangerous to have a human operator present

- High-precision operations that are beyond human capability
- Complex operations with many inputs and outputs

In all of these cases, please observe that a computer-automated system makes practical an operation or experiment that you might not otherwise attempt. And automation may offer additional advantages:

- Reduces data transcription errors. The old "graphite data acquisition system" (a pencil) is prone to many error sources not present in a computer data acquisition system. Indeed, more reliable data often leads to better quality control of products and new discoveries in experimental situations.
- Eliminates operator-induced variations in the process or data collection methods. Repeatability is drastically improved because the computer never gets tired and it always does things the same way.
- Increases data throughput because you can operate a system at computer speed rather than human speed.

There are some disadvantages hiding in this process of computer automation, however:

- May introduce new sources of error, through improper use of sensors, signal conditioning, and data conversion, and occasionally through computational (e.g., round-off) errors.
- Misapplication of any hardware or software system is a ticket for trouble. For instance, attempting to collect data at excessively high rates results in data recording errors.
- Reliability is always a question with computer systems. System failures (crashes) and software bugs plague every high-tech installation known, and they will plague yours as well.

Always consider the cost-effectiveness of a potential automation solution. It seems like everything these days is driven by money. If you can do it cheaper-better-faster, it is likely to be accepted by the owner, the shareholders, or whoever pays the bills. But is a computer guaranteed to save you money or time? If I have a one-time experiment where I can adequately record the data on a single strip-chart recorder, an oscilloscope, or with my pencil, then taking two days to write a special program makes no sense whatsoever.

One way to automate (or at least computerize) simple, one-time experiments is to build what I call a LabVIEW *crash cart* much like the doctor's crash cart in an emergency room. When someone has a short-term measurement problem, I can roll in my portable rack of equipment. It contains a Macintosh with LabVIEW, analog interface hardware, and some programmable instruments. I can quickly configure the general-purpose data acquisition program, record data, and analyze it, all within a few hours. You might want to consider this concept if you work in an area that has a need for versatile data acquisition. Use whatever spare equipment you may have, recycle some tried-and-true LabVIEW programs, and pile them on a cart. It doesn't even matter what kind of computer you have since LabVIEW runs on Windows (3.1, 95, and NT), Macintosh (68K and PPC), Sun SPARCstations, Concurrent PowerMAX systems, and HP workstations. The crash cart concept is simple and marvelously effective.

Automation is expensive: the cost of sensors, computers, software, and the programmer's effort quickly add up. But in the end, a marvelous new capability can arise. The researcher is suddenly freed from the labor of logging and interpreting data. The operator no longer has to orchestrate so many critical adjustments. And data quality and product quality rise. If your situation fits the basic requirements where automation is appropriate, then by all means consider LabVIEW as a solution.

Virtual instruments: LabVIEW's foundation

LabVIEW made the concept of the **virtual instrument (VI)** a practical reality. The objective in virtual instrumentation is to use a general-purpose computer to mimic real instruments with their dedicated controls and displays, but with the added versatility that comes with software. (See Fig. 1.1.) Instead of buying a strip-chart recorder, an oscilloscope, and a spectrum analyzer, you can buy one high-performance analog-to-digital converter and use a computer running LabVIEW to simulate all of these instruments and more. The VI concept is so fundamental to the way that LabVIEW works that the programs you write in LabVIEW are in fact called **VIs**. You use simple instruments **(subVIs)** to build more complex instruments just as you use subprograms to build a more complex main program in a conventional programming language.

Virtual versus real instrumentation.   Virtual instrumentation systems such as LabVIEW inevitably invite comparison to real physical instrumentation. The major drawback in using a personal computer for implementing virtual instruments is that the computer has only one central microprocessor. An application that uses multiple instruments can easily overburden the processor. A stand-alone instrument, however, may contain any number of processors, each dedicated to specific processing tasks. In addition, these multiple processors can operate in

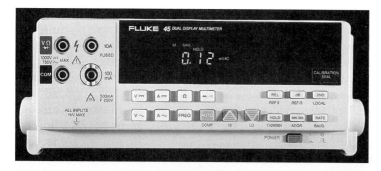

Figure 1.1 This virtual instrument (*bottom*) is a customized version of the real instrument, but having only the features that you need.

parallel, providing a great increase in overall performance. But this increase in performance results in the expensive price tag accompanying many dedicated instruments, as well as a decrease in flexibility.

The technology in plug-in boards is advancing to address these issues, however. Many boards now contain their own processors and are available at a more reasonable price. Digital signal processors are a good example of special-purpose processors that find their way onto plug-in boards. Many plug-in data acquisition boards also have sophisticated direct memory access (DMA), timing, and triggering capabilities that can span multiple boards, resulting in improved synchronization and signal coupling between boards. These developments, along with the development of more capable operating systems and computer architectures, have brought parallel processing capabilities to personal computers, making them more sophisticated platforms for instrumentation and data acquisition applications. Sophistication comes at the expense of complexity, however, because you must have greater knowledge of these hardware components and their interconnection than is required to use a stand-alone instrument with similar capabilities. Virtual instrumentation software is essential for turning these sophisticated hardware combinations into usable instrumentation systems.

Virtual instrumentation offers the greatest benefit over real instruments in the areas of price/performance, flexibility, and customization. For the price of a dedicated high-performance instrument, you can assemble a personal computer–based system with the fundamental hardware and software components to design virtual instruments targeted for specific applications. The hardware may be plug-in boards, external instruments, or a combination of both. In either case, a software interface can be as complicated or as simple as necessary to serve the application. You can simplify the operation of a complex stand-alone instrument with virtual instruments that focus on controlling only subsets of the instrument's full capabilities. I, for one, get lost in the buttons and menus on the panels of many modern instruments and find a simple VI a welcome relief.

Although LabVIEW has existed since 1986, the virtual instrumentation and block diagram concepts embodied in its design are still at the leading edge of instrumentation and computer science technology today. The cost of developing test program software continues to rise with the increasing complexity of the devices being tested and the instruments needed to test them. Software modularity, maintainability, and reusability, key benefits of LabVIEW's hierarchical and homogeneous structure, are critically important to reducing the burden of individual software developers. Reusing routines that you have written and sharing them with others can save a great deal of time and make programs more reliable.

Virtual instrumentation is becoming increasingly important in the instrument control world. **VMEbus Extensions for Instrumentation (VXI)**, a major development in instrumentation, is a standard that defines physical and electrical parameters, as well as software protocols, for implementing instrument-on-a-card test systems. A *VXI instrument* is a card that plugs into a chassis containing several cards. Because they are plug-in cards and not stand-alone boxes, individual VXI instruments do not have front panel user interfaces. Users cannot interact with a VXI instrument by pressing buttons or reading displays on a front panel. Instead, VXI systems must be controlled by a computer or other processor-based device, placing new demands on computer software for controlling instrumentation.

VXI instruments are natural candidates for virtual instrumentation implementations. In the area of user interaction, software front panels offer a visual means of controlling a faceless VXI instrument. In addition, the combination of plug-in modules and high-performance timing and communications capabilities of the VXIbus makes the configuration of a VXI test system much more complex than that of a GPIB test system. LabVIEW's method of graphically connecting virtual instruments into a block diagram accelerates the configuring and programming of VXI test systems.

Why Use LabVIEW?

I use LabVIEW because it has significant advantages over conventional languages and other control and data acquisition packages.

- My productivity is simply better in LabVIEW than with conventional programming languages. I've measured a factor of five compared with C on a small project. Others have reported improvements of 15 times.* Quick prototypes as well as finished systems are now routinely delivered in what used to be record time.

- The graphical user interface is built in, intuitive in operation, simple to apply, and, as a bonus, nice to look at.

- LabVIEW's graphical language—G—is a *real* programming language, not a specialized application. It has few intrinsic limitations.

- There is only a minimal performance penalty when compared with conventional programming languages, and LabVIEW does some things better. No other graphical programming system can make this claim.

- Programmer frustration is reduced because annoying syntax errors are eliminated. Ever gotten yourself into an argument with a C compiler over what is considered "legal"? Made a seemingly minor error with a pointer and had your machine crash?

- Many important high-level operations have been encapsulated in convenient VI libraries for quick application. Most of them are included with the program or are otherwise available free or at reasonable prices from third parties.

- Programming in LabVIEW is fun. I would *never* say that about C (challenging, yes, but fun, no).

Like any other tool, LabVIEW is only useful if you know how to use it. And the more skilled you are in the use of that tool, the more you will use it. After 10 years of practice, let's just say that I'm *really comfortable* with LabVIEW. It's gotten to the point where it is at least as important as a word processor, a multimeter, or a desktop calculator in my daily work as an engineer.

---

* *Telemetry Monitoring and Display Using LabVIEW,* by George Wells, Member of Technical Staff, and Edmund C. Baroth, Ph.D, Manager of the Measurement Technology Center, Jet Propulsion Laboratory, California Institute of Technology. Paper given at the National Instruments User Symposium, March 1993, Austin, Texas.

The Origin of LabVIEW

A computer scientist friend of mine relates this pseudobiblical history of the computer programming world:

> In the beginning, there was only machine language, and all was darkness. But soon, assembly language was invented, and there was a glimmer of light in the Programming World. Then came Fortran, *and the light went out.*

This verse conveys the feeling that traditional computer languages, even high-level languages, leave much to be desired. You spend a lot of time learning all kinds of syntactical subtleties, metaphors, compiler and linker commands, and so forth, just to say "Hello, world." And heaven forbid that you should want to draw a graph or make something move across the screen or send a message to another computer. We're talking about many days or weeks of work here. It's no wonder that it took so many years to make the computer a useful servant of the common person. Indeed, even now it requires at least a moderate education and plenty of experience to do anything significant in computer programming. For the working scientist or engineer, these classical battles with programming languages have been most counterproductive. All you wanted to do is make the darned thing display a temperature measurement from your experiment, and what did you get?

```
(beep)    SYNTAX ERROR AT LINE 1326
```

Thanks a lot, oh mighty compiler. Well, times have changed in a big way because LabVIEW has arrived. At last, working troops like us have a programming language that eliminates that arcane syntax, hides the compiler, and builds the graphical user interface right in. No fooling around, just wire up some icons and run. And yet, the thought of actually *programming with pictures* is so incredible when contrasted with ordinary computer languages. How did they do it? Who came up with this idea?

Here is a most enlightening story of the origins of LabVIEW. It's a saga of vision; of fear and loathing in the cruel world of computer programming; of hard work and long hours; and of breakthroughs, invention, and ultimate success. The original story, *An Instrument That Isn't Really,* was written by Michael Santori of National Instruments and has been updated for this book.*

---

* © 1990 IEEE. Reprinted, with permission, from *IEEE Spectrum*, vol. 27, no. 8, pp. 36–39, August 1990.

Introduction

Prior to the introduction of personal computers in the early 1980s, nearly all laboratories using programmable instrumentation controlled their test systems using dedicated instrument controllers. These expensive, single-purpose controllers had integral communication ports for controlling instrumentation using the *IEEE-488* bus, also known as the *General Purpose Interface Bus (GPIB)*. With the arrival of personal computers, however, engineers and scientists began looking for a way to use these cost-effective, general-purpose computers to control benchtop instruments. This development fueled the growth of National Instruments, which by 1983 was the dominant supplier of GPIB hardware interfaces for personal computers (as well as for minicomputers and other machines not dedicated solely to controlling instruments).

So, by 1983, GPIB was firmly established as the practical mechanism for electrically connecting instruments to computers. Except for dealing with some differing interpretations of the IEEE-488 specification by instrument manufacturers, users had few problems physically configuring their systems. The software to control the instruments, however, was not in such a good state. Almost 100 percent of all instrument control programs developed at this time were written in the BASIC programming language because BASIC was the dominant language used on the large installed base of dedicated instrument controllers. Although BASIC had advantages (including a simple and readable command set and interactive capabilities), it had one fundamental problem: like any other text-based programming language, it required engineers, scientists, and technicians who used the instruments to become programmers. These users had to translate their knowledge of their applications and their instruments into the lines of text required to produce a test program. This process, more often than not, proved to be a cumbersome and tedious chore, especially for those with little or no prior programming experience.

A vision emerges

National Instruments, which had its own team of programmers struggling to develop BASIC programs to control instrumentation, was sensitive to the burden that instrumentation programming placed on engineers and scientists. A new tool for developing instrumentation software programs was clearly needed. But what form would it take? Dr. Jim Truchard and Jeff Kodosky, two of the founders of National Instruments, along with Jack MacCrisken, who was then a consultant, began the task of inventing this tool. (See Fig. 1.2.) Truchard was in search of a software tool that would markedly change the way engineers and scientists approached their test development needs. A model software product that came to mind was the electronic spreadsheet. The spreadsheet addressed the same general problem Truchard, Kodosky, and MacCrisken faced—making the computer accessible to nonprogrammer computer users. Whereas the spreadsheet addressed the needs of financial planners, this entrepreneurial trio wanted to help engineers and scientists. They had their rallying cry—they would invent a software tool that had the same impact for scientists and engineers that the spreadsheet had on the financial community.

In 1984, the company, still relatively small in terms of revenue, decided to embark on a journey that would ultimately take several years. Truchard committed research and development funding to this phantom product and named Kodosky as the person to make it materialize. MacCrisken proved to be the catalyst—an amplifier for innovation on the part of Kodosky—while Truchard served as the facilitator and primary user. Dr. T, as he is affectionately known at National Instruments, has a knack for knowing when the product is *right*.

Figure 1.2 (*Left to right*): Jack MacCrisken, Jeff Kodosky, and Jim Truchard, LabVIEW inventors.

Kodosky wanted to move to an office away from the rest of the company, so he could get away from the day-to-day distractions of the office and create an environment ripe for inspiration and innovation. He also wanted a site close to the University of Texas at Austin, so he could access the many resources available at UT, including libraries for research purposes and, later, student programmers to staff his project. There were two offices available in the desired vicinity. One office was on the ground floor with floor-to-ceiling windows overlooking the pool at an apartment complex. The other office was on the second floor of the building and had no windows at all. He chose the latter. It would prove to be a fortuitous decision.

All the world's an instrument

The first fundamental concept behind LabVIEW was rooted in a large test system that Truchard and Kodosky had worked on at the Applied Research Laboratory in the late 1970s. Shipyard technicians used this system to test Navy sonar transducers. However, engineers and researchers also had access to the system for conducting underwater acoustics experiments. The system was flexible because Kodosky incorporated several levels of user interaction into its design. A technician could operate the system and run specific test procedures with predefined limits on parameters while an acoustics engineer had access to the lower-level facilities for actually designing the test procedures. The most flexibility was given to the researchers, who had access to all the programmable hardware in the system to configure as they desired (they could also blow up the equipment if they weren't careful). Two major drawbacks to the system were that it was an incredible investment in programming time—over 18 work-years—and that users had to understand the complicated mnemonics in menus in order to change anything.

Over several years, Kodosky refined the concept of this test system to the notion of instrumentation software as a hierarchy of virtual instruments. A virtual instrument (VI) would be composed of lower-level virtual instruments, much like a real instrument was composed of printed circuit boards and boards composed of integrated circuits (ICs). The bottom-level VIs represented the most fundamental software building blocks: computational and input/output (I/O) operations. Kodosky gave particular emphasis to the interconnection and nesting of multiple software layers. Specifically, he envisioned VIs as having the same type of construction at all levels. In the hardware domain, the techniques for assembling ICs into boards are dramatically different than assembling boards into a chassis. In the software domain, assembling statements into subroutines differs from assembling subroutines into programs, and these activities differ greatly from assembling concurrent programs into systems. The VI model of homogeneous structure and interface, at all levels, greatly simplifies the construction of software—a necessary achievement for improving design productivity. From a practical point of view, it was essential that VIs have a superset of the properties of the analogous software components they were replacing. Thus, LabVIEW had to have the computational ability of a programming language and the parallelism of concurrent programs.

Another major design characteristic of the virtual instrument model was that each VI had a user interface component. Using traditional programming approaches, even a simple command line user interface for a typical test program was a complex maze of input and output statements often added after the core of the program was written. With a VI, the user interface was an integral part of the software model. An engineer could interact with any VI at any level in the system simply by opening the VI's user interface. The user interface would make it easy to test software modules incrementally and interactively during system development. In addition, because the user interface was an integral part of every VI, it was always available for troubleshooting a system when a fault occurred. (The virtual instrument concept was so central to LabVIEW's incarnation that it eventually became embodied in the name of the product. Although Kodosky's initial concerns did not extend to the naming of the product, much thought would ultimately go into the name LabVIEW, which is an acronym for *Laboratory Virtual Instrument Engineering Workbench.*)

A hard-core UNIX guy won over by the Macintosh

The next fundamental concept of LabVIEW was more of a breakthrough than a slow evolution over time. Kodosky had never been interested in personal computers because they didn't have megabytes of memory and disk storage, and they didn't run UNIX. About the time Kodosky started his research on LabVIEW, however, his brother-in-law introduced him to the new Apple Macintosh personal computer. Kodosky's recollection of the incident was that "after playing with MacPaint for over three hours, I realized it was time to leave and I hadn't even said hello to my sister." He promptly bought his own Macintosh. After playing with the Macintosh, Kodosky came to the conclusion that the most intuitive user interface for a VI would be a facsimile of a real instrument front panel. (The Macintosh was a revelation because DOS and UNIX systems in 1983 did not have the requisite graphical user interface.) Most engineers learn about an instrument by studying its front panel and experimenting with it. With its mouse, menus, scroll bars, and icons, the

Macintosh proved that the right interface would also allow someone to learn software by experimentation. VIs with graphical front panels that could be operated using the mouse would be simple to operate. A user could discover how they work, minimizing documentation requirements (although people rarely documented their BASIC programs anyway).

Putting it all together with pictures

The final conceptual piece of LabVIEW was the programming technique. A VI with an easy-to-use graphical front panel programmed in BASIC or C would simplify operation, but would make the development of a VI more difficult. The code necessary to construct and operate a graphical panel is considerably more complex than that required to communicate with an instrument.

To begin addressing the programming problem, Kodosky went back to his model software product, the spreadsheet. Spreadsheet programs are so successful because they display data and programs as rows and columns of numbers and formulas. The presentation is simple and familiar to businesspeople. What do engineers do when they design a system? They draw a block diagram. Block diagrams help an engineer visualize the problem but only suggest a design. Translation of a block diagram to a schematic or computer program, however, requires a great deal of skill. What Kodosky wanted was a software-diagramming technique that would be easy to use for conceptualizing a system, yet flexible and powerful enough to actually serve as a programming language for developing instrumentation software.

Two visual tools Kodosky considered were flowcharts and state diagrams. It was obvious that flowcharts could not help. These charts offered a visualization of a process, but to really understand them you have to read the fine print in the boxes on the chart. Thus, the chart occupies too much space relative to the fine print yet adds very little information to a well-formatted program. The other option, a state diagram, is flexible and powerful but the perspective is very different from that of a block diagram. Representing a system as a collection of state diagrams requires a great amount of skill. Even after completion, the diagrams must be augmented with textual descriptions of the transitions and actions before they can be understood.

Another approach Kodosky considered was *dataflow diagrams*. Dataflow diagrams, long recommended as a top-level software design tool, have much in common with engineering block diagrams. Their one major weakness is the difficulty involved in making them powerful enough to represent iterative and conditional computations. Special nodes and feedback cycles have to be introduced into the diagram to represent these computations, making it extremely difficult to design or even understand a dataflow diagram for anything but the simplest computations. Kodosky felt strongly, however, that dataflow had some potential for his new software system.

By the end of 1984, Kodosky had experimented with most of the diagramming techniques, but they were all lacking in some way. Dataflow diagrams were the easiest to work with up until the point where loops were needed. Considering a typical test scenario, however, such as "take 10 measurements and average them," it's obvious that loops and iteration are at the heart of most instrumentation applications. In desperation, Kodosky began to make ad hoc sketches to depict loops specifically for these types of operations. *Loops* are basic building blocks of modern structured programming languages, but it was not clear how or if they could be drawn in a dataflow concept. The answer that emerged was a box; a box in a dataflow diagram could represent a loop. From the outside, the box would behave as any other node in the diagram, but inside it would contain another diagram, a *subdiagram,* representing the contents of the loop. All the semantics of the loop behavior could be encapsulated in the border of the box. In fact, all the common structures of structured programming languages could be represented by different types of boxes. His *structured dataflow* diagrams were inherently parallel because they were based on dataflow. In 1990, the first two U.S. patents were issued, covering structured dataflow diagrams and virtual instrument panels. (See Fig. 1.3.)

Kodosky was convinced he had achieved a major breakthrough but he was still troubled by a nagging point. There are times when it is important to force operations to take place sequentially—even when there is no dataflow requiring it. For example, a signal generator must provide a stimulus before a voltmeter can measure a response, even though there isn't an explicit data dependency between the instruments. A special box to represent sequential operations, however, would be cumber-

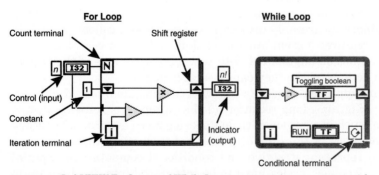

Figure 1.3 LabVIEW For Loop and While Loop programming structures with Shift Registers to recirculate data from previous iterations.

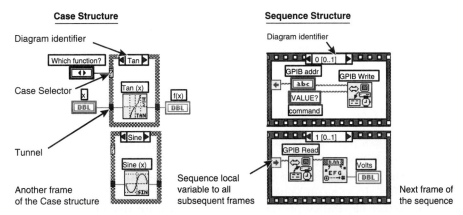

Figure 1.4 LabVIEW Case Structures are used for branching or decision operations, and Sequence Structures are used for explicit flow control.

some and take up extra space. During one of their design discussions, Truchard suggested that steps in a sequence were like frames in a movie. This comment led to the notion of having several sequential subdiagrams share the same screen space. It also led to the distinctive graphic style of the **Sequence Structure**, as shown in Fig. 1.4.

After inventing the fundamentals of LabVIEW block diagramming, it was a simple matter of using MacPaint to produce pictures of VI panels and diagrams for several common applications. When Kodosky showed them to some engineers at NI, the impact was dramatic. The engineers understood the meaning of the diagrams and correctly guessed how to operate the front panel. Of equal importance, the reviewers expressed great confidence that they would be able to easily construct such diagrams to do other applications. Now, the only remaining task was to write the software, facetiously known as *SMOP: small matter of programming.*

Favoring the underdog platform
for system design

Although Kodosky felt that the graphics tools on the Macintosh made it the computer of choice for developing LabVIEW, the clearer marketing choice was the DOS-based IBM PC. The Macintosh could never be the final platform for the product because it wasn't an open machine, and salespeople would never be able to sell it because the Macintosh was considered a toy by many scientists and engineers. Politics and marketing aside, it wasn't at all clear that you could build a system in which a user draws a picture and the system *runs* it. Even if such a system could be built, would it be fast enough to be useful? Putting marketing concerns aside momentarily, Kodosky decided to build a prototype on the Macintosh prior to building the *real* system on a PC.

Kodosky's affinity for the Macintosh was not for aesthetic reasons alone. The Macintosh system ROM contains high-performance graphics routines collectively known as QuickDraw functions. The Macintosh's most significant graphics capability is its ability to manipulate arbitrarily shaped regions quickly. This capability makes animated, interactive graphics possible. The graphics region algebra performed by the Macintosh is fast because of the unique coordinate system built into QuickDraw: the pixels are between, not on, the gridlines. In addition, the graphics display of the Macintosh uses square pixels, which simplifies drawing in general and rotations of bitmaps in particular. This latter capability proves especially useful for displaying rotating knobs and indicators on a VI front panel.

The operating system of the Macintosh is well integrated. It contains graphics, event management, input/output, memory management, resource and file management, and more—all tuned to the hardware environment for fast and efficient operation. Also, the Macintosh uses Motorola's 68000 family of microprocessors. These processors are an excellent base for large applications because they have large uniform address space (handling large arrays of data is easy) and a uniform instruction set (compiler-generated code is efficient). Remember that this was 1985: the IBM PC compatibles were still battling to break the 640-kilobyte barrier and had no intrinsic graphics support. It wasn't until Microsoft released Windows 3.0 in 1991 that a version of LabVIEW for the PC became feasible.

Ramping up development

Kodosky hired several people just out of school (and some part-time people still in school) to staff the development team. Without much experience, none of the team members was daunted by the size and complexity of the software project they were undertaking and instead they jumped into it with enthusiasm.

The team bought 10 Macintoshes equipped with 512 kilobytes of memory and internal hard-disk drives called *HyperDrives*. They connected all of the computers to a large temperamental disk server. The team took up residence in the same office near campus used by Kodosky for his brainstorming. The choice of location resulted in 11 people crammed into 800 square feet. As it turned out, the working conditions were almost ideal for the project. There were the occasional distractions with that many people in one room but the level of communication was tremendous. When a discussion erupted between two team members, it would invariably have some impact on another aspect of the system they were inventing. The other members working on aspects of the project affected by the proposed change would enter the discussion and quickly resolve the issue. The lack of windows and a clock also helped the team stay focused. (As it turned out, the developers were so impressed with the productivity of the one-room team concept that the LabVIEW group is still located in one large room, although it now has windows with a great view.)

They worked long hours and couldn't afford to worry about the time. All-nighters were the rule rather than the exception and lunch break often didn't happen until 3 P.M. There was a refrigerator and a microwave in the room so the team could eat and work at the same time. The main nutritional staples during development were double-stuff Oreo cookies and popcorn, and an occasional mass exodus to Armin's for Middle Eastern food.

The early development proceeded at an incredible pace. In four months time, Kodosky had put together a team and the team had learned how to program the Macintosh. MacCrisken contributed his project management skills and devised crucial data structure and software entity relationship diagrams that served as an overall road map for software development. They soon produced a proof-of-concept prototype that could control a GPIB instrument (through a serial port adapter), take multiple measurements, and display the average of the measurements. In proving the concept, however, it also became clear that there was a severe problem with the software speed. It would take two more development iterations and a year before the team would produce a viable product. (See Fig. 1.5.)

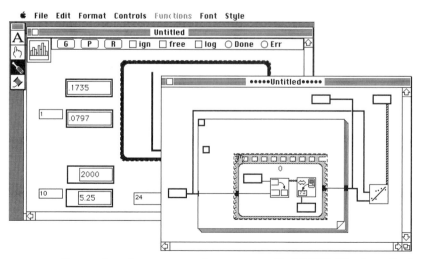

Figure 1.5   Screen shots from a very early prototype of LabVIEW. (*Thanks to Paul Daley of LLNL who discovered these old LabVIEW versions deep in his diskette archive.*)

Stretching the limits of tools and machine

After finishing the first prototype, Kodosky decided to continue working on the Macintosh because he felt the team still had much to learn before they were ready to begin the *real* product. It was at this time that the team began encountering the realities of developing such a large software system. The first problems they encountered were in the development tools. The software overflowed some of the internal tables, first in the C compiler and then in the linker. The team worked with the vendor to remedy the problem. Each time it occurred, the vendor expanded the tables. These fixes would last for a couple months until the project grew to overflow them again. The project continued to challenge the capabilities of the development tools for the duration of the project.

The next obstacle encountered was the Macintosh jump table. The project made heavy use of object-oriented techniques, which resulted in lots of functions, causing the jump tables to overflow. The only solution was to compromise on design principles and work within the limits imposed by the platform. As it turned out, such compromises would become more commonplace in the pursuit of acceptable performance.

The last major obstacle was memory. The project was already getting too large for the 512-kilobyte capacity of Macintosh and the team still hadn't implemented all the required functions, let alone the desirable ones they had been hoping to include. The prospects looked dim for implementing the complete system on a DOS-based PC, even with extensive use of overlaying techniques. This situation almost proved fatal to the project. The team was at a dead end and morale was at an all-time low. It was at this opportune time that Apple came to the rescue by introducing the Macintosh Plus in January 1986. The Macintosh Plus was essentially identical to the existing Macintosh except that it had a memory capacity of one megabyte. Suddenly, there was enough memory to implement and run the product with most of the features the team wanted.

Once again, the issue of the marketability of the Macintosh arose. A quick perusal of the DOS-based PC market showed that the software and hardware technology had not advanced very much. Kodosky decided (with approval by Dr. Truchard after some persuasion) that, having come this far on the Macintosh, they would go ahead and build the first version of LabVIEW on the Macintosh. By the time the first version of LabVIEW was complete, there would surely, they thought, be a new PC that could run large programs.

Facing reality on estimated development times

The initial estimates of the remaining development effort were grossly inaccurate. The April 1986 introduction date passed without a formal software release. In May, in anticipation of an imminent shipping date, the team moved from their campus workroom to the main office, where they could be close to the application engineers who did customer support. This event caused much excitement but still no product.

It was at this point that the company became over-anxious and tried to force the issue by prematurely starting beta testing. The testing was a fiasco. The software was far from complete. There were many bugs encountered in doing even the most simple and common operations. Development nearly ground to a halt as the developers spent their time listening to beta testers calling in the same problems. (See Fig. 1.6.)

As the overall design neared completion, the team began focusing more on details, especially performance. One of the original design goals was to match the performance of interpreted BASIC. It was not at all clear how much invention or redesign it would require to achieve this performance target, making it impossible to predict when the team would achieve this goal. On most computational benchmarks, the software was competitive with BASIC. There was one particular benchmark, the Sieve of Eratosthenes, that posed, by nature of its algorithm and design, particular problems for dataflow implementations. The performance numbers the team measured for the sieve benchmark were particularly horrendous and discouraging—a fraction of a second for a compiled C program, two minutes for interpreted BASIC, and over eight hours for LabVIEW.

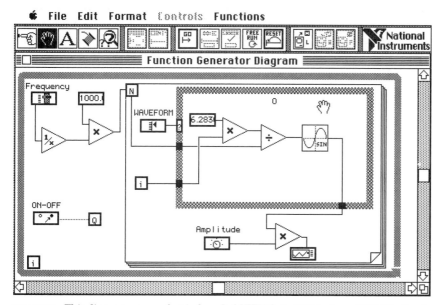

Figure 1.6   This diagram screen shot is from LabVIEW beta 0.36 in June 1986. The familiar structures (While and For Loops, and a Case Structure) had appeared by this time.

Kodosky did his best to predict when the software would be complete, based on the number of bugs, but was not sure how the major bugs would be found, much less fixed. Efficiently testing such a complex interactive program was a vexing and complex problem. The team finally settled on the *bug day* approach. They picked a day when the entire team would stop working on the source code and simply use Lab-VIEW. They would try all types of editing operations, build as many and varied VIs as they could, and write down all the problems they encountered until the white boards on every wall were full. The first bug day lasted only three hours. The team sorted the list and for the next five weeks fixed all the fatal flaws and as many minor flaws as possible. Then they had another bug day. They repeated this process until they couldn't generate even one fatal flaw during an entire day. The product wasn't perfect, but at least it would not be an embarrassment.

Shipping the first version

In October 1986, the team figured out how to bypass some of the overhead in calling a subVI, producing some improvement in performance (for all but the sieve benchmark, which was better, but still 20 times slower than BASIC). The decision was made to ship the product. The team personally duplicated and packaged the first 50 disks and hand-carried them to shipping. Version 1.0 was on the streets.

The reaction to LabVIEW was, in a word, startling. The product received worldwide acclaim as the first viable *visual,* or graphical, language. There were many compliments for a well-designed product, especially from research and development groups who had had their Macintosh-based projects canceled by less-adventurous CEOs and marketing departments. Interestingly enough, the anticipated demand of the targeted BASIC users did not materialize. These people were apparently content to continue programming as they had been doing. Instead, LabVIEW was attracting and eliciting demands from customers who had never programmed at all but who were trying to develop systems considered extremely difficult by experienced programmers in any language. Yet these customers believed they could successfully accomplish their application goals with LabVIEW.

Apple catches up with the potential offered by LabVIEW

Shortly after shipment of LabVIEW began, the company received its first prototype of the Macintosh II. This new version of the Macintosh had many design features that promised to legitimize the Macintosh in the scientific and engineering community. The most important of these features was the open architecture of the new machine. Previous Macintosh versions did not have the capability to accept plug-in expansion boards. The only mechanisms available for I/O were RS-422 serial and SCSI (Small Computer Systems Interface) ports. National Instruments sold stand-alone interface box products that converted these ports to IEEE-488 control ports, but performance suffered greatly.

The Macintosh II's open architecture made it possible to add not only IEEE-488 support but also other much-needed I/O capabilities, such as analog-to-digital conversion and digital I/O. The Macintosh II used the NuBus architecture, an IEEE standard bus that gave the new machine high-performance 32-bit capabilities for instrumentation and data acquisition that were unmatched by any computer short of a minicomputer (the PC's bus was 16 bits). With the flexibility and performance afforded by the new Macintosh, users now had access to the hardware capabilities needed to take full advantage of Lab-VIEW's virtual instrumentation capabilities. Audrey Harvey (now a system architect at National Instruments) led the hardware development team that produced the first Macintosh II NuBus interface boards, and Lynda Gruggett (now a LabVIEW consultant) wrote the original *LabDriver* VIs that supported this new high-performance I/O. With such impressive new capabilities and little news from the PC world, National Instruments found itself embarking on another iteration of LabVIEW development, still on the Macintosh.

Effective memory management turned out to be the key to making this graphical language competitive with ordinary interpreted languages. The development team had used a literal interpretation of dataflow programming. Each time data (a wire) leaves a source (a node), the Macintosh Memory Manager is called to allocate space for the new data, adding tremendous overhead. Other performance factors involved effective interpretation of the VI and diagram hierarchy and the scheduling of execution among nodes on the diagram. It became obvious that memory reuse was vital, but a suitable algorithm was far from obvious. Kodosky and MacCrisken spent about four intensive weekend brainstorming sessions juggling the various factors, eventually arriving at a vague algorithm that appeared to address everything. The whiteboard was covered with all sorts of instantiation diagrams with "little yellow arrows and blue dots" showing the prescribed flow of data. Then, one Monday morning, they called in Jeff Parker (now a LabVIEW consultant) and Steve Rogers (still a LabVIEW developer at National Instruments) and introduced them to this magnificent algorithm. The two of them proceeded to implement the algorithm (to the point that Kodosky and MacCrisken admittedly don't understand it anymore!). They kept the famous whiteboard around for about a year, occasionally referring to it to make sure everything was right. LabVIEW 1.1 included these concepts, known collectively as *inplaceness*.

While the development team was working with the new Macintosh, they were also scrambling to meet some of the demands made by customers. They were simultaneously making incremental improvements in performance, fixing flaws that came to light after shipment began, and trying to plan future developments. As a result of this process, LabVIEW progressed from version 1.0 to version 1.2 (and the sieve progressed to 23 seconds). LabVIEW 1.2 was a very reliable and robust product. I, for one, wrote a lot of useful programs in version 1.2 and I can't recall crashing. (See Figs. 1.7 and 1.8.)

The Macintosh II gave LabVIEW a much-needed and significant boost in performance. The improvement, however, was short-lived. The internal architecture of LabVIEW 1.2 was showing signs of distress and the software was apparently abusing the Macintosh resource manager as well as its memory manager. It was becoming clear that the only real way to enhance capabilities was with a complete redesign. At the least, a redesign could incorporate new diagram analysis algorithms and a fast built-in compiler that would eliminate performance problems once and for all. The major objective of the redesign was to achieve execution performance within a factor of two of compiled C.

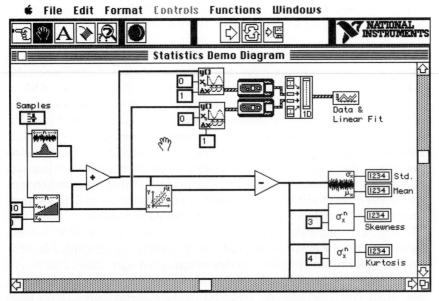

Figure 1.7 This is LabVIEW 1.2. It ran only in black and white and you couldn't move an object once it was wired. Somehow, we early users managed to get a *lot* accomplished and enjoyed ourselves, at that.

Figure 1.8 This is how we got to know the LabVIEW 1 development team: the *About LabVIEW* dialog box had these way-cool portraits.

LabVIEW 2: A first-rate instrument control product becomes a world-class programming system

Even as the plans for the next-generation LabVIEW were becoming firm, customers were fast approaching, and exceeding, the limits of Lab-VIEW 1.2. Some users were building systems of VIs using up to 8 MB of memory (then the limit on a Macintosh II). The *mega-applications* took up to 30 minutes to load into memory. Users reeled at the nefarious *Too many objects* error message. And members of the development team often shuddered when they thought of the huge number of allocated structures and the complexity of their interconnection needed to make such a system work.

The decision to redesign LabVIEW brought with it a new set of pressures. In responding to some of the customer demands, the company had to admit that version 1.2 was at its design limits. As a result, work began on a new version, already becoming known as LabVIEW 2. Once the word was out, the development team was pressured into predicting a release date. Despite Kodosky's best intentions, the scope of the redesign resulted in several missed shipping deadlines. Realize that the design of a hierarchical dataflow compiler with polymorphic functions and sophisticated memory management was new science—and it took awhile.

LabVIEW 2 was designed with formalized object-oriented programming (OOP) techniques, on the insistence of Jeff Parker. OOP has many advantages over common procedural languages, and in fact it was an enabling technology in this case. Unfortunately, OOP tools for C language development were in a rather primitive state in the 1988 time frame, so the team wrote their own spreadsheet-based development tools to automatically generate source code files and to keep track of objects and methods. These tools remain in use because they are more efficient than C++ in terms of code size and performance, though Kodosky reports that C++ is under serious consideration now for reasons of future support and portability.

The development team released an alpha version of the software in late 1988. Cosmetically, this version appeared to be in excellent shape. The compiler was working well and showed great increases in performance. There were also many enhancements in the editing capabilities of the product. All these positive signs resulted in an air of excitement and of imminent release. Unfortunately, the team had a long list of items they knew had to be fixed to produce a technically sound product. Over a year elapsed before the team released the final product. In January 1990, LabVIEW 2 shipped to the first eager customers. I have to say that being a beta tester was a real thrill: the improvement in speed and flexibility was astounding.

LabVIEW 2's compiler is especially notable not only for its performance but for its integration into the development system. Developing in a standard programming language normally requires separate compilation and linking steps to produce an executable program. The LabVIEW 2 compiler is an integral and invisible part of the LabVIEW system, compiling diagrams in a fraction of the time required by standard compilers. From a user's point of view, the compiler is so fast and invisible that LabVIEW 2 is every bit as interactive as the previous interpreted versions. (See Fig. 1.9.)

The port to Windows and Sun

The next major quest in the development of LabVIEW was the portable, or platform-independent version. Dr. Truchard (and thousands of users) had always wanted LabVIEW to run on the PC, but until Windows 3.0 came along, there was little hope of doing so because of the lack of 32-bit addressing support that is vital to the operation of such a large, sophisticated application. UNIX workstations, on the other hand, are well suited to such development, but the workstation market alone was not big enough to warrant the effort required. These reasons made Kodosky somewhat resistant to the whole idea of programming on the PC, but MacCrisken finally convinced him that

Figure 1.9 The team that delivered LabVIEW 2 into the hands of engineers and scientists (*clockwise from upper left*): Jack Barber, Karen Austin, Henry Velick, Jeff Kodosky, Tom Chamberlain, Deborah Batto, Paul Austin, Wei Tian, Steve Chall, Meg Fletcher, Rob Dye, Steve Rogers, and Brian Powell. Not shown: Jeff Parker, Jack MacCrisken, and Monnie Anderson.

portability itself—the isolation of the machine-dependent layer—is the real challenge. So, *the port* was on.

Microsoft Windows 3 turned out to be a major kludge with regard to 32-bit applications (Windows, itself, and DOS are 16-bit applications). Only in Appendix E of the Windows programming guide was there any mention whatsoever of 32-bit techniques. And most of the information contained in that appendix referred to storage of data, not applications. Finally, only one C compiler—Watcom C—was suited to LabVIEW development. But before Watcom C became available, Steve Rogers created a set of glue routines that translates 32-bit information back and forth to the 16-bit system function calls (in accordance with Appendix E). He managed to successfully debug these low-level routines without so much as a symbolic debugger, living instead with hexadecimal dumps. This gave the development team a six-month head start. Rogers summed up the entire situation: "It's ugly."

Development on the Sun SPARCstation, in contrast, was a relative breeze. Like all good workstations, the Sun supports a full range of professional development tools with few compromises—a programmer's dream. However, the X Windows environment that was selected for the LabVIEW graphical interface was totally different from the Macintosh or Windows toolbox environments. A great deal of effort was expended on the low-level graphics routines, but the long-term payoff is in the portability of X Windows–based programs. Development on the Sun was so convenient, in fact, that when a bug was encountered in the Windows version, the programmer would often do his or her debugging on the Sun rather than suffering along on the PC. Kodosky reports, "The Sun port made the PC port much easier and faster."

LabVIEW 2.5, which was released in August 1992, required rewriting about 80 percent of LabVIEW 2 to break out the machine-dependent, or *manager*, layer. Creating this manager layer required some compromises with regard to the look and feel of the particular platforms. For instance, creating *floating windows* (such as the LabVIEW Help window) are trivial on the Macintosh, difficult on the PC, and impossible under X Windows. The result is some degree of least-common-denominator programming, but the situation has continued to improve in later versions through the use of some additional machine-dependent programming. (See Fig. 1.10.)

LabVIEW 3

The LabVIEW 2.5 development effort established a new and flexible architecture that made the unification of all three versions in LabVIEW 3 relatively easy. LabVIEW 3, which shipped in July of 1993,

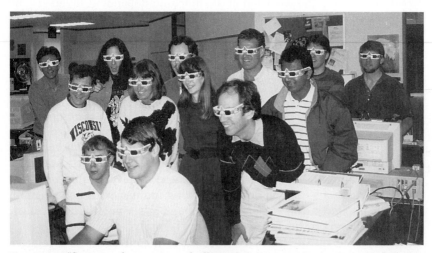

Figure 1.10 *"Some new features are so brilliant that eye protection is recommended when viewing."* The team that delivered LabVIEW 2.5 and 3.0 includes (*left to right, rear*) Steve Rogers, Thad Engeling, Duncan Hudson, Keving Woram, Greg Richardson, Greg McKaskle; (*middle*) Dean Luick, Meg Kay, Deborah Batto-Bryant, Paul Austin, Darshan Shah; (*seated*) Brian Powell, Bruce Mihura. Not pictured: Gregg Fowler, Apostolos Karmirantzos, Ron Stuart, Rob Dye, Jeff Kodosky, Jack MacCrisken, Stepan Riha.

included a number of new features beyond those introduced in version 2.5. Many of these important features were the suggestions of users accumulated over several years. Kodosky and his team, after the long and painful port, finally had the time to do some really creative programming. For instance, there had long been requests for a method by which the characteristics of controls and indicators could be changed programmatically. The *Attribute Node* addressed this need. Similarly, *Local Variables* made it possible to both read from and write to controls and indicators. This is an extension of strict dataflow programming, but it is a convenient way to solve many tricky problems. Many subtle compiler improvements were also made that enhance performance, robustness, and extensibility. Additional U.S. patents were issued in 1994 covering these extensions to structured dataflow diagrams such as globals and locals, occurrences, attribute nodes, execution highlighting, and so forth.

LabVIEW 3 has been a grand success, both for National Instruments and for the user community worldwide. Very large applications and systems have been assembled—I'm tentatively going to give the record to Kirk Fertitta of Sedona Systems with over 2000 VIs in a semiconductor fabrication control system. The *LabVIEW Application Builder* permits the compilation of true stand-alone applications for distribution. Important add-on toolkits are now offered by National Instruments and third parties, covering such areas as process control, imaging, and database access. Hundreds of consultants and corporations have made LabVIEW their core competency; speaking as one of them, the phones just keep on ringing.

LabVIEW 4 and beyond

Like many sophisticated software packages, LabVIEW has both benefited and suffered from *feature creep:* the designers respond to every user request, the package bulks up, and pretty soon the beginner is overwhelmed. April 1996 brought LabVIEW 4 to the masses, and, with it, some solutions to perceived ease-of-use issues. Controls, functions, and tools were moved into customizable floating palettes, menus were reorganized, and elaborate online help was added. Tip strips appear whenever you point to icons, buttons, or other objects. Debugging became much more powerful. And even the manuals received an infusion of valuable new information. I've heard significant, positive feedback from new users on many of these features. (Some old-timers are nonplussed: "Those youngsters in Austin can't leave well enough alone! Gimme back my old list-style menus!") I, for one, have sympathy for the beginner and firmly believe that every software package needs to be approachable and intuitive while maintaining significant underlying power and expandability. Version 4.0 is certainly a step in that direction.

Experienced users gained some editing shortcuts, new functions, additional control attributes, and more. Most importantly, a new Project menu appeared, loaded with features that support development of large applications. The Find command locates text, subVIs, functions, and so forth. The Hierarchy window is now quite flexible, allowing you to quickly navigate and maintain applications with hundreds of sub-VIs. And there's a Profiler to tell you which VIs are using up your precious CPU and memory resources. The serious developer will find that LabVIEW 4 saves work on big jobs. And you can take that to the bank.

Many new features are still in the planning stages. (See Fig. 1.11.) Here are a few teasers to keep you interested in future versions of LabVIEW:

- *Undo* (at last!).   The seemingly trivial act of undoing a mistaken action while editing a LabVIEW diagram is a programmer's nightmare. Undo turns out to be a very difficult problem in LabVIEW because of the complexity of its internal data structures. A solution is at hand, however: it *almost* made it into LabVIEW 4.

- *Improved support for large projects.*   LabVIEW has moved into the world of serious program development, where teams of programmers use strict software quality assurance and software engineering tech-

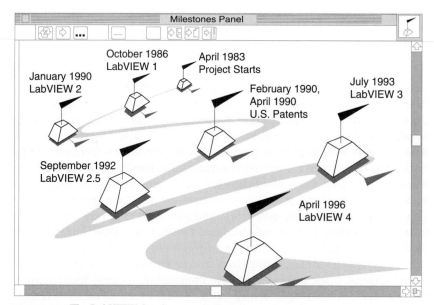

Figure 1.11   The LabVIEW development milestones.

niques. New tools to manage large projects have appeared in Lab-VIEW 4, and more are under development.

- *Multithreaded LabVIEW.*   *Multithreading* means that various parts of LabVIEW can run with greater independence under the auspices of the operating system's task scheduler. For instance, the drawing of a complex graphic can be preempted by an important numerical calculation, which in turn is preempted by an I/O operation. This enhances overall performance.

- *Distributed LabVIEW.*   In the future, you will be able to compile and download parts of your LabVIEW programs to other processors. For instance, you could have several processors on plug-in boards, at remote locations on a network, or running in outboard I/O interface boxes. This will drastically improve real-time performance and free you from having to use several languages to build a distributed processing system.

- *More connectivity.*   LabVIEW can be a VI server where other applications call LabVIEW to perform specified operations. Related topics are OLE Automation and World Wide Web services. These technologies are changing rapidly; expect rapid advances in LabVIEW support for all types of networking.

LabVIEW branches to BridgeVIEW

National Instruments decided to target the industrial process control market—initially with LabVIEW extensions—and ended up launching a new product, **BridgeVIEW**. It's important to make a distinction between LabVIEW the development environment and *G,* the underlying programming language. The two are indeed separable. Bridge-VIEW is an independent development environment that uses the G language and compiler, but is optimized for process control applications. Primary differences between the two products include some changes in the menus, the inclusion of a real-time process control database, extensive system configuration tools, a new driver concept, and a reduction in the amount of programming required to create a substantial process control application. The result is a ready-to-use process control package that you can freely extend with G language diagrammatic programming. This contrasts sharply with other process control packages that *do what they do,* and no more. LabVIEW users with a control application will find BridgeVIEW very comfortable.

Many of the original development team members continue to maintain the product while researching future extensions and directions. Several of them, including Lynda Gruggett and Jeff Parker, have gone on to start successful businesses of their own, specializing in LabVIEW programming. As you might expect with a project of such a large scope, LabVIEW continues to introduce National Instruments to many new applications and markets. Meanwhile, meeting the demanding needs of engineers and scientists will continue to make LabVIEW significant both as a product and as a standard for measuring software innovation.

LabVIEW influences other software products

The concepts found in LabVIEW have already influenced the design of many other instrumentation products, especially in the areas of software front panels and iconic programming. Such products exist for Macintosh, DOS, Windows, and UNIX-based computers. Although at first glance, these products are easily confused with LabVIEW, the differences are many.

Like LabVIEW, most instrumentation software products now offer some form of front panel–oriented user interface. The role of a LabVIEW front panel is unique, however, in comparison to other products. A graphical front panel in most instrumentation software products is simply a display/user interface mechanism introduced into an otherwise conventional, textual language–based programming system. National Instruments' *LabWindows CVI* is such a package. The sole purpose of the panel in such a system is to serve as a top-level interface to an instrument or plug-in board. In some packages, users don't have the flexibility to customize their own front panel; it's merely a user-friendly tool supplied by the vendor. These panels are either not applicable to or not available as an interface for use within an application program.

In LabVIEW, a front panel is an integral component of every software module (or VI). A LabVIEW front panel can serve as the interface to any type of program, whether it is a GPIB instrument driver program, a data acquisition program, or simply a VI that performs computations and displays graphs. The methodology of using and building front panels is fundamental to the design and operation of LabVIEW; for every front panel, there is an associated block diagram program and vice versa. Front panels can appear at any level in a LabVIEW VI and are not restricted to the highest level.

Another aspect of LabVIEW that finds its way into other software products is **iconic programming**. As with front panels, the iconic programming systems found in other products are largely add-on shells used to hide some of the details of systems based on conventional programming methodologies. Such products provide a predefined, set number of operations that can be used in iconic form. While generally quite simple to use because of their turnkey nature, these systems are not readily expanded because adding new functions is either impossible or requires a user to revert back to a standard programming language to create new icons. These iconic programming systems address organization of the high-level aspects of a test but do not have graphical constructs for specifying programming operations such as execution order, iteration, or branching. In addition, these systems typically do not support building a module that can be used in iconic form at a higher level. Finally, and perhaps most importantly, LabVIEW is a compiled language, whereas all other iconic packages are interpreted. A hundredfold increase in performance is typically demonstrated.

LabVIEW's iconic programming language is not simply an organizational tool. It is a true programming language complete with multiple data types, programming structures, and a sophisticated compiler. LabVIEW is unique for its hierarchy and expandability. VIs have the same construction at all levels so the creation of a new high-level VI is simply a matter of combining several lower-level VIs and putting a front panel on the new combination. Because LabVIEW's graphical programming system offers the functionality and performance of conventional programming languages, users can implement and add new functions to the system without having to resort to the use of another programming language.

How to Assemble a System

So, you have a job to do, something to automate, and you wonder where to begin. I call this the blank canvas syndrome, where you have an infinite set of possibilities and probably more than one that will do the job. What you need to do is list all the requirements and constraints for your project, discuss the situation with your colleagues, and make some decisions.

Having a list of requirements or objectives is such a fundamental first step, and yet we skip this step more often than not. I like to spend an appropriate amount of time with the project managers, designers, and prospective users to find out what they *really* need. For most projects, you can just scribble down notes, making sure that you completely understand the problem. Then, go back to your office (or garage, or whatever), and try to write a **requirements document**. This may or may not be a formal exercise with strict format specifications, depending on your company's policies. I like to draw pictures of the physical plant, floor plans, and a good overall block diagram of the system, along with some words that describe what the whole thing does. Then, I make a list of the proposed sensors and signals, required performance specifications, and other features. You can never have too much information this early in a project. Hopefully, there is a project manager involved who understands the scope of work. It is vital that your project doesn't fall prey to underestimation of the instrumentation and control efforts. Do you need more help? Get it. Is the schedule realistic? If not, then either the cost, the performance specifications, or the schedule will have to change. Chapter 4, "Building an Application," will lead you through the entire development process.

Use equipment that's familiar

Using hardware and software with which you are familiar gives you a quicker start and shorter learning curve. I hate seeing someone forced to use a Brand X computer when he or she is already an expert with Brand Y because so much time will be spent fiddling with the system instead of getting useful work accomplished. Of course, there are many reasons for choosing a particular computer or I/O system. You must consider the big picture.

The deciding factor on choosing a computer or I/O system is often a matter of complying with standards within your company or work area. If yours is a Sun world, you probably will stay with Sun, unless there is some overriding reason to look elsewhere. If your lab uses a standard such as VXI, stick with it. On the other hand, if nobody is there to force the decision, then you are a kid in a candy store, with many choices to make.

Picking an I/O system

LabVIEW is amenable to most any I/O interface known to the world of instrumentation, so you are generally free to shop around. Figure 1.12 shows the most common interfaces: plug-in data acquisition boards, video frame grabbers, GPIB, VXI, and serial instruments. Using network connections, it is also possible to communicate with remote, intelligent devices or computers, running LabVIEW and other programs, that add another dimension to data acquisition and control. I've found that the biggest determining factors in choosing an I/O system are as follows:

- Previous (positive) experience with the equipment or recommendations from someone you trust.

- Immediate availability of hardware. I'm more likely to use something that is left over from another project or something that I can order and have delivered in short order.

- Suitability for the purpose. It doesn't do much good to have lots of the *wrong* hardware available. Compare specifications and requirements carefully before committing to any hardware solution.

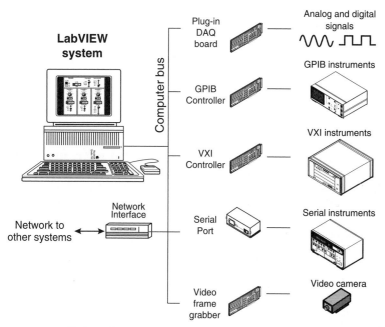

Plug-in
DAQ
board

Analog and digital
signals

**LabVIEW
system**

GPIB instruments

GPIB
Controller

VXI instruments

Computer bus

VXI
Controller

Network
Interface

Serial instruments

Serial
Port

Network to
other systems

Video
frame
grabber

Video camera

Figure 1.12 Choices, choices. Your system will consist of one or more computers running LabVIEW, one or more types of I/O hardware, and probably some network connections.

- Drivers—the low-level interface software for an instrument—are important. If there is a LabVIEW driver available for a given instrument, that will save time and effort because writing a driver is sometimes as complex as writing a major application.

- Reliability and safety. Requirements for very high reliability or personnel safety should strongly influence your choice of hardware (and software).

- Cost per I/O channel.

Plug-in boards.   Plug-in data acquisition boards have made a major impact on the instrumentation world because they turn a general-purpose computer into an instrument that connects directly to signals in the outside world. They are versatile and cost-effective. For instance, the MIO series of boards from National Instruments gives you up to 64 analog inputs, 2 analog outputs, and 8 digital input/output channels. The MIO-16 is, by the way, the most popular multifunction board in the world and is very well supported by LabVIEW. Chapter 7, "Writing a Data Acquisition Program," is devoted to using the LabVIEW data acquisition (DAQ) library, and much of that information applies directly to the MIO-16. With the addition of appropriate signal conditioning and external multiplexers, you can handle hundreds of inputs and outputs while using only one slot in your computer. You can choose among boards that offer maximum sampling rates from 25 kHz to 20 MHz with 8 to 16 bits of resolution. Most support direct memory access (DMA) data transfers to improve performance. Boards with more advanced features are being introduced constantly. A wide range of boards is available for the PC, Macintosh, and Sun. All major buses are supported.

You can use modern programmable instruments to augment the performance of your LabVIEW system. While plug-in boards do accommodate a wide variety of signals, they don't solve every problem. As an example, a digital oscilloscope can acquire very high frequency waveforms (well beyond the capability of any plug-in board) that you can upload, analyze, display, and store. Similarly, the plethora of functions available in the modular VXI (VME Extensions for Instrumentation) format makes it possible to build a custom high-performance test and measurement system with LabVIEW orchestrating the operation. And serial instruments represent the lowest-cost solution to remote-control interfacing.

GPIB, VXI, and serial instruments.   GPIB interfaces are particularly versatile and easy to use, thanks to the thoughtful design of the hardware standards and boards and to the built-in support in the LabVIEW GPIB and VISA (Virtual Instrument Standard Architecture) library. For the Sun, IBM PC, and Macintosh, National Instruments makes plug-in boards that offer high-performance DMA transfers and IEEE-488.2 compliance. You can also use external GPIB interfaces. For instance, on a computer that does not have a free slot for a plug-in interface, you can use the GPIB-SCSI-A box, which plugs into the SCSI port. For a longer reach, consider the GPIB-ENET, a GPIB interface that permits the control of instruments over a TCP/IP Ethernet link. The regular LabVIEW drivers work with both of these special interfaces transparently.

VXI interface boards, using the MXIbus, are available from National Instruments with full LabVIEW driver support at all levels for the Sun, IBM PC, and Macintosh. You can program everything from the lowest register-level operations on up—whatever the job requires. The MXIbus offers very high throughput. You can also control VXI systems with GPIB.

Serial port communications are supported by the serial port functions built into LabVIEW. Keep in mind, however, that serial protocols are so poorly standardized that you generally end up putting more effort into writing serial drivers than you would with GPIB or VXI.

By the way, all of the DAQ, GPIB, and serial functions are portable over all of the platforms, so long as the appropriate interface hardware is installed. It's pretty amazing to write a GPIB driver on a Mac, then e-mail it to a Sun user who proceeds to run it unmodified. Also note that LabVIEW can simultaneously communicate with any mix of I/O hardware, regardless of type, without any serious restrictions.

Special-purpose I/O systems.   For every industry or environment, there are specialized instruments, interface standards, and communications protocols. Regardless of the situation, you should have no fear of using LabVIEW to accommodate those unusual standards. In fact, if you ask around, you will probably find a reasonable combination of hardware and LabVIEW drivers to do the job. Here are a few examples.

In the commercial aircraft industry, modern flight control systems often use the Digital Information Transfer System (DITS), a specialized local area network (LAN) that uses the ARINC protocol. Another LAN, used mostly on military aircraft, is MIL-STD-1553A/B. If you wanted to test something that was connected to one of these systems, you would find that several manufacturers make VXI modules that transmit or receive data using the appropriate protocols. The modules plug into a standard VXI mainframe and connect to the LAN using the required connectors. On-board intelligence handles all the low-level timing and protocol generation, so your program can easily exchange messages with other nodes on the network. LabVIEW drivers are available for several of these modules.

Biomedical applications have some different requirements. Notably, it is very dangerous to connect anything electrical to a living specimen, because leakage currents can be lethal. For this reason, U.S. and international laws state that you may only use hardware designated for the application when connecting to human subjects (and it's right to be careful with our other animal friends, as well!). One company that makes a line of affordable analog interface equipment for life science research is Biopac Systems. Its data acquisition and stimulus-response units are modular, multichannel devices with a high-speed serial interface for use with PCs and Macintoshes. Dedicated software is provided, and LabVIEW drivers are available as well.

Industrial process control applications call for robust and reliable low-speed analog and digital I/O interfaces and controllers, often in the form of programmable logic controllers (PLCs). The physical plant is usually spread out over a large area and is filled with equipment that induces noise in analog signals. For this reason, a LAN or other communications scheme is desirable. PLCs use proprietary serial protocols, many of which are supported by LabVIEW drivers available from third-party developers. Another type of I/O hardware in wide use is made by Opto-22. This is a low-cost, modular interface that supports a wide range of analog and digital input and output signal types, from millivolt inputs to 220 VAC outputs. A local *brain board* scans the I/O modules and communicates with the remote host computer over a serial line. LabVIEW drivers are available for Opto-22 Optomux protocol, as well (I know—I wrote the package).

Sometimes you need to go mobile with your measurements. Laptop PCs and Macintosh PowerBooks, when combined with battery-operated I/O hardware, make LabVIEW a mobile solution. The aforementioned Biopac equipment has a battery-power option to support its MP100-series modules in the field. Dana Redington, a LabVIEW consultant with Redwolf Enterprises, took such a system to India to study the effects of meditation on the nervous systems of highly trained yoga masters. He collected electrocardiogram, skin temperature, respiration, and hand sweating data while the subjects underwent their behavioral maneuvers. I suspect that's about as far afield as LabVIEW can get without leaving the Earth, as LabVIEW did on the space shuttle *Columbia* in 1993. You can also build your own battery power source for some kinds of I/O hardware that may not already offer the option. I did it with Opto-22, by connecting a gel-cell battery to a DC-to-DC converter that supplied the required voltages. With LabVIEW running on a PowerBook, we were able to record electrochemical measurements while sitting in a small boat in the Pacific Ocean.

Limitations to consider.   It's important that you learn the limitations of a LabVIEW-based system and its associated hardware. Throughout this book you will find discussions of performance issues. But in the final analysis, there are few hard limits that will absolutely rule out a particular system configuration. I find it wise to obtain benchmarks, recommendations, and examples from others who have tackled similar projects. Learn from other people's experiences and mistakes. See the section entitled "Sources for Help and Answers," later in this chapter, for tips on making contact with the outside world.

Perhaps the biggest concern with the general-purpose platforms that LabVIEW runs on is its real-time response limitations. Realize that Windows, UNIX, and the Macintosh operating system are quite complex and are not really optimized for real-time applications. By the way, we need to set some guidelines for *real time* here and now. The precise definition of real time depends on your application's temporal response. This includes both the cycle time or sampling rate and the computer system's *latency*—the time it takes to respond to an external occurrence. Real-time control of your home heating system requires a response time of about one minute. High-pressure regulators often need to respond in something less than one second. Real-time flight controls in an F-16 fighter are sampled at 45 Hz. And real-time sequencers in an inertial confinement fusion experiment at Lawrence Livermore National Laboratory have to respond in something under a nanosecond. Now, that's quite a range. Which *real time* applies to your situation, and which requirements do you think that LabVIEW has a chance of meeting?

With the software timing functions available in LabVIEW, I generally draw the line at about 0.1 s. Faster than that, you will generally see excessive timing uncertainty or *jitter*. At 1-s cycle rates, you will rarely encounter any significant problems. However, there are other activities that take place on your computer that can upset even a 1-s operation:

- Drawing graphical items on the screen cannot be interrupted (*preempted,* in modern computer lingo). Drawing a graph with thousands of data points can take quite a long time, during which your LabVIEW program is unable to do anything else.

- LabVIEW makes intensive use of *memory management* to allocate space for data. If you are handling large arrays or strings, memory management operations can suddenly induce large nonpreemptable delays.

- Virtual memory augments physical RAM by swapping segments of memory to and from the hard disk as needed. This swapping operation adds unpredictable delays and should generally be avoided by installing more RAM for time-critical applications.

- All I/O devices—including plug-in DAQ boards, GPIB interfaces, serial devices, and network connections—add overhead to each operation. Do not expect a physical I/O device to return data instantaneously.

- Running other applications in the background reduces CPU availability and may add even more unpredictable delays.

- On a Macintosh, inserting a floppy disk will noticeably interrupt the system.

- Under Windows and on the Macintosh, mouse activity, especially holding the mouse button down while the cursor is in a scroll bar, effectively freezes the machine.

- On a Sun SPARCstation, it has been noted that incoming mail stops everything for a moment.

These and other unpredictable effects can be obtrusive in many real-time systems and you must learn how to deal with them.

One thing you can do is network several LabVIEW systems to divide the workload between real-time activity and user interface activity. With the networking VIs in LabVIEW, you can have a front-end machine that handles the I/O hardware, collects and preprocesses raw data, and does any real-time control. You might not even have a keyboard, mouse, or monitor connected. Another machine can periodically communicate with the real-time machine to upload and download information. Then the operator is free to use this man-machine interface (MMI) computer without fear of interrupting a time-critical task.

Using an external "smart" controller is the best choice when fast, repeatable, real-time response is important. PLCs, discussed in Chap. 8, "Process Control Applications," are widely used for industrial process control because they are fast, reliable, and easy to use. With a PLC and LabVIEW as the man-machine interface, you can build an excellent control system with true millisecond response. Similarly, packaged data acquisition units such as the Hewlett-Packard HP3852A make it possible to gather data at high speeds (perhaps in a remote or hazardous location), reduce the data, and transmit it to the LabVIEW host for display. Plug-in digital signal processing (DSP) boards and low-cost single-board computers can be programmed to do high-speed control algorithms without interruption from the host computer. Almost any device can be integrated nicely into your overall strategy to improve real-time performance. Your job is to choose the *right* devices.

Picking a computer

At the time of this writing, LabVIEW runs on the following computer systems:

- Macintosh and Power Macintosh running System 7
- IBM PC compatibles running Windows 3.1, Windows 95, or Windows NT
- Sun SPARCstations running Solaris 1.1 or 2.3 with X Windows
- Hewlett-Packard series 700 workstations running HP-UX 9.0.3

If you're expecting me to recommend particular models, you're out of luck. New versions of CPUs and operating systems come out so quickly these days that almost anything I say here is born obsolete. Therefore, I'll just give you some general guidance and a few benchmarks where available.

System configurations. LabVIEW is graphics-intensive. For those of you who grew up with simple command-line operating systems, the burden of all those graphics on the CPU seems immense. Fortunately, the latest generation of computers rise to the task without undue expense. For most applications, I recommend the fastest, most completely outfitted system that you can afford. Though you might get by with less, I consider a minimal LabVIEW machine to look like this:

- *Macintosh:* 68040—33 MHz with FPU, 16 MB RAM, 500-MB hard disk, CD-ROM, 13-inch color monitor
- *PC with Windows 3.1 or 95:* 80486DX2—66 MHz, 16 MB RAM, 500-MB hard disk, SVGA monitor, CD-ROM, 3.5-inch floppy disk
- *Sun:* SPARCstation 2 with 32 MB of main memory, 32 MB of disk swap space, 200 MB free disk space, and CD-ROM

Serious LabVIEW applications demand serious hardware. If you expect to handle large data sets (megasamples of data), do image processing, or display data at high speeds, then a faster system is mandatory. Developing a large LabVIEW application is faster and more enjoyable when the system responds quickly, so there is a productivity factor here, as well: buying a more expensive system pays off in the long run. A high-performance system would include the fastest available CPU, at least 32 MB of RAM, and a 19-inch color monitor with a video accelerator.

I'm also going to recommend that you consider moving to the newer operating systems, especially on the PC. Politely stated, Windows 3.1 is one enormous compromise, especially for a 32-bit application like LabVIEW. The 32-to-16 bit conversion process (called *thunking*) leads to numerous instabilities which appear in the form of *general protection faults* (GPFs) and much rebooting. Windows 95 and especially NT have proven more reliable and easier to maintain. Windows NT is an extremely reliable LabVIEW platform, and version 4 features the eminently usable Windows 95 shell, or user interface. The only disadvantage of NT may be a (temporary) shortage of drivers, since that platform is somewhat more complex when it comes to driver development. Plug-and-play capability is another feature that should not be overlooked—it saves much setup time, but requires new machines and new operating systems. Meanwhile, the Mac remains the most integrated and easy-to-maintain platform available, which partially explains its continuing popularity.

Memory and disk capacity. Your LabVIEW system will need plenty of memory. While UNIX workstations are almost always configured with large memories, you will have to upgrade your Macintosh or PC to make it really useful. The recommended 8 MB of RAM is really a bare minimum; 16 MB is much more practical, and you can *never* have too much. Applications which demand very large amounts of memory include image processing, multidimensional data visualization (graphing), and some waveform acquisition situations. It's fairly hard to calculate the exact amount of memory you will need because of the way that LabVIEW allocates data structures and the ever increasing complexity of your application (feature creep) as it develops. For signals like waveforms, you can count on using at least 4 bytes per sample and sometimes as many as 16 depending on the processing that you do. Think about this: one million data points may require 16 million bytes of memory! Monochrome images, which are generally 1 byte per pixel, actually end up consuming at least twice that much when displayed and several times more if they are converted to other data types for computations. *Virtual memory,* where the disk drive augments physical RAM memory, is available on all of LabVIEW's platforms but it won't solve all of your problems. Real-time performance of virtual memory is poor, and large, contiguous data structures typically cannot be broken up for swapping out to disk.

Disk capacity is also important. LabVIEW itself requires between 20 and 80 MB of disk space (64 MB on the Sun and HP), depending upon which features you choose to install, and the applications you write will occupy even more. Acquired data is often the determining factor when choosing the capacity of your disk drive. Capacity is fairly easy to calculate, assuming that you know what kind of data you are saving and how many samples are to be stored. For instance, ordinary single-precision floating point numbers, when stored in binary format, require 4 bytes per sample. If those numbers are converted to text format, they may require as many as 12 bytes per sample—a good reason for saving data in binary format. Most images occupy 1 byte per pixel, assuming 256 gray levels or colors. Thus, a typical 640 by 480 pixel image requires 307K of disk space. If you expect to store lots of data, plan to buy high-capacity removable media, such as magneto-optical disks. Most facilities that I've seen use them.

LabVIEW uses lots of scratch files and makes great demands on the file system when editing VIs, especially when they are located in VI libraries (files with a *.11b* extension). Greatly improved performance can be obtained by configuring a RAM disk for these scratch files. When you run LabVIEW, open the Preferences, select the Paths option, and set the Temporary Directory to the RAM disk. To set up a RAM disk on the Macintosh, use the *Memory* control panel or install a third-party RAM disk utility such as Maxima. On the PC, from the MS-DOS command prompt, enter the command Help ramdisk.sys for information on how you can create a ramdisk. Ramdisk.sys is a device driver that must be loaded with a device or devicehigh command in your Config.sys file. Make your RAM disk as large as possible—2 MB is the absolute minimum.

Expansion slots (and bus problems).   One of the best ways to add I/O interface capability to your computer is to install a plug-in board. GPIB interfaces, multifunction analog and digital I/O interfaces, and DSP accelerators are in widespread use on Macs and PCs. By planning ahead, you can determine how many and what type of expansion slots you might need. I've also included some of the dirty laundry for each platform, because the same questions and problems keep rearing their heads.

Macintosh. A typical configuration on a Macintosh includes an MIO-series multifunction board and a GPIB board. For the NuBus, get a GPIB board with DMA support such as the NB-GPIB/TNT (all boards mentioned here are from National Instruments). For newer Macs with the Peripheral Component Interconnect (PCI) bus, the PCI-GPIB does the job. This setup will support the world of GPIB instruments and provide some analog and digital I/O connections as well. Many of the new Macs include video and networking support, so these may be the only two boards you need to install. I've always considered a 3-slot Mac to be the minimum for serious LabVIEW systems, and the big 5- or 6-slot machines desirable when you are unsure what the future may hold.

The first PowerMacs, such as the 6100, 7100, and 8100, still used the NuBus, whereas all subsequent PowerMacs use PCI. There is a problem with those early models: Apple built a few DMA bugs into the bus interface. National Instruments discovered said bugs and responded by offering updated plug-in boards. If you want to use one of these problematic machines with an older board, check with National Instruments. A similar problem appeared on the later PCI PowerMacs, again regarding DMA, but thankfully it has been solved in the driver software.

National Instruments remains firmly committed to the Macintosh. Trust me on this one. It does much of its development on the Mac and works closely with Apple on technical issues. However, the vast Windows market clearly defines the development priority. Therefore, we Macintosh users usually have to wait awhile for the latest hardware and software products.

Windows. In the PC world, most desktop machines come with many expansion slots, though several of those slots may be consumed by disk, video, sound, serial, printer, and network interfaces. Newer PCs build in most of this functionality, which opens up some slots for data acquisition boards, GPIB interface boards, or whatever. Just beware of "pizza-box" configurations with few slots. The *type* of bus your PC has can make a big difference in performance and availability of plug-in boards. By far, the most common bus is the PC/AT, or Industry Standard Architecture (ISA) bus. Sadly, it offers about the lowest performance available, being only 16 bits wide and operating no faster than 8 MHz. (Realistically, this turns out to be a fairly minor limitation; the speed of the CPU when number crunching is more likely to limit your system's overall performance.) Much better is the Extended ISA (EISA) bus, which offers a 32-bit data path and much higher transfer rates. The Microchannel bus, which is also 16 bits, falls somewhere in between. The newer PCI bus offers the very best performance. Look carefully in the catalogs to determine which bus structure best fits your application. One guide that may help is National Instruments Application Note AN011, *DMA Fundamentals on Various PC Platforms.*

Speaking of DMA, a serious limitation of the ISA bus is that it only provides 24 address lines, and consequently, the bus is incapable of addressing more than 16 MB. If your application attempts to use a DMA buffer that is loaded at a higher address, serious trouble can result. Such problems may appear when you configure buffered data acquisition with a plug-in board. Please note that this is not a problem if you do not have more than 16 MB of memory installed. Also note that there is nothing you can do to force the NI-DAQ driver to locate the DMA buffer within the lower 16-MB zone. One solution is to avoid buffered I/O operations. A better solution is to use a computer with an EISA or PCI backplane and the appropriate boards.

Sun.   For GPIB on the Sun SPARCstation, you can use an SBus plug-in board (GPIB-SPRC-B), a TCP/IP Ethernet interface (GPIB/ENET/Sun), or a SCSI port GPIB adapter (GPIB-SPRC-S). National Instruments also offers data acquisition boards for the SBus.

HP series 700 workstations have an EISA bus, for which you can use a GPIB-HP700-EISA board. There are currently no compatible DAQ boards.

Networking.   In this well-connected era, no computer should be an island. With network hardware and software, most computers today can share printers, access file servers, and exchange electronic mail. With a LabVIEW system, this opens the possibility of sharing data between two or more computers. By using the TCP/IP networking protocol VIs in LabVIEW and the **Internet Toolkit**, you can exchange data with other computers over wide areas and even those not necessarily running LabVIEW. Having access to file servers is a big plus because you can easily archive data remotely. You can even talk to a GPIB instrument out on Ethernet by using an interface such as the GPIB-ENET. Beware, though, of real-time data logging via Ethernet and similar networks. They are notorious for adding unpredictable delays that are unacceptable in real-time applications.

All computers of recent vintage generally have built-in networking support, or you can add it by plugging in an interface board and installing some software. Ethernet connections are probably the most versatile because nearly all computers can access Ethernet and it offers reasonable performance. On all platforms, you can use LabVIEW's built-in TCP/IP functions to establish connections and transfer data. LabVIEW also has drivers for higher-level protocols that are useful for controlling other programs and/or transferring data. LabVIEW on the Macintosh supports AppleEvents. Under Windows, LabVIEW has Dynamic Data Exchange (DDE) which may be extended transnetwork by using NetDDE and OLE Automation capability. So far, LabVIEW for the Sun and HP only supports TCP/IP.

Macintosh networking is about as painless as it gets. TCP/IP is included with System 7.5 and is available as a free Control Panel for earlier versions. Just throw it at your System Folder, reboot, and you're on the air. Windows 3.1 allows you to add TCP/IP by installing a compatible Windows Socket TCP/IP network driver, such as Trumpet WinSock, but be prepared for the usual installation adventures and incompatibilities. Windows 95 and NT include TCP/IP and are much easier to configure for networking. Sun and HP workstations are *built* around TCP/IP, so that's a no-brainer. What is important is to decide what your goals are, seek out some of the third-party LabVIEW networking support packages, and work with a network manager. These things get complicated in a hurry!

Other software to consider

In addition to LabVIEW and all the usual applications you probably have on your computer, here are a few items worth considering.

Compiler for CINs. Some advanced LabVIEW users eventually want to write Code Interface Nodes (CINs). CINs allow you to call external code from a LabVIEW diagram with relative ease. You generally use them to access system functions, special hardware, or advanced analysis routines. CINs must be written in C, although in principle any compiler that can conform to a C calling interface could work. Be warned that CINs are not for the casual user; you must be a moderately skilled C programmer. Be sure to study the *LabVIEW Code Interface Node* manual very carefully. The preferred compilers are as follows:

- *Macintosh.* Think C or C++ (Symantec Corporation) and CodeWarrior (MetroWerks).

- *Windows 3.1.* Watcom C (Watcom Corporation), which properly handles the conversion, known as *thunking,* between the 32-bit LabVIEW world and the 16-bit DOS world lurking behind Windows.

- *Windows 95 and NT.* Visual C++ is the official compiler. The CIN is actually a DLL that is copied to a temporary directory when loaded. Other compilers should work, too, but they must be able to link with labview.lib or lvsb.lib and produce a DLL without mangled function names.

- *Sun Solaris.*   The unbundled C compiler (acc) is the official compiler and gcc usually works.
- *HP.*   The HP-UX C/ANSI C compiler.

Drawing applications.   Sometimes you will want to add custom graphics to your LabVIEW panels. This requires the use of a graphics application, which may be as simple as a shareware paint or draw application or as complex as a professional CAD package. On the Mac, you can import almost anything via the clipboard and paste it on the front panel or into custom controls. LabVIEW understands bitmaps as well as PICT format. On the PC, bitmaps and Enhanced Metafiles (not unlike PICT on the Mac) are acceptable. For the UNIX machines, the .xwd (X Window Dump) format is the only supported format.

Analysis and graphing applications.   There are many, many applications available for data analysis, graphing, and reporting, assuming that you don't do these operations in LabVIEW. Such applications as Igor and the Spyglass products (Mac only), PVWave, IDL, SPlus, HI-Q, Matlab, and Mathematica (all platforms) are extremely powerful and produce publication-quality graphs. Special LabVIEW drivers are available for Hi-Q, Igor, Matlab, and Mathematica that support each application's proprietary file formats and/or allow the application to be connected to LabVIEW. Sometimes, all you need is an ordinary spreadsheet, and that's fine. LabVIEW is perfectly happy to exchange data with other applications in delimited text format, which is typical for spreadsheets.

Networking applications and services.   You will probably get yourself connected to the Internet sooner or later—something that is highly advisable these days, considering the availability of additional Lab-VIEW help and other resources on the Net. As a minimum, subscribe to an Internet service provider or online service. Get yourself an e-mail address, a World Wide Web browser such as Netscape Navigator, and perhaps a file transfer protocol (FTP) application for downloading files (most Web browsers include FTP capability). I'm not recommending that you get *addicted* to all this Internet stuff, just have it available as a useful resource. Throughout this book, I'll list specific e-mail, FTP, and WWW addresses where you can obtain information and VIs.

Sources for Help and Answers

LabVIEW is a complex product and nobody expects you to puzzle through everything on your own. Lots of people come to me with questions about getting started with and using LabVIEW, so here are some of my shrink-wrapped answers.

Get trained

The first thing I suggest is that you take the courses provided by National Instruments. The introductory course is three days well-spent. You learn how to navigate LabVIEW and use the tools, how to build simple applications and drivers, and how to debug and document your work. Many users (including me) took this course with essentially no prior knowledge of LabVIEW, or even the particular computer it runs on, and immediately set to work on an actual application. In fact, it's important that your first application start soon after the course to reinforce what you learn. You can also take the advanced courses, but I usually recommend that you do so only after using LabVIEW for a while—maybe a couple of months or so. National Instruments also sells the workbooks that go with its classes, and there is a low-cost Lab-VIEW video that covers the basics. Finally, there is computer-based training available: the **LabVIEW Basics-Interactive CD-ROM**. These might be options if you can't make it to a class. Look in the back of the National Instruments catalog for information on these and other training aids. Also, those of you who work for larger companies may even have in-house training facilities or consultants who can help you get started.

This book is not intended as a tutorial, but there are some other publications targeted to the beginner:

- The *LabVIEW Tutorial* manual, included with every new copy of LabVIEW, is an excellent starting-out guide that walks you through the basics of creating VIs.

- *LabVIEW for Everyone* by Lisa Wells and Jeff Travis (1996) is an excellent book for beginners. It begins by assuming you know nothing about LabVIEW and leads you step-by-step through the learning process. It encompasses basic through advanced programming techniques and uses a series of hands-on examples to reinforce the learning process. Includes demonstration versions of LabVIEW (all platforms) plus example code on a CD-ROM.

- The *LabVIEW Student Edition* (1995) is a simplified version of Lab-VIEW primarily intended for use by students at the high school and college level. This low-cost package includes a single manual that serves as a tutorial and as a user's guide. It's an inexpensive way to get your feet wet, but probably not something you'd want to use for major projects. Includes student versions of LabVIEW on diskettes (Mac or Windows versions available).

- *LabTutor* by Dr. John Eaton of Stanford University (1996), teaches concepts and techniques of computer-based data acquisition, laboratory system control, and data analysis. LabTutor includes a Hyper-Card-based textbook (hardcopy plus software that runs on Windows or Macintosh), extensive programming examples, and practice exercises developed in LabVIEW. It was designed for use in college-level courseware or as a self-paced tutorial.

Use the example VIs

LabVIEW comes with many, many example VIs. National Instruments also has additional examples, utilities, and libraries available via mail or electronic communications (see the "Get It on the Net" section, next). It is important for you to spend time browsing the examples because they demonstrate so many common programming techniques. Some of the examples are real, working systems. For instance, in the data acquisition examples you will find programs that use National Instruments' plug-in boards to acquire data at high speeds, store it on disk, and read it for display. All of this is free, and you are free to copy these programs and modify them for your own applications.

Major example topics include:

Analysis.   DSP, statistics, signal generation, measurements

Applications.   ATE, simple data acquisition, and control techniques

Communications.   Networking and interapplication communication

CIN.   Basics of Code Interface Nodes

Data acquisition (DAQ).   Analog and digital I/O and counter/timer examples

Files.   Basic text and binary file I/O, data logging, spreadsheet formats

General.   Tips, programming structures, graphs, attributes, VI setup options, and so forth

GPIB.   Using GPIB instruments; basic drivers

Networking.   TCP/IP, DDE, OLE, AppleEvents

Serial.   Communicating via the serial port

In the Examples directory, you will find a VI called **Readme**. Run it, and you will see that it is an efficient browser for all the examples.

When all else fails, read the directions

Better yet, read the directions *first*. Do you have any idea how many phone calls to software companies are simple-minded questions that are easily solved by perusing the index of the user manual? The Lab-VIEW manuals are written by the developers and some major in-house users at National Instruments, then edited by a Tech Pubs team. They really know what they're talking about, the writing is clear, and the indexes have improved dramatically over the years. I've found the user manual to be one of the keys to becoming a proficient LabVIEW user because it contains all the details you could ever want to know. An effective way to learn something is to read, practice, then read again. Throw in some formal training, and you too can become a high-paid consultant.

In addition to the user manual, there are, of course, all the specialty manuals that come with LabVIEW—the communications VI reference manual, the data acquisition VI reference manual, and so forth. These are truly indispensable because they help to explain the *big picture*. For instance, what is the difference between a datalog file and a byte stream file? You can find that in the function reference manual under file I/O functions. And the data acquisition library is sufficiently complex that you need to read the background information in the first few chapters before doing anything serious.

 **platform\ appnotes**

A great deal of supplementary information is available (free!) from National Instruments in the form of application notes and technical notes. Application notes describe major topics pertaining to LabVIEW and the related use of various National Instruments products. Some of my favorites are Application Note 006, *Developing a LabVIEW Instrument Driver,* and Application Note 043, *Measuring Temperature with Thermocouples.* Technical notes are more limited in scope and are intended to explain subtle details of LabVIEW operation. They go out of date quickly because every time there is a new version of the program, the details change. Technical notes are of particular interest to advanced users who want to make fullest use of LabVIEW capabilities. All of the application notes and technical notes can be obtained by contacting National Instruments via its Internet site or bulletin board and also on its **Instrupedia** CD-ROM (available free). I've included all of the LabVIEW, DAQ, GPIB, and VXI-related notes on this book's CD-ROM, as well.

Get it on the Net

Speaking of bulletin boards, if you have a modem, you can call up the National Instruments user bulletin board at any time to download a variety of files, from instrument drivers to example programs. You may also upload your own files to the bulletin board system (BBS) so that the applications engineers can help solve your problems quickly and efficiently.

Using the National Instruments BBS.   You will need a modem, preferably a fast one if you plan to transfer many VIs, and you will need a communications program that supports xmodem, ymodem, or zmodem. The telephone number is (512) 794-5422. Communications settings are: 8 data bits, 1 stop bit, no parity, and any speed up to 14,400 baud. You will find information on GPIB and DAQ hardware products, LabVIEW (all platforms), LabWindows, and other products in various directories. Contact National Instruments for complete instructions. Those of you who are familiar with bulletin board operations can probably figure it out after a brief hacking session.

FTP file servers for LabVIEW users.   In addition to the dial-in bulletin board, those of you who have access to the Internet with an application that supports **File Transfer Protocol (FTP)** can access LabVIEW-related servers. National Instruments has one, with the Internet alias ftp.natinst.com. On it you will find much of the same information that is available on the regular bulletin board. The advantage, of course, is that FTP transfers are generally faster—effectively 50K baud or greater—depending on the physical connection that you have and the amount of traffic on the network. You log in with user name *anonymous* and enter your Internet address for the password.

Another server is ftp.pica.army.mil which is sponsored by the U.S. Army's Picatinny Arsenal and is used in conjunction with the info-labview mailgroup which is described in a following section. The regular anonymous login applies. Hundreds of LabVIEW users regularly access this server and most of the contributions are written by the users. Utility VIs, small applications, relevant documents, and demo versions of commercial LabVIEW add-on packages are available on this server.

LabVIEW on the Web

Since the last edition of this book, the World Wide Web has exploded in popularity, and LabVIEW has not been left out in the cold. Though the list is constantly expanding, I can at least give you a few primary sites that serve as jump-off points to other LabVIEW-related resources.

- *http://www.viewpointusa.com* is the home page for Viewpoint Software Solutions, which maintains a page with links to many other LabVIEW-related sites. Start here.

- *http://www.natinst.com* is the home page for National Instruments (Fig. 1.13). You can obtain information on products and support, download files from the the FTP site, and more.

- *http://k-whiner.pica.army.mil/info-labview* is associated with the info-labview mailgroup (see next section) and is another good

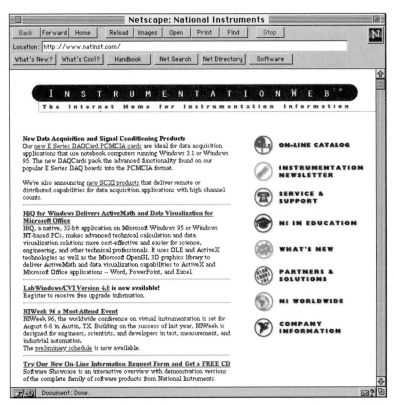

Figure 1.13 The National Instruments home page is a source of information on LabVIEW, hardware, and the world of computer-based instrumentation.

jumping-off point to other LabVIEW sites. Also links to the info-labview FTP site.

Also located on the National Instruments Web site is its searchable **KnowledgeBase** containing the latest support information from its applications engineering department. This KnowledgeBase is updated daily with an average of 40 new documents added every week. This makes the KnowledgeBase a dynamic repository reflecting the current issues brought up by LabVIEW users. It has a nice search engine that makes it easy to find answers to common problems, recently reported bugs, and installation difficulties.

The Internet mailgroup

Most of you probably have electronic mail (e-mail) access through one method or another. If your mail service, like most, is linked to the Internet, then you can join in the fun on the LabVIEW mailgroup. Mail-groups use ordinary e-mail to automatically distribute contributed messages to all subscribers. You send a message, and everyone on the list (now over 2000 users worldwide) will see it and have a chance to respond. Several application engineers and developers at National Instruments monitor the traffic and sometimes join in the free-for-all. There are all kinds of requests posted. Many messages are from users in search of special instrument drivers; there are lots of people who have written incomplete drivers that aren't necessarily suited to wide-spread distribution, but are useful just the same. Another popular area is application-specific questions. For instance, if you are planning to write a LabVIEW program to do some specialized measurements or analysis, just post a message describing your problem, and see who is doing similar work. There is a great deal of information sharing going on in the mailgroup. I've made many friends in the mailgroup, some of whom contributed to this book. The mailgroup is also a forum for, "Gee, I wish LabVIEW could do so-and-so." Many of these suggestions are actually incorporated into LabVIEW after a public discussion. And I've seen some rather lively discussions ensue when someone's hot-button gets pressed.

To join, send a message to info-labview-request@pica.army.mil and tell the list maintainer (Tom Corradeschi) that you would like to sign up. If you have a preferred e-mail address, give that to him; otherwise, he'll use the return path from your message. To post a message for all to see, send it to info-labview@pica.army.mil. Remember to be consid-erate to others. Don't send a message intended for a particular person to the whole group; use that person's e-mail address, not info-labview's. For the same reason, be careful when using the *reply* command in your e-mail program because that routes your reply back through the whole system. Please be brief and remember to proofread your text! Also, remember that others can't see your facial expressions or hear your tone of voice. The best advice I've heard is, what you type into an e-mail message should be suitable for viewing by your mother. For more insight on this subject, read "E-mail Etiquette" by Guy Kawasaki in the November 1991 issue of *MacUser*.

E-mail help from National Instruments

You can submit questions regarding LabVIEW directly to National Instruments via e-mail. Always include a detailed description of the problem and what seems to cause it (not just, "My computer keeps crashing!"), a list of the installed software versions including Lab-VIEW, the operating system and any other related software, and a description of your hardware configuration. Include your return e-mail address and phone number. Bundle it all up and send it to lv.support

@natinst.com. If you have questions related directly to data acquisition hardware or the NI-DAQ drivers, e-mail daq.support@natinst.com. For GPIB hardware and NI-GPIB driver problems, e-mail gpib.support @natinst.com. In my experience, answers come back in a matter of hours.

Frequently asked questions (FAQ) document

The concept of a FAQs (*Frequently Asked Questions*) document originated with online groups that cooperatively compiled the most common questions and answers into an indexed text document. In this case, National Instruments started one, but later decided that its Web-based **KnowledgeBase**, searchable from its Web site, www.natinst. com, was more effective. It includes the kind of information you might expect in a FAQs document, plus details regarding obscure **bugs** and system incompatibilities.

LabVIEW Technical Resource (LTR)

LabVIEW Technical Resource is a quarterly newsletter that is a gold mine of information for LabVIEW system developers. It was created by Lynda Gruggett and Jeff Parker who were both on the original LabVIEW development team and now run their own consulting businesses. Feature articles in each issue explain LabVIEW programming methodology, tips and techniques, and include in-depth technical case studies of user applications. Each issue also includes a diskette with the latest nifty example VIs. In the future, they're likely to come up with even more interesting tidbits to accompany the newsletter. Like this book, it's full of practical hands-on information, and I highly recommend that you subscribe if you can. It is published by LTR Publishing and currently costs $95 per year. See App. B, "Sources," for ordering information.

User groups and the VI UserNet

There is no substitute for direct human contact in any endeavor. Ever take any music lessons? You learn more in the first hour with a teacher than you will in two months of fooling around on your own. LabVIEW is the same way. Learning this complex, visual language is much easier with live teachers and demonstrations. That's why I recommend taking the LabVIEW class. But you can also benefit from working with other users at all experience levels.

Because LabVIEW is so popular, National Instruments has helped to form user groups all over the world. In the San Francisco area, for instance, we have two user groups that meet every two months. The meetings are based on user presentations, which are most enlightening. It's fun to see how others solve their automation problems and to compare their techniques with your own. At most meetings, there is also a presentation by a National Instruments representative, showing LabVIEW techniques and applications or new products. It's also a good place to meet other users with common interests. (Actually, I just go because there's usually free food.) And remember that user group meetings of a sort can take place in your area, your plant, and even in your office on a smaller scale. All you need is two or more people with a common interest and good things will surely happen. Show one another what you're working on and ask questions. Learn not to be afraid to show your work and accept positive criticism. Sharing and synergy are two of the most valuable assets that any project can have.

As of 1996, the user groups are coordinated. The **VI UserNet** is organized by National Instruments and consists of registered user groups worldwide and a support program that provides information and assistance to those groups and their members. You can be a part of the VI UserNet simply by attending ongoing user group meetings in your area or by registering over the Internet at www.natinst.com/viusernet. Once you register, you will automatically be notified of any upcoming meetings in your area. If you are interested in organizing and running user group meetings in your company, area, or university, you can join the VI UserNet as a *VIexpert*. Becoming a VIexpert in the program means that you receive periodic mailings with ready-to-go presentation materials in the form of slides, notes on each slide, and demonstration programs and instructions, if applicable. As a VIexpert, you will receive assistance from your sponsor, usually the local sales representative, as well as the VI UserNet program itself. If you wish to become a VIexpert, you can register online from the Web page at www.natinst.com/viusernet.

The alliance program: consultants

If you get involved with an application where you think you may need outside help, call National Instruments and ask for National Instruments *Solutions*, a guide to third-party products and consultants. This guide, which is updated periodically, contains information about developers whose products are based on National Instruments products (both hardware and software), as well as consultants who recommend National Instruments products. In it you will find descriptions of many useful products, some of which are mentioned in this book. It's worth reading through the guide because you may discover that someone has already written a package that solves a major part of your current problem. Consultants (like me) are also listed with descriptions of their areas of expertise. We can help with everything from writing drivers, to system configuration, to the production of complete turnkey systems.

If you are an experienced LabVIEW user or developer who has a product or service that you would like to offer to the rest of the world, call National Instruments and talk to the Alliance Program manager for more information.

Educational applications

For those of you in the realm of education, National Instruments has a literature kit available entitled *National Instruments in Education,* an informative resource for professors and researchers. It gives lists of contact names, article reprints, data sheets, and other related information. Another publication is the *National Instruments in Academia* directory, which is similar to the *Solutions* guide, but lists hundreds of academic users of LabVIEW and other National Instruments products. You might also look into the *LabVIEW Student Edition* (Wells 1995), a low-cost alternative to the full, professional development system. For about $65, registered students and staff can obtain a Macintosh or Windows version of LabVIEW with plenty of capability; it doesn't even require a floating point unit (FPU), so you can run it on low-cost computers.

(800) IEEE 488

For information or assistance with any National Instruments product, including LabVIEW, call **(800) 433-3488** or **(512) 794-0100**. It wrote the program and it designed the interface hardware, so by golly it had better have all the answers. Please use this as a last resort for simple programming problems because even though it has an army of people answering the phones, they are usually swamped. Also remember to find out who the field engineer in your area is; he or she can answer lots of questions regarding system configurations, pricing, delivery, local user groups, and so forth.

Compared with other, simpler, data acquisition programs, LabVIEW may take somewhat longer to learn. But consider this quote from Thijs Bolhuis, a research engineer on the faculty of the University of Twente in the Netherlands: "So it's more like comparing a car with a Boeing 757. It's easy to learn driving a car, but flying it is still impossible."

Bibliography

Eaton, John, and Laura Eaton, *LabTutor,* Oxford University Press, 1996. (ISBN 0-19-509162-0.)

Wells, Lisa K. *LabVIEW Student Edition,* Prentice-Hall, Englewood Cliffs, New Jersey, 1995. (ISBN 0-13-210683-3. Call Prentice-Hall at (800) 947-7700 or (201) 767-4990.)

Wells, Lisa K., and J. Travis, *LabVIEW for Everyone,* Prentice-Hall, Englewood Cliffs, New Jersey, 1996. (ISBN 0-13-268194-3. Call Prentice-Hall at (800) 947-7700 or (201) 767-4990.)

2

Inputs and Outputs

To automate your lab, one of the first things you will have to tackle is **data acquisition**—the process of making measurements of physical phenomena and storing them in some coherent fashion. It's a vast technical field with thousands of practitioners, most of whom are hackers like us. How did I learn about data acquisition? By *doing it,* plain and simple. Having a formal background in engineering or some kind of science is awfully helpful, but schools rarely teach the practical aspects of sensors and signals and so on. I think that it's most important that you get the big picture—learn the pitfalls and common solutions to data acquisition problems—and then try to see where your situation fits into the Grand Scheme.

This chapter should be of some help because the information presented here is hard-won, practical advice, for the most part. The most unusual feature of this chapter is that it contains no LabVIEW programming information. There is much more to a LabVIEW system than LabVIEW programming! If you plan to write applications that support any kind of input/output (I/O) interface hardware, read on.

Origins of Signals

Data acquisition deals with the elements shown in Fig. 2.1. The physical phenomenon may be electrical, optical, mechanical, or something else that you need to measure. The sensor changes that phenomenon into a signal that is easier to transmit, record, and analyze—usually a voltage or current. Signal conditioning amplifies and filters the raw signal to prepare it for analog to digital (ADC) conversion, which transforms the signal into a digital pattern suitable for use by your computer.

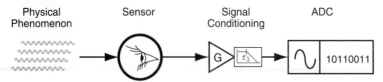

Figure 2.1   Elements of the data acquisition process.

Transducers and sensors

A **transducer** converts one physical phenomenon to another; in our case, we're mostly interested in an electrical signal as the output. For instance, a thermocouple produces a voltage that is related to temperature. An example of a transducer with a nonelectrical output is a liquid-in-glass thermometer. It converts temperature changes to visible changes in the volume of fluid. An elaboration on a transducer might be called a **sensor**. It starts with a transducer as the front end, but then adds signal conditioning (such as an amplifier), computations (such as linearization), and a means of transmitting the signal over some distance without degradation. Some industries call this a **transmitter**. Regardless of what you call it, the added signal conditioning is a great advantage in practical terms, because you don't have to worry so much about noise pickup when dealing with small signals. Of course, this added capability costs money and may add weight and bulk.

Figure 2.2 is a general model of all the world's sensors. If your instrument only seems to have the first couple of blocks, then it's probably a transducer. Table 2.1 contains examples of some sensors. The first example, a temperature transmitter, uses a thermocouple with some built-in signal conditioning. Many times you can handle thermocouples without a transmitter, but as we'll see later, you always need some form of signal conditioning. The second example, a pressure transmitter, is a slightly more complex instrument. I came across the third example, a magnetic field sensor, while doing some research. It uses an optical principle called *Faraday rotation* where the polarization of light is affected by magnetic fields.

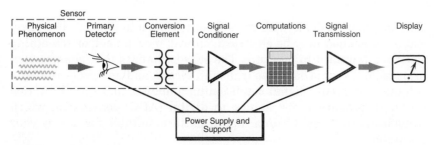

Figure 2.2   A completely general sensor model. Many times, your sensor is just a *transducer* which ends after the conversion element.

TABLE 2.1   **Three Practical Examples of Sensor Systems**

Block	Example A	Example B	Example C
Phenomenon	Temperature	Pressure	Magnetic field
Detector	—	Diaphragm displacement	Faraday rotation
Transducer	Thermocouple	LVDT	Laser and photodiode
Signal conditioner	Cold junction; amplifier	Demodulator	ADC
Computations	Linearize	Linearize; scale	Ratio; log; scale
Transmission	0–10 VDC	4–20 mA	RS-232 serial
Display	Analog meter	Analog meter	Computer system
Support	DC	DC (2-wire current loop)	DC; cooling

Example A: Temperature transmitter using a thermocouple, with cold-junction compensation, linearization, and analog output.

Example B: A pressure sensor using a linear variable differential transformer (LVDT) to detect diaphragm displacement, with analog output.

Example C: Magnetic field measurement using an optical technique with direct signal transmission to a computer. This represents a sophisticated state-of-the-art sensor system (3M Specialty Optical Fibers).

A detailed discussion of sensor technology is beyond the scope of this book. The references cover all aspects of the physics of transducers and the practical matters of selecting the right sensor. For the purposes of data acquisition, there are several important things you need to know about each of your sensors:

- The nature of the signal it produces—voltage, amplitude range, frequency response, impedance, accuracy requirement, and so on—determines what kind of signal conditioning, analog to digital converter (ADC), or other hardware you might need.

- How susceptible the sensor is to noise pickup or loading effects from data acquisition hardware.

- How the sensor is calibrated with respect to the physical phenomenon. In particular, you need to know if it's nonlinear or if it has problems with repeatability, overload, or other aberrant behavior.

- What kind of power or other utilities it might require. This is often overlooked and sometimes becomes a showstopper for complex instruments!

- What happens if you turn off your data acquisition equipment while the sensor still has power applied? Will there be damage to any components?

When you start to set up your system, try to pick sensors and design the data acquisition system in tandem. They are highly interdependent. The world's greatest sensor, when monitored by the wrong ADC, is of little value. It is important that you understand the details of how your sensors work. Try them out under known conditions if you have doubts. If something doesn't seem right, investigate. When you call the manufacturer for help, it may well turn out that you know more about the equipment than the designers, at least in your particular application. In a later section, we'll look at a holistic approach to signals and systems.

Modern trends are toward *smart sensors* containing onboard microprocessors that compensate for many of the errors that plague transducers, such as nonlinearity and drift. Such instruments are well worth the extra cost because they tend to be more accurate and remove much of the burden of error correction from you, the user. For low-frequency measurements of pressure, temperature, flow, and level, the process control industry is rapidly moving in this direction. Companies such as Rosemount, Foxboro, and Honeywell make complete lines of smart sensors.

More complex instruments can also be considered sensors in a broader way. For instance, a digital oscilloscope is a sensor of voltages that vary over time. Your LabVIEW program can interpret this voltage waveform in many different ways, depending upon what the 'scope is connected to. Note that the interface to a sensor like this is probably GPIB or RS-232 communications rather than an analog voltage. That's the beauty of using a computer to acquire data: once you get the hardware hooked up properly, all that is important is the signal itself and how you digitally process it.

Actuators

The opposite of a sensor, an **actuator** converts a signal (perhaps created by your LabVIEW program) into a physical phenomenon. Examples include electrically actuated valves, heating elements, power supplies, and motion control devices such as servo motors. Actuators are required any time you wish to **control** something such as temperature, pressure, or position. It turns out that we spend most of our time measuring things (the data acquisition phase) rather than controlling them, at least in the world of research. But control does come up from time to time, and you need to know how to use those analog and digital outputs so conveniently available on your interface boards.

Almost invariably, you will see actuators associated with **feedback control loops**. The reason is simple. Most actuators produce responses in the physical system that are more than just a little bit nonlinear and are sometimes unpredictable. For example, a valve with an electropneumatic actuator is often used to control fluid flow. The problem is that the flow varies in some nonlinear way with respect to the valve's position. Also, most valves have varying degrees of nonrepeatability. They creak and groan and get stuck—**hysteresis** and **deadband** are formal terms for this behavior. These are real-world problems that simply can't be ignored. Putting feedback around such actuators helps the situation greatly. The principle is simple. Add a sensor that measures the quantity that you need to control. Compare this measurement with the desired value (the difference is called the error) and adjust the actuator in such a way as to minimize the error. Chapter 9, "Process Control Applications," delves more deeply into this subject. The combination of LabVIEW and external loop controllers makes this whole situation easy to manage.

An important consideration for actuators is what sort of voltage or power they require. There are some industrial standards that are fairly easy to meet, such as 0–10 VDC or 4–20 mA—modest voltages and currents. But even these simple ranges can have added requirements, such as isolated grounds, where the signal ground is not the chassis of your computer. If you want to turn on a big heater, you may need large relays or contactors to handle the required current; the same is true for most high-voltage AC loads. Your computer doesn't have that kind of output, nor should it. Running lots of high power or high voltage into the back of your computer is not a pleasant thought! Try to think about these requirements ahead of time.

Categories of signals

You measure a signal because it contains some type of useful information. Therefore, the first questions you should ask are what information does the signal contain, and how is it conveyed? Generally, information is conveyed by a signal through one or more of the following signal parameters: state, rate, level, shape, or frequency content. These parameters will determine what kind of I/O interface equipment and analysis techniques you will need.

Any signal can generally be classified as **analog** or **digital**. A digital, or *binary,* signal has only two possible discrete levels of interest—an active level and an inactive level. They're typically found in computer logic circuits and in switching devices. An analog signal, on the other hand, contains information in the continuous variation of the signal with respect to time. In general, you can categorize digital signals as either **on-off** signals, where the state (on or off) is most important, or **pulse train** signals which contain a time series of pulses. On-off signals are easily acquired with a digital input port, perhaps with some signal conditioning to match the signal level to that of the port. Pulse trains are often applied to digital counters to measure frequency, period, pulse width, or duty cycle. It's important to keep in mind that digital signals are just special cases of analog signals, which leads me to an important idea:

Tip: You can use analog techniques to measure and generate digital signals. This is useful when (1) you don't have any digital I/O hardware handy; (2) you need to accurately correlate digital signals and analog signals; or (3) you need to generate a continuous but changing pattern of bits.

Among analog signal types are the DC signal and the AC signal. Analog *DC signals* are static or vary slowly with time. The most important characteristic of the DC signal is that information of interest is conveyed in the level, or amplitude, of the signal at a given instant. When measuring a DC signal, you need an instrument that can detect the level of the signal. The timing of the measurement is not difficult as long as the signal varies slowly. Therefore, the fundamental operation of the DC instrument is an ADC, which converts the analog electrical signal into a digital number that the computer interprets. Common examples of DC signals include temperature, pressure, battery voltage, strain gauge outputs, flow rate, and level measurements. In each case, the instrument monitors the signal and returns a single value indicating the magnitude of the signal at a given time. Therefore, DC instruments often report the information through devices such as meters, gauges, strip charts, and numerical readouts.

Tip: When you analyze your system, map each sensor to an appropriate LabVIEW indicator type.

Analog **AC time domain** signals are distinguished by the fact that they convey useful information not only in the level of the signal, but also in how this level varies with time. When measuring a time domain signal, often referred to as a **waveform**, you are interested in some characteristics of the shape of the waveform, such as slope, locations and shapes of peaks, and so on. You may also be interested in its frequency content.

To measure the shape of a time domain signal with a digital computer, you must take a precisely timed sequence of individual amplitude measurements, or **samples**. These measurements must be taken close enough together to adequately reproduce those characteristics of the waveform shape you want to measure. Also, the series of measurements should start and stop at the proper time to guarantee that the useful part of the waveform is acquired. Therefore, the instrument used to measure time domain signals consists of an ADC, a sample clock, and a trigger. A sample clock accurately times the occurrence of each ADC conversion.

Figure 2.3 illustrates the timing relationship between an analog waveform, a sampling clock, and a trigger pulse. To ensure that the desired portion of the waveform is acquired, you can use a trigger to start and/or stop the waveform measurement at the proper time according to some external condition. For instance, you may want to start acquisition when the signal voltage is moving in a positive direction through 0 V. Plug-in boards and oscilloscopes generally have trigger circuits that respond to such conditions.

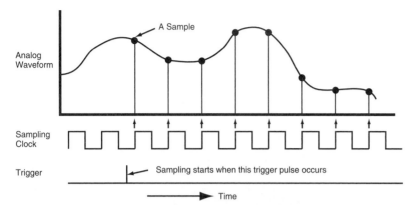

Figure 2.3 An illustration of the relationship between an analog waveform and the sampling clock and trigger that synchronize an ADC.

Another way that you can look at an analog signal is to convert the waveform data to the **frequency domain**. Information extracted from frequency domain analysis is based on the frequency content of the signal, as opposed to the shape, or time-based characteristics, of the waveform. Conversion from the time domain to the frequency domain on a digital computer is carried out through the use of a **Fast Fourier Transform (FFT)**, a standard function in the LabVIEW digital signal processing (DSP) function library. The *Inverse Fast Fourier Transform (IFFT)* converts frequency domain information back to the time domain. In the frequency domain, you can use DSP functions to observe the frequencies that make up a signal, the distribution of noise, and many other useful parameters that are otherwise not apparent in the time domain waveform. Digital signal processing can be performed by LabVIEW software routines or by special DSP hardware designed to do the analysis quickly and efficiently.

There is one more way to look at analog signals, and that is in the **joint time-frequency (JTF) domain** (Qian and Chen 1996). This is a combination of the two preceding techniques. JTF signals have an interesting frequency spectrum that varies with time. Examples are speech, sonar, and advanced modulation techniques for communication systems. The classic display technique for JTF analysis is the **spectrogram**, a plot of frequency versus time, for which LabVIEW has one of the very best, the Gabor spectrogram algorithm (Fig. 2.4). You can order the **Joint Time-Frequency Analysis Toolkit** for LabVIEW, which includes a compiled application as well as the necessary VIs to do your own processing with the Gabor spectrogram, short-time fast-Fourier transform, and several others. It works with live data from a data acquisition board or any other source.

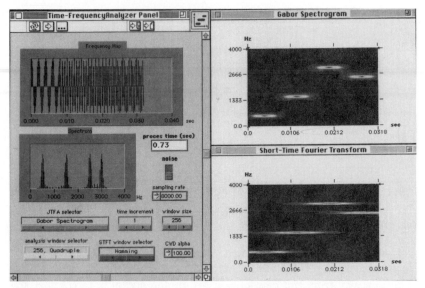

Figure 2.4 These plots illustrate the striking differences between a joint time-frequency analysis plot of a chirp signal analyzed with the short-time fast-Fourier transform spectrogram and the same chirp signal analyzed with the Gabor spectrogram.

As Fig. 2.5 shows, the signal classifications described in this section are not mutually exclusive. A single signal may convey more than one type of information. In fact, the digital on-off, pulse train, and DC signals are just simpler cases of the analog time domain signals that allow simpler measuring techniques.

The preceding example demonstrates how one signal can belong to many classes. The same signal can be measured with different types of

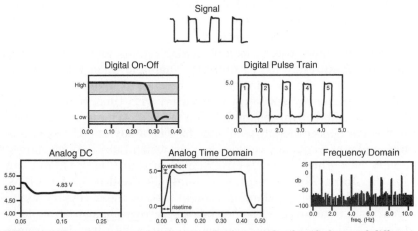

Figure 2.5 Five views of a signal. A series of pulses can be classified several different ways depending on the significance of its time, amplitude, and frequency characteristics.

instruments, ranging from a simple digital state detector to a complex frequency analysis instrument. This greatly affects how you choose signal conditioning equipment.

For most signals, you can follow the logical road map in Fig. 2.6 to determine its classification, typical interface hardware, processing requirements, and display techniques. As we'll see in coming sections, you need to characterize each signal to properly determine the kind of I/O hardware you'll need. Next, think about the signal attributes you need to measure or generate with the help of numerical methods. Then, there's the user interface issue—the part where LabVIEW controls and indicators come into play. Finally, you may have data storage requirements. Each of these items is directly affected by the signal characteristics.

Connections

Professor John Frisbee is hard at work in his lab, trying to make a pressure measurement with his brand-new computer:

Let's see here. . . . This pressure transducer says it has a 0–10 VDC output, positive on the red wire, minus on the black. The manual for my data

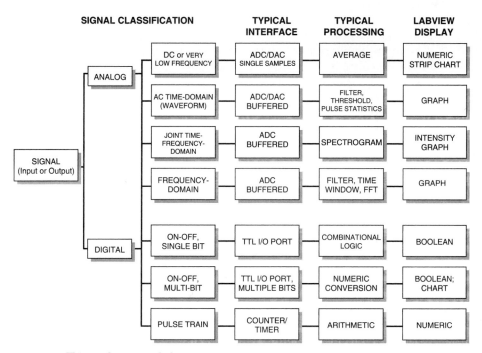

Figure 2.6 This road map can help you organize your information about each signal to logically design your LabVIEW system.

acquisition board says it can handle 0–10 VDC. No sweat. Just hook the input up to channel 1 on terminals 5 and 6. Twist a couple of wires together . . . tighten the screws . . . run the data acquisition demo program, and. . . . *Voila!* But what's this? My signal looks like . . . *crap!* My voltmeter says the input is DC, 1.23 V, and LabVIEW seems to be working OK, but the display is *really noisy*. What's going on here?

Poor John. He obviously didn't read this chapter. If he had, he would have said, "Aha! I need to put a lowpass filter on this signal and then make sure that everything is properly grounded and shielded." What he needs is **signal conditioning**, and believe me, so do you. This world is chock-full of noise sources and complex signals—all of them guaranteed to corrupt your data if you don't take care to separate the good from the bad.

There are several steps in designing the right signal conditioning approach for your application. First, remember that you need to know all about your sensors and what kind of signals they are supposed to produce. Then, you need to consider grounding and shielding. You may also need amplifiers and filters. Finally, you can list your specifications and go shopping for the right data acquisition hardware.

Grounding and shielding

Noise sources are lurking everywhere, but by following some simple principles of grounding and shielding, you can eliminate most noise-related problems right at the source—the wiring. In fact, how you connect a sensor to its associated data acquisition hardware greatly affects the overall performance of the system (Gunn 1987; Morrison 1986; Ott 1988; White 1986). Another point on the subject: measurements are inherently inaccurate. A good system design minimizes the distortion of the signal that takes place when trying to measure it: noise, nonlinear components, distortion, and so on. The wire between sensor and data acquisition can never improve the signal quality. You can only minimize the negatives with good technique. Without getting too involved with electromagnetic theory, I'll show you some of the recommended practices that instrumentation engineers everywhere use. Let's start with some definitions.

Ground.   Absolutely the most overused, misapplied, and misunderstood term in all of electronics. First of all, there is the most hallowed *Earth ground* that is represented by the electrical potential of the soil underneath your feet. The green wire on every power cord, along with any metal framework or chassis with 120 VAC mains power applied, is required by the National Electrical Code to be connected through a low-resistance path to the aforementioned dirt. There is exactly one reason for its existence: *safety*. Sadly, we somehow come to believe that *ground-*

ing our equipment will magically siphon away all sources of noise, as well as evil spirits. Baloney! Electricity flows only in closed circuits, or loops. You and your equipment sit upon Earth ground like a bird sits upon a high-voltage wire. Does the bird know it's living at 34,000 V? Of course not; there is no complete circuit. This is not to say that connections to Earth ground (which I will refer to as **safety ground** from here on) are unnecessary. You should always make sure that there is a reliable path from all of your equipment to safety ground as required by code. This prevents accidental connections between power sources and metallic objects from becoming hazards. Such fault currents are shunted away by the safety ground system.

What we really need to know about is a reference potential referred to as **signal common**, or sometimes as a **return** path. Every time you see a signal or measure a voltage, always ask the question, "Voltage . . . with respect to what reference?" That reference is the signal common, which in most situations is *not* the same as safety ground. A good example is the negative side of the battery in your car. Everything electrical in the vehicle has a return connection to this common, which is also connected to the chassis. Note that there is no connection whatsoever to Earth ground—the car has rubber tires that make fair insulators—and yet, the electrical system works just fine (except if it's very old or British).

In my labs, we run heavy copper braid, welding cable, or copper sheet between all the racks and experimental apparatus according to a grounding plan (Fig. 2.7). A well-designed signal common can even be effective at higher frequencies where second-order effects like **skin effect** and **self-inductance** become important. See the references Gunn 1987; Morrison 1986; Ott 1988; and White 1986 for instructions on designing a quality grounding system—it's worth its weight in Excedrin.

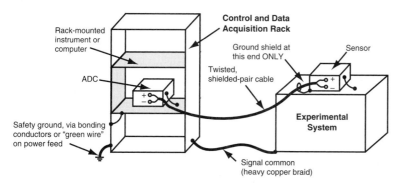

Figure 2.7 Taking the system approach to grounding in a laboratory. Note the use of a signal common (in the form of heavy copper braid or cable) to tie everything together. All items are connected to this signal common.

Electromagnetic fields.   Noise may be injected into your measurement system by **electromagnetic fields**, which are all around us. Without delving into Maxwell's equations, here are a few simple principles of electromagnetism that you use when connecting your data acquisition system.

Principle 1.   Two conductors that are separated by an insulator form a **capacitor**. An electric field exists between the conductors. If the potential (voltage) of one conductor changes with time, a proportional change in potential will appear in the other. This is called *capacitive coupling* and is one way noise is coupled into a circuit. Moving things apart reduces capacitive coupling.

Principle 2.   An electric field cannot enter a closed, conductive surface. That's why sitting in your car during a thunderstorm is better than sitting outside. The lightning's field cannot get inside. This kind of enclosure is also called a *Faraday cage,* or **electrostatic shield**, and is commonly implemented by a sheet of metal, screen, or braid surrounding a sensitive circuit. Electrostatic shields reduce capacitive coupling.

Principle 3.   A time-varying magnetic field will induce an electrical current only when a closed, conductive loop is present. Furthermore, the magnitude of the induced current is proportional to the intensity of the magnetic field and the area of the loop. This property is called *inductive coupling,* or **inductance**. Open the loop, and the current goes away.

Principle 4.   Sadly, **magnetic shielding** is not so easy to design for most situations. This is because the magnetic fields that we are most concerned about (low frequency, 50/60 Hz) are very penetrating and require very thick shields of iron or even better magnetic materials, such as expensive mu-metal.

Here are some basic practices you need to follow in order to block the effects of these electromagnetic noise sources:

- Put sensitive, high-impedance circuitry and connections inside a metallic shield that is connected to the common-mode voltage (usually the low side, or common) of the signal source. This will block capacitive coupling to the circuit (Principle 1), as well as the entry of any stray electric fields (Principle 2).

- Avoid closed, conductive loops—intentional or unintentional—often known as **ground loops**. Such loops act as pickups for stray magnetic fields (Principle 3). If a high current is induced in, for instance, the shield on a piece of coaxial cable, the resulting voltage drop along the shield will then appear in series with the measured voltage.

- Avoid placing sensitive circuits near sources of intense magnetic fields, such as transformers, motors, and power supplies. This will reduce the likelihood of magnetic pickup that you would otherwise have trouble shielding against (Principle 4).

Another unsuspected source of interference is your lovely color monitor on your PC. It is among the greatest sources of electrical interference known. Near the screen itself, there are intense electric fields due to the high voltages that accelerate the electron beam. Near the back, there are intense magnetic fields caused by the flyback transformer which is used to generate high voltage. Even the interface cards in your computer, for instance the video adapter and the computer's digital logic circuits, are sources of high-frequency noise. And *never* trust a fluorescent light fixture (or a politician).

Radio-frequency interference (RFI) is possible when there is a moderately intense RF source nearby. Common sources of RFI are transmitting devices such as walkie-talkies, cellular phones, commercial broadcast transmitters of all kinds, and RF induction heating equipment. Radio frequencies radiate for great distances through most nonmetallic structures, and really high (microwave) frequencies can even sneak in and out through cracks in metal enclosures. You might not think that a 75-MHz signal would be relevant to a 1-kHz-bandwidth data acquisition system, but there is a phenomenon known as *parasitic detection* or *demodulation* that occurs in many places. Any time that an RF signal passes through a diode (a rectifying device), it turns into DC plus any low frequencies that may be riding on (modulating) the RF carrier. Likely parasitic detectors include all of the solid-state devices in your system, plus any metal-oxide interfaces (such as dirty connections). As a licensed radio amateur, I know that parasitic detection can occur in metal rain gutter joints, TV antenna connections, and stereo amplifier output stages. This results in neighbors screaming at me about how I cut up their TV or stereo.

When RFI strikes your data acquisition system, it results in unexplained noise of varying amplitude and frequency. Sometimes you can observe stray RF signals by connecting a wide-bandwidth oscilloscope to signal lines. If you see more than a few mV of high-frequency noise, suspect a problem. Some solutions to RFI are as follows:

- Shield all the cables into and out of your equipment.
- Add RF-rejection filters on all signal and power leads.
- Put equipment in well-shielded enclosures and racks.

- Keep known RF sources and cables far away from sensitive equipment.

- Keep the person with the walkie-talkie or cellular phone *out of your lab.*

Other error sources.   **Thermojunction** voltages are generated any time two dissimilar metals come in contact with one another in the presence of a temperature gradient. This principle, known as the *Seebeck effect,* is the way a thermocouple generates its tiny signal. Problems occur in data acquisition when you attempt to measure DC signals that are in the microvolt to millivolt range, such as those from thermocouples and strain gauges. If you connect your instruments with wires, connectors, and terminal screws made of different metals or alloys, then you run the risk of adding uncontrolled thermojunction voltages to the signals—possibly to the tune of hundreds of microvolts. The most common case of thermojunction error that I see occurs when operators hook up thermocouples inside an experimental chamber and bring the wires out through a connector with pins made of copper or stainless steel. The thermocouple alloy wire meets the connector pin and forms a junction. Then, they turn on a big heater inside the chamber, creating a huge temperature gradient across the connector. Soon afterward, they notice that their temperature readouts are *way off.* Those parasitic thermojunction voltages inside the connector are added to the data in an unpredictable fashion. Here are some ways to kill the thermojunction bugs:

- Make all connections with the same metallic alloy as the wires they connect.

- Keep all connections at the same temperature.

- Minimize the number of connections in all low-level signal situations.

$$V_{out} = G(V_{in})$$

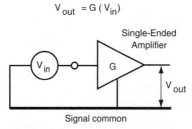

Single-Ended
Amplifier

V_{in}

G

V_{out}

Signal common

Figure 2.8   A single-ended amplifier has no intrinsic noise rejection properties. You need to carefully shield signal cables and make sure that the signal common is noise-free as well.

Differential and single-ended connections.   The means by which you connect a signal to your data acquisition can make a difference in system performance, especially in respect to noise rejection. **Single-ended** connections are the simplest and most obvious way to connect a signal source to an amplifier or other measurement device (Fig. 2.8). The significant hazard of this connection is that it is highly susceptible to noise pickup. Noise induced on any of the input wires, including the signal common, is added to the desired signal. Shielding the signal cable and being careful where you make connections to the signal common can help the situation. Single-ended connections are most often used in wide-bandwidth systems such as oscilloscopes, video, RF, and fast pulse measurements where low-impedance coaxial cables are the preferred means of transmission. They're also practical and trouble-free with higher-magnitude signals (say, 1 V or greater) that only need to travel short distances.

Differential connections depend on a pair of conductors where the voltage you want to measure (called the **normal-mode signal**) is the difference between the voltages on the individual conductors. The reason that differential connections are used is that noise pickup usually occurs equally on any two conductors that are closely spaced, such as a twisted pair of wires. That way, when you take the difference between the two voltages, the noise cancels but the difference signal remains. An **instrumentation amplifier** is optimized for use with differential signals, as shown in Fig. 2.9. The output is equal to the gain of the amplifier times the difference between the inputs. If you add another voltage in series with both inputs (called the **common-mode signal**), it cancels just like the noise pickup. The optimum signal source is a

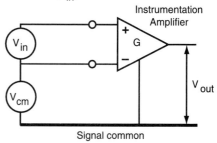

Proper differential amplifier application

$$V_{out} = G\,((V_{in} + V_{cm}) - (V_{cm}))$$
$$= G\,(V_{in})$$

**More common application
(Poorer common-mode rejection)**

$$V_{out} = G\,((V_{in} + V_{cm}) - (V_{cm}))$$
$$= G\,(V_{in})$$

Figure 2.9   Instrumentation amplifiers effectively reject common-mode (V_{cm}) signals, such as noise pickup, through cancellation. The normal-mode (differential) signal is amplified.

balanced signal where the signal voltage swings symmetrically with respect to the common-mode voltage. Wheatstone bridge circuits and transformers are the most common balanced sources.

The common-mode voltage can't be infinitely large, though, since every amplifier has some kind of maximum input voltage limit, which is usually less than 10 V—watch out for overloads! Also, beware that the common-mode rejection ratio (CMRR) of an amplifier generally decreases with frequency. Don't count on an ordinary amplifier to reject very intense RF signals, for instance. Differential inputs are available on most low-frequency instrumentation such as voltmeters, chart recorders, and plug-in boards such as those made by National Instruments. *Rule: Always use differential connections,* except when you can't.

In Fig. 2.10, you can see some typical signal connection schemes. Shielded cable is always recommended to reduce capacitive coupling

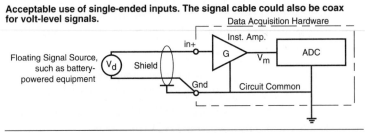

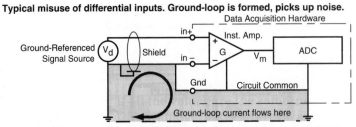

Figure 2.10   Proper use of differential and single-ended signal connections is shown in the top two figures. The bottom one is that all-too-common case where a ground loop is formed, enhancing the pickup of noise borne by magnetic fields.

and electric field pickup. Twisted, shielded pairs are best, but coaxial cable will do in situations where you are careful not to create the dreaded ground loop that appears in the bottom segment of the figure.

Why use amplifiers or other signal conditioning?

As you can see, the way you hook up your sensors can affect the overall performance of your data acquisition system. But even if the grounding and shielding are properly done, you should consider **signal conditioning**, which includes **amplifiers** and **filters**, among other things to reduce the noise relative to the signal level.

Amplifiers improve the quality of the input signal in several ways. They boost the amplitude of smaller signals, improving the resolution of the measurements. Second, they offer increased driving power (lower output impedance) which keeps such things as ADCs from loading the sensor. Third, they provide differential inputs, a technique known to help reject noise. An improvement on differential inputs, an **isolation amplifier**, requires no signal common at the input whatsoever.* Isolation amplifiers are available with common-mode voltage ranges up to thousands of volts.

Amplifiers are usually essential for microvolt signals such as those from thermocouples and strain gauges. In general, you should try to amplify your low-level signal as close to the physical phenomenon itself as possible. Doing this will help you increase the **signal-to-noise ratio (SNR)**. Signal-to-noise ratio is defined as

$$SNR = 20 \log \left(\frac{V_{sig}}{V_{noise}} \right)$$

where V_{sig} is the signal amplitude and V_{noise} is the noise amplitude, both measured in volts rms. The 20 log() operation converts the simple ratio to **decibels (dB)**, a ratiometric system used in electrical engineering, signal processing, and other fields. Decibels are convenient units for gain and loss computations. For instance, an SNR or gain of 20 dB is the same as a ratio of 10 to 1, 40 dB is 100 to 1, and so forth. Note that the zero noise condition results in an infinite SNR. May you one day achieve this. . . .

---

* Manufacturers *say* you don't need a ground reference, but experience in the field says it ain't so. George Wells of JPL reports that Analog Devices 5B modules sometimes couple large common-mode voltages to adjacent modules. This may be because of internal transformer orientation. Other brands may have their own problems. Your best bet is to provide a proper ground to all signals.

Amplifiers are available in stand-alone modular form, such as those from Action Instruments and Moore Products that mount on DIN rails, or in chassis-mounted modules, available from Preston and Ectron. Another choice is a module such as the National Instruments SCXI-1120, which includes an isolation amplifier and a lowpass filter on each of eight channels, followed by a multiplexer that routes the selected channel to a common ADC input. Most plug-in data acquisition boards include a programmable-gain instrumentation amplifier (PGIA). You change the gain by sending a command to the board, and the gain can be changed at any time—even while rapidly scanning through a set of channels. The difference between an on-board amplifier and an external amplifier is that the on-board amplifier must respond quickly to large changes in signal level (and perhaps gain setting) between channels. Errors can arise due to **settling time**: the time that it takes for the amplifier output to stabilize within a prescribed error tolerance of the final value. If you scan a set of channels at top speed with the amplifier at high gain, there is the possibility of lost accuracy. National Instruments has gone to great pains to assure that its custom-designed PGIAs settle very rapidly, and it guarantees full accuracy at all gains and scanning speeds. But if you can afford it, the amplifier-per-channel approach remains the best choice for high-accuracy data acquisition.

Filters are needed to reject undesired signals, such as high-frequency noise, and to provide **antialiasing** (discussed later in this chapter). Most of the time, you need lowpass filters which reject high frequencies while passing low frequencies including DC. The simplest filters are made from resistors and capacitors (and sometimes, inductors). **Active filters** combine resistors and capacitors with operational amplifiers to enhance performance. **Switched capacitor filters** are a modern alternative to these ordinary analog filters. They use arrays of small capacitors that are switched rapidly in and out of the circuit, simulating large resistors on a much smaller (integrated circuit) scale.

A wide variety of external filters are available in modular form for mounting on printed circuit boards and DIN rails. They are also available in plug-in modules, such as the National Instruments SCXI-1141 9-channel elliptic lowpass filter module, or in rack-mounted enclosures, such as those made by Frequency Devices, Precision Filters, and TTE. Alternatively, you can use the aforementioned SCXI-1120 with an amplifier and filter for each channel. (You might have guessed by now that I like the 1120 module. I use it a lot because it has excellent common-mode rejection, filtering, and accuracy.) A good overview of the subject of filters is available in Application Note AN058, *Programmable Lowpass Filters for PC-Based Data Acquisition (DAQ) Boards,* available from National Instruments.

Using a signal conditioning system outside of your computer also enhances safety. If a large overload should appear, the signal conditioner will take the hit rather than passing it directly to the backplane of your computer (and maybe all the way to the mouse or keyboard!). A robust amplifier package can easily be protected against severe overloads through the use of transient absorption components (such as varistors, zener diodes, and spark gaps), limiting resistors, and fuses. Medical systems are covered by federal and international regulations regarding isolation from stray currents. *Never connect electronic instruments to a live subject (human or otherwise) without a properly certified isolation amplifier and correct grounding.*

Special transducers may require **excitation**. Examples are resistance temperature detectors (RTDs), thermistors, potentiometers, and strain gauges as depicted in Fig. 2.11. All of these devices produce an output that is proportional to an excitation voltage or current as well as the physical phenomenon they are intended to measure. Thus, the excitation source can be a source of noise and drift and must be carefully designed. Modular signal conditioners, such as the Analog Devices 5B series, and SCXI hardware from National Instruments include high-quality voltage or current references for this purpose.

Some signal conditioning equipment may also have built-in **multiplexing**, which is an array of switching elements (relays or solid-state analog switches) that route many input signals to one common output. For instance, using SCXI equipment, you can have hundreds of analog inputs connected to one multiplexer at a location near the experiment. Then only one cable needs to be run back to a plug-in board in your computer. This drastically reduces the number and length of cables. Most plug-in boards include multiplexers.

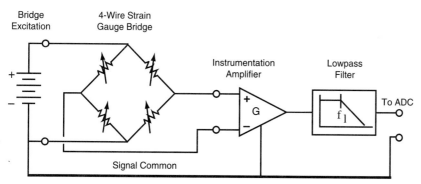

Figure 2.11 Schematic of a signal conditioner for a strain gauge, a bridge-based transducer that requires excitation. This signal conditioner has an instrumentation amplifier with high gain, followed by a lowpass filter to reject noise.

Multiplexing can cause some interesting problems when not properly applied, as I mentioned in regards to amplifier settling time. Compare the two signal configurations in Fig. 2.12. In the upper configuration, there is an amplifier and filter per channel, followed by the multiplexer which ultimately feeds the ADC. The SCXI-1120, SCXI-1102, and many packaged data acquisition systems are designed this way. It is the preferred arrangement because each filter output faithfully follows its respective input signal without disturbances from switching transients. But in the lower configuration, the amplifier and filter are located *after* the multiplexer. This saves money but is undesirable because each time the multiplexer changes channels, the very sluggish lowpass filter must settle to the voltage present at the new channel. As a result, you must scan the channels at a very slow rate unless you disable the lowpass filter, thus giving up its otherwise useful properties. The SCXI-1100 32-channel multiplexer amplifier module is designed this way and has caught some users unaware.

Practical tips on connecting input signals.   Let's look at a few common input signal connection situations that you're likely to come across. I recommend that you refer to the manual for your signal conditioning or plug-in board before making any connections. There may be particular options or requirements that differ from this tutorial.

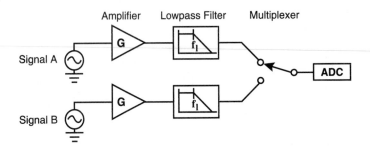

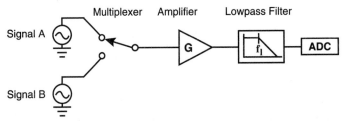

Figure 2.12   The preferred amplifier and filter per channel configuration (*above*). An undesirable, but cheaper, topology (*below*). Watch your step if your system looks like the latter.

Ground-referenced analog inputs. If one side of your signal has a direct connection to a reliable ground, use a differential input to avoid ground loops and provide common-mode noise rejection.

Floating analog inputs. Battery-powered equipment and instruments with isolated outputs do not supply a return connection to signal ground. This is generally good, since a ground loop is easy to avoid. You can connect such a signal to a *referenced single-ended* input (Fig. 2.13a), an input configuration available on most data acquisition boards, and called *RSE* in the National Instruments manuals. Common-mode noise rejection will be acceptable in this case. You can also use differential inputs, but note that they require the addition of a pair of *leak resistors*

a. Referenced single-ended connection

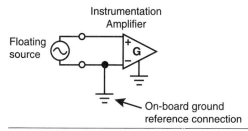

b. Differential connection – DC-coupled source

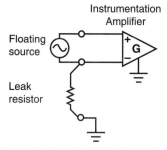

c. Differential connection – AC-coupled source

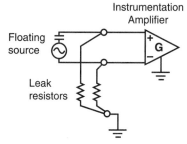

Figure 2.13 Floating source connections: (*a*) This is the simplest and most economical; (*b*) this is similar but may have noise rejection advantages; and (*c*) this is required for AC-coupled sources.

(Fig. 2.13*b* and *c*). Every amplifier injects a small *bias current* from its inputs back into the signal connections. If there is no path to ground, as is the case for a true floating source, the input voltage at one or both inputs will float to the amplifier's power supply rail voltage. The result is erratic operation because the amplifier is frequently saturated—operating out of its linear range. This is a sneaky problem! Sometimes the source is floating and you don't even know it. Perhaps the system will function normally for a few minutes after power is turned on, and then misbehave later on. Or, touching the leads together or touching them with your fingers may discharge the circuit, leading you to believe that there is an intermittent connection. Yikes! *Rule:* Use an ohmmeter to verify the presence of a resistive path to ground on all signals sources.

What is the proper value for a leak resistor? The manual for your input device may have a recommendation. In general, if the value is too low, you lose the advantage of a differential input because the input is tightly coupled to ground through the resistor. You may also overload the source in the case where leak resistors are connected to both inputs. If the value is too high, additional DC error voltages may arise due to *input offset current drift* (the input bias currents on the two inputs differ and may vary with temperature). A safe value is generally in the range of 1 kΩ to 100 kΩ. If the source is truly floating—such as battery-powered equipment—then go ahead and directly ground one side.

Thermocouples: Thermocouples have very low source impedance, low signal voltage, and may have either floating or grounded junctions. For an excellent tutorial on thermocouples, refer to the Omega Engineering *Temperature Handbook* (1997). For general information on connecting thermocouples to computer I/O, consult Application Note AN043, *Measuring Temperature with Thermocouples,* and AN056, *How to Use Thermocouples with an SCXI-1102 Module.* I generally prefer floating junctions, where the welded joint between the thermocouple wires is isolated from the surrounding sheath or other nearby metallic items. This removes any chance of a ground loop and results in a floating DC-coupled source as previously described. Always use differential connections to reject noise on this and other low-level signals, and be sure to use a leak resistor—perhaps 1 kΩ or so—on one of the inputs. You must also take care to use extension wire and connectors of the same alloy as the thermocouple element. Finally, the connections to the signal conditioning must be *isothermal,* that is, all connections are at the same temperature.

Thermocouples also require a *reference junction* measurement to compensate for the voltage produced at the junction between the thermocouple wires and copper connections. This may be provided by an additional thermocouple junction immersed in a reference temperature bath or, more commonly, by measuring the temperature at the reference temperature block, where the thermocouple alloy transitions to copper, typically near the amplifier. All modern signal conditioners include an isothermal reference temperature feature. The LabVIEW DAQ library includes VIs for making the corrections and performing linearization.

AC signals.   If you want to measure the RMS value of an AC wave-form, you have two choices: use an external AC-to-DC converter or digitize the waveform at high speed and do some signal processing in LabVIEW. For low-frequency voltage measurements, your best bet is a true RMS (TRMS) converter module, such as those made by Action Instruments and Ohio Semitronics (which also make single- and three-phase AC power transmitters). The input can be any AC waveform up to a few kHz and with amplitudes as high as 240 V RMS. For higher frequencies, a more sophisticated converter is required, and you may well have to build it yourself using an IC such as the Linear Technology LT1088 RMS to DC converter, which operates from DC to 100 MHz. To measure low-frequency AC current, use a current transformer and an AC converter module as before. If the frequency is very high, special current transformers made by Pearson Electronics are available and can feed a wideband RMS to DC converter. All of these transformers and AC converters give you signals that are isolated from the source, making connections to your DAQ board simple. When the shape of the waveform is of interest, you generally connect the signal directly to the input of a sufficiently fast ADC or digital oscilloscope, then acquire large buffers of data for analysis.

Digital inputs.   Digital on-off signals may require conditioning, depending upon their source. If the source is an electronic digital device, it probably has TTL-compatible outputs and can be connected directly to the digital I/O port of a plug-in board. Check the manuals for the devices at both ends to assure that both the levels and current requirements match. Detecting a contact closure (a switch) requires a *pull-up resistor* at the input (Fig. 2.14) to provide the high level when the switch is open. If your source produces a voltage outside of the 0–5 VDC range

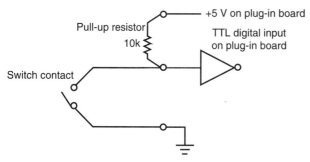

Figure 2.14   Contact closures are sensed by a TTL input with the help of an external pull-up resistor.

of a typical plug-in board, additional signal conditioning is required. You can buy a board such as the National Instruments SSR series which is compatible with high AC and DC voltages. Even better, the SCXI-1162HV gives you 32 channels of isolated high-voltage inputs.

Outputs need signal conditioning, too.   To drive actuators of one type or another, you may need signal conditioning. As with input signals, isolation is one of the major considerations, along with requirements for extra drive capability that many simple output devices can't handle directly.

For digital outputs, most plug-in boards offer simple TTL logic drivers, which swing from 0 to about +3 volts, depending on the load (you need to consult the specifications for your hardware to make sure). If you want to drive a solenoid valve, for instance, much more current is needed—perhaps several amperes at 24 VDC or even 120 VAC. In such cases, you need a relay of some type. Electromechanical relays are simple and cheap with good contact ratings, but sometimes they require more coil current than a TTL output can supply. Sensitive relays, such as reed relays, are often acceptable. Solid-state relays use SCRs (silicon-controlled rectifiers) or triacs to control heavier loads with minimal control current requirements. Their main limitation is that most units are only usable for AC circuits. Many types of modular I/O systems have options for these higher voltages and currents, such as the SCXI-1161 with eight power relays, which you can connect directly to your plug-in board. If you need to drive other types of logic or require large output voltages and/or currents at high speed, a special interface circuit may have to be custom-designed. Figure 2.15 shows a couple of simple options for driving LEDs and heavier DC loads, such as solenoids, using MOSFETs to handle the power. National Instruments sells a variety of digital signal conditioners that plug right into its boards; I'd use them first because they're convenient.

One warning is in order regarding digital outputs. When you turn on a digital output device, be it a plug-in board or external module, which

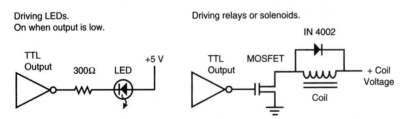

Figure 2.15   Simple circuits you can use with digital outputs on MIO- and DIO-series boards. Drive low-current loads like LEDs directly (*left*). MOSFETs are available in a wide range of current and voltage ratings for driving heavy DC loads (*right*).

output state will it produce? On, off, or high-impedance (disconnected)? Can it produce a brief but rapid pulse train? I've seen everything, and you will, too, given time. Connect an oscilloscope to each output and see what happens when you turn the system on and off. If the result is unsatisfactory (or unsafe!), you may need a switch or relay to temporarily connect the load to the proper source. This warning applies to *analog* outputs, too.

Most of the analog world gets by with control voltages in the range of ±10 V or less and control currents of 20 mA or less. These outputs are commonly available from most I/O boards and modular signal conditioners. If you need more current and/or voltage, you can use a power amplifier. Audio amplifiers are a quick and easy solution to some of these problems, though most of them have a highpass filter that rolls off the DC response (that is, they can produce no DC output current). Many commercial DC power supplies have analog inputs and are good for low-frequency applications. To control big AC heaters, motors, and other heavy loads, look to triac-based power controllers. They permit an ordinary analog voltage or current input to control tens or even hundreds of kilowatts with reasonable cost and efficiency. One thing to watch out for is the need for isolation when you get near high-power equipment. An isolation amplifier could save your equipment if a fault occurs; it may also eliminate grounding problems which are so prevalent around high-power systems.

Choosing the right I/O subsystem

As soon as your project gets under way, make a list of the sensors you need to monitor along with any actuators you need to drive. Exact specifications on sensors and actuators will make your job much easier. As an instrumentation engineer, I spend a large part of my time on any project just collecting data sheets, calling manufacturers, and peering into little black boxes trying to elucidate the important details I need for interfacing. Understanding the application is important, too. Just because a pressure transducer will respond in 1 μs doesn't mean that your system will actually have microsecond dynamic conditions to measure. On the other hand, that superfast transducer may surprise you by putting out all kinds of fast pulses because there are some little bubbles whizzing by in the soup. Using the wrong signal conditioner in either case can result in a phenomenon known as *bogus data*.

Since you are a computer expert, fire up your favorite spreadsheet or database application and make up an instrument list. The process control industry goes so far as to standardize on a format known as *instrument data sheets,* which are used to specify, procure, install, and finally document all aspects of each sensor and actuator. Others working on your project, particularly the quality assurance staff, will be very happy to see this kind of documentation. For the purposes of designing an I/O subsystem, your database might include these items:

- Instrument name or identifier
- Location, purpose, and references to other drawings such as wiring and installation details
- Calibration information: engineering units (such as PSIG) and full-scale range
- Accuracy, resolution, linearity, and noise, if significant
- Signal current, voltage, or frequency range
- Signal bandwidth
- Isolation requirements
- Excitation or power requirements: current and voltage

To choose your I/O subsystem, begin by sorting the instrument list according to the types of signals and other basic requirements. Remember to add plenty of spare channels! Consider the relative importance of each instrument. If you have 99 thermocouples and 1 pressure gauge, your I/O design choice will certainly lean toward accommodating thermocouples. But that pressure signal may be the single most important measurement in the whole system; don't try to adapt its 0-10 V output to work with an input channel that is optimized for microvolt thermocouple signals. For each signal, determine the minimum specifications for its associated signal conditioner. Important specs are as follows:

- Adjustability of zero offset and gain
- Bandwidth—minimum and maximum frequencies to pass
- Filtering—usually antialiasing lowpass filters
- Settling time and phase shift characteristics
- Accuracy
- Gain and offset drift with time and temperature (very important)
- Excitation—built in or external?
- For thermocouples, cold junction compensation
- Linearization—may be better performed in software

Next, consider the physical requirements. Exposure to weather, high temperatures, moisture and other contamination, or intense electromagnetic interference may cause damage to unprotected equipment. Will the equipment have to work in a hostile environment? If so, it must be in a suitable enclosure. If the channel count is very high, having many channels per module could save both space and money. Convenience should not be overlooked: ever work on a tiny module with itty-bitty terminal screws that are deeply recessed into an overstuffed terminal box? This is a practical matter; if you have lots of signals to hook up, talk this over with the people who will do the installation.

If your company already has many installations of a certain type or I/O, that may be an overriding factor, so long as the specifications are met. The bottom line is always cost. Using excess or borrowed equipment should always be considered when money is tight. You can do a cost-per-channel analysis, if that makes sense. For instance, using a multifunction board in your computer with just a few channels hooked up through Analog Devices 5B series signal conditioners is very cost-effective. But if you need 100 channels, using SCXI would certainly save money over the 5Bs. (See Fig. 2.16.) You might even consider a multipurpose data acquisition and control unit, such as Hewlett-Packard's HP3852A which is competitive for larger channel counts and offers stand-alone programmability.

Remote and distributed I/O. Your sensors may not be located close to your computer system, or they may be in an inaccessible area—a hazardous enclosure or associated with a high-voltage source. In such cases, **remote I/O** hardware is appropriate. It makes sense to locate the acquisition hardware close to groups of sensors—*remote* from the

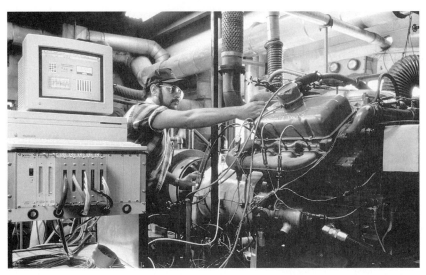

Figure 2.16 EG&G Automotive Research (San Antonio, Texas) has the type of industrial environment that makes effective use of SCXI signal conditioning products. (*Photo courtesy of National Instruments and EG&G Automotive Research.*)

computer—because it saves much signal wiring which in turn reduces cost and reduces the chance of noise pickup. Many remote I/O systems are commercially available with a variety of communication interfaces. If more than one I/O subsystem can be connected to a common communication line, it is often referred to as **distributed I/O**.

National Instruments carries the **Analog Devices 6B series** distributed I/O system. This family includes a wide variety of analog and digital I/O modules that plug into backplanes that hold 1, 4, or 16 modules. Backplanes are connected to the host computer via RS-232 or RS-485 serial lines as shown in Fig. 2.17. Most computers have RS-232 built in, and it is adequate for short distances. For RS-485, you can install an AT-485 RS-485 interface and gain the ability to extend your reach to 4000 feet. LabVIEW drivers are available for all platforms. See the National Instruments catalog for details.

A similar distributed I/O system is made by **Opto-22**. As with the 6B series, you choose from a variety of analog and digital I/O modules that are installed in backplanes of various types and sizes. A *brain board* (model B1 for digital and B2 for analog I/O) connects one or more backplanes to an RS-422 serial line running the *Optomux* protocol. Macintosh users can connect directly to this RS-422 party line; other

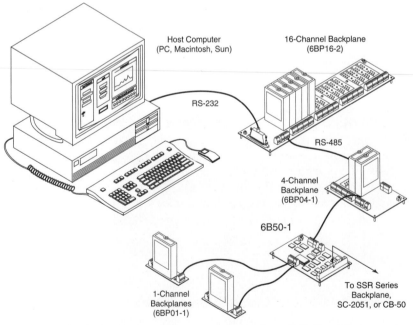

Figure 2.17 The Analog Devices 6B series, available through National Instruments, provides distributed I/O capability with serial communications.

platforms require an RS-422 converter or serial card. A free LabVIEW driver, written by yours truly, is available from National Instruments. I've found Optomux equipment to be a simple, reliable, low-cost solution for connecting remote sensors and systems around the lab.

If you need high-voltage isolation—and I mean *really* high voltage—with high throughput, consider **ControlNet** hardware from **Group3 Technology**. This distributed I/O system features a fiber-optic network, providing excellent noise immunity and isolation along with high communications speeds. You install a *Loop Controller* board in your PC (ISA bus) which then connects to one or more *Device Interface* modules via fiber-optic cable. Each Device Interface can house any combination of up to three I/O cards, each handling many types of analog and digital I/O, including such special devices as stepper motors, DC motors, encoders, and GPIB devices. Group3 offers a comprehensive LabVIEW driver for Windows.

National Instruments adds remote serial-link capability to its SCXI line of modular signal conditioning with the SCXI-2000 chassis or the SCXI-2400 module. With these systems, you connect up to 32 chassis to your computer via RS-232 or RS-485, then plug in any combination of the available SCXI signal conditioning modules. Programming is a snap: you use the standard NI-DAQ LabVIEW driver libraries in the same manner as you would a plug-in board and the traditional parallel connection to SCXI modules.

Regardless of perceived complexity, careful analysis of your system's needs in the beginning will result in money and aggravation saved in the end. Trust me; I've been there.

Acquiring the Signal

Up until now, we've been discussing the real (mostly analog) world of signals. Now it's time to digitize those signals for use in LabVIEW. By definition, **analog** signals are **continuous-time, continuous-value** functions. That means they can take on any possible value and are defined over all possible time resolutions. (By the way: don't think that digital pulses are special; they're just analog signals that happen to be square waves. If you look closely, they have all kinds of ringing, noise, and slew rate limits—all the characteristics of analog signals.)

An **analog to digital converter** (ADC) samples your analog signals on a regular basis and converts the amplitude at each sample time to a digital value with finite resolution. These are termed **discrete-time, discrete-value** functions. Unlike their analog counterparts, discrete functions are defined only at times specified by the sample interval and may only have values determined by the resolution of the ADC. In other words, when you digitize an analog signal, you *have to approxi-*

mate. How *much* you can throw out depends on your signal and your specifications for data analysis. Is 1 percent resolution acceptable? Or is 0.0001 percent required? And how fine does the temporal resolution need to be? One second? Or one nanosecond? Please be realistic. Additional amplitude and temporal resolution can be *expensive*. To answer these questions, we need to look at this business of sampling more closely.

Sampling theorem

A fundamental rule of sampled data systems is that the input signal must be sampled at a rate greater than twice the highest frequency component in the signal. This is known as the **Shannon sampling theorem**, and the critical sampling rate is call the **Nyquist rate**. Stated as a formula, it says that $f_s/2 > f_a$, where f_s is the sampling frequency and f_a is the maximum frequency of the signal being sampled. Violating the Nyquist criterion is called **undersampling** and results in **aliasing**. Look at Fig. 2.18 which simulates a sampled data system. I started out with a simple 1-kHz sine wave (dotted lines), and then sampled it at two different frequencies, 1.2 kHz and 5.5 kHz. At 5.5 kHz, the signal is safely below the Nyquist rate, which would be 2.75 kHz, and the data points look something like the original (with a little bit of information thrown out, of course). But the data with a 1.2-kHz sampling rate is aliased: it looks as if the signal is 200 Hz, not 1 kHz. This effect is also called **frequency fold back**: everything above $f_s/2$ is folded back into the sub-$f_s/2$ range. If you undersample your signal and get stuck with aliasing in your data, can you undo the aliasing? In most cases, no.

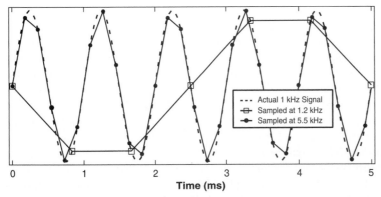

Figure 2.18 Graphical display of the effects of sampling rates. When the original 1-kHz sine wave is sampled at 1.2 kHz (too slow), it is totally unrecognizable in the data samples. Sampling at 5.5 kHz yields a much better representation. What would happen if there was a lot of really high frequency noise?

As a rule, you should not undersample if you hope to make sense of waveform data. Exceptions do occur in certain *controlled* situations. An example is **equivalent-time sampling** in digital oscilloscopes, where a repetitive waveform is sampled at a low rate, but with careful control of the sampling delay with respect to a precise trigger.

Let's go a step further and consider a nice 1-kHz sine wave, but this time add some high-frequency noise to it. We already know that a 5.5-kHz sample rate will represent the sine wave all right, but any noise that is beyond $f_s/2$ (2.75 kHz) will alias. Is this a disaster? That depends on the **power spectrum** (amplitude squared versus frequency) of the noise or interfering signal. Say that the noise is very, very small in amplitude—much less than the resolution of your ADC. In that case it will be undetectable, even though it violates the Nyquist criterion. The real problems are medium-amplitude noise or spurious signals. In Fig. 2.19, I simulated a 1-kHz sine wave with lowpass-filtered white noise added to it. If we use a 16-bit ADC, the specs say its spectral noise floor is about –115 dB below full-scale when displayed as a power spectrum. (This corresponds to an rms signal-to-noise ratio of 98.08 dB for all frequencies up to the Nyquist limit.) Assuming that the signal is sampled at 5.5 kHz as before, the Nyquist limit is 2.75 kHz.

Looking at the power spectrum, you can see that some of the noise power is above the floor for the ADC, and there is also noise present at frequencies above 2.75 kHz. The shaded triangle represents aliased energy and gives you a qualitative feel for how much contamination you can expect. Exactly what the contamination will look like is anybody's guess; it depends on the nature of the out-of-band noise. In this case, you can be pretty sure that none of the aliased energy will be above –65 dB, though. The good news is that this is just plain old uncor-

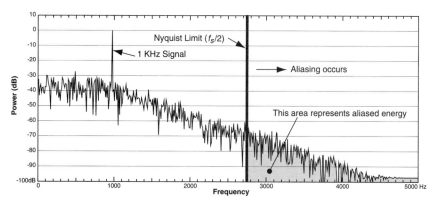

Figure 2.19 Power spectrum of a 1-kHz sine wave with lowpass-filtered noise added. If the ADC resolves 16 bits, its spectral noise floor is –115 dB. Assuming that we sample at 5.5 kHz, any energy appearing above $f_s/2$ (2.75 kHz) and above –115 dB will be aliased.

related noise, so its aliased version will also be plain old uncorrelated noise. Not a disaster, just another noise source.

Filtering and averaging

To get rid of aliasing problems, you need to use a **lowpass filter**, known in this case as an **antialiasing filter**. Analog filters are mandatory, regardless of sampling rate, unless you know the signal's frequency characteristics and can live with the aliased noise. There has to be *something* to limit the bandwidth of the raw signal to $f_s/2$. The analog filter can be in the transducer, the signal conditioner, on the ADC board, or in all three places. One problem with analog filters is that they can become very complex and expensive. If the desired signal is fairly close to the Nyquist limit, the filter needs to cut off very quickly, implying lots of stages (this is more formally known as the **order** of the filter's **transfer function**). High-performance antialiasing filters, such as the SCXI-1141, have such high-order designs and meet the requirements of most situations.

Digital filters can augment, but not replace, analog filters. Digital filter VIs are included with the LabVIEW analysis library, and they are functionally equivalent to analog filters. The simplest type of digital filter is a **moving averager** (examples of which are available with Lab-VIEW) which has the advantage of being usable in real time on a sample-by-sample basis. One way to simplify the antialiasing filter problem is to **oversample** the input. If your ADC hardware is fast enough, just turn the sampling rate way up, then use a digital filter to eliminate the higher frequencies that are of no interest. This makes the analog filtering problem much simpler because the Nyquist frequency has been raised much higher, so the analog filter doesn't have to be so sharp. A compromise is always necessary: you need to sample at a rate high enough to avoid significant aliasing with a modest analog filter; but sampling at too high a rate may not be practical because the hardware is too expensive and/or the flood of extra data may overload your poor CPU.

A potential problem with averaging comes up when you handle nonlinear data. The process of averaging is defined to be the summation of several values, divided by the number of values. If your data is, for instance, exponential in nature, then averaging values (a linear operation) will tend to bias the data. (Consider the fact that $e^x + e^y$ is not equal to $e^{(x+y)}$). One solution is to linearize the data before averaging. In the case of exponential data, you should take the logarithm first. You may also be able to ignore this problem if the values are closely spaced—small pieces of a curve are effectively linear. It's vital that you understand your signals qualitatively and quantitatively before applying *any* numerical processing, no matter how innocuous it may seem.

If your main concern is rejecting 60-Hz line frequency interference, an old trick is to average an array of samples over one line period (16.66 ms in the United States). For instance, you could acquire data at 600 Hz and average groups of 10, 20, 30, and so on, up to 600 samples. You should do this for every channel. Using plug-in boards with Lab-VIEW's data acquisition drivers permits you to adjust the sampling interval with high precision, making this a reasonable option. Set up a simple experiment to acquire and average data from a noisy input. Vary the sampling period and see if there isn't a null in the noise level at each 16.66-ms multiple.

If you are attempting to average recurrent waveforms to reduce noise, remember that the arrays of data that you acquire must be perfectly in-phase. If a phase shift occurs during acquisition, then your waveforms will partially cancel each other or cause distortion. **Triggered** data acquisition (discussed later) is the normal solution because it helps to guarantee that each buffer of data is acquired at the same part of the signal's cycle.

Some other aspects of filtering that may be important for some of your applications are **impulse response** and **phase response**. For ordinary data logging, these factors are generally ignored. But if you are doing dynamic testing such as vibration analysis, acoustics, or seismology, impulse and phase response can be very important. As a rule of thumb, when filters become very complex (high-order), they cut off sharper, have more radical phase shifts around the cutoff frequency, and, depending on the filter type, exhibit more ringing on transients. Overall, filtering is a rather complex topic that is best left to the references; the *Active Filter Cookbook* is one of my favorites. Even with an electrical engineering degree and lots of experience with filters, I still use it to get a quick answer to practical filtering problems.

The best way to analyze your filtering needs is to use a spectrum analyzer. That way, you know exactly what signals are present and what has to be filtered out. You can use a dedicated spectrum analyzer instrument (*very* expensive), a digital oscilloscope with FFT capability (or let LabVIEW do the power spectrum), or even a multifunction I/O board running as fast as possible with LabVIEW doing the power spectrum. Spectrum analyzers are included in the Data Acquisition examples distributed with LabVIEW and they work quite well.

About ADCs, DACs, and multiplexers

Important characteristics of an ADC or D/A converter (DAC) are resolution, range, speed, and sources of error. (For a detailed look at all of these parameters, consult the *Analog-Digital Conversion Handbook,* available from Analog Devices.)

Resolution is the number of bits that the ADC uses to represent the analog signal. The greater the number of bits, the finer the resolution of the converter. Figure 2.20 demonstrates the resolution of a hypothetical 3-bit converter, which can resolve 2^3, or 8, different levels. The sine wave in this figure is not well represented because of the rather coarse **quantization** levels available. Common ADCs have resolutions of 8, 12, and 16 bits, corresponding to 256, 4096, and 65,536 quantization levels. Using high-resolution converters is generally desirable, though they tend to be somewhat slower.

Range refers to the maximum and minimum voltage levels that the ADC can quantize. Exceeding the input range results in what is variously termed clipping, saturation, or overflow/underflow, where the ADC gets stuck at its largest or smallest output code. The **code width** of an ADC is defined as the change of voltage between two adjacent quantization levels or, as a formula,

$$\text{Code width} = \frac{\text{range}}{2^N}$$

where N is the number of bits and code width and range are measured in volts. A high-resolution converter (lots of bits) has a small code width. The intrinsic range, resolution, and code width of an ADC can be modified by preceding it with an amplifier that adds gain. The code width expression then becomes

$$\text{Code width} = \frac{\text{range}}{\text{gain} \times 2^N}$$

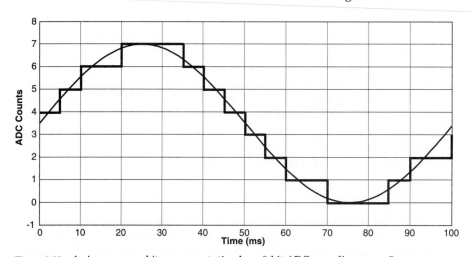

Figure 2.20   A sine wave and its representation by a 3-bit ADC sampling every 5 ms.

High gain thus narrows the code width and enhances the resolution while reducing effective range. For instance, a common 12-bit ADC with a range of 0–10 V has a code width of 2.44 mV. By adding a gain of 100, the code width becomes 24.4 μV, but the effective range becomes 10/100 = 0.1 V. It is important to note the trade-off between resolution and range when you change the gain. High gain means that overflow may occur at a much lower voltage.

Conversion speed is determined by the technology used in designing the ADC and associated components, particularly the **sample-and-hold** amplifier that freezes the analog signal just long enough to do the conversion. Speed is measured in time per conversion or samples per second. Figure 2.21 compares some common ADC technologies, typical resolutions, and conversion speeds. A very common trade-off is resolution versus speed; it simply takes more time or is more costly to precisely determine the exact voltage. In fact, high-speed ADCs, such as flash converters that are often used in digital oscilloscopes, decrease in effective resolution as the conversion rate is increased. Your application determines what conversion speed is required.

There are many sources of **error** in ADCs, some of which are a little hard to quantify; in fact, if you look at the spec sheets for ADCs from different manufacturers, you may not be able to directly compare the error magnitudes because of the varying techniques the manufacturers may have used.

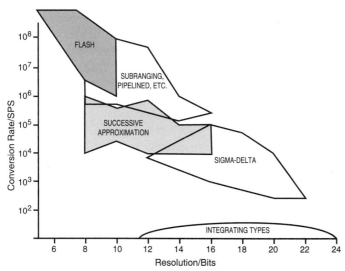

Figure 2.21 Some representative analog to digital converter performance characteristics. *(Courtesy of Analog Devices.)*

Simple errors are **gain** and **offset** errors. An ideal ADC follows the equation for a straight line, $y = mx + b$, where y is the input voltage, x is the output code, and m is the code width. Gain errors change the slope (m) of this equation, which is a change in the code width. Offset errors change the intercept (b), which means that zero volts input doesn't give you zero counts at the output. These errors are easily corrected through calibration. Either you can adjust some trimmer potentiometers so that zero and full-scale match a calibration standard, or you can make measurements of calibration voltages and fix the data through a simple straight-line expression in software. Fancy ADC systems, like the E-series plug-in boards from National Instruments, include self-calibration right on the board.

Linearity is another problem. Ideally, all the code widths are the same. Real ADCs have some linearity errors that make them deviate from the ideal. One of the measures of this error is **differential nonlinearity**, which tells you the worst-case deviation in code width. **Integral nonlinearity** is a measure of the ADC transfer function. It is measured as the worst-case deviation from a straight line drawn through the center of the first and last code widths. An ideal converter would have zero integral nonlinearity. Nonlinearity problems are much more difficult to calibrate out of your system. To do so would mean taking a calibration measurement at each and every quantization level and using that data to correct each value. In practice, you just make sure that the ADC is tightly specified and that the manufacturer delivers the goods, as promised.

If a **multiplexer** is used before an ADC to scan many channels, **timing skew** will occur (Fig. 2.22). Since the ADC is being switched between several inputs, it is impossible for it to make all the measurements simultaneously. A delay between the conversion of each channel results, and this is called *skew*. If your measurements depend on critical timing (phase matching) between channels, you need to know exactly how much skew there is in your ADC system.

Multiplexers are used as cost-saving devices, since ADCs tend to be among the most expensive parts in the system, but the skew problem can be intolerable in some applications. Then, multiple ADCs or sample-and-hold amplifiers (one per channel) are recommended. This is the approach taken by the National Instruments SCXI-1140 and A2000-series boards, respectively.

You can remove the timing skew in software as long as you know exactly what the skew is. Most plug-in DAQ boards work like this: by default, the multiplexer scans through the channel list at the top speed of the ADC. For instance, if you have a 100-kHz ADC, there will be a skew of approximately 10 μs between channels. However, the hardware and/or the driver software may increase this value somewhat due to all the

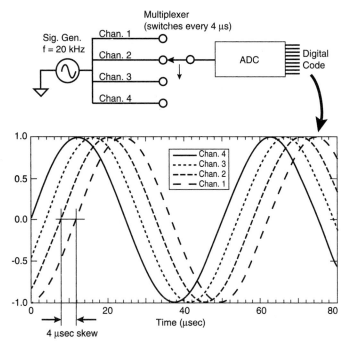

Figure 2.22   Demonstration of skew in an ADC with a multiplexer. Ideally, there would be zero switching time between channels on the multiplexer; this one has 4 μs. Since the inputs are all the same signal, the plotted data shows an apparent phase shift.

extra settling time. For best results, you probably will have to acquire some test data to be sure. You can also choose to adjust the **interchannel delay** (i.e., the skew) with the DAQ VIs in LabVIEW. That feature lets *you* specify the skew, which makes it easier to correct the data's timebase. But the chances are, even with your adjustments and corrections, the results won't be quite as accurate as the multiple ADC approach, and that's the reason we prefer to use an optimum hardware solution.

One misconception about ADCs is that they always do some averaging of the input signal between conversions. For instance, if you are sampling every millisecond, you might expect the converted value to represent the average value over the last millisecond of time. This is true only for certain classes of ADCs, namely dual-slope integrators and voltage-to-frequency converters. Ubiquitous high-speed ADCs, as found on most multifunction boards, are always preceded by sample-and-hold (S/H) amplifiers.

The S/H samples the incoming signal for an extremely brief period of time (the **aperture time**) and stores the voltage on a capacitor for measurement by the ADC. The aperture time depends on the resolution of the ADC and is in the nanosecond range for 16-bit converters. Therefore, if a noise spike should occur during the aperture time, you will get an accurate measurement of the *spike,* not the real waveform. This is one more reason for using a lowpass filter.

When a multiplexer changes from one channel to another, there is a period of time during which the output is in transition, known as the **settling time**. Because of the complex nature of the circuitry in these systems, the transition may not be as clean as you might expect. There may be an overshoot with some damped sinusoidal ringing. Since your objective is to obtain an accurate representation of the input signal, you must wait for these aberrations to decay away. Settling time is the amount of time required for the output voltage to begin tracking the input voltage within a specified error band after a change of channels has occurred. It is clearly specified on all ADC system data sheets. You should not attempt to acquire data faster than the rate determined by settling time plus ADC conversion time.

Another unexpected source of input error is sometimes referred to as **charge pumpout**. When a multiplexer switches from one channel to the next, the input capacitance of the multiplexer (and the next circuit element, such as the sample-and-hold) must charge or discharge to match the voltage of the new input signal. The result is a small glitch induced on the input signal, either positive or negative, depending upon the relative magnitude of the voltage on the preceding channel. If the signal lines are long, you may also see ringing. Charge pumpout effects add to settling time in an unpredictable manner, and may cause momentary overloading or gross errors in high-impedance sources. This is another reason to use signal conditioning; an input amplifier provides a buffering action to reduce the glitches.

Many systems precede the ADC with a programmable-gain instrumentation amplifier (PGIA). Under software control, you can change the gain to suit the amplitude of the signal on each channel. A true instrumentation amplifier with its inherent differential connections is the predominant type. You may have options, through software registers or hardware jumpers, to defeat the differential mode or use various signal grounding schemes, as on the National Instruments MIO-16 series multifunction boards. Study the available configurations and find the one best suited to your application. The one downside to having a PGIA in the signal chain is that it invariably adds some error to the acquisition process in the form of offset voltage drift, gain inaccuracy, noise, and bandwidth. These errors are at their worst at high-gain settings, so study the specifications carefully. An old axiom in analog design is that high gain and high speed are difficult to obtain simultaneously.

Digital to analog converters.   Digital to analog converters (DACs) perform the reverse action of ADCs: a digital code is scaled to a proportional analog voltage. We use DACs to generate analog stimuli, such as test waveforms and actuator control signals. By and large, they have the same general performance characteristics as ADCs. Their main limitations, besides the things we've already discussed, are **settling time** and **slew rate**. When you make a change in the digital code, the output is expected to change instantaneously to the desired voltage. How fast the change actually occurs (measured in volts per second) is the *slew rate*. Hopefully, a clean, crisp step will be produced. In actuality, the output may overshoot and ring for awhile or may take a more leisurely, underdamped approach to the final value. This represents *settling time*. If you are generating high-frequency signals (audio or above), you need faster settling times and slew rates. If you are controlling the current delivered to a heating element, these specs probably aren't much of a concern.

When a DAC is used for waveform generation, it must be followed by a lowpass filter, called a **reconstruction filter**, that performs an anti-aliasing function in reverse. Each time the D/A output is updated (at an interval determined by the timebase) a step in output voltage is produced. This step contains a theoretically infinite number of harmonic frequencies. For high-quality waveforms, this out-of-band energy must be filtered out by the reconstruction filter. DACs for audio and dynamic signal applications, such as National Instruments' A2100 series dynamic signal I/O boards, include such filters and have a spectrally pure output. Ordinary data acquisition boards generally have no such filtering and will produce lots of spurious energy. If spectral purity and transient fidelity are important in your application, be mindful of this fact.

Digital codes.   The pattern of bits—the digital *word*—used to exchange information with an ADC or DAC may have one of several coding schemes, some of which aren't intuitive. If you ever have to deal directly with the I/O hardware (especially in lower-level driver programs), you will need to study these schemes. If the converter is set up for **unipolar** inputs (all-positive or all-negative analog voltages), the binary coding is straightforward, as in Table 2.2. But to represent both polarities of numbers for a **bipolar** converter, a **sign bit** is needed to indicate the signal's polarity. The bipolar coding schemes shown in Table 2.3 are widely used. Each has advantages, depending on the application.

Triggering and timing

Triggering refers to any method by which you synchronize an ADC or DAC to some event. If there is a regular event that causes each individual ADC conversion, it's called the **timebase**, or *clock,* and is usually generated by a crystal-controlled clock oscillator. For this discussion, we'll define triggering as an event that starts or stops a *series* of conversions which are individually paced by a timebase.

TABLE 2.2   Straight Binary Coding Scheme for Unipolar, 3-Bit Converter

Decimal equivalent	Decimal fraction of full-scale		Straight binary
	Positive	Negative	
7	$7/8$	$-7/8$	111
6	$6/8$	$-6/8$	110
5	$5/8$	$-5/8$	101
4	$4/8$	$-4/8$	100
3	$3/8$	$-3/8$	011
2	$2/8$	$-2/8$	010
1	$1/8$	$-1/8$	001
0	$0/8$	$-0/8$	000

TABLE 2.3   Some Commonly Used Coding Schemes for Bipolar Converters, a 4-Bit Example

Decimal equivalent	Fraction of full-scale	Sign and magnitude	Two's complement	Offset binary
7	$7/8$	0111	0111	1111
6	$6/8$	0110	0110	1110
5	$5/8$	0101	0101	1101
4	$4/8$	0100	0100	1100
3	$3/8$	0011	0011	1011
2	$2/8$	0010	0010	1010
1	$1/8$	0001	0001	1001
0	0+	0000	0000	1000
0	0−	1000	0000	1000
−1	$-1/8$	1001	1111	0111
−2	$-2/8$	1010	1110	0110
−3	$-3/8$	1011	1101	0101
−4	$-4/8$	1100	1100	0100
−5	$-5/8$	1101	1011	0011
−6	$-6/8$	1110	1010	0010
−7	$-7/8$	1111	1001	0001
−8	$-8/8$	Not represented	1000	0000

NOTE: The sign and magnitude scheme has two representations for zero, but can't represent −8. Also, the only difference between offset binary and two's complement is the polarity of the sign bit.

When should you bother with triggering? One situation is when you are waiting for a transient event to occur—a single pulse. It would be wasteful (or maybe impossible) to run your ADC for a long period of time, filling up memory and/or disk space, when all you are interested in is a short burst of data before and/or after the trigger event. Another use for triggering is to force your data acquisition to be in-phase with the signal. Signal analysis may be simplified if the waveform always starts with the same polarity and level. Or, you may want to acquire many buffers of data from a recurrent waveform (such as a sine wave) in order to average them, thus reducing the noise. Trigger sources come in three flavors: external, internal, or software-generated.

External triggers are digital pulses, usually produced by specialized hardware or a signal coming from the equipment that you are interfacing with. An example is a function generator that has a connector on it called *sync* which produces a TTL pulse every time output waveform crosses 0 V in the positive direction. Sometimes you have to build your own trigger generator. When dealing with pulsed light sources (such as some lasers), an optical detector such as a photodiode can be used to trigger a short but high-speed burst of data acquisition. Signal conditioning is generally required for external triggers because most data acquisition hardware demands a clean pulse with a limited amplitude range. Chapter 9, "Physics Applications," goes into some detail on external triggering.

Internal triggering is built into many data acquisition devices, including oscilloscopes, transient recorders, and multifunction boards. It is basically an analog function where a device called a **comparator** or **discriminator** detects the signal's crossing of a specified level. The slope of the signal may also be part of the triggering criteria. Really sophisticated instruments permit triggering on specified patterns, which is especially useful in digital logic and communications signal analysis. The on-board triggering features of National Instruments' boards are easy to use in LabVIEW, courtesy of the data acquisition VIs. Newer boards include an advanced system timing controller chip, the DAQ-STC, with programmable function inputs that solve some of the more difficult triggering problems you may encounter.

Software-generated triggers require a program that evaluates an incoming signal or some other status information and decides when to begin saving data or generating an output. A trivial example is the Run button in LabVIEW that starts up a simple data acquisition program. On-the-fly signal analysis is a bit more complex and quickly runs into performance problems if you need to look at fast signals. For instance, you may want to save data from a spectrum analyzer only when the process temperature gets above a certain limit. That should be no problem, since the temperature probably doesn't change very fast. A difficult problem would be to evaluate the distortion of an incoming audio signal and save only the waveforms that are defective. That might require DSP hardware; it might not be practical at all, at least in real time. The NI-DAQ driver includes basic software trigger functionality, such as level and slope detection, that works with many plug-in boards and is very easy to use.

A little noise can be a good thing

Performance of an A/D or D/A system can be enhanced by adding a small amount of noise and by averaging (Lipshitz, Wannamaker, and Vanderkooy 1992). Any time the input voltage is somewhere between two quantization levels of the A/D and there is some **dither** noise present, the least-significant bit (LSB) tends to toggle among a few codes. For instance, the duty cycle of this toggling action is exactly 50 percent if the voltage is exactly between the two quantization levels. Duty cycle and input voltage track each other in a nice, proportional manner (except if the converter demonstrates some kind of nonlinear behavior). All you have to do is filter out the noise, which can be accomplished by averaging or other forms of digital filtering.

A source of uncorrelated dither noise, about 1 LSB peak-to-peak or greater, is required to make this technique work. Some high-performance A/D and D/A systems include dither noise generators; digital audio systems and the National Instruments dynamic signal acquisition boards (A2100, A2150) are examples. High-resolution converters (16 bits and greater) generally have enough thermal noise present to supply the necessary dithering. Incidentally, this resolution enhancement occurs even if you don't apply a filter; filtering simply reduces the noise level.

Figure 2.23 demonstrates the effect of dither noise on the quantization of a slow, low-amplitude ramp signal. To make this realistic, say that the total change in voltage is only about 4 LSBs over a period of 10 s (graph A). The vertical axis is scaled in LSBs for clarity. The sampling rate is 20 Hz. In graph B, you can see the coarse quantization steps expected from an ideal noise-free A/D. Much imagination is

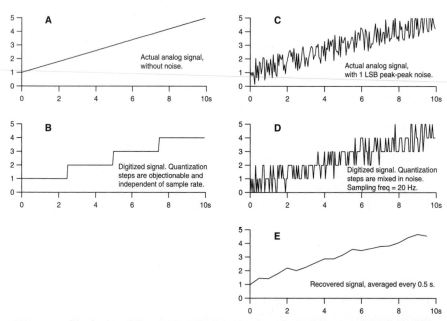

Figure 2.23 Graphs A and B represent digitization of an ideal analog ramp of 4-LSB amplitude which results in objectionable quantization steps. Adding 1 LSB peak-peak dither noise and lowpass filtering (graphs C–E) improves results.

required to see a smooth ramp in this graph. In graph C, dither noise with an amplitude of 1 LSB peak-to-peak has been added to the analog ramp. Graph D is the raw digitized version of this noisy ramp. Contrast this with graph B, the no-noise case with its coarse steps. To eliminate the random noise, I applied a simple *boxcar* filter where every 10 samples (0.5 s worth of data) is averaged into a single value; more elaborate digital filtering might improve the result. Graph E is the recovered signal. Clearly, this is an improvement over the ideal, noiseless case, and it is very easy to implement in LabVIEW. In Chap. 7, "Writing a Data Acquisition Program," I'll show you how to oversample and average to improve your measurements.

Low-frequency analog signals give you some opportunities to further improve the quality of your acquired data. At first glance, that thermocouple signal with a sub-1-Hz bandwidth and little noise could be adequately sampled at 2 or 3 Hz. But by **oversampling**—sampling at a rate several times higher than the minimum specified by the Nyquist rate—you can enhance resolution and noise rejection.

Noise is reduced in proportion to the square root of the number of samples that are averaged. For example, if you average 100 samples, the standard deviation of the average value will be reduced by a factor of 10 when compared to a single measurement. Another way of expressing this result is that you get a 20-dB improvement in signal-to-noise ratio when you average 100 times as many samples. This condition is true so long as the A/D converter has good linearity and a small amount of dither noise. This same improvement occurs with repetitive signals, such as our 1-kHz sine wave with dither noise. If you synchronize your ADC with the waveform by triggering, you can average several waveforms. Since the noise is not correlated with the signal, the noise once again averages to zero according to the square-root rule. How you do this in LabVIEW is discussed in Chap. 7, "Writing a Data Acquisition Program."

Throughput

A final consideration in your choice of converters is the **throughput** of the system, a yardstick for overall performance, usually measured in samples per second. Major factors determining throughput are as follows:

- A/D or D/A conversion speed
- Use of multiplexers and amplifiers, which may add delays between channels
- Disk system performance, if streaming data to or from disk
- Use of DMA, which speeds data transfer

- CPU speed, especially if a lot of data processing is required

- Operating system overhead

The glossy brochure or data sheet you get with your I/O hardware rarely addresses these very real system-oriented limitations. Maximum performance is achieved when the controlling program is written in assembly language, one channel is being sampled with the amplifier gain at minimum, and data is being stored in memory with no analysis or display of any kind. Your application will always be somewhat removed from this particular benchmark.

Practical disk systems have many throughput limitations. The disk itself takes awhile to move the recording heads around and can only transfer so many bytes per second. The file system, and any data conversion you have to do in LabVIEW, are added as overhead. If everything is working well, a stream-to-disk LabVIEW VI will continuously run in excess of 100 kHz. For really fast I/O, you simply have to live within the limits of available memory. But memory is cheap these days, and the performance is much better than that of any disk system. If you really need 256 MB of RAM to perform your experiment, then don't fool around, *just buy it*. Tell the purchasing manager that Gary said so.

Double-buffered DMA for acquisition and waveform generation is built into the LabVIEW support for many I/O boards and offers many advantages in speed because the hardware does all the real-time work of transferring data from the I/O to main memory. Your program can perform analysis, display, and archiving tasks while the I/O is in progress (you can't do *too* much processing though . . .). Refer to your LabVIEW data acquisition VI library reference manual for details on this technique. Chapter 6, "Using the DAQ Library," also discusses all aspects of high-speed buffered I/O.

Performance without DMA is quite limited. Each time you send a command to a plug-in board, the command is processed by the NI-DAQ driver, which in turn must get permission from the operating system to perform an I/O operation. There is a great deal of overhead in this process. On the Macintosh, it takes approximately 0.5 ms, and under Windows 3.1, it's about 3.5 ms. That means you can read one sample at a time from an input at about 2 kHz on a Mac and at about 300 Hz on a PC without DMA. Clearly, this technique is not very efficient and should be used only for infrequent I/O operations.

If you need to do very much on-the-fly analysis, adding a **DSP board** can augment the power of your computer's CPU by off-loading tasks such as FFT computations. Using a DSP board as a general-purpose computer is another story; actually another *book!* Programming such a machine to orchestrate data transfers, do control algorithms, and so on, requires programming in C or assembly language using the support tools for your particular DSP board. If you are an experienced programmer, this is a high-performance alternative. The rest of us have to stick to post-run analysis or simply get more and/or faster computers.

Bibliography

Beckwith, Thomas G. and R. D. Marangoni, *Mechanical Measurements,* Addison-Wesley, Reading, Massachusetts, 1990. (ISBN 0-201-17866-4)

Gunn, Ronald, "Designing System Grounds and Signal Returns," *Control Engineering,* May, 1987.

Lancaster, Donald, *Active Filter Cookbook,* Howard W. Sams & Co., Indianapolis, 1975. (ISBN 0-672-21168-8)

Lipshitz, Stanley P., R. A. Wannamaker, and J. Vanderkooy, "Quantization and Diter: A Theoretical Survey," *J. Audio Eng. Soc.,* 40:(5):355–375 (1992).

Morrison, Ralph, *Grounding and Shielding Techniques in Instrumentation,* Wiley-Interscience, New York, 1986.

Norton, Harry R. *Electronic Analysis Instruments,* Prentice-Hall, Englewood Cliffs, New Jersey, 1992. (ISBN 0-13-249426-4)

Omega Engineering, Inc., *Temperature Handbook,* Stamford, Connecticut, 1997. (Available free by calling 203-359-1660 or 800-222-2665.)

Ott, Henry W., *Noise Reduction Techniques in Electronic Systems,* John Wiley & Sons, New York, 1988. (ISBN 0-471-85068-3)

Pallas-Areny, Ramon and J. G. Webster, *Sensors and Signal Conditioning,* John Wiley & Sons, New York, 1991. (ISBN 0-471-54565-1)

Qian, Shie and Dapang Chen, *Joint Time-Frequency Analysis—Methods and Applications,* Prentice-Hall, Englewood Cliffs, New Jersey, 1996. (ISBN 0-13-254384-2. Call Prentice-Hall at 800-947-7700 or 201-767-4990.)

Sheingold, Daniel H., *Analog-Digital Conversion Handbook,* Prentice-Hall, Englewood Cliffs, New Jersey, 1986. (ISBN 0-13-032848-0)

Steer, Robert W., Jr., "Anti-aliasing Filters Reduce Errors in ADC Converters," *EDN,* March 30, 1989.

3M Specialty Optical Fibers, *Fiber Optic Current Sensor Module* (product information and application note), West Haven, Connecticut, (203) 934-7961.

White, Donald R. J. *Shielding Design Methodology and Procedures,* Interference Control Technologies, Gainesville, Virginia, 1986. (ISBN 0-932263-26-7)

LabVIEW Programming Techniques

This chapter is devoted to the nuts and bolts of LabVIEW programming. Make no mistake about it: LabVIEW is a programming language, and a sophisticated one at that. It takes time to learn how to use it effectively. When I went for that first LabVIEW test-drive, I was certainly impressed with the ease at which we made a spectrum analyzer out of an oscilloscope. After I bought the program, I went through the tutorial manual and that helped. But soon, I started asking questions like, "How do you get data into a spreadsheet, and format a command string for GPIB, and run my test every 3.7 seconds, and . . ." and all kinds of things. It became apparent that I needed help getting started, so I took the LabVIEW class, and later, the Advanced LabVIEW class.

And you should, too, even though it costs money and takes time. It's *worth* it. Ask any of the MBAs in the front office; they know the value of training in terms of dollars and cents as well as worker productivity. The LabVIEW tutorial that comes with the package is very helpful for beginners. It's a combination of a getting started manual and the training manual. Don't rush through it too quickly. There is a great deal of information to absorb. I like to read, experiment, and then read some more, when I'm learning a new application like this. If you can't make it to a class, consider buying the LabVIEW video from National Instruments. It's roughly equivalent to the tutorial and besides, everyone likes to watch TV. Another do-it-yourself training aid is the virtual training CD-ROM, also from National Instruments. Or get Lisa and Jeff's book, *LabVIEW for Everyone* (1996). It's an excellent starter book. For the purpose of this chapter, I assume that you've been working with LabVIEW for awhile and know the basic concepts.

Another thing you should do is spend plenty of time looking at the example VIs that come with the LabVIEW package. Collectively, the examples contain about 80 percent of the basic concepts that you really need to do an effective job, plus a lot of ready-to-use drivers and special functions. The rest you can get right here. Remember that this book is not a replacement for the user manual. Yeah, I know, you don't read user manuals either, but it might be a good idea to crack the manuals next time you get stuck. I think they are pretty well-written. What I want to cover here are some important concepts that should make your programming more effective. My examples are based on the analysis of real applications. Chapter 4, "Building an Application," goes into more detail on the process of high-level application development.

About the Diagrams in This Book

It's hard to present LabVIEW through printed media. After all, it's an interactive graphical language, and the static nature of paper can obscure the workings of the underlying structure. In this book, I've used some accepted conventions regarding images of LabVIEW diagrams and panels. One such convention is shown in Fig. 3.1. Sequence structures and Case structures appear on the screen as single frames, but may in fact have several hidden frames, or **subdiagrams**. You view the subdiagrams by operating the control bar at the top ◀ 2 [0..2] ▶. Too bad I can't let you click on these pages. . . . Instead, I'll just spread the subdiagrams out in a logical manner that should not cause too much confusion. For details on how you, too, can print and otherwise document LabVIEW programs, refer to the end of Chap. 4 under "Printing LabVIEW Diagrams and Panels."

Sequencing and Dataflow

Regular textual programming languages (and most computers) are based on a concept called **control flow**, which is geared toward making

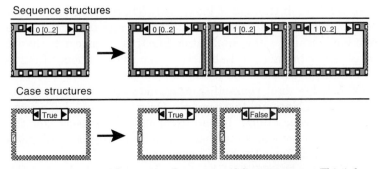

Figure 3.1   A standard for printing Sequence and Case structures. This is but one compromise we must make when displaying LabVIEW programs on paper.

things happen one step at a time with explicit ordering. The LabVIEW language, **G**, on the other hand, is known formally as a **dataflow** language. All it cares about is that each **node** (an object that takes inputs and processes them into outputs) has all its inputs available before executing. This is a new way of programming—one that you have to get used to before declaring yourself a qualified LabVIEW programmer. The Dataflow concept should be used to its best advantage at all times. This section discusses some of the concepts of dataflow programming with which you should be familiar.

Figure 3.2 compares ordinary procedural programming (such as Basic or C) with dataflow programming. In all cases, the PROCESS A AND B step can execute only after GET A and GET B are completed. In the procedural language, we have forced GET A to happen before GET B. What if the source of data for B was actually ready to go before A? Then you would end up wasting time waiting for A. The dataflow version says nothing about whether GET A or GET B must go first. If the underlying code (courtesy of the LabVIEW compiler) is intelligent enough, the two GET tasks will overlap in time as required, enhancing throughput for this imaginary system.

LabVIEW permits you to have any number of different nodes on a diagram all executing in parallel. Furthermore, the LabVIEW environment supports parallel execution, or multitasking, between multiple VIs, regardless of the capability of the operating system or computer.

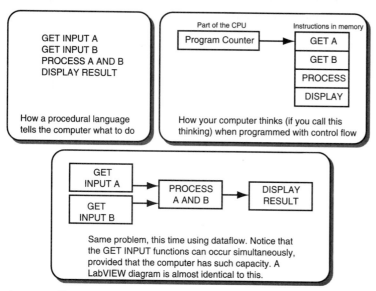

Figure 3.2   Compare and contrast control flow programming in a procedural language with dataflow programming in LabVIEW.

These capabilities give you great freedom to run various tasks asynchronously with one another without doing any special programming yourself. On the other hand, you sometimes need to force the sequence of execution to guarantee that operations occur in the proper order. For that, LabVIEW has several methods.

Sequence structures

The simplest way to force the order of execution is to use a Sequence structure as in the upper example of Fig. 3.3. Data from one frame is passed to succeeding frames through **Sequence local variables**, which you create through a pop-up menu on the border of the Sequence structure. In a sense, this method avoids the use of (and advantages of) dataflow programming. You should try to avoid the overuse of sequence structures. LabVIEW has a great deal of inherent parallelism, like our previous example where GET A and GET B could be processed simultaneously. (Future computers with multiprocessor architectures could make good use of this feature.) Using a sequence guarantees the order of execution but prohibits parallel operations. For instance, asynchronous tasks that use I/O devices (such as GPIB and serial communications and plug-in boards) can run concurrently with CPU-bound number crunching tasks. Your program may actually execute faster if you can add parallelism by reducing the use of Sequence structures. Note that sequence structures add *no code or execution overhead* of their own. Perhaps the worst features of Sequence structures are that they tend to hide parts of the program and that they interrupt the natural left-to-right visual flow. The lower example in Fig. 3.3 is much easier to understand and permits parallel execution of GET A and GET B.

Zealots may consider the Sequence structure something to avoid at all costs. Not so. Sequencing is mandatory in many problems and can clarify the program structure by grouping logically connected operations into neat frames. They should also be used to conserve screen

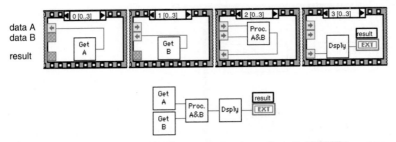

Figure 3.3 In the upper example, Sequence structures force LabVIEW to *not* use dataflow. Do this only when you have a good reason. The lower example shows the preferred method.

space. Don't get carried away with the *avoidance* of Sequence structures. A contrived "pure dataflow" diagram that uses no Sequence structures may obscure the intentions of your code as badly as the overuse of Sequences. Good use of dataflow results in a clear, single-page main program that is easy to understand. Similarly, you can encapsulate major parts of your main program in frames of a Sequence structure to enhance its readability. Try not to use too many local variables in the Sequence structure, because they can make it difficult to follow the flow of data.

Data dependency

A fundamental concept of dataflow programming is **data dependency**, which says that a given node can't execute until *all* of its inputs are available. So in fact, you can write a program using dataflow or not. Let's look at an example that is very easy to do with a sequence, but is better done without. Consider Fig. 3.4, which shows four possible solutions to the problem where you need to open a file, read from it, and then close it.

Solution A uses a sequence. Almost everybody does it this way the first time. Its main disadvantage is that you have to flip through the subdiagrams to see what's going on. Now, let's do it with dataflow, where all the functions are linked by wires in some logical order. A problem arises in solution B that may not be obvious, especially in a more com-

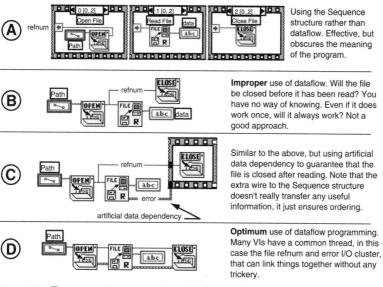

(A) Using the Sequence structure rather than dataflow. Effective, but obscures the meaning of the program.

(B) **Improper** use of dataflow. Will the file be closed before it has been read? You have no way of knowing. Even if it does work once, will it always work? Not a good approach.

(C) Similar to the above, but using artificial data dependency to guarantee that the file is closed after reading. Note that the extra wire to the Sequence structure doesn't really transfer any useful information, it just ensures ordering.

(D) **Optimum** use of dataflow programming. Many VIs have a common thread, in this case the file refnum and error I/O cluster, that can link things together without any trickery.

Figure 3.4 Four ways to open, read, and close a file, using either Sequence or dataflow programming methods. Example D is preferred.

plicated program: will the file be read before it is closed? Which function executes first? Don't assume top-to-bottom or left-to-right execution when no data dependency exists! Make sure that the sequence of events is explicitly defined when necessary. A solution is to create **artificial data dependency** between the **Read File** and the **Close File** functions, as shown in example C. I just connected one of the outputs of the **Read File** function (any output will do) to the border of the Sequence structure enclosing the **Close File**. That single-frame sequence could also have been a Case structure or a While Loop—no matter: it's just a container for the next event. The advantage to this style of programming is clarity: the entire program is visible at first glance. Once you get good at it, you can write many of your programs this way.

Adding common threads

Going further with the idea of data dependency, you can build flow control right into your subVIs as demonstrated in example D. If you make a collection of subVIs that are frequently used together, give them all a common input/output terminal pair so that they can be chained together without requiring Sequence structures. In the case of LabVIEW's file I/O functions, it turns out that the file refnum is duplicated by the **Read File** function, and it can be passed along to the **Close File** function. Thus, the read operation has to be completed before it permits the file to be closed. Problem solved and very neatly.

A good common thread is an error code, since just about every operation that you devise probably has some kind of error checking built into it, particularly those that do I/O operations. Each VI should test the incoming error and not execute its function if there is an existing error, then pass that error (or its own error) to the output. You can assemble this error information into a cluster containing a numeric error code, a string containing the name of the function that generated the error, and an error Boolean for quick testing. This technique, which is a universal standard first promoted by Monnie Anderson at National Instruments, is called **Error I/O**. Particular examples are the data acquisition (DAQ) library functions (Fig. 3.5), GPIB, VISA, serial, and file I/O. Error I/O is discussed in detail in Chap. 5, "Instrument Drivers."

Looping

Most of your VIs will contain one or more of the two available loop structures, the **For Loop** and the **While Loop**. Besides the obvious use—doing an operation many times—there are many nonobvious ways to use a loop (particularly the While Loop) that are helpful to know about. We'll start with some details about looping that are often overlooked.

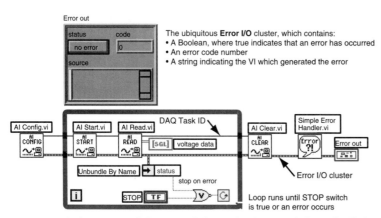

Figure 3.5 A cluster containing error information is passed through all the important subVIs in this program that uses the DAQ library. The While Loop stops if an error is detected, and the user ultimately sees the source of the error displayed by the Simple Error Handler VI. Note the clean appearance of this style of programming.

Subtleties of the For Loop

Use the **For Loop** when you definitely know how many times a subdiagram needs to be executed. Examples are building and processing arrays and repeating an operation a fixed number of times. Most of the time, you process arrays with a For Loop because LabVIEW already knows how many elements there are, and the **autoindexing** feature takes care of the iteration count for you automatically: all you have to do is wire the array to the loop, and the number of iterations (count) will be equal to the number of elements in the array. But what happens when you hook up more than one array to the For Loop, each with a different number of elements? What if the count terminal, **N**, is also wired, but to yet a different number? Figure 3.6 should help clear up some of these questions. *Rule: The smaller count always wins.* If an empty array is hooked up to a For Loop, that loop will *never* execute.

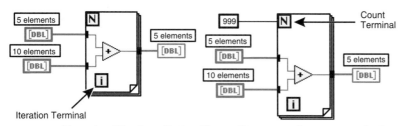

Figure 3.6 The rule of For Loop limits: *The smallest count always wins,* whether it's the N terminal or one of several arrays.

Also, note that there is no way to abort a For Loop. In most programming languages, there is a GOTO or an EXIT command that can force the program to jump out of the loop. Such a mechanism was never included in LabVIEW because it destroys the dataflow continuity. Suppose you just bailed out of a For Loop from inside a nested Case structure. To what values should the outputs of the Case, let alone the loop, be set? Every situation would have a different answer; it is wiser to simply enforce good programming habits. If you need to escape from a For Loop, use a While Loop instead! By the way, try popping up (see your tutorial manual for instructions on popping up on your platform) on the border of a For Loop, and use the Replace operation; you can instantly change it to a While Loop, with no rewiring. The reverse operation also works. You can even swap between Sequence and Case structures, and LabVIEW preserves the frame numbers. Loops and other structures can be removed entirely, leaving their contents wired in place so far as possible, by the same process (for example, try the Remove For Loop operation). See the LabVIEW User Manual for these and other cool editing tricks that can save you time.

Wonderful Whiles

The While Loop is one of the most versatile structures in LabVIEW. With it, you can iterate an unlimited number of times then suddenly quit when the Boolean **conditional terminal**, ⟳, becomes false.

If the conditional terminal is left unwired, the loop executes exactly *one time*. If you put uninitialized shift registers on one of these one-trip loops and then construct your entire subVI inside it, the shift registers become a memory element between calls to the VI. You can retain all sorts of status information this way, such as knowing how long it's been since this subVI was last called (see the section on Shift Registers that follows).

Pretest While Loop.   What if you need a While Loop that does not execute *at all* if some condition is false? We call this a *pretest* While, and it's really easy to do (Fig. 3.7). Just use a Case structure to contain the code that you might not want to execute.

Graceful stops.   It's considered bad form to write an infinite loop in LabVIEW (or any other language, for that matter). Infinite loops run forever, generally because the programmer told it to stop only when $2 + 2 = 5$, or something like that. I remember running Fortran programs on the old Cyber 175 back at school, where an infinite loop was rather hard to detect from a time-sharing terminal—there was always an unpredictable delay before the friendly prompt came back, regardless

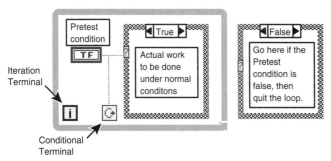

Figure 3.7 A pretest While Loop. If the pretest condition is false, the False frame of the Case structure is executed, skipping the actual work to be done that resides in the True case.

of how long your program took to execute. Trouble was, some folks had to pay real money for computer time, and that computer cost about $1000 per hour to run! The hazard in LabVIEW is that the only way to stop an infinite loop is to click the Abort icon, ▣, in the toolbar. I/O hardware could be left in an indeterminate state. As a minimum, you need to put a Boolean switch on the front panel, name it RUN, and wire it to ⟳. There's a really cool stop sign I've been using that's pasted into a boolean; the Boolean control palette even has buttons prelabeled STOP. Use whatever is appropriate for your experiment.

A funny thing happens when you have a whole bunch of stuff going on in a While Loop: it sometimes takes a long time to stop when you turn off that RUN Boolean you so thoughtfully included. The problem (and its solution) are shown in Fig. 3.8. What happens in the left frame is that there is no data dependency between the guts of the loop and the RUN switch, so the switch may be read before the rest of the diagram executes. If that happens, the loop will go around one more time before actually stopping. If one cycle of the loop takes 10 minutes, the

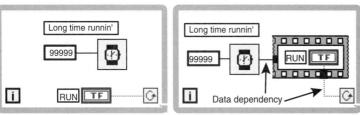

Figure 3.8 The left example may run an extra cycle after the RUN switch is turned off. Forcing the switch to be evaluated as the last item (*right*) guarantees that the loop will exit promptly.

user is going to wonder why the RUN switch doesn't seem to do anything. Forcing the RUN Boolean to be evaluated as the last thing in the While Loop cures this extra-cycle problem.

Shift Registers

Shift registers are special local variables or memory elements available in For and While Loops that transfer values from the completion of one iteration to the beginning of the next. You create them by popping up on the border of a loop. When an iteration of the loop completes, a value is written to the shift register—call this the nth value. On the next iteration, that value is available as a source of data and is now known as the $(n - 1)$th value. Also, you can add as many terminals as you like to the left side, thus returning not only the $(n - 1)$th value, but $(n - 2)$, $(n - 3)$, and so on. This gives you the ability to do digital filtering, modeling of discrete systems, and other algorithms that require a short history of the values of some variable. Any kind of data can be stored in a shift register—they are **polymorphic**. Figure 3.9 is an implementation of a simple *finite impulse response* (FIR) *filter,* in this case a moving averager that computes the average of the last four values. You can see from the strip charts how the random numbers have been smoothed over time in the filtered case. National Instruments application note AN023, *Digital Signal Processing Fundamentals,* discusses difference equations, Z transforms, and signal flow diagrams in detail.

Besides purely mathematical applications like this one, there are many other things you can do with shift registers. Figure 3.10 is a very

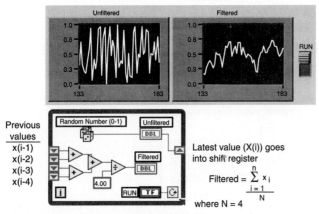

Figure 3.9 Using a shift register to perform a simple moving average on random numbers. Note the difference in the graphs of filtered and unfiltered data. This is a very simple case of a finite impulse response filter.

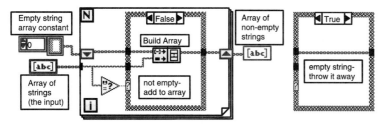

Figure 3.10 Weeding out empty strings with a shift register. A similar program might be used to select special numeric values. Notice that we had to use Build Array inside a loop, a relatively slow construct, but also unavoidable.

common construct where an array is assembled based on some conditional testing of the incoming data. In this case, it's weeding out empty strings from an incoming array. This program is frequently seen in configuration management programs (see Chap. 7, "Writing a Data Acquisition Program"). In that case, a user is filling out a big cluster array that contains information about the various channels in the system. Leaving a channel name empty implies that the channel is unused and should be deleted from the output array. The Build Array function is located inside a Case structure that checks to see if the current string array element is empty. To initialize the shift register, I created a one-dimensional (1D) string array constant on the diagram by popping up on the shift register terminal and selecting Create Constant.

Uninitialized shift registers

In Fig. 3.10, what would happen if that empty string array constant already had something in it? That data would appear in the output array *ahead* of the desired data. That's why we want an *empty* array for initialization. What happens if it is left out altogether? The answer is that the first time the program runs after being loaded, the shift register is in fact empty and works as expected. But it then *retains its previous contents until the next execution.* Every time you run this modified VI, the output string would get bigger and bigger (a good way to make LabVIEW run out of memory, by the way). All shift registers are initialized at compile time as well: arrays and strings are empty, numerics are zero, and Booleans are False. There are some important uses for uninitialized shift registers that you need to know about.

First, you can use uninitialized shift registers to keep track of state information between calls to a subVI. This is an extremely powerful technique and should be studied closely. You will see it dozens of times in this book. In Fig. 3.11, a shift register saves the previous value of the Setpoint front-panel control and compares it to the current setting. If a

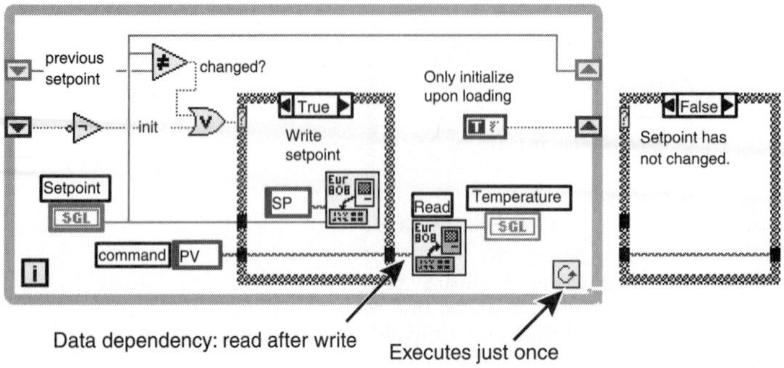

Figure 3.11 This VI writes a new setpoint to a Eurotherm 808 temperature controller only when the user has changed the value. It then reads the current temperature. The upper shift register saves the previous setpoint value for change-of-state detection. The lower shift register is used for initialization to guarantee that a setpoint will always be written when the VI is first run.

change of value has occurred, the new setting is sent to a temperature controller via the serial port. By transmitting only when the value has changed, you can reduce the communications traffic. This technique, known as **change-of-state detection**, can make a VI act more intelligently toward operator inputs. Use a second (Boolean) shift register to force the transmission of the setpoint the first time this VI is run. Since the Boolean shift register is False when loaded, you can test for that condition as shown here. Then, write True to the shift register to keep the VI from performing the initialization operation again.

Note that the ⟳ terminal is unwired which means that the contents of the loop execute only once each time the VI is called. Such a construct is of little use as a top-level VI. Instead, its intended use is as a more intelligent subVI—one with **state memory**. That is, each time this subVI is called, the contents of the shift register provide it with logical information regarding conditions at the end of the previous iteration. This allows you to program the subVI to take action based not only on the current inputs, but on previous inputs as well. This concept will be extrapolated into powerful **state machines** in subsequent chapters.

The shift register in Fig. 3.12 keeps track of the elapsed time since the subVI was last called. If you compare the elapsed time with a desired value, you could use this to trigger a periodic function such as data logging or a watchdog timing. This technique is also used in the PID (proportional integral derivative) Toolkit control blocks whose algorithms are time-dependent.

Global and Local Variables

Another, very important use for uninitialized shift registers is where you create **global variable VIs**. In G, a variable is a wire connecting

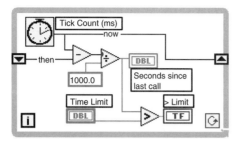

Figure 3.12 This example shows how to use an uninitialized shift register to determine how long it's been since this subVI was last called. This makes the subVI *time aware* and useful for data logging, watchdog timing, or time-dependent calculations.

two objects on a diagram. Since it exists only on one diagram, it is by definition a local variable. By using an uninitialized shift register in a subVI, two or more calling VIs can share information by reading from and writing to the shift register in the subVI. This is a kind of global variable, and it's a very powerful notion. Figure 3.13 shows what the basic model looks like.

If **Set Value** is True (write mode), the input value is loaded into the shift register and copied to the output. If **Set Value** is False (read mode), the old value is read out and recycled in the shift register. The **Valid** indicator tells you that something has been written; it would be a bad idea to read from this global and get nothing when you expect a number. Important note: for each global variable VI, you must create a distinct VI with a *unique name.*

There are several really nice features of global variables. First, they can be read or written any time, any place, and all callers will access the same data. This includes multiple copies on the same diagram and, of course, communications between top-level VIs. This permits asynchronous tasks to share information. For instance, you could have one

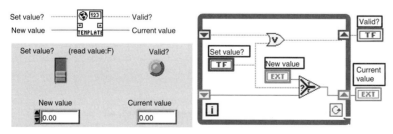

Figure 3.13 A global variable VI that stores a single numeric value. You could easily change the input and output data type to an array, a cluster, or anything else.

top-level VI that just scans your input hardware to collect readings at some rate. It writes the data to a global array. Independently, you could have another top-level VI that displays those readings from the global at another rate, and yet another VI that stores the values. This is like having a global database or a client-server relationship among VIs.

Because these global variables are VIs, they are more than just memory locations. They can perform processing on the data, such as filtering or selection, and they can keep track of time like the **Interval Timer VI** in Fig. 3.14. Each channel of this interval timer compares the present time with the time stored in the shift register the last time that the channel's **Event** output was True. When the **Iteration** input is equal to zero, all of the timers are synchronized and are forced to trigger. This technique of initialization is another common trick. It's convenient because you can wire the **Iteration** input to the iteration terminal, [i], in the calling VI, which then initializes the subVI on the first iteration. I use this timer in many applications throughout this book, and it's available on the book's CD-ROM in the timing library.

platform\ timing\interval timer.vi

As you can see, one global variable can store multiple elements of different types. Just add more shift registers and input/output terminals. Using clusters or arrays, the storage capacity is virtually unlimited.

LabVIEW has built-in global variables, as well (discussed in the next section). They are faster and more efficient than these shift register–based globals and should be used preferentially. However, you can't embed any intelligence in them since they have no diagram; they are merely data storage devices.

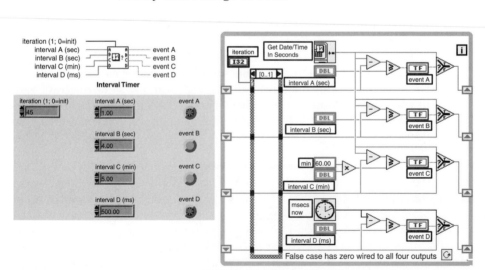

Figure 3.14   A time interval generator based on uninitialized shift registers. Call this subVI with one of the *Event* Booleans connected to a Case structure that contains a function you wish to perform periodically. For instance, you could place a strip chart or file storage function in the True frame of the Case structure.

There is one more issue with these global variables: performance. Scalar types including numerics and Booleans are very fast and limited only by LabVIEW's subVI calling overhead, which is on the order of microseconds. Arrays or clusters of numerics and Booleans are a little slower, but the number of elements is what is most important. The real killer is when your global carries clusters or arrays that contain strings. This requires the services of the memory manager every time it is called, and thus the performance is relatively poor (almost 100 times slower than a comparably sized collection of numerics).

Built-in global variables—and their hazards

Starting with LabVIEW 3, global variables are built in. To create a global variable, you select it from the Structures subpalette of the function palette, place it on the diagram, and then double-click on it to open and edit its front panel, exactly like any subVI. You can place any number of controls on the panel, name them, and then save the global with a name—again, just like any subVI. Back on your main diagram, pop up on the global, and select one of the controls that you put in the global, and then choose whether you wish to read or write data. Finally, wire it to the appropriate source or destination. At any time, you can open the panel of the global variable to view or change its contents. That can be very helpful during a debugging session.

The difference between built-in globals and the kind you make yourself with a subVI is that the built-in ones are not true VIs and as such cannot be programmed to do anything besides simple data storage. However, built-in globals are about 10 times faster for most data types. Another advantage of the built-in globals is that you can have all the global data for your entire program present in just one global variable but access them separately with no penalty in performance. With subVI-based globals, you can combine many variables into one global, but you must read and write them all at once, which increases execution time and memory management overhead. Thus, built-in globals are preferred for most applications for performance reasons.

A hazard you need to be aware of when using either type of global variable is the potential for **race conditions**. A race condition exists when two or more events can occur in any order, but you rely on them occurring in a *particular* order. While you're developing your VI, or under normal conditions, the order may be as expected and all is well. But under different conditions the order will vary, causing the program to misbehave. Sequence structures and data dependency prevent race conditions from being a general problem in LabVIEW, but global variables provide a way to violate strict dataflow programming. Therefore, it's up to you to understand the pitfalls of race conditions.

In Fig. 3.15, two While Loops are executing at the same time (they don't necessarily have to be on the same diagram). Both loops write a value to a global number, and one of the loops reads the value. The trouble is, which value will the global contain when it's time to read it? The value from Loop A or the value from Loop B? Note that there can be any number of data writers out there, adding to the uncertainty. You might have to add an elaborate handshaking, timing, or sequencing scheme to this simple example in order to force things to occur in a predictable fashion.

An all-around safe approach to avoiding race conditions is to write your overall hierarchy in such a way that a global can only be written from one location. This condition would be met, for instance, by the client-server architecture where there is one data source (a data acquisition VI) with multiple data readers (display, archive, etc.). You must also make sure that you never read from a global before it is initialized. This is one of the first rules taught for traditional languages: initialize the variables, then start running the main program. For example, it would be improper for the data display VI to run before the data acquisition VI because the global variable is initially empty or contains garbage. *Rule: Enforce the order of execution in all situations that use global variables.*

If your application has a global array, there is a risk of excessive data duplication. When an array is passed along through wires on a single diagram, LabVIEW does an admirable job of avoiding array duplication, thus saving memory. This is particularly important when you want to access a single element, by indexing, adding, or replacing an element. But if the data comes from a global variable, your program has to read the data, make a local copy, index or modify the array, and then write it back. If you do this process at many different locations, you end up making many copies of the data. This wastes memory and adds execution overhead. A solution is to create a subVI that encapsulates the global, providing whatever access the rest of your program

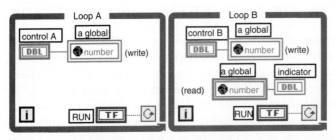

Figure 3.15 Race conditions are a hazard associated with all global variables. The global gets written in two places. Which value will it contain when it's read?

requires. It might have single-element inputs and outputs, addressing the array by element number. In this way, the subVI has the only direct access to the global, guaranteeing that there is only one copy of the data. This implementation is realized automatically when you create global variable VIs built from shift registers.

Global variables, while handy, can quickly become a programmer's nightmare because they hide the flow of data. For instance, you could write a LabVIEW program where there are several subVIs sitting on a diagram with no wires interconnecting them and no flow control structures. Global variables make this possible: the subVIs all run until a global Boolean is set to False, and all of the data is passed among the subVIs in global variables. The problem is nobody can understand what is happening since all data transfers are hidden. Similar things happen in regular programming languages where most of the data is passed in global variables rather than being part of the subroutine calls. This data hiding is not only confusing, it is dangerous. All you have to do is access the wrong item in a global at the wrong time, and things will go nuts. How do you troubleshoot your program when you can't even figure out where the data is coming from or going to?

The answer is another *rule: Use global variables only where there is no other dataflow alternative.* Using global variables to synchronize or exchange information between parallel loops or top-level VIs is perfectly reasonable. Using globals to carry data from one side of a diagram to the other "because the wires would be too long" is asking for trouble. You are in effect making your data accessible to the entire LabVIEW hierarchy. One more helpful tip with any global variable: use the Show . . . Label pop-up item (whether it's a built-in or VI-based global) to display its name. When there are many global variables in a program, it's difficult to keep track of which is which, so labeling helps. Finally, if you need to locate all instances of a global variable, you can use the **Find** command from the Project menu, or you can pop up on the global variable and choose **Find:Global References**.

Multiple, asynchronous loops in one diagram.   Here is a classic application for global variables. Recall that objects on a LabVIEW diagram run in parallel, within the constraints of dataflow. (Technically, this is referred to as *arbitrary interleaving* on a single-processor system.) A diagram can therefore have more than one loop running at a time, at totally unrelated speeds or intervals. This has some interesting applications that are most useful.

In Fig. 3.16, there are two While Loops that perform independent functions. The upper loop, which might be called the master, runs at a fixed 100-ms cycle time and uses the **AI Sample Channel VI** (from the DAQ library) to read an analog input and display it on a waveform chart. The master loop runs until the user turns off the RUN Boolean control. Note that the state of the RUN control is written to a global Boolean when the loop is finished.

The lower loop, the slave, runs until the global Boolean becomes False. Note that there are no timing functions in this loop; it runs as fast as LabVIEW will permit—a rate significantly faster than the master loop. Inside the slave loop, there is a Case structure connected to a Boolean control called *Open the SubVI*. When it is True, a subVI inside the True frame of the Case is called. The subVI has been set to **Show front panel when called**. This is a setup item available through a pop-up item on the subVI called **SubVI Node Setup**. Thus, when the user clicks the Open button, the subVI panel appears, then continues to run until some condition internal to that subVI is satisfied, at which time control returns to the slave loop, which is free to run once again. Note that while the subVI is running the slave loop is suspended. Lab-VIEW demands that *all* nodes inside a loop structure must be finished before the loop can cycle again.

What would happen if the contents of the slave loop were placed inside the master loop? When the subVI opens, the main loop would be suspended and it could not collect any data until the subVI is through. In our master-slave example, the main loop continues to run at its nominal rate at all times. That is the utility of multiple, independent loops.

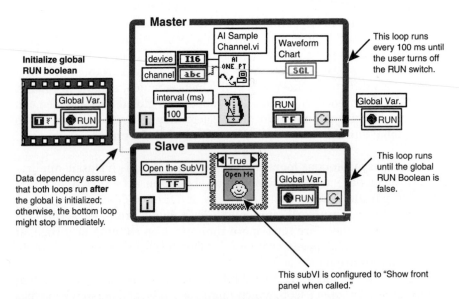

Figure 3.16 Independent, asynchronous While Loops. The RUN global Boolean terminates both loops from one RUN switch. You can expand this technique to control as many independent loops as you need, and they don't even have to be within the same diagram.

There is a required initialization action. At the left side of the diagram, the RUN global variable is initialized to True (run), and wires to both loops force the loops to wait until the global has been initialized. If this were not done, the slave loop might stop immediately if the global Boolean was initially False. The Boolean constant and the global variable must be encased in a structure of some kind to guarantee that the initialization is completed before the loops start up.

Since the RUN state is carried in a global variable, you have even more options for interacting with external VIs. The VI discussed here can signal another top-level VI to stop. Or, another top-level VI could set the RUN global variable to False and stop the slave loop in this VI. By adding Boolean logic, you can extrapolate this concept to synchronize any number of parallel loops or VIs.

Local variables

Another way to manipulate data within the scope of a LabVIEW diagram is with **local variables**. A local variable allows you to read data from or write data to controls and indicators without directly wiring to the usual control or indicator terminal. This means you have unlimited read-write access from multiple locations on the diagram. To create a local variable, select a Local variable from the Structures palette and drop it on the diagram. Pop up on the local variable node and select the item you wish to access. The list contains the names of every control and indicator defined. (If you change the name of a control or indicator that is accessed by a local variable, you will have to reselect it from the local.) Then, choose whether you want to read or write data. The local variable then behaves exactly the same as the control or indicator's terminal, other than the fact that you are free to read *or* write. Here are some important facts about local variables.

- Local variables act only on the controls and indicators that reside on the same diagram. You can't use a local variable to access a control that resides in another VI. Use global variables, or better, regular wired connections to subVIs to transfer data outside of the current diagram.

- You can have as many local variables as you want for each control or indicator. Note how confusing this can become: imagine your controls changing state mysteriously because you accidentally selected the wrong item in one or more local variables. Danger!

- Like global variables, you should use local variables only when there is no other reasonable dataflow alternative. They bypass the explicit flow of data, obscuring the relationships between data sources (controls) and data sinks (indicators).

■ Each instance of a local variable requires a copy of the associated data. This can be significant for arrays and other data types that contain large amounts of data. This is another reason that it's better to use wires than local variables whenever possible.

There are three basic uses for local variables: control initialization, control adjustment or interaction, and for temporary storage.

Figure 3.17 demonstrates control initialization, a simple, safe, and common use for a local variable. When you start up a top-level VI, it is important that the controls be preset to their required states. In this example, a Boolean control opens and closes a valve via a digital output line on a plug-in board. At startup, a local variable sets the Boolean control to False before starting the While Loop. If you have many controls to initialize in this manner, you will need just as many local variables. Note the Sequence structure surrounding the initialization part of the program. This guarantees that the local variable has done its work before the While Loop starts. Otherwise, a race condition might arise.

The same technique is useful at all levels in a hierarchy, but please note that you can initialize the controls in a subVI by assigning them to terminals on the subVI's icon, then wiring in the desired values from the calling VI. This is a case where there is a dataflow alternative. However, if you intend to use a VI at the top level, there is no such alternative, and you can use local variables with my blessing.

Another problem that is solved by local variables is one we have visited before: stopping a parallel While Loop. This is a case where the local variable is a temporary storage device with a scope that extends throughout the diagram of a single VI. Contrast this with a global variable, whose scope is all VIs currently in memory. In Fig. 3.16, I used a global variable to stop the slave loop. You can also use a local variable in a similar manner, as shown in Fig. 3.18. There is one catch: you can't use a local variable with a Boolean control that has its mechanical

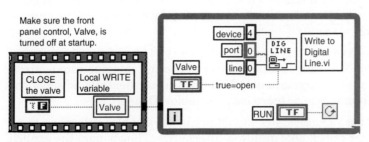

Figure 3.17   Local variables are a convenient way to initialize front panel controls. The Sequence structure guarantees that the initialization is completed before the While Loop starts.

action set to one of the *latch* modes. Those are the modes you would normally use for a *stop switch,* where the switch resets to its off position after it is read by the program. Why this limitation? Because there is an ambiguous situation: if the user throws a Boolean into its temporary (latched) position, should it reset after being read directly from its regular terminal or when it is read by a local variable, or both? There is no universal answer to this situation, so it is not allowed. Figure 3.18 has a solution, though. After the two loops stop, another local variable resets the switch for you.

Managing controls that interact is another cool use for local variables. For instance, the example VI **Simulating Radio Buttons** gives the user a set of exclusive options, where only one option can be selected at a time. In that example, the diagram uses local variables to reset the old selection to False.

You will surely dream up many uses for local variables. But a word of caution is in order regarding race conditions. It is very easy to write a program that acts in an unpredictable or undesirable manner because there is more than one source for the data displayed in a control or indicator. What you must do is explicitly define the order of execution in such a way that the action of a local variable cannot interfere with other data sources, whether they are user inputs, control terminals, or other local variables on the same diagram. It's difficult to give you a more precise description of the potential problems because there are so many situations. Just think carefully before using local variables and always test your program thoroughly.

To show you how easy it is to create unnerving activity with local variables, another apparently simple example of interactive controls is

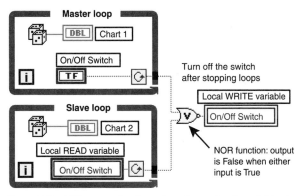

Figure 3.18   This example shows how to use local variables to stop a parallel While Loop. The switch is programmatically reset because latching modes are not permitted for Boolean controls that are also accessed by local variables.

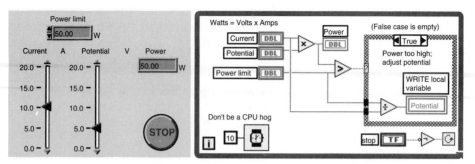

Figure 3.19   A first try at limiting the product of two numeric controls. But it acts funny when the user drags and holds the Potential slider to a high value.

shown in Fig. 3.19. I have two numeric slider controls, for **Potential** (volts) and **Current** (amps), and I want to limit the product of the two (**Power**, in watts) to a value that my power supply can handle. In this solution, the product is compared with a maximum power limit, and if it's too high, a local variable forces the **Potential** control to an appropriate value. (I could have limited the **Current** control as easily.) This program works, but it has one quirk: if the user sets the **Current** way up and then drags and holds the **Potential** slider too high, the local variable keeps resetting the **Potential** slider to a valid value. However, since the user keeps holding it at the illegal value, the slider oscillates between the legal and illegal value as fast as the loop can run.

This was such an interesting problem that I posted it as a challenge to the info-labview mailgroup. Of 29 answers, only 2 looked anything like what I expected: simple and proper use of a couple of local variables. The others varied in approach and complexity to a surprising degree. Alternatives include change-of-value detectors, scale readjustments using Attribute nodes, and some rather esoteric solutions such as state machines. My favorite example using local variables was submitted by Abner Bello, a graduate student working at Lawrence Livermore National Laboratory (a coincidence—honest!) and the essence of his entry appears in Fig. 3.20. It turns out that all you have to do is add a second local variable inside the Case structure. In this way, the controls are cross-coupled. However, there is now a more subtle race condition present. Depending upon how fast your computer is and what kind of slider control you have placed on the front panel, you may see a tiny bit of jitter in the slider's pointer as you move it upward. It's caused by the fact that *both* controls are updated by local variables simultaneously. To completely eliminate this problem, some very complex solutions (still based on local variables) were designed. Other approaches using Attribute nodes to adjust the control scales are efficient solutions.

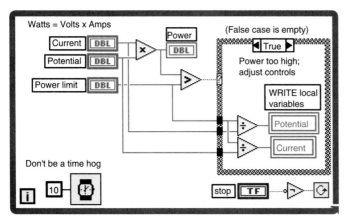

Figure 3.20   A solution to the local variable challenge. If you raise one control too high, the other is reduced. This works pretty good. The panel is identical to that of Fig. 3.19.

Strings

Every programmer spends a lot of time putting **strings** of characters together and taking them apart. Strings are useful for indicators where you need to say something to the operator, for communications with GPIB and serial instruments, and for reading and writing data files that other applications will access. If you've had the displeasure of using *old* FORTRAN (say, the 1966 vintage), you know what it's like to deal with strings in a language that didn't even have a string or character *type,* let alone string functions. We LabVIEW users are in much better shape, with a nice set of string-wrangling functions built right in. If you know anything about the C language, some of these functions will be familiar. Let's look at some common string problems and their solutions.

Building strings

Instrument drivers are the classic case study for string building. The problem is to assemble a command for an instrument (usually GPIB) based on several control settings. Figure 3.21 was taken from the Tektronix 370A driver which uses most of the tricks you need to know. Here's how it works.

1. The **Pick Line & Append** function is driven by a ring control named **Pulse** that supplies a number (0, 1, or 2) that is mapped into the words *OFF, SHORT,* or *LONG.* These key words are appended to the initial command string, STPGEN PUL:.

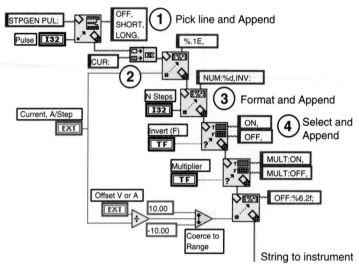

Figure 3.21   String building in a driver VI. This one uses most of the major string-building functions in a classic diagonal layout common to many drivers.

2. The **Concatenate Strings** function tacks on a substring, CUR:. If you need to concatenate several strings, you can resize Concatenate Strings (by dragging at any corner) to obtain more inputs.

3. The **Format & Append** function is most versatile for appending numeric values. You need to learn a little about C-style formatting commands (see the LabVIEW manual for details) to use this function. The percent sign tells it that the next few characters are a formatting instruction. What is nice about this function is that it not only formats the number in a predictable way, but you can also tack on other characters before or after the value. This saves space and gets rid of a lot of Concatenate Strings functions. In this example, the format string NUM:%d, INV: translates to a prefix, NUM:, a decimal value specified by %d, and finally a suffix, INV:. A newer function is available with enhanced capability: **Format Into String**. You can pop up on this function and select Edit Format String to obtain an interactive dialog box where you build the otherwise cryptic formatting commands. As a bonus, Format Into String can be resized to handle more than one numeric input.

4. The **Select & Append** function uses a Boolean control to pick one of two choices, such as ON or OFF, which is then appended to the string. This string-building process may continue as needed to build an elaborate instrument command.

One function missing from this example is **Index & Append**. It's much like Pick Line & Append, but it chooses from an array of strings. It's very handy if there are a large number of choices; just fill up an array control with the desired settings and pick from them.

A very powerful function for general-purpose string building is **Format Into String** (Fig. 3.22). If you happen to know C, you'll recognize it as the *printf* function. You can resize the function (drag any corner) to accommodate any number of numeric or string inputs. Pop up on the function and select Edit Format String to ease the job of constructing a valid format string constant. Note that you can also use a control or other string to determine the format. In that case, there could be run-time errors in the format string, so the function includes error I/O clusters. The *LabVIEW Function Manual* or the online help gives you details on the myriad possibilities of syntax for this powerful function.

Taking 'em apart

The other half of the instrument driver world involves interpreting messages. The message may contain all sorts of headers, delimiters, flags, and who-knows-what, plus a few numbers or important letters that you actually want. Breaking down such a string is known as **parsing**. It's a classic exercise in computer science and linguistics as well. Remember how challenging it was to study our own language back in fifth grade—parsing sentences into nouns, verbs, and all that? I thought that was tough; then I tackled the reply messages that some instrument manufacturers come up with! Figure 3.23 comes from one of the easier instruments, again the Tektronix 370A driver. A typical response message would look like this:

```
STPGEN NUMBER:18;PULSE:SHORT;OFFSET:-1.37;INVERT:OFF;MULT:ON;
```

Let's examine the diagram that parses this message.

1. The top row is based on the versatile **Match Pattern** function. Nothing fancy is being done with it here, other than searching for a

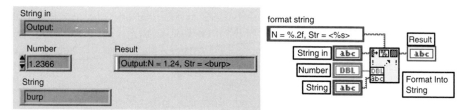

Figure 3.22 Format Into String accepts any number of polymorphic inputs and builds an arbitrarily formatted output string. It's just like the C *printf* function.

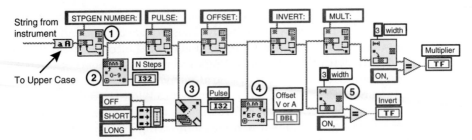

Figure 3.23 Using string functions to parse the response message from a GPIB instrument. This is typical of many instruments you may actually encounter.

desired keyword. The manual fully describes the functions of the many special characters you can type into the **regular expression** input that controls Match Pattern. One other thing I did is pass the incoming string through the **To Upper Case** function. Otherwise, the pattern keys would have to contain both upper- and lowercase letters. The output from each pattern match is known as **after substring**. It contains the remainder of the original string immediately following the pattern, assuming that the pattern was found. If there is any chance that your pattern might not be found, test the **offset past match** output; if it's less than zero, there was no match, and you can handle things at that point with a Case structure.

2. Each of the **after substrings** in this example is then passed to another level of parsing. The first one uses the **From Decimal** function, one of several number extractors; others handle octal, hexadecimal, and fraction/scientific notation. These are very robust functions. If the incoming string starts with a valid numeric character, the expected value is returned. The only problem you can run into is cases where several values are run together such as [123.E3-.567.89]. Then you need to use the **Format & Strip** function to break it down, provided that the format is fixed. That is, you know exactly where to split it up. You could also use Match Pattern again if there are any other known, embedded flags, even if the flag is only a space character.

3. After locating the keyword PULSE, we expect one of three possible strings: OFF, SHORT, or LONG. **Index & Strip** searches a string array containing these words and returns the index of the one that matches (0, 1, or 2). The index is wired to a ring indicator named **Pulse** that displays the status.

4. Keyword OFFSET is located, and the substring is passed to the **From Exponential/Fract/Sci** function to extract the number, which in this case is in fractional form.

5. INVERT is located next, followed by one of two possible strings, ON or OFF. When I wrote this VI, I first used Index & Strip again, with its search array containing ON and OFF. But a bug cropped up! It turned out that another keyword farther along in the string (MULT) also used ON and OFF. Since Match Pattern passes us the *entire remainder* of the string, Index and Strip happily went out and found the *wrong* ON word—the one which belonged to MULT. Things were OK if the INVERT state was ON, since we found that right away. The solution I chose was to use the String Subset function, split off the first three characters, and test only those. You could also look for the entire command, INVERT:ON or INVERT:OFF. Moral of story: test thoroughly before shipping.

The **Scan From String** function, like the C *scanf* function, can save much effort when parsing strings (Fig. 3.24). Like its complement, Format Into String, this function produces one or more polymorphic outputs (numeric or string), depending upon the contents of the Format String input. Input terminals allow you to determine the data format of numeric outputs and set default values as well.

Other difficult parsing problems arise when you attempt to extract information from text files. If the person who designed the file format is kind and thoughtful, all you will have to do is search for a keyword, then read a number. I've seen other situations that border on the intractable; you need to be a computer science whiz to write a reliable parser in the worst cases. These are very challenging problems, so don't feel ashamed if it takes you a long time to write a successful LabVIEW string-parsing VI.

Dealing with unprintables

Sometimes you need to create or display a string that contains some of the unprintable ASCII characters, such as Control-X or the escape

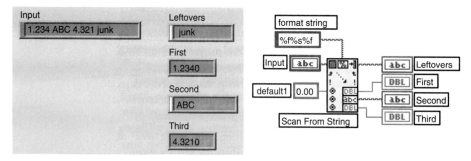

Figure 3.24 The Scan From String function is great for parsing simple strings.

TABLE 3.1 Escape Sequences (\ Codes) for Strings

Escape codes	Interpreted as
\00-\FF	Hexadecimal value of an 8-bit character
\b	Backspace (ASCII BS or equivalent to \08)
\f	Formfeed (ASCII FF or equivalent to \0C)
\n	Newline (ASCII LF or equivalent to \0A)
\r	Return (ASCII CR or equivalent to \0D)
\t	Tab (ASCII HT or equivalent to \09)
\s	Space (equivalent to \20)
\\	Backslash (ASCII \ or equivalent to \5C)

character. The trick is to use the pop-up item, **'\' Codes Display**, which works on front panel control and indicators as well as diagram string constants. LabVIEW will interpret one- or two-character codes following the backslash character as shown in Table 3.1. You can also enter unprintables by simply typing them into the string. Control characters, carriage returns, and so on, all work fine . . . except for the Tab (Control-I)—LabVIEW uses the Tab key to switch tools, so you have to type \t. Note that the hexadecimal codes require uppercase letters. One other disconcerting feature of these escape codes: if you enter a code that can be translated into a printable character (for instance, \41 = A), the printable character will appear as soon as you run the VI.

There are many conversion functions in the String palette. Figure 3.25 shows just a few of them in action. These string converters are the equivalent of functions such as ASC() and CHR() in Basic, where you convert numbers to and from strings. The **Scan From String** function is particularly powerful and not limited to hexadecimal conversion. You expand it to suit the number of variables in the source string, then enter an appropriate number of format specifiers in the format string.

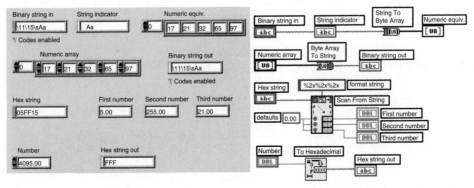

Figure 3.25 Here are some of the ways you can convert to and from strings that contain unprintable characters. All of these functions are found in the String palette.

Like its complement, **Format Into String**, you can pop up on this function and select Edit Format String to build formatting commands.

Spreadsheets, strings, and arrays

Frequently you will need to write your data to disk for later use by spreadsheet programs and other applications that prefer tab-delimited text. Such a string looks like this:

```
value <tab> value <tab> value <cr>
```

(Sometimes the delimiter is a comma or other character. No matter—LabVIEW handles all delimiters.) A very important portability note is in order here. Most platforms are different with respect to their end-of-line character. A platform-independent constant, End of Line () is available from the String function palette that automatically generates the proper character when ported. The proper characters are:

Macintosh: Carriage return (\r)

PC: Carriage return, then line feed (\r\n)

UNIX: Line feed (\n)

A really interesting problem crops up with string controls when the user types a carriage return into the string: LabVIEW always inserts a *line feed*. For the examples in this book, I generally use a carriage return, since I'm a Mac user. But remember this portability issue if you plan to carry your VIs from one machine to another.

To convert arrays of numerics to strings, the easiest technique is to use the **Array to Spreadsheet String** function. Just wire your array into it along with a format specifier, and out pops a tab-delimited string, ready to write to a file. For a one-dimensional (1D) array (Fig. 3.26), tab characters are inserted between each value and a carriage return at the end. This looks like one horizontal row of numbers in a spreadsheet. If you don't want the default tab characters between values, you can wire a different string to the **delimiter** input.

You can read the data back in from a file (simulated here) and convert it back into an array by using the **Spreadsheet String to Array** function. It has an additional requirement that you supply a **type specifier** (such as a 1D array) to give it a hint as to what layout the data might have. The format specifier doesn't have to show the exact field width and decimal precision; plain *%e* or *%d* generally does the job for floating point or integer values, respectively.

In Fig. 3.27, a two-dimensional (2D) array, also known as a **matrix**, is easily converted to and from a spreadsheet string. In this case, you

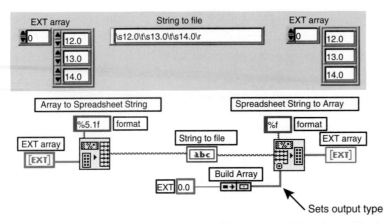

Figure 3.26 Converting a 1D array to a spreadsheet-compatible string and back.

get a tab between values in a row and a carriage return at the end of each row. If the rows and columns appear swapped in your spreadsheet program, insert the array function Transpose 2D Array before converting the array to text. Notice that I hooked up Spreadsheet String to Array to a different type specifier, this time a long integer (I32). Resolution was lost because integers don't have a fractional part; this is to demonstrate that you need to be careful when mixing data types. I also obtained that type specifier by a different method: an **array constant**, which is another of those new LabVIEW 4 features that I keep forgetting to use. You can create constants of *any* data type on the diagram. Look through the function palettes, and you'll see constants everywhere. In this case, I chose an array constant, and then dragged a

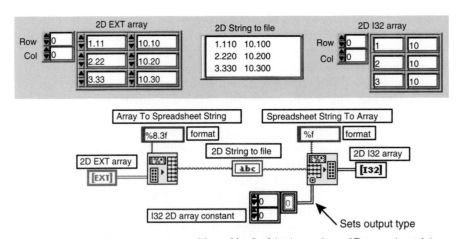

Figure 3.27 Converting an array to a table and back, this time using a 2D array (matrix).

numeric constant into it. This produced a 1D numeric array. I then popped up on the array and selected Add Dimension to make it 2D.

A more general solution for converting arrays to strings is to use a For Loop with a shift register containing one of the string conversion functions and Concatenate Strings. Sometimes, this is needed for more complicated situations where you need to intermingle data from several arrays, when you need many columns, or when you need other information within rows. Figure 3.28 uses these techniques in a situation where you have a 2D data array (several channels and many samples per channel), another array with timestamps, and a string array with channel names.

The names are used to build a header in the upper For Loop, which is then concatenated to a large string that contains the data. This business can be a real memory burner (and *slow,* as well) if your arrays are large. The strings compound the speed and memory efficiency problem. This is one of the few cases where I've reverted to writing a Code Interface Node, which was the only way to obtain acceptable performance

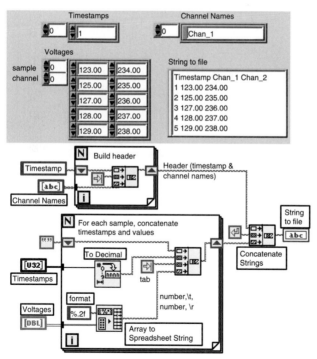

Figure 3.28   A realistic example of building a spreadsheet string from a 2D data array, a timestamp array, and a string array containing channel names for the file's header. If this solution is still too slow for your application, you have to implement it in C code through a Code Interface Node.

with large arrays and complex formatting requirements. If you're doing a data acquisition system, try writing out the data as you collect it—processing and writing out one row at a time—rather than saving it all up until the end. On the other hand, file I/O operations are pretty slow, too, so some optimization is in order. See Chap. 7, "Writing a Data Acquisition Program," for in-depth coverage. Film at eleven.

Arrays

Any time you have a series of numbers that need to be handled as a unit, they probably belong in an **array**. Most arrays are one-dimensional (1D, a column or vector), a few are 2D (a matrix), and hardly any are 3D or greater. LabVIEW permits you to create arrays of numerics, strings, Booleans, and pretty much any other data type (except for arrays of arrays). Arrays are often created by loops as shown in Fig. 3.29. For Loops are the best because they preallocate the required memory when they start. While Loops can't; LabVIEW has no way of knowing how many times a While Loop will cycle, so the Memory Manager will have to be called occasionally, slowing execution somewhat.

You can also create an array by using the **Build Array** function (Fig. 3.30). Notice the versatility of Build Array: it lets you concatenate entire arrays to other arrays or just tack on single elements. There's a pop-up menu on each input terminal that lets you set the type to Array Input or Element Input. If the input type is *Element,* the output will be an array of those elements. If the input type is *Array,* the output will be similar to the input. For instance, if the input is 2D, the output will also be 2D. To handle more than one input, you can resize the function by dragging at a corner. Note the **coercion dots** where the SGL (single-precision floating point) and I16 (two-byte integer) numeric types are wired to the top Build Array function. This indicates a change of data type because an array cannot contain a mix of data types. LabVIEW

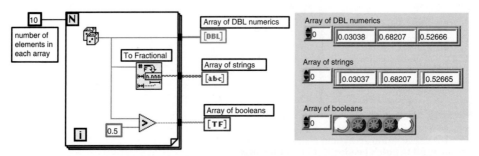

Figure 3.29   Creating arrays using a For Loop. A While Loop would do the same thing. This is an efficient way to build arrays with many elements.

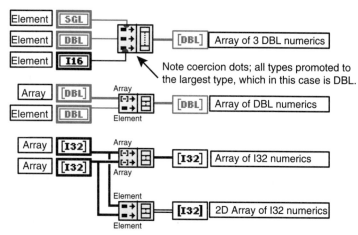

Figure 3.30   Using the Build Array function. Use the pop-up menu on its input terminals to determine whether the input is an element or an array. Note the various results.

must promote all types to the one with the greatest numeric range, which in this case is DBL (double-precision floating point). This also implies that you can't build an array of, say, numerics and strings. For such intermixing, you must turn to **clusters**, which we'll look at a bit later.

Figure 3.31 shows how to find out how many elements are in an array by using the **Array Size** function. Note that an empty array has zero elements. You can use **Index Array** to extract a single element. Like most LabVIEW functions, Index Array is polymorphic and will return a scalar of the same type as the array.

If you have a multidimensional array, these same functions still work, but you have more dimensions to keep track of (Fig. 3.32). Array Size

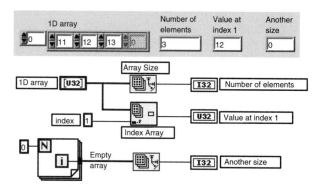

Figure 3.31   How to get the size of an array and fetch a single value. Remember that all array indexing is based on zero, not one.

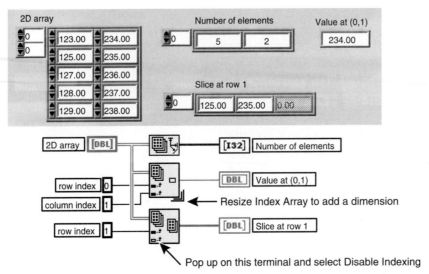

Figure 3.32 Sizing, indexing, and slicing 2D arrays is a little different, since you have two indexes to manipulate at all steps.

returns an array of values, one per dimension. Index Array can be resized by dragging at a corner to accommodate more dimensions. You have to supply an indexing value for each dimension. An exception is when you wish to slice the array, extracting a column or row of data, as in the bottom example. You use a pop-up item on the indexing terminal called Disable Indexing to change to this mode of operation. Supply one indexing value and the output is an array with one less dimension than the input array. If I'm doing a lot of work with multidimensional arrays, I create special subVIs to do the slicing, indexing, and sizing. That way, the inputs to the subVI have names associated with each dimension, rather than forcing me to keep track of each row or column's purpose.

Initializing arrays

Sometimes you need an array that is initialized when your program starts, say, for a lookup table. There are many ways to do this, as shown in Fig. 3.33.

- If all the values are the same, use a For Loop with a constant inside. Disadvantage: takes a certain amount of time to create the array.

- Use the **Initialize Array** function with the **dimension size** input connected to a constant numeric set to the number of elements. This is equivalent to the previous method, but more compact.

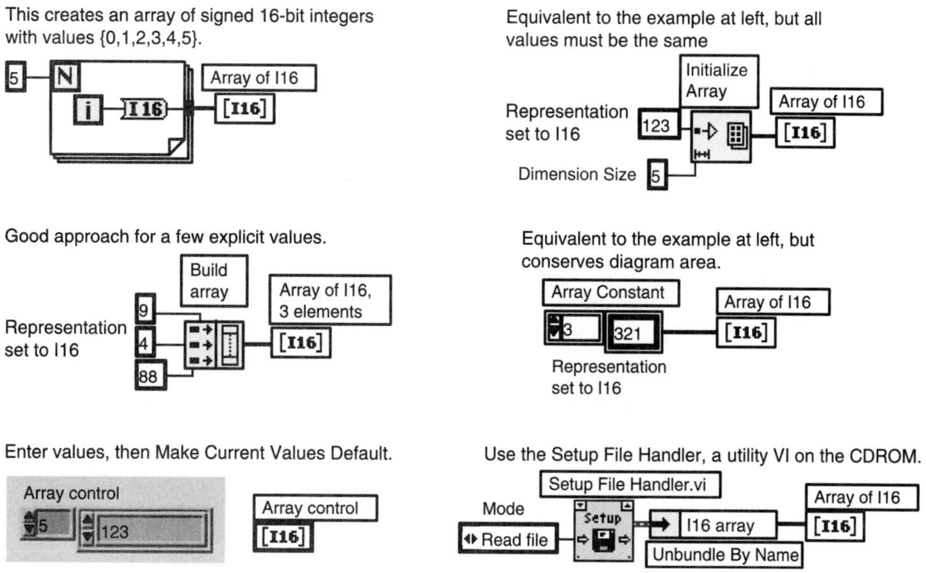

This creates an array of signed 16-bit integers with values {0,1,2,3,4,5}.

Equivalent to the example at left, but all values must be the same

Good approach for a few explicit values.

Equivalent to the example at left, but conserves diagram area.

Enter values, then Make Current Values Default.

Use the Setup File Handler, a utility VI on the CDROM.

Figure 3.33 Several ways of programmatically initializing arrays. For large amounts of data, there are trade-offs between data storage on disk and speed of execution.

- Similarly, if the values can be calculated in some straightforward way, put the formula in a For Loop instead of a constant. For instance, a special waveform or function could be created this way.

- Create a diagram array constant and manually enter the desired values. Disadvantage: tedious and uses memory on disk when the VI is saved.

- Create a front panel array control and manually type in the values. Select **Make Current Value Default** from the control's Data Operations pop-up menu. From now on, that array will always have those values unless you change them. From the diagram, you can select **Hide Front Panel Control** or position the control off-screen to keep anyone from modifying the data. Disadvantage: data takes up extra space on disk when you save the VI.

- If there is much data, you could save it in a file and load it at startup. The utility VI, **Setup File Handler**, included on the CD-ROM, is handy for this. Its operation is discussed in Chap. 7, "Writing a Data Acquisition Program."

 platform\ setup file handler.llb

A special case of initialization is that of an **empty array**. This is *not* an array with one or more values set to zero, false, empty string, or the like! It contains *zero* elements. In C or Pascal, this corresponds to creating a new pointer to an array. The most frequent use of an empty array is to initialize a shift register that is used to hold an array (see the section on shift registers). Here are some ways to create an empty array:

- Create a front panel array control. Select **Empty Array**, from its Data Operations pop-up, and then **Make Current Value Default** from the control's pop-up menu. This is, by definition, an empty array.

- Create a For Loop with the count terminal, $\boxed{N}$, wired to zero. Place a diagram constant of an appropriate type inside the loop and wire outside the loop. The loop will execute zero times (i.e., not at all), but the array that is created at the loop border tunnel will have the proper type.

- Use the **Initialize Array** function with the **dimension size** input unconnected. This is functionally equivalent to the For Loop with $N = 0$.

- Use a diagram array constant. Select **Empty Array** from its Data Operations pop-up menu.

Note that you can't use the Build Array function. Its output always contains at least one element.

Array memory usage and performance

Perhaps more than any other structure in LabVIEW, arrays are responsible for a great deal of memory usage (see Chap. 9, "Physics Applications," for some examples). It's not unusual to collect thousands or even millions of data points from an experiment and then try to analyze or display them all at once. Ultimately, you may see a little bulldozer cursor and/or a cheerful dialog box informing you that LabVIEW has run out of memory. There are some things you can do to prevent this occurrence.

First, read the LabVIEW Technical Note TN020, *Minimizing the Number of Data Buffers;* I'll summarize it here. LabVIEW does its best to conserve memory. When an array is created, LabVIEW has to allocate a contiguous area of memory called a **data buffer** in which to store the array. (By the way, every data type is subject to the same rules for memory allocation; arrays and strings, in particular, just take up more space.) Figure 3.34 contains a sampling of functions that do and do not reuse memory in a predictable way. If you do a simple operation such as multiplying a scalar by an array, no extra memory management is required. An array that is indexed on the boundary of a For Loop, processed, then rebuilt, also requires no memory management. The Build Array function, on the other hand always creates a new data buffer. It's better to use **Replace Array Element** on an existing array as shown in Fig. 3.35. This is one of the few cases where you can

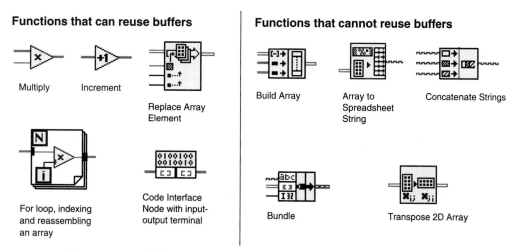

Figure 3.34 Here are some of the operations that you can count on for predictable reuse or non-reuse of memory. If you deal with large arrays or strings, think about these differences.

explicitly control the allocation of memory in LabVIEW, and it's highly advisable when you handle large arrays or you require maximum performance.

One confusing issue about multidimensional arrays is keeping track of the indices. Which one is the row and which one is the column?

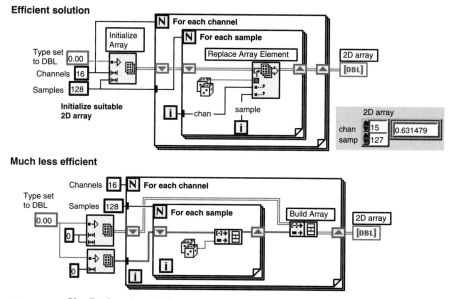

Figure 3.35 Use Replace Array Element inside a For Loop instead of Build Array to permit reuse of an existing data buffer. This is much faster.

Which one does a nested loop structure act upon first? I keep track of this by looking at the indicator on the panel, like the one in Fig. 3.35. The top index (called *channel,* in this example) is also the top index on the Replace Array Element function; this is also true on the Index Array function. So, at least you can keep track of *that* much. By the way, it is considered good form to label your array controls and wires on the diagram as I did in this example. When you access a multidimensional array with nested loops as in the previous example, the outer loop accesses the top index, and the inner loop accesses the bottom index. Figure 3.36 summarizes this array index information.

All this memory reuse business also adds overhead at execution time because the **memory manager** has to be called. Talk about an overworked manager. . . . The poor thing has to go searching around in RAM looking for whatever-sized chunk the program happens to need. If a space can't be found directly, the manager has to shuffle other blocks around until a suitable hole opens up. This can take time, especially when memory is getting tight. This is also the reason your VIs sometimes execute faster the *second* time you run them: most of the allocation phase of memory management is done on the first iteration or run. Similarly, when an array is created in a For Loop, LabVIEW can usually predict how much space is needed and call the memory manager just once. Not so in a While Loop, since there is no way to know in advance how many times you're going to loop. It's also not so when building arrays or concatenating strings inside a loop—two more situations to avoid when performance is paramount. The best source of information on memory management is the LabVIEW user's manual, in the chapter called "Performance Issues." That chapter is recommended reading for all LabVIEW users, as is the chapter, "Understanding How LabVIEW Executes VIs."

Loop	1D array	2D array	3D array
Outer	column	row	page
Middle		column	row
Inner			column

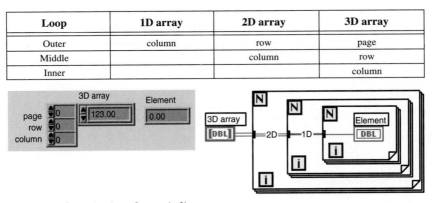

Figure 3.36 Organization of array indices.

Clusters

You can gather several different data types into a single, more manageable unit called a **cluster**. It is conceptually the same as a *record* in Pascal or a *struct* in C. Clusters are normally used to group related data elements that are used in multiple places on a diagram. This reduces wiring clutter: many items are carried along in a single wire. They also reduce the number of terminals required on a subVI. When saved as a custom control with the **typedef** or **strict typedef** option (use the **Control Editor**), clusters serve as data type definitions which are important in managing large LabVIEW applications. Using clusters is good programming practice, but it does require a little insight as to when and where they are best employed. If you're a novice programmer, look at the LabVIEW examples and the figures in this book to see how clusters are used in real life.

An important fact about a cluster is it can contain only controls or indicators but not a mixture of both. This precludes the use of a cluster to group a set of controls and indicators on a panel. Use graphical elements from the Decorations palette to group controls and indicators. If you really need to read *and* write values in a cluster, local variables can certainly do the job. I would not recommend using locals to continuously read and write a cluster because the chance for a race condition is very high. It's much safer to use a local variable to initialize the cluster (just once) or perhaps to correct an errant input or reflect a change of mode. *Rule: For highly interactive panels, don't use a cluster as an input and output element.*

Clusters are assembled on the diagram by using either the **Bundle** function (Fig. 3.37) or the **Bundle by Name** function (Fig. 3.38). The

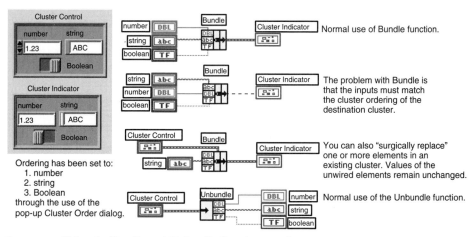

Figure 3.37   Using the Bundle and Unbundle functions on clusters.

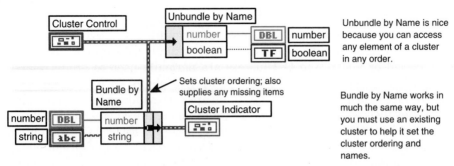

Figure 3.38 Use Bundle by Name and Unbundle by Name in preference to their no-name counterparts.

data types that you connect to these functions must match the data types in the destination cluster (numeric types are polymorphic; for instance, you can safely connect an integer type to a floating point type). The Bundle function has one further restriction: the elements must be connected in the proper order. There is a pop-up menu available on the cluster border called **Cluster Order** that you use to set the ordering of elements. You must carefully watch cluster ordering. Two otherwise identical clusters with different element orderings can't be connected. An exception to this rule, one which causes bugs that are difficult to trace, is where the misordered elements are of similar data type (for instance, all are numerics). You can connect the misordered clusters, but element A of one cluster may actually be passed to element B of the other. This blunder is far too common and is one of the reasons for using Bundle by Name.

To disassemble a cluster, you can use the **Unbundle** or **Unbundle by Name** functions. When you create a cluster control, give each element a reasonably short name. Then, when you use Bundle by Name or Unbundle by Name, the name doesn't take up too much space on the diagram. There is a pop-up menu on each of these functions (**Select Item**) with which you select the items to access. Named access has the additional advantage that adding an item to the related cluster control or indicator doesn't break any wires like it does with the unnamed method. *Rule: Always use named cluster access except when there is some compelling reason not to.*

When you use Bundle by Name, its middle terminal *must* be wired. The functions of the middle terminal on Bundle by Name are to determine the element ordering, the data types, and to set the item names. Even if you have wired all input elements, you must wire the middle terminal because the input elements only determine the data types. The Bundle function does not have this limitation; you need only wire to its middle terminal when you wish to access a limited set of a cluster's elements.

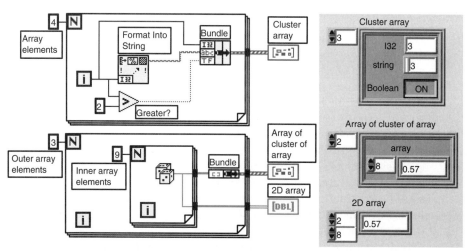

Figure 3.39 Building a cluster array (*top*). Building an array of clusters which contain an array (*bottom*). This is distinctly different from a 2D array.

Clusters are often incorporated into arrays (we call them cluster arrays) as shown in Fig. 3.39. It's a convenient way to package large collections of data such as I/O configurations where you have many different pieces of data to describe a channel in a cluster and many channels (clusters) in an array. Cluster arrays are also used to define many of the graph and chart types in LabVIEW, a subject discussed in detail in Chap. 10, "Data Visualization, Imaging, and Sound." Figure 3.39 also shows the LabVIEW equivalent of an *array of arrays,* which is implemented as an array of clusters of arrays. Note the difference between this construct and a simple 2D array, or matrix. Use these arrays of cluster arrays when you want to combine arrays with different sizes; multidimensional LabVIEW arrays are always rectangular.

Timing

Depending on your needs, LabVIEW's timing functions can be simple and effective or totally inadequate. And the problems are not all the fault of LabVIEW itself; there are fundamental limitations on all general-purpose computer systems with regards to real-time response, whatever *that* means (1 second? 0.01 second? 1 nanosecond?). Most applications I've seen work comfortably with the available LabVIEW time measurements that resolve milliseconds, and many more operate with 1-second resolution. A few applications demand sub-milli-second resolution and response time, which is problematic due primarily to operating system issues. Those cases require special attention. So, what's with all this timing stuff, anyway?

Where do little timers come from?

When LabVIEW was born on the Macintosh, the only timer available was based on the 60-Hz line frequency. Interrupts to the CPU occur every 1/60th of a second and are counted as long as the Mac is powered on. This timer, still emulated on all Macs, is called the *tick count,* though it is no longer directly accessible in LabVIEW. The modern timer actually uses a 20-µs resolution counter that is based on a crystal-controlled oscillator on the Mac's motherboard. The actual resolution you get depends on whether or not you have the QuickTime extension installed. QuickTime, which of course handles multimedia on the Mac, requires a 1-ms timer to guarantee smooth video and sound reproduction. Without QuickTime, the system reverts to an emulation of the old 60-Hz (16.66-ms resolution) timer. By all means, install QuickTime on your Mac.

It is possible to do high-precision timing on a Macintosh if you call the appropriate Macintosh Time Manager toolbox functions through the use of CINs. Dirk Demol of Measurex Corporation wrote a CIN-based VI that reads the 20-µs-resolution timer. It's useful for determining the elapsed time between software events where 1-ms resolution is not sufficient. However, it can't be used as an interrupt timer in a loop like some of the other LabVIEW timing functions. That is, you must poll this timer and see if the desired time has passed if you wish to use it to regulate time intervals. You can find it at ftp.pica.army.mil in a file called *lvtimer.sea.* Christophe Salzmann at EPFL in Switzerland wrote some elaborate CIN-based VIs for real-time control for the Macintosh. He used the high-resolution timer for interrupt-driven operations but had to write all of the time-critical code as CINs. You can check out his work at http://iawww.epfl.ch/Software/IA_Software.html.

On IBM PC compatibles, the hardware that keeps track of time is not well standardized, though all modern machines use a crystal clock on the motherboard, much like the Macintosh. The resolution is operating system–dependent. Under Windows 3.x, resolution is normally limited to 55 ms. There is an option, however, that you can access through the LabVIEW Preferences that sets the resolution to a genuine 1 ms (see the LabVIEW manual for configuration instructions). There is one problem with the high-resolution mode that you need to be aware of. Under Windows, the processor receives an interrupt at each tick of the clock—1000 times every second, with 1-ms resolution selected. That's a *lot* of interrupts, though it doesn't normally cause any problems . . . except (sometimes) when you are using the DAQ library. Most DAQ operations that access plug-in boards generate some interrupts. (If you don't have DMA support, an interrupt is generated for every A/D conversion.) Sometimes, a DAQ interrupt occurs while the processor is servicing a clock interrupt, and disaster strikes: you may miss data, find yourself at the DOS prompt, or simply crash. But in fact these failures are rare. You just need to be aware of the problem, do lots of testing, and switch back to the default 55-ms mode if you have a case of nerves.

On the Sun SPARCstation, time is derived from a hardware clock that resolves 100 μs, and LabVIEW obtains an accurate 1 ms. No funny business there. As you can imagine, these platform-dependent differences in resolution are important in any application that requires timing information much better than about 1 s.

On the HP workstations, 1-ms resolution is standard.

Three fine-resolution timers are available within LabVIEW: **Wait (ms)**, **Wait Until Next ms Multiple**, and **Tick Count (ms)**. These functions attempt to resolve milliseconds with the aforementioned limitations of the operating systems.

Another kind of timer that is available in LabVIEW is the system clock/calendar which is maintained by a battery-backed crystal oscillator and counter chip. This timer has a platform-dependent resolution: 1 s on the Macintosh, $\frac{1}{55}$ s on Windows, and 1 ms on the UNIX platforms. Most computers have a clock/calendar timer of this kind. The timing functions that get the system time are **Get Date/Time In Seconds**, **Get Date/Time String**, and **Seconds To Date/Time**. These functions are as accurate as your system clock. You can verify this by observing the drift in the clock/calendar displayed on your screen. It's probably within a minute per month or so.

Are you curious about the timing resolution of your system? Then write a simple timer test VI like the one shown in Fig. 3.40. A For Loop runs at maximum speed, calling the timing function under test. The initial time is subtracted from the current time, and each value is appended to an array for plotting. You can see the results for my Macintosh Quadra 950 running Mac OS 7.5.

Using the built-in timing functions

There are two things you probably want to do with timers. First, you want to make things happen at regular intervals. Second, you want to record when events occur.

Intervals. If you want a loop to run at a nice, regular interval, the function to use is Wait Until Next ms Multiple. Just place it inside the loop structure and wire it to a number that's scaled in milliseconds. It waits until the tick count in milliseconds becomes an exact multiple of the value that you supply. If several VIs need to be synchronized, this function will help there, as well. For instance, two independent VIs can be forced to run with harmonically related periods such as 100 ms and

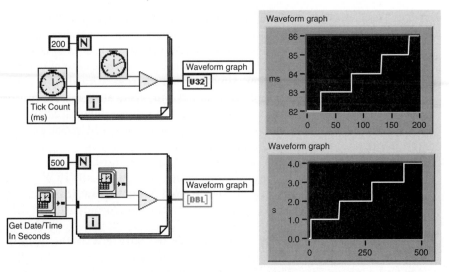

Figure 3.40   Write a simple timer test VI to check the resolution of your system's LabVIEW ticker. These results are for my Macintosh Quadra 950 with Mac OS 7.5.

200 ms as shown in Fig. 3.41. In this case, every 200 ms, you would find that both VIs are in sync. The effect is exactly like the action of a metronome and a group of musicians—it's their heartbeat. This is not the case if you use the simpler Wait (ms) function; it just guarantees that a certain amount of time has passed, without regard to *absolute* time. Note that both of these timers work by *adding* activity to the loop. That is, the loop can't go on to the next cycle until everything in the loop has finished, and that includes the timer. Since LabVIEW executes everything inside the loop in parallel, the timer is presumably started at the same time as everything else. Note that "everything else" must be completed in *less* time than the desired interval. The timer

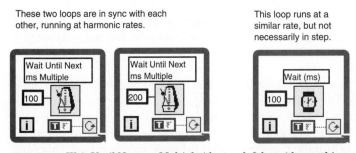

Figure 3.41   Wait Until Next ms Multiple (the two left loops) keeps things in sync. The right loop runs every 100 ms, but may be out of phase with the others.

does not have a magic ability to speed up or abort other functions. Wait Till Next ms Multiple will add on extra delay as necessary to make the tick count come out even, but not if the other tasks overrun the desired interval.

Both of these loop timers are asynchronous; that is, they do not tie up the entire machine while waiting for time to pass. Any time a call to Wait (ms) is encountered, LabVIEW puts the calling VI into a *scheduler queue* until the timer expires. This guarantees that other VIs have a chance to run. Other applications running in the background on the Macintosh or under Windows will also be more likely to get a chance to run as well. UNIX users don't have this concern since that operating system automatically gives each task a time slice. (Note that UNIX does not change the behavior of LabVIEW timers themselves; it only affects the distribution of time slices between LabVIEW and other programs.)

Here's when to use each of the timers:

- Highly regular loop timing—use Wait Till Next ms Multiple

- Many parallel loops with regular timing—use Wait Till Next ms Multiple

- Arbitrary, asynchronous time delay to give other tasks some time to execute—use Wait (ms)

- Single-shot delays (as opposed to cyclic operations, like loops)—use Wait (ms)

What time is it?   To find out what time it is with 1-second resolution, use one of the system time functions with whatever format you need.

- **Get Date/Time In Seconds** returns the number of seconds since midnight January 1, 1904. This *epoch* time standard is used on many computer systems because you can easily scale it to hours, days, or whatever. It conveniently carries date and time in one double-precision (DBL) value. *Notes:* The absolute time reported by this function depends on the time zone to which the computer was set. Also, some platforms (UNIX) only recognize times starting at midnight January 1, 1970, for which the value is 2,082,844,800.

- **Get Date/Time String** returns formatted strings containing time and date. Nice for screen displays or printing in reports. It has several formatting options.

- **Seconds To Date/Time** returns a **date time rec** cluster that's useful for extracting individual time and date values, such as finding the current month. I also use this function when I want to build a specially formatted time and date string.

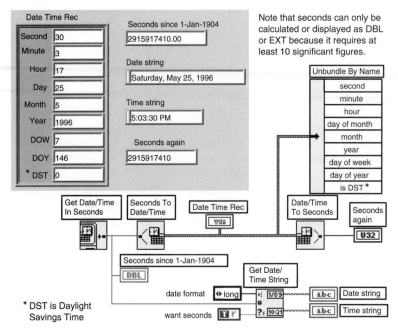

Figure 3.42 How to switch between the various formats for system time, particularly getting in and out of the date time rec cluster.

■ **Date/Time to Seconds** converts the date time rec back to seconds. It's useful when you want to combine individual time and date items, such as letting the user sift through data by the day of the week.

Figure 3.42 shows how all of these functions can be connected together. An important fact you must know about is that time in seconds requires 10 significant figures (requiring a U32 integer) and as many as 13 if you wish to maintain millisecond precision. The latter resolution can be carried by only two of LabVIEW's data types: double (DBL) or extended-precision (EXT) floating point. If it ever gets converted to any other type, or if it gets printed out as a string with less than 10 (or 13) decimal digits, resolution will be lost. This is also a problem when importing these time values into other applications that permit single-precision floating point data, which only offers 7 significant figures.

Sending timing data to other applications.   Many graphing and spreadsheet programs do a lousy job of importing timestamps of the form, *23-Jun-1990 10:03:17*. Epoch seconds are OK, but then the other program has to know how to compute the date and time, which requires a big algorithm. Most spreadsheet programs can handle epoch seconds if you give them a little help. In Microsoft Excel, for instance, you must divide the epoch seconds value by 86,400, which is the number of seconds in a day. The result is what Excel calls a *Serial Number* where the integer part is the number of days since the zero year, and the fractional part is a fraction of a day. Then, you just format the number as date and time. Again, watch out for the numeric precision problem if you're importing epoch seconds.

Something I found very useful in data logging is to save the time in **decimal hours**. For instance, if it's 3:30 P.M., decimal hours equal 15.50. Thus, you know what time of day things were started, and you can easily plot your data versus this simple number. The VI shown in Fig. 3.43 does the trick. It uses two uninitialized shift registers to keep track of the starting time (in hours and seconds), which are saved when the VI is first run. From then on, the time reads out in decimal hours. If the VI gets called after midnight, the hours keep incrementing. After

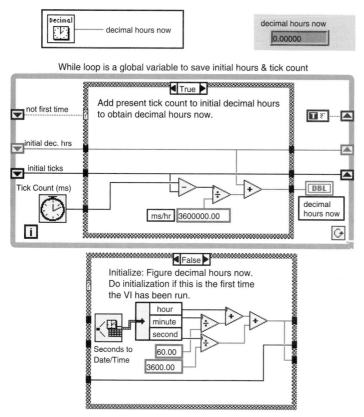

Figure 3.43   The Decimal Hours VI returns the time in hours, but as a floating point number, with millisecond resolution. It doesn't roll over to zero when you go through midnight.

a week, for instance, it will return 168.00 hours. Resolution is limited by your operating system.

platform\g\Decimal Hours.vi

You UNIX users are lucky: the Decimal Hours VI will return time with a resolution of 1 ms. Windows and (especially) Mac users must live with less resolution. But I have a solution for you on the CD-ROM: the **High-Res Seconds** VI combines the Seconds To Date/Time function with the Tick Count (ms) function to obtain the best available resolution for your platform. The code is similar to the Decimal Hours VI in that when you initialize it, it stores the current epoch time, but it also stores the tick count. Though these two values are not truly synchronized, for short durations they don't drift apart very fast; besides, you can reinitialize the VI any time you want to resynchronize the two timers. There is also a control that switches between high resolution and the more accurate (but poorer resolution) date/time function.

platform\g\High-Res Seconds.vi

High-resolution and high-accuracy timing. If your application requires higher accuracy or resolution than the built-in timing functions can supply, then you will have to use some additional hardware. I know of at least two solutions. First, you can use one of the National Instruments data acquisition (DAQ) boards as a timekeeper. DAQ boards include a stable timebase with microsecond resolution that is used to time A/D conversions and drive various counter-timers. Through the DAQ VI library, you can use these timers to regulate the cycle time of loops or as a high-resolution clock for timing short-term events. Chapter 6, "Using the DAQ Library," discusses these techniques in detail under the topic Hardware Timed I/O.

You can also read the time from an external clock if your lab has a suitable timing source. For instance, timebase generators for use with analog tape instrumentation recorders are based on a standard called **IRIG** (*InterRange Instrumentation Group*) that uses a serial interface with up to 0.1-μs resolution. Another source of absolute timing information is the National Institute of Standards and Technology (NIST) time services which offer encoded time, date, and a precision frequency reference via radio station WWV. And the new Global Positioning System (**GPS**) receivers can resolve absolute time to 0.1 μs anywhere on Earth. The key to using one of these timing sources is to obtain a suitable interface to your computer and a LabVIEW driver. Keep in mind the ultimate limitation for precision timing applications: software latency. It takes a finite amount of time to call the CIN that fetches the time measurement or that triggers the timing hardware. If you can set up the hardware in such a way that there is no software in the loop, very high precision is feasible.

One maker of such interfaces is Bancomm. It makes VME, VXI, and ISA-bus time code processors and clocks, as well as GPS satellite receivers, displays, and an Ethernet-based time server. One board of particular interest to PC users is the bc630AT Real Time Clock. It decodes

IRIG-A and IRIG-B time code formats and has an access latency of less than 150 µs. You can synchronize multiple computers via an RS422 link between bc630AT boards. A LabVIEW driver for Windows is available from Bancomm. Contact the company for more information about any of these products.

The Trimble Navigation model Goldcard 115 is a PCMCIA GPS interface for laptop computers. Trimble offers a software development kit which allows you to interface to LabVIEW for Windows using the **Call Library** function (Trimble supplies the dynamic link library). The GPS receiver is very compact and LabVIEW user Leo Breton (lbreton@ mnsinc.com) reports that he is very impressed with its performance.

Absolute Time Corporation manufactures several GPS receiver modules and frequency reference modules with RS-232 interfaces that would appear to be easy to handle within LabVIEW. Its model 103 GPS Synchronized Time Code Generator provides formats including IRIG A,B,D,E,G,H, and NASA 36, all software selectable via RS-232.

Dennis Erickson, senior electronics engineer at Bonneville Power Administration, designed a Macintosh-based LabVIEW system called the Portable Power System Monitor (PPSM) that measures disturbances in the electrical distribution system over the western half of the United States and Canada (Erickson and Albright 1993). Many PPSMs are networked together via modems and other network connections to provide the ability to trace disturbance origins through the use of time correlation. One challenge he had to overcome is the fact that these widely separated machines had to maintain absolute time synchronization to a fraction of a second over very long periods of time. The Macintosh system clock is insufficiently stable for this application, so he turned to a hardware solution. TrueTime Corporation makes a NuBus board, the Model 560-5701 MAC II-SG Generator/Synchronizer board, that reads IRIG-B time code. Dennis already has access to IRIG sources at most of his locations, but if required, it's also available from GPS or WWV receivers. He has a LabVIEW driver that reads the time from the board and adjusts it to local or universal (UTC) time. TrueTime also supplies a utility program that sets the Macintosh clock.

Another requirement that Dennis has is that the sampling clock for his MIO-16 A/D board must be very stable. An option on the MAC II-SG board is a 1-MHz clock output that can be connected to the sample clock input of the A/D. This avoids any long-term drift in synchronization between analog samples and the master clock. With this method, he can now time tag his data to 1 µs with excellent accuracy.

Files

Sooner, not later, you're going to be saving data in disk files for future analysis. Perhaps the files will be read by LabVIEW or another application on your computer or on another machine of different manufacture. In any case, that data is (hopefully) important to someone, so you need to study the techniques available in LabVIEW for getting the data on disk reliably and without too much grief.

Before you start shoveling data into files, make sure that you understand the requirements of the application(s) that will be reading your files. Every application has preferred formats that are described in the appropriate manuals. If all else fails, it's usually a safe bet to write out numbers as **ASCII text** files, but even that simple format can cause problems at import time—things including strange header information, incorrect combinations of carriage returns and/or line feeds, unequal column lengths, too many columns, or wrong numeric formats. **Binary** files are even worse, requiring tight specifications for both the writer and the reader. They are much faster to write or read and more compact than text files though, so learn to handle them as well. This section includes discussions of some common formats and techniques that you can use to handle them.

Study and understand your computer's file system. In the LabVIEW Function Reference Manual there is a nice discussion of some important details such as path names and file reference numbers (refnums). If things really get gritty, you can also refer to the system reference manuals, such as *Inside Macintosh* or one of the many UNIX, DOS, or Windows programming guides you can pick up at the bookstore.

Accessing files

File operations are a three-step process. First, you create or open a file. Then you write data to the file and/or read data from the file. Finally, you close the file. When creating or opening a file, you must specify its location, or **path**. Modern computing systems employ a hierarchical file system, which imposes a directory structure on the storage medium. You store files inside directories, which can in turn contain other directories. To locate a file within the file system, LabVIEW uses a path-naming scheme that works consistently across all operating systems. On the Macintosh and DOS/Windows, you can have multiple drives attached to your machine and each drive is explicitly referenced. On the Sun and HP, UNIX hides the physical implementation from you. Here are some examples of absolute path names:

Macintosh

```
HD80:My Data Folder:Data 123
```

Windows 3.x (95 and NT similar, but permit long file names)

```
C:\JOE\PROGS\DATA\DATA123.DAT
```

UNIX

```
/usr/johnny/labview/examples/data_123.dat
```

LabVIEW's **Path** control (from the Path & Refnum palette) automatically checks the format of the path name that you enter and attempts to coerce it into something valid for your operating system. Paths can be built and parsed, just like strings. In fact, you can convert strings to paths and back using the conversion functions, **String to Path** and **Path to String**. There are also several functions in the File I/O function palette to assist you in this. Figure 3.44 shows how the **Build Path** function can append a string to an existing path. You might use this if you had a predefined directory where a file should be created and a file name determined by your program. Given a valid path, you can also parse off the last item in the path by using the **Strip Path** function. In the example of Fig. 3.44, the path is parsed until you get an empty path. Constants, such as **Empty Path** and **Not A Path**, are useful for evaluating the contents of a path name. The **Default Directory constant** leads you to a location in the file system specified through the LabVIEW preferences. You can also obtain a path name from the user by calling the **File Dialog** function. This function allows you to prompt the user and determine whether the chosen file exists.

Once you have selected a valid path name, you can use either the **New File** function to create a file or the **Open File** function to gain access to an existing one. Both of these functions return a **file refnum**, a magic number that LabVIEW uses internally to keep track of the file's status. This refnum is then passed to the other file I/O functions rather than the path name. When the file is finally closed, the refnum no longer has any meaning and any further attempt at using it will result in an error.

You can navigate and directly manipulate your computer's file system from within LabVIEW. In the Advanced file palette are several useful functions, such as **File/Directory Info**, **List Directory**, **Copy**, **Move**, and **Delete**. This is a pretty comprehensive set of tools, though the methods by which you combine them and manipulate the data

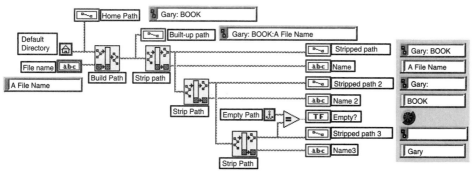

Figure 3.44 LabVIEW has functions to build, parse, and compare path names. These are useful when programmatically manipulating file names.

(which is mostly strings) can be quite complex. For an elaborate example, check out the **Readme VI** in the LabVIEW examples directory.

File types

LabVIEW's file I/O functions can read and write virtually any file format. The three most common formats are:

- ASCII text-format byte stream files
- Binary-format byte stream files
- LabVIEW datalog-format files

ASCII text files are readable in almost any application and are the closest thing to a universal interchange format available at this time. Your data must be formatted into strings before writing. The resulting file can be viewed with a word processor and printed, so it makes sense for report generation problems as well. A parsing process, as described in the strings section, must be used to recover data values after reading a text file. The disadvantages of text files are that all this conversion takes extra time and the files tend to be somewhat bulky when used to store numeric data.

Binary-format byte stream files typically contain a bit-for-bit image of the data that resides in your computer's memory. They cannot be viewed by word processors, nor can they be read by any program without detailed knowledge of the files' format. The advantage of a binary file is that little or no data conversion is required during read and write operations, so you get maximum performance. Binary files are usually much smaller than text files. For instance, a 1000-value record of data from a data acquisition board may be stored in its raw 16-bit binary file, occupying 2000 bytes on disk. Converted to text, it may take up to 10,000 bytes, or five times as much. The disadvantage of binary files is their lack of portability—always a serious concern.

LabVIEW offers another option, the **datalog-format file**, which is a special binary format. This format stores data as a sequence of records of a single arbitrary data type that you specify when you create the file. LabVIEW indexes data in a datalog file in terms of these records. Notice that these records can be a complex type, such as a cluster, which contains many types of data. LabVIEW permits random read access to datalog files, and timestamps are included with each record. Datalog format is discussed in detail in an appendix of the LabVIEW manual in case you need to read datalogs with other applications.

Writing text files

Here's the basic procedure for most situations that write data to text files:

1. Determine the path name.

2. Open or create the file.

3. Convert the data to a string if it's not already in string format.

4. Write the string to the file.

5. Close the file.

The upper example in Fig. 3.45 uses several of the built-in file I/O functions to perform these steps. First, the user receives a dialog box requesting the name and location of a new file. The **File Dialog** function has a **select mode** input that restricts the possible selections to existing files, nonexisting files, or both. In this example, I wanted to create a new data file, so I set the mode to new file (2) which forces the user to choose a new name. An output from the File Dialog function, **canceled**, is True if the user clicks the Cancel button. I wired it to a Case structure—its True case is empty—to skip the file I/O process if the operation was canceled. Next, the **New File** function creates the desired file on the specified path. It returns a refnum for use by the **Write File** function which does the real work in this program. Assume that the string to write is already formatted. After writing, the **Close File** function flushes the data to disk and closes the file. Finally, I call **Simple Error Handler** (from the Time & Dialog function palette) to notify the user if an error occurs. Note the clean appearance of this example, thanks to the use of the flow-through refnum and error I/O parameters. *Rule: Always include an error handler VI to do something sensible when an I/O error occurs.*

Each of the file I/O functions returns an error code in its error I/O cluster. Not handling errors is a risky proposition for file I/O activity. Lots of things can go wrong. For instance, the disk might be full or a

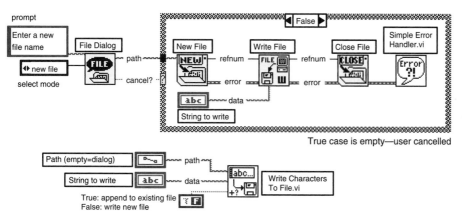

Figure 3.45 The upper example uses the built-in file I/O functions to create, open, and write text data to a file. The Case structure takes care of user cancellations in the file dialog. The lower example uses one of the utility functions, which includes internal error handling.

bad path could be generated if your path selection technique is complicated. *Rule: Always use error I/O (error chaining) for file I/O operations, when available.*

Your VIs need not be cluttered with lots of file management functions. Furthermore, you should not have to write much code to do 90 percent of all file I/O. The utilities and examples supplied with LabVIEW are quite helpful in this regard. In the bottom half of Fig. 3.45, the utility VI, **Write Characters To File**, replaces the collection of functions in the upper example, and it includes error checking. You will want to open that VI and see how it's built from lower-level file I/O utility functions. If the incoming path name is empty, the File Dialog function asks you for a file name then creates the file to be written. If the path name is not empty, the VI attempts to create the file using that path name. A Boolean input, **append to file?**, lets you choose between append mode (for preexisting files) or file creation. If no errors are detected, the data string is written to the file, and then the file is closed. If the operation of this utility isn't exactly what you need, you can always modify it and save it under a different name.

A practical example that uses this file utility, a simple data logger, is shown in Fig. 3.46. When Write Characters To File is first called, it creates a data file and writes some header information. Since the VI has an output containing the path of the file chosen, the path is available for use in later operations on that file without reprompting the user. Inside the While Loop, a subVI reads data from some source and returns it in text format. Again, Write Characters To File is called, but with the mode set to append. The loop executes once per second, regulated by Wait Until Next ms Multiple. The result is a file containing a header followed by records of data at 1-second intervals.

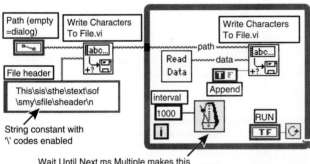

Figure 3.46 A simple data logger that uses the Write Characters to File utility for all the file management. In the loop, data is acquired, formatted into a suitable string, and saved by Write Characters to File. Simple, eh?

This text-based scheme has some performance limitations. If you need to save data at really high rates (such as thousands of samples per second), the first thing to consider is binary-format files, which are very fast. If you must use text files, one way to speed things up is to avoid closing the file after writing each record. The file system maintains a memory-based file buffer, called a *disk cache*, that increases disk performance. Closing the file flushes the file buffer to disk. This forces the disk to move the heads around (called *seeking*), then write the data, a time-consuming process that limits throughput. If you avoid closing the file until you are done, the disk cache can keep a moderate amount of data in memory, flushing to disk only when it becomes full. The disadvantage to using the disk cache is that if your computer crashes during data collection, data in the disk cache will be lost. For this reason, LabVIEW has a file I/O function, **Flush File**, that intentionally writes the output buffer to disk. You call Flush File occasionally to limit the amount of data in the buffer.

Figure 3.47 shows a rewrite of the simple data logging example. This example uses the standard file functions with error I/O and an error dialog. This is the preferred level at which you should work because errors are so common with file access. The file VI **Open/Create/ Replace File** has many handy features such as file replacement dialogs and is generally more useful than the simpler File Dialog function from the advanced file palette. As before, a new file is created and a header is written outside the loop. Inside the loop, data is appended to the file every 1.0 s. The Write File function has its **pos mode** input set to End, which means that it will write data starting at the end of the file; data will be appended at each call. If the Read Data VI requires little execution time, this VI can log data at rates as high as thousands of records per second.

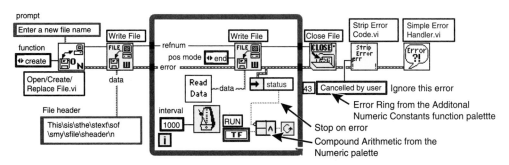

Figure 3.47 A more elaborate version of the simple data logger using file operations with error handling. Strip Error Code is a utility I created to eliminate the annoying error dialog when the user cancels file creation.

When the user stops the loop or an error occurs, the file is closed, then an error dialog is produced if an error occurred. Note the presence of the **Strip Error Code VI**, a utility that I wrote to clear undesired error codes. I included two versions on the CD-ROM, one with file refnums as flow-through parameters, and the other with DAQ taskIDs for use in DAQ applications.

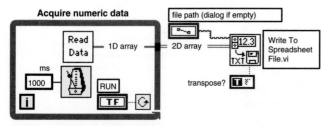

platform\ drivers\driver utilities\Strip Error Code.vi

In this case, the **Canceled by User** error is removed because an error dialog is not needed in that case. Note the use of **enum constants** in three places. You should use these descriptive constants in place of simple numeric constants whenever possible. To create an enum constant, drag one in from the Numeric Constant palette or pop up on the terminal to which you want it connected and select **Create Constant**.

Another file utility VI, **Write To Spreadsheet File**, can simplify your life when your objective is writing spreadsheet-compatible text. You often collect data in 1D or 2D numeric arrays, and you need to convert that to tab-delimited text. As shown in Fig. 3.48 you can accumulate 1D arrays by indexing on the border of a loop, then wire it right into Write To Spreadsheet File. This is really convenient for exporting data from simulations that create 1D or 2D arrays. The **Transpose** option swaps rows and columns; I've found that I almost always need to transpose. The risk of using this VI as shown here is that LabVIEW may run out of memory if you let the While Loop run for a sufficiently long time. Instead, you can put Write To Spreadsheet File inside the acquisition loop: the VI will also accept 1D arrays, in which case it writes a single line of data values, separated by tabs and with a trailing end-of-line marker.

Reading text files

Reading data from a text file is similar to writing it:

1. Determine the path name.
2. Open the file.

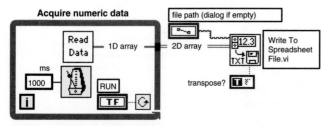

Figure 3.48   Here's another simple way to log data to spreadsheet-compatible files using a file utility.

3. Read the string from the file.

4. Close the file.

5. Convert the string to a suitable format, if necessary.

Figure 3.49 shows two examples that are symmetrical with the previous ones. The main difference is that the Read File function can read any number of bytes (the **count** input) starting at any location in the file (the **pos offset** input). By default, Read File starts reading at the beginning of the file (which is what you would normally do) and **count** is zero (it reads no data). For the simple case where you wish to read the entire file, just wire a constant to **count** and set it to a number larger than the expected amount of data. The upper example in Fig. 3.49 shows another method where the EOF (end of file) function returns the number of bytes in the file which is then wired to **count**. I normally use the constant.

As before, you can use a utility VI, **Read Characters From File**, to save much programming effort. It has two inputs of particular interest: **number of characters** and **start of read offset** that function similarly to the Read File inputs **count** and **pos offset**. To read the whole file, you can set **number of characters** to −1, which is also the default.

Looking further through the file utility VIs, you will find other useful VIs such as **Read From Spreadsheet File**, shown in simplified form in Fig. 3.50. This VI loads one or more lines of text data from a file and interprets it as a 2D array of numbers. You can call it with **number of rows** set to one to read just one line of data at a time, in which case you can use the **first row** output (a 1D array). If the rows and columns need to be exchanged, set **transpose** to True. By default, it assumes that the tab character delimits values on each line. If your for-

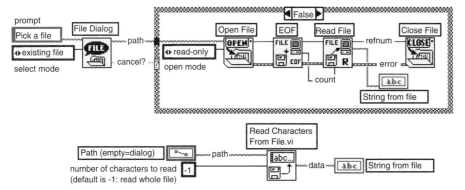

Figure 3.49 The upper example uses the built-in file I/O functions to open an existing file and read text data from it. The lower example uses one of the utility functions.

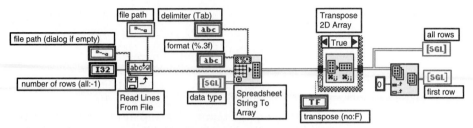

Figure 3.50 File utility VI Read From Spreadsheet File interprets a text file containing rows and columns of numbers as a matrix (2D array). This is a simplified diagram.

mat is different, you can enter the appropriate character in the **delimiter** string. Like many of the utilities, this one is based on another utility subVI, **Read Lines From File**, that understands the concept of a line of text. The end-of-line character(s), which varies from system to system, is properly handled. This functionality is actually built into the Read File function. Read Lines From File goes on to read multiple lines until the end of the file is encountered.

Words of wisdom: Always remember that you can edit the diagram of a utility VI such as this to accommodate your special requirements. It's a powerful way to program because the groundwork is all done for you. But also remember to save the modified version with a new name, and save it someplace besides the vi.lib directory. If you don't, your next LabVIEW upgrade will overwrite your changes.

Binary files

The main reasons for using **binary files** as opposed to ASCII text are that they are faster for both reading and writing operations and they are generally smaller in size. They are faster because they are smaller and because no data conversion needs to be performed (see the section on conversions.) Instead, an image of the data in memory is copied byte for byte out to the disk and then back in again when it's read. Converting to ASCII also requires more bytes to maintain numerical precision. For example, a single-precision floating point number (SGL; 4 bytes) has 7 significant figures. Add to that the exponent field and some ± signs, and you need about 13 characters, plus a delimiter, to represent it as ASCII. In binary you need only store the 4 bytes, a savings of more than three to one. Byte stream binary files (as opposed to datalog files) are also **randomly accessible**. That means you can tell the disk drive to read or write particular areas or individual bytes in the file. Random access is a bit tricky, however, as we shall see.

One small problem: the program that reads the data must know every little detail about how the file was written. Data types, byte counts, headers, and so forth have to be specified. You can't view it like an ASCII text string, so there's little hope of deciphering such a file without plenty of information. Even LabVIEW datalog files (a special type of binary file, discussed later) are not immune to this problem. If you can't tell the file I/O functions what data type the datalog file contains, it can't be accessed. On the other hand, consider the fact that parsing an arbitrary ASCII text file is also nontrivial, as we discussed in the section on strings. That's why there aren't any universal text file interpreters VIs. You should consider using binary files when

- Real-time performance is crucial. Avoiding the numeric-to-text conversion and the extra amount of data that accompanies an ASCII text file will definitely speed things up.

- You already have a requirement for a certain binary format. For instance, you may be writing files in the native format of another application.

- Random read-write access is required.

To make a binary file readable, you have several options. First, you can plan to read the file back in with LabVIEW because the person who wrote it should darned well be able to read it. Within LabVIEW, the data could then be translated and written to another file format or just analyzed right there. Second, you can write the file in a format specified by another application. Third, you can work closely with the programmer on another application or use an application with the ability to import arbitrary binary formatted files. Applications such as Igor, S, IDL, and Spyglass Transform do a credible job of importing arbitrary binary files. They still require full information about the file format, however. Here are several common data organization techniques I've seen used with binary files:

1. One file, with a header block at the start that contains indexing information such as: number of channels, data offsets, and data lengths. An example of this is the Continuous Acquisition to File (Binary) examples in the Data Acquisition Examples library. It is also used by many commercial graphing and analysis programs.

2. One file, organized as a *linked list*. Each record (say, a channel of data) is written with its own header that tells the reader where this record begins and ends and also tells the reader where to find the next record in the file (this is called a *link*.) This technique is used by some graphing and database programs.

3. Two files, one containing only the actual binary data, and another containing an index to the data, perhaps in ASCII format. My HIST trending package uses this technique with an index file that is

also binary. I once worked on another binary file set (the format came from VAX-land) that used an ASCII index file. That was nice because you could figure out what was in the binary file just by printing out the index.

In all of these formats, the index or header information is likely to include such things as channel names, calibration information, and other items you need to make sense of the data. Binary files are much more than a big bag of bytes. There was an excellent article in *LTR* by Jeff Parker (1996) on the subject of preventing obsolescence in binary file structures. He created a set of VIs that manages what he called FlexFiles, which contain an ASCII text header with keywords followed by binary data. The file structure is defined by the header, so you don't have to worry about unraveling the file encoding later on. I think it's a great general-purpose solution to what is otherwise a very application-specific problem. If you order the back issue of *LTR,* you get the diskette with the FlexFile VIs, too.

Writing binary files.   LabVIEW's file I/O functions make it easy to access binary files. The effort, as with text files, is all in the data formatting. You have to figure out how to deal with your particular header or index format, and of course the data itself. Sorry, but that's *your* problem, since no two formats are the same. The best I can do is show you the basics of random-access files.

Figure 3.51 is a simple driver VI for a binary file format that I just made up. This format has a header containing one I32 (4 bytes) that is the number of data samples to follow. The data follows immediately afterward and is in SGL floating point format. Each time this driver is

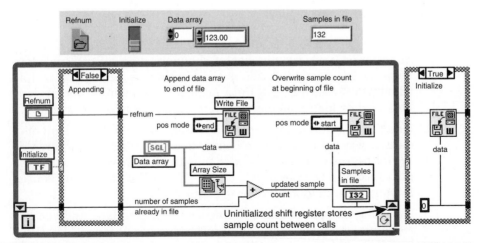

Figure 3.51   This subVI appends an array of SGL floats to a binary file and updates the sample count, an I32 integer, located at the beginning of the file. (Error handling omitted for clarity.)

called, the data array is appended to the file and the header is updated to reflect the total sample count.

An important concept in file access is the **file mark**, which is a pointer to the current location in the file, measured in bytes. It is maintained invisibly by the file system. The **pos mode** and **pos offset** inputs on the Write File, Read File, and Seek functions permit you to place the mark anywhere you wish. This is how you achieve random access: figure out where you are, then move to where you need to be. If the mark is at the end of the file (EOF) and you call Write File, then data is appended. If the mark is in the middle of the file, then Write File will overwrite existing data, starting at the mark.

In this example, the calling VI opens and closes the data file and passes the file's refnum via a **Byte Stream refnum** control. (If you ever need to pass the refnum for a datalog-format file, you have to use a **Data Log refnum** control.) There are no special tricks to opening or creating a byte stream binary file; LabVIEW does not differentiate between binary and text files with regards to file type—it's only how you interpret the data that makes a difference. On the first call to this VI, **Initialize** should be set to true, which results in the sample count being set to zero and written to the file. An uninitialized shift register stores the sample count for use on subsequent calls.

After initialization, Write File is called with **pos mode** set to 1, which means append data to the end of the file. Since Write File is polymorphic, I just wired the incoming data array to the **data** input. The size of the array is added to the previous sample count. Then, Write File is called again but this time with **pos mode** set to 0, which forces it to begin writing at the start of the file. The data in this case is our updated sample count, an I32 integer, which overwrites the previous value without bothering data elsewhere in the file.

Reading binary files. Reading the data is even easier, at least for this simple example, as shown in Fig. 3.52. Read File is called with the **type**

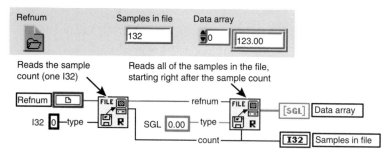

Figure 3.52 Reading the simple binary file created in the previous example. All you have to do is read the first 4 bytes, which represents the number of samples to follow, then read that number of data points. (Error handling omitted for clarity.)

input wired to an I32 constant so that it returns the sample count with the appropriate interpretation. This is another example of polymorphism at work. If you do not wire to **type**, the default type, *string,* is used, and your data is returned as a string. Next, Read File is called again to read the data, which is in SGL format. Because **count** is wired, Read File returns an array of the specified type. No special positioning of the file marker was required in this example because everything was in order. Things are more complex when you have multiple data arrays and/or headers in one file.

These binary file I/O examples have so far used the basic file functions, but you can also do it with some easier VIs from the Binary File function palette. For integer types, there are **Write To I16 File** and **Read From I16 File**. For floating point types, there are **Write To SGL File** and **Read From SGL File**. They handle 1D and 2D arrays, and any of these can be modified to suit other numeric formats. Their biggest limitation is lack of random-access control when writing data.

Random-access reading is, as I said earlier, a bit tricky because you have to keep track of the file mark, and that's a function of the data in the file. To illustrate, I created a fairly simple VI that allows you to read random blocks of data from a file created by the LabVIEW DAQ example VI, **Cont Acq to File (scaled)**, located in the directory examples/daq/analogin/strmdisk.llb/. The binary file created by that example contains an I32 header whose value is the number of channels, followed by scans of SGL-format data. A scan consists of one value for each channel. The objective is to read and display several scans (I'm calling this a *block* of data), starting at an arbitrary location in the file. Figure 3.53 is a solution (not the best, most feature-packed solution, I assure you, but it's simple enough to explain). Here's how it works.

1. The binary file is opened.

2. A single I32 integer is read by the Read File function. Its value is the number of channels in each scan. For computation of file offset, it is multiplied by four, the number of bytes in a value of type SGL. Already, you can see the dependency on prior knowledge of the file's contents.

3. The program idles in a While Loop. On each iteration, a new file offset is computed. **Offset** equals scans per block, times the number of bytes per scan, times the desired block number, plus 4 bytes (which accounts for the I32 header). Read From SGL File is set up to read relative to the start of the file with the computed offset. I used another cool feature of this high-level file VI: it understands the concept of rows and columns when reading 2D arrays. You can see the **row** and **col** values on the diagram.

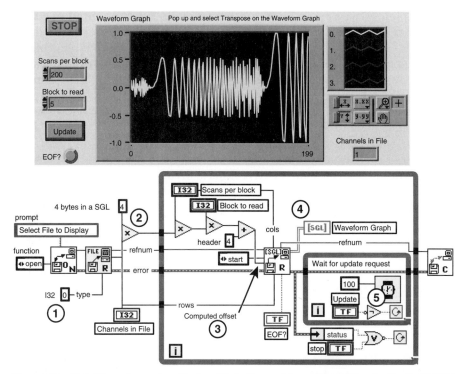

Figure 3.53   This VI reads random blocks of data from a binary file written by the LabVIEW DAQ example VI, Cont Acq to File (scaled). I couldn't make it much simpler than this.

4. The data is loaded and displayed on a waveform graph. You must pop up on the graph and select **Transpose**; otherwise, the x and y axes are swapped.

5. A small While Loop runs until the user clicks the Update button. This is a standard way of suspending execution pending operator intervention.

When the program is done, the file is closed and errors are checked. As you can see, even this simple example is rather tricky. That's the way it always is with binary files. A much better user interface is feasible but we'll cover that in a later chapter.

Writing datalog files

LabVIEW datalog files conveniently store data in binary format one record at a time. A record can be any LabVIEW data type, though you will usually use a cluster containing several data types. To access datalog files, you make use of the fact that the file I/O functions are polymorphic. Whenever you make a connection to the **type** input of a New File or Open File function, it assumes that you intend to access a data-log file containing records of the type you just connected. When the file is opened, the refnum (properly called a **datalog refnum**) carries information that describes the type of data in the file. The Read File and Write File functions then adapt to the appropriate type. A broken wire will result if you attempt to wire the **data** terminal to a source or destination of the wrong type.

Figure 3.54 is a rework of our simple data logger using LabVIEW datalog files. At the lower left, the data type is specified as a cluster containing a string and a SGL numeric array. By wiring it to the **type** input of the File Dialog function, you limit the user's choice of file types to those with this particular type (you don't *have* to wire it; it's just a convenience). Similarly, New File responds by creating a file with a datalog refnum that corresponds to this type. In the While Loop, Write File appends one record per iteration, containing a string with the current time and an array of values. The datalog refnum tells Write File what data type to expect. Note that datalog files are effectively *append*

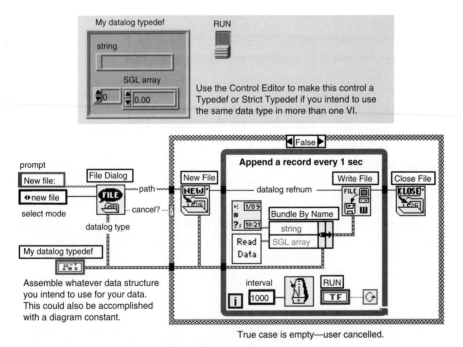

Figure 3.54 Writing data to a datalog file. The data type in this case is a cluster containing a string and a numeric array. Records are appended every second. (Error handling removed for clarity.)

only; you cannot overwrite selected datalogs in an existing file. To edit the contents of a datalog file, you must open the file and copy the desired records to another, similar datalog file.

Note the use of a **typedef** control for determination of data type in this example. By wiring such a type specifier to all dependent objects (File Dialog, New File, and Bundle By Name), you can guarantee that the program will work properly with no broken wires, even if you change the constituents of the control. This is extremely important for code maintenance in large projects and is a good habit to get into. For this simple example, you wouldn't have to edit or save the control as a typedef, but at least it's properly wired and easy to change if necessary.

You can also create datalog files by using **front panel data logging** functions under the Operate menu. Front panel data logging appends a record containing a timestamp and all of the front panel data to a file of your choosing. In the Data Logging submenu, you create a file (**Change Log File Binding ...**), then manually log the panel at any time (the **Log ...** command) or enable **Log At Completion** to automatically append a record when execution of the VI ends. The VI need not have its front panel displayed in order for Log At Completion to function. This is a handy way to do data logging without programming in the usual sense. Just create a subVI with a set of controls you wish to log (it does not need any wiring on its diagram). Set it up to Log At Completion, wire it into the diagram of a calling VI, and every time the subVI is called, a data snapshot is recorded. The format of this kind of datalog is a cluster containing two things: a timestamp and a cluster with all front panel controls. The cluster order is the same as the Panel Order, which you set in the **Edit>>Panel Order ...** menu item.

Front panel data logging creates standard datalog files, readable by the methods described in the following section. You can also view the contents of each record right on the panel by choosing **Retrieve ...** from the Data Logging submenu. This is a convenient way of storing and manually retrieving VI setups. You can also place the VI from which you logged data onto a diagram, pop up on it and select **Enable Database Access**. A halo that looks like a file cabinet appears around the icon of the subVI. It has terminals for programmatically accessing specified records and for reading timestamps and data.

Reading datalog files

You can read one or more records at a time from a datalog file. Figure 3.55 shows the basic method by which you read a single record. The **EOF function** reports the number of records in the file, rather than the number of bytes, as it did with a byte stream text file. Similarly, Read File responds to its **pos offset** input by seeking the desired

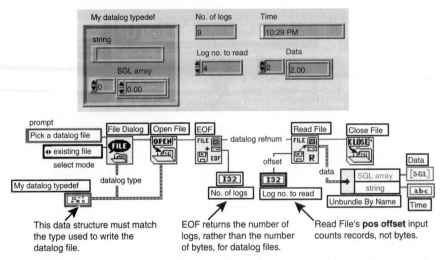

Figure 3.55 This VI reads a single datalog of the format written by the previous example. Note the value of creating a typedef control to set the datalog type. (Error handling removed for clarity.)

record number (starting with zero) rather than a byte number. In this example, one record containing the expected bundle of data is returned. Note how Read File's data output is of the same type as the datalog typedef wired to Open File. The type information is carried in the datalog refnum.

If you want to read more than one record at a time, just connect a numeric value to the **count** terminal of Read File as shown in Fig. 3.56. Its output will then be an array of the data type previously defined. You

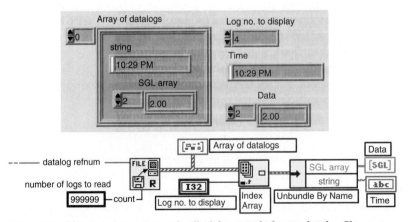

Figure 3.56 This code fragment reads all of the records from a datalog file.

can also wire the **pos offset** input to select which record is the first to be read. With these two controls, you can read any number of records (in sequence) from any location in the file.

Datalog file utilities.   An easy way to get started with datalog files is to use the utility VIs in the LabVIEW examples (path: labview/examples/file/datalog.llb). These VIs are modeled after some of the other file utilities and include functions to open, read, write, and close files containing datalogs with a data type of your choice. The examples simulate common usage, and there is a handy example that reads one record at a time when you click a button. For an all-in-one solution to the problem of reading and writing datalog files, see the description of the **Datalog Handler VI** in Chap. 7, "Writing a Data Acquisition Program."

Data Types and Conversions

One thing that proves that LabVIEW is a complete programming language is its support for essentially all data types. Numbers can be floating point or integer, with various degrees of precision. Booleans, bytes, strings, and numerics can be combined freely into various structures, giving you total freedom to make the data type suit the problem. **Polymorphism** makes this potentially complicated world of data types into something that even the novice can manage without much study. Polymorphism is the ability to adjust to input data of different types. Most built-in LabVIEW functions are polymorphic. VIs that you write are not truly polymorphic—they can adapt between numeric types, but not between other data types such as strings to numerics. Most of the time, you can just wire from source to destination without much care since the functions adapt to the kind of data that you supply. For instance, in Fig. 3.57, a constant is added to each value in an array. Amazing! Most other languages would require you to write a loop to do that. How does LabVIEW know what to do? The key is object-oriented programming, where polymorphism is but one of the novel concepts that make this new programming technology so desirable. There are of course limits to polymorphism, as the bottom example in the figure shows. The result of adding a Boolean to string is a little hard to define, so the natural polymorphism in LabVIEW doesn't permit these operations. But what if you actually *needed* to perform such an operation? That's where **conversions** and **type casting** come in.

Conversion and coercion

Data in LabVIEW has two components, the **data** itself and its **type descriptor**. You can't see the type descriptor; it is used internally to

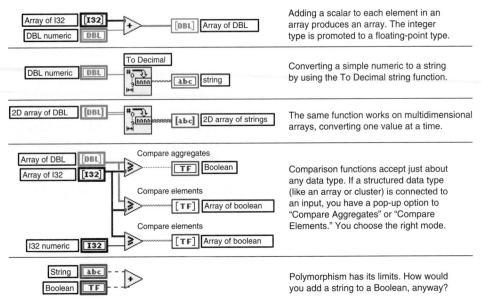

Figure 3.57   Polymorphism in action. Think how complicated this would be if the functions didn't adapt automatically. The lower example shows the limits of polymorphism. How in the world could you add a Boolean or a string? If there *was* a way, it would be included in LabVIEW.

give LabVIEW directions on how to handle the associated data—that's how polymorphic functions know what kind of data is connected. A type descriptor identifies the type of the data (such as a DBL floating point array) and the number of bytes in the data. When data is **converted** from one type to another, both the data component and the type descriptor are modified in some fashion. For example: [I32]—[DBL]—[DBL], where an I32 (signed integer with 32 bits, or 4 bytes) is converted to a DBL (64-bit, or 8-byte floating point), the value contained in the I32 is changed into a *characteristic* and an *exponent*. The type descriptor is changed accordingly, and this new data type takes up a bit more memory. For conversion between scalar numeric types, the process is very simple, generally requiring only one CPU instruction. But if aggregate types are involved (strings, clusters, etc.), this conversion process takes some time. First, the value has to be interpreted in some way, requiring that a special conversion program be run. Second, the new data type may require more or less memory, so the system's memory manager may need to be called. By now you should be getting the idea that conversion is something you may want to avoid, if only for performance reasons.

Conversion is explicitly performed by using one of the functions from the Conversion menu. They are polymorphic, so you can feed them scalars (simple numbers or Booleans), arrays, clusters, and so on, as long as the input makes some sense. There is another place that conversions occur, sometimes without your being aware. When you make a connection, sometimes a little gray dot appears at the destination's terminal: **I32**—▸**DBL**. This is called a **coercion** dot and performs exactly the same operation as an explicit conversion function. One other warning about conversion and coercion: *be wary of lost precision.* A DBL or EXT floating point can take on values up to $10^{\pm 237}$ or thereabouts. If you converted such a big number to an unsigned byte (U8), with a range of only 0–255, then clearly the original value could be lost. It is generally good practice to modify numeric data types to eliminate coercion because it reduces memory usage and increases speed. Use the **Representation** pop-up menu item on controls, indicators, and diagram constants to adjust the representation.

Intricate conversions and type casting

Besides simple numeric type conversions, there are some more advanced ones that you might use in special situations. This is an advanced topic, so I've saved it for last.

Figure 3.58 uses an intertype conversion to make a cluster of Booleans into an array. **Cluster to Array** works on any cluster that

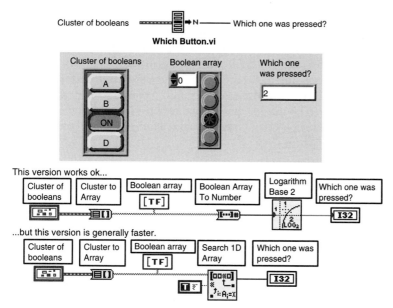

Figure 3.58 A cluster of Booleans makes a nice user interface item, but it's hard to interpret. Here are two solutions that find the true bit. The bottom solution is my final solution.

contains only controls of the same type (you can't arbitrarily mix strings, numerics, etc.). Once you have an array of Booleans, the figure shows two ways to find the element that is True. In the upper solution, the **Boolean Array to Number** function returns a value in the range of $0–2^{32} - 1$ based on the bit pattern in the Boolean array. Since the bit that is set must correspond to a power of two, I then take the Log_2 of that number, which returns a number between 0 and 32 for each button, and −1 for no buttons pressed. Pretty crafty, eh? But the bottom solution turns out to be faster (I benchmarked it and wrote an article about it in the *LTR*). Starting with the Boolean array, use **Search 1D Array** to find the first element that is true. Search 1D Array returns the element number, which is again a number between 0 and 32 or a large negative number for no buttons. This number could then be passed to the selection terminal in a Case structure to take some action based on which switch was pressed. This utility, the **Which Button VI**, has been a popular one and is included in the utility library on the CD-ROM.

platform\ utility\Which Button.vi

Figure 3.59 shows a way to use a nice-looking set of **Ring Indicators** in a cluster as a status indicator. An array of I32 numerics is converted to a cluster by using the **Array to Cluster** function. A funny thing happens with this function: how does LabVIEW know how many elements belong in the output cluster (the array can have any number of elements)? For this reason, a pop-up item on Array to Cluster called **Set Cluster Size** was added. You have to set the number to match the indicator (five, in this case) or you'll get a broken wire.

One of the most powerful ways to change one data type to another is **type casting**. As opposed to conversions, type casting only changes the type descriptor. *The data component is unchanged.* The data is in no way rescaled or rearranged; it is merely interpreted in a different way. The good news is that this process is very fast, though a new copy of the incoming data has to be made, requiring a call to the memory manager. The bad news is that you have to know what you're doing! Type casting

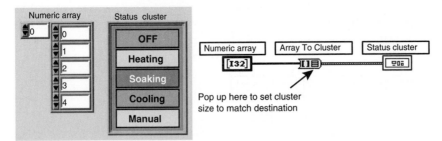

Figure 3.59 A numeric array is converted to a cluster of Ring indicators (which are of type I32) by using Array to Cluster. Remember to use the pop-up item on this conversion function called Set Cluster Size for the number of cluster elements. In this case, the size is five.

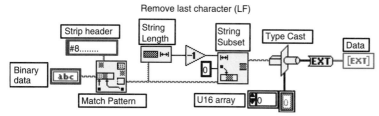

Figure 3.60 Lifted from the HP 54510 driver, this code segment strips the header off a data string, removes a trailing line feed character, then type casts the data to a U16 integer array, which is finally converted to an EXT array.

is a specialized operation that you will very rarely need; that's why it was banished to the Advanced function palette. LabVIEW has enough polymorphism and conversion functions built-in so that you rarely need the Type Cast function.

The most common use for the Type Cast function is shown in Fig. 3.60, where a binary data string returned from an oscilloscope is type cast to an array of integers. Notice that some header information and a trailing character had to be removed from the string before casting. Failure to do so would leave extra garbage values in the resultant array. Worse yet, what would happen if the incoming string were off by plus or minus one byte at the beginning? Byte pairs, used to make up I16 integers, would then be incorrectly paired. Results would be very strange. Note that the Type Cast function will accept most data types except for clusters that contain arrays or strings.

Warning: The Type Cast function expects a certain byte ordering, namely big-endian, or most-significant byte first to guarantee portability between platforms running LabVIEW. But there are problems interpreting this data *outside* of LabVIEW. Big-endian is the normal ordering for the Macintosh and Sun. But not so on the PC! This is an example where your code, or the data you save in a binary file, may not be machine-independent.

Indeed, there is much trouble in type casting land, and you should try to use polymorphism and conversion functions whenever possible. Consider Fig. 3.61. The first example uses the Type Cast function, whereas the second example accomplishes exactly the same operation—writing a binary image of an array to disk—in a much clearer, more concise way. Keep looking through the function palettes if the particular data type compatibility that you need is not apparent. The bottom example shows how flexible the LabVIEW primitives are. In this case, Write File accommodates any imaginable data type without putting you through Type Casting obfuscation.

If you get into serious data conversion and type casting exercises, be careful, be patient, and prepare to explore the other data conversion functions in the Advanced palette. Sometimes the bytes are out of

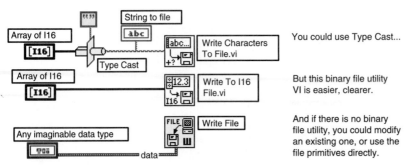

Figure 3.61 "Eschew obfuscation," the English teacher said. Look for ways to avoid type casting and simplify your diagrams. Easy-level functions and primitives are extremely flexible.

order, as in the PC versus Mac situation. In that case, try **Swap Bytes** or **Swap Words** and display the data in a string with its format set to hexadecimal, octal, or binary (use the pop-up menu, **Format and Precision**). Some instruments go so far as to send the data backward, that is, the first value arrives last. You can use **Reverse Array** or **Reverse String** to cure that nasty situation. **Split Number** and **Join Number** are two other functions that allow you to directly manipulate the ordering of bytes in a machine-independent manner. Such are the adventures of writing instrument drivers, a topic covered in detail in Chap. 5, "Instrument Drivers."

Flatten to string (. . . do *what*?).   I mentioned before that the Type Cast function can't handle certain complicated data types. That's because LabVIEW stores strings and arrays in *handle blocks,* which are discontiguous segments of memory organized in a tree structure. When such data types are placed in a cluster, the data may be physically stored in many areas of memory. Type Cast expects all the data to be located in a single contiguous area so that it can perform its simple and fast transformation. You can read all about LabVIEW data storage details in the appendix to the LabVIEW user manual.

Occasionally, you need to transmit arbitrarily complex data types over a serial link. The link may be a serial port, a network connection using a protocol such as TCP/IP, or even a binary file on disk, which is in fact a serial storage method. Type Cast can't do it, but the **Flatten To String** function can (so can the file primitives; they use the same algorithms as Flatten To String when creating datalog files). What this function does is copy all discontiguous data into one contiguous buffer called the **data string**. The data string also contains embedded header information for nonscalar items (strings and arrays) which are useful when trying to reconstruct that flattened data. Figure 3.62 shows Flat-

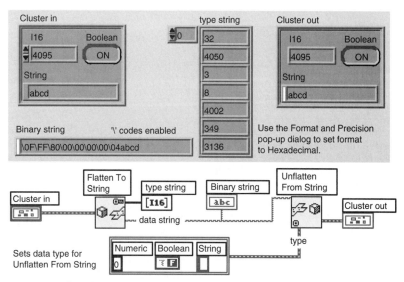

Figure 3.62   Use *flattened* data when you need to transmit complicated data types over a communications link or store them in a binary file.

ten To String in action, along with its counterpart **Unflatten From String**. The data string could be transmitted over a network, or stored in a file, and then could be read and reconstructed by Unflatten From String. As with all binary formats, you must describe the underlying data format to the reading program. Unflatten From String requires a data **type** to properly reconstruct the original data.

The most common uses for flattened data are transmission over a network or storage to a binary file. My utility VI, Setup File Handler (included on the CD-ROM), uses this technique to store and retrieve clusters on disk as a means of maintaining front-panel setup information. Perhaps the most esoteric use of Flatten To String that I've seen is as a means of obtaining type descriptor information. All data in LabVIEW carries a type descriptor along with the data, but you never see it. But there is a way: Flatten To String returns a **type string** (actually, an I16 array) containing information about the flattened data. I have seen a use for this in a LabVIEW add-on package called Virtual Panel from Sedona Systems. It wrote a parser for the type string that determines the makeup of a front-panel control or indicator. With this parser, you can permit a user to add arbitrary items to a cluster, and then, *without editing the diagram,* interpret the contents of the cluster. The programming behind this is something you have to see to believe.

Get carried away department.   Here's a grand finale for conversion and type casting. Say that you need to fix the length of a string at three

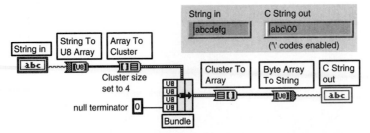

Figure 3.63 Making a fixed-length, null-terminated string for compatibility with the C language. The key is the Array to Cluster conversion that produces a fixed number of elements. This is a really obscure example.

characters and add on a *null* (zero) terminator. I actually had to do this for compatibility with another application that expected a C-style string, which requires the addition of a null terminator. Let's use everything we know about the conversion functions and do it like Fig. 3.63.

This trick (courtesy of Rob Dye, a member of the LabVIEW development team) uses the Set Cluster Size pop-up setting in an **Array to Cluster** conversion function to force the string length to be four characters, total. The bundler allows parallel access to the whole string, so it's easy to change one character, in this case the last one. It turns out that this program is very fast because all of the conversions performed here are actually type-casting operations underneath. The disadvantage of this technique, as compared to using a few string functions, is that it is hard to understand. I know; it took me a few minutes to figure out.

Bibliography

Erickson, Dennis C. and Robert J. Albright, *"Design of a LabVIEW-Based Portable Power System Disturbance Monitor,"* paper presented at the 1993 National Instruments User Symposium. (Available from National Instruments.)

LabVIEW Technical Note TN020, *"Minimizing the Number of Data Buffers."* (Available from National Instruments or on the CD-ROM.)

Parker, Jeff, "Flexing Your LabVIEW Datalogging Muscle!" *LabVIEW Technical Resource,* vol. 4, no. 2, Spring 1996. (Back issues available from LTR Publishing.)

Wells, Lisa K. and J. Travis, *LabVIEW for Everyone,* Prentice-Hall, Englewood Cliffs, New Jersey, 1996. (ISBN 0-13-268194-3. Call Prentice-Hall at (800) 947-7700 or (201) 767-4990.)

4

Building an Application

Most of the real programming applications I've looked at over the years seemed as though they had just happened. Be it Fortran, Pascal, or LabVIEW, it was as if the programmer had no real goals in mind—no sense of mission or understanding of the big picture. No planning. I actually had to use an old data acquisition system that started life as a hardware test program. One of the techs sat down to test some new I/O interface hardware one day, so he wrote a simple program to collect measurements. Someone saw what was going on and asked him if he could store the data on disk. He hammered away for a few days, and, by golly, it worked. The same scenario was repeated over and over for several years, culminating in a full-featured . . . *mess*. It collected data, but nobody could understand the program, let alone modify or maintain it. By default, this contrivance became a standard data acquisition system for a whole bunch of small labs. It took years to finally replace it, mainly because it was a daunting task. But LabVIEW made it easy. These days, we start by writing programs in LabVIEW, but the same old scenario keeps repeating itself: hack something together, then try to fix it up and document it sometime later.

Haphazard programming need not be the rule. Computer scientists have come up with an arsenal of program design, analysis, and quality management techniques over the years, all of them based on common sense, and all of them applicable to LabVIEW. If you happen to be familiar with such formalisms, such as structured design, by all means use those methods. But you don't need to be a computer scientist to design a quality application. Rather, you need to think ahead, analyze the problem, and generally be methodical. This chapter should help you see the big picture and design a better application. Here are the steps I use to build a LabVIEW application:

1. Define and understand the problem.

2. Specify the type of I/O hardware you will need.

3. Prototype the user interface.

4. Design, then write, the program.

5. Test and debug the program.

6. Write the documentation (*please!*).

To make this whole process clearer, I'm going to go through a real example: a LabVIEW-based control and data-logging system for Larry's Vacuum Brazing Lab (call it **VBL**, for short). At each step, I'll outline the general approach then illustrate my particular tactics and the problems I discovered in the VBL project.

Define the Problem

If you, the system designer, can't understand the problem, all is lost! You will stumble about in the dark, hoping to accidentally solve your customer's problems through blind luck or divine intervention. Sorry, but that's not going to happen. What you need to do is spend a significant amount of time just understanding the problem. At this point, you don't need a computer at all, just a pencil and maybe a voltmeter or an oscilloscope, and the desire to find out what is really going on.

Analyze the user's needs

I like to interview the end users in several sessions. Talk to everyone involved with particular attention to the operators—the ones who actually have to interact with the VIs you write. Even if *you* are the customer, you still have to go through this step to make sure that you have all the important specifications on paper. How else will you know when you're done?

Tell your customers about LabVIEW. Show them what it can do in a live demonstration. That way, you can speak a common language—you can speak of controls, indicators, files, and subVIs. In return, your customer should show you the system that needs to be monitored or controlled. Perhaps there's an existing measurement and control system that has shortcomings—find out what's wrong with that existing system. Learn the proper terminology. Maybe you need to read up on the technology if it's something you've never worked with before. I didn't know what vacuum brazing was until I spent a couple of hours with Larry. Here's what I learned:

The principle of vacuum brazing is simple (Fig. 4.1). *Brazing* involves joining two materials (usually, but not always, metal) by melting a filler metal (such as brass) and allowing it to wet the materials to be joined. Soldering (like we do in electronics) is similar. The idea is *not* to melt the materials being joined, and that means carefully controlling the temperature. Another complication is that the base metals sometimes react with the air or other contaminants at high temperatures, forming an impervious oxide layer that inhibits joining. Larry's solution is to put everything in a vacuum chamber where there is no oxygen, or anything else for that matter. Thus, we call it *vacuum brazing*. The VBL has five similar electric furnaces, each with its own vacuum bell jar. The heater is controlled by a Eurotherm model 847 digital controller, which measures the temperature with a thermocouple and adjusts the power applied to the big electric heater until the measured temperature matches the setpoint that Larry has entered.

Gather specifications

As you interview the customers, start making a list of basic **functional requirements and specifications**. Watch out for the old standoff where the user keeps asking what your proposed system can provide. You don't even *have* a proposed system yet! Just concentrate on getting the real needs on paper. You can negotiate practical limitations later.

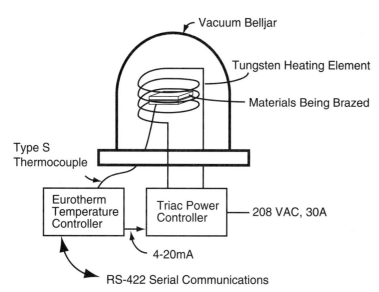

Figure 4.1   A simplified vacuum brazing furnace. The temperature controller adjusts power to the heating element until the measured temperature matches the desired setpoint. Not shown is the vacuum pump and other support equipment. Serial communications make it possible for LabVIEW to run this furnace.

Ask probing questions that take into consideration his or her actual understanding of the problem, his or her knowledge of instrumentation, and LabVIEW's capabilities. If there is an existing computer system (not necessarily in the same lab, but one with a similar purpose), use that as a starting point. As the project progresses, keep referring to this original list to make sure that everything has been addressed. (It's amazing, but every time I think I'm finished, I check the requirements document and find out I've missed at least one important feature.) Review the specifications with the user when you think you understand the problem. In formal software engineering, the requirements document may adhere to some standards, such as those published by IEEE, which can be quite involved. In that case, you will have formal design reviews where the customer and perhaps some outside experts will review your proposed system design. While beyond the scope of this chapter, this topic will be addressed in a future book. In any case, here are some important requirements to consider:

- Characterize each signal. Is it digital or analog? Low or high frequency? What kind of I/O hardware is proposed or required for proper interfacing? Are LabVIEW drivers available?

- What are the basic operations, steps, event sequences, and procedures that the software needs to perform? This determines much of the overall structure of the program.

- Are there critical performance specifications? For example, rapid response time may be required in a control loop, or very high accuracy and noise rejection are desired. Make sure that the hardware, LabVIEW, and your programming expertise are up to the task.

- What displays and controls are required? Break down displays by type, such as charts, graphs, numerics, strings, and Booleans. Consider which screen object controls or displays which signals.

- Determine the signal analysis needs such as statistics, linearization, peak detection, frequency transforms, filtering, and so on. If unusual algorithms are required, seek details early in the project. What needs to be done in real time versus post-run analysis? This may drastically affect your choice of computer and the system's overall performance.

- What will be done with the data that will be collected? Compatibility with other applications (sometimes on other computers) is an important issue. You must always save the data in a suitable format, and you should be involved with the development of analysis tools. Various options for real-time exchange with other programs also may be considered (Dynamic Data Exchange; Interapplication Communication; networking).

■ What other information needs to be recorded besides acquired data? Often, users like to save run setup information or comments in a running log format with time stamps.

■ How much of this is *really* necessary? Separate needs from wants. Prioritize the tasks. Realize that there are *always* constraints on budget and/or time and you have to work within these constraints. Speaking of which, get commitment on the budget and schedule early in the project!

The major requirements for the VBL project I divided into *must-haves* and *future additions,* which prioritized the jobs nicely. Larry was really short of funding on this job, so the future additions are low priority.

Must-Haves

1. All five systems may operate simultaneously.
2. Procedure: ramp up to a soak setpoint, then go to manual control so user can tweak temperature up to melting point. Resume ramp on command.
3. LabVIEW will generate the temperature ramp profiles. User needs a nice way to enter parameters and maintain recipes.
4. Strip-chart indicators for real-time temperature trends.
5. Notify user (beep and/or dialog) when the soak temp is reached.
6. Alarm (beep and dialog) when temperature exceeds upper limit in controller.
7. Make post-run trend plots to paste into Microsoft Word report document.

Future Additions

1. Control vacuum pump-down controller. This will require many RS-232 ports.
2. Trend vacuum measurement. This will require even more RS-232 ports.

Draw a block diagram

Draw a preliminary **block diagram** of the system. Think in terms of signal flow all the way from I/O hardware to computer screen and back out again. What are the inputs and outputs? This will define the signals, and the signals will define the kind of I/O hardware and data presentation that you will need. List the characteristics of each signal. Some of the items to consider are as follows:

- Sensor and actuator types, manufacturers, model numbers, and so forth
- Number of channels, categorized by signal type
- Signal characteristics: voltage, current, pulse rate, and so forth
- Frequency content—determines sampling rates and filtering requirements
- Isolation and grounding requirements
- Type of analysis to be performed—influences acquisition and storage techniques

Get as much detail as possible right now. This information is vital if you hope to design a really successful automation package. It would be a shame to mis-specify I/O hardware or write a program that simply doesn't account for the needs of all the instruments you plan to support.

For VBL, I learned that there would only be two basic signals running between the computer and each furnace: the measured temperature from the controller and the setpoint going to the controller (Fig. 4.2). In their raw forms, both are DC analog signals. The Eurotherm controller converts the signals to and from digital commands that are transmitted over an RS-422 serial communications line. RS-422 permits *multidrop connections,* meaning that multiple controllers can share a single communications line. Therefore, I knew that no signal conditioning of the usual type was needed, but a driver for this particular Eurotherm controller would have to be written. As a bonus, the communications hardware uses differential connections to enhance noise rejection—very thoughtful, these engineers.

Collect details on any special equipment proposed for use in the system. Technical manuals are needed to figure out how to hook up the signal lines and will also give you signal specifications. For all but the simplest instruments there may be a significant driver development effort required (especially for GPIB or serial communications), so you will need to get a copy of the programming manual as well. Sometimes one major instrument *is* the I/O system, as I discovered with VBL.

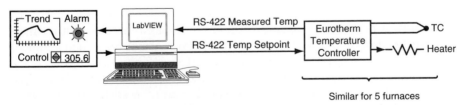

Figure 4.2 Draw a block diagram of your project to make sure you know how the pieces fit together. This one was really simple, with only one input and one output for each of five furnaces.

When you have all the information together, write up a system requirements document. Even if it's only one page. Even if your company does not require it. Even if it seems like too much work at the moment. Why? *Because it will pay off in the form of a higher quality product.*

Specify the I/O Hardware

Now that you know which instruments will be used on your project, follow the steps outlined in Chap. 2, "Inputs and Outputs," to determine what kind of I/O hardware to use. The signals your instruments produce will define the hardware. There are many factors to consider, so choose wisely.

Since you have to write a LabVIEW program to support the I/O, having examples of completed **drivers** available will save you much time and effort. The LabVIEW instrument library contains hundreds of ready-to-use drivers, all available for free. Even if your instrument isn't in the library, there may be something very close—a different model by the same manufacturer—that is easily modified. If you plan to use any of the National Instruments multifunction boards, prowl through the DAQ example VIs to find relevant demonstration programs that you can use as starting points. For simple projects, it's surprising how quickly the examples can be modified to become the final application. LabVIEW 4 includes some help on this, the **DAQ Example Navigator**, found in the Help menu. Future versions of LabVIEW will include more and better tools to help you choose or design an initial application architecture or technique. With any luck, one day you may have Gary In A Box.

Availability and performance of drivers is one more consideration in your choice of I/O hardware. You may need to do some preliminary testing with the actual instruments and data acquisition equipment before you commit to a final list of specifications. Be absolutely sure that you can meet the user's needs for overall **throughput**: the rate at which data can be acquired, processed, displayed, and stored. Write some simple test VIs at this point and rest better at night. The **Speed Tester** VI in Fig. 4.3 is useful when you have a subVI that you want to exercise at top speed. You can put anything inside the For Loop and get a fairly accurate measure of its execution time. Make sure that the speed tester does plenty of iterations so that you get enough timing resolution. As you learned in Chap. 3, "LabVIEW Programming Techniques," there are limitations on the timing precision of some computers. If you want to benchmark events with microsecond precision, use the timing example VI, examples/daq/counter.llb/Timer Template, which makes use of the timing hardware on an MIO-16 board.

**platform\
benchmark\
speed tester.vi**

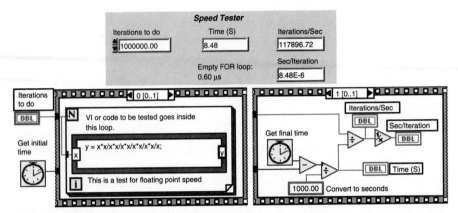

Figure 4.3 A general-purpose speed tester VI that is used when you need to check the throughput or iteration rate of a subVI or segment of code. In this example, I did 10 floating point operations. The speed of my Macintosh Quadra 950 was 1.3 megaflops, after subtracting LabVIEW's overhead for doing the For Loop.

In most cases you can't write the application unless you know what hardware will be used. For instance, in a high-throughput data acquisition application where many thousands of samples per second of data are streamed to disk, you probably can't do much on-the-fly analysis, graphics, or changing of windows because of the extreme performance demands on the CPU. On the other hand, programming a low-speed temperature recorder has no such demands and permits a substantial amount of real-time processing and display.

The Eurotherm controllers use the serial port for communications. Even though Larry was only asking for one sample per second top speed, I suspected that there could be an upper limit to the total throughput lurking close by. Serial instruments are notorious for adding lots of header and trailer information to otherwise simple messages, which compounds the problem of an already-slow communications link. The bad news was that there was no driver available, so I had to write one from scratch before any testing was possible. The good news was that it only took 30 ms to exchange a message with a controller. That means I could move about 33 messages per second, distributed among the five controllers, or about 6 messages per controller per second. Not a problem, unless he ever wants to triple the number of furnaces.

Prototype the User Interface

An effective and fun way to start designing your application is to create prototype front panels that you can show to the users. The panels don't have to work at all, or maybe you can just hook up random number generators to animate the graphs and other indicators. Don't spend much time programming; concentrate on designing panels that meet the specifications. Consider the best types of controls and indicators for each signal. Make a list of inputs and outputs, grouped in some logical categories, and pair them up with the most sensible control and indicator types. If you have to write a formal software requirements document, you can paste images of your mock front panels into the document. That makes your intentions clearer.

User interface design

Making a front panel easy to understand while satisfying complex requirements is one of the keys to successful virtual instrument development. LabVIEW, like other modern graphical presentation programs, has nearly unlimited flexibility in graphical user interface design. But to quote the manager of a large graphic arts department, "We don't have a shortage of technology, we have a shortage of *talent!*" I wish that I could refer you to a concise and appropriate design guide for user interface design, but that is not possible at this time. The best thing I've seen are the Apple Computer user interface guidelines in *Inside Macintosh.* Some industries, such as the nuclear power industry, have formal user interface guidelines that are extremely rigid. If you are involved with a project in such an area, be sure to consult the required documents. Otherwise, you are very much on your own.

Take the time to look at high-quality computer applications and see how they manage objects on the screen. Decide which features you would prefer to emulate or avoid. Try working with someone else's LabVIEW application without getting any instructions. Is it easy to understand and use, or are you bewildered by dozens of illogical, unlabeled controls, 173 different colors, and lots of blinking lights? Observe your customer as he or she tries to use *your* VI. Don't butt in; just watch. You'll learn a lot from the experience, and fast! If the user gets stuck, you must fix the user interface and/or the programming problems. Form a picture in your own mind of good and bad user interface design.

One surefire way to create a bad GUI is to get carried away with colors, fonts, and pictures. They quickly become distracting to the operator when overused. (Please don't emulate the glitzy screens you see in advertising; they are exactly what you *don't* want.) Instead, stick to some common themes. Pick a few text styles and assign them to certain purposes. Similarly, use a standard background color (like gray or a really light pastel), a standard highlight color, and a couple of status colors such as bright green and red. Human factors specialists tell us that **consistency** and **simplicity** really are the keys to designing quality man-machine interfaces (MMI). Operators will be less likely to make mistakes if the layouts among various panels are similar.

Group logically related controls in the same area of the screen, perhaps with a surrounding box with a subtly different background color. You can see this technique on the panels of high-quality instruments from companies such as Tektronix and Hewlett-Packard. Speaking of which, those *real* instruments are excellent models for your *virtual* instruments.

The *LabVIEW Style Guide* (Johnson and Kay 1995) contains some additional tips on designing panels, if you want to pursue this matter further. An informal document, the *Style Guide* was written by Meg Kay (one of the LabVIEW developers) and me. In it, we discuss the basic elements of LabVIEW programming style. It is currently available from the National Instruments FTP server ftp.natinst.com, or the info-labview mailgroup server ftp.pica.army.mil, or this book's CD-ROM. You are free to use it as a basis for your own in-house development standards—another way to enhance the quality of your development process.

**platform\
style guide\
LV_Style.pdf**

Panel possibilities

Remember that you have an arsenal of graphical controls available; don't just use simple numerics where a slider or ring control would be more intuitive. Import pictures from a drawing application and paste them into **Pict Ring** controls or as states in Boolean controls, and so forth, as shown in Fig. 4.4. Color is fully supported (except in this book). Deal with indicators the same way. Use the **Control Editor** to do detailed customization. The Control Editor is accessed by first selecting a control on the panel then choosing **Edit Control** from the Edit menu. You can resize and color all of the parts of any control and paste in pictures for any part, then save the control under a chosen name for later reuse. Be creative, but always try to choose the appropriate graphic design, not just the one with the most glitz. After all, the operator needs information, not entertainment.

Booleans with pictures pasted in are especially useful as indicators. For instance, if the True state contains a warning message and the False state has both the foreground and background color set to transparent (**T**, an invisible pen pattern in the color palette when using the coloring tool), then the warning message will appear as if by magic when the state is set to True. Similarly, an item can appear to move, change color, or change size based on its state through the use of these pasted-in pictures. Starting with LabVIEW 4, the built-in LabVIEW controls and indicators can be made to move or change size programmatically through the use of **Attribute Nodes**.

Attribute Nodes are an extremely flexible way to manipulate the appearance and behavior of the user interface. You create an Attribute

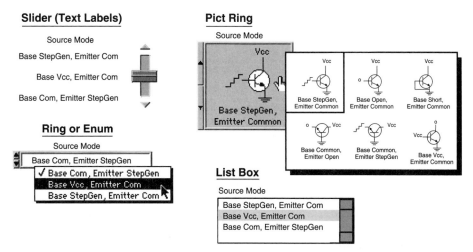

Figure 4.4 Controls can be highly customized with various text styles and imported pictures. Here are four sensible numeric controls that could be used for the same function. Pick your favorite.

Node by popping up on a control or indicator and choosing **Create ... Attribute Node**. Every control and indicator has a long list of attributes that you can read or write. There can be multiple Attribute Nodes for any given front panel item, but the Attribute Nodes must remain within the diagram of the VI where the control or indicator resides. (Perhaps a future version of LabVIEW will allow you to access attributes directly from subVIs.) A given Attribute Node can be resized by dragging at a corner to permit access to multiple attributes at one time. Each item in the list can be either read or write, and items are accessed sequentially from top to bottom. I'm not going to spend a great deal of time on Attribute Nodes because their usage is highly dependent upon the particular control and its application. But you will see them throughout this book in the various examples. Suffice it to say that you can change almost any visible characteristic of a panel item, and it's worth your time exploring the possibilities.

Real-time trending is best handled by the various charts, which are designed to update displayed data one point or one buffer at a time. Arrays of data acquired periodically are best displayed on a graph, which repaints its entire display when updated. Note that graphs and charts, have many features that you can customize, such as axis labels, grids, colors, and so forth. If you have a special data display problem that is beyond the capability of an ordinary graph or chart, also consider the **Picture Control Toolkit**, available from National Instruments. It allows you to draw just about anything in a rectangular window placed on the Front Panel. There are other, more advanced data display toolkits available from third parties. Chapter 10, "Data Visualization, Imaging, and Sound," discusses all these aspects of graphical display in detail.

Simple applications may be handled with a single panel, but more complex situations call for multiple VIs to avoid overcrowding the screen. Subdivide the controls and indicators according to function or mode of operation. See if there is a way to group them such that the user can press a button that activates a subVI that is set to **Show front panel when called** (part of the VI Setup menu, available by popping up on the icon). The subVI opens and presents the user with some logically related information and controls, and stays around until an Exit button is pressed, after which its window closes—like a dialog box, but much more versatile. Look at the Window options in the VI Setup menu. It contains many useful options for customizing the look of the VI window. Functions for configuration management, special control modes, alarm reporting, and alternative data presentations are all candidates for these dynamic windows. Examples of dynamic windows and programming tricks illustrating their use are discussed in Chap. 8, "Process Control Applications." For demonstration purposes, these dynamic windows can be quickly prototyped and made to operate in a realistic manner.

Your next step is to show your mock-up panels to the users and collect their comments. If there are only one or two people who need to see the demonstration, just gather them around your computer and do it live. Animation really helps the users visualize the end result. Also, you can edit the panels while they watch (Fig. 4.5).

If the audience is bigger than your office can handle, try using a projection screen for your computer down in the conference room. LCD panels and RGB projectors are widely available now and offer reasonable quality. That way, you can still do the live demonstration. As a backup, take screen shots of the LabVIEW panels that you can edit in a draw/paint application and add descriptive notes. Besides making a nice handout, hard copies are especially useful for projects that require quality assurance plans and formal design reviews. Gotta have things in print, you know.

> The Vacuum Brazing Lab had only a few things to display during normal operation: the five furnace temperatures, their setpoints, and their status (heating, soaking, cooling, etc.). That made one nice front panel with a big strip chart and a few other indicators. Next, I needed a panel through which Larry could edit the ramp-and-soak temperature recipe for each furnace—an ideal application for a dynamic window. Finally, there had to be a panel for manual control of the furnace. That panel needed such controls as auto/manual, recipe start/stop, and manual setpoint entry. It, too, was to be a dynamic window that appeared whenever a button on the

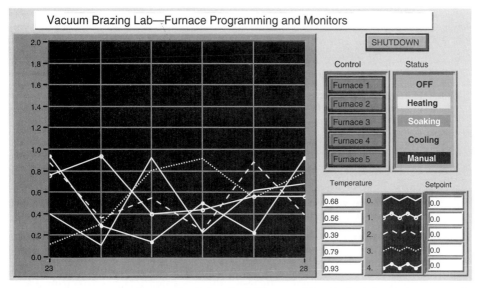

Figure 4.5   Can you make that graph a little taller? "No sweat," I replied, while calmly resizing the graph.

main panel was pressed. I created rough versions of the three panels, made some dummy connections that animated it all, and showed it to Larry.

Iterate on your preliminary panel design. Big projects may require several demonstrations to satisfy the more critical users. This is especially true if you have collected additional requirements because of the impact of your presentation. People start seeing alternatives they previously had not imagined. Take notes during the demonstrations and add to your requirements list. Discuss the new ideas and requirements with your cohorts and try to come up with likely programming solutions to the more difficult problems. Remember to keep the users in the loop during all phases of the review process. They will be the ultimate judges of your work and you certainly don't want to surprise them on the day of final delivery.

Design, Then Write Your Program

Don't be stymied by the "Blank Screen Syndrome." The same effect occurs in many fields when it's time to create something: the writer with a blank sheet of paper or the painter with an empty canvas. Prototyping the user interface takes care of the panel, but the diagram starts as a big collection of unconnected controls and indicators. Where to start?

Modern software engineering starts a project in the same way as any other engineering discipline: with a **design**—a plan of attack. You must do the same. The alternative is to sit in front of your computer hoping for divine inspiration to somehow guide you toward the optimum program. Most likely, you'll end up with another of those little test programs that balloon into full-featured, unmaintainable disasters. Instead, let's try using some design practices that work well in the LabVIEW environment.

In case you're wondering why designing and writing the program are wrapped into this one section instead of being separated, I have a good reason: most LabVIEW VIs run nicely on their own, with no main program. This is an important LabVIEW advantage that is often overlooked. Once you get past the most general stages of design, you start writing subVIs that beg to be run, tested, and optimized as you go. No need to write elaborate test programs. No need to wait until the entire application is assembled, complete with a bunch of buried bugs.

The ability to do **rapid prototyping** in LabVIEW is one of the major reasons for the product's success. You can quickly throw together a test program that improves your understanding of the underlying hardware and the ways in which LabVIEW behaves in your particular situation. These prototype programs are extremely valuable in the overall development process because they allow you to test important hypotheses and assumptions before committing yourself to a certain approach. Your first try at solving a problem may be ugly, but functional; it's the *later iterations* of this initial program that you actually deliver. This concept of **iterative design** is often the only practical approach to solving laboratory problems where the requirements change as fast as you can modify the program. If you can't seem to arrive at a concrete list of requirements, just do the best you can to design a flexible application that you can update and extend on short notice. Many of the architectures shown in the chapter are based on such practical needs and are indeed flexible and extensible.

If you're an experienced programmer, be sure to use your hard-learned experience. After all, LabVIEW is a programming language. All the sophisticated tools of structured analysis can be applied (if you're comfortable with that sort of thing), or you can just draw pictures and block diagrams until the functional requirements seem to match. This world is too full of overly rigid people and theorists producing more heat than light; let's get the job done!

Ask a Wizard

To help you get started, National Instruments added a **Solution Wizard** to LabVIEW version 4.1. The Wizard leads you through a list of questions regarding your application in the same way that you might interview your customer. Then, it draws from a library of example VIs, suggesting possible solutions that are ready to run. From that point, you continue by customizing the user interface and adding special features. As a design assistant, it's particularly valuable for DAQ-based applications, but it can also suggest basic program designs that are useful for ordinary applications. As time goes on, the Wizard's database will expand to encompass a broader range of programs.

Top-down or bottom-up?

There are two classic ways to attack a programming problem: from the top down and from the bottom up, and everyone has an opinion—an opinion that may well change from one project to the next—on which way is best.

Top-down structured design begins with the big picture: "I'm going to control this airplane; I'll start with the cockpit layout." When you have a big project to tackle, top-down works most naturally. LabVIEW has a big advantage over other languages when it comes to top-down design: it's easy to start with the final user interface and then animate it. A top-down LabVIEW design implies creation of dummy subVIs, each with a definite purpose and interrelationship to adjacent subVIs, callers, and callees, but at first without any programming. You define the front panel objects, data types, and the connector pane and its terminal layout. When the hierarchy is complete, then you start filling in the code. This method offers great flexibility when you have teams of programmers because you tend to break the project into parts (VIs) that you can assign to different people.

Bottom-up structured design begins by solving those difficult low-level bit manipulation, number-crunching, and timing problems right from the start. Writing an instrument driver tends to be this way. You can't do anything until you know how to pass messages back and forth to the instrument, and that implies programming at the lowest level as step one. Each of these lower-level subVIs can be written in complete and final form and tested as a stand-alone program. Your only other concern is that the right kind of inputs and outputs are available to link with the calling VIs.

Keeping track of inputs and outputs implies the creation of a **data dictionary**, a hierarchical table in which you list important data types that need to be passed among various subVIs. Data dictionaries are mandatory when using formal software design methods, but are quite useful on any project that involves more than a few VIs. I maintain a data dictionary as a word processing document that is always open in the background while I'm doing development. A spreadsheet or database might be even better; if you use a computer-aided software engineering (CASE) tool, it will of course include a data dictionary utility. I list the controls and indicators by name, thus keeping their names consistent throughout the VI hierarchy. Sometimes, I paste in screen shots of the actual front panel items to remind me what they contain. This is also a chance to get a head start on documentation, which is always easier to write at the moment you're involved with the nuts and bolts of the problem. Many items that make it to the dictionary are saved as **typedefs** or **strict typedefs**. This saves countless hours of editing when, for instance, a cluster needs just one more element.

Don't be afraid to use both top-down and bottom-up techniques at once, thus ending up in the middle, if that feels right. Indeed, you need to know *something* about the I/O hardware and how the drivers work before you can possibly link the raw data to the final data display.

> That Eurotherm controller had to be attacked before I could proceed with the main program design for VBL; I had to know what kind of information would be exchanged with it. The Eurotherm temperature controller driver was definitely bottom-up design because it required the formatting of some pretty cryptic string commands plus the handling of serial port time-outs and other errors. When the driver was done, I could attack the main programming task from the top down by animating my dummy panels. The driver just acted as a data *source* or *sink*.

Modularity

Break the problem into modular pieces that you can understand. I call this the divide and conquer technique and it works in every imaginable situation from designing a computer to planning a party. The modules in this case are **subVIs**. Each subVI handles a specific **task**—a function or operation that needs to be performed. Link all the tasks together, and an **application** is born as shown in Fig. 4.6.

One of the tricks is knowing *when* to create a subVI. Don't just lasso a big chunk of a diagram and stick it in a subVI because you ran out of space; that only proves a lack of forethought. Wouldn't you know, LabVIEW 4 makes it easy to do: select part of your diagram, and choose **SubVI from Selection** from the Edit menu, and poof! Instant subVI, with labeled controls and connector pane, all wired into place. Easy as this may be, you should instead always think in terms of tasks. Design and develop each task as if it were a stand-alone application. That makes it easier to test and promotes reuse in other problems. Each task, in turn, is made up of smaller tasks . . . the essence of top-down hierarchical design.

Task Level	Task Type		
Highest	*Application*	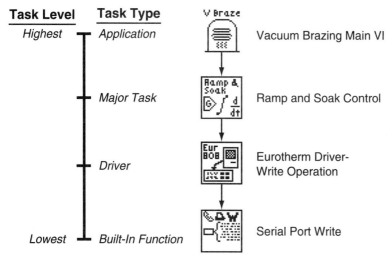	Vacuum Brazing Main VI
	Major Task		Ramp and Soak Control
	Driver		Eurotherm Driver-Write Operation
Lowest	*Built-In Function*		Serial Port Write

Figure 4.6 Using modularity in your program design makes it much easier to understand. This is one slice through the VI hierarchy of my VBL project.

Any properly designed task has a clear purpose. Think of a one-sentence thesis statement that clearly summarizes the purpose of the subVI: "This VI loads data from a series of transient recorders and places the data in an output array." (A good place to put this thesis statement is in the VI Description dialog.) If you can't write a simple statement like that, you may be creating a catchall subVI. Also consider the reusability of the subVIs you create. Can the function be used in several locations in your program? If so, you definitely have a reusable module, saving disk space and memory. If the subVI requirements are *almost* identical in several locations, it's probably worth writing it in such a way that it becomes a universal solution—perhaps it just needs a mode control. On the other hand, excessive modularity can lead to inefficiency because each subVI adds calling overhead at execution time (a few microseconds per VI) and takes up more space on disk.

There are additional advantages to writing a modular program. First, a simple diagram is easier to understand. Other programmers will be able to figure out a diagram that has a few subVIs much more readily than a complex diagram with level upon level of nested loops and Sequence structures. This is like writing a 10,000-line main program in a procedural language. Second, it is generally easier to modify a modular program. For instance, you might want to change from one brand of digital voltmeter to another. By incorporating well-written, modular drivers, you would just substitute Brand X for Brand Y and be running again in minutes. Finally, a simpler diagram compiles faster (I *hate* to wait) and is less likely to induce file system and memory problems when loading or saving. One goal in LabVIEW programming is to make your diagrams fit on a standard screen (whatever size is most common for computers like yours). This forces you to design and lay out diagrams in a thoughtful manner. Another goal is to limit the diagram memory usage of a subVI to about 200K. Use the **Get Info** command from the File menu to see how big each component of a VI is. These are not strict rules, however. Main VIs with complex user interfaces, especially those with many Attribute Nodes, invariably take up much screen space and memory.

Choose an architecture: Canonical VIs

Your initial objective is to decide on an overall **architecture**, or programming strategy, which determines how you want your application to work in the broadest sense. Here are some models, which I call **Canonical VIs**, that represent the fundamental structure of actual LabVIEW applications that I've seen. This list continues to grow as the years go by, and they are all reliable approaches. Choosing an appropriate architecture is a mix of analysis, intuition, and experience. I know that my first application (in LabVIEW 1.1!) would look silly to me today because there was nobody to show me the *possible* architectures, let alone the optimum one. Study these canonical VI architectures, memorize their basic attributes, and see if your next application doesn't go together a little more smoothly.

Initialize, then loop (sequence version). The simplest applications initialize then loop. You perform some initialization, such as setting up files and starting the hardware, then drop into a While Loop that does the main task several times. The main loop usually consists of four steps that are repeated at a rate that matches the requirements of your signals:

1. Acquire
2. Analyze
3. Display
4. Store

In a well-written program, these steps would be encapsulated in sub-VIs. After the main loop has terminated, there may also be a shutdown or cleanup task that closes files or turns off something in the hardware. This strategy is a classic for the top-level VI in ordinary data acquisition. The first two Canonical VIs, which follow, work this way.

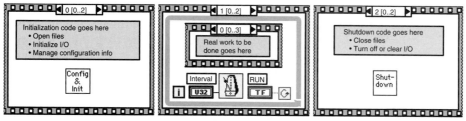

Figure 4.7 Canonical VI No. 1: A sequence containing frames for starting up, doing the work, and shutting down. A classic for data acquisition programs. The While Loop runs until the operation is finished. The Sequence inside contains the real work to be accomplished.

Canonical VI No. 1 (Fig. 4.7) is by far the most commonly used program structure in all of LabVIEW, primarily because it is an obvious solution. An overall Sequence structure forces the order of initialize, main operation, and shutdown. The main While Loop runs at a regular interval until the user stops the operation or some other event occurs. Frequently found inside the main loop is another Sequence structure that contains the operations to be performed: acquire, analyze, display, and then store.

Initialize, then loop (dataflow version).   An improvement on the previous example, shown in Fig. 4.8, makes effective use of dataflow programming and can be somewhat easier to understand. Connections between the three major operations (initialize, main operation, and shutdown) force the order of execution in the same way that an overall sequence structure does, only there is no obscuring of the overall program. The same methodology can and should be applied inside the main While Loop by using common threads between the functions employed there. The net result is a clearer program, explainable with just one page. This concept is used by most advanced LabVIEW users, like you. The example shown here is in every way a real, working LabVIEW program.

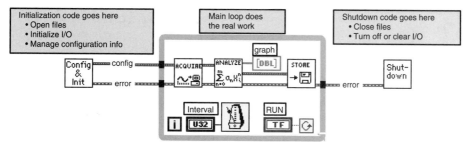

Figure 4.8 Canonical VI No. 2: Same functionality as No. 1, but this time using dataflow instead of Sequence structures to enhance readability, which is desirable. Note that the connections between tasks (subVIs) are not optional: they force the order of execution.

Independent parallel loops. Any time you have two tasks that you need to do at different speeds or priorities, consider using multiple independent While Loops that operate in parallel on one diagram (Fig. 4.9). I also use independent loops when there is a main task that needs to run regularly and one or more secondary tasks that run only when the operator throws a switch. If data needs to be exchanged between the loops, as it often does, use local or global variables. In this example, a Boolean control with a local variable stops the loops at the appropriate time, and a smart global variable (operating like a little database) carries a cluster of settings between the two loops. This is another top-level VI architecture.

Remember to initialize the RUN Boolean before it is to be read anywhere else. If you are using a loop similar to the bottom one shown in this example, put a time delay inside the loop to keep if from hogging CPU time when nothing is happening. I usually pick a time such as 100 or 200 ms because that's about the threshold of human perception.

Global variables tend to hide the flow of data if they are buried inside subVIs. To make your programs easier to understand, a good policy is to place all global variables out on the diagram where they are easily spotted. In this example, the Manual Control subVI reads settings information from a global, changes that information, then writes it back to the global. I could have hidden the global operations inside the subVI, but then you wouldn't have a clue as to how that subVI acts on the settings information, which is also used by the Ramp/Soak Con-

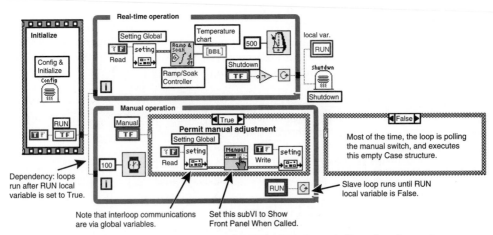

Figure 4.9 Canonical VI No. 3: Parallel loops. For VBL, I used two independent loops: the upper one for the actual control, and the lower one to handle manual operation (shown simplified here). This way, the main control loop always runs at a constant interval regardless of the state of the manual loop. A Boolean local variable stops the bottom loop and status information is passed between the loops in a global variable.

troller subVI. It also helps to show the name of the global variable so that the reader knows where the data is being stored.

The lower loop can be replicated for any number of independent tasks. They can be launched when the user clicks a button, as in the VBL example, or when a logical condition occurs, such as an alarm. This is called **polled** operation, where a loop cycles rapidly, checking for some condition. Polling of controls is very common in LabVIEW because we do not (as yet) have a simple **interrupt-based** front panel trigger technique. Such a technique would work like an **Occurrence**, which you must trigger programmatically, but instead would be triggered by a front panel event such as a mouse click. All of this doesn't worry me much because polling is simple to understand and implement and is not very expensive in terms of CPU time (costing only tens of microseconds per iteration) so long as you put a timer in the loop. Use it with confidence.

I also want to point out what an incredibly powerful yet simple technique this is. Go ahead: implement parallel tasks in C or Pascal. I hope you have a compiler and/or operating system that handles *multi-threaded* execution, and the knowledge to do so. In LabVIEW, we have intrinsic parallel execution capability, and it requires no particular effort on your part. Future versions of LabVIEW may extrapolate this concept across multiple processors. Imagine assigning subVIs to various CPUs in your computer, in an external box, or across the network. I can hardly wait, because that will enable really high-performance real-time applications, but without the hassle of low-level programming in a specialized programming environment.

Client-server.   I stole the term **client-server** from the world of distributed computing where a central host has all the disk drives and shared resources (the **server**), and a number of users out on the network access those resources as required (the **clients**). Here is how it works in a LabVIEW application: you write a server VI that is solely responsible for, say, acquiring data from the hardware. Acquired data is prepared and then written to one or more global variables that act like a database. Then, you design one or more client VIs that read the data in the global variable(s), as shown in Fig. 4.10. This is a very powerful concept, one that you will see throughout this book and in many advanced examples.

A good use for this might be process control (Chap. 8, "Process Control Applications") where the client tasks are such things as alarm generation, real-time trending, historical trending to disk, and several different operator interface VIs. The beauty of the client-server concept is that the clients can be:

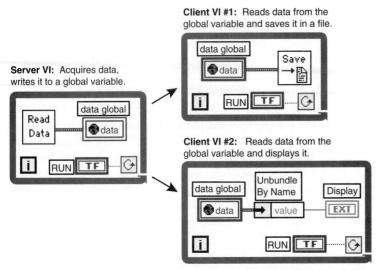

Figure 4.10   Canonical VI No. 4: Client-server systems. Client VIs receive data from a server VI through the use of a global variable. This permits time-independence between several VIs or loops.

- Independent loops on one diagram
- Completely independent top-level VIs in different windows
- Running at different rates
- Running on different machines if you use a network

If you want one button to shut down everything, add a RUN Boolean control to a global variable and wire that into all the clients. You can also set the **priority** of execution for each VI by two different means. First, you can put a timer in each loop and make the high-priority loops run more often. This is simple and foolproof and is generally the recommended technique. Second, you can adjust the execution priority through the VI Setup dialog. Typically, the server would have slightly higher priority to guarantee fresh data and good response to the I/O systems while the clients would run at lower priority. Use execution priority with caution and a good dose of understanding about how LabVIEW schedules VI execution. In a nutshell, high-priority VIs cut in line ahead of low-priority VIs. If a high-priority VI needs service too often, it may starve out all other VIs, and your whole hierarchy will grind to a halt. You can read more about this topic in the LabVIEW user's manual, in the chapter on performance issues. Other references on this topic are listed in the bibliography.

Race conditions are a risk with the client-server architecture because global variables may be accessed without explicit ordering. The most hazardous situation is where you have two or more locations where data is *written* to a global variable. Which location wrote the latest data? Do you care? If so, you must enforce execution order by some means. Another kind of race condition surrounds the issue of data aging. For example, in Fig. 4.10, the first client VI periodically stores data in a file. How does that client know that fresh data is available? Can it store the same data more than once, or can it miss new data? This may be a problem. The best way to synchronize clients and servers by using a global **queue.** A *queue* is like people waiting in line. The server puts new data in the queue (data is *enqueued*), and the clients dequeue the data at a later time. If the queue is empty, the client must wait until there's new data. For a good example of the queue technique, see the LabVIEW examples in the directory examples/general/queue.llb.

Client-server (with autonomous VIs).   Autonomous client or server VIs can be launched by a master VI to run independently without being placed in a While Loop on the diagram of the master VI. Figure 4.11 shows how. Operation of the autonomous Read Data Server VI is quite similar to the previous example in that it acquires data at an independent rate and transmits it to the master (client) VI through a global variable. The server VI is stopped by a global Boolean when commanded by the master VI. Note that the server VI is placed *outside* the While Loop in the master VI because the server is called only once and is intended to run until the master VI terminates. If the server were placed *inside* the While Loop, that loop would not even finish its first cycle; it would wait (forever) until the server VI finishes.

There can be multiple autonomous VIs, and their panels may or may not appear when the VIs are called. For instance, an alarm display VI would certainly be displayed, while a VI that simply logs data to disk probably would not. What if an error occurs in the autonomous VI? You have several options. You can do nothing, as in my simple example, or maybe return an error cluster when execution is finished. You could have the VI generate a dialog box, but what happens after that? A versatile solution is to have the autonomous VI set the Run global Boolean to False and wire the master VI in such a way that it is forced to stop when the Run global becomes False. That way, any VI in the hierarchy could potentially stop everything. Be careful. Don't have the application come to a screeching halt without telling the user *why* it just halted.

As presented in the example, there is no particular advantage to the autonomous VI solution when compared to placing While Loops on the main diagram. In fact, I think it's more obscure because unless you place a message on the diagram, there is no way to tell what that autonomous VI is doing or where the data is going. However, it is use-

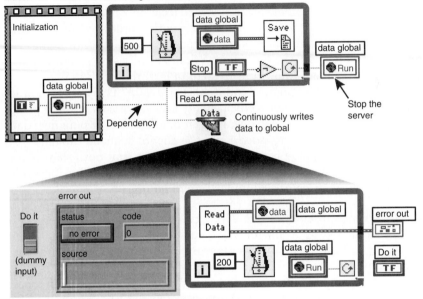

Master VI: Reads data from the global variable and saves it in a file.

Initialization

data global

500

data global

Save

Stop   TF

data global

Run

data global

Run

Stop the server

Read Data server

Data

Dependency

Continuously writes data to global

error out

status

no error

code

0

Do it

(dummy input)

source

Read Data

data

data global

error out

200

data global

Run

Do it

TF

Server VI: Acquires data, writes it to a global variable.
Runs until global Run is False. Front panel is never shown.

Figure 4.11 Canonical VI No. 5: the upper diagram is a master VI (and client) that launches the lower VI, which is an autonomous server.

ful when you are really launching something external, perhaps over a network, or when there is some driving reason for the VI to be called just once.

Pop-up windows. Sometimes you want a single panel that the operator uses as a main menu to access various modes of operation. A good example is automatic test applications where the operator decides which test to perform by clicking a button. That button starts a subVI that does the work. When it's done, control returns to the main menu. While running, the VI appears, and then disappears when done.

Back in Fig. 4.9, the lower While Loop (the manual control loop) contains a Case structure that is controlled by a button on the panel. When the button is pressed (True state), the Manual Control VI inside the case is called. That VI is set to **Show front panel when called**, so its panel appears and remains visible until execution terminates, at which time it closes again, providing that you set it to **Close afterwards if previously closed**. Both of these options are available in the VI Setup menu or the **SubVI Node Setup dialog**, which is available by popping up on the icon of a VI on a diagram. Several Case structures could be placed inside one While Loop to permit the user to call various subVIs, but only one at a time. Alternatively, you can place each subVI in its own While Loop and permit them all to be open simultaneously. The structure of a typical subVI called by this method is shown in Fig. 4.12. Advanced versions of these schemes are discussed in greater detail in Chap. 7, "Writing a Data Acquisition Program," and Chap. 8, "Process Control Applications."

It's worth exploring the window options in the VI Setup menu (Fig. 4.13) for this type of VI. You will typically disable closing the window; otherwise, if the user clicks the close box while the VI is still running, there is no way to stop it! For clarity in the user interface, you might turn off the menus, toolbar, and scroll bars. The Abort button is another dangerous control to think about for any user interface VI. It's usually better to hide it and instead give the user an exit, return, cancel, or stop Boolean as appropriate. You should also select the Dialog Box option. This prevents the user from accidentally clicking on another window and bringing it to the front. Once your pop-up window is hidden, the user may become hopelessly confused in a sea of windows!

State machines.   There is a very powerful and versatile alternative to the sequence structure, called a **state machine**, as described in the advanced LabVIEW training course. The general concept of a state machine originates in the world of digital (Boolean) logic design where it is a formal method of system design. In LabVIEW, a state machine uses a Case structure wired to a counter that's maintained in a shift register in a While Loop. This technique allows you to jump around in the sequence by manipulating the counter. For instance, any frame can jump directly to an error-handling frame. This technique is widely used in drivers, sequencers, and complex user interfaces and is also applicable to situations that require extensive error checking. Any time you

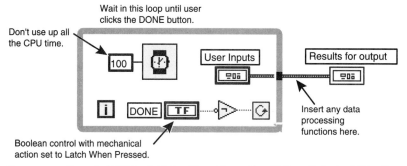

Figure 4.12   Canonical VI No. 6: Using Show Front Panel When Called subVIs. Sits around in the While Loop until the user clicks the DONE button, then sends the output back to the calling VI. Enhancements are to put data validation inside the loop and additional data processing after the loop.

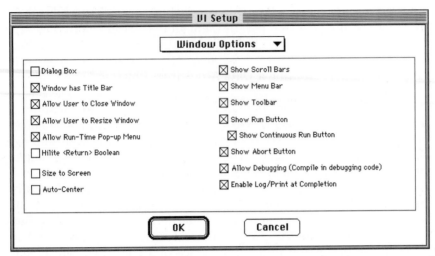

Figure 4.13 The Window Options in the VI Setup dialog can optimize the presentation of an interactive VI.

have a chain of events where one operation depends on the status of a previous operation, or where there are many modes of operation, a state machine is a good way to do the job.

Figure 4.14 is an example of the structure of a state machine. The objective is to read a valid sample of data, do some calculations, and then quit. If anything goes wrong at any step, it jumps to frame zero where an error handler will report what went wrong. The **state number** is maintained as a numeric value in a shift register, so any frame can jump to any other frame. Shift registers or local variables must also be used for any data that needs to be passed between frames, such as the **Results** of the two activity subVIs in this example. One of the configuration tricks you will want to remember is to use frame zero for errors. That way, if you add a frame later on, the error frame number doesn't change; otherwise, you would have to edit every frame to update the error frame's new address.

Each frame that contains an activity also checks for errors (or some other condition) to see where the program should go next. In driver VIs, you commonly have to respond to a variety of error conditions where you may want to retry communications, abort, or do something else depending on the condition detected. Similarly, in a complex user interface, you may have to handle major changes in display configuration (using Attribute Nodes), or handle errors arising from user data entries. The state machine lets you handle these complex situations. In this example, the program starts in frame 1 where data is acquired. If the data is no good, the program jumps to frame 0, reports the problem,

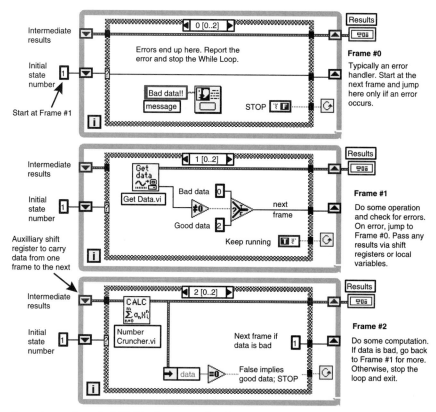

Figure 4.14 Canonical VI No. 7: a generalized state machine. Any frame of the case can jump to any other by manipulating the state number shift register. Results are passed from one frame to another in another shift register. Normal execution proceeds from frame 1 through frame 2. Frame 0 or frame 2 can stop execution. An exceptionally versatile concept, well worth studying.

and stops the While Loop. If the data is OK, it gets analyzed in frame 2. If the analysis results are no good, it jumps back to frame 1 for more data. Note that an infinite loop could occur here; additional conditions should be added in a practical program to guarantee stopping after some number of retries.

Tip: I always forget to stop the While Loop after the final frame. The program will execute the last frame over and over, often with very strange results. Remember to put the little False Boolean constant where it belongs: in the error handler frame *and* in the last frame of the sequence.

A state machine can be the diagram behind a flexible user interface, or it can be called as a subVI. In a user interface, the state machine manages various modes of operation. For instance, the user may have a series of mode selections when configuring an experiment. A mode selector switch may directly drive the Case structure, or you may use Attribute Nodes to selectively hide and show valid mode selection buttons. Depending upon which button is then pressed, the state machine jumps to an appropriate frame to handle that selection.

My favorite use for state machines is intelligent subVIs in such applications as sequencers and profile generators. In those situations, the state machine subVI is called periodically in the main While Loop. Each time it's called, information from the last cycle is available in the shift register, providing the required history: where have I been? Data passed in through the connector pane provides the current information: where am I now? And computation within the state machine subVI determines the future: where should I go next? Those values may drive an I/O device through a subVI within the state machine, or they may be passed back to the calling VI through the connector pane. Figure 4.15 is another example from VBL, and it works as I've just described. This VI is called every second from the VBL main While Loop. Inside, it calls a state machine, Recipe Control Logic, which keeps

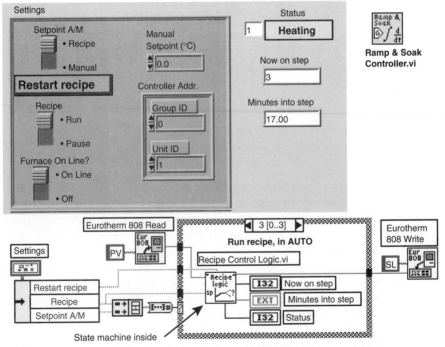

Figure 4.15 A peek inside the Ramp-and-Soak Controller VI (simplified), which is called from the VBL main VI. A state machine, Recipe Control Logic, keeps track of complex temperature profile recipes.

track of the state of a complex ramp-and-soak temperature recipe. On each iteration, the state machine receives the current process variable (temperature) measurement and some commands regarding whether or not to continue running the recipe. It computes a new controller setpoint, which is returned and then transmitted to the Eurotherm 808 controller.

Great confusion can arise when developing a state machine. Imagine how quickly the number of frames can accumulate in a situation with many logical paths. Then imagine what happens when one of those numeric constants that points to the next frame has the *wrong number.* Or even worse, what if you have about 17 frames and you need to add one in the middle? You may have to *edit* dozens of little numeric constants. And just wait until you have to explain to a novice user how it all works!

Thankfully, creative LabVIEW developers have come up with an easy solution to these complex situations: use **enumerated constants** (also called *enums*) instead of numbers. Take a look at Fig. 4.16, showing an improved version of our previous state machine example. You can see the enumerated constant, with three possible values (error, get data, calculate), has replaced the more cryptic numeric constants. The Case structure now tells you in English which frame you're on, and the enums more clearly state where the program will go next.

A maintenance problem still exists with this improved state machine, however. If you add a new state, you must edit (or replace) each enumerated constant. This is tedious, and comes with the attendant risk of injecting an error into your code. (In a future version of LabVIEW, you will be able to save enumerated constant as typedefs; that will elegantly solve this problem.) A good solution appeared in *LTR* (Fowler 1996) where Gregg Fowler of National Instruments designed an architecture

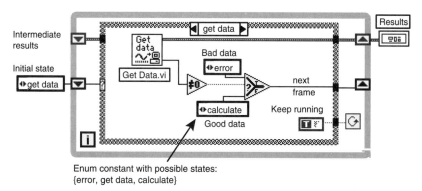

Enum constant with possible states:
{error, get data, calculate}

Figure 4.16 A recommended way to write state machines, using enumerated constants.

for interactive applications based on an event handler in a state machine. His solution uses subVIs that select the desired state from an array of strings. Each string corresponds exactly to an item in a front panel enum control. Figure 4.17 shows the data conversion trick he used, where the Scan From String function locates the proper enum item based on the string in a shift register. Note that you still have to add or remove frames from the Case structure when you change the number of items in the enumerated constant.

The VI hierarchy as a design tool

A good way to start mapping out your application is to sketch a preliminary **VI hierarchy**. To see what this might look like, open a LabVIEW example VI and select **Show VI Hierarchy** from the Project menu. You don't need to start off with lots of detail. Just scribble out a map showing the way you would like things to flow and the likely interactions between various subVIs, as in Fig. 4.18. Modular decomposition in many languages looks like this figure. There's a main program at the top, several major tasks in the middle level, and system support or I/O drivers at the lowest level. You could also draw this as a nested list, much the way file systems are often diagrammed.

Each **node** or item in the hierarchy represents a task, which then becomes a subVI. Use your list of functional requirements as a checklist to see that each feature has a home somewhere in the hierarchy. As you add features, you can keep adding nodes to this main sketch, or make separate sketches for each major task. Modularity again! No need to worry about the programming details inside a low-level task; just make sure you know what it needs to do in a general way. Remember that the hierarchy is a design tool that should be referred to and updated continuously as you write your programs.

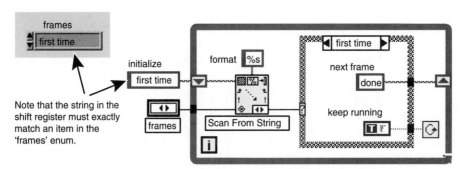

Figure 4.17 Another way of maintaining state machines, using strings to choose the right enumerated value. A clever solution by Gregg Fowler of National Instruments.

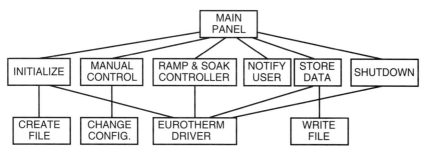

Figure 4.18 A preliminary VI hierarchy for VBL. At this point, I really didn't know what was going to happen inside each subVI, but at least I had an idea about the division of labor.

The ramp-and-soak controller (one of the major subVIs in VBL) looked simple enough at first, but turned out to be one of the trickiest routines I've ever written. Without a healthy respect for modularity, I would have had a much more difficult time. The problems stemmed from interactions between various modes of operation, such as manual control, ramping, and soaking. My hierarchy sketch was a real mess by the time I was through, but it was the only easy way to track those modes and interactions.

If you have experience with formal software engineering techniques, including **computer-aided software engineering (CASE) tools**, by all means use them. The methods recommended by software engineers are all applicable to LabVIEW. In particular, *entity diagrams* and *state diagrams* map nicely into the VI hierarchy, while *dataflow diagrams* can map directly into LabVIEW block diagrams.

Programming by plagiarizing

A secret weapon for LabVIEW programming is using available example VIs as starting points. Many of your problems have already been solved by someone else, but the trick is to get hold of that code. The examples and driver libraries that come with LabVIEW are a gold mine, especially for the beginner. Start prowling these directories, looking for tidbits that may be useful. If you have access to a local LabVIEW user group, be sure to make some contacts and discuss your more difficult problems. The online world is a similarly valuable resource. I simply could not do my job any more without these resources.

You can start with some of the canonical VIs as we have discussed. These structures are found in just about every application, sometimes in combination. The simplest VIs don't require any fancy structures or programming tricks. Instead, you just plop down some built-in functions, wire them up, and that's it. This book contains many programming constructs that you will see over and over. Some of them are included on the CD-ROM that accompanies this book.

The examples, utilities, and drivers can often be linked together to form a usable application in no time at all. Data acquisition using plug-in multifunction boards is one area where I rarely have to write my own code. Using the examples and utilities pays off for file I/O as well. I mention this because everyone writes their own file handlers for their first application. It's rarely necessary, because 90 percent of your needs are probably met by a pair of file utility VIs that are already on your hard disk: **Write Characters to File** and **Read Characters From File**. The other 10 percent you can get by modifying an example or utility to meet your requirements. Little effort on your part and lots of bang for the buck for the customer. That's the way it's supposed to work.

Pay attention to your data

Consider the information that has to be passed from one part of the program to another. Any time you write a subVI that performs some task, make a list of the inputs and outputs. How do these inputs and outputs relate to other VIs in the hierarchy that have to access these items? Do the best you can to think of everything ahead of time. At least, try not to miss the obvious such as a channel number or error cluster that needs to be passed just about everywhere.

Think about the number of terminals available on the connector pane and how you would like the connections to be laid out. Is there enough room for all your items? If not, use **clusters** to group related items together. Always leave a few uncommitted terminals on the connector pane in case you need to add an item later. That way, you don't have to rewire everything. Clusters make sense for other reasons. For instance, passing the name and calibration information for a signal along with its data in one cluster makes a nice unit that clarifies the program. Clustered data minimizes the number of wires on the diagram, too.

Data structures such as clusters and arrays also make handling of data more efficient when closely coupled to the **algorithms** that you choose. An *algorithm* is a stepwise procedure that acts upon some associated data. Conversely, a well-chosen data structure reflects the organization of its associated algorithm. Getting them to work in harmony results in a clear LabVIEW diagram that runs at top speed. And as a bonus, the computer scientists will think you're one of *them*.

A sample of this idea is shown in Fig. 4.19. If there are many channels to process, keep them in an array. Having an array implies using a For or While Loop to process that array. After processing inside a loop, the logical output structure is another array. If the array needs to carry more information than simple numerics, make it a cluster array, as in the figure. The snippet of code shown here could readily stand on its own as a subVI, doing a task of data acquisition. Furthermore, it could easily be enhanced by adding more items to the clusters, such as channel calibration information. Thinking ahead to relate algorithms and data structures can certainly make your program easier to understand and modify.

The only drawback to complicated data structures may be performance. All that bundling, unbundling, and indexing of arrays does take some extra time and memory. An old rule for writing high-performance programs dictates that you do the smallest possible amount of data shuffling in high-speed loops and real-time VIs. For example, it may be worth splitting out the required data from a highly nested structure of clusters and arrays before it's time to enter a For Loop for processing.

An important feature of LabVIEW that can help you manage complicated data structures is the **Type Definition** which performs the

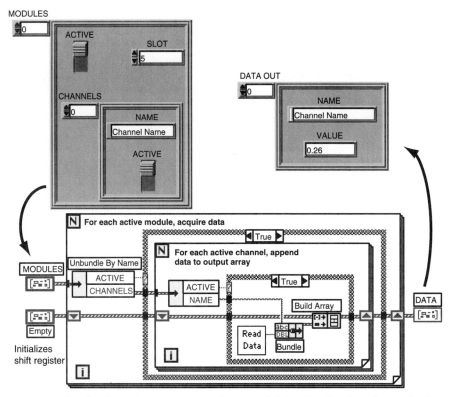

Figure 4.19 The Modules data structure at the upper left implies the algorithm at the bottom because the way that the cluster arrays are nested is related to the way the For Loops are nested.

same function as a typedef in C and a Type statement in Pascal. You edit a control using the LabVIEW **Control Editor**, in which you can make detailed changes to the built-in controls. Add all of the items that you need in the data structure. Then, you can save your new control with a custom name. An option in the Control Editor window is **Type Definition**. If you select this item, the control can't be reconfigured from the panel of any VI in which it appears; it can only be modified through the Control Editor. The beauty of this scheme is that the control itself now defines a data type and changing it in one place (the Control Editor) automatically changes it in every location where it is used. If you don't use a Type Definition and you decide to change one item in the control, then you must manually edit every VI in which that control appears. Otherwise, broken wires would result throughout the hierarchy—a major source of suffering back in the LabVIEW 2 days, I might add. As you can see, Type Definitions can save you much work and raise the quality of the final product.

> Since VBL had five similar furnaces to control, it was obvious that they should be processed in a For Loop with $\boxed{\text{N}}$ set to 5. The data I had to act on was basically the status of each temperature controller and its associated recipe for ramping and soaking. Since my program had several ways to access the data (manual control, recipe editor, automatic controller, etc.), the best solution was to create a smart global variable, as shown in Fig. 4.20. This is actually a **global named set** where the *name* is the furnace number to access. It's a kind of database with the furnace number as the key. Because there is just one cluster to keep track of, each subVI that accesses this global is similar in form.

Sketching program structure

I use a really powerful, visual tool to design my LabVIEW programs. It's called **LabVIEW sketching** and it requires sophisticated hardware: *a pencil and paper*. The idea is to "think in LabVIEW" and put your conceptual program design on paper. You can work at any level of detail. At first, you'll be attacking the main VI, trying to make the major steps happen in the right order. Later on, you will need to figure out exactly where the data comes from, how it needs to be processed, and where it needs to go. Representing this information graphically is a powerful notion. What's even better is that you can implement these sketches directly as LabVIEW diagrams without an intermediate translation step. Figure 4.21 shows my first sketch of the VBL application.

You can also do sketching on your computer with LabVIEW. This has the advantage of permitting you to try out programming techniques that might simplify the problem. Then, your test diagram can be

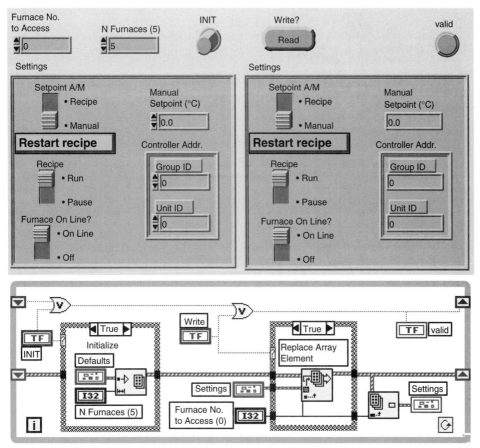

Figure 4.20   The Controller Settings Global contains a cluster with all the information needed to keep track of each furnace's status in VBL. The left one is a control, for writing to the global, and the right one is an indicator for readout from the selected furnace.

pasted right into the real VI. I do this a lot when I'm not sure how a built-in function works. I hook it into a simple test VI and fiddle with it until I really understand. It's a much better approach than to bury a mysterious function deep inside an important VI, then have to figure out why things aren't working later on. This scheme works great with top-down design where you have *stub* VIs without diagrams. You simply paste the final results of your experimental development into the diagram of the stub VI.

Show your sketches to other LabVIEW users. Exchange ideas as you do the design. It's a vastly underused resource, this synergy thing. Everyone has something to contribute—a new way of looking at the problem, a trick they heard about, or sometimes a ready-to-use VI that

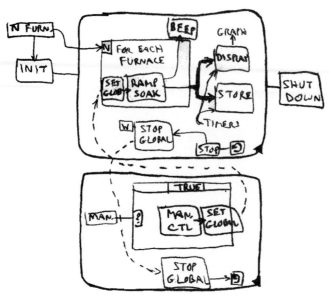

Figure 4.21   Sketch for the main VI used in VBL. Not very detailed at this point, but it sure gets the point across.

fills the bill. To quote from Brad Hedstrom of Advanced Measurements, "If you can't draw it with a pencil and paper, how can you draw it in *G?*"

Pseudocoding

If you are an experienced programmer, you may find that it's easier to write some parts of your program in a procedural language or **pseudocode**. Of course, you should only do this if it comes naturally. Translating Pascalese to LabVIEW may or may not be obvious or efficient, but I sometimes use this technique instead of LabVIEW sketching when I have a really tough numerical algorithm to hammer out. Fig. 4.22 shows a likely mapping between some example pseudocode and a LabVIEW data structure, and Fig. 4.23 shows the associated LabVIEW diagram that is a translation of the same code.

There's something that bothers me about this translation process. The folks who thought up LabVIEW in the first place were trying to free us from the necessity of writing procedural code with all its unforgiving syntactical rules. Normally, LabVIEW makes complicated things simple, but sometimes it also make simple things complicated. Making an oscilloscope into a spectrum analyzer using virtual instruments is really easy, but making a character-by-character string parser is a real mess. In such cases, we choose the best tool for the job at hand, and be happy.

Pseudo-code   **LabVIEW Data Structure**

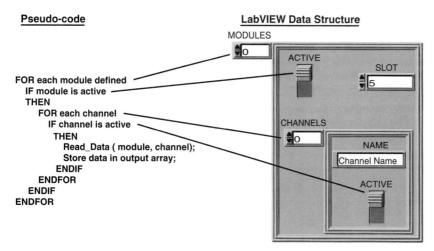

```
FOR each module defined
   IF module is active
   THEN
      FOR each channel
         IF channel is active
         THEN
            Read_Data ( module, channel);
            Store data in output array;
         ENDIF
      ENDFOR
   ENDIF
ENDFOR
```

Figure 4.22   A mapping between a pseudocode segment and a LabVIEW data structure.

To design the difficult ramp-and-soak control logic in VBL, I found that a pseudocode approach was easier. I didn't have to look far to recover the example that appears in Fig. 4.24; it was pasted into a diagram string constant in the subVI called *Recipe Control Logic*. I won't bother to reproduce the entire VI diagram here because it has too many nested Case structures to print in a reasonable space.

Language translation

Sometimes, programming in C is simply the best way to solve a problem. In that case, you can use **Code Interface Nodes (CINs)** which are written in C and link nicely into LabVIEW (see Chap. 1, "Roots," for information about appropriate compilers for CINs). They are ideal in cases where you want to import an existing code because you can do so

Pseudo-code   **G (LabVIEW) code**

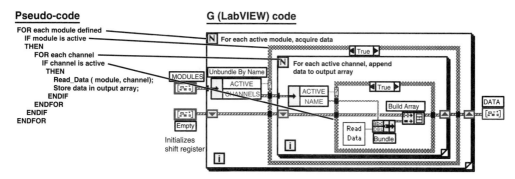

Figure 4.23   The same pseudocode translated into a LabVIEW diagram, which acts on the data structure from the previous figure. If this is your cup of tea, by all means use this approach.

Psuedo-code for this VI

```
if setpoint==manual
   freeze ramp timer
   do manual updates
else
   if recipe==pause
      freeze setpoint
   else
      if step <= Nsteps
         if slope > 0 && sp < target
```

Figure 4.24 If you do decide to use pseudocode to design your program, include it right on the diagram by pasting it into a String constant like this.

almost directly. CINs are also needed for direct access to your computer's system routines, graphics toolbox, and the like. I've used them mostly for the conversion of large arrays of numbers into strings with intricate formatting. That's a case where you are forced to chain several string functions together inside a loop with several string concatenations for each iteration. In that case, LabVIEW has to call the memory manager on every iteration of the loop (maybe several times on each iteration), and the resultant process is very slow. In C, you can compute the final string size, allocate memory just once, and write to the output string very efficiently. The problem with CINs is that the average user can't maintain them because they require a compiler for, and knowledge of, another language. Furthermore, CINs must be recompiled before they can run on a different computer. That's why I call them *sins*. They do make a great escape hatch for situations where you have no other choice.

Another way to access external code modules is through the **Call Library** node. It looks like a CIN on the diagram, but it's configured through a pop-up dialog through which you define the data type and other attributes of each input and output. The inputs and outputs of the Call Library node have a one-to-one correspondence with the inputs and outputs of the external module that you are calling. Windows makes extensive use of **Dynamic Link Libraries (DLLs)** to encapsulate drivers and various system functions. The Macintosh, starting with System 7.5, uses **Code Fragments** as a new method for adding more system functionality. Almost any compiler can generate a DLL or Code Fragment—and you're not limited to C. As long as you know what the parameters are, Call Library will make the connection.

Ranges, coercion, and default values

Expect users to supply ridiculous inputs at every possible opportunity. A program that does not self-destruct under such abuse is said to be **robust**. Quick-and-dirty test programs are rarely robust. Commercial applications such as word processors are highly robust, lest the publisher go out of business. You may need to put appreciable effort into bullet-proofing your LabVIEW application.

On numeric controls, use the **Data Range . . .** pop-up dialog to *coerce* values into the desired range (minimum, maximum, and increment). If the values are not evenly spaced (such as a 1-2-5 sequence) use a function similar to the **Range Finder VI** shown in Fig. 4.25. Don't, as a rule, choose *Suspend* in the Data Range dialog, because the front panel of the VI then has to be memory-resident all the time in case it needs to be opened.

platform\ drivers\driver utilities\Range Finder.vi

Note that there is no way to tell if a control has Data Range limits set just by looking at the control; you must open the pop-up dialog. For this reason, some LabVIEW programmers prefer to use the **Coerce To Range VI** (Fig. 4.26) that applies limits programmatically. It's also useful when you wish to dynamically change the limits—something you can't do with an Attribute Node. For instance, many GPIB instruments limit the permissible settings of one control based upon the settings of another: a voltmeter might permit a range setting of 2000 V for DC, but only 1000 V for AC. If the affected controls (e.g., Range and Mode) reside in the same VI, put the interlock logic there. If one or more of the controls are not readily available, you can request the present settings from the instrument to make sure that you don't ask for an invalid combination.

platform\ drivers\driver utilities\Coerce to Range.vi

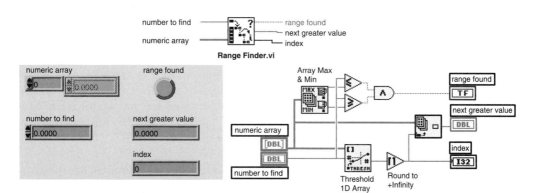

Figure 4.25 My version of the Range Finder utility VI. This one looks through an array of permissible values and finds the one that is greater than or equal to the value you wish to find. It returns that value and the index into the number to find array.

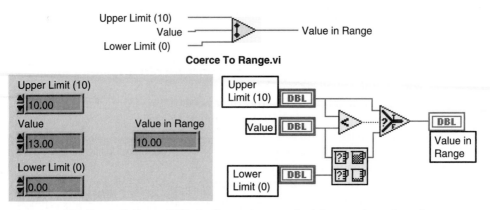

Figure 4.26 The Coerce To Range VI limits the maximum and minimum values of a scalar.

String controls and tables are particularly obnoxious because the user can (and will) type just about anything into one. Think about the consequences of this for every string in your program. You may need to apply a filter of some type to remove or replace unacceptable characters. For instance, other applications may not like a data file where the name of a signal has embedded blanks or nonalphanumeric characters. String length may need adjustment. On the CD-ROM that accompanies this book, there is a VI called **Fix String Length** that truncates long strings and pads short ones.

platform\ utility\Fix String Length.vi

One nefarious character is the carriage return or **end-of-line (EOL)** character for your platform. Users sometimes hit the *Return* key rather than the *Enter* key to complete the entry of text into a LabVIEW string control, thus appending EOL to the string. Note that training users will not solve the problem! You have two options. In the LabVIEW Preferences, under Front Panel, there is an option to treat Return the same as Enter in string controls. If selected, the two keys act the same and no EOL character is stored. The other alternative is to write a subVI to search for EOL and kill it. The Preferences method is nice, but what happens when you install your VI on another machine? Will that preference be properly set? And what about all the other preferences that you so carefully tuned for you application? If a setting is very important, you must explicitly tell the user to update the preferences when installing your VI.

Controls should have reasonable default values. It's nice to have a VI that does not fail when run *as-opened* with default values. After entering the values you desire, select **Make Current Value Default** from the control's pop up or from the Operate menu. Remember to show the default in parentheses in the control's label so that it appears in the Help window. But don't make the data in graphs and arrays into default values (unless it's really required); that just wastes disk space when the VI is saved.

Make intelligent use of default values. In the case of a utility VI Write Characters to File, the default path is empty, which forces a file dialog. This can save the use of a Boolean switch in many cases.

Handling errors

Another aspect of robust programs is the way they handle run-time errors. Commercial software contains an incredible amount of code devoted to error handling, so don't feel silly when half your diagram is devoted to testing values and generating error clusters or dialogs. Most problems occur during the initial setup of a system, but may rarely occur thereafter. It may seem wasteful to have so much code lying around that is used only 0.01 percent of the time. But it's the startup phase where users need the most information about what is going wrong. Put in the error routines and *leave them there*. If you want, add a Boolean control to turn off dialog generation. Realize that dialog boxes tie up the VI from which they are called until the user responds. This is not a good mode of operation for an unattended system, but you may still want the option of viewing dialogs during a troubleshooting session.

Every call to an I/O driver or file service VI should be followed by an **error handler** of some kind. You should expect such actions to fail at any time because of several major reasons:

- A system configuration error has been made. For instance, some equipment has not been properly installed or connected. Also, with plug-in boards, you must install the correct I/O handler in your operating system.

- Improper parameters have been supplied, such as channel numbers or file path names.

- A programming error has occurred on the diagram. Typically, you forget to wire an important parameter.

- LabVIEW bugs crop up (incredible, but true).

A good error handler tells the user the following:

- Where the error came from
- What might have caused the error
- What actions he or she might take to fix and/or avoid recurrence
- One or more appropriate options for escape (continue, stop, abort, etc.)

Errors should always be reported in plain language, though an error code number is usually displayed in addition in case a system guru wants to dig deeper. Dialog boxes are a logical choice when the error is severe enough that user intervention is required. A string indicator on the panel of a VI will suffice when the message is more of an informative nature.

Error handler VIs are included with LabVIEW in the Time and Dialog functions. My favorite is called **Simple Error Handler** and it works for just about any purpose. You can feed it an error code number or a standard Error I/O cluster and it will generate a formatted message and an optional dialog. Error I/O has become very popular in LabVIEW programming because it solves one of those universal needs, and as such, it works as a common dataflow thread between many VIs, as you have already seen in many examples in this book. The file I/O functions, data acquisition library, and all of the newer driver VIs use it. If the error handlers supplied don't suit your needs, use them as a foundation for your own customized version. The **General Error Handler VI** permits you to enter custom error codes and messages. For complex applications, I include a modified version of the General Error Handler with my special messages. Throughout the application hierarchy, I can then generate my own error codes and the user will see a plain-language message.

If an error condition is severe enough that execution of the VI must not continue, you can call the Stop function (the one in the Advanced functions that looks like a stop sign). However, calling it can be risky if any I/O activity is pending. Realize that the Stop function causes the entire hierarchy of VIs to abort immediately. If a buffered data acquisition operation is in progress, it keeps going. Analog and digital outputs retain their last values. It may be difficult to clear up these conditions. Therefore, use the Stop function with caution.

VBL had to run reliably when unattended. Therefore, I had to avoid any error dialogs that would lock up the system. When you call one of the dialog subVIs, the calling VI must wait for the user to dismiss the dialog before it can continue execution. That's the reason you should never generate an error dialog from within a driver VI; do it at the top level only. My solution was to add a switch to enable dialog generation only for test purposes. If a communications error occurred during normal operation, the driver would retry the I/O operation several times. If that failed, the main program would simply go on as if nothing had happened. This was a judgment call based on the criticality of the operation. I decided that no harm would come to any of the furnaces because even the worst-case error (total communications failure) would only result in a *really long* constant temperature soak. This has proven to be the correct choice after several years of continuous operation.

Putting it all together

Keep hammering away at your application, one VI at a time. Use all the tools we have discussed for each step of the process. Remember that each VI can and should be treated as a stand-alone program. Break it down into pieces you understand (more subVIs) and tackle those one at a time. Then, build up the hierarchy, testing as you go. It's a reliable path to success. Never write your program as one huge VI—the Lab-VIEW equivalent of a 40,000-line main program—because it will be very difficult to troubleshoot, let alone understand. Documenting as you go can also save time in the long run because it's easier to write about what you've done while you're doing it. The same is true for quality assurance documents such as test procedures. If formal testing is required, do a dry run of the formal testing as early as possible in the development process. That means the procedure is complete and any required test software is written and validated.

One of the LabVIEW inventors, Jack MacCrisken, is a firm believer in iterative design after watching many users go through the development process over the years. His rule of thumb is that every application should be written twice. The first time, it's ugly, but it gets the job done and establishes a viable hierarchical approach. The second time, you sweep through and optimize, clean up, and document each VI, along with redesigning any parts of your program that no longer suit the overall requirements.

Check your user requirements document from time to time to make sure that everything has been addressed. Keep the users in the loop by demonstrating parts of your application as they are completed. It's amazing what an operator will say when shown a LabVIEW panel that mimics real laboratory equipment. You need this feedback at all stages of development as a form of reality check. In the real world of science, requirements change. If the experiment succeeds, the requirements grow. If it produces unexpected results, requirements change. And users change, too! You and your programs need to be flexible and ready to accept change. An excellent article on this subject, written by Ted Brunzie of JPL, appears in *LTR* (1995).

Testing and Debugging Your Program

If you have designed your program in a modular fashion, testing will *almost* take care of itself: you are able to test each subVI independently, greatly increasing your chances of success. It's comforting to know that each module has been thoroughly thrashed and shows no signs of aberrant behavior. Nonmodular programming will come back to haunt you because a big, complicated diagram is much harder to debug than a collection of smaller, simpler ones.

Debugging is a part of life for all programmers (hopefully not *too* big a part). LabVIEW has some tools and techniques that can speed up the debugging process. Read over the chapter of the LabVIEW manual on *executing and debugging VIs*. It has a whole list of debugging techniques. Here are a few of the important ones.

See what the subVIs are up to

The first debugging technique is to open any subVIs that might be of interest in finding your problem. While a top-level VI executes, open and observe the lower-level VIs. Their panels will update each time they are called, allowing you to see any intermediate results. This is a good way to find errors such as swapped cluster elements or out-of-range values. If the value on one panel doesn't agree with the value on another panel, you have your wires crossed somewhere. It's another reason for using Type Definitions on all your clusters.

There is one special trick to viewing the panels while running: if a subVI is set up to be **reentrant**, then you must double-click that subVI node on the diagram it is called from *while the caller is running*. Otherwise, you will just be looking at another copy of the reentrant code. Reentrant VIs have independent data storage areas allocated for each instance in which the VI is used. Examples of reentrant VIs are the GPIB library and some of the data acquisition VIs.

You will also note that execution slows way down when panels are open. This is caused by extra graphics updates. On a panel that is not displayed, the graphics don't have to be drawn and that saves much execution time. There is also a saving in memory on VIs that are not displayed because LabVIEW must duplicate all data that is displayed in an indicator. If you are running a fast application where timing is critical, having extra panels open may murder your real-time response, so this debugging technique may not be feasible. I've actually used this very fact as a debugging tool in driver development. Sometimes, an instrument doesn't respond to commands as fast as you think and your VI can get out of sync. Having a lower-level VI's panel open can add just enough delay that the system starts working. Then you have a clue as to where to add some additional delay or logic.

Peeking at data

It is often helpful to look inside a VI at intermediate values that are not otherwise displayed. Even if no problems are evident, this can be valuable—one of those lessons that you can only learn the hard way, by having a VI that appears to be working, but only for the particular test cases that you have been using. I like to connect extra, temporary indicators at various points around the diagram as a sanity check. Look at such things as the iteration counter in a loop or the intermediate results of a complicated string search. If the values you see don't make sense, find out why not. Otherwise, the problem will come back to haunt you.

Versions of LabVIEW starting with 2.5 also have a **probe** tool ⊕. While a VI is executing you can click on any wire with the probe tool, or pop up on any wire and select *Probe* from the pop-up menu (Fig. 4.27). A *windoid* (little window) appears that displays the value flowing through that wire. It works for all data types—even clusters and arrays—and you can even pop up on data in the probe window to prowl through arrays. You can have as many probe windows as you like, floating all over the screen, and the probes can be custom controls to display the data just the way you like. If the VI executes too fast, the values may become a blur; you may need to single-step the VI in that case (see the following section). I like the probe because I don't have to create, wire, and then later delete all kinds of temporary indicators.

One step at a time

Sometimes you just can't figure out what's happening when the VI runs at full speed. In that case, try **single stepping** the execution of your program. Single-stepping mode is entered by clicking on the **Pause button** ▐▐. When the VI runs, the diagram will open with the single-stepping controls displayed in the toolbar, and execution will be paused with some part of the diagram flashing. You then control execution with the following buttons:

⎌ **Step Into** allows the next node to execute. If the node is a subVI, the subVI opens in pause mode, and its diagram is displayed with

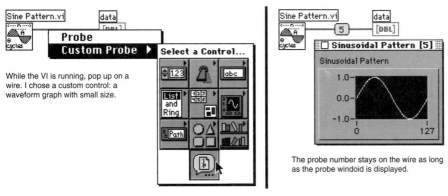

Figure 4.27   To use the data probe, pop up on any wire while the VI is executing. Select *Probe* or *Custom Probe* from the pop up. The little window that appears contains live data.

part of its diagram flashing. This is a recursive type of debugging, allowing you to burrow down through the hierarchy.

Step Over lets you execute subVIs without opening them. For built-in functions, Step Over and Step Into are equivalent. This is my most-used button when stepping through a big diagram.

Step Out Of lets you finish quickly. You can use this button to complete a loop (even if it has 10,000 iterations to go) or a Sequence structure without taking the VI out of pause mode. If you hold down the mouse button, you can control how many levels it steps out of.

If you have trouble remembering what each button does, turn on **Tip Strips** (use the Miscellaneous Preferences dialog). They tell you in a clear and context-sensitive manner what will happen with messages such as *Step into subVI "Get Data."* During these single-stepping operations, you're free to create probes anywhere in the hierarchy. For that matter, you can freely open subVIs, view panels, and do just about anything except edit a running VI.

Execution highlighting

Another way to see exactly what is happening in a diagram is to enable **execution highlighting**. Click on the execution highlighting button , and notice that it changes to . Run the VI while viewing the diagram. When execution starts, you can watch the flow of data. In the Debugging Preferences, you can enable data bubbles to animate the flow. Each time the output of a node generates a value, that value is displayed in a little box if you select the auto-probe feature in the Debugging Preferences. Execution highlighting is most useful in conjunction with single stepping: you can carefully compare your expectations of how the VI works against what actually occurs.

My favorite use for execution highlighting is to find an infinite loop or a loop that doesn't terminate after the expected number of iterations. While Loops are especially prone to execute forever. All you have to do is accidentally invert the Boolean condition that terminates the loop, and you're stuck. If this happens in a subVI, the calling VI may be in a nonresponsive state. When you turn on execution highlighting or single stepping, any subVI that is running will have a green arrow embedded in its icon: .

Sometimes a VI tries to run forever even though it contains no loop structures. One cause may be a subVI calling a CIN that contains an infinite loop. Reading from a serial port is another way to get stuck because that operation has no time-out feature. If no characters are present at the port, the VI will wait forever. (The solution to that problem is to call **Bytes at Serial Port** to see how many characters to read, then read that many. If nothing shows up after a period of time, you can quit without attempting to read. See Chap. 5, "Instrument Drivers," for more information). That is why you must always design low-level I/O routines and drivers with time-outs. In any case, execution highlighting will let you know which node is "hung."

> Since VBL used the serial port to communicate with the Eurotherm temperature controllers, I had to write a robust serial port driver with timeouts. Chapter 5, "Instrument Drivers," discusses this exact problem and solves it with a state machine and Bytes at Serial Port.

Be warned that highlighting greatly reduces performance because of all the graphical activity. I don't know how many times I've gone through a debugging session, accidentally leaving highlighting turned on. Then I wonder why the machine is so slow. To keep users from accidentally turning on execution highlighting or the other debugging features, you can disable these features. To do this, use the VI Setup . . . dialog and deselect the debugging option.

Setting breakpoints

A **breakpoint** is a marker you set in a computer program to pause execution when the program reaches it. Breakpoints can be set on any subVI, node, or wire in the hierarchy by clicking on them with the breakpoint tool, 🔘. A bold, red dot appears on the selected object. When the breakpoint is encountered during execution, the VI automatically enters pause mode and highlights the node the program will execute next. You can click pause or one of the other single-stepping buttons to continue. To clear a breakpoint, point at it with the breakpoint tool and you'll notice that the tool changes to ⊙. Click, and the breakpoint is removed.

Another kind of breakpoint that works only with subVIs is **Suspend when called**. You access this option through the VI Setup . . . dialog or through the **SubVI Setup . . .** dialog, accessed by popping up on the icon of a VI on a diagram. If a subVI's panel is not open when the breakpoint occurs, it will open automatically. The same thing happens when you have a numeric control or indicator set to suspend on a range error—a kind of conditional breakpoint. You might use this feature when something disastrous would happen if somebody entered an illegal value.

Once the subVI is suspended, it will not proceed until you click one of the following buttons on the control bar:

⏩ Is the **run** button, which runs the subVI as if it were a top-level VI being run on its own. You can run it over and over again, changing the input values and observing the results. A really cool thing you can do while in this state (and no other) is to edit the values of *indicators*. If the VI runs for a long time and you need to abort it, you can click the abort button ⬛, and it will stop the entire hierarchy.

⬛ Is the **return to caller** button. Click this after you are finished fiddling with any values on the panel. Control returns to the calling VI, whether or not you have clicked the run button (remember to do so if you wish to have the subVI compute new values). The combination of these two buttons permits you to completely override the action of a subVI, which is handy when you want to perform a test with artificial data without modifying any diagrams.

Debugging global variables

If your program uses many global variables or VIs that use uninitialized shift registers for internal state memory, you have an extra layer of complexity and many more opportunities for bugs to crop up. Here's a brief list of common mistakes associated with global variables and state memory:

- Accidentally writing data to the wrong global variable. It's easy to do; just select the wrong item on one of LabVIEW's built-in globals, and you're in trouble.

- Forgetting to initialize shift-register-based memory. Most of the examples in this book that use uninitialized shift registers have a Case structure inside the loop that writes appropriate data into the shift register at initialization time. If you expect a shift register to be empty each time the program starts, you must initialize it as such. It will automatically be empty when the VI is loaded, but will no longer be empty after the first run.

- Calling a subVI with state memory from multiple locations without making the subVI **reentrant** when required. You need to use reentrancy whenever you want the independent calls *not* to share data, for instance when computing a running average. Reentrant execution is selected from the VI Setup menu.

- Conversely, setting up a subVI with state memory as reentrant when you *do* want multiple calls to share data. Remember that calls to reentrant VIs from different locations don't share data. For instance, a file management subVI that creates a data file in one location and then writes data to the file in another location might keep the file path in an uninitialized shift register. Such a subVI won't work if it is made reentrant.

- Race conditions. You must be absolutely certain that every global variable is accessed in the proper order by its various calling VIs.

The most common case is where you attempt to write and read a global variable on the same diagram without forcing the execution sequence. Race conditions are absolutely the most difficult bugs to find and are the main reason you should avoid using globals haphazardly.

- Try to avoid situations where a global variable is written to in more than one location in the hierarchy. It may be hard to figure out which location supplied the latest value.

How do you debug these global variables? The first thing you must do is locate all of the global variable's callers. Open the global variable's panel and select *This VI's Callers* from the Project menu. Note every location where the global is accessed, then audit the list and see if it makes sense. Alternatively, you can use the Find command in the Project menu. Keep the panel of the global open while you run the main VI. Observe changes in the displayed data if you can. You may want to single step one or more calling VIs to more carefully observe data. One trick I've used is to add a new string control called **info** to the global variable. At every location where the global is called to read or write data, I add another call that writes a message to the **info** string. It might say, "SubVI abc writing xyz array from inner Case structure." You can also wire the Call Chain function (in the Advanced function palette) to the **info** string. (Actually, it has to be a string array in this case.) Call Chain returns a string array containing an ordered list of the VI calling chain, from top-level VI on down. Either of these methods makes it abundantly clear who is accessing what.

Debugging local variables and attribute nodes

Everything I've said regarding global variables is true to a great degree for local variables. Race conditions, in particular, can be very difficult to diagnose. *This is reason enough to avoid using local variables except when absolutely necessary!* (See Chap. 3, "Programming Techniques," for more warnings about local and global variables.) Execution highlighting and/or single stepping are probably your best debugging tools because you can usually see in what order the local variables are being executed. However, if your VI has a complicated architecture with parallel loops and timers, the relative ordering of events is time-dependent and cannot be duplicated in the slow motion of execution highlighting.

In difficult cases, you must first make sure that you have not inadvertently selected the wrong item in a local variable. Pop up on the problematic control or indicator, and select **Find>>Local Variables**. This will lead you to each local variable associated with that control. Be sure that each instance is logically correct: is it read or write mode, and is it the proper place to access this variable? Your only other recourse is to patiently walk through the logic of your diagram, just like you would in any programming language. See? I told you that local variables are a violation of LabVIEW's otherwise strict dataflow concepts. And what did they get you? The same old problems we have with traditional languages.

Attribute nodes can be a source of bugs similar to local variables. Controls disappear at the wrong time, scales get adjusted to bizarre values, and control sliders jiggle up and down. The pop-up Find command can also locate Attribute nodes, and you should always go through that exercise as a first step in debugging. Make sure that you have forced the execution sequence for each Attribute node, and that the sequence makes sense. Complex user interfaces make extensive use of Attribute nodes, and it's easy to forget to connect an item or two, leaving a control in an inconsistent condition. After a heavy editing session, mistakes are bound to crop up. Again, you must patiently walk through your code.

> The bugs I found in the VBL project were mostly due to unforeseen conditions. Changing operating modes in midstream created misbehavior because I did not plan for situations where the system was not initialized or used in the normal sequence. Another insidious bug was a couple of swapped cluster elements. The pop-up menu on clusters called **cluster order** can be important. I managed to exchange a setpoint with a measured value in one location, and this error could not be detected until the whole application was wired up. I found that error by having several subVI panels open at once. Since VBL was developed in LabVIEW 2.2, Type Definitions and Unbundle By Name were unavailable; they would have saved me some time.

Tracing execution

Many procedural languages contain a **trace** command or mode of operation, where you can record a history of values for a given variable. This is very useful when you're not sure in which order events occurred or in which order values were computed. An idea I got from Dan Snider, who wrote the Motion Toolbox for Parker Compumotor, is a **trace VI** that you can insert in your program to record important events. Values can be recorded in two ways: to disk or by appending to an array. The VI can record values each time it's called, like a simple data logger, or it can watch for changes in a particular value and record only the changes. This implementation is not perfect, however. If you have a race condition on a diagram where you are writing to a global variable at two locations almost simultaneously, the trace VI may not be quick enough to separate the two updates. This is where a built-in LabVIEW trace command would save the day. Perhaps a future version of Lab-VIEW will have this feature.

platform\ utility\Trace.vi

Figure 4.28 shows the connector pane and front panel of the Trace VI that's on the CD-ROM. Like many of the utilities included with this book, this one is only a starting point. I made it versatile, but you will certainly want to customize it or start all over with something that fits your needs a bit better. In this example, trace information may be appended to a file or to a string displayed on the panel of the VI. Each trace message contains a timestamp, the value being traced, an optional message string, and the error code. A single numeric value is traced, but you can replace it with whatever data you may have. Edit the diagram to change the formatting of the string as desired.

The **When to log** control determines when a trace record will be logged to the file or string. *Log always* means a record will be saved every time the VI is called. *Log on change* means only record data if **Value** has changed since the last time the VI was called. The **Mode** control determines what operation to perform. You can clear the string, choose a new file, log to the string, or log to the file. If you are routing trace information to the string, you may open the VI to display the trace summary. I also include a mode called *nothing,* which makes the VI do exactly that. Why include such a mode? So that you can leave the Trace VI in place on a diagram but in a disabled condition.

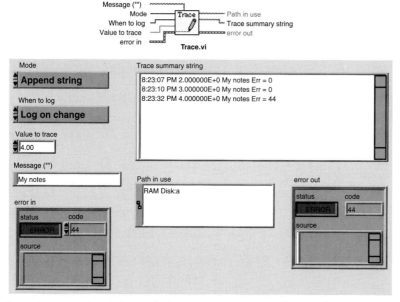

Figure 4.28 The Trace VI can help debug some applications by recording changes in important variables. You can record to the string indicator on the panel or to a file.

This VI is usually wired into a diagram to monitor a specific variable. You can also place it in an independent While Loop, perhaps in its own top-level VI, and have it monitor a global variable for any changes. It's important to remember that the Trace VI takes some time to do its job. Appending to the string starts out by taking a few milliseconds, but it gradually slows down as the string grows. Logging to a file will also take some milliseconds, but it's a constant delay. Displaying the panel while logging to the string can seriously degrade performance. You may want to modify the VI for higher performance by stripping out all the extra features you don't need. In particular, to trace a single numeric value, all you have to do is see if its value has changed, then append it to an array. That's much faster than all the string handling, but it's not quite as informative.

Checking performance

During development, you should occasionally check the performance of your application to make sure that it meets any specifications for speed or response time. You should also check memory usage and make sure that your customers will have sufficient memory and CPU speed for the application. LabVIEW has a VI performance profiler that makes it much easier to verify speed and memory usage for a hierarchy.

Select **Show Profile Window** from the Project menu to open the Profile Window and start a profiling session. There are check boxes for selecting timing statistics, timing details, and memory usage. I usually turn everything on. Click the **Start** button to enable the collection of performance data, then run your VI and use it in a normal manner. The Profile Window must stay open in the background to collect data. At any time, you can click the **Snapshot** button to view the current statistics. Statistics are presented in a large table, with one row for each VI. You can save this data in a tab-delimited text file by clicking the **Save** button.

Scroll through the table and note the almost-overwhelming bounty of information. (See the LabVIEW user's manual for details on the meaning of each value.) Click on any column header to sort the information by that statistic. For instance, you will probably want to know which VIs use the most memory. If you see something surprising in the list, such as a subVI using a large amount of memory or taking up too much time, it's time to investigate. Note that the memory and timing values are relative—the profiler itself uses some memory and CPU time—but the comparisons are accurate.

Documentation

Most programmers hold documentation in the same regard as root canal surgery. Meanwhile, users hold documentation dear to their hearts. The only resolution is for you, the LabVIEW programmer, to make a concerted effort to get that vital documentation on disk and perhaps on paper. This section describes some of the documentation tools and formats that have been accepted in commercial LabVIEW software.

The key to good documentation is to generate it as you go. For instance, when you finish constructing a new subVI, fill in the Get Info VI description item, described later. Then, when you want to put together a software maintenance document, you can just copy and paste that information into your word processor. It's much easier to explain the function of a VI or control when you have just finished working on it. Come back in a month, and you won't remember any of the details.

If you want to write commercial-grade LabVIEW applications, you will find that documentation is at least as important as having a well-designed program. As a benchmark, I spend at least 25 percent of my time on a given contract entering information into various parts of VIs and in the production of the final document.

VI descriptions

The VI description in the **Get Info** dialog box from the File menu is often a user's only source of information about a VI. Think about the way that you find out how someone else's VIs work, or even how the ones in the LabVIEW libraries work. Isn't it nice when there's online help, rather than having to dig out the manual? Important items to include in the description are

- An overview of the VI's function, followed by as much detail about the operation of the VI as you can supply
- Instructions for use
- Description of inputs and outputs
- Author's name and date

Information can be cut and pasted into and out of this window. If you need to create a formal document, you can copy the contents of this description into your document. This is how I manage to deliver a really nice looking document with each driver that I write without doing lots of extra work. I just write the description as if I were writing that formal document. You can also use the **VI List** application as described in the following section on Formal Documents to extract these comments automatically.

You can also display the VI description by

- Selecting the *Connector Pane and Description* option when using the Print Documentation command from the File menu
- Showing the Help window and placing the wiring tool on a subVI's icon on the block diagram

Control descriptions

Every control and indicator should have a description entered through the **Data Operations>>Description** pop-up menu. You can display this information by showing the Help window and placing the cursor on the control (Fig. 4.29). You can also display it by placing the wiring tool on the control's terminal on the block diagram. This is very handy when you are starting to wire up a very complex VI with many front panel items. The description should contain the following general information, where applicable:

- Purpose or function of the control or indicator.
- Limits on numeric values. (I usually write *Range: 0–128.*)
- Default values.
- Special interactions with other control settings.

This is the most underused feature of LabVIEW. When confronted with a new VI, a user typically has no alternative but to guess the function of each control and indicator. It is a welcome sight to have a brief message show up in the LabVIEW Help window just by pointing at the object. Get in the habit of entering a description as soon as you create the object. Then, if you copy the object to other VIs, the description follows along. It's much easier than saving the documentation for later. Remember to tell users about this feature.

Custom online help

LabVIEW has an online help system that serves as a replacement for most of the manuals. You can add your own reference documents to this

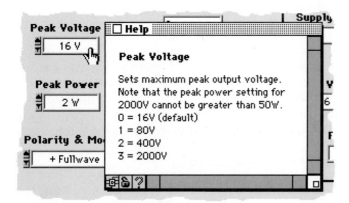

Figure 4.29 Control descriptions are really helpful, but only if you remember to type them in!

help system. The documents could describe the usage of individual VIs or serve as a user manual. The key is to create a document (it can contain both graphics and text), and then use a specialized help compiler for your platform to generate a source file in Windows Help format. The following compilers are available:*

- *Windows:* RoboHelp from Blue Sky Software
- *Windows:* Doc-To-Help from WexTech Systems
- *Macintosh:* QuickView from Altura Software
- *UNIX:* HyperHelp from Bristol Technologies

Once you have a help document compiled, you link it to a particular VI through the Documentation section of the VI Setup menu. Particular keywords (Help Tags) in a help file can be linked as well. That makes it easy for the user to search for a topic or VI name and jump directly to the proper part of your spiffy online help document. Developers are encouraged to place their help files in the Help directory and to use the *<helpdir>:* pseudopath in VIs that reference help in this directory. When you enter a path in VI Setup's Help Path, use the current platform's path conventions. As with other paths in LabVIEW, the path will be formatted correctly when you move to another platform.

Additionally, you can place VIs and LLBs in the Help directory and top-level VIs will be automatically listed in the Help menu. When the user selects a VI from the menu, it will be loaded (and if you configure VI Setup to execute upon load, it will start executing immediately).

You can programmatically access the online help system through the Control Online Help function from the Advanced function palette. This function lets you open and close the online help system, display the main Contents menu, or search for a specific keyword. It's a way to make a Help button on a LabVIEW panel do something more than display a dialog box.

Documenting the diagram

While the overall VI description provides adequate coverage of the purpose and function of a VI, it leaves something to be desired when it comes to explaining the diagram. There are many helpful items that you can add to a diagram to make it easier to understand (assuming that you have laid it out in a neat and orderly fashion). Many of these techniques appear in the examples in this book.

---

* Blue Sky Software: (800) 677-4946 or (619) 459-6365; WexTech Systems, Inc., (800) 939-8324; Altura Software, (408) 655-8005; Bristol Technologies, (203) 438-6969.

- Label every loop and every frame of Case and Sequence structures. Place a free label (using the text tool) inside each frame that states the objective of that frame, for example, "Read data from all configured channels." Sometimes it helps to use a larger font or set the style to bold to make the label stand out.

- Label important wires, especially when the wire is very long or its source is somehow obscured. I like to make the foreground color transparent (T) and the background color white, then place the label right on the wire: ~~~path~~~.

- Use large, bold key numbers located near important parts of the diagram, then use a scrolling diagram string constant (located off to the side or bottom of the diagram) to explain each key item. This technique reduces clutter within the diagram but provides much information nearby. (Monnie Anderson, formerly an analyst at National Instruments, promoted this one; I've started to use it more and more.)

- Add an index to sequence structures. If you have a sequence with more than two or three frames, create a list outside the structure that helps the user quickly locate the desired frame.

VI history

During development, you can track changes to VIs through the History Window, which you display by selecting the **Show History** item from the Windows menu. In the History Window, you can enter descriptions of important changes to the VI, then add your comments to the history log. Revision numbers are kept for each VI, and you can reset the revision number (which also erases all history entries) by clicking the **Reset** button in the History Window.

Some kinds of information can be automatically added to this historical record. From the LabVIEW Preferences dialog, you have access to a number of settings associated with History logging. For instance, you can have LabVIEW automatically add an entry every time the VI is saved or prompt the user for an entry at that time. Settings made through the Preferences dialog are the default settings for new VIs. You can also customize the History settings for individual VIs through the VI Setup menu.

History information can be printed though the **Print Documentation** command in the File menu. Of course, this only prints the history for a single VI. Eventually, LabVIEW will have a command that extracts history information for all the VIs in a hierarchy or directory.

This capability is included with LabVIEW as a tool for formal software development. There is great demand from professional LabVIEW developers for more capability in such areas. That's why the Project menu appeared in the first place. Expect more features in the History Window in future versions.

Other ways to document

One foolproof way of getting important instructions to the user is to place a block of text right on the front panel where it can't be missed. Like a pilot's checklist, a concise enumerated list of important steps can be invaluable. You might even put a suggestion there that says, "Select Get Info from the File menu for instructions."

If a front panel has a large string indicator, have it do double duty by putting instructions in it, then *Make Current Value Default.* Note that you can type into an indicator as long as the VI is in edit mode.

Printing LabVIEW panels and diagrams

I don't believe in printing LabVIEW panels and diagrams for the purpose of basic documentation—and I'm not alone in my position. The interactive, layered, hierarchical nature of LabVIEW is at best poorly represented on paper. "But my Quality Assurance manager requires printouts," you say. Well, mine did, too, but I talked him into accepting floppy disks instead. What use is a big, unreadable stack of paper anyway? My point is this: *the LabVIEW paradigm is completely different from procedural languages and should not be forced into that same old mold.* Nobody is going to stop you from printing out your code, but please think before you kill another tree.

Despite my pleading, you may still have to print a few panels or diagrams. Perhaps you need to show someone your work where there is no computer running LabVIEW. Or maybe you're writing a paper (or a book!) about your LabVIEW project and you need images of various screens. In those cases, you can and should print those images. Here are some of the methods.

The **Print Window** command (from the File menu) does just that: whichever LabVIEW window is on top gets sent to the printer, using the current page setup. Limited customization of the printout is available through the **Execution Options** in the VI Setup menu. In particular, you can request *scale-to-fit,* which really helps if the panel is large. When printing a front panel, note that *all* items on the panel will be printed, including those you have scrolled out of the usual viewing area. To avoid printing those items, you should hide them (choose **Hide Front Panel Control** by popping up on the control's terminal).

The **Print Documentation** command is quite flexible, though it only prints one VI at a time. You can choose which parts of the VI you wish to print (panel, diagram, connector pane, description, etc.) through the feature-laden Print Documentation dialog box. Printouts are autoscaled (if desired), which means that reasonably large panels and diagrams will fit on a single sheet of paper.

Automated documentation is possible with the **printing utility VIs**, available from ftp.natinst.com. These VIs use the features of the Print Documentation command programmatically, thus saving you from manually configuring and printing each VI. You can print documentation for all VIs in memory or those in a directory. There's also a VI that permits you to programmatically print the panel of any VI in memory, whether its panel is displayed or not. The results are identical to the VI Setup feature, Print Panel When VI Completes Execution, but the VI does not have to run.

Putting LabVIEW screen images into other documents. There are several ways to electronically place an image of a LabVIEW screen in another application:

- Copy and paste items directly
- Use a screen-capture utility
- Print to encapsulated PostScript (EPS) files

On the Macintosh, you can select objects from a LabVIEW panel or diagram, copy them to the clipboard, and then paste them into any application that displays PICT objects, including word processors. If you paste them into a drawing application, such as MacDraw or Canvas, the objects are accurately colored and fully editable. Diagrams look pretty good, though you do lose some wire textures, such as the zigzag pattern for strings and the dotted lines for Booleans.

LabVIEW for Windows isn't quite as simple. By default, selected objects are copied as bitmaps, and this works reliably. By turning on a LabVIEW preference item, they may be copied as *Enhanced Metafiles,* which are object-oriented graphics similar to PICT format on the Mac. However, there are some scaling problems, resulting in very large metafile images.

Screen captures are another quick way to obtain a bitmap image of anything on your computer's screen, including LabVIEW panels and diagrams. Both Macintosh and Windows machines have a built-in screen capture capability. On the Macintosh, use Command-Shift-3, which saves a bitmap image of the entire screen to a file on the startup disk. On Windows, the Print Screen key copies the complete screen image to the clipboard, and Alt-Print Screen copies the top window (the one you clicked last) to the clipboard.

Alternatively, you can obtain one of several screen-capture utilities that can grab a selected area of the screen and save it to the clipboard or to a file. On the Macintosh, some utilities are Digital Camera, Screenshot, or Capture. (I use Screenshot for many of my documents.) For Windows, there are many choices recommended by LabVIEW users: Corel Capture, Hijaak, Paintshop Pro, HyperSnap, Screen Thief, and Snappro. The last three are available as shareware from many bulletin boards and FTP sites and as commercial packages. The commercial versions offer more features, as a rule. The nice thing about many of these utilities is that you can capture pulled menus and cursors, which is really helpful for user documentation.

What if you're creating a really formal document or presentation and you want the very finest quality images of your LabVIEW screens? Here's Gary's secret recipe, using the PostScript printing feature of LabVIEW. It works on any Macintosh and on some Windows systems with certain printer drivers, such as the one for the HP LaserJet 4m; check your driver to see if it has an EPS file generation feature. You must have LabVIEW 4.01 or later, LaserWriter driver 8.0 (for the Mac), and Adobe Illustrator 6.0 to edit the resulting images. Here are the steps:

1. Use LabVIEW's Print Documentation feature with a custom setup to print whatever is desired. Your life will be simpler if you use the **scale to fit** option to get everything on one page. Otherwise, objects will be clipped or lost since EPS only records one page worth of information. *Note:* In the LabVIEW Preferences, under Printing, select *PostScript printing, level 1.*

2. In the print dialog, print to a file. Make the file type EPS with a preview.

3. Open the resulting file with Illustrator 6.0 (prior versions will fail to properly parse the EPS file). The panel and diagram are fully editable, color PostScript objects. You will need to ungroup and delete some of the surrounding boxes. Also, many items are masked and use PostScript patterns. Be careful what you change or delete.

4. Save the file as Illustrator EPS for importing into a page layout program. *Note:* If you send the file to a service bureau, make sure you take along any strange fonts that you might have chosen in LabVIEW.

While it takes several steps, the results are gorgeous when printed at high resolution, such as 1200 dpi. This book is an example of the results.

Writing formal documents

If you need to prepare a formal document describing your LabVIEW project, try to follow the conventions described here. The final product should end up looking much like the LabVIEW data acquisition VI library reference manual. My objective here is to help propagate a consistent style of documentation so users can more quickly understand what you have written. If you work for a big company, it may have a style guide for technical writers that should be consulted as well. General document style is beyond the scope of this book; only the specifics of content and format as they pertain to VI descriptions will be discussed.

Document outline.   For an instrument driver or similar package, a document might consist of the following basic elements:

1. Cover page
2. Table of contents
3. Introduction—"About this Package"
4. Programming notes—help the user apply the lower-level function VIs
5. Using the demonstration VI
6. Detailed description of each lower-level function VI

The first five items are general in nature. Use your best judgment as to what they should contain. The last item, the detailed description of a particular VI, is the subject of the rest of this section. For major applications, I usually write a user manual and a programmer manual. In the user manual, I begin with a *quick start* section. This I limit to only a few pages because most users have the attention span of a two-year-old. In that section, I put annotated screen shots that describe the important controls and explain how to start up and shut down the system. Next, I go into detail about the various LabVIEW panels and modes of operation. In general, you should model your manuals after those of other commercial packages that you think are effective.

Connector pane picture.   Use the methods described under "Putting LabVIEW Screen Images into Other Documents" to import an image of the connector pane into your word processor as shown in Fig. 4.30. This gives the reader a handy key to the VI's connections, just like you find in the LabVIEW manuals.

Note the different styles of text in the figure. This is achieved by setting the **required connections** on the VI's connector pane. While editing a VI and showing the connector pane, pop up on a terminal

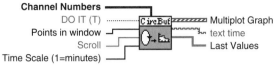

CircBuf to Multiplot Graph.vi

Figure 4.30 The connector pane is an important part of the document for any VI. Different text styles can indicate relative importance of each terminal.

point and select **This Connection Is**. The choices available are *Required, Recommended,* or *Optional.* Required terminals will automatically be displayed in the Help window (and in printouts) in boldface. These terminals must be wired when the VI is placed on a diagram, or the calling VI will be broken. Recommended terminals (the default setting) are displayed in normal face. Optional terminals are those that the user will rarely have to access, and they are grayed out. In the Help window, the user can select **simple diagram help** or **detailed diagram help**. In the simple mode, optional terminals are not shown. This simplifies the life of novice users.

platform\ vi_list.llb

VI description. If you have already entered a description of the VI in the Get Info box with the VI, open it, select all the text and copy it to the clipboard to import it into a document in your word processor. There is a utility VI called **VI List** (available on the CD-ROM that accompanies this book) that copies all of the VI description strings from directories and libraries of VIs into a new text document. This automates the process for you. Just run the top-level VI (VI List) and follow the directions. Since it's a LabVIEW program, you can modify it to reformat the text as you like.

Names of input and output terminals should be in bold face. If your word processor can do page layouts, the description can flow around the connector pane picture. Here is the text that goes with the connector pane shown in Fig. 4.30:

A handy multichannel plotter for use with the Circular Buffer trending VI. Calls the Circular Buffer driver to return the desired quantity of data for one or more channels. Displays data as a multiplot graph and returns the last values for the specified channels. All channels share a common time base. Supports all the features of the Circular Buffer VI. To see this VI in action, run the Circ Buf Example VI, then run this VI. Since the Circular Buffer is a kind of global variable, its data can be shared between these independent, top-level VIs.

Terminal descriptions. Every input and output needs a description that includes the following information.

- The data type
- What it does
- Valid range (for inputs)
- Default value (for inputs)

This may be the same information that you entered in the control's description dialog box. A recommended standard for terminal labeling makes use of text style to indicate how frequently you need to change each item. When you create the VI, modify the font for each front panel item's label as follows: use boldface for items that you will have to change often, use the normal font for items that you plan to use less often, and put square brackets [label] around the labels of items where the default value usually suffices. This method maps directly to the required connections behavior previously described. When you write the terminal descriptions into a document, put them in this prioritized order so the user will see the most-used items first. I like to start each line with a picture of the appropriate LabVIEW terminal data type, followed by the terminal's name, then its description, range, and defaults:

[I32] **Peak Voltage** sets the maximum peak output voltage. Note that the peak power setting for 2000 V cannot be greater than 50 W. The possible values are as follows:

0: 16 V   (Default)
1: 80 V
2: 400 V
3: 2000 V

Make a complete set of terminal icons that can be kept in a separate document, open at the same time as your project document. Just copy and paste the icons. I made such a document in Microsoft Word that I call "LabVIEW Document Helpers." It also includes preformatted document sections and styles that speed up and standardize my work. If you can't handle all this graphical stuff, at least show the data type in text format. Examples:

I32	I32 integer
[DBL]	Array of DBL numerics
[[DBL]]	2D array of DBL numerics
cluster	Cluster
ABC	String

platform\
style guide\
LV Document
Helper

The "LabVIEW Document Helpers" document is on the CD-ROM in several formats. Try it out, and feel free to add your favorite documentation tidbits.

Programming examples. If you are producing a commercial package, it's a good idea to include some examples using your VIs. Show how the VI is used in a loop or in conjunction with graphs or an analysis operation. Above all, have a "try me first" example that is guaranteed to work! This will give the user higher confidence that the rest of the package is similarly functional. Put completed examples on disk where the interested user can find them and try them out. Make prominent mention of the existence of these examples in your documentation, perhaps in the *quick start* section.

Distributing documents

In this modern age, more and more documents are distributed in electronic form. Except for commercially marketed software packages, the user is expected to download some kind of document for personal viewing and/or printing. Text files are of course the least-common-denominator format, but they leave much to be desired: you can't include graphics at all. Word processors and page layout programs can create nice documents, but they are not generally portable (though Microsoft has done a good job of Mac-PC portability with Word, except for graphic items). Besides text and word processor files, there are some good formats available nowadays, thanks to the explosion of the World Wide Web.

Portable Document Format (PDF) was created by Adobe Systems to provide cross-platform portability of elaborate documents. It based PDF on PostScript technology, which supports embedded fonts and graphics. You can buy Adobe Acrobat for almost any computer and use it to translate documents from word processors and page layout applications into this universal format. Users can obtain a free copy of Adobe Acrobat Reader from online sources (National Instruments has it on its FTP site, ftp.natinst.com, and its Web site, http://www.natinst.com), or you can include it on your distribution media. Again, Acrobat Reader is available for many platforms. Except for the fact that the files are sometimes bulky, I think this is the best way to distribute high-quality documentation.

HyperText Markup Language (HTML) is the native format for many items on the World Wide Web, and all Web browsers can read files in this format—including local files on disk. The file itself is just ASCII text, but it contains a complex coding scheme that allows documents to contain not only text, but links to other files, including graphics and sound. You can use Web authoring software, such as Adobe PageMill, to create HTML documents. It provides a WYSIWYG editor where you can paste text and graphics. When you save the document, it automatically creates the graphic files and puts the links in the HTML file. There is even discussion of including the ability for LabVIEW to automatically generate portable documentation in HTML or some other portable format. Keep watching the National Instruments announcements.

Custom online help is another viable way to distribute documents. By definition, all LabVIEW users have a way to view such documents. They can be searched by keyword and of course you can include graphics. See the previous section, "Custom Online Help," or the LabVIEW user manual for more information on creating these files.

Final Touches

If you follow the directions discussed here, you will end up with a well-designed LabVIEW application that meets the specifications determined early in the process. A few final chores may remain.

Test and verify your program. First, compare your application with the original specifications one more time. Make sure that all the needs are fulfilled—controls and indicators are all in place, data files contain the correct formats, throughput is acceptable, and so forth. Second, you should abuse your program in a big way. Try pressing buttons in the wrong order and entering ridiculous values in all controls (your users will!). Where data files are involved, I like to go out and modify, delete, or otherwise mangle the files without LabVIEW's knowledge, just to see what happens. Remember that error handling is the name of the game in robust programming. If you are operating under the auspices of formal software quality assurance, you will have to write a detailed validation and verification plan, followed by a report of the test results. A phenomenal amount of paperwork will be generated.

Train your users. Depending on the complexity of the application, this may require anything from a few minutes to several hours. I once developed a big general-purpose data acquisition package and I had about 15 people to train to use it. The package had lots of features and most of the users were unfamiliar with LabVIEW. My strategy was to personally train two people at a time in front of a live workstation. The user's manual that I wrote was the only other teaching aid. After going through the basic operations section of the manual in order during the training session, the students could see that the manual was a good reference when they had questions later. It took about two hours for each training session, much of which consisted of demonstration by me, with hands-on practice by the users at each major step. Simple reinforcement exercises really help the students to retain what you have taught them. I learned afterward that everyone really appreciated these training sessions because they helped them get a jump start in the use of the new system.

Last, but not least, make several **backup** copies of all of your VIs and associated documents. Hopefully, you have been making some kind of backups for safety's sake all along. It's an important habit to get into because system failures and foul-ups on your part should never become major setbacks. I like to keep the working copy on my hard disk, a daily backup on another (removable) hard disk, and a safety copy on floppies or some other media, perhaps a file server. When you make up a deliverable package, you can put a set of master floppies in one of those clear plastic diskette holders in the back of the user's manual. Looks really "pro."

VBL epilogue

It turns out that it took longer to get the equipment fabricated and installed in Larry's lab than it did for me to write the application. I did all the testing in my office with a Eurotherm controller next to my Mac, including all the demonstrations. Since there was plenty of time, I finished off the documentation and delivered a copy in advance—Larry was pleasantly surprised. Training was spread out over several sessions, giving him plenty of time to try out all the features. We tested the package thoroughly without power applied to the furnaces for safety's sake. Only a few final modifications and debugging sessions were needed before the package was ready for real brazing runs. It's been running constantly since the end of 1992 with excellent results. Larry is another happy LabVIEW customer.

Bibliography

Brunzie, Ted J., "Aging Gracefully: Writing Software that Takes Changes in Stride," *LabVIEW Technical Resource,* vol. 3, no. 4, Fall 1995.

Fowler, Gregg, "Interactive Architectures Revisited," *LabVIEW Technical Resource,* vol. 4, no. 2, spring 1996.

Gruggett, Lynda, "Getting Your Priorities Straight," *LabVIEW Technical Resource,* vol. 1, no. 2, Summer 1993. (Back issues available from LTR Publishing.)

Johnson, Gary, and Meg Kay, *LabVIEW Style Guide,* National Instruments FTP server ftp://ftp.natinst.com/support/labview/documents/style-guide and on this book's CD-ROM in directory platform\style guide, 1995.

Instrument Drivers

A LabVIEW **instrument driver** is a collection of VIs that controls a programmable instrument. Each routine handles a specific operation such as reading data, writing data, or configuring the instrument. A well-written driver makes it easy to access an instrument because it encapsulates the complex, low-level hardware setup and communications protocols. You are presented with a set of driver VIs which are easy to understand, modify, and apply to the problem at hand.

The key to writing drivers lies in a simple pronouncement: **RTFM**—*Read the Fine Manual.* I'm talking about the *LabVIEW Instrument I/O VI Reference Manual* and the programming manual that goes with the instrument you're writing the driver for. Without these references, you may end up frustrated, or at best, with a really bizarre driver. The guidelines on writing drivers were incorporated into the manual because they are critically important to the creation of logically and stylistically correct drivers. Originally, this information was available only as Application Note AN006, *Writing a LabVIEW Instrument Driver.* It's one of my all-time favorite programming guides. (For a long time, it was the *only* programming guide to LabVIEW; Kevin Schmeisser of National Instruments deserves a lot of credit for forging ahead and writing it in the first place.) I won't duplicate here what it already says so well. Instead, I'll concentrate on design techniques and some of the tricks I've learned by writing a dozen or so major drivers. Many of the utility VIs mentioned in this chapter are on the CD-ROM, so you won't have to look far when you start writing your own drivers.

About the Instrument Library

One of the reasons that LabVIEW has been so widely accepted is because of the way it incorporates instrument drivers. Unlike many competing applications, LabVIEW drivers are written in LabVIEW—complete with the usual panels and diagrams—instead of arriving as precompiled black boxes that only the manufacturer can modify. That means you can start with an existing driver and adapt it to your needs as you see fit. Another important asset is the National Instruments **instrument library**. It contains drivers for hundreds of instruments using a variety of hardware standards such as GPIB, RS-232/422, VXI, and CAMAC. Each driver is fully supported by National Instruments. They are also *free*. Obtaining drivers from the library is easy:

- All LabVIEW distribution CD-ROMs include the complete instrument library.

- The instrument library is available on its own CD-ROM from National Instruments.

- Use the Internet FTP server (ftp.natinst.com) or the National Instruments Web site (http://www.natinst.com) if you have access to Internet services.

- Use the dial-up bulletin board (512-794-5422) if you have a modem. It offers the same files as the FTP server.

- Call your local National Instruments representative. Representatives have copies of the driver library locally.

- Call National Instruments (800-433-3488) and it will mail you diskettes.

Many of the drivers are commercial-grade software, meaning that they are thoroughly tested, fairly robust, documented, and supported. They are also one of your best resources for instrument programming examples (particularly the more recent ones). Whenever you need to write a new driver, always look at an existing driver that is related to your new project. Programming by plagiarizing is very productive and promotes standardization among drivers. Ideally, every instrument should be a drop-in replacement for every other instrument of its genre. No need to reinvent the wheel!

If your instrument is not in the library, start by looking on ftp. natinst.com in the **beta** and **donated** instrument directories. Here, you will find formal drivers that are not fully tested and informal drivers written by other users, but with no guarantee as to their reliability. Also, look at the info-labview mailgroup FTP site (ftp.pica.army.mil) where many donated instrument drivers reside. Finally, consider posting a message to the info-labview mailgroup (see Chap. 1, "Roots," for information on this mailgroup) and ask the world if they have or know of a driver for your instrument. Any of these solutions is, in my experience, better than starting from scratch.

National Instruments welcomes contributions to the instrument library. If you have written a new driver that others might be interested in using, consider submitting it. Consultants who are skilled in writing instrument drivers can join the Alliance Program and become Certified Instrument Driver Developers. If you have that entrepreneurial spirit, you could even *sell* your driver package, providing that there's a market. Software Engineering Group (SEG) was probably the first to do this with its HighwayView package that supports Allen-Bradley programmable logic controllers (PLCs). It's been a successful venture. Many other manufacturers of programmable instruments also sell their drivers rather than placing them in the library. If you can't find the driver you need in the library, you might call the manufacturer of the instrument.

Driver Basics

Writing a driver can be trivial or traumatic; it depends on your programming experience, the complexity of the instrument, and the approach you take. Start by reading the first few chapters of the *LabVIEW Instrument I/O Reference Manual,* which will give you an overview of the preferred way to write a driver. Then, spend time with your instrument and the programming manual. Figure out how everything is supposed to work. Then decide what your objectives are. Do you just need to read a single data value, or do you need to implement every command? This has implications with respect to the complexity of the project.

Communication standards

The kinds of instruments you are most likely to use are "smart," stand-alone devices that use one of several communication standards, notably **serial**, **GPIB**, and **VXI**. These are the ones we'll tackle (see Fig. 5.1). Plug-in data acquisition boards are also extremely common. If you are using boards made by National Instruments, the drivers are already written and are supplied with LabVIEW in the form of example VIs and the DAQ function library; they are discussed in Chap. 6, "Using the DAQ Library." A very good overview of GPIB and serial interfaces is available in the *Instrument Communication Handbook* (IOTech 1991).

Programming for other manufacturer's plug-in boards and special hardware I/O subsystems can be accomplished in a procedural language like C and implemented as Code Interface Nodes (CINs) in LabVIEW. Though CIN programming is beyond the scope of this book, the general principles discussed in this chapter are still relevant. Some manufacturers include Windows Dynamic Link Libraries (DLLs) as low-level interfaces to their drivers. These you can access with the **Call**

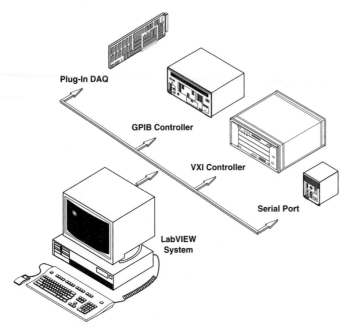

Plug-In DAQ

GPIB Controller

VXI Controller

Serial Port

LabVIEW
System

Figure 5.1 GPIB, VXI, and serial communications are very common and are simplified by using instrument drivers. Plug-in data acquisition cards require special, low-level drivers. Drivers for National Instruments' boards are supplied with LabVIEW.

Library function, available from the Advanced function palette. In fact, writing DLLs is often easier than writing CINs and can simplify maintenance since the DLL is an external module. Again, this is an advanced topic, but there are two useful application notes available: AN057, *An Introduction to Using Windows Dynamic Link Libraries (DLLs) from LabVIEW* and AN072, *Calling Dynamic Link Libraries (DLLs) from LabVIEW—Detailed Procedures.* The Call Library function has a pop-up configuration dialog that makes it pretty easy to exchange commands and data with a DLL, and it requires no special programming.

Some users have attempted, with some success, to access plug-in boards with **peek** and **poke** commands from LabVIEW. This is a slightly hazardous method where you directly access registers on a board without a DLL, driver, or other operating system interface. As such, it can be very fast—no operating system overhead—but is highly dependent upon knowledge of the exact hardware configuration. For instance, the base address of a plug-in board may change when installed in a different slot. Peek and Poke functions are included with LabVIEW for Macintosh (Advanced function palette), but not with Windows. For Windows, you can download PeekPoke library from ftp.pica.army.mil. Written by Joe Travis, these free VIs access real-mode memory (below 1 MB). A more sophisticated package called **Peek/Poke** is available from Viewpoint Software Solutions (http://www.viewpointusa.com). It includes about 40 VIs that can read and write a variety of data formats, including large blocks of data.

Serial instruments.   Popular serial communication interface standards include **RS-232C**, **RS-422A**, and **RS-485A**. These standards are defined by the Electronics Industries Association (EIA) and include specifications for cabling, connector pinouts, signal levels, and timing. *Note that none of these standards say anything about the protocol or message formats.* This is a popular misconception. Protocols are covered by independent standards, or, more often, by the will and whim of the instrument manufacturer. The advantages of serial communication are simplicity and low cost. RS-232, for instance, has been around for a long time, so there is plenty of cheap hardware available and it's built into almost every computer. The disadvantage is that serial systems tend to be slow (you can move only one bit of data at a time), and the protocols are sometimes burdensome in terms of programming.

RS-232C is the most common standard, supported by virtually all computer systems and most serial instruments. It uses the familiar 25-pin D-style connector for most equipment, or a 9-pin version on IBM PC systems. The standard defines functions for all the pins, though you will most often see just a few of the lines used: transmit data, receive data, and ground. The other pins are used for handshaking, with such functions as *Clear to Send* and *Ready to Send.* These functions are supported by the LabVIEW serial port functions, if your instrument requires their use. The main limitation of RS-232 is that it is electrically single-ended which results in poor noise rejection. The standard also limits the maximum distance to 100 meters, though this is frequently violated in practice. The top data rate is normally 19,200 baud (bits per second), but some systems support higher speeds. It's also the most abused and ignored standard in the industry. Manufacturers take many liberties regarding signal levels, baud rate, connectors, and so forth. Not all RS-232-compliant devices are actually compatible. Beware!

RS-422A is similar to RS-232, but uses differential drivers and receivers, thus requiring two pairs of wires plus a ground as the minimum connection. Because of its superior noise rejection and drive capability, RS-422 is usable to 1200 meters at speeds below 9600 baud, and up to 1 Mbaud at shorter distances. Macintosh serial ports are RS-422A-compliant.

Other standards in this series are **RS-432A** and **RS-485A**. RS-423A is identical to RS-232C, except that the electrical characteristics are improved to support higher transmission rates over longer distances. RS-485A is an extension of RS-422A that specifies greater drive current and supports *multidrop* systems (multiple talkers and listeners on one set of wires). Generally, your computer will need an adapter box or plug-in board to properly support these standards. National Instruments makes a plug-in board for the ISA bus, the AT-485, with two or four RS-485 ports. You can buy adapter boxes that provide electrical compatibility between all of these standards from companies such as Black Box.

A few instruments use a specialized **9-bit protocol** with an RS-485 multidrop system. I mention it here because a number of LabVIEW users have inquired about it on the info-labview mailgroup. This protocol was designed by Intel Corporation as a means of communicating between microcontrollers and various peripheral devices; Intel called it the **Intel MicroLAN** protocol. In addition to the standard eight data bits found in each data frame, these protocols use a ninth bit (in what would normally be the parity position) as an address flag. When the ninth bit is asserted, it tells the listeners that the other eight bits are a device address. That makes it easy for hardware to sift through message traffic on the network and pick out only those messages directed at a particular node. The downside is, you must have a special UART (universal asynchronous receiver-transmitter), or serial interface chip, to perform this 9-bit address filtering. Standard computers do not include this special UART; they are available only on after-market serial interfaces designed specifically for the 9-bit protocol, and they are only available for the PC. (I tried very hard to make this work on the Mac. Maybe one day there will be a suitable PCI board and driver.) To my knowledge, only a few users have implemented this protocol in LabVIEW for their proprietary applications, and only one has a commercial product: Cimetrics Technology offers its Nine-Bit Solution μLAN for LabVIEW for Windows NT. It's intended for PC networking as opposed to instrument drivers, but clearly Cimetrics knows what it's doing. I also understand that National Instruments is considering the development of drivers that will solve some 9-bit problems. By all means, contact it and see what's up.

Adding serial ports. If you need more serial ports on your computer, consider a multiport plug-in board. For a Macintosh with NuBus slots, the one I usually recommend is the Hurdler series from Creative Solutions. I like the Hurdlers because they are very easy to configure and offer up to 16 ports. If you are using the regular serial I/O VIs in LabVIEW, you must edit the subVI, Open Serial Driver, which you can find on the diagram of the Serial Port Init VI. On its panel, you will see two string array controls with input and output driver names. The default input names are *.aIn* and *.bIn,* and the default output names are *.aOut* and *.bOut.* To add to your Hurdler ports, add similar names to these arrays, starting with *.cIn* and *.cOut,* and continuing for as many ports as your board has. When you're done, *Make Current Values Default* and save the VI. It's a good idea to save a backup copy outside of vi.lib because it will otherwise be overwritten during the next LabVIEW upgrade. A board for PCI-bus PowerMacs is the Smart Serial 6 from Keyspan featuring 6 RS-232/422 ports and onboard intelligence to offload the host CPU. Users report that it works just fine with LabVIEW. Other PCI boards include the VersalLink Pro from Advanced Logic Integration, the Fenris from MegaWolf (with up to 64 ports on one board), and the MultiPort/PCI from Silicon Valley Bus Company, which adds not only serial ports but a PC-style parallel port as well.

For Windows, there are several good solutions. Many companies make low-cost serial boards for RS-232; these you install per the manufacturer's instructions, and the ports appear as additional Comm ports without special configuration in LabVIEW. One important feature to look for is a *16550-compatible UART.* This piece of hardware includes a 16-byte buffer to prevent data loss (the nefarious *overrun* error), which otherwise will surely occur under Windows. The National Instruments AT-232 board has this UART and is available with two or four ports. Viewpoint Software Solutions (http://www.viewpointusa.com) offers the MultiCom multichannel RS-232/422 board and driver software for LabVIEW. It supports up to 16 ports per board, with a maximum of 96 ports per PC, and has an onboard processor to reduce software overhead. If you're doing high-speed communications or high port count applications, consider something like the MultiCom in preference to a really cheap, less-capable board.

Troubleshooting serial interfaces. There is great likelihood that you will encounter problems when setting up RS-232-style serial communications systems. Here are a few of the more common problems and solutions.

- Swapped transmit and receive lines. Though the standards clearly define which is which, manufacturers seem to take liberties. I always manage to hook things up backward the first time, and the whole system is dead. The answer is to use a *null modem* cable that swaps these critical lines. You can use a voltmeter to figure out which pins are transmit and receive. *Transmit* lines will deliver a steady voltage, on the order of 3 V for RS-232 and ±1.5 V for RS-422 and RS-485. *Receive* lines generally stick around zero volts.

- Failure to properly connect the hardware handshaking lines. For instance, some instruments won't transmit until the **Clear to Send**

(CTS) line is asserted. Study your instrument's manual and try to find out which lines need to be connected.

- Wrong speed, parity, or stop bits settings. Obviously, all parties must agree on these low-level protocol settings. The **Serial Port Init** VI (Serial Instrument I/O function palette) sets these parameters for most serial interfaces.

- When in doubt, a serial line activity indicator from Radio Shack is a very useful tool for verifying serial line connections and activity. If you do a lot of serial cable debugging, then a full RS-232 breakout box from Black Box or equivalent will allow for rapid troubleshooting of serial cables.

- Multiple applications or devices trying to access the serial port. If the Serial Port Init VI returns an error, make sure that there are no other programs running on your computer that might be using the same serial port. For instance, AppleTalk on a Macintosh seizes the printer port and you must disable it if you wish to use that port. Also, some terminal emulators and fax software either seize the modem port at boot time or won't release it when you quit the application. A common headache under Windows is devices that share an interrupt request (IRQ) line. Typically, odd-numbered serial ports (Comm1 and Comm3) share IRQ3 and even-numbered ports IRQ4. I had a lap-top with a pointing device that was assigned to Comm3, and every time I moved the mouse, my LabVIEW application using Comm1 would go crazy. The solution was to reconfigure the pointing device (through a low-level setup utility or Control Panel) to use a different Comm port. If you're running a Plug-and-Play system (such as Windows 95) then your job is easier, because the IRQs are shown for all the world to see in the device registry. The system also tries to keep track of conflicts and displays them in the Resources tab of the System:Device Manager display under Control Panels.

GPIB instruments.   Hewlett-Packard Corporation gets credit for inventing this popular communications and control technique back in 1965, calling it the *HP Interface Bus* (*HP-IB*), a name it uses to this day. The Institute of Electrical and Electronics Engineers (IEEE) formalized it as **IEEE 488** in 1978, afterwhich its common name, **General-Purpose Interface Bus (GPIB)** was adopted. It's a powerful, flexible, and popular communications standard supported by thousands of commercial instruments and computer systems. Right now, LabVIEW has more GPIB drivers than any other type. The most important characteristics of GPIB are as follows:

- It is a parallel, or bus-based, standard capable of transferring one byte (eight bits) per cycle.

- It is fairly fast, transferring up to about 800 Kbytes/s.[†]

- Hardware takes care of timing and handshaking.

- It requires significantly more expensive and complex hardware than serial interfaces.

- Distance is limited to 20 meters unless special bus extender units are added.

- Up to 15 devices can coexist on one bus; up to 31 with a bus expander unit.

There is also a newer version of this standard, **IEEE 488.2**, established in 1987. The original standard didn't address data formats, status reporting, error handling, and so forth. The new standard does. It standardizes many of these lower-level protocol issues, simplifying your programming task. Of course, only the most recently designed instruments are 488.2-compliant, and your GPIB interface installed in your computer must also be up-to-date. The newer National Instruments GPIB boards support 488.2, and the LabVIEW GPIB library is based on it.

Even after the 488.2 standard was implemented, chaos reigned in the area of instrument command languages. A consortium of instrumentation companies convened in 1990 to define the **Standard Commands for Programmable Instrumentation (SCPI)** and programmers' lives became much easier. SCPI defines:

- Commands required by IEEE 488.2. Example: *IDN?* (send instrument identification)

- Commands required by SCPI. Example: *ERR?* (send next entry from instrument's error queue)

- Optional commands. Example: *DISP* (controls selection and presentation of display information)

Commands are structured as a hierarchical command tree. You specify a function, a subfunction, a sub-sub-function, and so on, separated by a colon (:) character. For instance, the SCPI message for an autoranging voltage measurement would be

---

[†] In 1993, National Instruments developed HS488, an extension to IEEE 488 which increases throughput up to 8 Mbytes/s by eliminating extra handshaking steps. HS488 has been recognized by several major manufacturers and is now under consideration for IEEE standardization.

```
SENSE:VOLTAGE:RANGE:AUTO
```

The first time I programmed a SCPI-compliant instrument (the HP 54510A Digitizing Oscilloscope), it was a pleasant surprise because the command set . . . *made sense!* Also, the SCPI model (Fig. 5.2) covers instruments of all kinds with a general model, so the programs you write tend to be reusable. By all means, feel welcome to borrow code directly from drivers for other SCPI instruments and save yourself some time.

The bad news is, GPIB is a fairly complex communications standard. The good news is, 95 percent of the time all you need to do is write a simple command string and read back a reply string. However, there are times when you need to use some of the more sophisticated aspects of GPIB, such as the device and controller functions. To really be successful in applying advanced functions, you will probably want to read up on the GPIB standard or maybe even take an IEEE 488 course, such as the one that National Instruments offers.

VXI instruments.   One of the newer industry-standard computer busses, VME, has been extended to support an instrument-on-a-card architecture. **VME Extensions for Instrumentation (VXI)** is a standard that was first established in 1987 by the VXI Consortium and has been formalized as IEEE standard 1155-1993. The goals of the consortium are to bring the following benefits to test and measurement scientists and engineers: increased test throughput, smaller instrument and system size, reduced cost, more precise timing and synchronization, and a standardized hardware system for programming and configuration. This

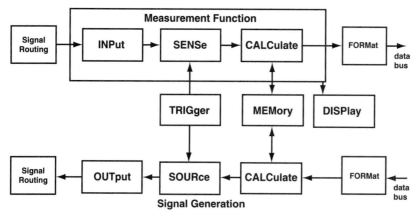

Figure 5.2   The SCPI instrument model. Each block, or subsystem, is represented by a command hierarchy.

standard is intended to take instrument systems into the next generation. Dozens of manufacturers are producing VXI instruments, interface equipment, and software, including Tektronix, Hewlett-Packard, Racal-Dana, Wavetek, and National Instruments.

VXI modules plug into a mainframe with up to 20 slots. The leftmost slot, called *Slot 0,* has special hardware features. The module that goes there is responsible for certain system resources: backplane clocks, trigger signals, and configuration signals. Typically, the Slot 0 module is either the system controller or is directly connected to an external system controller.

VXI is a modern computer architecture that fully supports multiple processors and shared main memory—up to 4 gigabytes, thanks to its 32-bit bus—Slot 0 may or may not be the *only* controller. Included in the VXI specification is a commander/servant hierarchy for module-to-module communication. For instance, a digitizer module can control a trigger generator, then directly store the acquired data in the main, shared memory for use by the controller. A subtlety of this specification is that you must maintain a quasirigid hierarchy when communicating amongst several modules. For instance, if A is a commander of B which is a commander of C, then A should only communicate to C through module B. If A and B try to talk to C simultaneously, then module C will get confused when it receives *interlaced* protocol packets from modules A and B. This really has implications only for software design, but they can be considerable; it must be considered and dealt with up front at the initial system design time.

An important feature of VXI systems is that most modules have no front panel controls, just I/O connectors and (sometimes) indicator lamps. A decade ago this would have been impractical because the complete burden of control is shifted to the software. But now, we have LabVIEW and the concept of virtual instruments where, as the National Instruments banner says, *The Software is the Instrument.* Instead of buying expensive specialty instruments, you combine a number of generic instruments. VXI was designed from the ground up to offer high performance in this software-dominated architecture. All you have to do is readjust your thinking with regards to solving instrumentation problems from real instrument to virtual instrument.

Overall, I'd say the manufacturers have been very successful in establishing the VXI standard. Sometimes cost comes into question. For small systems, the modules, mainframes, and interfaces are pretty expensive. The situation improves quickly for large channel counts; VXI can actually save you money on a per-channel basis. Also consider the fact that VXI system performance is hard to beat, the level of integration is very high, and the software support is excellent. The new **VXI *plug&play* Systems Alliance**, formed in 1993, goes beyond the basic VXI specification to coordinate the software interface for every module and controller marketed as *VXI plug&play compliant.* Such standardization benefits users like us by reducing development costs. What you get with a compliant instrument is

- An executable, virtual instrument front panel that allows you to start using the instrument immediately (Windows only, as a rule)
- Drivers for LabVIEW, LabWindows/CVI, and C, and as Windows DLLs callable from Basic and other applications
- A knowledge base file with online information about the device
- Standardized installation disks

The majority of VXI devices can be classified as either **register-based** or **message-based**. Register-based and message-based devices differ in their control interface. Some VXI devices are capable of both modes of control.

Register-based devices are programmed at a low level using binary information. You read and write directly to and from hardware registers on the device. The obvious advantage of this is speed: there is essentially no overhead at the destination as there would be for parsing command strings. The disadvantage is that each device requires customized manipulation of its registers and the programming is quite tedious. If you want to see what I mean by tedious, look at the driver for the Hewlett-Packard E1411A multimeter.

Message-based devices, in contrast, communicate at a high level using ASCII characters—just like GPIB. The strings you send to message-based devices must be in the device's specific language, but you don't have to be concerned with module-specific registers, binary transfers, and so on. Many VXI message-based instruments are SCPI compliant, which means you can use parts of drivers that were written for other SCPI instruments, most likely GPIB. The disadvantage of message-based instruments is that the data transfers are somewhat slower due to the overhead of creating, parsing, and sending ASCII messages.

There are several ways to configure the intelligence in a VXI system (Fig. 5.3). The simplest way is to use a **GPIB-to-VXI interface module** in slot 0. The interface module effectively puts a GPIB front end on a VXI chassis so that each VXI module appears to be a separate GPIB instrument. This is an advantage if you already understand GPIB and have a GPIB interface in your computer. The module takes care of all the resource manager duties to configure and initialize the instruments. Each instrument is assigned a unique GPIB address. Then, the GPIB-to-VXI interface translates GPIB messages to VXI message-

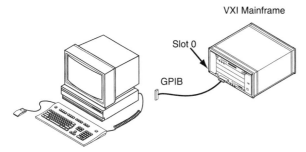

External Controller using GPIB communications
and an embedded GPIB-VXI interface module

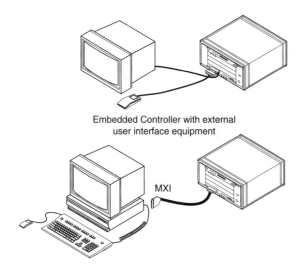

Embedded Controller with external
user interface equipment

External Controller using MXI and an
embedded VXI-MXI interface module

Figure 5.3   Three ways to run a VXI system: with an external controller using GPIB or MXI communications or with an embedded controller (which might be running LabVIEW).

based commands and passes them to the appropriate module. Your GPIB-based host computer simply communicates using standard GPIB protocol (read, write, poll, etc.). Additional functionality (such as access to register-based control and high-speed memory transfers) is available by addressing the GPIB-to-VXI interface module itself.

The second way to configure a VXI system is to use an **embedded controller**. An embedded controller is a custom computer designed specifically for VXI and packaged in a VXI module. It occupies a special slot—slot 0. Embedded computers offer the smallest physical size and the highest performance because they communicate directly with the VXI backplane. Many types of embedded controllers are available, most notably the 80486 and Pentium family. These are complete computers, including memory, disks, video display interfaces, network connections, and so on. Therefore, you can run LabVIEW on one of these machines, right in the VXI mainframe—a tidy, high-performance package. Naturally, you could also write your programs using other languages, but who would ever want to do *that?*

National Instruments invented a third configuration: **Multisystem Extension Interface (MXIbus)**, a high-performance parallel communication link that interconnects devices using multiconductor cables. MXI (pronounced *mixie*) works like a regular computer bus, but is cabled for high-speed communication between physically separate devices. It provides direct control and shared memory between devices and matches the data transfer rates of high-performance computers and peripherals. You plug a MXI interface board into your computer's backplane, and a MXI controller into Slot 0 of a VXI mainframe, and connect them with a special cable. Performance is nearly as good as that of an embedded controller. The latest version of the MXI standard, MXI-2, adds synchronous block mode transfers for higher throughput. MXI-1 and MXI-2 interfaces are available for PCI, ISA, NuBus, and SBus computer buses.

From the user's perspective, a desktop PC connected to the VXIbus via the VXI-MXI interface is identical to using a dedicated VXI embedded controller. The National Instruments NI-VXI bus interface software is a comprehensive software package for configuring, communicating with, and troubleshooting a VXI system. The NI-VXI bus interface software includes a **Resource Manager (RM)** program for initializing your system, a library of software routines for programming your system, a Resource Editor program (VXIedit) for configuring your VXI system resources, and a VXI Interactive Control program (VIC) for interacting with and troubleshooting the VXIbus.

The Resource Manager duties are part of the VXI specification and provide a surprisingly useful amount of functionality and configuration information to the developer. The VME specification provided no mechanism for allocating system resources, such as logical addresses or address space in the memory map. Thus, managing several modules' resources manually would quickly become burdensome and unwieldy. The RM program simplifies your life, especially if it has autoconfiguration, like the NI-RM. With it, one can determine the location and capabilities of every VXI module in the system at start up. This is often useful in, for example, ATE applications where having the proper combination of modules installed in the chassis at a particular time can be critical. The VXI examples include sample code for invoking the NI-RM at startup.

The choice of interface and the protocol for each module make a difference in overall performance. In particular, register-based operation may or may not be significantly faster than message-based operation. Using a GPIB-to-VXI interface under LabVIEW adds sufficient overhead to each transaction that it becomes the dominant factor in system performance. Meanwhile, embedded controllers require only microseconds to access a module, making register-based operation vastly superior. Lately, the best instruments are resorting to using message-based commands for configuration and register-based commands for acquiring data and performing control in real time. This is an excellent compromise between ease of programming for setup and performance where it counts.

To use LabVIEW to program a VXI system with either an embedded controller or a VXI-MXI interface, you will need the VXI VIs available with the LabVIEW VXI Development System. Registered LabVIEW users can order an upgrade to obtain the VIs free of charge, or you can download them from ftp.natinst.com. If you don't have the real VXI VIs, you can temporarily use the set of stub VIs which is included in the VXI driver library. The stub VIs have names identical to the real ones and allow you to build a hierarchy that will compile and run, but won't do any real I/O. Also included in the stub VI directory is a library called _VXITLS.LLB_ that you will want to add to your working VXI library. It contains some important and useful high-level utility VIs for opening and closing VXI instruments and for reading and writing messages. Later in this chapter I'll discuss the use of these utilities.

If you're lucky, you can use the VISA interface VIs to communicate with VXI instruments. Some of the VXI drivers were written with a VISA core, which is included with every copy of LabVIEW.

Parallel port interfaces (PC only).   Just about every IBM PC–compatible computer includes an 8-bit bidirectional parallel port, also known as a Centronics port, which you most often use for printers. There are two hardware versions available on newer PCs: the classic version and the **Enhanced Parallel Port (EPP)**. LabVIEW can access the parallel port by several techniques.

The Serial Port Read and Serial Port Write functions access the parallel port when you set the port number to 10 or above, with 10 referring to LPT1. There are some tricks, however, as pointed out by Brad Hedstrom in an article in _LTR_ (Hedstrom 1994). The parallel port expects three handshaking lines—BUSY, PE, and SLCT—to be grounded. Otherwise, LabVIEW will return an _out of paper_ error.

You can also use the **in port** and **out port** VIs which are intended for fast direct access to I/O-mapped hardware such as the parallel port. However, there are some disadvantages to this method. These low-level functions expect you to supply a base I/O address, which is not guaranteed to be the same from one machine to the next. Also, Inport and Outport can't be used under Windows NT due to that system's memory protection features.

Some instruments are designed for the parallel port and include a proper driver, usually in the form of a DLL that you can access with the Call Library function. An example is the DAQBook series from IOTech, which is the equivalent of a plug-in multifunction board. Be aware that you won't be able to use the port for printing as long as the instrument is operating. Printers don't know how to share the port, and they end up trying to print everything that comes down the line.

Learn about your instrument

You can't program it if you don't understand it. When I receive a new instrument for a driver project, I'm not always familiar with its purpose or its modes of operation. I fully expect that it will take several hours of experimenting with the controls and reading the user manual before I'm comfortable with the fundamentals. It's also a good idea to connect the instrument to some kind of signal source or output monitor. That way, you can stimulate inputs and observe outputs. I have a function generator, a voltmeter, and an oscilloscope, plus test leads and accessories to accommodate most instruments. Sometimes, I need to borrow more exotic equipment. Take my advice: don't spend too much time trying to write a driver without access to the actual instrument. You can certainly learn the basics of the command set offline, but it's amazing how soon you will have questions that can only be answered by exchanging some messages.

VXI instruments are a little more challenging to learn to use because they don't have front panels. Regular GPIB rack-and-stack instruments let you fiddle with the knobs, which helps a lot during the get-acquainted phase. VXI requires you to hook up the communications link, get it working, then use some kind of software tool to poke commands at the instrument and read the returned values. At least VXI *plug&play* instruments come with a compiled application that you can use for test purposes.

Obtain and study the programming manual. Some companies write programming manuals that border on works of art, as you will find with the newer HP and Tektronix instruments. Other manuals are little more than lists of commands with terse explanations. (I'll be a nice guy and leave those companies anonymous.) Pray that you don't end up with one of the latter. By the way, programming manuals are notorious for errors and omissions. I think it's because so few people actually *do* any low-level programming; they rely on people like us to do the dirty chore of writing a driver. If you find mistakes in a manual, by all means tell the manufacturer so it can fix them in the next revision.

Even the best manuals can be kind of scary—some complex instruments have really big manuals. What you have to do is skim through a couple of times to get a feel for the overall structure of the command set. Pay attention to the basic communications protocol, which is especially important for instruments that use the serial port. Also, figure out how the instrument responds to and reports errors. Take notes, draw pictures, and make lists of important discoveries.

Interactions between settings need special attention. For instance, changing from volts to amps on a DMM probably implies that the Range control takes on a different set of legal values. Sending an illegal range command may cause the meter to go to the nearest range, do nothing, or simply *lock up!* (Newer instruments are getting better about these sorts of things; in the old days, *rebooting* an instrument was sometimes required.) Your driver will need to arbitrate these control interactions, so note them as soon as they're discovered.

Determine which functions to program

Nothing is quite so overwhelming as opening the programming manual and finding out that your instrument has *4378 commands!* Obviously, you're not going to implement them all; you need to decide which commands are needed for your project.

If you are hired specifically to write an instrument driver, like those of us in the consulting world, the customer will probably supply a list of commands that you are required to support. If the list is long, you simply take more time, charge more money, and become rich. But if you are writing a driver for your own specific application, you probably don't have the time to develop a comprehensive driver package. Instead, you must determine the scope of the job and decide exactly which functions you need to implement. Here are some functions that most simple driver packages should support:

- *Basic communications.* The ability to write to and read from the instrument, with some form of error handling. Easy with GPIB or VXI, somewhat more complicated with serial devices.

- *Sending commands.* The ability to tell the instrument to perform a function or change a setting.

- *Transferring data.* If the instrument is a measurement device such as a voltmeter or oscilloscope, you probably need to fetch data, scale it, and present it in some useful fashion. If the instrument generates outputs such as a waveform generator, you need to write blocks of data representing waveforms.

- *Configuration management.*   The ability to load and store the settings of many of the instrument's important controls all at once. Some instruments have internal setup memory, while others let you read and write long strings of setup commands with ease. Others offer no help whatsoever, making this task really difficult.

- *Important controls.*   There are always a few basic controls that you simply *must* support, such as the mode and range on a DMM. More extensive drivers support more controls.

The basic question to ask is, will the user do most of the setup manually through the instrument's front panel, or will LabVIEW have to do most of the work? With VXI, the answer is easy: there are *no* front panel controls, so your LabVIEW driver has to implement most, if not all, of the available control functions. If I'm using LabVIEW on the test bench next to an oscilloscope, I manually adjust the 'scope until the waveform looks OK, then just have LabVIEW grab the data for later analysis. No software control functions are required in this case, and all I want is a Read Data VI. If the application is in the area of automated test equipment (ATE), instrument setups have to be controlled to guarantee that the setups are identical from test to test. In that case, configuration management will be very important and your driver will have access to many control functions.

Think about the intended application, then look through the programming manual again and pick out the important functions. Make a checklist and get ready to talk to your instrument.

Establish communications

After studying the problem, your next step is to establish communications with the instrument. You may need to install communications hardware (such as a GPIB interface board); then you need to assemble the proper cables and try a few simple test commands to verify that the instrument hears you. If you are setting up your computer or interface hardware for the first time, consider borrowing an instrument with an available LabVIEW driver to try out. It's nice to know that there are no problems in your development system. I'm going to assume these initial communications tests will use the simplest forms of communication, such as traditional GPIB and serial. More advanced methods of driver development are discussed later.

Looking into plug on
cable that plugs into
CPU jack.

Pin	Function
1	DTR
2	CTS
3	XMIT (-)
4	GND
5	RCV (-)
6	XMIT (+)
7	GPi *
8	RCV (+)

Serial cable
connections for the
Macintosh II and
Quadra series using
mini DIN-8 connector.

Signal levels are specified
by RS-422A.

* General-purpose input. Can be set in
software to be a second external clock.

Pin	Function
1	DTR
2	CTS
3	XMIT (-)
4	GND
5	RCV (-)
6	XMIT (+)
7	GPi *
8	RCV (+)
9	+5 V, .1 A

Serial cable connections for
Power Macintosh with
GeoPort mini DIN-9
connector.

NOTE:
DIN-8 connectors will fit into
and work with this jack.

* General-purpose input. Can be set in
software to be a second external clock, or
wake up CPU, or DMA handshake.

Wiring for DIN-8 (or 9) to DB-25 for RS-232 compatibility

DIN-8 male		DB-25 male
1	——————	4 RTS
2	——————	5 CTS
3	——————	2 XMIT
4 & 8	——————	1 & 7 GND
5	——————	3 RCV

Figure 5.4 Serial port wiring for Macintosh. Use an off-the-shelf modem cable for RS-232 devices. For custom cables, I usually butcher an ImageWriter cable because it has the DIN8 connector with all eight wires ready to go.

Hardware and wiring

Serial: Problematic because the standards are so often violated (non-standard standards?), serial hardware is more challenging to hook up than the other types. Figure 5.4 shows wiring diagrams for the older Macintosh models that use standard 8-pin DIN plugs and newer PowerMac models with a 9-pin GeoPort connector. It turns out the GeoPort is backward-compatible: in the middle of an 8-pin plug, they stuck in another pin (number 9). The ninth pin is a source of +5 VDC at 0.1 A for powering external devices, such as network interfaces and modems. For RS-232 applications, go to the computer store and buy a Macintosh modem cable, which has a DB-25 male at the free end. For RS-422 applications, start with an ImageWriter cable, and cut off one end. All eight wires are available, and you can connect them as required.

Figure 5.5 shows serial port connections for the very common IBM PC/AT version. Cables are available with the required DB-9 on one end

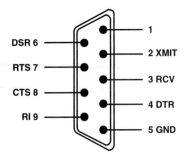

Serial cable connections for IBM compatibles using a DB-9 connector.

If you need a DB-25 connection, use a DB-9 to DB-25 adapter.

Figure 5.5 For IBM PCs using a DB-9 connector, you can get cables and connectors like this at your local electronics emporium. DB-9 to DB-25 adapters are also handy.

and a DB-9 or DB-25 on the free end to mate with most instruments. If you install a board with extra serial ports or with special interfaces (such as RS-422 or RS-485), special connectors may be required.

If you must extend the serial cable beyond a few feet, it is important to use the right kind of cable. Transmit and receive lines should reside in separate twisted, shielded pairs to prevent crosstalk (I usually use Belden 8723). If you don't, the capacitive coupling will yield puzzling results: every character you transmit will appear in the receive buffer.

Your instrument's manual has to supply information about connector pinouts and the requirements for connections to hardware handshaking lines (such as CTS and RTS). The usual wiring error is to swap transmit and receive lines on RS-232. RS-422 adds to the problem by permitting you to swap the positive and negative lines as well. One trick I use to sort out the wires is to test each pin with a voltmeter. The negative lead of the meter should go to the ground pin. Transmit lines will be driven to a nice, solid voltage (such as +3 V), while receive lines will be zero, or floating randomly. You can also use an oscilloscope to look for bursts of data if you can force the instrument to go into *talk* mode. A **null modem** cable or adapter usually does the trick for RS-232 signal mix-ups. It effectively swaps the transmit and receive lines and provides jumpers for CTS and RTS. Be sure to have one handy, along with some gender changers (male-to-male and female-to-female connectors), when you start plugging together serial equipment.

GPIB: You need some kind of IEEE 488 interface in your computer. Plug-in boards from National Instruments are the logical choice since they are all supported by LabVIEW and they offer high performance. External interface boxes (SCSI, RS-232, or Ethernet to GPIB) also use the same NI-488 driver. Cabling is generally easy with GPIB because the connectors are all standard. Just make sure that you don't violate the 20-meter maximum length; otherwise, you may see unexplained errors and/or outright communication failures. Incredibly, people have trouble hooking up GPIB instruments. Their main problem is making sure that the connector is pushed all the way in at both ends. Always start your testing with just one instrument on the bus to avoid unexpected addressing clashes.

VXI: If you are using a GPIB interface to your VXI equipment, refer to the preceding GPIB setup information. If you are using VXI-MXI, you need to make sure your MXI card is properly installed in your PC, and that your VXI-MXI interface is in slot 0 of your chassis. If you are using an embedded controller, you need only plug it into slot 0 and you are ready to boot.

Because there are no cables associated with the VXIbus (exception: MXI cable), connecting your instruments is generally a simple matter of setting unique logical addresses on each instrument and plugging them into your VXI chassis. Depending on your chassis, however, you may have to configure some jumpers. Some models (particularly older ones) require you to physically install or remove Bus Grant, Interrupt Acknowledge, and ACFAIL jumpers on the VXIbus backplane depending on whether or not you will be installing an instrument in a particular slot. The BG* and IACK* daisy-chain jumpers propagate the bus grant and interrupt acknowledge signals across unused slots or for slots with installed modules that do not propagate these signals. These signals are normally propagated by each installed module from the appropriate input pin BGxIN* or IACKIN* on its P1 connector to the appropriate output pin (BGxOUT* or IACKOUT*). The continuity of BG0*-BG3* and IACK* from slot 0 must be maintained for proper system operation. Normally, then, these jumpers should be removed for each slot in which a module is installed and replaced when the module is removed. Newer VXI chassis models have jumperless backplanes and automatically connect and disconnect these signals as you install and remove modules. Check your mainframe's user manual to see if you need to configure jumpers in your mainframe.

Protocols and basic message passing

GPIB: Figure out how to set the GPIB address of your instrument, or at least find out what the address is. From the instrument's manual, determine what the command terminator is (carriage return, linefeed, EOI asserted, or a combination), and pick out a simple command to try out. The **GPIB Read** and **GPIB Write** VIs both have an input called **Mode** that controls EOI, carriage return, and linefeed actions. Make sure that this mode setting is appropriate to your instrument. The default (Mode = zero) works for most instruments, in my experience. The **GPIB Test VI** shown in Fig. 5.6 is an interactive general-purpose GPIB instrument controller that you can use to test commands one at

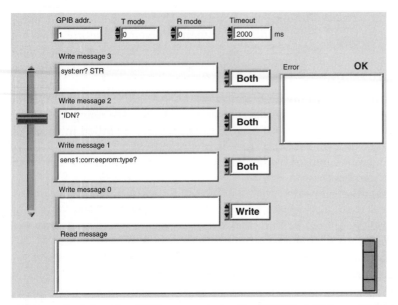

Figure 5.6   An interactive GPIB communicator, the GPIB Test VI is useful for testing commands. You can write and/or read as desired. It's easy to switch among the four messages for transmission.

 platform\ drivers\comm test vis\GPIB Test.vi

a time. For convenience, there are four write messages so you can quickly send a sequence of messages. Type in your commands, and move the big selector switch to the first command you wish to send. With the ring controls, choose *Write, Read,* or *Both* (write then read) and run the VI. See how the instrument reacts. Look at the **error** window and see if there are any unexpected errors reported.

On the first try, you may get a time-out because the GPIB address is incorrect. If all else fails, go through all the addresses from 1 to 31 (zero is the controller) until you get a response. You can use the **FindLstn** function (in the 488.2 library) to find all listeners on the bus; it returns an array of addresses. In really tough cases, you may have to use a GPIB bus analyzer (HP, Tektronix, National Instruments, and IOTech all make them) to examine the bus traffic. Always verify the command terminator. If the instrument expects the end or identify (EOI) signal or a special character and you don't send it, nothing will happen. The GPIB Test VI has numeric controls to set the read and write modes, which determine the EOI behavior.

Another classic hang-up with GPIB involves the issue of **repeat addressing**. When the controller (your computer) talks to another device on the bus (an instrument), the first thing the controller has to do is *address* the instrument. If the controller wishes to communicate with the same device again, it may take advantage of the fact that many (but not all) instruments remember that they are still addressed. If the instrument doesn't remember that it is still addressed, then you need to enable the repeat addressing action in your system's GPIB driver. On the Macintosh, this is a checkbox called *Repeat Addressing* in the NI-488 Control Panel. Under Windows, you set it from ibconf. On the Sun, it can't be set directly. On all platforms, you can use the **GPIB Initialize** VI to set repeat addressing. (GPIB Initialize also cures a variety of ills when your GPIB interface suddenly ceases to function.) I get calls all the time regarding drivers I've written that don't work reliably, and this is the first thing I tell the user to check (after seeing that the cable is plugged in and the address is properly set).

Serial: Unlike GPIB, serial instruments have little in common with each other since there are essentially no standards in use. Some instruments are individually addressed so that they can be used in multi-drop networks such as RS-422A. Others have no addressing and are designed for use on a dedicated link. Protocols vary from a GPIB-like ASCII message exchange to pure binary with complex handshaking. Study your instrument's programming manual and figure out what protocol it uses. If it's a simple ASCII-based scheme, you can use a terminal emulator application (the same one you use with a modem) to test out commands. Or, you can use the **Serial Test VI**, included on the CD-ROM. Like its GPIB cousin, you can write and read strings to and from the instrument. The VI includes serial port initialization and time-outs and error reports in case something is amiss. The underlying subVI, **Serial Port Receive Message**, watches for an optional end-of-message character in addition to a byte count.

platform\ drivers\comm test vis\Serial Test.vi

Be sure to set the basic serial parameters: speed (baud rate), bits per character, stop bits, parity, and XON/XOFF action. LabVIEW's **Serial Port Init** function sets these parameters and more. If you use a terminal emulator, you will have to do the same thing in that program. Check these parameters very carefully. Next to swapped transmit and receive lines, setting one of these items improperly is the easiest way to fail to establish communication.

Instruments that use those nasty binary protocols with handshaking are nearly impossible to test by hand. The problem is that they require you to type lots of escape codes (\ codes in LabVIEW strings) because most of the characters are non-ASCII, unsigned bytes. Also, there may be two or more message exchange phases for just one command, which is rather tedious. For these instruments, I try to muddle through at least one command just to find out if the link is properly connected, then plunge right in and write the LabVIEW code to handle the protocol. Hopefully, I'm 90 percent successful on the first try because debugging is difficult. Modifying the Serial Test VI is also a good way to get started. Add frames to the Sequence structure that do the operations your instrument needs.

As with GPIB, you can use a serial line analyzer (made by HP, Tektronix, and National Instruments) to eavesdrop on the communications process. The analyzer stores lots of characters and decodes them to whatever format you like (ASCII, hex, octal, etc.). This really helps when your driver *almost* works but still has reliability problems.

platform
drivers\\comm
test vis
VXI Test.vi

VXI: Setting up a VXI system is quite similar to a GPIB system; in fact, GPIB is the most frequently used communications interface for VXI. Again, like a pure GPIB system, start by making sure that you know your system configuration and that everything is properly connected. The utility VI, **VXI Test**, is just like GPIB Test, sharing most of the basic controls. The one difference is that you must select the communications platform, either GPIB or MXI.

In starting up the VXI system when using either an embedded controller or VXI-MXI, you must first run VXIinit. This program, included in the NI-VXI software, initializes the registers on your hardware. You may wish to make this program run automatically at system startup time. Next, you need to run the **Resource Manager (RM)**, whose responsibilities include identifying all devices in the system, managing the system self-tests and diagnostics, configuring address maps, configuring the system's commander/servant hierarchy, allocating interrupt lines, and initiating normal system operation. In LabVIEW, you should call the **InitVXIlibrary** VI at the start of your application. This VI is the application startup initialization routine and performs all necessary installation and initialization procedures to make the NI-VXI interface functional. This includes copying all of the RM device information into the data structures in the NI-VXI library. The **Open VXI Instrument** VI, found in the VXI Instrument Driver Support library, calls the InitVXIlibrary VI when you initialize an instrument driver; you should use the Open VXI Instrument VI in all VXI instrument driver initialization VIs.

When using the GPIB-VXI interface, you do not need to perform any of these steps. You do, however, need to identify the GPIB secondary address that the GPIB-VXI assigns to your particular VXI instrument. The Open VXI Instrument VI performs this secondary address query, storing the full GPIB address (primary + secondary) of your instrument in a global VI which returns an instrument ID. Using the VXI Instrument Driver Support VIs, you will pass in the instrument ID to communicate with your instrument. If you are not using the VXI Instrument Driver Support VIs and wish to communicate using the GPIB Write/Read primitives, you will still need to know the secondary address. You can obtain this by issuing the *LaSaddr? <la>* query to the National Instruments GPIB-VXI. For more information, consult your GPIB-VXI user manual.

Driver Design Techniques

Building instrument drivers is no different from any other LabVIEW project. All the techniques discussed in Chap. 4, "Building an Application," are fully applicable. You still need to define the problem, do some preliminary testing and prototyping, then follow good design and programming practices. Iterate on your design until you have something clean and reliable. Follow up with thorough testing and documentation, and you will have a versatile product that is easy to use and easy to maintain.

To help you get started in the right direction, I've assembled some recommendations and working examples that represent good driver design techniques.

Driver architectures

With every major release of LabVIEW, I've watched the general architecture of instrument drivers change significantly. Back in the time of LabVIEW 1, about the only I/O functions we had were GPIB read and write, and serial port read and write. Because the product was so new, driver architectures weren't really defined, and there was a degree of chaos in the blossoming driver library. With LabVIEW 2, we gained IEEE-488.2 functions and the important application note, *Writing a LabVIEW 2 Instrument Driver,* which gave developers directions regarding hierarchical program design. In the time of LabVIEW 3, those of us involved in driver (and DAQ) development standardized on **error I/O** as a common thread. It really cleaned up our diagrams, eliminated many Sequence structures, and unified error handling. VXI instruments appeared, as did the initial **VISA Transition Library (VTL)**. (VTL was implemented as a wrapper around the existing GPIB functions, rather than as native functions.) Many consultants launched their careers by writing drivers for VXI instruments, some of them using VTL as the foundation. Now, with LabVIEW 4, VISA is the primary platform for driver development—in LabVIEW and in many other instrumentation control languages.

The **Virtual Instrument Software Architecture (VISA)** is a driver software architecture developed by National Instruments to handle all forms of instrument I/O. It has been accepted as a standard for VXI by the VXI *plug&play* Alliance and is an integral part of LabVIEW. The principle is simple: a consistent interface to all instruments based on the concept of *open, read/write,* and *close,* much like file operations. When an instrument in opened, a **VISA session** identifier (like a file refnum) is created to uniquely identify that instrument. Data is exchanged in string format for message-based instruments or as words or bytes for register-level access as you might find in some VXI instruments. Events, such as triggers and service requests, are a part of the standard as is error handling. Learning how to use the VISA functions will save you time in the long run because you only have one low-level driver library to deal with.

LabVIEW 4 still gives you a choice when it's time to write a driver. You can jump directly into the VISA library, or you can work with the traditional GPIB, VXI, and serial libraries. I can think of a few reasons why you might stay with the older libraries. First, you are adapting an older driver to a new instrument, and it's easier to keep the old-style code than it is to convert to VISA. Second, you are writing a quick, informal driver for your own use, and you could care less about compatibility with future LabVIEW releases, portability, or other long-term goals. Third, you are more comfortable with the old-style functions, having learned them years ago. Fourth, there is currently more overhead associated with a VISA call than, say, a traditional GPIB function call (this situation may change in future releases). Because there is a great deal of legacy code around, and because some of you still want to operate in the old regime, I'll spend some time discussing traditional as well as VISA driver architectures. Eventually, though, I would advise you to make a total conversion to VISA because that's where LabVIEW is going, and performance and portability will be enhanced. Future versions will include compatibility VIs for GPIB and serial I/O, with VISA as the core, much the same way as VTL used to have GPIB as its core.

Modularity by grouping of functions

I've seen two extremes of **modularity** applied to LabVIEW instrument drivers: *too much* and *none*. Naturally, I'm going to preach for something in between. Too much modularity is where there is one subVI for every individual command. There are several problems with this approach. One, the interaction between control settings is really hard to arbitrate because each function has to query the instrument to see what state it's in, rather than just comparing a few control settings on the VI's panel. Two, the user has to plow through the directories and libraries, searching for the desired command. And three, there are just too darned many VIs, which becomes a nightmare for the poor person who has to maintain the library. Guess what happens when you find a mistake that is common to all 352 VIs? *You get to edit every single one of 'em.*

Having no modularity is the other extreme. You may find it in trivial drivers where there are only a couple of commands and hence, just one VI. In that case, it's probably OK. You may also find a lack of modularity in complex drivers written by a novice, in which case it's a disaster. There is nothing quite like a diagram with sequences inside of sequences inside of sequences that won't even fit on a 19-inch monitor.

In fact, these aren't really drivers at all. They are actually dedicated applications that happen to implement the commands of a particular instrument. This kind of driver is of little use to anyone else.

A better way to modularize a driver in LabVIEW is to build VIs that group the various commands by function. Like the SCPI model, you might have a VI for triggering functions, a VI for input channel selection, one for timebase setup, and so forth. Another model is the front panel of a modern oscilloscope. It has dozens of knobs and switches, but they are logically grouped, both by physical layout and (usually) by artwork on the panel. These intuitive control groupings make an instrument easier to learn and increase the operator's efficiency. That's how we want our LabVIEW drivers to work, too.

The top-level hierarchy for the HP54510A Digitizing Oscilloscope driver shown in Fig. 5.7 is representative of a moderately complex driver package. Of the hundred or so commands available, I selected the ones that seemed most useful and grouped them according to function. A typical function VI, from the Tektronix TDS-520A driver, is shown in Fig. 5.8. It concisely implements the basic capabilities of the instrument's delay trigger section. This VI is organized in canonical form and is typical of all good driver VIs. Note some of its important attributes: error I/O clusters, VISA session refnums as input and output common threads, and a simple dataflow diagram that builds a command string for transmission to the instrument. If a user needs to add a more advanced command, there is plenty of panel and diagram space to do so.

Moderate modularity yields to excess modularity when you have to implement miscellaneous commands. Sometimes a command doesn't fit with anything else, and it is normally used by itself—for instance, a master reset switch. It would be illogical to throw such a switch in with other unrelated functions.

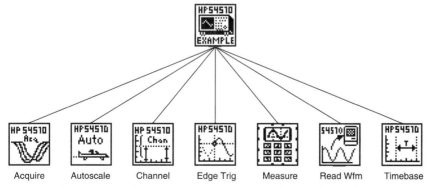

Figure 5.7 Hierarchy for the HP54510A Digitizing Oscilloscope driver. Commands are nicely grouped by function, making them easy to access.

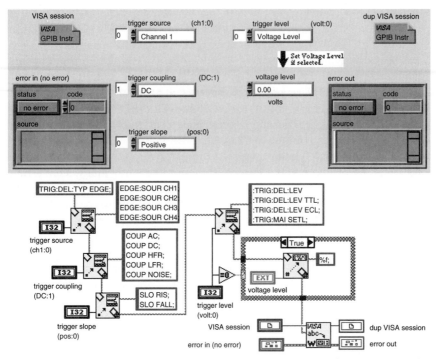

Figure 5.8 Front panel and diagram for the Tektronix TDS-520A Delay Trigger VI. This driver uses VISA to communicate via GPIB.

Read and write in the same subVI

On most instruments, commands have both a read and a write mode. That allows you to remotely set a control (such as the operator turning a knob) or to read the current setting of a control (such as the operator looking at a knob). Which action(s) should a driver VI implement? Like so many other design questions, the answer to this read/write problem depends on the application. (Note that we're talking about controls only; you almost always have to read data from the instrument.)

Many drivers are designed to write control settings (commands) but not to read back the settings. It's simpler to write such a program—it takes only about half the amount of programming—and it's generally sufficient for most applications. But there are some situations where you will want to read the settings. Occasionally, a setting needs to be read back because settings on some controls interact in a complex or ill-defined manner. It may be difficult to keep track of *all* control settings inside your program, in which case it's reasonable to go out and fetch the actual state of the instrument. Or, you may want to do a control readback as a safety measure to confirm that an important setting was accepted.

A truly complete driver package includes full read/write capability. This comes at the expense of time and effort in writing the package plus the extra code that has to be carried along. It is, however, the most versatile scheme. If you wish to implement both read and write modes in a single VI, here is a scheme that I've found effective.

The driver VI in Fig. 5.9 has a switch called **Set** that permits you to write a setting then read it back or to only read the current setting of the instrument's **Measure Mode** control. For this instrument, the command for the measure mode setting is *MEA* followed by a keyword, such as *REP* (repetitive). If you put a question mark after the command, the present setting is returned. In the diagram, you can see a Case structure controlled by the **Set** switch. If the switch is true (the *set,* or write mode), a GPIB command is generated that sets the instrument's measure mode. Then, the query command (*MEA?*) is appended to read the current state of the control, regardless of whether or not a new state was sent. The 370A/371A GPIB Comm subVI writes the command, then reads the response, which is decoded and displayed in a Ring indicator, **Measure Mode**. If the **Set** switch is False, new settings are not sent; only the *MEA?* command is sent, then the response is decoded as before.

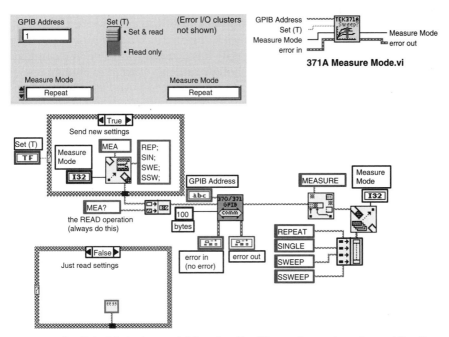

Figure 5.9 A call to this instrument driver function VI permits you to write a setting then read it back, or to only read the current setting. The 370A/371A GPIB Comm subVI handles all the communications.

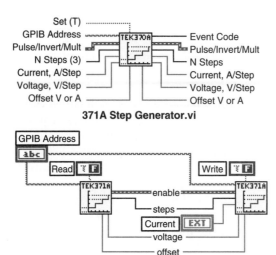

Figure 5.10 Applying one of the read/write VIs, the 370A Step Generator. Here, the user wishes to adjust a single control (current) while maintaining the values of all the others.

This VI only handles a single command, but the scheme is readily extended to support an arbitrary number of commands.

An application showing the versatility of the read/write technique, the 370A Step Generator, appears in Fig. 5.10. When a single function VI sets many controls, you normally have to keep track of, and send, all of the commands at once even though you only intend to change one of them. By using a read-only call to the subVI followed by a write-then-read call, you can avoid this problem. Because the outputs of the VI are an exact image of the inputs, you can wire them straight across, with the insertion of the particular control(s) that need to be updated. For large numbers of controls, consider grouping them in a cluster and using the Unbundle By Name and Bundle By Name functions to access the desired items. That saves wiring.

The alternative to reading and writing in the same subVI is to keep track of all the settings within your main program. You might use global variables as a storage location or perhaps a set of shift registers in a While Loop. Or, you can use the **Setup File Handler VI** that I wrote for this purpose. It maintains multiple setups in uninitialized shift registers and on disk for nonvolatile setup storage. The Setup File Handler is described in detail in Chap. 7, "Writing a Data Acquisition Program."

Many functions in one driver VI

Here's an efficient way to write a driver VI that reads and writes data for many individual commands. I came up with this architecture when developing TranspectorView, an elaborate driver/application for the

Transpector residual gas analyzer (RGA) manufactured by Leybold Inficon. An RGA is a mass spectrometer that is designed specially for analyzing trace gasses in vacuum systems. The Transpector uses a serial interface and has hundreds of commands, most of which are read/write (or query/update as the manufacturer calls it).

Because many of the commands exchange a single numeric value, it made sense to group them into a single driver VI that has a numeric input and a numeric output with an enum control to select the particular command. To make the driver more robust, I needed to enforce minimum and maximum limits. Also, each command required that the value be formatted in a particular way—various integer and floating point types—and most commands had units specified. Clearly, this is a lot of command-specific information. Writing one VI per command would be simple, but wasteful. Instead, I created a cluster array, called **Program**, containing all of this information. It's on the front panel, but normally scrolled off-screen because the user doesn't need to see it. Figure 5.11 shows the panel and diagram of one of the TranspectorView driver VIs.

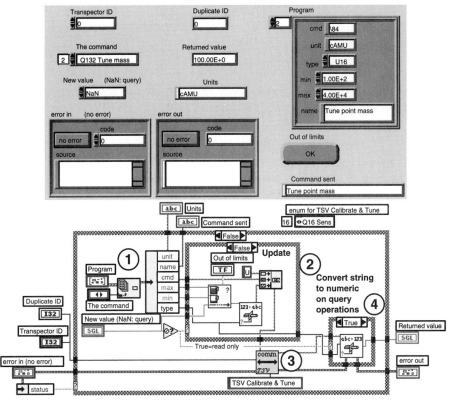

Figure 5.11   This TranspectorView driver VI can send or receive data for many commands. The Program cluster array determines attributes for each command.

Every VI in the TranspectorView hierarchy has standard flow-through parameters: a Transpector ID—a kind of refnum—and error I/O terminals. The command to be sent is determined by an enum control. On the diagram, I include an enum constant that is configured to match the front panel control as a convenience to the driver user. When you run the VI, it always reads the value for the selected command. If you do not wire to the **New value** input, its default value (NaN) tells the VI that you are only reading data. If you supply a value, that value is written to the instrument, and then the value is read back for confirmation.

Here's a rundown on the diagram:

1. The **Program** cluster array is indexed by the **Command** enum, then the cluster elements are broken out by Unbundle By Name. You could put all kinds of command-specific information in such a cluster.

2. A Case structure determines what kind of command string to format. For update (write) operations, it uses all of the items from the **Program** cluster to enforce limits on the **New value** and to format that value appropriately. For query (read) operations, a simple two-character command is generated.

3. The Trans Comm subVI sends the command and receives the response.

4. The numeric response is decoded.

If any errors are detected, they are returned in the **error out** cluster, which is the subject of the next section.

Error I/O flow control

Another characteristic of a robust driver is that it handles error conditions well. Any time you connect your computer to the outside world, unexpected conditions are sure to generate errors, and the instrument driver software is the place to trap those errors. Your response depends on the nature and severity of the error, the state of the overall system, and options for recovery.

The most straightforward error response is a **dialog box**. Assuming that an operator is always available to respond, the dialog box can present a clear statement about the error: who, what, when, where, and why. Dialogs are always appropriate for fundamental errors such as basic setup conflicts ("No GPIB board in slot 3") and for catastrophic errors where the program simply cannot continue without operator intervention ("The power supply reported a self-test failure and has shut down"). It's also helpful to receive informative dialogs when you are setting up an instrument for the first time. For complicated instrument systems, you might consider adding extra dialog boxes that can be disabled with a switch once the system is up and running. A new concept in driver development uses an **error query global variable** that stores a Boolean value for each instrument that determines whether or not errors should be checked and displayed. Each driver subVI reads this global variable and acts accordingly. By turning off error checking, you save some execution time. Using a global variable saves you from having to wire a *dialog error* Boolean to every driver subVI.

Automatic error recovery is used often in serial communications systems, particularly those that span great distances and/or run at high speeds. Local area networks typically have sophisticated means of error detection and automatic message retransmission. For a serial instrument, you may be able to attempt retransmission of data if a time-out occurs or if a message is garbled. Retransmission can be added to a state machine–based driver without too much trouble. If a message is invalid, or if a time-out occurs, you could jump back to the first frame of the sequence and send the command again, hoping for success on the second try. An important feature to include there would be a limit on the number of retransmissions; otherwise, you would end up in an infinite loop if the instrument never responds (Fig. 5.12). Such automatic actions should be limited to the lowest levels of a driver package, as in the example of a serial interface. Serious measurement and control applications are designed to report *any* error that is detected to guarantee data quality and system reliability. Therefore, you should think carefully before making your program so smart that it "fixes" or ignores potentially dangerous error conditions.

You can use error handling to promote dataflow programming and simplify applications of a driver package. As described in Chap. 4, "Building an Application," you create an error I/O cluster containing error information and pass it from one VI to the next. If an error is generated by one VI, the next one will be notified of the error and be able to take appropriate action. For instance, if a function that initializes the instrument fails, it probably makes no sense to continue sending commands. The error I/O chaining scheme can manage this decision at the driver

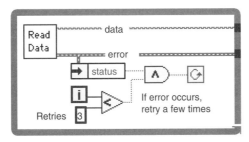

Figure 5.12 One way of implementing retry logic is to place a low-level driver subVI in a While Loop and check for errors. Remember to limit the number of retries.

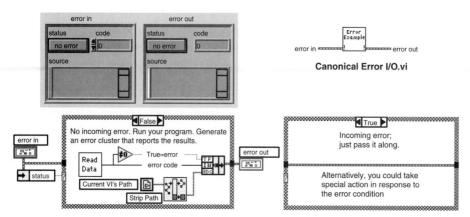

Figure 5.13   The Canonical error I/O VI. You can encapsulate any program inside the False case.

level, rather than forcing the user to add Case structures to the top-level VI. Most VIs respond to an incoming error by skipping all activity and simply passing the incoming error through.

A canonical VI with error I/O is shown in Fig. 5.13. The **error in** and **error out** clusters always appear in the connector pane as shown. Doing so permits all users of error I/O to line up their VIs in an even row. These clusters are available as standard controls in the Array & Cluster control menu. The cluster contents are always the same:

Item Number 1: **Status** (Boolean).   *True* means an error occurred. *False* implies a warning if the error code number is non-zero.

Item Number 2: **Code** (I32).   An error code number used for message generation.

Item Number 3: **Source** (string).   Contains the name of the VI calling chain that generated the error.

On the diagram, the **error in** boolean is tested, and if it's True, you may run a special error response program or simply pass the error along to the **error out** indicator and do nothing else. If no incoming error is detected, then it's up to your program to generate an error cluster of its own, depending on the outcome of the operation that it performs. Figure 5.13 shows a couple of tricks in case your subVI doesn't generate an error cluster. Generate the **Status** Boolean with the help of the Not Equal comparison function. Enter the name of the VI into the **Source** string automatically by using the Current VI's Path constant and the Strip Path function, both from the File I/O function menu.

Figure 5.14 is an example of error I/O in action in the driver for a VXI instrument. Error I/O is a part of the VXI utility VIs that are included in _VXITLS.LLB in the VXI instrument library. This technique makes

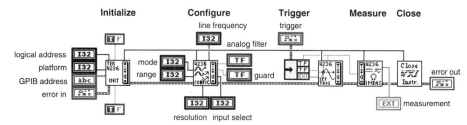

Figure 5.14 An example of error in/error out, the Tektronix VX4236 DVM, a VXI instrument. Note how clear and simple this application is, with no need for flow control structures. Error I/O is included in the VXI driver support, and you can build on it as shown here.

it easy to do your error handling in a consistent fashion all the way from the bottom to the top of the hierarchy. As you can see from the diagram, applying the Tektronix VX4236 DVM driver is very easy because of the use of error I/O.

At some point in your application, usually at the end of a chain of I/O operations, the error cluster is submitted to an error handler. The error handler decodes the *code* number into plain language and appends the *source* string. That way, the user will understand what the error is and where it came from without resorting to an error message table or a lot of debugging. The message is generally displayed in a dialog box.

Error codes are somewhat standardized. Zero generally means no error. Many error codes that are generated by LabVIEW are available from the **Error Ring** diagram constant. You choose it from the Additional Numeric Constants palette, drop it on the diagram, and choose one of the many available error codes by name. Its output is an I32 integer. For instance, selecting *Bad path* returns 71. Table 5.1 lists

TABLE 5.1 Predefined LabVIEW Error Codes for Generic Driver VIs

−1210	LabVIEW: Parameter out of range
−1220	LabVIEW: Unable to open instrument
−1221	LabVIEW: Unable to close instrument
−1223	LabVIEW: Instrument identification query failed
−1225	LabVIEW: Error triggering instrument
−1226	LabVIEW: Error polling instrument
−1228	LabVIEW: Error writing to instrument from file
−1229	LabVIEW: Error reading from instrument to file
−1230	LabVIEW: Error writing to instrument
−1231	LabVIEW: Error reading from instrument
−1232	LabVIEW: Instrument not initialized
−1234	LabVIEW: Error placing instrument in local mode
−1236	LabVIEW: Error interpreting instrument response
−1239	LabVIEW: Error in configuring time-out
−1240	LabVIEW: Instrument timed out
−1300	LabVIEW: Instrument-specific error

some of the error codes that are reserved for use with generic instrument driver VIs; there are many more codes defined by the VISA driver, as well. If you use one of these codes in your own drivers, the General Error Handler VI that comes with LabVIEW will be able to interpret them. (Codes from 5000 to 9999 are reserved for miscellaneous user-defined errors; they are not automatically interpreted by the error handlers.)

The **General Error Handler** utility VI (Fig. 5.15) accepts the standard error cluster or the individual items from an error cluster and decodes the code numbers into a message that it can display in an error dialog and in an output string. A useful feature of this handler is its ability to decode user-defined error codes. You supply two arrays: *user-defined codes* and *user-defined descriptions*. The arrays have a one-to-one correspondence between code numbers and messages. With this handler, you can automatically decode both predefined errors (such as GPIB and VXI), plus your own special cases. I would suggest using the

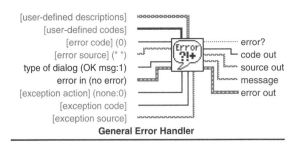

General Error Handler

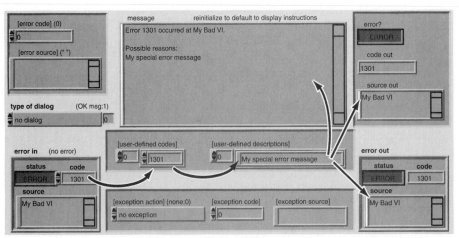

Figure 5.15 The General Error Handler utility VI is all you need to decode and display errors. The arrows indicate how the VI can decode user-defined error codes and messages that you supply, in addition to the predefined error codes.

codes starting at 1301 because those are reserved for instrument-specific errors.

Error I/O is popular for error handling and also because it simplifies diagrams by eliminating the need for many flow control structures. By all means, use it in all of your drivers and other projects.

Using a communications subVI—traditional methods

The simple act of exchanging messages with an instrument is not always so simple. Serial instruments are the most complex, often requiring that special headers, checksums, and end-of-message flags be added to the basic message. Many GPIB instruments require you to perform a Serial Poll to check for errors, then fetch the error code if one is detected. The list goes on and on. If you duplicate this programming in each of your driver's function VIs, it will be much harder to understand and maintain, not to mention that it will take up more disk space. Instead, create one or two **communications subVIs** that encapsulate this low-level programming. It's good programming practice —a proper use of modularity—that also enables you to easily update your driver if there is a change in a lower-level communications specification or technique. In this section, we'll look at some examples of *comm* VIs for GPIB, serial, and VXI instruments.

The coming of VISA has combined more and more communications functionality into high-level VIs. For instance, all forms of serial, GPIB, and VXI communications may be handled by just a few VISA functions that are built into LabVIEW—in much the same way that all file I/O operations are handled. The intent is to help you avoid having to work at the lowest levels of communications interfacing whenever possible. This is consistent with the high-level nature of LabVIEW. When you create your *comm* subVIs, you make the choice: VISA or something else. If you change your mind in the future, all you have to modify are the diagrams of the *comm* subVIs. Clearly, this kind of modularity pays off.

GPIB communications subVI. Let's start off with the most common type of instrument interface, GPIB, beginning with traditional GPIB functions. The typical steps that need to be performed when communicating with a GPIB instrument are:

1. Send a command using **GPIB Write** and check for GPIB bus errors.

2. If a response is expected, call **GPIB Read** with the expected number of bytes, and check for GPIB bus errors.

3. If the instrument is capable of reporting command execution errors, see if the last command generated an error.

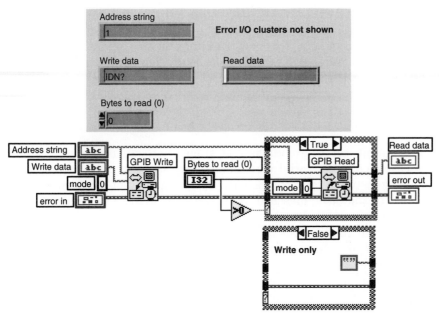

Figure 5.16 GPIB Write and GPIB Read combined into a general-purpose communications subVI.

GPIB Write (along with GPIB Read) is shown in Fig. 5.16. The main inputs are **address string**, containing the address (and subaddress, if required) of the target instrument, and **data**, a string containing the message to send. Errors are returned in the **error out** cluster. **Mode** determines how the message should be terminated as listed in Table 5.2. The default is zero, where the hardware EOI signal is sent with the last character in the string. Many instruments use this mode. If your instrument requires a carriage return or linefeed, you have the choice of using the appropriate mode, or you can explicitly append the right character(s) to each message and set the mode to zero or seven; the result will be the same.

TABLE 5.2 Termination Modes for the GPIB Write Function

0: Send EOI with last character of string
1: Append CR to string and send EOI with CR
2: Append LF to string and send EOI with LF
3: Append CR LF to string and send EOI with LF
4: Append CR to string but do not send EOI
5: Append LF to string but do not send EOI
6: Append CR LF to string but do not send EOI
7: Do not send EOI

GPIB Read is the complementary function, with similar attributes as shown in Fig. 5.16. The trick when reading data is to decide when the message is complete. GPIB Read can make that decision two ways: when the specified **byte count** is reached, when the EOI signal is asserted, or when a specified terminator character, such as CR, is received. The **mode** input specifies termination conditions other than reaching **byte count**. By default, **mode** is zero and termination characters are ignored. This mode has worked for every GPIB instrument I've ever programmed.

An interesting option is available on the GPIB Read and Write functions: you can choose to do I/O **synchronously** or **asynchronously** through a pop-up item on each function. Why should you care? Typically, it's preferable to do all I/O asynchronously because that implies independent, parallel execution of various parts of your LabVIEW hierarchy. Synchronous I/O prevents any other VIs or functions from executing until the I/O operation is complete. There is one situation when the synchronous mode may be required. If you use any GPIB drivers that were created with the LabWindows/CVI Function Panel Converter, be warned that those drivers are all synchronous because they use the Call Library function to access a DLL. In turn, the NI-GPIB driver is accessed through a synchronous call from the DLL. Because of the way the NI-GPIB driver is written, you cannot issue an asynchronous GPIB call from LabVIEW that might overlap in time with the synchronous GPIB call from the DLL. You can either make all your LabVIEW GPIB operations synchronous or make sure that you never cause the overlap situation to occur—perhaps by careful sequencing among drivers.

You can start with GPIB Read and GPIB Write, then add features or combine them into one, unified, **comm** VI, as I usually name it. The typical comm VI sends a command, then, if the number of bytes to read is greater than zero, it reads a reply message as shown in Fig. 5.16. Some instruments, especially older ones, require extra characters in every command message and/or they include extra characters in reply messages. In such cases, you can incorporate string handling functions in the comm VI. This technique cleans up the diagrams of all higher-level driver VIs and prevents duplication of code.

platform\
drivers\driver
utilities\
**Read SCPI
Error Queue.vi**

If you are programming a SCPI-compliant instrument, you can read errors from the standardized SCPI error queue. A driver support VI, **Read SCPI Error Queue**, polls the instrument and returns a string containing any error messages via the regular error out cluster. You could add this function to your comm VI, as well. Events are stored in a queue—oldest events are read out first—so you need to read events out after every command to keep from filling the queue with old, uninteresting events. The disadvantage of this technique is that it adds additional communications overhead. Read SCPI Error Queue checks the state of the Error Query Global Variable at each call, enabling you to turn off error checking dynamically.

Serial communications subVI. Just about every instrument that uses serial communications has its own unique protocol. As a result, it's hard to write a truly general-purpose communication subVI. What I *have* managed to do is put together a reasonably versatile model that you can use as a starting point for other serial instruments. The example is from the Eurotherm 808 Digital Controller driver, which you can get from the driver library or from the CD-ROM. The instrument is a single-loop PID (proportional integral derivative) controller used to regulate feedback loops in industrial processes. It has an option for RS-232 or RS-422 communications, permitting read/write access to almost all of its settings. After fumbling around with separate VIs for reading data and writing commands, I finally decided that a single *comm* VI, was the right thing to use. It turned out to be useful in other serial port projects as well. Its panel is shown in Fig. 5.17. I wrote it in LabVIEW 2 but I've kept updating it over the years. The current version (on the CD-ROM) includes everything I know about serial port drivers and is completely revised. There's also a VISA-based version that we'll look at a bit later.

The Eurotherm 808 protocol is fairly complicated (it's defined by ANSI X3.28 Rev. 1976), allowing you to do such things as avoid read-

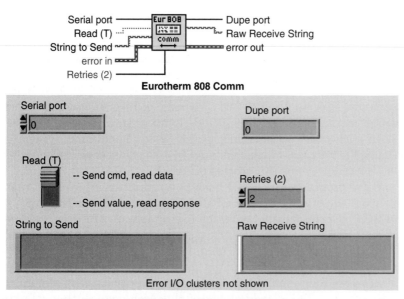

Figure 5.17 The Eurotherm 808 Comm VI is typical of serial port communications handlers. It arbitrates message passing and error responses.

dressing an instrument if you just finished talking to it. While this saves a few bytes in the message, it also complicates the heck out of the programming, so I decided not to bother with that feature. You may have to make similar decisions with the protocol for your instrument. This VI handles the lowest level of message exchange in a straightforward manner. Higher-level VIs take care of such things as formatting the command, tacking on a header, and adding a checksum. You could easily add those other tasks to this VI, if appropriate. The steps performed are as follows:

1. Flush the receive buffer in case extraneous characters are present.

2. Write the command string.

3. If the **Read** switch is set to True, a reply message containing data is expected. Read one character at a time, appending it to a string carried in a shift register, until an end-of-message character is encountered.

4. If the **Read** switch is set to False, just one character is expected, indicating acknowledgment of the command. Read and verify that character.

5. To close out the message exchange, send an end-of-transmission character. Flush the receive buffer in case extraneous characters are present.

6. If an error has occurred, retry the message exchange by jumping to step 1 (Initialize). Keep retrying until **Retries** is reached, then exit and report any errors.

In the old version of this driver, discussed in the first edition, I used a **state machine**, a technique described in Chap. 4, "Building an Application." It permits you to jump around between steps in the program depending on the conditions at the end of each step. The state machine technique is powerful and flexible—just the ticket for the more difficult serial port drivers. However, after recent development efforts, I decided to use a more straightforward sequential-style driver where the steps of the protocol are implemented from left to right on the LabVIEW diagram.

Figure 5.18 shows the diagram for the Eurotherm 808 Comm VI. Learn from it, copy it, and adapt it as you see fit. Messages are formatted by higher-level VIs, though it might be possible to include the formatting in this VI. Typical of serial instruments, Eurotherm uses a binary message format with start and end-of-message characters and a data checksum for error detection.

First, the serial port receive buffer is flushed in case any extraneous characters are present. Second, the **String To Write** is written to the

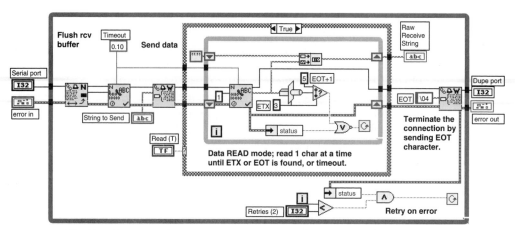

Figure 5.18 The Eurotherm 808 Comm VI, a robust serial port communications handler. Special serial I/O subVIs were written to add error I/O to the regular VIs supplied with LabVIEW.

serial port. Third, data is read from the port one character at a time until an end-of-message is detected or a time-out occurs. Finally, a termination character is sent to the instrument.

I wrote some special subVIs for this driver that are very helpful. If you look at the serial VIs, they do not include error I/O, so a *wrapper* VI that adds error handling makes sense. In the Eurotherm driver library, you will find the **Bytes At Serial Port+** and **Serial Port Write+** VIs. Another very important fact about the serial library is that, unlike GPIB Read, there is no time-out on Serial Port Read. Instead, you should use the LabVIEW example VI, **Serial Read with Timeout** or **Serial Port Receive Message**, which is included on the CD-ROM, or the hopped-up version of Serial Port Read With Timeout that I included in the Eurotherm driver (it has error I/O). Otherwise, any communications failure will cause your VI to hang. The trick used in these utility VIs is a call to **Bytes At Serial Port**, which returns the number of bytes in the serial port receive buffer. If and only if there is one or more bytes in the buffer, Serial Port Read can be called.

After flushing the read buffer and writing the command, a Boolean Case structure determines whether a data message is expected (True case, shown) or if a simple one-character acknowledgment is expected (False case, not shown). For data messages, there are two valid termination characters (EOT and ETX). Again, the simple serial port VIs do not include built-in termination character detection, so a While Loop is required where one character at a time is read and evaluated. The received message string is assembled in a shift register. There is a great deal of overhead in this process since there is one I/O call per

 platform\ drivers\driver utilities\Serial Port Receive Message.vi

character. On the Mac, that takes about 0.5 ms. On the PC, it's about 3 ms. If this is excessive, your only alternative is to wait until the expected amount of data is available (periodically call **Bytes At Serial Port**), then read a large amount of data into a string, and finally sift through that string to locate the valid part of the message. For the Eurotherm controller, the messages are quite short and the controller is not normally called very frequently, so the performance is adequate. After reading the message, a termination character is sent.

If errors are detected, retry logic is triggered, the overall While Loop continues to run, and the entire process repeats as if the VI were being called again. A limited number of retries are permitted; it is uncool to end up in an infinite loop whenever an error occurs!

Flushing the receive buffer. A problem that often occurs with serial drivers is that the incoming data buffer may fill with characters that you don't expect. Then, when you send a command to the instrument and sit around waiting for a special response character, what you will actually be reading is old data. A solution is to begin the sequence of events with the simple piece of code shown in Fig. 5.19. This is a *flush buffer* procedure that reads all the bytes that are present in the serial port receive buffer. After flushing, go ahead and send a command, and you will have more confidence that the data you receive is in response to that command. In the Eurotherm driver, the flush is done in the Write and Error frames. This empties the buffer before and after every message exchange, guaranteeing a clear buffer for the next message exchange.

The Eurotherm driver is a bit slow because of the single-character read operations which add lots of overhead. This becomes a serious problem when the messages are long. One improvement you could make is to read lots of characters into an intermediate buffer, then parse out messages from that buffer. Albert Geven (geven@natlab. research.philips.com), a member of the Philips Research, Test & Measurement Automation team, implemented such a serial library for gen-

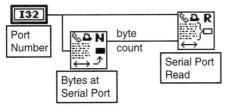

Figure 5.19 A simple bit of code that flushes the serial port buffer. Use it before sending any commands or any time that you want to make sure the buffer has been emptied.

eral use. He includes error I/O and all the usual serial functions. You can get his serial library from ftp.pica.army.mil. Some instruments send a header containing a value that tells you how many bytes follow. In that case, you may only have to read a few bytes in single-character mode, then tell the serial port read VI to return the expected number of characters. The Transpector is such an instrument, and reading its large buffers is very fast.

The ultimate way to improve performance is to write a system-level driver such as a DLL for Windows, DRVR resource for Mac, or driver for UNIX. Such a driver would run continuously in the background with high priority and would take care of all the low-level message passing. LabVIEW could then call the driver—probably through a CIN or Call Library node—to exchange data with the driver. Please note that this is a significant development effort for serious programmers only! The performance, however, is much better than we can achieve with a simple LabVIEW diagram. National Instruments is considering development of a toolkit that could make the programming easier, but even so, it's going to require experience with C.

VXI communications subVIs.   The VXI standard came along later in the life of LabVIEW, and as a result the VXI driver library is highly standardized with a well-designed hierarchy. (Older GPIB instrument drivers could benefit from insertion of these new standards, but it would be rather costly to rewrite all those old drivers.) A communications subVI for a word-serial VXI instrument is quite similar to the GPIB example previously discussed. Register-based instruments can be more complex, but you may find enough similarity between commands for your instrument to allow the design of a *comm* subVI.

Given the complexity caused by the number of controller options, VXI functions, and instrument types available to VXI users, National Instruments has developed a set of high-level VIs for use in VXI instrument drivers to help simplify development. The VXI Instrument Driver Support Library is controller-independent and works with both message-based and register-based VXI instruments. Instrument drivers built from the VXI Support Library work with National Instruments PC-based VXIpc embedded controllers, MXI interfaces for the PC AT, EISA, PS/2, Sbus, and Macintosh computers, and the GPIB-VXI Slot 0 controller. The LabVIEW VXI Instrument Driver Support VIs are distributed with the LabVIEW VXI Instrument Library. You must have these VIs in order to use the LabVIEW VXI instrument drivers.

In order for an instrument driver to communicate with a particular VXI instrument, it must know the logical address of the instrument and also the type of controller that is serving as its master. In the case of VXI-MXI or embedded controllers, VXI word serial communication is required, while in the case of GPIB-VXI controller, GPIB reads/writes are needed. Generally, the type of I/O operation required does not affect the contents of the actual message sent to the instrument; therefore, the same instrument driver message building routines can be used with either Word Serial or GPIB communications. With that in mind, to make an instrument driver work with either type of controller, at least three controls are required on the front panel to specify the information needed to address the instrument: a control that identifies the controller as one requiring either NI-VXI or NI-488 calls, a control for the unique logical address of that particular instrument, and a control for the GPIB primary address of the GPIB-VXI and the secondary GPIB address it assigns to the instrument (in the case of GPIB-VXI controlled instruments). Not only would these controls take up a significant amount of front panel space, but users would be required to remember a great deal of information to communicate with their VXI instruments. A solution to this problem is an instrument identifier (much like a file refnum) through which the driver VIs can obtain the required instrument information.

To use the concept of instrument identifiers with VXI, you must first run the **Open VXI Instrument** VI to open the instrument and generate an instrument ID. For subsequent operations with the instrument, only this instrument ID is needed. In other words, one addressing control (instrument ID) replaces the three controls previously needed for addressing. Information about each instrument is stored in a global storage VI, **VXI Instrument Global**, which is called by the **VXI Receive Message**, **VXI Send Message**, **VXI Read Register**, and **VXI Write Register** VIs. One additional step is required: you must call the **Close VXI Instrument** VI to take an instrument out of VXI Instrument Global when you are finished. These VIs and more are included in the VXI Instrument Driver Support Library in vxitls.llb.

The VXI communications library is highly ordered and is easy to understand and use. Figure 5.20 is a simple VXI *comm* VI that calls VXI Send Message and VXI Receive Message for word serial instruments. At the highest level of the hierarchy, you call Open VXI Instrument, then call your individual driver subVIs (with VXI Comm at their core), and finally Close VXI Instrument. Since error I/O is used throughout the hierarchy, you can pass the error cluster to the General Error Handler at the end of the chain to report any errors that might have occurred. For register-based instruments, the VXI utilities library also includes VXI Read Register and VXI Write Register to neatly encapsulate register I/O, if that approach makes sense for your instrument.

VISA—The new solution

VISA is the New Age of LabVIEW instrument drivers and is the preferred development platform for new projects. In fact, if you want to

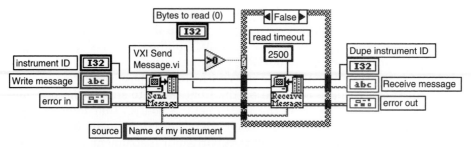

Figure 5.20   A communications subVI for VXI word serial instruments. It uses VXI Send and Receive Message VIs in a manner similar to the GPIB example in Fig. 5.16.

formally submit a driver to the LabVIEW Instrument Driver Library, it *must* be VISA-based. Even though VISA requires you to use a separate set of low-level VIs, all the knowledge that you have of GPIB, serial, and VXI drivers is still applicable. In principle, you can replace GPIB Write in your old driver with VISA Write, change a few connections, and your driver will work just like before. Of course, there are other procedural differences, and that's what we'll look at here.

If you're creating a driver from scratch, please start with the **instrument driver template VIs**. They are located in the directory examples\instr\insttmpl.llb and are described in detail in the *LabVIEW I/O VI Reference Manual*. The template VIs include such operations as Initialize, Close, Reset, and communications VIs for message-based and register-based instruments. Icons are standardized, too (there's a whole set of VIs in the library examples\instr\insticon.llb that you can copy for other functions). You open a template VI, edit as required, and save it with a customized name. The default name starts with *PREFIX* which you should replace with a mnemonic for your instrument, such as *TEK380*. This technique will save you much time and promotes standardization among drivers. Most of the newer drivers in the library, especially VXI, are based on these templates.

Getting connected to VISA.   Before you can actually communicate using VISA protocols and functions, you must be sure you have the VISA driver installed in your system. There is an **NI-VISA Installer** included in the LabVIEW distribution kit that you must run in addition to the regular LabVIEW installer.

All of the VISA functions are accessed through the **Instrument I/O>>VISA** function palette. The basic procedure for doing instrument I/O with the VISA library is as follows:

1. Open a session with the instrument by calling **VISA Open**. It returns a **VISA session** refnum that is required by all subsequent

VISA function calls. This is much like opening a file and obtaining a file refnum.

2. Use **VISA Attribute nodes** to read or change parameters associated with a VISA session. For instance, you can set serial port speed and stop bits or set the GPIB termination character. This special attribute node is also found on the VISA function palette. It's similar to normal attribute nodes, but you have to wire it to a VISA session.

3. Use **VISA Read** and **VISA Write** for conventional string-based message exchange. This is just like traditional GPIB, serial, or file I/O functions.

4. Use **VISA Close** to terminate communications and dispose of memory associated with a VISA session.

**platform\
drivers\driver
utilities\
Find VISA
Resources.vi>**

The first thing you should do is find the devices associated with your particular interface. On the CD-ROM I've included a handy VI, **Find VISA Resources**, that makes it easy. You can choose serial, GPIB, VXI, or all available devices. If it's out there, this VI will find it. Even better, it returns the complete and correct **resource name** for each device. A valid resource name is required when you call VISA Open. I don't know about you, but I can never get the syntax right on these strings. Some examples you might see are

ASRL1::INSTR—Serial instrument on serial port 1.

GPIB::3::1::INSTR—GPIB instrument at primary adr. 3, secondary adr. 1.

GPIB-VXI::2::INSTR—VXI device at logical adr. 2 with GPIB-VXI controller.

Now that you have the name of the device, you can call VISA Open. One more bit of information will be required, however. Each VISA session has an associated **class**. A class can be serial, GPIB, VXI, or GPIB-VXI (there could be more in future versions). It tells the VISA driver what kind of I/O operations are associated with the session (Fig. 5.21). To set the class, you wire a **VISA Session** control (from the Path & Refnum control palette) to VISA Open, then pop up on the Session control and select the VISA class. If you think about it, this could be pretty slick when you change from, say, GPIB-VXI to an embedded VXI controller. Just change the class, and you're ready to run. The default class is INSTR, and it is actually a superclass containing all the others. For subVIs, you can use this default with the knowledge that any session class can be wired to it without error. The only time you need to set the class is for the VISA Open function and to limit the number of choices available for a VISA Attribute node.

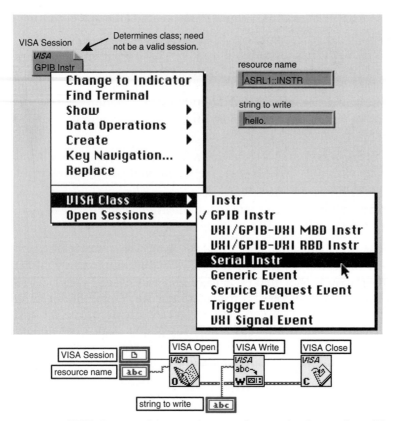

Figure 5.21 VISA Open requires a session control to set the class and a valid resource name. Its session output is wired to all subsequent VISA functions.

The VISA Open function only needs to be called once for each instrument, and you can leave the instrument open forever, unless you want to free up a few bytes of system resources by calling VISA Close. You should open the instrument from an initialization VI in the driver hierarchy and wire the VISA session to other communications VIs. The initialization VI should also take care of any special VISA attribute settings, such as serial port speed, and it should also perform any instrument initialization operations, such as resetting to power-up defaults or clearing memory.

Rule: Every VISA-based driver VI should include, as a minimum, four basic terminals: VISA session in and out, and error in and out. The template VIs enforce this rule. I usually choose the eight-terminal connector pane for simple driver VIs or the 12-terminal one for more complex VIs. Either one makes the session and error I/O terminals line up nicely with 98 percent of the other driver VIs you'll ever see.

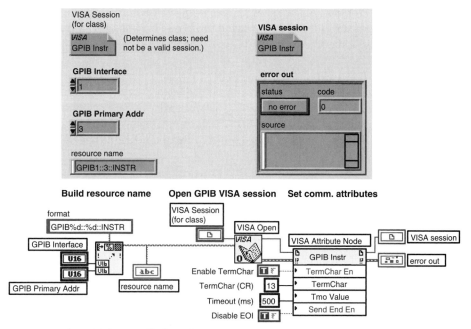

Figure 5.22   An initialization VI for a GPIB instrument with VISA communications. I used Format Into String to build the resource name. VISA Attribute node is only required to change default communications settings.

GPIB drivers with VISA.   To communicate with a GPIB instrument using VISA, start out with an initialization VI like the one shown in Fig. 5.22. For this example, I used the **Format Into String** function to build the resource name for VISA Open. This simplifies the user interface by requiring only the GPIB interface board number and the GPIB primary address. (Seriously, how many casual users could remember to type *GPIB1::3::INSTR*?) Use the pop up on the VISA session control to set the class to *GPIB Instr.* You must also set the class on the VISA session indicator or you'll get a broken wire.

The VISA attribute node is inserted if you need to change the default communication parameters. I selected a few of the common ones related to message termination. Note that there is no distinction between read and write termination action. The good news is that most instruments are symmetrical: they require the same termination character and EOI action for both read and write operations. If your instrument is asymmetrical, you must include a VISA attribute node before each VISA Read and VISA Write function to switch the appropriate termination attributes.

Once the session is opened, you can use VISA Write and VISA Read in the usual manner to exchange string-based messages with the instrument. You can of course write a *comm* VI for instruments that need extra characters added or removed from each message. And all driver VIs should have the standard VISA session and error cluster inputs and outputs.

Serial drivers with VISA.   Serial instruments work even better with VISA than they do with the traditional serial VIs because there is a bit less overhead and because VISA ASRL (serial) has read time-outs built in! (This has long been a shortcoming of the traditional serial VIs and I'm glad a solution is at hand.)

To try my hand at this new driver development technique, I wrote a VISA version of the driver for that old war horse, the Eurotherm 808 controller. Figure 5.23 shows the panel and diagram of the Eurotherm 808 Initialize VI. It's quite similar to the GPIB initialization VI, except for the important communications attributes. There is a key difference between traditional and VISA serial port specifiers: VISA ports start with *one,* while the old ones start with *zero.*

 **platform\ drivers\ eurotherm 808\ euro808v.llb**

Take a look at the rest of the Eurotherm 808 driver on the CD-ROM and you'll see how easy it is to implement VISA serial drivers. I spent a good deal of time making the traditional and VISA versions of this driver identical as far as possible. As a result, I simply replaced the Serial Port Read With Timeout VI with VISA Read and all the connec-

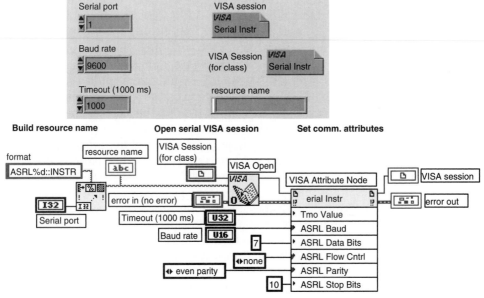

Figure 5.23   VISA version of the Eurotherm 808 Initialize VI.

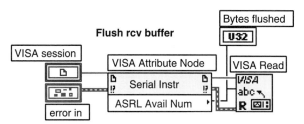

Figure 5.24 Flushing the serial port receive buffer, VISA-style.

tions matched. One other small change has to be made: Bytes At Serial Port VI is replaced by a VISA Attribute when you need to flush the receive buffer, as shown in Fig. 5.24.

VXI drivers with VISA. VISA was designed with VXI as its major application, so every imaginable feature is included. You can access the advanced memory manipulation operations of VXI, exchange register-level data, and read resource information. The newer drivers in the VXI library are VISA-based, so you have a gold mine of examples to peruse when developing your own drivers. In fact, there is no reason for starting from scratch on VXI drivers; just locate a similar instrument and make the needed modifications. The instrument driver template VIs—built on VXI with VISA—are also an excellent place to start development.

For an example of a register-based VXI instrument with both traditional and VISA drivers, look at the HP1411 (VISA) and the HPE1326 (traditional VXI) drivers. The example VIs are identical except that the VISA instrument resource descriptor (a string control) replaces three controls on the older driver: platform, GPIB address, and logical address. Program flow of the driver proceeds in exactly the same manner as other VISA instruments, starting with VISA Open, followed by various VISA register I/O functions, and finally VISA Close.

By now, you should be seeing signs of the overall consistency and universality of VISA as a driver architecture. The traditional instrument I/O functions in LabVIEW will soon be built on top of VISA as a means of backward compatibility. To obtain maximum advantage in terms of performance and simplicity, plan to write your new drivers with VISA as the core and the template VIs as the model whenever possible.

Timing, handshaking, and triggering

What happens when your 500-MHz 986ZX computer sends a bunch of commands in rapid-fire mode to a poor, unsuspecting instrument? Will the commands be buffered up in high-speed memory for later processing? Or will the instrument simply halt and catch fire? What if there is a communications error? Instruments are *not* infinitely fast—they require some time to respond to commands—and your driver must synchronize itself to the needs of the instrument. Timing and handshaking techniques, both hardware and software, are available and necessary to manage these situations.

GPIB handshaking.   An important feature of the IEEE 488 standard is that the exchange of individual bytes is arbitrated by hardware **handshaking** signals. The talker makes sure that the listener is ready to receive the next byte. The talker then places the data on the bus, tells the listener that the data is ready, and then waits for an acknowledgment—and all of this is done by hardware. Therefore, no matter how fast or how slow the various devices on the bus may be, you have reasonable assurance that the individual bytes will be successfully transmitted. Only in cases where there is an electrical problem with the bus will you see low-level communications errors. Using cables that are too long or poorly shielded may corrupt the signals. Nevertheless, low-level timing is not your problem, unless you happen to be designing GPIB interface hardware.

As an aside, this issue of data integrity on GPIB raises some interesting questions. Please note that there is no hardware verification for data integrity in the GPIB standard. Thus, there is a potential for data corruption, and your run-of-the-mill driver software will never know it, particularly if the corrupted data is inside of a waveform or binary data stream. (Invalid commands are another story: instruments reject them.) You can cause such errors to occur—I have—by using defective cables and improperly installed GPIB extenders. If the error rate is fairly low (say, one bad bit in 10,000,000), *most* information will be transferred intact. But occasionally, there will be an (undetected?) error. How can you fix this problem? The only way I know of is adding error detection or correction bytes to the data stream. A checksum or an exotic cyclic redundancy check (CRC) code are likely candidates. Note, however, that the code must be generated and decoded by all devices on the bus. Seen any oscilloscopes with a CRC byte in the waveform data? I haven't. Apparently, this problem will not soon be solved, at least for older communication standards like GPIB. Just be aware that it exists, and if you are working on a *really* critical system, be prepared to justify your choice of communication technique.

Even though the individual bytes make it through, low-level communication problems can still occur. The culprit is usually the EOI signal and special termination characters that may be required to flag the end of each message. The **mode** controls on GPIB Read and GPIB write, and the VISA Attribute Node termination items determine this end-of-data behavior. You should check your instrument's manual to find the correct mode setting. Sometimes a bit of experimentation with the GPIB Test utility VI can clear up any uncertainties.

Another catch is that some instruments require repeat addressing as described earlier in this chapter. Make sure you clearly specify in your driver documentation what the proper setting is for repeat addressing and/or unaddressing.

Sending commands at the wrong time can be a problem. Any command that initiates a time-consuming operation has the potential for putting the instrument offline for awhile. For instance, if you tell your instrument to perform an extensive self-diagnostic test, it may ignore all GPIB activity until the test is completed, or it might buffer the commands for later execution. Also, the *rate* at which commands are sent can be important. Most instruments permit you to send many commands in one string. The question is, will all the commands in the string be received before the first one is executed? Most times, the answer is yes, but there may be dire implications if the instrument ignores half the commands you just sent. Experience indicates that testing is the only way to be sure.

There are two ways to solve these timing problems. First, you can add delays between commands by sending them one at a time in a sequence structure where every other frame of the sequence contains a LabVIEW timer. A dataflow alternative is to use the **Wait+ (ms)** utility VI (from the function palette DAQ>>Counter>>Advanced Counter), which has error I/O so it's easy to link it into a sequence of GPIB operations as shown in Fig. 5.25. The second method is to find out if the previous operation is complete. If you enable **service requests (SRQ)** for your instrument, you can use the **Wait for GPIB RQS** VI for traditional GPIB drivers to tell you when the operation is complete. For VISA-based GPIB, use **Wait for RQS**, from the VISA>>Event handling function palette. This technique is often used with digital oscilloscopes; simplified examples are shown in Fig. 5.26. (This figure also shows the symmetry between traditional GPIB and VISA drivers. You can see how easy it is to convert to VISA.) If your instrument is SCPI-compliant,

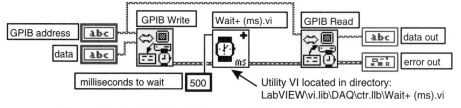

Figure 5.25 Insert this handy delay VI between GPIB operations to avoid timing problems with some instruments.

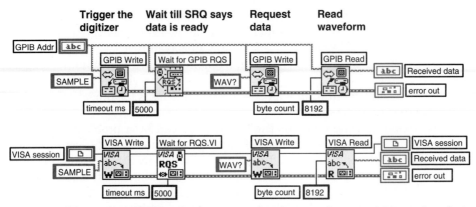

Figure 5.26 Waiting for a GPIB service request synchronizes waveform acquisition and readout. Top example is traditional GPIB, bottom example is VISA GPIB. Digitizer is triggered, then the VI waits until SRQ is asserted before requesting and reading data.

there is an Operation Complete (*OPC?) command that gives you a status report.

An important and useful aspect of SRQ-based synchronization is that you can wait for multiple SRQ events from multiple instruments in parallel. For instance, you could duplicate the code in Fig. 5.26 for as many digitizers as you have. Since the Wait for RQS functions and VIs are reentrant, and they know which GPIB address the SRQ must come from, each instance of the VI will hold off until the *correct* instrument asserts SRQ.

Serial handshaking. Serial instruments use various combinations of software and hardware techniques to perform handshaking. Unlike GPIB, there are no standardized triggers, per se, though some instruments simulate this behavior. As usual, it's important to find out what methods your instrument understands.

Hardware handshaking uses the extra control lines that are part of the RS-232C standard. Using the **Serial Port Init** VI, you can configure LabVIEW to support Clear to Send (CTS), Ready to Send (RTS), Data Terminal Ready (DTR), and Data Set Ready (DSR) handshaking. CTS/RTS handshaking is the most common, and the Serial Port Init VI refers to this as the normal hardware handshaking. If CTS handshaking is enabled, the remote device asserts CTS whenever it is ready to receive data. This is also known as input handshaking. If DTR handshaking is enabled, the computer asserts the DTR line when it is ready to receive data. This is also known as output handshaking. Wiring for a typical CTS/DTR arrangement is shown in Fig. 5.27. I've found very few commercial instruments that use this protocol. By and large, the

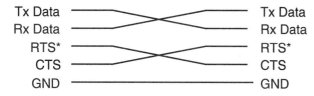

*Some devices use DTR instead of RTS.

Figure 5.27 Typical wiring for an RS-232 serial device using null-modem hardware handshaking. Just to make things interesting, some devices use RTS and some use DTR for a similar function. Hopefully, your manuals sort this out.

manufacturer just tells you to connect only the data lines (transmit and receive data, and ground), and ignore the other connections. If any of the special hardware handshake lines are needed, your computer must have the appropriate terminals. Notably, the Mac only has CTS/RTS (which Apple calls CTS/DTR just to make things more confusing). On some instruments, you don't have to supply *dynamic* signals to the handshake terminals; a simple jumper will do. Usually, the instrument manual will tell you which pins to interconnect to bring the instrument to life.

The most common technique for software handshaking is called **XON/XOFF protocol**. If you have ever used a standard ASCII terminal connected to a modem or mainframe computer, you probably have used this protocol to pause screen scrolling. When the receiver can no longer accept data, it sends XOFF (usually Control-S) to tell the sender to stop sending data. When the receiver is again ready, it sends XON (usually Control-Q) to indicate that transmission can begin again. The XON and XOFF characters can be independently enabled through the Serial Port Init VI. An important thing to remember about this protocol is that the XON and XOFF characters are *always* interpreted as XON and XOFF functions. Therefore, you should not send binary data with this protocol because the data may contain bytes with values equal to XON or XOFF. Another hazard of this protocol crops up when a receiving device forgets to send XON, in which case the sender ends up waiting forever to transmit data. Keep this in mind when you write a driver; make sure that the VI times out if this deadlock condition should arise.

Other forms of software handshaking have been devised by various manufacturers. Some use characters other than XON/XOFF, so the Serial Port Init VI permits you to choose the special character. Alternatively, your driver can watch for the magic character and respond accordingly. Another technique uses multiple exchanges of special characters to force the sender and receiver to agree that they are both ready for an upcoming data transfer. Needless to say, there is a large amount of overhead and complexity associated with such a driver. The state machine architecture is about the only way to arbitrate such complex protocols.

VXI interrupts and triggers.   The VXI library allows direct access to all of the interrupt and trigger lines defined by the VXI standard. The function of each line can be independently defined, and once you set it up, LabVIEW can wait for interrupts from other VXI modules or generate triggers that initiate all sorts of events. Here are a couple of examples, supplied by Kirk Fertitta of Sedona Visual Controls. Kirk designed an elaborate VXI/LabVIEW process control system for semiconductor fabrication equipment, where he found the flexibility of VXI triggers and interrupts indispensable. His system consists of a 100-MHz 80486 embedded controller for real-time functions plus a desktop 66-MHz 80486 system with an MXI interface serving as a user interface.

In the first example, he needed to synchronize the operation of many valves that were connected to several VXI digital output modules, each with 96 channels. To do so, he connected the trigger lines from the embedded controller to front panel connectors on the interface modules. Once connected, a large number of valves could be simultaneously actuated with nanosecond hardware timing. Trigger signals could be generated from the LabVIEW program with the **AssertVXIInt** VI or could come from external events if suitably configured with the **TrigAssertConfig** VI.

In a second case, Kirk was using ADC modules and a circular buffer for data. When the buffer is half-full, the module asserts one of the seven VXI interrupt lines, which is monitored in LabVIEW by the **Wait for Interrupt** VI—much like the Wait for RQS VI that you've probably seen in the GPIB world. When the interrupt is detected, the LabVIEW diagram wakes up and empties the buffer by transferring data with the **VXIMove** VI. Some modules may also have the capability to assert a different interrupt (still one of the seven you can use in VXI) when the buffer is totally full. In that case, the LabVIEW program would certainly respond differently than in the half-full case, since this is really an error and data is about to be lost due to buffer overrun. Having so many interrupts to choose from really gives you a lot of flexibility.

An interesting application for triggers is in waveform generation. Some DAC modules have buffers and clocked outputs which can be tied to any of the VXI trigger lines. You load the buffer with a waveform and then clock successive data points out to the DAC based on a trigger signal rather than a simple hardware clock. The trigger can be controlled by another module through the VXI backplane or it can be routed into the front panel Trigger In connector on the DAC. That way, an external sequencer could control the waveform pace.

Range checking

An important part of making your driver robust is expecting the user to enter unexpected values into every control. One way to handle these situations is by setting the limits on numeric controls through the use of the **Data Range** dialog from the control's pop-up menu (Fig. 5.28). Enter minimum, maximum, and increment limits, then select **Coerce** from the menu to force the user's input into range. If you choose **Suspend** for the range error action, the VI's front panel is kept in memory and opens up if a range error occurs. This uses extra memory, but may be the best way to respond to some situations. Selecting **Ignore** (the default) turns off range checking. The disadvantages of using the Data Range dialog items is you get no feedback to tell you that coercion is occurring. Also, if you copy the control, the Data Range setup goes with it. If you forget to change the setup for the new control, it may behave improperly.

The alternative to the Data Range dialog is to write your own range-checking code. A favorite utility VI of mine is **Coerce To Range**, which was described in Chap. 4 and is included on the CD-ROM. The various **platform** comparison functions are also candidates for range checking. If the val-**drivers\driver** ues are not evenly spaced (such as a 1-2-5 sequence) use a function sim-**utilities\Coerce** ilar to the Range Finder VI also described in Chap. 4.
To Range.vi Changing the **representation** of a numeric control or indicator may also limit the range of the input, particularly for integer types. For

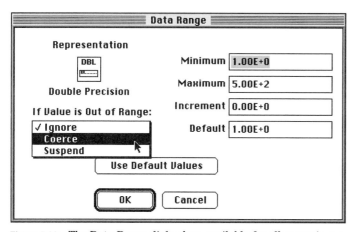

Figure 5.28 The Data Range dialog box, available for all numeric controls and indicators through a pop-up menu. Use this to limit unexpected input values to a more reasonable range.

instance, a U8 control can only represent integers between 0 and 255. Anything greater than 255 is coerced to 255 and anything less than 0 is coerced to 0.

Other difficult situations must be handled programmatically. Many instruments limit the permissible settings of one control based upon the settings of another. For example, a voltmeter might permit a range setting of 2000 V for DC, but only 1000 V for AC. If the affected controls (e.g., Range and Mode) reside in the same VI, put the interlock logic there. If one or more of the controls are not readily available, you can request the present settings from the instrument to make sure that you don't ask for an invalid combination. This may seem like a lot of work, but I've seen too many instruments that go *stark, raving bonkers* when a bad value is sent.

String controls don't have a feature analogous to the Data Range dialog; all the checking has to be done by your program. LabVIEW has several string comparison functions that are helpful. You can use **Empty String/Path?** to test for empty strings and path names, which are probably the most common out-of-range string entries. The other string comparison functions (**Decimal Digit?**, **Hex Digit?**, **Octal Digit?**, **Printable?**, **White Space?**, and **Lexical Class**) give you important attributes for the first character in a string. Being polymorphic, they also act on the ASCII equivalent of a number. For instance, if you wire the integer number zero to the **Printable?** function, the function would return *False,* since the ASCII equivalent of zero is *NUL,* which is not printable. Figure 5.29 shows how you might check to see that all characters of a string are decimal digits.

platform\ drivers\driver utilities\Read SCPI Error Queue.vi

There is one other method of range checking, *instrument error queries,* that relies on the instrument to detect and correct error conditions and report them back to LabVIEW. Only possible with instruments featuring this capability, the error query method simplifies both VI development and VI use when properly implemented. The **Read SCPI Error Queue** VI provides this service when used with SCPI-compliant instruments. Each time you send a series of com-

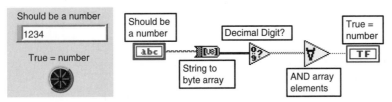

Figure 5.29   This VI checks to see that all characters in a string are decimal digits. The comparison function Decimal Digit? tests one character at a time, building a Boolean output array. The logical AND of all these values is True if all the characters are OK.

mands to the instrument, call Read SCPI Error Queue to report any problems. A well-designed instrument will respond with an informative message ("Timebase out of range for this mode") if a clash occurs among settings.

Boundary conditions—values such as zero, infinity (Inf), not-a-number (NaN) and empty string—cause lots of trouble in instrument drivers. Use the Data Range setup and comparison functions to prevent defective values from finding their way to the instrument and always *test* your drivers to make sure that ridiculous inputs don't stop the show.

Setup management

An important part of software that supports smart instruments is **setup management**. A good driver package allows you to save and recall collections of control settings, which are usually called *instrument setups*. This saves much time, considering how many controls are present on the front panels of some instruments.

> *Historical note:* Digital storage oscilloscopes (DSOs) gradually became so complex and feature-laden that it was considered a badge of honor for a technician to obtain a usable trace in less than five minutes . . . all those buttons and lights and menus and submenus were really boggling! The solution was to provide an *auto-setup* button that got something visible on the display. Manufacturers also added some means by which to store and recall setups. All the good DSOs have these features, nowadays.

Sophisticated instruments usually have built-in, nonvolatile storage for several settings, and your driver should have a feature that accesses those setup memories. If the instrument has no such memory, then write a program to upload and save setups on disk for cataloging and later downloading. You may want to provide this local storage even if the instrument *has* setup memory: what if the memory fails or is accidentally overwritten? Also, you may want to carry setups around on a diskette for use with similar instruments in other locations.

Figures 5.30 through 5.33 show how I managed setups for the Tektronix 370A/371A curve tracers, which are fairly complicated GPIB instruments. This setup management VI has a total of seven functions, as you can see by the **Action** control. It supports uploading and downloading of setups to files on your LabVIEW system and local storage and recall of settings on the instrument's internal disk drive. Other functions are initialize, check instrument ID, and test memory. To save space, I'll just show the setup management functions here. You can get this driver from the instrument library if you want to copy from it. The figure captions explain the function of each frame of the Case structure that is connected to the **Action** control.

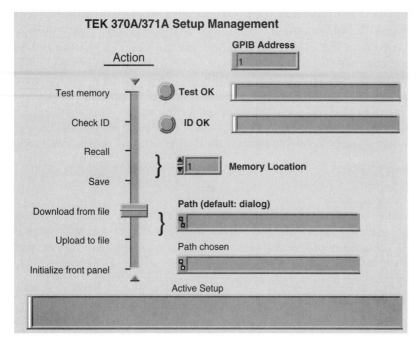

Figure 5.30 Panel for the Tektronix 370A/371A Setup Management VI. It allows you to load and save complete instrument setups, to check the instrument's ID, and test its memory. Figures 5.31 through 5.33 show the parts of the diagram that manage setups. Error I/O clusters are not shown.

It was really nice of Tektronix to include the *SET?* command, which responds with a long ASCII string that contains a series of valid setup commands. You can look at the string (it's displayed in the **Active Setup** string indicator), edit it (if you're careful!), and save it to a file as I did in this driver. Then, it's a simple matter of writing the whole

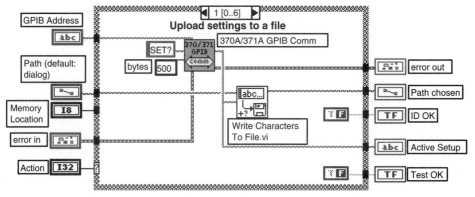

Figure 5.31 Frame 1 requests the present setup then writes it to a file. Since the setup is just a long ASCII string containing GPIB commands, you can read it back from the file and send it to the instrument to restore all of the settings.

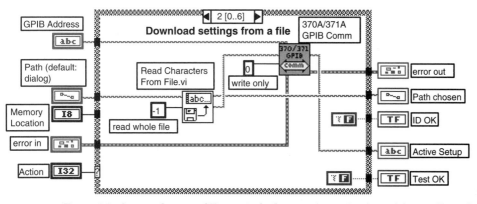

Figure 5.32 Frame 2 is the complement of Frame 1: the long setting string is read from a file and written to the instrument. Since the instrument created all the commands, one would expect them to all be valid.

string back to the instrument to restore all the settings. Having built-in setup memory in the instrument is even easier to use; just tell it to store and recall setups from the desired memory location, or file number, in the case of the 370A/371A.

Other instruments are not so nicely equipped. If it won't send you one long string of commands, you may be stuck with the task of requesting each individual control setting, saving the settings, then building valid commands to send the setup back again. This can be pretty involved; I've only done it once, and I think that's the last time. Instead, you probably will want to use the instrument's built-in setup storage. If it doesn't even have *that,* write a letter to the manufacturer and tell them what you think of their interface software.

If your driver function VIs support reading and writing in the same VIs, you have another option. The values returned by each VI can be

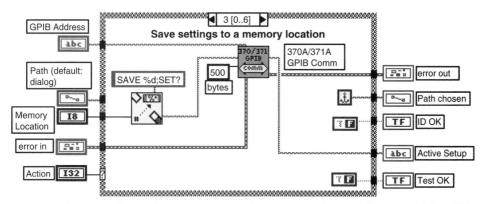

Figure 5.33 Frame 3 tells the instrument to save the present settings to a file on the built-in disk drive. Many instruments use nonvolatile RAM or EEPROM memory instead of magnetic media.

saved in binary or datalog files for later recall, at which time the values are sent to the instrument by the same VI that read them. LabVIEW file functions can read and write an image of a cluster in binary format; all you have to do is combine all the important settings into a cluster. After reading the data from the file, unbundle the values and send them to the instrument using the reverse procedure. The utility VI, **Setup File Handler**, included on the CD-ROM, is handy for this. Its operation is discussed in Chap. 7, "Writing a Data Acquisition Program." Figure 5.34 shows an example where settings from a couple of the Tek 370/371 functions are stored on disk using the Setup File Handler. The setup data is assembled into a cluster whose contents are defined by a typedef control. The same typedef is used in the Setup File Handler VI.

**platform\
Setup File
Handler.llb**

Documentation

One measure of quality in instrument driver software is the documentation. Drivers tend to have many obscure functions and special appli-

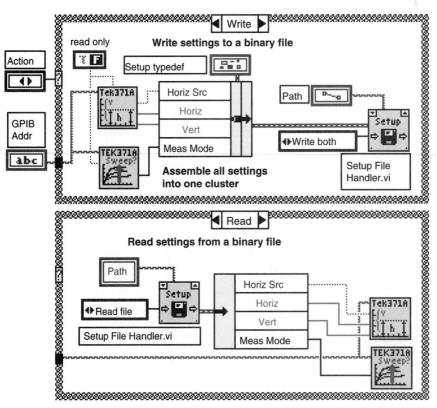

Figure 5.34   Use the Setup File Handler utility VI to store and retrieve instrument setups on disk.

cation requirements, all of which need some explanation. A driver that implements more than a few commands may even need a function index so that the user can find out which VI is needed to perform a desired operation. And establishing communications may not be trivial, especially for serial instruments. Good documentation is the key to happy users. Review the documentation section near the end of Chap. 4, "Writing an Application." It describes most of the techniques and recommended practices that you should try to use.

When you start writing the first subVI for a driver, type in control and indicator descriptions through the **Description** pop-up menu. This information can be displayed by showing the Help window and is the easiest way for a user to learn about the function of each control. If you enter this information right at the start, then any time you copy the control or indicator, the description goes with it. Besides, when you're writing the VI, you probably know everything there is to know about the function, so the description is really easy to write. I like to copy text right out of the programming manual, if it's appropriate. It pays to document as you go.

The VI description in the **Get Info** dialog box from the File menu is often a user's only source of information about a VI. Try to explain the purpose of the VI, how it works, and how it should be used. This text can also be copied and pasted into the final document.

Try to include some kind of document on disk with your driver. Drivers that are part of the instrument library should have a really complete writeup, with illustrations. The issue of platform portability of documents was mentioned in Chap. 4, and with drivers, it's almost a certainty that users of other systems will want to read your documents. When LabVIEW only ran on the Macintosh, we created all documents in MacWrite or Microsoft Word and everyone was happy. When LabVIEW went to Windows, the instrument library collapsed into .llb files and all documentation was lost! As a result, I've had to field dozens of calls from users who can't figure out how some of my older drivers worked. If only they'd had those documents. . . . For now, my recommendation is this: as a minimum, paste all vital information into the Get Info box or a string control on a top-level example VI that is easy to find. Alternatively, create a simple text document. If you're energetic and you want illustrations, generate a PDF (Portable Document Format) document using Adobe Acrobat and make sure it stays with your driver VIs, or create a LabVIEW Help document using one of the Windows Help utilities. (If you do use Help, place a note on the front panel of each VI that has help links; otherwise, users might not remember to look at it.) Hopefully, National Instruments will decide on a policy regarding instrument driver documentation standards and add that to the driver development application note.

If you're just doing an in-house driver, think about your coworkers who will one day need to use or modify your driver when you are not available. Also, remember that the stranger who looks at your program six months from now may well be *you*. Include such things as: how to connect the instrument, how to get it to "talk," problems you have discovered (and their resolutions), and of course a description of each function VI. Such information is not only useful, but it may make you *famous* rather than *infamous*.

Bibliography

Application Note No. AN006, *Developing a LabVIEW Instrument Driver.* Available from National Instruments Web site http://www.natinst.com/labview/applnote/ or via FTP ftp://ftp.natinst.com/support/support_notes/labview/pdf/ or on this book's CD-ROM.

Application Note No. AN057, *An Introduction to Using Windows Dynamic Link Libraries (DLLs) from LabVIEW.* Available from National Instruments Web site http://www. natinst.com/labview/applnote/ or via FTP ftp://ftp.natinst.com/support/support_notes/ labview/pdf/ or on this book's CD-ROM.

Application Note No. AN072, *Calling Dynamic Link Libraries (DLLs) from LabVIEW— Detailed Procedures.* Available from National Instruments Web site http://www. natinst.com/labview/applnote/ or via FTP ftp://ftp.natinst.com/support/support_notes/ labview/pdf/ or on this book's CD-ROM.

Hedstrom, Brad, "Free 8-bit Digital Output Port in LabVIEW for Windows," *LabVIEW Technical Resource,* vol. 2, no. 4, fall 1994. (Back issues available from LTR Publishing.)

Instrument Communication Handbook, IOTech, Inc., 25971 Cannon Road, Cleveland, OH 44146, 1991.

Using the DAQ Library

One reason for the success of LabVIEW is the **data acquisition (DAQ) library** for programming plug-in boards made by National Instruments. Analog, digital, and timing I/O boards are available for all popular buses on the PC, Macintosh, and Sun. You can add external signal conditioning and multiplexers, particularly SCXI (Signal Conditioning eXtensions for Instrumentation), to improve signal quality and expand the number of channels. Multiple boards can be interconnected by the RTSI (Real Time System Integration) bus, using a ribbon cable that routes timing and trigger signals between boards to synchronize various operations. Direct memory access (DMA) is available to improve data transfer speeds. And all of these features are directly accessible through the DAQ library, which is distributed with every copy of LabVIEW and is 99 percent portable among platforms. It's a popular and cost-effective combination for modern instrumentation systems.

The data acquisition VI reference manual, part of the LabVIEW manual set, is the primary source for information about the DAQ library. It contains details about every DAQ function, information on basic applications, and the board-specific details that affect some operations. You should spend time becoming familiar with this important manual. This chapter is by no means a replacement for the manual; it merely amplifies the basic concepts. The good news about the DAQ library is, it's really easy once you understand the general idea.

Almost any situation can be handled with plug-in boards, as long as you have the right boards, signal conditioning, and multiplexers (such as SCXI) available. Chapter 2, "Inputs and Outputs," discusses the basics of hardware interfaces and system design trade-offs. A free software package for Windows from National Instruments, **DAQ Designer**, can help you choose hardware. It uses a question-and-answer approach that leads you through the system configuration maze.

The NI-DAQ Driver

An underappreciated part of the LabVIEW data acquisition world is the **NI-DAQ driver**, which is the system-level interface between user software (LabVIEW, C, Basic, etc.) and the plug-in boards. The core VIs in the LabVIEW DAQ library call Code Interface Nodes (CINs) that in turn call the NI-DAQ driver. NI-DAQ is a very complex piece of code; there are about as many programmers on the NI-DAQ project and about as many lines of code as there are for LabVIEW! There is a different NI-DAQ driver for each platform (though they are trying to write more common modules to save time and effort), so you can imagine the effort required to maintain the drivers. National Instruments works very, very hard on these drivers to promote their consistency, flexibility, and reliability. Frequent revisions are issued to fix bugs, support new products, and handle changes in the various computer models and systems. You can download new driver versions from ftp.natinst.com or the bulletin board.

During a normal LabVIEW installation, the NI-DAQ driver for your platform will be installed automatically. Before using a DAQ board, you should run the **NI-DAQ configuration utility** program. The configuration utility lets you verify and/or change hardware settings on plug-in boards, PCMCIA interfaces, SCXI signal conditioning, and any other devices supported by NI-DAQ. The utility also lets you test the operation of some I/O functions, at least on the PC. Starting with NI-DAQ version 5.0, a separate configuration program called the **DAQ Channel Wizard** (description follows) helps you assign names, scale factors, and other information to various I/O channels. Details on these utilities are discussed in the *Data Acquisition Basics Manual,* which also covers a lot of other fundamentals regarding the DAQ library. (In fact, I think that the DAQ basics manual is so good that I hardly needed to write this chapter.) If you have trouble or questions regarding the NI-DAQ drivers, call National Instruments or e-mail daq_support@natinst.com.

What about boards made by other manufacturers? Most importantly, none are supported by the DAQ library, unless someone happens to build an exact clone of a National Instrument product. Other boards are certainly usable with LabVIEW; you just need a suitable driver. Companies that definitely offer LabVIEW drivers for some of their products include Computer Boards, Data Translation, IO Tech, Strawberry Tree, United Electronics Industries, and Analog Devices. These are some of the trade-offs to consider when using third-party boards:

- You won't have the consistent interface offered by the DAQ library. Most foreign boards that I've seen have really strange LabVIEW drivers. I used one that had nearly all of the board's functions called by a single driver VI with about 50 controls on the panel—what a mess! By all means, encourage third parties to develop drivers that look something like the DAQ library or at least follow some of the programming guidelines in this book. Data Translation did.

- Unlike the DAQ library, many third-party drivers do not support **asynchronous** or parallel operations (nearly all operations in the DAQ library can operate asynchronously, increasing throughput and ease of use). This may or may not affect your particular project, but should be considered. Hopefully, the manufacturer can at least tell you whether or not its driver has asynchronous features.

- Third parties don't use the RTSI bus to synchronize various boards, so you may have to find another technique (perhaps external trigger signals) to do synchronization, if required.

- Third-party drivers based on external libraries may not work after upgrading LabVIEW; NI-DAQ is guaranteed to remain compatible.

- If there is no LabVIEW driver available from the manufacturer, see if someone has written one. Consider posting to the info-labview mailgroup. For Windows, the manufacturer may supply a DLL that you can link into LabVIEW by using the **Call Library** function. If it supplies low-level C sources, you can build those into CINs (with suitable programming expertise and plenty of time).

- If you have to start from scratch writing a driver, you have either (1) too much time on your hands, (2) such a huge investment in foreign hardware that you can't afford *not* to write a driver, or (3) National Instruments doesn't offer the functionality of your board (yet). For my money, it's cheaper to buy a new plug-and-play board than it is to write software.

The NI-DAQ Channel Wizard

The **NI-DAQ Channel Wizard** is an important feature that was added to NI-DAQ version 5.0. It greatly simplifies the process of defining I/O channels by supplying a convenient graphical user interface through which you define hardware devices, channel specifications, and scale factors. All the information is saved in a configuration file that the NI-DAQ driver reads when it's time to access the hardware. You can also export the contents of the configuration file to a text file to document your DAQ setup. From a LabVIEW perspective, a key feature of the Channel Wizard is that it permits you to access I/O channels by *name* rather than by hardware channel number. It also removes the burden of maintaining channel configuration data within LabVIEW, a subject that's covered extensively in the next chapter, "Writing a Data Acquisition Program."

If you don't have NI-DAQ 5.0, fear not. This chapter deals with the general nature of the DAQ library and everything here is useful whether or not you use the newer named access feature.

Hardware Options

National Instruments offers dozens of products that you can assemble into a full-featured instrumentation system in conjunction with LabVIEW—its catalog lists dozens of plug-in boards and different kinds of signal conditioning hardware. Let's take a quick look at some of your options.

Multifunction I/O boards

The quickest way to get a LabVIEW system into operation in a laboratory situation is to buy a multifunction I/O interface. National Instruments has several lines of multifunction interfaces: the full-featured **MIO** series plug-in boards, the low-cost **Lab** series, the **DAQCard** series based on PCMCIA cards for portable use, and the **DAQPad** series for parallel ports. Almost every interface has the following general features:

- Up to 64 analog inputs, with a multiplexer and programmable-gain amplifier
- A 12- or 16-bit ADC with available sampling rates to 1 MHz
- Two analog outputs with separate DAC converters
- One or more 8-bit bidirectional digital I/O ports
- Several programmable counter-timers

Connections to the outside world are made with a ribbon cable, which you plug into a terminal block (like the model CB-50 connector) or a cable adapter that connects to a variety of signal conditioning devices like the Analog Devices 5B series modules for analog signals. These simple hardware setups pretty well cover the basic requirements of routine, low-speed, data acquisition and control with low channel counts.

If you need more channels, you can add an analog multiplexer, such as the AMUX-64T, or connect your multifunction board to SCXI modules (described later), which offer a very large channel count. For low-level signals such as thermocouples, you need to choose a board with high gain and/or use an external amplifier or signal conditioner. The DAQ library knows all about the multifunction boards, the AMUX-64T, and SCXI modules, making them very easy to use. Using external signal conditioning means that you may have to keep track of some additional scale factors when you write your LabVIEW program.

Specialized analog I/O boards

For specialized analog applications, you can buy a dedicated analog I/O board. The first board in this series, the A2000, has four channels with 12-bit, 1-MHz, simultaneous sampling. You would choose this board in preference to an MIO-series board where any delay or timing skew between channels caused by a multiplexer is undesirable. The A2000 also has true analog triggering, much like that of an oscilloscope.

For high-accuracy, dynamic signal acquisition, such as audio and vibration analysis, the A2100 and A2150 boards are recommended. They use 16-bit sigma-delta ADCs originally intended for digital audio applications, with some enhancements to optimize their absolute accuracy and DC performance. Maximum sampling rates are 48 kHz for the A2100 and 51.2 kHz for the A2150. The A2100 has two inputs and two outputs; the output specifications are similar to those of the inputs. The A2150 has four inputs.

If you need more analog outputs, the AO series offers up to ten 12-bit DACs with the ability to directly drive either voltage (± 10 V) or current (0–20 mA) loads.

Digital and timing I/O boards

For purely digital I/O applications, you can buy the DIO-series boards which offer up to 96 TTL-compatible input/output bits. You can use each line individually to sense contact closures or to drive relays, for instance, or you can use an entire 8- or 16-bit port as a parallel interface to other computer-based equipment. The DAQ library supports everything from single-bit operations to block mode DMA parallel transfers. Note that you will usually need some kind of signal conditioning to interface the relatively sensitive TTL I/O ports to real-world loads that require higher voltage or current. National Instruments offers the SSR series signal conditioning modules for AC and DC loads, complete with optical isolation. Or, you can build your own interface circuits as required.

A unique interface, the TIO series, features 10 general-purpose counter/timers plus 16 digital I/O bits. With a TIO board, you can set up fairly complex arrangements of event counters, delays, and timers to control and measure various time-dependent events. Again, these boards have TTL-level signals, requiring some form of signal conditioning for most applications.

SCXI

A cost-effective way to add lots of I/O channels to your computer is to use SCXI hardware with a multifunction board. The SCXI line encompasses an array of analog and digital input and output modules with built-in multiplexing so that one plug-in board can access hundreds of channels. You install one or more modules in a SCXI chassis and connect one of the modules directly to the plug-in board via a ribbon cable or to the parallel port of a PC if you use the SCXI-1200 multifunction module. The chassis has a power supply and a backplane with analog and digital buses that permit communication and synchronization among modules. (See Fig. 6.1.) Up to eight SCXI-1001 chassis with a total of 96 modules can be combined into one system. And, like the plug-in boards, the DAQ library handles SCXI channels transparently. Just specify the chassis, module, and channel numbers that you want to access.

The SCXI line is very popular and is growing rapidly. Analog modules include low-cost solid-state and relay multiplexers, isolated inputs with optional excitation for transducers such as RTDs and strain gauges, and isolated analog outputs. All analog inputs are differential and have available lowpass filtering and programmable-gain amplifiers. Digital I/O modules are available for TTL input and output, optically isolated inputs, and various relay outputs that handle higher voltages and currents.

The basic SCXI hardware, using a plug-in DAQ board, is limited to a maximum 10-m cable run from the chassis to the computer. Other modules, such as the SCXI-1200, incorporate the functionality of a plug-in board right on the module. The SCXI-1200 uses a PC-compatible par-

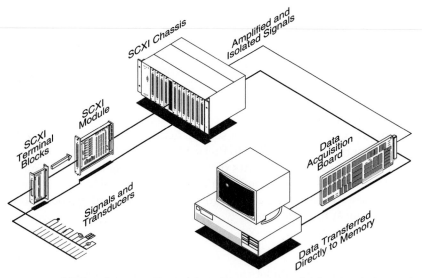

Figure 6.1 SCXI modules provide signal conditioning and multiplex signals into and out of plug-in data acquisition boards.

allel port to extend the link up to 100 m while providing good throughput. Remote SCXI equipment, such as the SCXI-2000 chassis or the SCXI-2400 module, feature local intelligence and high-performance serial communications links for remote operation, while maintaining the consistent software interface of the DAQ library. With these systems, you connect up to 32 chassis to your computer via RS-232 or RS-485, then plug in any combination of the available SCXI signal conditioning modules. With RS-485, you can reach out 1200 m (4000 ft).

Portable DAQ

For portable DAQ applications using notebook or laptop computers, you use one of the products that require no plug-in slots at all. The DAQCard series are Personal Computer Memory Card International Association cards (PCMCIA cards, or PC cards for short*) with I/O capabilities similar to the regular plug-in boards. Another alternative is the DAQPad series that plugs into the parallel port. They require modest amounts of DC power that can be supplied by batteries.

Direct memory access (DMA)

Here are a few notes regarding DMA and the DAQ library.

- DMA is highly desirable because it improves the rate of data transfer from the plug-in board to your computer's main memory. In fact, high-speed operations are often impossible without it. The alternative is interrupt-driven transfers, where the CPU has to laboriously move each and every word of data. Most PCs can handle several thousand interrupts per second, and no more.

- A DMA controller is built into the motherboard of every IBM-compatible PC, and all but the lowest-cost plug-in boards (such as the PC-LPM-16) include a DMA interface.

- Macintosh models with NuBus slots do not have built-in DMA. Instead, you must buy another interface board with a DMA controller, such as the NB-GPIB/TNT or the older NB-DMA2800, and attach a RTSI cable between it and the I/O board. Otherwise, you're stuck with (much slower) interrupt-driven transfers.

- On the Macintosh, the DAQ library will *automatically* use DMA any time the required hardware is available (remember to connect the RTSI cable or all I/O operations will fail). On the PC, you have control over whether DMA is employed.

---

* This acronym business is getting out of hand. I believe that PCMCIA actually stands for People Can't Memorize Computer Industry Acronyms.

- The latest PCI-based E-series MIO boards have multiple DMA channels and *bus mastering* capability. When a board is allowed to take over as bus master (in place of the host CPU), throughput can increase even more because less work has to be done at interrupt time.

Basics of the DAQ Library

Two words describe the LabVIEW DAQ library: *consistent* and *integrated.* Every DAQ function uses a consistent set of input and output parameters, and the functions work consistently among the various I/O boards, even across LabVIEW's platforms. You can write a program for an NB-MIO-16 multifunction board on a Macintosh, carry a floppy disk over to a Windows machine with an AT-MIO-16, and the program will work there without modification. Because the DAQ library has been an important part of LabVIEW for many years, you can be assured that the two are tightly integrated. For instance, you can wire a data array from an analog acquisition DAQ operation directly to a Waveform Graph, and you can intermix the DAQ error I/O chain with the error I/O chain for the file functions. These facts make the library relatively easy to apply, once you understand the organization, conventions, and terminology.

DAQ library hierarchy

Like all good LabVIEW projects, the DAQ library is thoughtfully organized in a hierarchical manner from an easy top level to a sophisticated bottom level. With the new LabVIEW 4 **FlexView** function palettes, you can display the DAQ VIs with any organization you wish. I'll use the default palette layout for illustration purposes, but you may prefer the daq_view setup that ships with LabVIEW; it puts priority on the DAQ functions in the palette layout. The function palette for the analog input part of the DAQ library in Fig. 6.2 shows a sample of the overall hierarchy. **Easy I/O** is great for getting started, but is rather limited in its functionality. The **intermediate** level is where you will do most of your work once you get to know the library. **Advanced** VIs are only used when you need to access certain less-frequently used features of the library. Easy I/O VIs are built from intermediate VIs, and intermediate VIs are built from advanced VIs. There are also calibration, configuration, and signal conditioning utility VIs. From top to bottom, the library is consistent in its use of common input and output terminal names.

Easy I/O. The easy I/O VIs were created with the express purpose of simplifying your life as a developer. You need to know very little about the operation of the DAQ library or your particular I/O board in order

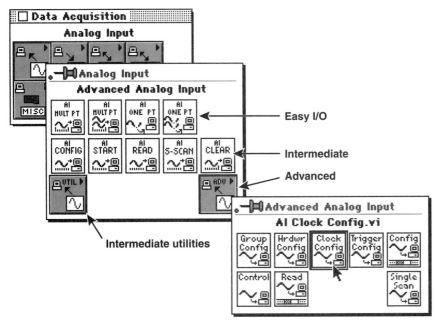

Figure 6.2 Hierarchy of the analog input DAQ library as displayed in the default view of the function palette.

to acquire analog data, drive analog outputs, access digital I/O, or do basic counting and timing operations with the easy I/O functions. They are written at the same high level as many of the example VIs, using the intermediate VIs and a built-in call to the error handler to notify you should anything go wrong. You are encouraged to use the easy I/O VIs or examples as a starting point for your applications, modifying them as required. Just remember to save your modified VI with a new name! Being an intrinsically lazy person, I use the easy I/O library whenever I can. The major capabilities missing from easy I/O are continuous buffered I/O operations, triggering, and the various utility operations. For these, you must use the intermediate VIs.

Intermediate. Serious DAQ applications typically require you to use the intermediate library. They offer much more functionality than the easy I/O library, but you will have to do more wiring and have a deeper understanding of the data acquisition hardware. Important features of the intermediate library that the easy I/O library lacks are

- Advanced buffer management, such as circular buffering
- External timing and triggering options
- Time-out limits

- Calibration and hardware configuration control
- Access to the RTSI bus interconnection functions
- Direct access to status information

Error handling is more flexible than that of the easy I/O VIs, too, because you have direct access to the error I/O clusters. This is a very flexible library and, like all the DAQ functions, is well documented in the *Data Acquisition VI Reference Manual.*

Advanced.   The advanced VIs provide access to the lowest level of programming in the DAQ library. They make direct calls to the NI-DAQ driver through CINs, so there is no lower-level programming for you to study or modify. Very few applications require that you use the advanced VIs; the intermediate VIs are the ones you should concentrate on for most applications. Here are a few of the capabilities of the advanced VIs that the intermediate VIs lack.

- Multiple buffering
- Full access to all status information
- Direct control of polarity and gain
- Sampling rate specifications in terms of sampling clock period and clock divisor
- Unscaled output data specification

We won't spend much time on the advanced library. You can see how it's applied by examining the diagrams of the intermediate VIs or by reading the manual.

Conventions used in the DAQ library

Signal names, parameter formats, and connector pane layouts are well standardized in the DAQ library. Figure 6.3 shows two intermediate VIs that are good examples. The first thing you should notice is the style of the control and indicator names. A boldface label means that the control or indicator is *required;* it must be wired or LabVIEW will give you a broken arrow. There are very few required terminals in the DAQ library at present, though. Labels appearing in plain text indicate *recommended* terminals that are generally important and you should definitely understand their operation. Grayed labels indicate *optional* terminals that you rarely need to use. Control labels also contain default input values where appropriate. For instance, the input label, **channels (0)**, means that the **channel** control will be set to channel zero if you leave it unwired. These labeling conventions are a really good idea and I highly recommend that you follow them when creating your own VIs.

AI Waveform Scan.vi

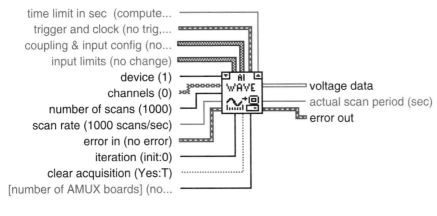

time limit in sec (compute...
trigger and clock (no trig,...
coupling & input config (no...
input limits (no change)
device (1)
channels (0)
number of scans (1000)
scan rate (1000 scans/sec)
error in (no error)
iteration (init:0)
clear acquisition (Yes:T)
[number of AMUX boards] (no...

voltage data
actual scan period (sec)
error out

DIO Read.vi

scan backlog
number read
taskID in
number of scans to read
time limit in sec (no chang...
error in (no error)
taskID out
port data
retrieval complete
error out

Figure 6.3 Connector panes for a couple of intermediate VIs, showing some of the most common signal names.

Defaults. The DAQ library uses several methods for the management of default values, all of which are intended to save you wiring. First is the notion of a **default input**: the default value of a front panel control, such as the zero value for **channels (0)**. If the default input suits your needs, you don't have to wire that control. Second, there is the **default setting**. Default settings are recorded by the driver. For instance, the trigger and clock settings for analog acquisition, once set, are retained until you cause them to change. On many inputs, you will see the notation (*no change:0*). The default value for such a control is zero, and it forces the driver to use whatever the default setting happens to be. Many default settings can also be set from the DAQ configuration utility.

Devices. Every DAQ VI that performs a configuration or initialization operation has a control called **device**. Device is a number that specifies the data acquisition board that you wish to access. On the Macintosh and on PCs with EISA and Microchannel busses, it is the physical slot number of the board. On PCs with ISA busses and on the Sun, it is a user-assigned number from 1 through 16, also known as a *logical slot number*. The DAQ configuration utility tells you what devices are installed.

Channel addressing.   Many of the analog I/O VIs have a **channel** control that you use to specify which physical inputs or outputs to access. It is a string control with a syntax that is clearly specified in the reference manual (and I'll throw in a few examples in a moment). You can type channel selections directly into a string and hope you have entered them correctly. Or, you can write a configuration program in LabVIEW that uses Ring controls and other handy techniques to generate a syntactically correct channel string. Generation and management of such strings are discussed in Chap. 7, "Writing a Data Acquisition Program."

Each channel you specify becomes a member of a **group**. The order of the channels in the list defines the order in which the channels are scanned during an input or output operation. To erase a group, you pass an empty channel list to the I/O configuration VI along with the group number. You can have up to 16 groups defined at any one time for a single group type. Available group types are analog input, analog output, digital I/O, and counter-timer.

The **channel** list is an array of strings, though it only needs to have one element, and that element can contain an arbitrarily complex list of channels. So, you can specify one channel per element of the array, specify an entire list of channels in just one array element, or use a combination of these two methods. Individual channels are specified by values separated by commas, for example, 2,3,7. To scan a sequence of channels, separate the values with a colon, for example, 2:7 would scan channels 2, 3, 4, 5, 6, 7 in order. You would preferentially use the array format to specify channels when simultaneously configuring other attributes of an I/O operation (for example channel gains and limits) that are also specified by array inputs.

There are three types of channels: onboard channels (literally, on the plug-in board), AMUX-64T channels, and SCXI channels. Some formats for onboard channels are shown in Fig. 6.4. The keyword *OB* is optional and indicates that the number following is an onboard channel.

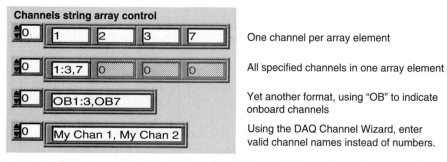

Figure 6.4 Some channel list formats for onboard channels. You can intermix formats freely in one string array.

If you're using the NI-DAQ Channel Wizard and NI-DAQ 5.0 or later, you can enter channel names into the channel list strings as shown in the bottom example of Fig. 6.4. Valid names are those that you entered through the Wizard. Note that you have to spell them correctly! Names are case-insensitive, but spaces count.

Channel specifiers (and the data returned) for AMUX-64T boards are quite a bit more complicated because of the way that the board scans channels and the fact that they can be used in either single-ended or differential mode. The key to sorting this out is the fact that each onboard channel is multiplexed to either 4, 8, or 16 physical channels depending upon whether 1, 2, or 4 AMUX boards are installed. If you have one AMUX board, and your channel list just has the number zero as a parameter, the DAQ VI will return four values, corresponding to the first four physical channels on input. If you only want to read the value of one physical channel, you must specify the AMUX number in the channel specifier. Figure 6.5 shows some simple examples, and many more examples may be found in the LabVIEW DAQ manual.

SCXI systems use a channel specifier that follows the general format: onboard channel, chassis ID, module slot, module channel. Most of the time, you can omit the onboard channel, and LabVIEW assumes that channel 0 is used. Figure 6.6 shows some basic examples of SCXI channel specifiers. The channel specifier can also send special commands to manage SCXI features, such as the calibration ground on an

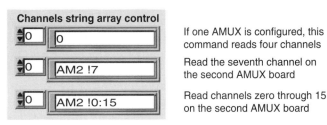

Figure 6.5 Channel list examples for systems using AMUX multiplexer boards.

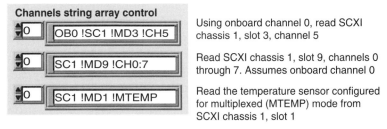

Figure 6.6 Channel list examples for SCXI systems.

SCXI-1100 and reading temperature references on some of the analog connector blocks. These are detailed in the LabVIEW DAQ manual.

Task ID.   When you use the intermediate or advanced VIs, you will see that each VI has an input and/or output called **task ID**. The task ID is a magic number created by a group configuration VI, such as **AI Config**. Like a file refnum, it carries information about a DAQ operation between the various VIs. Information includes such items as the device, type of operation, list of channels, group, size of the data buffer in memory, and status of the data acquisition operation. And, like a file refnum, you should never change the value of a task ID.

You can have an arbitrary number of tasks running concurrently. For instance, you might start an analog output waveform generation task, an analog acquisition task, and a digital output task. Make sure that you don't mix up the task IDs. Task IDs can be passed to subVIs as 32-bit unsigned integers (U32 integers), so you are not forced to have all of your DAQ VIs on one diagram.

Input limits.   Many of the analog acquisition VIs have an **input limits** control, which is a cluster array containing the upper (maximum) and lower (minimum) voltage limits for each channel. These limits are your best estimate of the maximum and minimum voltages that you wish to measure with an analog input channel given that channel's range, polarity, and gain settings. For instance, if you think your signal will range from –0.2 V to 4.4 V and you enter those values as lower and upper limits, the driver will probably adjust the hardware for a ±5-V range, the nearest practical setting. *Output limits* are defined as the upper and lower voltage outputs for an analog output channel. These limits are the maximum and minimum voltages that can be generated at an analog output channel given that channel's polarity and reference voltage. Instead of forcing you to think in terms of range, polarity, gain, and reference voltage settings, LabVIEW allows to you to specify these settings more naturally as a pair of voltages—the limit settings. If you enter a value that would seem to require a gain factor that your board does not support, fear not: the driver will choose the nearest value that accommodates the requested range.

LabVIEW uses limit settings to calculate the range, polarity, gain, and reference voltage settings you can use on a board. When a board uses jumpers or dip switches to select one of these properties and you have to change a jumper setting, you must enter the correct jumper setting in the DAQ configuration utility. All of National Instruments' data acquisition boards have programmable gains (no jumpers) but some SCXI modules do not (they use jumpers or dip switches). Many of the modules have jumpered ranges and polarities; therefore, you must enter these settings in the DAQ configuration utility. For most boards, you must also change the jumper configuration if you want to use an external analog output voltage reference.

Input limits are discussed in detail in the DAQ manual. If you still have trouble understanding the various gain interactions, by all means run one of the example VIs and connect your I/O hardware to some known signals to see what actually happens.

Error I/O. The intermediate and advanced VIs include error I/O connections, using the standard error cluster, for your convenience. Error I/O and the task IDs are common threads that make sequential DAQ operations really simple to wire up. Your diagram will probably contain more wiring to controls and indicators than it will between DAQ VIs.

Scans, buffering, and all that. There is a whole collection of terms that apply to acquisition and signal generation with the DAQ library. Here are the basics.

- **Sample.** A sample is one ADC or DAC conversion for one channel.

- **Scan.** A scan is a collection of one sample from each of one or more channels or ports in an analog or digital group. One sample from each of 100 channels, when taken in one operation, is a scan.

- **Waveform.** A waveform is a collection of samples associated with a single input or output channel.

- **Update.** An update is an output operation that corresponds to a scan on an input device.

- **Buffer.** A buffer is an area in memory that stores a series of scans for input or updates for output. The data may belong to one channel, such as a single waveform, or to several channels, representing several waveforms. Contrast with a scan or update, which contain only *one* sample per channel.

The concept of a buffer is very important because that is how you store quantities of data for direct access by the hardware—and that spells performance. If your LabVIEW program always had to generate or read each individual sample, there would be little hope of sampling at accurate rates much beyond 10 Hz. Instead, the data is shoveled into and out of an area of memory, usually via DMA, through hardware-timed transfers. With these techniques, you can (theoretically, at least) acquire data and generate waveforms nearly as fast as your computer's bus can move the data.

Immediate nonbuffered I/O. The simplest type of I/O operations don't use a buffer and are suited to low-speed acquisition and signal generation. These are the **nonbuffered I/O** operations. An **immediate non-buffered I/O** operation reads a scan from or writes an update to a group of channels when you call the appropriate DAQ VI. A group is accessed whenever you call the VI, under the control of software timing, as in the example of Fig. 6.7. There is some support from hardware timing in this operation: you can control the interchannel delay for channels within a scan. You should consider immediate nonbuffered I/O for the following:

- Simple test programs
- Low-speed data acquisition, up to a few samples per second
- Manual actuation of output devices through Boolean controls on a panel or low-speed, automatic sequencing

Timed nonbuffered I/O. The next step up with regards to timing is **timed nonbuffered I/O**. Also known as **hardware-timed I/O**, the DAQ VI sets up the onboard counter-timers to regulate the rate at which scans or updates are performed, instead of using a software timer. Your loop runs at a reliable rate, but your program still acquires or generates one scan or update per cycle of the loop. Depending on the amount of software overhead that you add, such as graphing of data or saving to files, a timed nonbuffered I/O loop can run reliably up to a hundred or more cycles per second. The big limitation is the overhead of each I/O call. On the Macintosh, it's about 0.5 ms, and with Windows, about 3 ms. That means the fastest you can acquire data would be less than about 2000 Hz and 300 Hz, respectively, for the two platforms. (Please note that, regardless of sample rate, you always have the risk of overburdening your system and missing some scans.) Figure 6.8

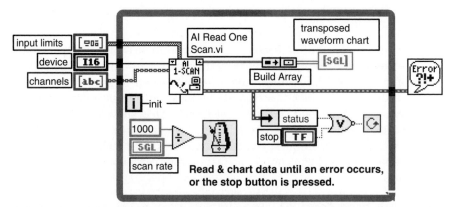

Figure 6.7   Immediate nonbuffered I/O, from the example VI, *ContAcq&Chart (easy immed).* The easy I/O function, AI Read One Scan, is called at a rate determined by the value you wire to a LabVIEW timer.

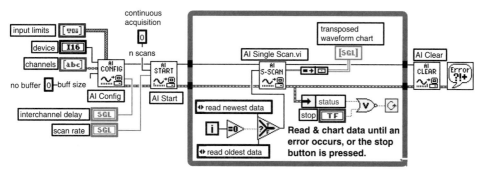

Figure 6.8 This diagram shows the intermediate VIs in a timed nonbuffered I/O arrangement, from the example VI, *Cont Acq&Chart (hw timed)*.

shows how you set up a simple application. Note that there are no software timers in the While Loop. The AI Single Scan VI waits until the next scan of data is available each time it is called. Applications for this DAQ technique are

- Feedback control operations where an algorithm acts on a measurement and generates a corresponding result on a regular basis

- Data acquisition and signal generation at moderate rates (up to 100 Hz or perhaps a little faster) where consistent sample interval is important

Timed buffered I/O. For DAQ applications running at high speeds, you must turn to **timed buffered I/O**. With buffered I/O, precision hardware timers control the real-time flow of data between memory buffers and the ADCs and DACs. LabVIEW transfers data between the plug-in board and a buffer whenever the buffer is full (for inputs) or empty (for outputs). These operations make maximal use of hardware: the on-board counter-timers, and any DMA hardware that your system may have. Buffered operations can be triggered by hardware or software events to start the process, thus synchronizing the process with the physical world. You must use the intermediate or advanced VIs to write buffered I/O applications. There are three types of buffered I/O, as described in the next sections.

By the way, you might be wondering where the buffers reside. They are, in fact, allocated in your *system's* memory space because that is where the low-level I/O handler is installed by NI-DAQ. Increasing the memory available to LabVIEW actually *decreases* the memory available to buffered I/O operations and any other system-related memory allocation activities as well. Be cautious when requesting very large buffers.

Simple buffered I/O. **Simple buffered I/O** uses a single buffer in memory big enough for all of your data. Space in memory is allocated by NI-DAQ when the data acquisition task is configured, so there are no memory management operations to slow you down during operation, unless you have turned on the **virtual memory (VM)** features that your system offers. (Virtual memory swaps blocks of memory back and forth to disk, causing brief interruptions in many operations; use it with caution in real-time applications. The same goes for some implementations of disk caching where the cache fills up and flushes to disk at unpredictable intervals.) The input or output task proceeds until the end of the buffer is reached, then it stops automatically. For a simple buffered output operation, you can load the buffer all at once or a piece at a time, as long as you keep up with the output process. For input operations, you can read the data out in pieces or just wait until the operation is complete. The buffer stays intact until you call **AI Clear** or you reboot your system. Note that the size of the buffer is limited by available memory. Consider using simple buffered I/O for the following:

- Single-shot data acquisition at high speed with moderate buffer sizes
- Single-shot waveform generation at high speed

Circular buffered I/O. If you want to continue your high-performance buffered I/O process indefinitely, or if you need to handle more data than memory will hold, use **circular buffered I/O**. A circular buffer is an area of memory that is reused sequentially. During a circular buffer input operation, you must read data from the buffer while the operation is in progress. Otherwise, old data will be overwritten when the next cycle starts. Similarly, an output operation can continue forever, but if you want the output waveform to change on-the-fly, you have to reload the buffer at an appropriate time. Figure 6.9 shows how easy it is to build a circular buffer acquisition application. For this example, I used the intermediate VI, **AI Continuous Scan**. If you want to see another more detailed and very flexible example, read on.

Circular buffered I/O is a powerful technique because the buffer has an apparently unlimited size, and the input or output operation proceeds *in the background with no software overhead*. The only burden on your program is that it must load or unload data from the buffer before it is overwritten. I really like circular buffered I/O because it makes the most effective use of available hardware and allows the software to process data in parallel with the acquisition activity. Use it whenever you require maximum overall performance.

Multibuffered I/O. Sometimes a circular buffer fills (or empties) too quickly for your software to keep up. In that case, you must use **multi-**

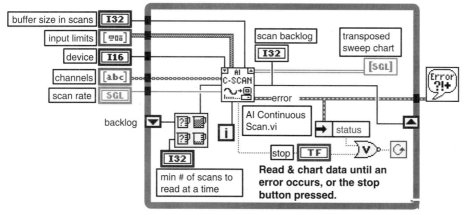

Figure 6.9   This simple VI uses circular buffered I/O to simultaneously acquire and chart data. It uses the upper-level intermediate VI, AI Continuous Scan, and it's very fast.

buffered I/O, which allocates more than one memory buffer. (Another common name is *double buffering,* which is really a misnomer.) Each trigger event starts acquisition and fills one buffer, then acquisition stops until the next trigger. Or, you can specify continuous acquisition, in which case the buffers fill continuously and sequentially. Since there are several buffers, your program has additional time to read data out of one buffer while the hardware is writing data into another, or vice versa. You must use the intermediate or advanced VIs to implement multibuffering. Multibuffering is generally required when you can't reuse a simple buffer or a circular buffer. For example, you are acquiring triggered waveforms and can't read the waveform data (empty the buffer) until the next trigger occurs.

DAQ examples and wizards

Like all the examples that come with LabVIEW, you are encouraged to use the DAQ examples as starting points for your applications—program by plagiarizing! Most of the samples presented here sprout from the examples; there's no reason to start from scratch all the time. Analog examples include all modes of buffered and nonbuffered input and output. There is a *stream to disk* library for high-speed recording of data directly to disk. Digital examples demonstrate various operations including I/O with handshaking. Counter-timer examples show you how to generate pulse trains and measure frequency. And finally, there are examples for various SCXI modules. Somewhere in this assemblage of over five megabytes of DAQ examples lurks a potential solution to *your* problem. Use the **readme** VI that is in the Examples directory to learn about the available VIs. It reads the contents of the VI description item for each VI and displays the text for your viewing pleasure. Open the VIs in the run_me.llb library in the DAQ examples directory. They are the simplest, cleanest diagrams of intermediate and advanced VIs that I've seen, and they demonstrate all forms of I/O at an elementary level.

LabVIEW 4.0 has a **DAQ Example Navigator** feature, available in the Help menu. It prompts you for basic information about your DAQ application, then suggests possible example VIs. Beginning with Lab-VIEW 4.1, you can also turn to the **Solution Wizard** to help you design your DAQ-based application. It's one of the choices you see when you launch LabVIEW. The Wizard leads you through a detailed list of questions regarding your application and then selects an appropriate example VI. Finally, it customizes the example VI by entering channel names you have previously defined through the DAQ Channel Wizard. Additional functionality will be added to the Solution Wizard with subsequent LabVIEW releases. Surrounded by all this wizardly software, how can you miss?

Analog Inputs

Analog acquisition represents about 80 percent of the real-world DAQ applications, so I'm going to spend a significant amount of time on the subject. The easy I/O VIs are pretty much self-explanatory, so the intermediate library will get most of our attention.

Configuration, starting, and stopping

AI Config (Fig. 6.10) is the name of the game when it comes to setting up an analog input operation. From the basic task specifications—device, channel, buffer size, and so forth—it checks the setup for errors, downloads settings to the target data acquisition board, allocates memory for any buffers, and returns a task ID number for use by subsequent DAQ VIs. Note that AI Config does not start any sampling—it only makes preparations. Perhaps the most confusing thing about DAQ configuration issues is that each plug-in board has slightly different specifications with regards to channel ranges, input limits, and scanning order. An appendix to the DAQ manual summarizes these requirements. If you get something wrong, AI Config will return an error, such as invalid or inconsistent numeric parameter. These error messages are sometimes nonspecific, so it's up to you to figure out which parameter is at fault.

You might also note from the connector pane of each DAQ VI that the intermediate and advanced VIs sometimes have a large number of terminals to permit access to the broad range of DAQ attributes and func-

AI Config

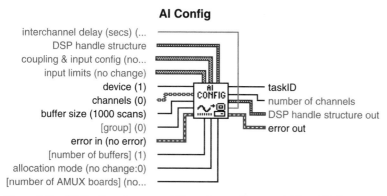

interchannel delay (secs) (...
DSP handle structure
coupling & input config (no...
input limits (no change)
device (1)
channels (0)
buffer size (1000 scans)
[group] (0)
error in (no error)
[number of buffers] (1)
allocation mode (no change:0)
[number of AMUX boards] (no...

taskID
number of channels
DSP handle structure out
error out

Figure 6.10 AI Config sets up conditions for analog acquisition. Of the many inputs, note that only a few are not grayed out: those are the ones you are most likely to use.

tions. To simplify your life, pay primary attention to the items that are not grayed out in the Help window, or try switching to **simple diagram help** (use the little icon in the lower-left corner of the Help window).

Once you have a task configured, you start buffered acquisition by calling **AI Start** (Fig. 6.11). Important inputs are the **number of scans to acquire** and **scan rate**. If you set **number of scans to acquire** to zero, continuous acquisition is requested. This VI is also the place where you specify triggering conditions. If your board supports it, you can choose various options such as digital or analog triggering with optional slope and level detection, much like an oscilloscope. If you have set up multibuffered acquisition using AI Config, then you need to set **number of buffers to acquire** to the same value supplied to AI Config.

Unbuffered acquisition doesn't require a call to AI Start. Rather, you can use **AI Single Scan** (Fig. 6.12). It reads a single scan of data from

AI Start

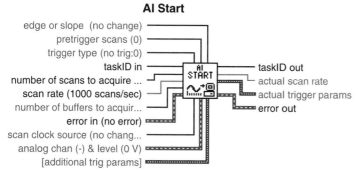

edge or slope (no change)
pretrigger scans (0)
trigger type (no trig:0)
taskID in
number of scans to acquire ...
scan rate (1000 scans/sec)
number of buffers to acquir...
error in (no error)
scan clock source (no chang...
analog chan (-) & level (0 V)
[additional trig params]

taskID out
actual scan rate
actual trigger params
error out

Figure 6.11 Call AI Start to start buffered data acquisition. This VI determines how much data to acquire and it sets triggering conditions.

AI Single Scan

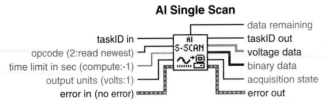

Figure 6.12 AI Single Scan fetches one scan of data from an analog input device.

the board and returns the data as voltage, raw binary, or both, depending on the setting of **output units**.

When you are through with all analog input operations, call **AI Clear** to stop any in-progress acquisition and release any resources such as buffers. AI Clear should be the last node in your DAQ VI chain before the error handler. It always clears the acquisition regardless of the error status. Easy VIs always clear the acquisition after every call. As a result, AI Config gets called every time and there is much extra overhead. Intermediate VIs include an input to tell the VI whether or not to call AI Config and AI Clear. Properly applied, you can get much better performance than with the easy VIs.

Those are the primary intermediate VIs you need to know about to get started and stopped. Next, you will want to read data.

Low-speed acquisition

Let's say you want to read one or more channels at a modest rate, up to perhaps 10 Hz, with the sampling interval regulated by the LabVIEW timer functions. You can read one scan, or better, you can read several scans and average the samples for each channel to reduce noise. Figure 6.13 shows a VI that performs the simple case of acquiring one scan. It's arranged as a subVI that stores the task ID in an uninitialized shift register between calls. There is no reason to call AI Config every time, since nothing has changed. You connect the **iteration** input of this VI to the iteration terminal, [i] of the calling VI, assuming that this VI is called repeatedly in the usual While Loop. On the first iteration, AI Config does its thing, but it is not called on subsequent iterations. Note that the buffer size is set to zero, so that no data buffer is allocated. Therefore, only one scan can be acquired at a time.

After the Case structure, the task ID and error cluster from AI Config are passed to AI Single Scan, which is the easy way to grab one sample from each channel (i.e., one scan). Since there is no buffer allocated and there is no continuous acquisition happening, you don't have to call AI Clear. Outputs of this VI are voltages for each channel and the error cluster.

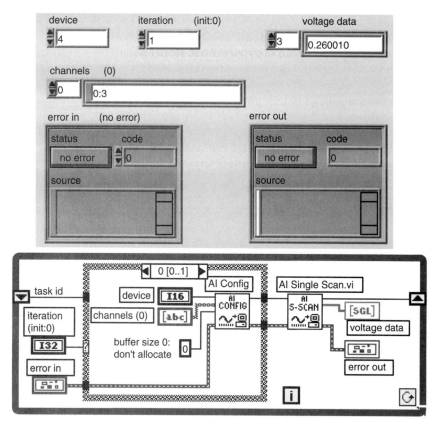

Figure 6.13 A simple subVI that reads one scan from a set of channels. It uses an uninitialized shift register to store the *task id* between calls. Case 1 has *task id* wired straight across and *error in* wired through to *error out*. This example was derived from the intermediate VI, AI Read One Scan.

This VI is a watered-down version of **AI Read One Scan**, an intermediate VI that has more input parameters such as input scaling and number of AMUX boards. Like most of the examples in this chapter, I've simplified it to show only the most important controls. Controls appearing here also appear in the original AI Read One Scan in the simple help view. An even simpler version of this VI is available in the easy I/O library as **AI Sample Channels**. To summarize, you can access this same functionality at three levels, not including the advanced VIs:

AI Sample Channels (easy I/O)

AI Read One Scan (upper-level intermediate)

AI Config; AI Single Scan (lower-level intermediate)

Figure 6.14 shows a simple top-level VI that calls the driver VI we've just discussed. A While Loop executes periodically, timed by the Wait Until Next ms Multiple function. The user can select one channel for display on the Waveform Chart. The data array returned by AI Read One Scan is indexed to extract the desired channel. The VI stops when the user clicks the Stop button or when an I/O error is detected.

One problem occurs with the initialization technique that uses an iteration counter. If there is any possibility that the While Loop will iterate more than 2^{31} times, the iteration counter will overflow to zero and reinitialize the subVI. In such cases, create a shift register on the While Loop and wire it as shown in Fig. 6.15. On the first iteration, the shift register will contain zero. On all subsequent iterations, it will contain one. (How big is 2^{31} anyway? If it's 2^{31} seconds, that's 69 years, since there are about $\pi \times 10^7$ seconds in a year. Therefore, your loop must be running much faster than 1 Hz in order to overflow.)

Now, how about an enhanced operation in which you grab several samples from each channel, then average them to reduce noise? I started with the previous example, then added a few more intermediate VIs and some controls to come up with the VI in Fig. 6.16. Looking at

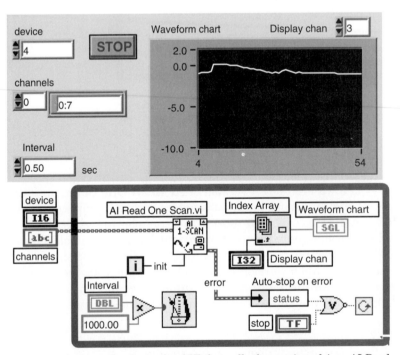

Figure 6.14 An example of a top-level VI that calls the previous driver, AI Read One Scan.

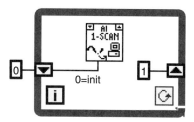

Figure 6.15 Another way to manage the iteration terminal, with no chance of overflow.

the diagram, AI Config is used in exactly the same way as before, except that a buffer is allocated, sized to hold the **number of scans**. Since this is a simple buffered acquisition, AI Start is called next to start the acquisition clocks on the plug-in board, running at the desired **scan rate**. Next, you have to fetch the data from the buffer, a job for **AI Read**. AI Read is an all-purpose DAQ VI for retrieving data, regardless of buffering, and it's embedded in most DAQ VIs that return data. The number of scans is passed to AI Read so that it reads all of the data; you could also read the data in pieces. AI Read returns a 2D array of voltages, representing each individual sample. You can use that data

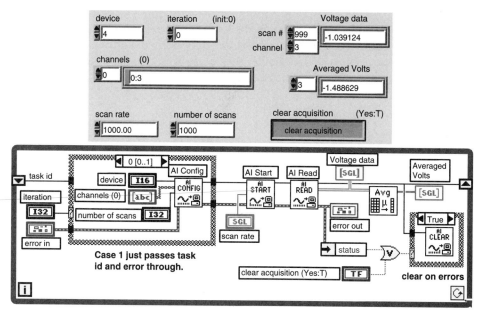

Figure 6.16 This example shows how to use the intermediate VIs to read multiple scans from multiple channels. Note the overall similarity with the example in Fig. 6.13. At the upper right is my utility subVI, Average Voltage.

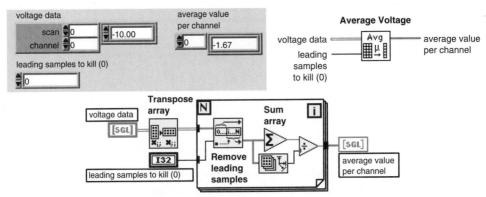

platform\ daq\Average Voltage.vi

directly, or, for this example, pass the 2D array to **Average Voltage**, a utility subVI that I wrote and included on this book's CD-ROM (see Fig. 6.17). It averages all the samples for each channel and returns a 1D array that you can display and store on disk. I've gotten a lot of mileage out of this utility VI; you'll see it in several upcoming examples.

Since a buffer was allocated in this VI, you should call AI Clear when you are done. The **clear acquisition** Boolean should be wired to the **Stop** button on the calling VI so that AI Clear is called only after the final iteration occurs. If you clear the acquisition then call this VI again (without Iteration = 0), the task ID will no longer be valid and an error results.

This example, like the previous one, is quite similar to something directly available in the upper intermediate library, in this case **AI Waveform Scan**. In turn, AI Waveform Scan is encapsulated in the easy I/O VI, **AI Acquire Waveforms**. It is also called by several of the DAQ examples, such as **Acquire N Scans**. Here is a summary of the VIs available to perform this immediate buffered I/O operation:

Acquire N Scans (examples)

AI Acquire Waveforms (easy I/O)

AI Waveform Scan (upper-level intermediate)

AI Config, AI Start, AI Read, AI Clear (lower-level intermediate)

My utility VI, Average Voltage, can be added to any of the higher-level VIs where you have 2D voltage data, including your top-level application. Speaking of which, what would a simple, top-level VI look like? Figure 6.18 shows one that calls AI Acquire Waveforms, displays one channel, and stores everything on disk in tab-delimited text format.

Figure 6.17 Average Voltage averages the samples for each channel into a single value. You can also have it remove a number of leading samples in case your signal conditioning has problems with settling time.

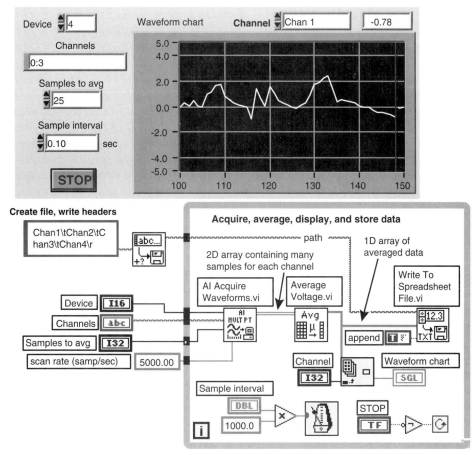

Figure 6.18 A low-speed data acquisition system with averaging, tab-delimited text storage, and a single-channel strip chart. Embellish as desired. The next chapter discusses an improved version of this example.

Sampling parameters are placed outside the While Loop so the user can't change them during the run. On the first call, the user receives a dialog for file creation, and a header is written by the file utility VI, Write Characters To File. Inside the While Loop, the averaged array of data is converted to text then appended to the file by another file utility, Write to Spreadsheet File. This example is useful for sampling rates up to about 10 Hz, beyond which the software timer is relatively imprecise. A more elaborate version of this example is discussed in the next chapter.

Medium-speed acquisition and processing

Many applications demand that you sample one or more analog channels at moderate speeds, on the order of tens to thousands of samples per second, which I'll call *medium-speed acquisition*. At these speeds, you must have the I/O hardware do more of the time-critical work. Let's look at some of these medium-speed DAQ techniques.

Hardware-timed loops.   Figure 6.8 shows the diagram of the example VI, **Cont Acq&Chart (hw timed)**, which is one way of doing hardware-timed loops. It uses the intermediate VI, AI Single Scan, to fetch data from the plug-in board using nonbuffered I/O. Funny that it's called *nonbuffered*. If you think about it, there actually *is* a buffer out there somewhere—there has to be, otherwise some data would be lost each time AI Single Scan returns data to the calling VI, a process that takes a finite amount of time. The mystery buffer is a piece of hardware called a **first-in, first-out (FIFO)** memory that is located on the plug-in board. Samples from the ADC are temporarily stored in the FIFO pending a bus transfer to your computer's main memory, giving the software extra time to take care of other business. An important piece of information is the size of the available FIFO, which varies among models of plug-in boards. For instance, an AT-MIO-16X has 512 words (a word is 16 bits, or one sample), an AT-MIO-16F-5 has 256 words, while an NB-MIO-16 has only 16 words. If you are collecting data at 100,000 samples per second, a 16 word FIFO will fill in just 160 µs—not much time for the driver to get around to uploading the data, and no time at all for a LabVIEW loop to come around again.

So you see, these hardware-timed loops, using nonbuffered I/O, are limited to moderate sampling rates. Testing the VI in Fig. 6.8 on my Quadra 950 with an NB-MIO-16X (with a 16-word FIFO), I can chart one channel at up to about 75 Hz without overflowing the FIFO (DAQ error number –10845, overflow error). If I make the graph smaller, change my monitor from 8-bit color to black and white, or do anything else that reduces graphics overhead, the maximum sampling rate goes up. Within these performance limits, hardware-timed loops are quite useful. Control algorithms are a great application for them because the real-world output device can't wait too long for an update, and the algorithm itself is probably time-dependent to the point that it becomes unstable in the presence of a timebase with excessive jitter. So, you can run several feedback algorithms inside a hardware-timed loop at 50 Hz, for instance, and display the present values, all with good timebase stability. About the only things that will mess up your timing are switching between windows, running too many VIs at once, or putting LabVIEW into the background in competition with another high-priority program running on your computer.

Circular buffers and parallel processing.   Circular buffered I/O adds a significant step in performance to your DAQ program because it can use hardware to continuously transfer data into your computer's main memory. Please note that DMA hardware must be present in order for this technique to work consistently beyond a few thousand samples per second.

The easiest way to set up a circular buffered acquisition is to use the AI Continuous Scan VI from the upper-level intermediate library. It has all the necessary controls for most applications, though you can copy parts from it and modify them to fit your requirements as needed. Figure 6.19 is an interesting example written by Mark Scrivener of Lawrence Livermore National Laboratory (LLNL). His objective was to monitor the current flowing in an electrochemical process and integrate that current over time to determine the total number of coulombs of ions deposited in the process. A *coulomb* is the amount of charge transferred by a current of 1 A flowing for 1 s. Therefore, the program must measure the current, multiply by the time since the last sample, then add the result to the previous sum. The operating equation is

$$Q = \sum_{n=0}^{N} I_n dt$$

where Q is the charge in coulombs, I_n is the latest current measurement, and dt is the interval since the last sample was taken. This constitutes a simple rectangular integration.

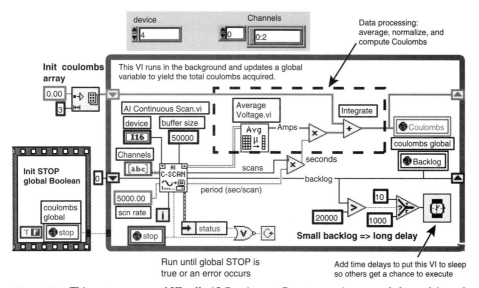

Figure 6.19   This autonomous subVI calls AI Continuous Scan to acquire several channels' worth of data using circular buffered acquisition. The data is processed and written to a global variable for use elsewhere. A delay in the loop gives other VIs a chance to execute.

This VI is set up as a kind of data server VI that communicates via global variables with several client VIs that display and store the calculated result. It runs until the global **stop** Boolean is set to True or a DAQ error occurs. Each time around the loop, the scan backlog from AI Continuous Scan is evaluated. If there is no appreciable amount of data remaining in the circular buffer, a 1-s delay is called for. Calling any of the delay functions allows other concurrently executing VIs to run while this VI sleeps and the hardware does the work of collecting the next buffer of data. If the backlog is very large, a small delay is requested to avoid overwriting the buffer. A large buffer size (50,000 scans) was specified to give ample time before overwriting occurs. At 5000 scans per second, it takes 10 seconds to fill the buffer. In that amount of time, you can do all sorts of background activity. Obviously, Mark must have lots of memory because that big buffer occupies 50,000 × 3 channels × 4 bytes per sample, for a total of 600,000 bytes. Duplication of the array elsewhere in the diagram can quickly lead to an out-of-memory condition. Keep this in mind when you start typing lots of zeroes into the **buffer size** control.

On the diagram, AI Continuous Scan acquires three channels of data at a 5-kHz scan rate. This high scan rate is required because the current waveform is pulsed. The 2D data array is averaged on a channel-by-channel basis by Average Voltage. Its output is an array of channels with units of amperes, courtesy of the scale factor applied during the acquisition process. Each current value is then multiplied by the actual scan period supplied by AI Continuous Scan, yielding results in units of coulombs. Summing the latest measurement with the previous total in the shift register yields an integrated value, which is written to a global variable for use elsewhere in a client VI.

With this arrangement, the acquisition server VI is asleep most of the time while the buffer is filling. When it wakes up, AI Continuous Scan will read the requested number of bytes (stored in the lower shift register). Then the data analysis happens and the VI goes back to sleep. Other VIs have plenty of time to use the collected data.

A possible enhancement to this VI would be to use the **Integrate** VI from the analysis library rather than performing a simple average on each buffer of data. Testing indicated that the difference between the two methods was very small because the average value of a simple square pulse is equal to the integral over the same time period.

High-speed disk streaming

Circular buffered I/O is the basis for **disk streaming**, recording to disk at high speed. When you run your analog input hardware at near-maximum speeds in a disk streaming application, it will probably be impossible to view very much of that data in real time because your computer will be very busy transferring data from memory to disk. On the other hand, you may be able to perform some real-time analysis, as in the previous example, that does not require extensive graphical displays. The disk streaming example in Fig. 6.20 includes a waveform graph, but it could easily be deleted for higher performance. I started with the example VI, **Cont Acq to File (Scaled)**, then added the programming for a graph that I stole from **Cont Acq&Graph (Buffered)**. (As I always say, program by plagiarizing.)

I tested this VI on my Quadra 950 with an NB-MIO-16XH-18 and a DMA-2800, the latter of which has DMA capability, which is required for these higher sampling rates. The settings shown in Fig. 6.20 are

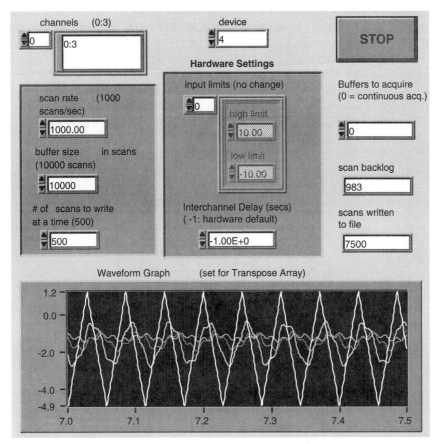

Figure 6.20 Panel for a VI that acquires data, graphs, and writes scaled (voltage) data directly to disk with maximum throughput. Adapted from the example VI, Cont Acq to File (Scaled).

typical of the maximum achievable performance with a graph: four channels displayed at 1 kHz per channel, including writing of scaled data to a file. Without the graph, I could run the VI right up to the full speed of the board, which is about 55 kHz. If you have a faster A/D board, such as an NB- or EISA-A2000 which samples at rates up to 1 MHz, you will find that the limiting factor is the throughput of your disk system. One million samples per second, multiplied by 4 bytes per sample, is 4,000,000 bytes per second—that's a pretty fast disk system. There is a way to cut down the volume of data by a factor of two: store the data as raw (I16 integer) binary. The other stream-to-disk example, **Cont Acq to File (Raw)**, does just that.

You will need to experiment a bit with the **scan rate**, **buffer size**, and **scans to write** controls to achieve maximum performance. As a rule, I like to make the buffer size at least twice, and preferably 10 times, the scan rate to give the VI time to catch up with any scan backlog that occurs due to other activity on the machine. The **scans to write** value is a bit more nebulous. Sometimes, you can find a performance peak when the number of bytes written each time corresponds to the size of a buffer, or cache memory, in your disk system. If you are graphing data, plan to update the graph no more than about 10 times per second to avoid excessive overhead. The same rule of thumb probably applies to file I/O. I usually shoot for one or two file writes and graph updates per second.

The diagram for this disk streaming VI, shown in Fig. 6.21, is fairly complex. But if you examine it from left to right one VI at a time, it's

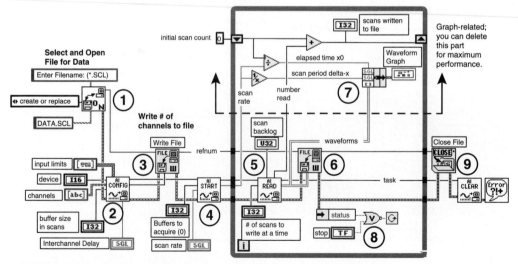

Figure 6.21 Diagram for the disk streaming example. File I/O utility VIs are combined with lower-level intermediate DAQ VIs to yield a flexible, high-performance data recording system.

not too hard to understand. There are really two parallel tasks happening in this diagram: data acquisition using the DAQ functions, and file I/O using some file utility VIs with error handling. The two tasks share error I/O as a common thread; you can see the error cluster zigzag through the diagram. The file refnum is passed from one file I/O VI to the next, while the DAQ task ID is passed between DAQ VIs. In general, the left part of the diagram is devoted to initialization, the loop contains the real-time acquisition, and the right part handles final cleanup. All of the DAQ VIs are from the lower-level intermediate library, and together they perform exactly the same function as AI Continuous Scan, which appears in the previous example. Let's go through the diagram step-by-step.

1. The **Open/Create/Replace File** VI opens or creates a new byte stream data file.

2. The **AI Config** VI allocates the data acquisition buffer and sets the A/D input limits.

3. The **Write File** function writes the **Number of Channels** output from AI Config to the data file. This value represents the number of channels and is needed when an analysis program attempts to read the data file.

4. The **AI Start** VI starts the buffered data acquisition operation. If **buffers to acquire** is zero, the operation will continue indefinitely. AI Start also sets the scan rate.

5. The **AI Read** VI waits until the requested **number of scans to write** is available from the circular buffer. It returns a 2D array containing that many scans of data, scaled to voltage. If there is more data in the buffer, **scan backlog** will be greater than zero.

6. The **Write File** function appends the 2D data array to the file.

7. The icons in this area support the waveform graph. Since AI Read returns the actual scan interval, that timing information is available for scaling the x axis in seconds. You can delete everything above the dashed line to increase the performance of this VI. Alternatively, the graph could be placed inside a Case structure so that you can turn off graphing if desired.

8. The While Loop stops if an error occurs or the **stop** button is pressed. This loop cycles at a rate determined by the amount of time that it takes to acquire **number of scans to write**.

9. Final cleanup is handled by the **Close File** function and **AI Clear** VI. If an error occurred, the **General Error Handler** VI displays a dialog.

Special sampling

Some analog acquisition applications demand very careful control over the timing of each sample. For instance, if you are measuring the phase shift between several analog signals, you need to know precisely when each sample is taken on each channel or use **simultaneous sampling** hardware that adds no interchannel delay. Other situations demand **triggering**, where the acquisition operation starts when a certain condition is met, such as the detection of a critical voltage level in a signal. There are many special sampling tools built into the DAQ library and various plug-in boards that make your life easier when these situations arise.

Simultaneous sampling.   When you use an ordinary MIO-series board or other analog input device that has a multiplexer, each sample arrives at a slightly different time than its neighbors. The time differential is determined by the sampling rate of the ADC. If this interchannel phase (timing skew) is important, you should consider buying hardware with multichannel, simultaneous sampling. Such hardware may have one ADC per channel, such as the A2150-series boards, or it may have one sample-and-hold amplifier per channel, such as the A2000-series boards and the SCXI-1140 module. (A *sample-and-hold* takes an instantaneous snapshot of the input voltage and stores it with a capacitor until the ADC gets around to reading the value. That way, one expensive ADC can be shared among several channels using cheaper sample-and-holds.) Simultaneous sampling is important in many time- and phase-sensitive applications, such as vibration analysis and acoustics.

For most operations, the DAQ library attempts to scan a group of channels by running the ADC of your I/O board at top speed, thus providing the minimum timing skew. This is called **near-simultaneous sampling**. Indeed, for many applications, the 10-µs skew provided by a 100-kHz ADC is negligible. If you wish to override this feature, you must use the **interchannel delay** control on AI Config. The default value for **interchannel delay** is preset to the minimum value permitted by the device you are configuring, which implies near-simultaneous sampling. For example, if you were to increase the delay to 1 ms, all I/O operations would be limited to a top speed of 1000 samples per second. Ten channels could be scanned no faster than 100 scans per second.

The good news about simultaneous sampling is that, once you buy the hardware, you don't have to do anything special with the DAQ software—the board does all the work. But if you don't have one of those fancy boards, you must correct the timing skew for each channel when you analyze the data. The best way to find out how much skew is in your data is to measure it. Connect all channels of interest to a common input signal, preferably a square wave because its rapid transitions are obvious time markers. Collect scans of data using your acquisition VI, then display the results with all channels on the same graph. The x axis of the graph must be calibrated in seconds (see the example VIs). Use the graph cursors to measure channel-to-channel timing skew. Since the amount of skew may vary with the sampling rate and the number of channels, you may need to examine the results for several sampling conditions. The timebase correction values may then be applied to your data by adjusting the X_0 (initial time value) when graphing each channel.

Triggering. The whole subject of triggering is discussed in more detail in Chap. 9, "Physics Applications." Here, we'll look at the options available in the DAQ world. First, there are two basic types of triggering: hardware and software. **Hardware triggering** relies on specialized hardware features included on a plug-in board. There are in turn two types of hardware triggers: analog and digital. *Analog* trigger circuitry generates a trigger when an input signal reaches a specified slope and level. This feature is identical to the familiar triggering controls on oscilloscopes. Analog triggering is only available on certain plug-in boards, such as the dynamic signal acquisition series (AT-A2150, NB-A2150, etc.) from National Instruments. *Digital* triggers are supplied through an external connector input to the board, such as the external trigger input to an oscilloscope. Digital triggers are available on all National Instruments plug-in boards. **Software triggering** uses a program (either deep inside the driver or one written in LabVIEW) that examines continuously acquired data to see if it meets the triggering criteria. Data is only processed if it meets the criteria, thus saving CPU time and/or disk space. In summary, hardware triggering acts directly on the analog signal; software triggering acts on the digitized data.

Another aspect of triggering that you need to understand is the difference between **pretrigger** and **posttrigger** sampling. Data acquired after a trigger pulse occurs is known as *posttrigger* data, while data acquired before the trigger is *pretrigger* data. Pretrigger data is useful when you need to record some baseline data before the main signal arrives, or in situations where there is some uncertainty as to the relationship between the main event and the trigger pulse.

The upper-level intermediate VI, **AI Waveform Scan**, is the single most useful DAQ function for triggered acquisition. It supports all types of hardware and software triggering, and it's used in all the example VIs that demonstrate the various trigger modes. It has enough features for most applications, but if there is something missing, you can always modify it and save it under a different name. The diagram for AI Waveform Scan is complex because it allows you to transparently switch between analog hardware triggering and software triggering—similar functions with completely different implementations.

Let's look at hardware triggering first. All hardware triggering parameters are entered through **AI Start**. Figure 6.22 explains their basic functions, and the DAQ manual discusses them in detail. In turn, AI Start calls the advanced VI, **AI Trigger Config**. For complicated triggering situations, refer to the DAQ manual under AI Trigger Config. If you are using AI Waveform Scan, only a few of these controls are available on its panel.

Digital hardware triggering.   Digital hardware triggering is easy to set up and use. You will need a TTL-compatible signal that is synchronized to the analog signal you wish to capture. On a standard MIO-series

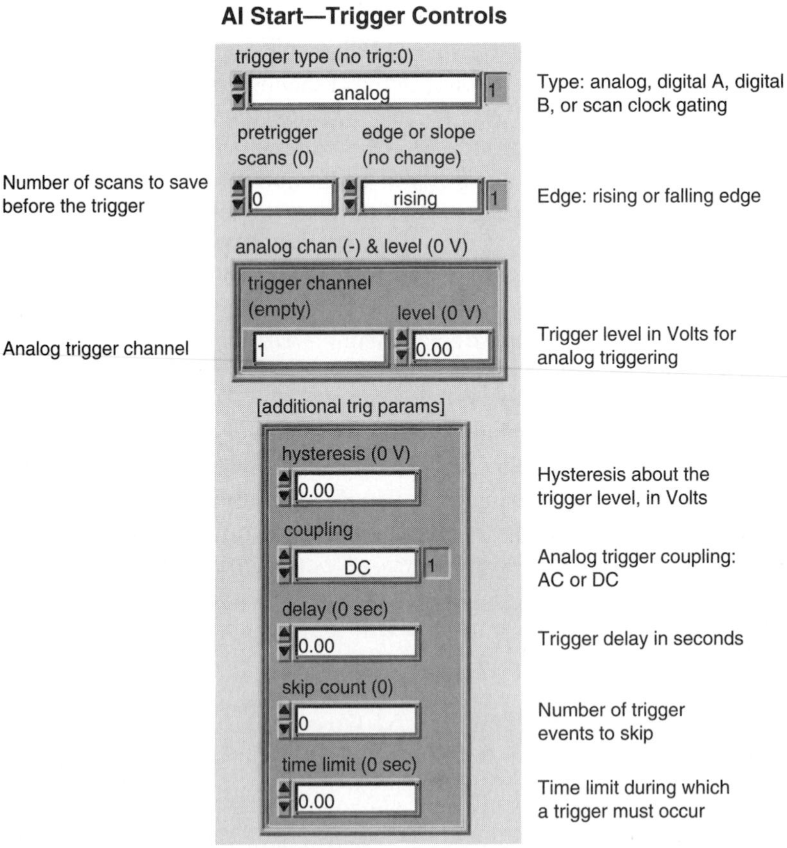

AI Start—Trigger Controls

trigger type (no trig:0)	
analog [1]	Type: analog, digital A, digital B, or scan clock gating
pretrigger scans (0) edge or slope (no change)	
Number of scans to save before the trigger [0] [rising] [1]	Edge: rising or falling edge
analog chan (-) & level (0 V)	
trigger channel (empty) level (0 V)	
Analog trigger channel [1] [0.00]	Trigger level in Volts for analog triggering
[additional trig params]	
hysteresis (0 V) [0.00]	Hysteresis about the trigger level, in Volts
coupling [DC] [1]	Analog trigger coupling: AC or DC
delay (0 sec) [0.00]	Trigger delay in seconds
skip count (0) [0]	Number of trigger events to skip
time limit (0 sec) [0.00]	Time limit during which a trigger must occur

Figure 6.22   Triggering controls available on the intermediate DAQ function, AI Start.

board, there are two digital inputs you may use for triggering a scan: STARTTRIG* and STOPTRIG. The asterisk (*) means that a TTL low level (ground) is required to assert the signal; otherwise, a high level (>2.5 V) is required. So, to generate a start trigger, you need to connect a TTL signal to STARTTRIG* that is high except at the moment you want to start acquiring posttrigger data. If you are collecting pretrigger data with an MIO board, you set STOPTTRIG high at the moment when you have collected sufficient pretrigger data. On the E-series multifunction boards, programmable function input (PFI) lines serve a variety of purposes with regards to triggering and timing. On other boards, such as the NB-A2100, there is only one external trigger input, and its action depends on the trigger mode set by the driver. Consult the hardware manual for details on your particular board, and refer to AI Trigger Config in the DAQ manual for more information on using special-purpose triggering pins. There are many ways to connect these versatile triggering pins; study the manuals carefully and plan to do some experiments with your board and LabVIEW.

For programming examples, see **Acquire N Scans-DTrig** or **Acquire N Scans-Multi-DTrig**. Both use AI Waveform Scan. A more elaborate example, **Acquire&Proc N Scans-Trig**, uses the lower-level intermediate VIs and allows on-the-fly processing of data. You might use this VI when you are measuring a recurrent waveform that is synchronized to a digital trigger, such as the output of a function generator. With synchronization, each acquired waveform is guaranteed to be locked in-phase with every other. Therefore, you can perform mathematical operations, such as waveform averaging or differencing, without errors due to phase mismatching.

Note that the trigger signal can be generated by the same plug-in board that you use for data acquisition. For instance, a counter-timer or DAC update clock can serve as a system synchronization signal. This permits you to simultaneously measure a response while generating a stimulus. In the DAQ examples, in the analog_io.llb library, there are some of these hardware-timed examples. Chapter 9, "Physics Applications," also has some examples of synchronized output and input.

Analog hardware triggering.   If you have one of the fancy plug-in boards with analog triggering hardware, you have the makings of a real triggered-sweep oscilloscope (albeit somewhat limited in bandwidth). No special external connections are required because onboard analog comparators and logic sample the analog signal and generate a hardware trigger signal when the requested conditions are present. Boards with hardware analog triggering include the E-series MIO boards, the dynamic signal acquisition boards (A2000 and A2150, etc.), and the new digital oscilloscope boards. To see how analog triggering works, try one of the ATrig example VIs, such as **Acquire N Scans-ATrig**, **Acquire N Scans-Multi-ATrig**, or **Acquire&Proc N Scans-Trig**, which are the analog versions of the examples used for digital triggers.

Software triggering. Software triggering is built into the NI-DAQ driver and is particularly useful with I/O boards that don't offer analog triggering hardware, such as the standard MIO series. You access software triggering through the **conditional retrieval** controls in **AI Read** (Fig. 6.23). These controls simulate the hardware options available in AI Start, but the action of conditional retrieval is different. The I/O board actually collects data in its free-running, untriggered mode. For each buffer of data acquired, the driver searches through the buffer, looking for the first part of the data that matches the trigger conditions. If a match is found, AI Read returns the data. If no match is found, no data is returned. This saves time because it requires less copying or moving of data in memory.

For software triggering applications, you can use the features of AI Waveform Scan, which is nicely packaged in the example **Acquire N Scans-SW Trig**. Or, you can use **Acquire&Proc Scans-SW Trig**, which uses the lower-level intermediate VIs for continuous processing. This last example continuously triggers off of data in a buffer without

AI Read—Conditional Retrieval Controls

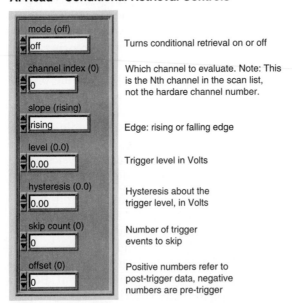

mode (off)	Turns conditional retrieval on or off
channel index (0)	Which channel to evaluate. Note: This is the Nth channel in the scan list, not the hardare channel number.
slope (rising)	Edge: rising or falling edge
level (0.0)	Trigger level in Volts
hysteresis (0.0)	Hysteresis about the trigger level, in Volts
skip count (0)	Number of trigger events to skip
offset (0)	Positive numbers refer to post-trigger data, negative numbers are pre-trigger

Figure 6.23 Condition retrieval controls, available from AI Read, simulate analog triggering for boards that don't have analog triggering hardware.

pausing acquisition. Furthermore, you can change the trigger parameters without stopping acquisition.

DAQ occurrences for asynchronous reading. Sometimes, something funny happens when you call AI Read to upload a bunch of scans from a continuous buffered acquisition: your whole LabVIEW application seems to lock up or act very erratic. The reason is that AI Read is waiting until the requested number of scans have been acquired. You would think that the DAQ library would wait asynchronously, allowing other parts of your diagrams to continue. But at the lowest level, AI Read is calling a CIN, and CINs execute synchronously, blocking out all other LabVIEW activity until the data is ready. This wastes CPU time and interferes with user interface activity.

If there were a DAQ Status VI, perhaps you could poll it in a loop to find out when the buffer is full before calling AI Read. But there is no such status VI. Instead, you can take one of two approaches. First, you can use one of the software timers, such as Wait (ms), to put the acquisition loop to sleep while data accumulates in the buffers. This gives other tasks some time. The trick is determining how long to wait. The magic number is something less than the expected scan time, which you can estimate by dividing the number of scans to read by the scan rate. I tested this method and found that the delay needed to be about 50 percent of this value. For instance, when scanning 1000 scans/sec and reading 500 scans per cycle of the loop, a safe timer setting was about 250 ms. Greater values resulted in a large (or growing) backlog. While simple, this technique has the risk of causing a backlog problem.

DAQ occurrences to the rescue! The **DAQ Occurrence Config** VI, located in the miscellaneous DAQ function palette, has the ability to monitor the status of a DAQ task and set an occurrence when a desired event has transpired. For instance, it can set the occurrence when a specified number of scans have been acquired, when a counter changes state, or when a DAQ error occurs. *Note:* As of this writing, DAQ occurrences work only for Windows, though support for other platforms is planned.

The diagram in Fig. 6.24 shows how to call AI Read only when the desired number of scans are ready. The **Wait On Occurrence** function holds off a While Loop containing AI Read until the number of scans equals **general value A**. As soon as the occurrence is set, AI Read quickly fetches the data, the data is graphed, and the loop pauses at the Wait On Occurrence function again. Since the acquisition loop is paused most of the time, you need to use parallel While Loops to manage other processing, such as the user interface. Data can be exchanged among loops with local variables or with global variables if the data is needed in other client VIs.

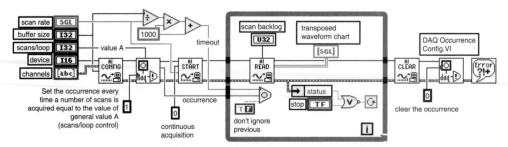

Figure 6.24 A DAQ occurrence is generated whenever a specified number of scans (scans/loop) are available. In the meantime, the While Loop is asleep and no time is wasted.

Different sampling rates on different channels. It's really easy to acquire data from several channels at the same speed, as we've already seen. But how do you set up a system that runs different sampling rates on different channels? One fundamental limitation of the DAQ library and the available plug-in boards is that you can only run one acquisition task on a given board at one time. That is, you can't do something simple like simultaneously calling AI Continuous Scan and AI Waveform Scan for the same board but with different channels and sampling parameters, expecting them to run in parallel. The first one to execute will start its operation, then the second one will mess up the register settings on the board, destroying the first operation. Instead of data, you get error messages. (Please note that you *can* run multiple tasks on a single board if they are of different types. For instance, a buffered input and a buffered output operation can run simultaneously.)

The best solution is to use a separate plug-in board for each acquisition task. The DAQ driver can manage many input tasks in parallel, so long as there is only one input task *per board*. For instance, you can run two of the continuous acquisition example VIs in parallel, with one of them scanning board A at 10 kHz and the other scanning board B at 1 Hz. System resources—buffer space, computations, file I/O, and overhead—are nicely allocated and scheduled, courtesy of the NI-DAQ driver and the LabVIEW scheduler. You still have to make sure, however, that your system doesn't get overloaded to the point where it can't keep up with the aggregate data rate. The only notable drawback of this approach is the cost of the extra board(s).

Upcoming versions of the NI-DAQ driver will probably include support for multirate scanning. The newer E-series DAQ boards have the hardware to do it, but the software drivers are a little behind. It turns out that the problem is nontrivial when you try to maintain backward compatibility with older boards and other DAQ VIs. Assuming that they are successful, you should gain the ability to acquire data with at least a 500-to-1 ratio in scan rate between channels.

If your objective is to save disk space or to avoid graphing too many data points at one time, then you have another option: sample all channels at the speed of the fastest channel, and then decimate the data for the slower channels. The LabVIEW analysis VI, **Decimate**, from the Digital Signal Processing function palette, is pretty fast and can be the foundation for more elaborate decimation operations. A quick benchmark indicates that a 10,000-element array can be decimated by a factor of 1000:1 in only a few milliseconds on an average PC. The Decimate VI can also average the decimated data rather than simply extracting every nth sample.

platform\ decimate\Decimate Selected Channels.vi

For a practical DAQ application where you acquire scans from several channels, the decimation problem is easier said than done. Figure 6.25 is one solution, a VI I call **Decimate Selected Channels**. Data arrives as **Mixed data**—both fast and slow channels—in a 2D array, which is the standard data format for DAQ waveform acquisition VIs. Within this array, let's assume that you arbitrarily choose some channels for decimation (the slow channels), while the others are to remain untouched (the fast channels). The **Channels to decimate** array is where you choose the slow channels. A For Loop sifts through the mixed data and builds two new output arrays, the fast and the slow. You can enter an arbitrary **Decimation factor** for the slow channels.

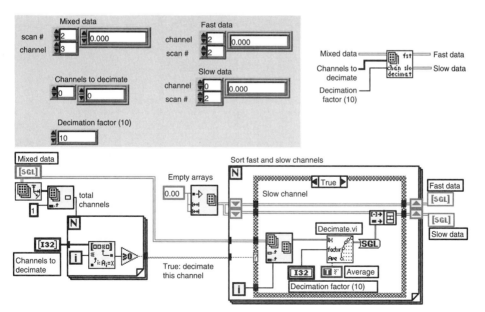

Figure 6.25 The Decimate Selected Channels VI lets you decimate your choice of channels from a 2D data array. The slow, or decimated, channels are more efficient for display and storage.

Figure 6.26 is an example of a continuous acquisition VI that calls the Decimate Selected Channels VI. AI Continuous Scan acquires all channels at the fast rate. Decimate Selected Channels divides the data into fast and slow arrays. You can select one channel for display from either of the arrays. Fast and slow data are appended to separate binary files by two calls to the Write File function. An error cluster propagates among the I/O VIs. If an error occurs, the While Loop stops. When I tried this on my Quadra 950, I could easily display the 100:1 decimated version of data acquired at 10 kHz. But directly graphing the 10-kHz waveform resulted in a buffer overflow; I don't have the CPU horsepower to display that much data in real time. In addition, the size of the data file for slow data is a factor of 100 smaller than that for the fast data. Clearly, decimation is an effective solution in this case.

Here's a benchmark on the Decimate Selected Channels VI, for comparison purposes: with mixed data consisting of 1000 scans and 16

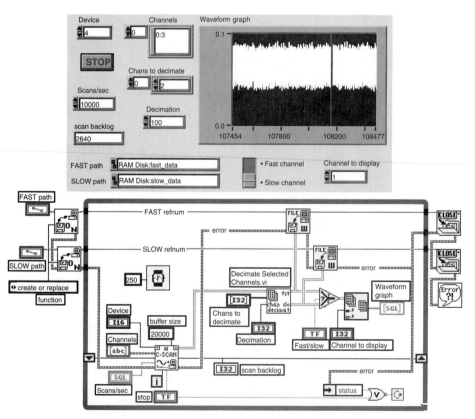

Figure 6.26   A demonstration of the Decimate Selected Channels VI. You can view either a fast or a slow (decimated) channel from continuously acquired data. The two data files segregate the results.

channels, with 8 channels selected for processing and a decimation factor of 10, the VI requires 180 ms on the Quadra 950. A really fast Pentium or PowerPC could probably do it in 20 ms or so.

 **platform\ decimate** I've included two other decimation VIs on the CD-ROM. The **Avg Selected Channels** VI works a bit like the Decimate Selected Channels VI, but returns slow data as a 1D array. That is, it takes all of the incoming waveform data for a slow channel and averages it into a single point. The VI also permits you to turn averaging on and off. When it's off, the VI returns the first sample and ignores the rest. This VI is about twice as fast as the decimation VI. The **Avg Sequential Channels** VI is similar to Avg Selected Channels, but it assumes that the mixed data is organized with fast channels first, followed by slow channels. All you do is tell the VI the number of fast channels. This VI is about four times as fast as the decimation VI.

These data averager VIs are faster because they do less processing than the decimation VI, and, in the case of the Avg Sequential Channels VI, because there is much less array manipulation. LabVIEW is at the mercy of the memory manager when it comes time to create arrays, and memory management always takes extra time. If you were to write your own decimation or averaging algorithm in C, you might be able to preallocate memory buffers and avoid this problem. For really high performance, it's an option, as long as you're comfortable with C. Otherwise, do some benchmarking and optimize your VIs to reduce array manipulation, particularly array building and array splitting.

For a turnkey approach to data logging at variant rates, take a look at the Multi-Rate VI published in *LTR* (LTR Publishing 1994). They use decimation and a custom binary file format that allows you to choose a different storage rate for each channel. Special VIs are included for reading and writing the files. Again, the ultimate speed limitation is the time LabVIEW takes to decimate waveforms and allocate memory.

Ignoring some data.   We spend a lot of time worrying about processing every single sample of data in a continuous stream. But is that really an *absolute* requirement for your application? I worked on an electrophysiology experiment where we needed to observe the power spectrum of brain waves in real time. I set up a VI that performs circular buffered acquisition with the data piped to a power spectrum VI, then to a graph. It quickly became apparent that my computer could not keep up with the required sampling rate because the FFT algorithms in the power spectrum were using up too much CPU time. AI Read would report a buffer overrun after only a few seconds, and the VI would give me an error dialog and stop. The important factor in this application is that I didn't really need to see all of the data samples. If I could view 50 to 75 percent of the data, that would be sufficient. To process any more data, I would need a much faster computer or maybe a DSP board.

Instead of going out and buying a faster computer or slaving over the program, I simply turned off the error handler! So what if the DAQ input buffer gets overwritten? I still see the latest power spectrum, even though I missed some fraction of a second of data. AI Read sometimes returns an overrun error, but the While Loop keeps on running. I added a switch to the front panel that enables or disables the stopping of the main loop on errors. It's handy to have full error handling when you are getting things set up. Another solution is to add a filter for the error code you wish to ignore. You can use the utility VI, **Strip Error Code (DAQ)**, on the CD-ROM.

platform\ daq\Strip Error Code (DAQ).vi

Figure 6.27 shows a more graceful technique (it's bad form to intentionally generate errors). You can prevent buffer overruns altogether by telling the AI Read VI to return only the latest data, ignoring the rest. Use the **read/search position** cluster setting the **position** to *relative to end of data*. AI Read will then return the number of scans selected by **scans to read**, with the last sample returned being the very latest sample in the buffer.

If you're wondering about the details behind this whole buffering, backlog, and overflow issue, read on. There was a big discussion on the info-labview mailgroup regarding the DAQ interrupt rate. It turns out

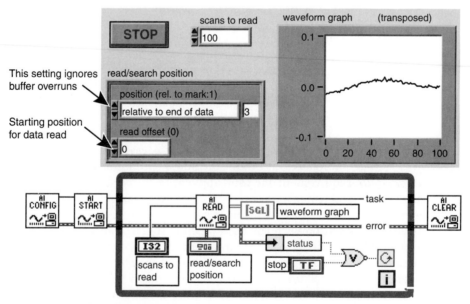

Figure 6.27 Use the read/search position cluster on AI Read, set as shown, to prevent buffer overrun errors by returning only the latest data.

that the interrupt rate for DMA operations isn't generally the point of failure. An interrupt occurs only when the DMA controller needs to be reset after transferring a block of data. The DMA hardware is transferring data from the board to an area of system memory reserved by the NI-DAQ driver. It's up to your LabVIEW program to issue AI Read calls to copy the data in that buffer to LabVIEW memory space for whatever purpose. The amount of data remaining in the system memory is the **backlog**. If you don't call AI Read often enough, the DMA buffer starts to overwrite old data and an error is reported. Setting the read/search position parameter in AI Read to *relative to end of data* tells NI-DAQ to ignore any older, backlogged data. You can easily modify the continuous acquisition examples to operate this way and have your virtual oscilloscope ripping along at tens of kHz per channel.

Analog Outputs

The analog output DAQ library is somewhat simpler than the input side—there aren't quite so many options on output devices. Like the input library, you can use the easy I/O VIs to get started or move into the intermediate VIs for additional features. And everything you learned about inputs applies symmetrically to outputs, thanks to the consistency of the DAQ library.

Configuring and stopping

All analog output operations begin with a call to **AO Config** (Fig. 6.28). Like AI Config, it accepts a list of channels on a given device to which data will be written. If you set the **buffer size** to zero, no buffer is allocated, and you will only be able to perform single-value updates. A nonzero buffer length implies **waveform generation**, where multiple updates are sequentially written to one or more output channels. AO Config creates a **taskID** for use by other analog output VIs.

AO Config

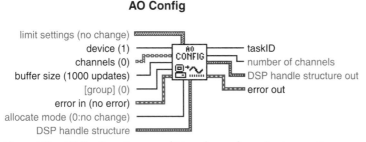

Figure 6.28 AO Config sets up conditions for analog output operations.

The last VI you call after stopping a buffered analog output task is **AO Clear**, which is similar to and just as simple as AI Clear. That's about all there is to setting up an analog output sequence, besides the writing of data.

Simple updates

If you're doing low-speed updates, say 10 Hz or less, an unbuffered analog output operation should be adequate. In the easy I/O library, there is the **AO Update Channel** VI, which writes a single value to a single channel, and its cousin, the **AO Update Channels** VI, which writes a single value to multiple channels. Both include a call to the error handler. In turn, both of them call the **AO Write One Update** VI from the upper-level intermediate library. That's the VI to use for simple applications like the two-channel DC voltage source VI in Fig. 6.29. AO Write One Update accepts the usual **device** and **channels** specifications and an array of voltages containing one value per channel. The data could just as well come from a measurement, a calculation, a global variable, or a preinitialized array containing low-speed waveforms.

Like the other, upper-level intermediate VIs, AO Write One Update contains an uninitialized shift register that stores the **taskID** between calls. When the VI is called with **iteration** equal to zero, AO Config is called to create a new taskID that references the specified device and channels. For all other values of **iteration**, the taskID circulates in the

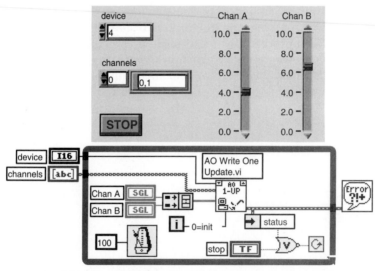

Figure 6.29   This VI calls AO Write One Update 10 times per second to create a manually operated, two-channel voltage source.

shift register and is used by **Analog Output Single Update**, an advanced VI that actually writes data. This method saves CPU time because a new task doesn't have to be configured each time. However, you must remember that the uninitialized shift register serves as global memory. That is, if you need to invoke AO Write One Update in more than one place in your diagram, be aware that all instances will share the same taskID. Is that what you want? If you want to initialize AO Write One Update in one location, then use it to write data in several other places (to the same output channels), then the default setup is fine. But, if you want to use it to write data to different sets of channels, then you must open it, and set the VI configuration to **reentrant** execution, and save the VI with a new name. Reentrant VIs create a separate set of storage locations for each instance of the VI, so the shift registers will no longer share data. This is the opposite of a global variable where you *want* the shift registers to store data between calls, regardless of who calls the subVI. To summarize, here is the hierarchy of VIs for simple analog outputs:

AO Update Channels (easy I/O)

AO Write One Update (upper-level intermediate)

AO Config (lower-level intermediate)

AO Single Update (advanced)

Analog outputs as digital attenuators.   Another interesting thing you can do with your analog outputs is use them as **digital attenuators**. Most of National Instruments' boards have an external reference option for each analog output. Instead of using the fixed, onboard DC reference voltage, you can supply your own external signal through the external reference input. What's interesting is that your signal can be either polarity of DC, or even an AC voltage. The output of the DAC is the product of the reference voltage (your signal) and the digital count sent to the analog output by one of the DAQ VIs. The circuit that does this is called a *multiplying DAC*. For unipolar setups, if you tell the DAC to go to 50 percent of its output range, the output signal amplitude will be 50 percent of the reference amplitude. For bipolar setups, a request for a negative output inverts the reference signal. Note, however, that National Instruments does not specify DAC performance with external references that are much different from the nominal 5 or 10 VDC. If you want to use very low DC voltages or AC signals, test first! There may be some nonlinearity, noise, or bandwidth limitations that you don't expect.

Digital attenuation is particularly useful when you need to control the amplitude of a signal that is generated by another instrument. For instance, your average multifunction board isn't fast enough to generate a clean 50-kHz sine wave, but the multiplying DAC is more than happy to pass such a signal from an external function generator. In fact, the preceding DC source example VI would serve nicely as a volume control for a stereo audio application. This technique also solves a sticky waveform generation problem: changing amplitude on the fly without causing discontinuities. It's easy: use one DAC channel to generate a continuous waveform (discussed later), and feed that signal into the external reference of a second DAC channel that serves as a digital attenuator.

There is only one setup trick to remember. If you are using one DAC channel for waveform generation, the second channel (the attenuator) must be assigned to a different group. To do this, you need to wire a different value to the **group** input on AO Config for one of the DACs. (If you want to generate waveforms on both DACs simultaneously, that's possible, but the two waveforms must be stored in the same 2D array and be part of the same waveform generation operation.)

Waveform generation

Above 10 Hz or so, you should consider using buffered waveform generation. This is much the same situation we saw with analog inputs, where software-timed loops lack the accuracy to run at higher speeds. The general steps you must perform are as follows:

1. Create a waveform—an array of values scaled to voltage. Determine how many samples the waveform needs and how fast you intend to send samples (updates) to the DAC.

2. Call **AO Write** (Fig. 6.30) to load the waveform into a buffer that you previously allocated with AO Config. The buffer should be at least as long as the waveform, though best performance is attained when the lengths are equal. You can also request waveform **regeneration**, where the buffer is automatically written to the DAC over and over again.

AO Write

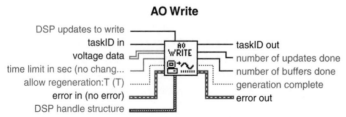

Figure 6.30   AO Write loads a waveform (an array of voltages) into a memory buffer.

3. Call **AO Start** (Fig. 6.31) to start the actual output operation. AO Start determines the update rate and the number of buffer iterations. If **buffer iterations** is zero, waveform regeneration is requested. The only way to stop regeneration is to call AO Clear.

4. If you are generating a single buffer, call **AO Wait** before calling AO Clear. AO Wait checks to see that the whole buffer has been written to the DAC and doesn't return until the operation is complete. If you call AO Clear too soon, you will abort the operation in midbuffer.

5. Always remember to call **AO Clear** when you are finished to free up memory.

There are upper-level intermediate VIs that make waveform generation easy. If you want to generate a single-shot waveform, use the **AO Waveform Gen** VI. It accepts a 2D array of data (the waveforms for each channel) and generates a timed, simple-buffered waveform for the given output channels at the specified update rate. It does not return until the generation is complete. Internally, it calls the expected sequence of lower-level intermediate VIs: configure, write, start, wait, and clear. The example in Fig. 6.32 uses AO Waveform Gen to produce a single-shot chirp waveform. The **Chirp Pattern** VI from the analysis library builds an array of data that is displayed with the Waveform Graph. Since I only wanted to drive one output, I had to use a Build Array function to make a 2D array—the data type required by AO Waveform Gen. However, the rows and columns turn out to be switched (lots of channels; only one sample!), so I used the **Transpose 1D Array** function to swap them.

Somewhat more challenging is the generation of continuously repeating waveforms. This requires **buffered waveform generation** where you copy LabVIEW data to an intermediate buffer managed by NI-DAQ prior to its being written to the DAC. For a simple, continuous waveform, you can use the upper-level intermediate VI, **AO Continuous Gen**, which works much like AO Waveform Gen. The example VI, **Continuous Generation**, shows how to use it. No problem there.

AO Start

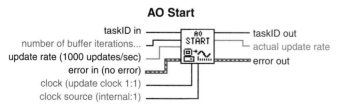

Figure 6.31 Call AO Start to initiate a buffered analog output operation.

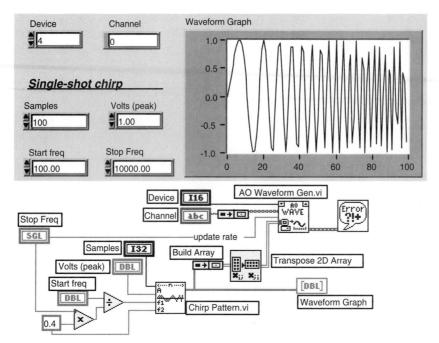

Figure 6.32 This example generates a single-shot chirp waveform with calibrated start and stop frequencies using the Chirp Pattern VI and AO Waveform Gen.

To change the waveform on the fly, you must turn to the lower-level intermediate VIs and **circular buffered waveform generation**, as shown in Fig. 6.33. For simplicity, I distilled this one from the example VI, **Function Generator**, which allows you to change many aspects of the waveform on the fly. The basic procedure for circular buffered waveform generation is as follows:

1. Call **AO Config** to allocate an output buffer.

2. Create your waveform, sized to fit the output buffer. Make it into a 2D array (use Build Array), then use Transpose 2D Array to swap the rows and columns for compatibility with AO Write.

3. Load your waveform into the buffer with **AO Write**.

4. Start waveform generation with **AO Start**. Set the **number of iterations** to zero to force continuous generation. The buffer will be written to the output channel over and over, until you call AO Clear.

5. To change the waveform during generation, pass a new 2D waveform array to AO Write. The buffer will be overwritten, but waveform generation will not be interrupted. Note, however, that this is

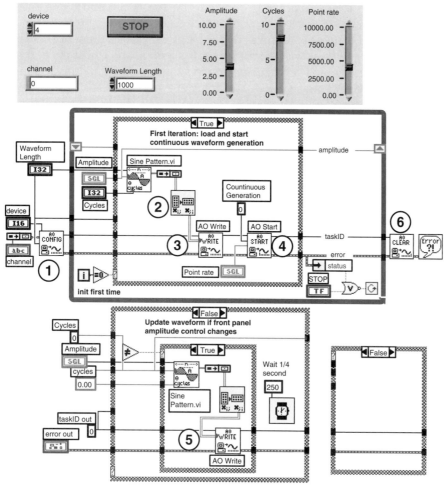

Figure 6.33 A simple example of continuous generation with on-the-fly waveform amplitude changes. This VI is a simplified version of the DAQ AO example, Function Generator.

not a synchronous operation; the new waveform data will appear in the output signal as soon as the data transfer process overwrites the part of the buffer that is presently being passed to the DAC.

6. When you're all done, call **AO Clear**.

In this example, the initial waveform is created and loaded and started on the first iteration of the While Loop. After the first iteration, a Not Equal comparison function checks to see if the **Amplitude** control has changed. If so, the True frame of the inner Case structure creates a new waveform and loads it into the buffer with AO Write. The

While Loop terminates when the Stop button is pressed or when an error occurs.

You could add lots of features to this VI. For instance, there are several interacting controls (**Waveform Length**, **Cycles**, and **Point rate**) that, together, determine the frequency of the sine wave. It would make sense to write a subVI that figures out optimum settings based on a single **Frequency** control on the panel. The subVI would have to vary all three of the parameters according to some schedule that results in an acceptably clean waveform without exceeding the capabilities of the hardware.

An important improvement to this on-the-fly change of data was provided by Jeff Parker, writing in *LTR* (Parker 1995). Jeff needed to generate a continuous sine wave with variable amplitude to drive a shaker table, with a feedback loop that regulated the waveform amplitude. The standard AO Continuous Generation VI is almost good enough for such a control problem, but it's missing one importation attribute. Lab-VIEW writes data to the waveform buffer at a location called the **write mark**. Meanwhile, the NI-DAQ driver copies data from the buffer to the DAC output at a location called the **output mark**. Normally, you will write ahead of the output operation and all is well. The problem is that you never know how far ahead the write mark is with respect to the output mark. So when you add new data to the buffer, there is an indeterminate delay before the new data actually appears at the output. Jeff's solution is a modified version of the regular VI, called *AO Continuous Gen for Control*. It minimizes the delay and, most important, keeps the delay relatively constant.

Streaming data from disk. The complement to a stream-to-disk operation is streaming data *from* disk files to analog outputs. I've found it useful as a means of playing back acquired data from events that are not easy to repeat. For instance, you may have a complex experiment that only provides one chance to acquire a long waveform, but you have lots of diagnostic equipment that you would like to expose to that data for test purposes. This turns out to be straightforward, using the intermediate DAQ analog output library. Basically, you repeatedly read blocks of data from disk and write them to the output buffer of a continuous waveform generation task. I wrote a VI, **AO Stream From Disk**, that does the job. It reads files created by the analog input example VI, Cont Acq to File (Scaled), which was described earlier in this chapter. Problem solved.

platform\ daq\AO Stream From Disk

Simultaneous analog input and output

The DAQ library allows you to run concurrent analog input and output tasks on a single board, so it's feasible to generate a stimulus while monitoring a response. In the DAQ examples, there are two simple examples where the acquisition process runs continuously with hardware timing or in immediate mode where a single sample is acquired. The analog output task in both examples is an immediate, or single-sample, update. Since the outputs are driven in immediate mode, the update limit will be defined by system overhead—on the order of 150 Hz for Windows and 1 kHz for Macintosh—if there is no additional LabVIEW overhead. Within these limits, the examples are easy to understand and apply.

Some applications require fast waveform generation that is accurately synchronized with the data acquisition task. This, too, is straightforward. In Chap. 9, "Physics Applications," there is such an example where a ramp waveform is generated while several analog input channels are monitored. The trick is to connect the DAC update clock to a suitable triggering input for the ADC. Every time the DAC produces a new output value, the ADC acquires a corresponding scan. You could get creative and use additional counter-timers to, for instance, acquire several samples for every DAC update or to delay the acquisition to permit the external system to settle.

What about the opposite case where you monitor an input signal and generate an analog output based on some condition? This can be tricky. The most obvious and flexible way is to acquire data (probably one sample at a time) and have LabVIEW determine when to update the DAC output. Simple process control applications work well when written this way. However, you are stuck with the usual speed limitations and it will be difficult to exceed a loop cycle rate of about 100 Hz without excessive timing jitter. You should definitely try some simple applications before committing to this approach if your timing requirements enter the 10-ms region.

For better performance, you must program either an onboard digital signal processor, a single-board computer, or embedded processor of some type. You have just entered the world of **real-time programming**, and rest assured that it requires programming in C or assembly language under the auspices of a real-time operating system. Some day, LabVIEW will be able to download code to specialized real-time processors, and this class of problem will be solved for us non-C programmers.

Digital I/O

There are two types of digital I/O that you can perform with the DAQ library: digital port I/O and buffered I/O with handshaking. The **digital port I/O** VIs let you read and write one or more bits at a time from the digital interfaces available on many plug-in boards using untimed, immediate digital I/O. These simple VIs accommodate the situations where you need to read or write a few bits at low data rates. For greater performance, you must turn to **buffered digital I/O**. Boards that support handshaking, such as the DIO series, can transfer buffers of digital data at high speed. The Digital Group VIs access these features using hardware-timed, buffered digital I/O.

Simple, bitwise I/O

Routine digital I/O operations, where a number of bits are read or written at low speeds, are handled by the digital port VIs in the intermediate library. The easy I/O library also has some VIs that simplify these operations, but we'll look at the intermediate VIs directly because they really are quite easy to use.

Like the analog I/O libraries, digital I/O operations begin with an (advanced level) configuration VI: **DIO Port Config**. Figure 6.34 shows how it's used. You choose a **device** in the usual manner: the board's slot number. **Port** refers to the digital I/O port number. Valid entries depend on the particular board you are using—refer to the LabVIEW DAQ manual for details. If you are using one of the SCXI digital modules, enter the usual SCXI specifier, such as *SC1!MD7*.

The other important input to DIO Port Config is the **line direction map**, an I32 control which specifies the direction of each line in the port.

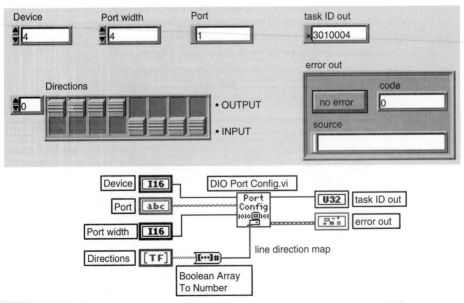

Figure 6.34   DIO Port Config sets up a digital port for untimed, immediate digital I/O.

If a bit is 0 in the line map, the line is an input line. If a bit is 1, the line is an output line. In this example, I created a Boolean array control, then used **Boolean Array to Number** to change the array to a number. You could also use a diagram constant or an integer numeric control. If you do, pop up on the constant or control and select *Show . . . Radix,* then from the Format and Precision dialog, set the Radix to Binary. You can then enter ones and zeros directly without trying to figure out decimal equivalents, such as this: `b11110000`. Please note that many boards do not permit you to mix inputs and outputs within one port. In those cases, you can wire the line direction map to a zero for all inputs, or to −1 for all outputs. (*Serious programmer's note:* If you display the data as binary, note that −1 decimal is the equivalent of all 1s in a binary number because LabVIEW uses two's complement arithmetic.)

Once the port is configured, you can use the advanced (but easy to understand) VIs, **DIO Port Read** to read a bit pattern or **DIO Port Write** to write a bit pattern. Input and output patterns are U32 integers that you can interpret as desired. In the example of Fig. 6.35, I defined two digital port tasks: one for inputs and one for outputs. DIO Port Config is called once for each task. Inside the While Loop, DIO Port Read reads the bit pattern from a port, then the pattern is con-

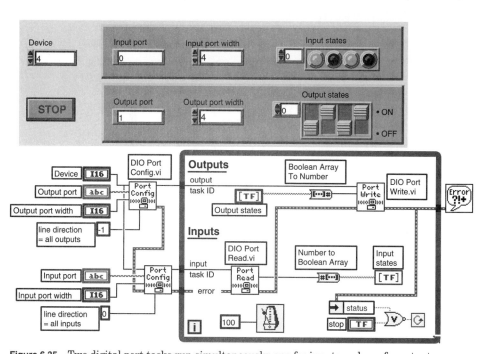

Figure 6.35 Two digital port tasks run simultaneously: one for inputs and one for outputs.

verted by **Number to Boolean Array** for display. Similarly, data from a Boolean array control is written to the other port by DIO Port Write. The error cluster wiring path determines the order in which the two I/O operations occur; in this case, reading occurs before writing.

In your application, various Boolean operations such as manual controls, interlocks, and pattern generators might determine output states. Note that there is nothing preventing you from reconfiguring port directions while you're running, which yields a **bidirectional** port. You can also read from a port that has bits configured as outputs, permitting you to read back the port settings for confirmation.

Another way you can do untimed immediate digital I/O is to use the intermediate VI, **DIO Single Read/Write**. It takes care of the port configuration, then reads or writes one or more scans. It has an **iteration**

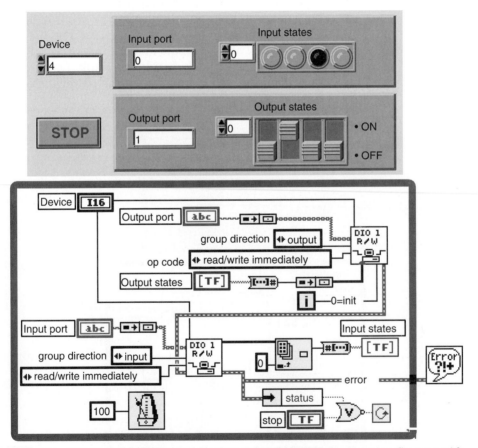

Figure 6.36   DIO Single Read/Write can simplify routine digital I/O programming. Compare with Fig. 6.35.

input that you connect to the iteration terminal of a loop in the calling VI. When iteration equals zero, DIO Config is called. Figure 6.36 does the same job as the previous example, but this time using DIO Single Read/ Write. Before running this VI, you must configure DIO Single Read/ Write as *reentrant* because it keeps track of the task ID in an uninitialized shift register. If you don't make it reentrant, both instances of the VI will end up sharing the same task ID, which is not what you want. Note that the data inputs and outputs for DIO Single Read/Write are arrays because it can do more than one update or scan per call.

Digital I/O with handshaking

Digital port I/O is limited to low-speed transfers because all operations occur in software-timed loops. You can transfer digital data at high speeds with precise timing and synchronization by using the **handshaking** features of certain plug-in boards (notably the DIO series) and the digital group I/O library. Handshaking may take one of three forms in the context of the DAQ library:

- **Internal** handshaking, where an onboard clock triggers each scan or update. Useful for fixed-rate sampling or pattern generation. (I think the rest of the world would call this *clocking* rather than handshaking.) The DIO-32F class of boards have this mode.

- **I/O connector** handshaking, where an external digital line triggers each scan or update. This mode permits an external hardware device to force data synchronization. A familiar example of this type of operation is the ubiquitous Centronics-standard parallel port used on PCs for printers and other peripherals.

- **RTSI** handshaking, where the trigger is carried by a RTSI line from another plug-in board. This mode is useful when you have several I/O operations that you wish to synchronize; they can even be mixed analog and digital operations.

Handshaking in the DAQ library implies the transfer of a buffer of data, so these are in fact buffered I/O operations. Because the DAQ library is consistent in its naming of function VIs, the buffered digital output example in Fig. 6.37 should remind you of a buffered analog waveform generation process. The objective here is to transfer an array of data to a digital port at a rate determined by hardware handshaking. The controls shown are set for internal handshaking with a clock frequency of 1 kHz. If you were to look at the affected output bits, you would see them update every 1.0 ms. *Note:* Buffered digital I/O is generally limited to the DIO-32 boards at this time because they are the only boards with digital I/O clocks and DMA capability.

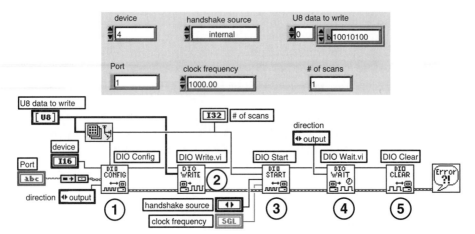

Figure 6.37 Using the intermediate digital VIs to write out an array of values at a controlled rate.

Here are the steps for buffered digital output:

1. The **DIO Config** VI allocates a buffer and sets the port direction to output. It has many other handshaking configuration options (see the manual) that are especially useful when the handshaking source is an external signal.

2. The **DIO Write** VI loads the array of data into the preallocated buffer. You can also set a time limit on the I/O operation to keep your system from "hanging." That's important when you are connected to external hardware that may or may not respond properly.

3. The handshaking mode is set, and the output operation starts when you call the **DIO Start** VI.

4. The **DIO Wait** VI puts the VI in suspense until the operation is complete. (I wish the analog DAQ library had a function like this.)

5. The buffer is released by the **DIO Clear** VI. You can also abort any digital I/O operation by calling DIO Clear at any time.

Buffered digital outputs have interesting applications besides exchanging parallel data with other instruments. A good example is a precision event **sequencer** or **pattern generator**. Say that you have a machine or experiment with a number of discrete (digital) devices that you need to actuate in particular combinations at precise times. In that case, each digital bit on your DAQ board is wired to an actuator. When you write a bit pattern to a port, you instantly set the states of all actuators. For low speeds where a bit of timing jitter is tolerable, you could do single updates with the Write To Digital Port VI, then start a LabVIEW timer, and keep doing this in a sequence. But for precise timing, a buffered digital output operation is ideal because the digital words are transferred from memory to the output at intervals determined by a crystal-controlled clock on the DAQ board.

The trick is to compile a long sequence (array) of integers representing the output states at each interval of time. The length of the array is determined by the finest timing resolution that you require. For instance, if one bit needs to change at 1-ms intervals while all others only change every 100 ms, you must create 100 copies of the slower data and clock port data out at the higher rate. Clearly, you will want to write a program to compile large arrays representing such sequences rather than entering all that data by hand.

Data can be stored in an array in memory if it's not too big or on disk, in which case you stream the data from disk in much the same way as with analog waveform generation. Continuous operation at 10 kHz has been reported, and of course you can also go very slow, but with high precision. Again, note that the DIO-32 boards are the right choice for these operations. To see how it's done, look at the **Digital DblBuffered Pattern Generator** VI in the digital I/O DAQ examples. It demonstrates both input and output, and the clock source can be internal (onboard), external, or from the RTSI bus. The latter option can lead to all kinds of cool synchronization solutions. For instance, you could generate an elaborate digital stimulus while observing the system response on some analog channels with a guaranteed time relationship. Or you could build a simple logic analyzer using two DIO boards, one for input and one for output.

Counters and Timers

While it *is* possible to count and time external events with LabVIEW software loops, these tasks are better accomplished with the counter-timer hardware included on the MIO, TIO, and LAB-series plug-in boards. For instance, LabVIEW does not have the performance required to count individual external events occurring at 1 MHz, nor does it have timers that resolve anything beyond 1 ms—but the hardware does. National Instruments hardware designers selected the Advanced Micro Devices Am9513 System Timing Controller (STC) chip—an exceptionally versatile device—for the MIO and TIO boards and an Intel 8253 counter-timer chip for the Lab-series boards and most of the PCMCIA cards. The newer E-series boards use a custom timing chip, the DAQ-STC. Several onboard clocks can be counted and divided to produce accurate timing intervals, or you can use an external or RTSI clock. With the DAQ counter-timer VIs and a little bit of wiring, you can configure this versatile hardware for a variety of tasks: generating accurately timed pulses, counting events, and measuring period and frequency.

With versatility comes complexity (which is why you might revert to software timers where appropriate, such as timing loops that run at 1 Hz or slower). These counter-timers have several modes and there are many, many ways that you can interconnect them. It helps to have some understanding of the STC itself, and that information is available from several sources. In the manual for your plug-in board is a general description of the STC, and in the back of the manual is a copy of the complete data sheet. Also, the DAQ manual appendix has reference information for each model of plug-in board. By all means spend some time trying to digest this information before embarking on any unusual counting and timing adventures. It's important to note that some of the counters on an MIO board are reserved for data acquisition timing (they aren't even wired to the connector), so you need to make sure that your counting application doesn't request a preassigned counter if you are also doing data acquisition at the same time. On the other hand, you can use the applications described in this chapter without too much studying of the hardware.

About the Am9513 system timing controller (STC)

Because it is the most versatile of the timing chips, I'll concentrate on the Am9513. (The DAQ-STC offers most of the functionality of the Am9513, but only has two counters. The 8253 is quite limited in its capability and requires special programming not covered in the example or easy VIs.) Each Am9513STC contains five independent 16-bit counters and a 4-bit programmable frequency output. The part we're mainly interested in is the counter module (Fig. 6.38) and its various modes of operation. Each counter has a **SOURCE** input, a **GATE** input, and an output called **OUT**. The SOURCE input is normally connected

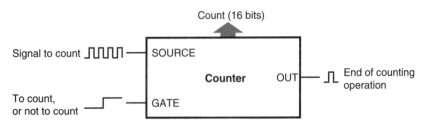

Figure 6.38   Each of the five counters in an Am9513 system timing controller looks like this. Signals come from a variety of sources, including other counters.

to a clock or a signal to be counted. The GATE input enables and disables counting. The output generates a pulse when a preprogrammed **terminal count (TC)** is reached. Your LabVIEW program can read the present count (a 16-bit value) and the state of the output at any time. Versatility is achieved not only through the variety of operating modes, but also through the many ways you can interconnect these signals among counters.

Here are the most useful operating modes, all of which are directly related to the function of the GATE signal. These modes are determined by the *gate parameters,* a cluster input to the **CTR Mode Config** VI.

- *No gating.* Software starts and stops the counting. Marginally useful because you're at the mercy of the response time of software.
- *Level gating.* Counting proceeds when GATE is high for high-level gating or low for low-level gating; otherwise, counting is suspended.
- *Edge-triggered gating.* Counting starts when a GATE transition occurs. Positive or negative edge triggering is selectable.
- *Terminal count gating.* Counting starts and/or stops when the next lower-order counter reaches its terminal count. Permits cascading of counters.

The terminal count action can also be programmed by the CTR Mode Config VI. There are two modes:

- *Toggled.* Each time the counter reaches its terminal count, the output state is complemented (i.e., it toggles). Terminal count can be 65,535 when counting up or zero when counting down.
- *Pulsed.* Each time the counter reaches its terminal count, a single pulse is generated. The pulse width is equal to one cycle of the SOURCE signal and is high during that interval and low otherwise.

The CTR Mode Config VI allows you to change the timebase configuration by effectively connecting the SOURCE input to one of several signals.

- *Internal frequency.* SOURCE connected to an onboard clock, with a choice of several frequencies depending upon your board. Useful in frequency and time measurements
- *SOURCE or GATE signal of another counter.* Useful for sharing one input pin among several counters
- *OUT signal of counter n − 1.* Allows cascading of counters. Especially useful when you need to count beyond 16 bits (65,535 counts)

As you can see, there are many possible interconnections and modes available. The way I set up a new application (assuming it's one that isn't in the examples) is to start with a timing diagram, a traditional tool for digital logic design. Then, I try to sketch out a schematic showing how the counters and signals should be interconnected. I make note of each counter's modes of operation, signal polarities, and clock sources. Finally, I study the options available in the configuration VIs and map my design into LabVIEW parameters. For each of the examples that follow, I'll show you a timing diagram and a simple schematic to help clarify the setup.

Historical note: A funny thing happened on the way to this chapter. Just about the time I finished the first edition of this book, Monnie Anderson at National Instruments got really enthused about improving the counter-timer library—partly because my examples were so complicated! As a result, it's much easier to set up a counting, timing, or pulse generation application than it was a few years ago, and I don't have as much explaining to do. Thanks, Monnie.

Event counter

Say that your job is to count Widgets coming down a conveyer belt, logging the running total to disk every minute. One solution uses a photoelectric switch and a **totalizing counter**. Figure 6.39 shows the

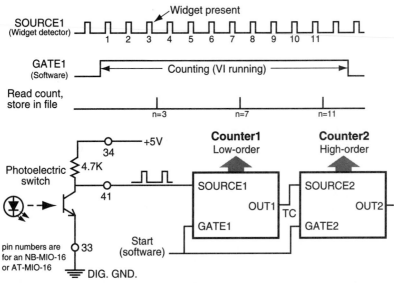

Figure 6.39 Timing diagram and block diagram for a cascaded, totalizing counter application.

timing diagram and schematic for this application. The transistor in the photoelectric switch turns off when the light beam is interrupted by a passing Widget, resulting in a high level (+5 V) input at pin 41, the SOURCE input of a counter. As long as the VI is running, the counters are enabled. Two counters are cascaded (TC from the first feeds the SOURCE of the second) to permit a maximum Widget count of $2^{32} - 1$, or about 4 billion, assuming use of the Am9513 with 16-bit counters. If you have a board with DAQ-STC chips, each counter is 24 bits so you may or may not need to cascade them. Every minute or so, the software should read the count and log it to disk. Interfacing for a simple transistor-output photoelectric switch is shown, along with the pin numbers for an NB- or AT-MIO-16 board.

Like most problems in LabVIEW, start your programming by looking in the DAQ examples and locate the **How to Count** VI. This comprehensive example demonstrates four ways to count events and four ways to count time using the easy, intermediate, and advanced counter VIs. There's also the **How to Count (8253)** VI that exercises just about every function of the 8253 chip. I start with these examples for most of the solutions in this section.

Figure 6.40 shows the panel and diagram for a VI that charts the accumulated number of Widgets versus time. I used the easy counter VI,

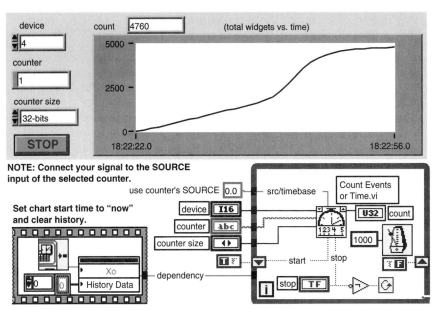

Figure 6.40   This totalizing counter application charts the total count retrieved from a cascaded pair of counters. I varied the source frequency during operation as you can see by the curve on the chart.

Count Events or Time. It runs until the user clicks the stop button or an error occurs (like all easy VIs, this one includes its own internal error handler). There are only a few setup tricks for this easy VI. To choose between counting events or time, use the **event source/timebase** input. If it's set to zero, as in this example, you apply your signal to the chosen counter's SOURCE input, just like I showed on the schematic. To make it measure time, you enter a valid value for an onboard clock frequency (see the DAQ manual appendix for valid frequencies). The Count Events or Time VI has two Boolean inputs to tell it when to start and stop counting, called **start/reset** and **stop**, respectively. In this example, I told it to start when the VI starts and to stop when the user clicks stop. You could also manipulate these inputs to responds to your process.

I used the **X Scale>>Formatting** pop-up dialog to make the Waveform Chart display x-axis data as time and date. When the VI starts, X_0 (the x-axis origin) is set to the present date and time value through an Attribute node. The chart is cleared by writing an empty array to the History Data attribute.

If you need more flexibility in your counting application, open the diagram of the easy VI and see how it uses intermediate VIs. The diagram is straightforward. One trick you'll see there is how it automatically determines which counter is next when you choose to cascade counters. The problem is interesting because the NI-DAQ driver and the hardware require that you choose *adjacent* counters when cascading. The counter utility VI, **Adjacent Counters**, has a little database that makes the decision. It also delivers a handy array containing a list of valid timebase frequencies for the STC chip you have chosen.

Interval, duration, and period timers

Another measurement that you might want to make on your Widget assembly line is the **interval** between Widgets, to make sure that they don't start crashing into one another. The timing diagram and schematic are shown in Fig. 6.41. An onboard clock with known frequency is applied to the SOURCE input, and the counter is configured for *period* mode. The gate mode is then configured for *low level,* so the counter accumulates clock pulses as long as the GATE signal is low. In our application, this condition is true so long as no Widgets are present. All you need to do is read the value in the counter and multiply by the period of the clock signal to obtain the time interval between Widgets.

This same circuit also measures duration or period, in addition to interval, depending upon how the counter responds to the GATE signal. If you set the gate mode to rising or falling edge, you will measure the *period* of the GATE signal. If you set the gate mode to high level, you will measure the *duration* of the GATE signal (the time that it is high). Using these semantics, interval plus duration equals period.

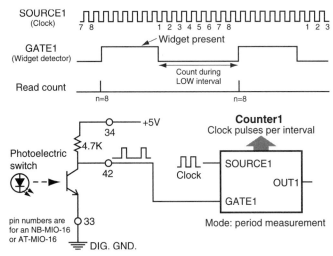

Figure 6.41   Timing diagram and schematic for an interval/duration/
period timer.

The VI that implements the interval/duration/period counter is
shown in Fig. 6.42 and uses the easy counter VI, **Measure Pulse
Width or Period**. Only one counter is required, though you can cascade them to count longer intervals. The input signal (Widget detector)
is connected to the GATE pin of the chosen counter. **Timebase freq**
must be set to one of the valid onboard clock settings. Selecting too high
a clock frequency may cause a counter overflow. The **Measurement**
enum control lets you choose the mode in which the counter operates.
Possible values are

- High level (duration)
- Low level (interval)
- Rising edge (period)
- Falling edge (period)

These map nicely into the gate mode settings permitted by **CTR Mode
Config**, the advanced VI called by our easy VI. The measurement is
scaled to seconds for the **Time** display.

You can use this VI for all kinds of interval and period measurements.
All you have to watch out for is counter overflow. A low-frequency signal, combined with a high-frequency clock, will eventually overflow the
16-bit counter. If that becomes a problem, you could either cascade
counters or add some really tricky logic that automatically chooses the
fastest usable clock speed—a king of autoranging operation. Also note
that you can make a simple frequency counter by selecting one of the
edge (period) modes. Take the reciprocal of period in seconds and you

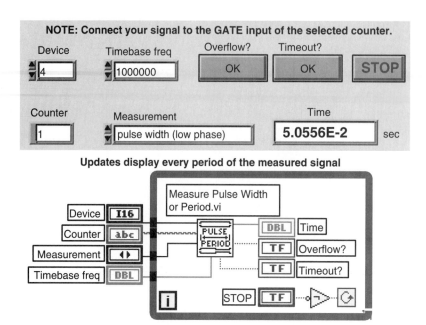

Figure 6.42 This VI measures intervals or durations, depending on the setting of the *Measurement* control. Resolution and range are determined by the *Timebase freq* setting. The panel shows the results obtained with a 10-Hz input signal, measuring the low-level interval which is 50 ms.

have frequency in Hz. Another frequency counter is discussed later in this chapter.

Recording intervals—fast!   Perhaps you need to record the interval between each and every Widget, and they come down the line very fast. How fast can you measure intervals with the DAQ library? The easy counter VI, **Measure Pulse Width or Period**, when called in a loop, will be at the mercy of NI-DAQ calling overhead. It has lots of subVI calls, including some timers to improve performance of other VIs running concurrently, and it stops and restarts the counting operation on each call. As a result, it is only be able to make about six measurements per second.

By switching to intermediate and advanced VIs, you can increase the performance by reducing the number of I/O calls to one per iteration. On the CD-ROM, I've included a VI that you can use to test your system, called **Interval Timer Speed Test**. It's also a nice interval timer in its own right; just delete the timing code on the diagram. On my Macintosh Quadra 950, I could make about 500 interval measurements per second. Under Windows, it may run a bit slower because the NI-DAQ calling overhead is about 3.5 ms versus 0.5 ms on the Mac. You will note that while this VI is running, other VIs are starved of CPU

platform\ timing\Interval Timer Speed Test.vi

time because the lowest-level counter VI calls a CIN that waits until fresh data is ready.

One other way to use the DAQ library to obtain pretty fast interval measurements is to use fast analog waveform acquisition. If you have a fast ADC, digitize the pulse signal, and then use some analysis functions to locate the step transitions and extract the time intervals. Timing resolution will be limited by the ADC sampling rate. The quantity of data will be limited by either available memory or by disk streaming performance. (Note that you must analyze the data after the experiment in order to obtain very high measurement rates.)

So, you want to go even faster? Then turn to specialized hardware. Such an instrument is called a **time interval analyzer (TIA) or time to digital converter (TDC)** in the world of physics diagnostics. At least one company, Guide Technology, makes a series of time interval analyzer plug-in boards with LabVIEW drivers. The boards can record up to 10 million events per second and timestamp those events with resolution as fine as 0.075 ns. Several models are available in ISA and PCI bus format. You could also use a modular TDC instrument, perhaps in VXI or CAMAC format, and upload the data from that.

Pulse generation

Another mode of operation for the counter/timers is **pulse generation**. You can generate single pulses (also known as *one-shot mode*) or continuous pulse trains. A tour de force in example VIs is "**How to Generate Pulses and Pulse Trains**" from the counter examples. In this one example, you can see solutions using easy, intermediate, and advanced VIs in every imaginable combination. There are two easy VIs that should cover 90 percent of your needs: **Generate Delayed Pulse** and **Generate Pulse Train**. I have little to add to these comprehensive examples.

You can have more than one pulse generator running simultaneously as long as they use separate counters. This makes it possible to combine counters as delay elements in complex timing and triggering schemes. For instance, an external trigger event is first delayed, and then the production of a series of pulses begins. Another good example is operating a **stepper motor**. Stepper motors require a good deal of current to operate, so they are accompanied by an interface box called a translator. The inputs to the simplest kind of translator are two TTL digital lines: *direction* and *step*. The direction line determines rotation (CW or CCW), and the step line causes the motor to move one step for each pulse. Paul Daley of Lawrence Livermore National Laboratory and I developed a simple driver based on the counter/timer functions back in the days of LabVIEW 2. I've updated the concept to LabVIEW 4, and this new **Stepper Motor DAQ Driver VI** (Fig. 6.43) is on the CD-ROM.

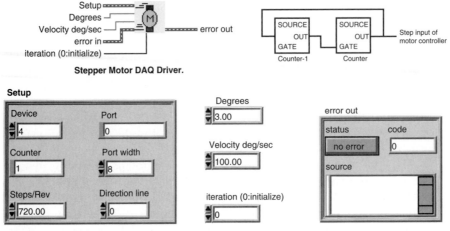

Stepper Motor DAQ Driver.

Figure 6.43   The Stepper Motor DAQ Driver VI uses code plagiarized from the *How to Generate Pulses and Pulse Trains* example to generate a specified number of pulses, which moves a motor through an exact angular displacement.

platform\ daq\Stepper Motor DAQ Driver.vi

Starting with the "How to Count example," I chose a solution that uses two counters: one to generate a gated pulse train that steps the motor, and another that counts the number of pulses and stops the first counter after the desired number of steps. A single update to a digital output line serves as the direction signal and the direction is determined by the sign of the **Degrees** control. Pulse rate is determined by the **Velocity** control. Like all good drivers, this one is calibrated in familiar units—angular motion in degrees—though you could rescale it for linear motion. One limitation of this particular VI is that the number of steps you can move is limited by 16-bit (Am2913) or 24-bit (DAQ-STC) counter overflow. Also, this VI only does *relative* moves, that is, it does not keep track of *absolute* or cumulative motor position. A calling VI could do that.

Frequency counting

Frequency counting is another application area where counter-timers are effective. There are several ways to implement a frequency counter, one of which was noted in the previous interval/period measurement example. That method—taking the reciprocal of one period—is very effective at low frequencies: You only have to wait for one period of the unknown signal to pass before you obtain a measurement. The disadvantage of that approach is, as the input frequency increases toward that of the clock frequency, resolution goes to zero.

Another technique, commonly found in benchtop frequency counters, uses a fixed *gate time* (for example, 1 s) during which edges of the unknown signal are counted. The reciprocal of the count is frequency.

This method works best at *high* frequencies; as frequency goes to zero, resolution goes to zero. A 10-s gate time yields 0.1-Hz resolution; a 1-s gate time yields 1.0-Hz resolution. Figure 6.44 shows the timing diagram and schematic for the high-frequency counting technique. It's really a combination of two basic counter-timer operations—a pulse generator to make the gate signal and a cascaded event counter. The unknown signal frequency can be as high as 6.9 MHz for the Am2913 and 20 MHz for the DAQ-STC. To go faster, you must add an outboard **prescaler**, a divide-by-*n* counter based on digital logic ICs with sufficient speed for your application. You might also want to add signal conditioning (an amplifier and comparator) to clean up the raw signal.

Let's take the easy road to frequency counting and use the **Measure Frequency** VI from the easy level of the counter library. A top-level VI that displays frequency versus time is shown in Fig. 6.45. Each time the Measure Frequency VI is called, it configures the various counters, then a single gate pulse is generated and the unknown input signal is counted for the duration of the gate. Like most of the easy VIs, this one has some performance limitations. Particularly, there is a latency when setting up and starting the counting operations—I measured 150 to 200 ms—so the duty cycle of this solution will be limited by that value. One way to go faster would be to configure (at the intermediate level)

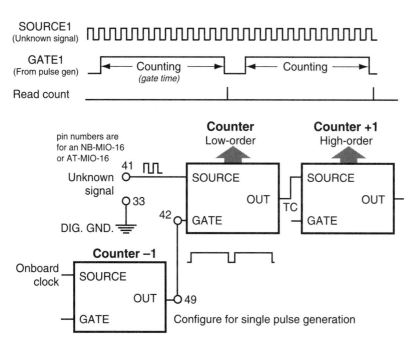

Figure 6.44 Timing diagram and schematic for a frequency counter with a fixed gate time. It requires a pulse generator for the gate and a cascaded event counter to count the unknown pulses during the gate high interval.

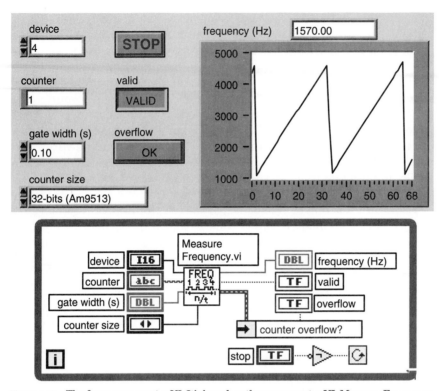

Figure 6.45   The frequency counter VI. It's based on the easy counter VI, Measure Frequency.

the gate pulse generator as a continuous pulse generator with a high duty cycle, such as 99 percent. Then your frequency counter could run continuously and spend 99 percent of its time measuring and only 1 percent of its time resetting hardware.

I hope this chapter has given you insight into the diverse applications of the DAQ library. Over the years, I've found that the library is very flexible, and that it keeps getting better with each release of LabVIEW. With a couple of plug-in boards, you can handle a very large number of applications. In the next chapter, we'll look at some designs for generic data acquisition applications, some of which use the DAQ library.

Bibliography

LTR Publishing, "How Do You Do That in Lab VIEW—Last Issue's Challenge," the Multi-Rate VI, *LabVIEW Technical Resource,* vol. 2, no. 2, spring. (Back issues available from LTR Publishing.)

Parker, Jeff, "Feeding a Hungry Waveform on the Go!" *LabVIEW Technical Resource,* vol. 3, no. 2, spring. (Back issues available from LTR Publishing.)

Writing a Data Acquisition Program

I'm going to bet that your first LabVIEW application was (or will be) some kind of data acquisition system. I say that because data acquisition is by far the most common LabVIEW application. Every experiment or process has signals to be measured, monitored, analyzed, and logged, and each signal has its own special requirements. While it's impossible to design a universal data acquisition system to fit every situation, there are plenty of common architectures that you can use, each containing elements that you can incorporate into your own problem-solving tool kit.

Speaking of tool kits, there are some third-party products for LabVIEW data acquisition on the market that will be discussed later in the chapter. Such a product can save you a great deal of time and money if your application fits the product's framework. In many cases, you will only need the most basic understanding of LabVIEW to start acquiring and displaying data. Even if it's not a perfect match, the support VIs in these commercial packages can certainly be adapted to your special needs. Also, National Instruments added a **Solution Wizard** to LabVIEW version 4.1 that addresses the needs of the user who wants to do *no programming whatsoever*. From a usability standpoint, these higher-level approaches put LabVIEW on par with other software products that require no programming but are otherwise limited in capability. As a result, you can now access the nearly unlimited flexibility of LabVIEW—a true programming language—while starting off with the no-programming approach. The best of both worlds!

As I mentioned in the Introduction, what you'll learn in this chapter are all the *other* things that the LabVIEW manuals and examples don't cover. The act of fetching data from an input device is the easy part, and it's a subject that is already well discussed. On the other hand, how do you keep track of channel assignments and other configuration information? And how does data analysis affect program design? These topics are important, yet rarely mentioned. Time to change all that.

Your data acquisition application might include some control (output) functionality as well. Most experiments have some things that need to be manipulated—some valves, a power supply setpoint, or maybe a motor. That should be no problem so long as you spend some time designing your program with the expectation that you will need some control features. If your situation requires a great deal of control functionality, read Chap. 8, "Process Control Applications," to see some methods that may work better than simply adding on to a data acquisition design.

Plan your application like any other, going through the recommended steps. I've added a few items to the procedure that emphasize special considerations for data acquisition: **data analysis**, **throughput**, and **configuration management** requirements. Here are the basic steps.

1. Define and understand the problem; define the signals and determine what the data analysis needs are.

2. Specify the type of I/O hardware you will need, and then determine sample rates and total throughput.

3. Prototype the user interface and decide how to manage configurations.

4. Design, then write the program.

If your system requires extra versatility, like the ability to quickly change channel assignments or types of I/O hardware, then you will need to include features to manage the system's **configuration**. Users should be able to access a few simple controls rather than having to edit the diagram when a configuration change is needed.

Data **throughput**, the aggregate sampling rate measured in samples per second, plays a dominant role in determining the architecture of your program. High sampling rates can severely limit your ability to do real-time analysis and graphics. Even low-speed systems can be problematic when you require accurate timing. Fortunately, there are plenty of hardware and software solutions available in the LabVIEW world.

The reason for assembling a data acquisition system is to **acquire** data, and the reason for acquiring data is to **analyze** it. Surprisingly, these facts are often overlooked. Planning to include analysis features and appropriate file formats will save you (and the recipients of your data) a lot of grief.

The canonical LabVIEW VI for a simple, yet complete, data acquisition program is shown in Fig. 7.1. It begins with a VI that handles I/O configuration and the opening of any data files. The rest of the program resides in a While Loop that cycles at a rate determined by the sample interval control. The Read Data VI communicates with hardware and returns the raw data, which is then analyzed for display and stored in files. All subVIs that can produce an error condition are linked by an error I/O cluster, and an error handler tells the user what went wrong. Simple as this diagram is, it could actually work, and do some rather sophisticated processing at that. Try simplifying your next data acquisition problem to this level. Add functionality as required, but keep things modular so that it's easy to understand and modify. This chapter is devoted to the building blocks shown in the diagram.

Data Analysis and Storage

Data analysis has a different meaning in every application. It depends on the kind of signals you are faced with. For many applications, it means calculating simple statistics (minimum, maximum, mean, standard deviation, etc.) over some period of time. In spectroscopy and chromatography, it means peak detection, curve fitting, and integration. In acoustics and vibration studies, it means Fourier transforms, filtering, and correlation. Each type of analysis affects your LabVIEW program design in some way. For instance, doing a Fast-Fourier Transform (FFT) on a large array in real time requires lots of processing power—your system could become so burdened that data collection may be disrupted. Such analysis drives the performance requirements of your VIs. And everyone worries about timing information, both for real-time analysis and when reading data from files. It's

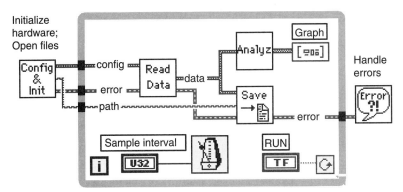

Figure 7.1 A generic data acquisition program includes the functions shown here.

obvious that your program has to measure and store time markers reliably and in a format that is useful to the analysis programs.

What you need to avoid is *analysis by accident.* Time and again I've seen LabVIEW programs that grab data from the hardware and stuff it into a file with no thought about compatibility with the analysis program. Then the poor analyst has to grind along, parsing the file into readable pieces, trying to reconstitute important features of the data set. Sometimes, the important information isn't available on disk at all, and you *hope* that it has been written down *somewhere.* Disaster! Gastric distress also occurs when a new real-time analysis need crops up and your program is so inflexible that the new features can't be added without major surgery.

I recommend a preemptive strike. When someone proposes a new data acquisition system, make it a point to force that person to describe, in detail, how the data will be analyzed. Make sure he or she understands the implications of storing the megabytes or gigabytes of data that an automated data acquisition system may collect. If there is a collective shrug of shoulders, ask them point-blank, ". . . then why are we collecting data at all?" *Do not write your data acquisition program until you understand the analysis requirements.*

Finally, you can get started. Divide the analysis job into real-time and post-run tasks, and determine how each aspect will affect your program.

Post-run analysis

You can analyze data with LabVIEW, another application, or a custom program written in some other language. Sometimes, more than one analysis program will have to read the same data file. In all cases, you need to decide on a suitable **data file format** that your data acquisition program has to write. The file type (typically text or binary), the structure of the data, and the inclusion of timing and configuration information are all important. If other people are involved in the analysis process, get them involved early in the design process. Write down clear file format specifications. Plan to generate sample data files and do plenty of testing so as to assure everyone that the real data will transfer without problems.

It's a good idea to structure your program so that a single *data saver* VI is responsible for writing a given data file type. Raw data and configuration information go in, and data files go out. You can easily test this data saver module as a stand-alone VI or call it from a test program before your final application is completed. The result is a module with a clear purpose that is reliable and reusable. LabVIEW can read and write any file format (refer to Chap. 3, "Programming Techniques," in the section on files, for a general discussion of file I/O). Which data format you use depends on the program that has to read it.

Datalog file format.   If you plan to analyze data only in LabVIEW, the easiest and most compact format is the **datalog file**, discussed in detail in Chap. 3. A datalog file contains a sequence of binary data **records**. All records in a given file are of the same type, but a record can be a complex data structure, for instance, a cluster containing strings and arrays. The record type is determined when you create the file. You can read records one at a time in a random-access fashion or read several at once, in which case they are returned as an array. This gives your analysis program the ability to use the data file like a simple database, searching for desired records based on one or more key fields in each record, such as a timestamp.

The disadvantage of datalog format files is that they can only be read by LabVIEW or by a custom-written program. However, you can easily write a translator in LabVIEW that reads your datalog format and writes out files with another format. Another hazard (common to all binary file formats) is that you must know the data type used when the file was written; otherwise, you may never be able to decipher the file.

You might be able to use the automatic front panel datalogging features of LabVIEW. They are very easy to use. All you have to do is turn on the datalogging by using the **Data Logging** submenu in the Operate menu for a subVI that displays the data you wish to save. Every time that the subVI finishes executing (even if its front panel is not displayed), the front panel data are appended to the current log file. The first time the subVI is called, you will receive a dialog asking for a new datalog file. You can also open the subVI and change log files through the Data Logging menu. To access logged data, you can use the file I/O functions, or you can place the subVI of interest in a new diagram and choose **Enable Database Access** from its pop-up menu. You can then read the datalog records one at a time. All of the front panel controls are available—they are in a cluster that is conveniently accessed by Unbundle By Name. But for maximum file performance, there's nothing better than wiring the file I/O functions directly into your diagram. Open the datalog file at the start of the experiment, and don't close it until you're done.

Datalog file handler VI makes it easy.   It seems like your diagrams always end up with a large number of file I/O functions scattered all over the place, with all the attendant wiring. One way to clean up the situation is to encapsulate all file I/O operations into a single **integrated VI**. This approach works for many other applications, as well, such as instrument drivers. The principle is simple: create a VI with a **Mode**

control wired to a Case structure containing the various operations you need to perform. For files, the modes might be Create, Write, and Read. I did exactly that for the **Datalog File Handler VI**, and it really makes datalog files easy to use (Johnson 1994).

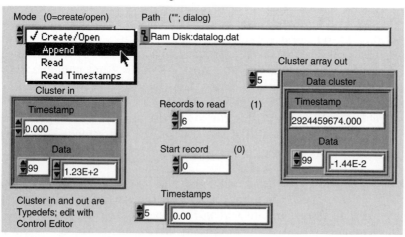

platform\datalog file handler.llb

On the panel in Fig. 7.2, you can see the **Mode** control and its four possible choices. You begin by creating a new file or opening an existing one. The file's path is saved in an uninitialized shift register, so you don't have to wire to the Path input for other I/O operations. *Append* mode appends data in the **Cluster in** control to the file. *Read* returns a selected range of data as a cluster array. You can choose the starting record number and the number of records to read. The last mode, *Read Timestamps,* returns an array of timestamp values for the entire file. This tells you the number of records in the file (equal to the number of elements in the **Timestamps** array). It's also a convenient way to locate a particular record of data based on time. The **Cluster in** and **Cluster array out** controls are typedefs. Modify them with the Control Editor to match your data type. *Note:* The Timestamp is a required item in the cluster.

To see how the Datalog File Handler VI works, check out the demonstration VI included on the CD-ROM. That example includes a data

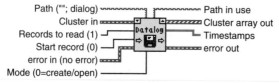

Datalog File Handler

Figure 7.2 The Datalog File Handler VI encapsulates datalog file I/O operations into a single, integrated VI.

analysis VI that you'll find useful. A really cool feature of the analysis VI is a little subVI called **Left-Right Buttons** that simulates a set of fast and slow buttons like you might find on a tape recorder. It allows the operator to quickly scroll through the data, viewing one record at a time on a graph. Use it in good health.

ASCII text format.   Good old **ASCII text** files are your best bet for portable data files. Almost every application can load data from a text file that has simple formatting. The ubiquitous **tab-delimited text** format is a likely choice. Format your data values as strings with a tab character between each value and place a carriage return at the end of the line; then write it out. The only other thing you need to determine is the type of header information. Simple graphing and spreadsheet applications are happy with column names as the first line in the file:

```
Date      Time       Channel_1    Channel_2
5-13-82   01:17:34   5.678        -13.43
5-13-82   01:17:44   5.665        -13.58
```

platform\ simple das\ String List Converter.vi

A spreadsheet could be programmed to interpret all kinds of header information, if you need to include more. Other applications are less versatile with respect to headers, so be sure you know who's going to be reading your file. Figure 7.3 shows a simple data logger that writes a text header, followed by tab-delimited text data. It uses the easy-level file VIs for simplicity. I wrote a little utility VI, **String List Converter**, to make it easier for the user to enter channel names. The names are typed into a string control, separated by carriage returns. String List Converter translates the list into a set of tab-delimited names for the file header and into a string array that you can wire to the *Strings[]* attribute for a ring control, as shown.

The disadvantages of ASCII text files are that they are bulkier than binary files, and they take much longer to read and write (often *several hundred times* longer) because each value has to be converted to and from strings of characters. For high-speed data recording applications, text files are out of the question. You *might* be able to store a few thousand samples per second as text on a fast computer, but be sure to benchmark carefully before committing yourself to text files.

Custom binary formats.   LabVIEW can write files with arbitrary binary formats to suit other applications. If you can handle the requisite programming, binary files are really worthwhile—high on performance and very compact. It's also nice to open a binary file with an analysis program and have it load without any special translation. Keep in mind the fact that LabVIEW datalog files are also binary format (and

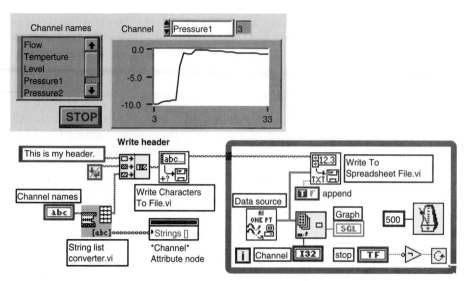

Figure 7.3   This simple data logger example writes a text header, then tab-delimited data. The String List Converter VI initializes the *Channels* control with all the channel names.

fast, too), but are significantly easier to use, at least within LabVIEW. If you don't really need a custom binary format, stick with datalogs for simplicity.

Binary file handlers require significant programming experience. Even if you have all the formatting information, be prepared to spend time working out the programming details. Software manufacturers will generally supply you with a description of their application's native binary file format if you ask the right person. Usually, you will get some kind of program listing that was lifted from their file I/O routines. If the company is interested in making its file format public, they will supply an application note and sometimes even machine-readable code. The folks at **Wavemetrics** supply all this information for **Igor** (their analysis and graphing package for the Macintosh) with the application. Because the information was available, the VIs to read and write Igor binary were easy to create and are now public domain. Figure 7.4 shows the panel for the VI that writes a single-precision floating point array to an Igor binary file. The diagram is very complex, so it's not shown. You can obtain these Igor support VIs from Wavemetrics, National Instruments, or the various FTP servers via the Internet. By the way, Igor can also read arbitrary binary formats (simple ones, at least) directly through an external operation (XOP) called GBLoadWave. With that capability, you can write your LabVIEW data as simple binary arrays then load it right into Igor with no special programming whatsoever.

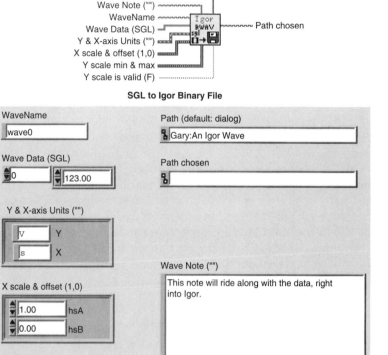

SGL to Igor Binary File

WaveName

> wave0

Wave Data (SGL)

> 0   123.00

Y & X-axis Units ("")

> V   Y
> s   X

X scale & offset (1,0)

> 1.00   hsA
> 0.00   hsB

Y scale min & max

> 0.00   max
> 0.00   min

Path (default: dialog)

> Gary:An Igor Wave

Path chosen

>

Wave Note ("")

> This note will ride along with the data, right into Igor.

Y scale is valid (F)

Figure 7.4   This VI creates a file suitable for direct loading with Wavemetrics' Igor.

Some binary formats such as the previously described Igor format are unsuitable for continuous data acquisition—where you would like to append records one at a time as the experiment proceeds. They are designed for single-shot experiments where the entire file is written at once. This is fine for single buffers of data from an oscilloscope, but less useful for a simple data logger. Buffering data in memory (in arrays) is one way to solve this problem, but if your computer should crash, that data might be lost. You could rewrite the entire file occasionally to avoid such a catastrophe if you are forced to use one of these single-shot formats. On the other hand, if you are *not* stuck with such a pre-defined format, it is easy and efficient to write continuously to a binary file as you can see by examining the techniques used in the DAQ disk streaming example VIs.

Direct links to other applications. Several other important analysis applications are available with LabVIEW links. National Instruments offers **HiQ**, an application for engineering math, simulation, and analysis. LabVIEW includes VIs for direct communication with HiQ via Apple Events, Program to Program Communication (PPC), Dynamic Data Exchange (DDE), Object Linking and Embedding (OLE) Automation, and via files. (You'll find the VIs in the **Communication** function palette.) The ability to write data directly to another application using DDE or PPC is very appealing since it makes background analysis without user intervention a reality; it also eliminates the intermediate file conversion hassle.

Microsoft Excel is another big name in data analysis, with its large installed base on both Windows and Macintosh. Besides loading tab-delimited text, DDE is a very common way to transfer data. Chapter 11, "ATE Applications," discusses this subject in detail and there are good example VIs in the LabVIEW example libraries. Similarly, you can use OLE commands to exchange data with Excel, and the LabVIEW examples are a good place to start. Jerry Levine (jslevine@dnai.com) has written a VI called **WriteXL** that directly writes Excel *binary* files. It records a two-dimensional array of data, with names for the columns, a comment which appears as a note to cell A1, and an array of named variables, all of which can be accessed by EXCEL macros. Since the VI uses no CINs, it is portable. Get it from ftp.pica.army.mil.

Matlab is a popular multiplatform mathematics and analysis program, and for the Windows version there is a DDE-based LabVIEW driver. The driver was written by Sergey Liberman of Raytheon (liberman@res1.rd.ray.com) and is available from ftp.pica.army.mil. It is nicely structured and allows you to open a conversation, send and receive matrix data, and send commands to Matlab.

For **KaleidaGraph** on the Macintosh, Joakim Pettersson (joakimp@ fy.chalmers.se) wrote a LabVIEW driver based on AppleEvents. Kaleida-Graph is fully AppleScript-compatible, and the driver includes an example that sends data and creates a new graph.

Timestamps. Most data that we collect is a function of time. Therefore, timing information needs to be stored along with the data in your files. The precision or resolution of these timestamps will be driven by the requirements of your experiment and the limitations of LabVIEW's timing functions. Requirements for formatting of the timestamps will be determined by the application that reads the data file.

Consider an ordinary data-logging application where a few dozen channels are stored to disk as ASCII text every few seconds. A resolution of one second is probably adequate, and a source for this timing information is **Get Date/Time In Seconds**, or one of the other built-in timing functions. You can then format the returned value as seconds relative to 1 Jan 1904, as seconds relative to the start of your experiment, or divide it by 60 to obtain minutes, and so forth. Saving a simple numeric timestamp has the advantage that it is easy to interpret. If you use a spreadsheet application that can manipulate time and date formats (such as mm/dd/yy hh:mm:ss), then **Get Date/Time String** may be appropriate.

For more resolution, you can use the **High-Res Seconds** VI, described in Chap. 3, "Programming Techniques." It has a resolution of one millisecond (limited by your computer's capability) and returns the time as a floating point value. You can get similar results by using the simple **Tick Count (ms)** function, which returns a relative number of milliseconds. The uncertainty of these higher-resolution timers depends on your machine and on LabVIEW's workload. You may want to do some testing if you need really accurate software-derived timestamps.

Data that is acquired at a constant rate (periodic sampling) needs a timestamp only at the beginning of the collection period because the time at any sample is easily calculated. This is certainly true of data acquired with hardware-timed I/O using the DAQ library. There is no reason to store a timestamp with every sample if you already know the sample interval with acceptable precision; it would just take up extra disk space. Only data that is taken aperiodically requires such detailed timestamp information.

Sampling rates higher than about 10 Hz usually are handled by data acquisition hardware (or smart I/O subsystems) because there is too much timing uncertainty in fast LabVIEW loops on general-purpose computers. Using hardware can simplify your timestamping requirements. Because you know that the hardware is sampling at a steady rate, there is no need to store a timestamp for every sample period. Rather, you need only save an initial time and a value for the sampling interval. The data analysis program should then be able to reconstruct the timebase from this simple scheme.

A technique used in *really* fast diagnostics is to add a timing **fiducial** pulse to one or more data channels. Also known as a *fid,* it is a pulse that occurs at some critical time during the experiment and is recorded on all systems (and maybe on all channels, as well). It's much the same as the room full of soldiers where the commander says, "Synchronize watches." For example, when testing explosives, a fiducial pulse is distributed to all of the diagnostic systems just before detonation. For analog data channels, the fiducial pulse can be coupled to each channel through a small capacitor, creating a small *glitch* in the data at the critical moment. You can even synchronize nonelectronic systems by generating a suitable stimulus, such as flashing a strobe in front of a movie or video camera. Fiducials are worth considering any time you need absolute synchronization among disparate systems.

If you need accurate time-of-day information, be sure to reset the computer clock before the experiment begins. Personal computer clocks are notorious for their long-term drift. If you are connected to the Internet, you can install a utility that will automatically reset your system clock to a standard time server. For Windows, there are several public-domain utilities, such as *WNSTIME* (available from sunsite.unc.edu), that you can install. For Macintosh, you can use the *Network Time* control panel program (available from sumex-aim.stanford.edu). These utilities even take into consideration the time zone and the daylight savings time settings for your machine. The only other trick is finding a suitable Network Time Protocol server. The one I've had good luck with is NASA's norad.arc.nasa.gov server.

In the section on timing in Chap. 3, I list a host of precision timing devices that you might consider, such as GPS and IRIG standards. Such hardware can provide absolute timing standards with accuracy as good as a few hundred nanoseconds. That's about as good as it gets.

Passing along configuration information. Your analysis program may need information about the configuration of the experiment or software that generated the data. In many cases, channel names are all that is needed, and you can pass them along as the column titles in a spreadsheet file. Beyond that, you have two basic choices: use a separate **configuration file** or add a **file header** to each data file. Both methods are highly dependent upon the ability of the analysis program to read and interpret the information.

If you're using the **NI-DAQ Channel Wizard**, it has a useful feature called *Export*. Export allows you to save the contents of the channel configuration file in tab-delimited text format. Available items include channel names and descriptions, scale factors, hardware device information, and sensor information. Almost any data analysis application (or another LabVIEW program) can read such a configuration file.

Binary files almost always have headers because the program that reads them needs information about the type and location of the data within. Here is a list of the kind of information contained in a binary file header:

Experiment identification

Channel name

Create time and date

Data type (single or double-precision)

Data file version (to avoid incompatibility with future versions)

Y-axis and x-axis units

Number of data points

Y-axis and x-axis scale factors

Flag to indicate whether user comments follow the data segment

As always, the format of this binary file header will be highly specified on a byte-by-byte basis. You need to make sure that each item is of the proper data type and length before writing the header out to the file. An effective way to do this is to assemble all the items into a cluster, **Type Cast** it (see Chap. 3, "Programming Techniques") to a string, then write it out using byte stream mode with the **Write File** function. Alternatively, the header can be text with flag characters or end-of-line characters to help the reading application parse the information.

For text files, generating a header is as simple as writing out a series of strings that have been formatted to contain the desired information. Reading and *decoding* a text-format header, on the other hand, can be quite challenging for any program. If you simply want an experimental record or free-form notepad header for purposes of documentation, that's no problem. But parsing information out of the header for programmatic use requires careful design of the header's format. Many graphing and analysis programs can do little more than read blocks of text into a long string for display purposes; they have little or no capacity for parsing the string. Spreadsheets (and of course programming languages) can search for patterns, extract numbers from strings, and so forth, but not if the format is poorly defined. Therefore, you need to work on both ends of the data analysis problem—reading as well as writing—to make sure that things will play together.

Another solution to this header problem is to use what I call an **index file** which is separate from the data file. The index file contains all the information necessary to successfully load the data including pointers into the data file. It can also contain configuration information. The data file can be binary or ASCII format, containing only the data values. I've used this technique on several projects, and it adds some versatility. If the index file is ASCII text, then you can print it out to see what's in the data file. Also, the data file may be more easily loaded into programs that would otherwise choke on header information. You still have the problem of loading the configuration, but at least the data can be loaded and the configuration is safely stored on disk. One caution: don't lose one of the files!

The configuration file can be formatted for direct import into a spreadsheet and used as a printable record of the experiment. This turns out to be quite useful. What I try to produce is a complete description of the hardware setup used for a given test, including mod-

ule types, channel assignments, gain settings, and so forth. Here's what
a simple configuration file might look like:

```
Source expt   RUN306   08-SEP-1992 21:18:51.00   HD:Data:RUN306
File        Module ID     Slot  Crate  Signal Name      Chan    Units
TEST0.T     Kinetic 3525  1     1      TC1              1       Deg C
TEST0.T     Kinetic 3525  1     1      TC2              2       Deg C
TEST0.T     Kinetic 3525  1     1      Upper src temp   4       Deg C
TEST0.T     Kinetic 3525  1     1      Lower src temp   5       Deg C
END
```

When the experimenter has a question regarding the signal connections, I can refer to this list, which is usually clipped into the laboratory
logbook. We'll discuss some methods for generating configuration files
later in this chapter.

Using a real database.   If your data management needs are more complex than the usual single-file-and-spreadsheet scheme can handle,
consider using a commercial **database** application for management of
configurations, experimental data, and other important information.
The advantages of a database are the abilities to index, search, and
sort data with concurrent access from several locations but with explicitly regulated access to the data, thus enhancing security and reliability. The **SQL Toolkit** from National Instruments enables LabVIEW
to directly communicate with any **Open Database Connectivity
(ODBC)**–compliant database application using **Structured Query
Language (SQL)** commands. The toolkit is available for all versions of
Windows as well as Macintosh and is compatible with nearly all major
databases. It was originally created by Ellipsis Products and marketed
as **DatabaseVIEW**.

The SQL Toolkit can directly access a database file on the local disk
using SQL commands to read or write information, or the database can
exist on a network—perhaps residing on a mainframe computer or
workstation. You begin by establishing a *session,* or connection to the
target database(s), then build SQL commands using LabVIEW string
functions. The commands are then executed by the SQL Toolkit if you
are connecting directly to a file or by a database application which
serves as a *database engine.* Multiple SQL transactions may be active
concurrently—an important feature, since it may take some time to
obtain results when using a complex SQL command to access a very
large database.

Figure 7.5 shows an example that simulates a year of weather in
Boston and inserts each day's statistics into a dBASE database. The
dataflow is pretty clear. First a connection is made to the database

using the Connect VI for the data source *DBV DEMO DBASE*. The first two frames of the sequence (not shown) create the empty climate table in the database. Next, frame 2 begins by creating the year of simulated data. A dynamic SQL INSERT statement is also created using wildcard characters (?) to designate the values that will be inserted later. In the For Loop, each field value is bound to its associated parameter in the wildcard list, and then the Execute Prepared SQL VI inserts data into the climate table. The dynamic SQL method can speed inserts up to four times over the standard convert, parse, and execute method. Finally, the SQL statement reference is discarded in the End SQL VI. When the loop is complete, the last frame of the Sequence structure (not shown) disconnects from the database.

If you're using Fourth Dimension (4D) as your primary database on Macintosh or Windows machines, a package called **4D Open for Lab-VIEW** is available from **CIT** of Belgium. Fourth Dimension has a simplified way of setting up relational databases that is somewhat easier than a full SQL database, and often runs faster as well. The 4D Open package includes high-level VIs that make access easy.

Real-time analysis and display

LabVIEW's extensive library of built-in analysis functions makes it easy to process and display your newly acquired data in real time. You

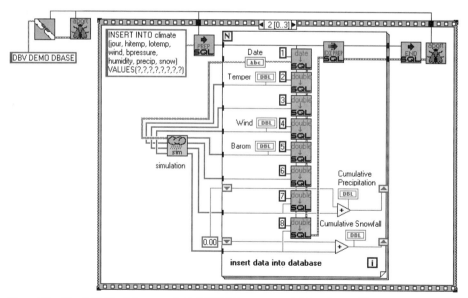

Figure 7.5 The SQL Toolkit connects LabVIEW to commercial databases. This example inserts simulated weather data into a climate database. (*Example courtesy of Ellipsis Products, Inc.*)

are limited by only two things: your system's performance and your imagination. Analysis and presentation are the things that make this whole business of virtual instrumentation useful. You can turn a voltmeter into a strip-chart recorder, an oscilloscope into a spectrum analyzer, and a multifunction plug-in board into . . . just about anything. Here, we'll look at the general problems and approaches to real-time analysis and display. Later chapters will discuss particular applications.

Once again, we've got the old battle over the precise definition of **real time**. It is wholly dependent upon your application. If one-minute updates for analysis and display are enough, then *one minute* is real time. If you need millisecond updates, then *that's* real time, too. What matters is that you understand the fundamental limitations of your computer, I/O hardware, and LabVIEW with regard to performance and response time.

platform\ benchmark

You want hard data on performance? Take a look at the **LabVIEW Benchmark** VIs, available on the CD-ROM or from ftp.natinst.com. The suite includes a comprehensive battery of tests including memory, file I/O, analysis, graphics, and numerical processing capabilities. You can run the test on your machine, and then compare your results with those of others with the **Compare** VI. Some of the results are unexpected; between platforms, you may find a machine that is fifty times faster at one task but three times slower at another. There are dependencies on system configuration, as well. The type of bus, the operating system version, amount of memory, video card, disk system, and so forth can all make major differences in performance.

For reference, Table 7.1 lists a few simple LabVIEW benchmarks that might help you decide what to include in your real-time VIs. I measured these values on my Macintosh Quadra 950, which is of

TABLE 7.1 LabVIEW for Macintosh Benchmark (in order of increasing execution time)*

Test	Execution time
Empty For Loop	0.393 μs
Calling an empty VI, subroutine priority	3.1 μs
Read a numeric from a global	4.0 μs
Read a DBL array global, (1000 values)	708 μs
Update numeric indicator I32 display (default size)	1.5 ms
Standard deviation (1000 values)	2.0 ms
Linear fit (1000 values)	1.7 ms
Read a string array global (1000 strings)	7.4 ms
Butterworth filter (1000 values)	10 ms
Real FFT (1024 values)	34 ms
Waveform graph (default size, 1000 SGL values)	50 ms
Amplitude and phase spectrum (1000 values)	564 ms

* Tests run on a Quadra 950.

course a 33-MHz 68040, running System 7.5. Newer, faster systems of all types will easily beat these numbers, sometimes by a factor of 10.

The kind of analysis you need to perform is determined by the nature of your signals and the information you want to extract (Table 7.2). Assuming that you purchase the full version of LabVIEW, there are about 200 analysis functions available. Other functions (and useful combinations of the regular ones) are available from the examples, the **G Math Toolkit** (from National Instruments), and from others who support LabVIEW through the Alliance Program. If you ever need an analysis function that seems obvious or generally useful, be sure to contact National Instruments to find out if it's already available. They also take suggestions—user input is really what makes this palette grow.

Continuous versus single-shot data analysis. Data acquisition may involve either **continuous data** or **single-shot data**. Continuous data generally arrives one sample at a time, like readings from a voltmeter. It is usually displayed on something such as a strip chart, and probably would be stored to disk as a time-dependent history. Single-shot data arrives as a big buffer or block of samples, like a waveform from an oscilloscope. It is usually displayed on a graph, and each shot would be stored as a complete unit, possibly in its own file. Analysis techniques for these two data types may have some significant differences.

TABLE 7.2 Signal Types and Analysis Examples

Signal type	Typical analysis
Analog—DC	Scaling
	Statistics
	Curve fitting
Analog–Time domain	Scaling
	Statistics
	Filtering
	Peak detection and counting
	Pulse parameters
Analog–Frequency domain	Filtering
	Windowing
	FFT/power spectrum
	Convolution/deconvolution
	Joint time frequency analysis
Digital on-off	Logic
Digital pulse train	Counting
	Statistics
	Time measurement
	Frequency measurement

There is a special form of continuous data that I call **block-mode continuous data** where you continuously acquire measurements, but only load them into your LabVIEW program as a block or buffer when some quantity of measurements have accumulated. Multiple buffering or circular buffering can be carried out by any smart instrument, including the DAQ library. The advantage of block-mode buffered operation is reduced I/O overhead: you only need to fetch data when a buffer is half full, rather than fetching each individual sample. The disadvantage is the added latency between acquisition of the oldest data in the buffer and the transfer of that data to the program for processing. For analysis purposes, you may treat this data as either continuous or single-shot since it has some properties of both.

Here is an example of the difference between processing continuous versus single-shot data. Say that your main interest is finding the mean and standard deviation of a time-variant analog signal. This is really easy to do, you notice, because LabVIEW just happens to have a statistical function called **Standard Deviation** which also computes the mean. So far so good.

Single-shot data.   A single buffer of data from the desired channel is acquired by using **AI Acquire Waveform** with a plug-in board. This subVI returns a numeric array containing a sequence of samples, or waveform, taken at a specified sample rate. To compute the statistics, wire the array to the Standard Deviation function and display the results (Fig. 7.6). You might note that there is a coercion dot on the input terminal to Standard Deviation. That's because the DAQ library uses single-precision floating point values, while the analysis library uses double-precision. The result is extra memory management and some loss of efficiency and speed, but it is currently unavoidable.

Continuous data.   You can collect one sample per cycle of the While Loop by calling **AI Single Scan** as shown in Fig. 7.7. If you want to use the built-in Standard Deviation function, you have to put all of the samples into an array and wait until the While Loop finishes run-

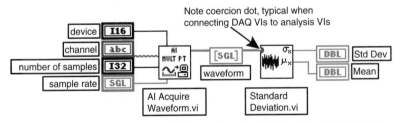

Figure 7.6   Statistics are easy to calculate using the built-in Standard Deviation function when data is acquired as a single-shot (or buffer), in this case using AI Acquire Waveform from the easy-I/O library.

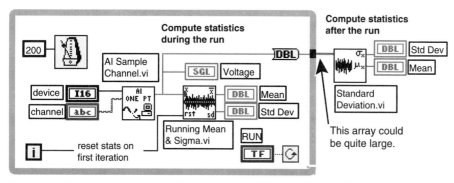

Figure 7.7   I had to write a special function, Running Mean & Sigma, that accumulated and calculated statistics during execution of a continuous data acquisition process. Building an array for postrun calculations consumes much memory.

ning—not exactly a real-time computation. Or, you could build the array one sample at a time in a shift register and call Standard Deviation each time. That may seem OK, but the array grows without limit until the loop stops—a waste of memory at best, or you may cause Lab-VIEW to run out of memory altogether. The best solution is to create a different version of the mean and standard deviation algorithm, one that uses an **incremental** calculation.

platform\ utility\Running Mean & Sigma.vi   I wrote a function called **Running Mean & Sigma** that recomputes the statistics each time it is called by maintaining intermediate computations in uninitialized shift registers (Fig. 7.8). It is fast and efficient, storing just three numbers in the shift registers. A **Reset** switch sets the intermediate values to zero to clear the function's memory. The idea came right out of the user manual for my HP-45 calculator, proving that inspiration is wherever you find it. Algorithms for this and hundreds of other problems are available in many textbooks and in the popular *Numerical Recipes* series (Press 1990). You can use the concept shown here for other continuous data analysis problems—it's on the CD-ROM.

Faster analysis and display.   Real-time analysis may involve significant amounts of mathematical computation. Digital Signal Processing (DSP) functions, such as the Fast Fourier Transform (FFT) and image processing functions, operate on large arrays of data and may require many seconds even on the fastest computers. If execution time becomes a problem, you can:

- Make sure that you are using the most efficient computation techniques. Try to simplify mathematical expressions and processes and seek alternative algorithms.

- Avoid excessive array manipulation and duplication.

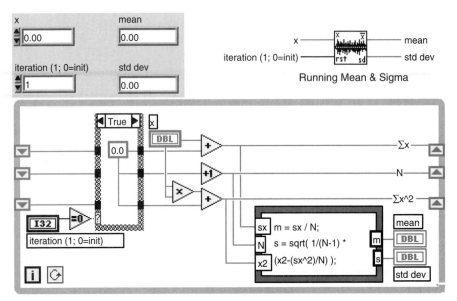

Figure 7.8 Running Mean & Sigma calculates statistics on an incremental basis by storing intermediate computations in uninitialized shift registers. The Reset switch clears the registers.

- Figure out ways to reduce the amount of data used in the calculations. Decimation is a possibility (see Chap. 6, "Using the DAQ Library" and the section entitled "Reducing the Volume of Data," which follows).

- Do the analysis postrun instead of in real time.

- Get a faster computer.

- Use a DSP coprocessor board.

Some of the options you may reject immediately, such as postprocessing, which is of little value when you are trying to do feedback control. On the other hand, if you really *need* that 8192-point power spectrum displayed at 15 Hz, then you had better be using something faster than the average PC. Always be sure that the analysis and display activities don't interfere with acquisition and storage of data.

DSP boards. A DSP board can speed up many analysis functions, particularly those that act on arrays of data. You should *not* consider them to be general-purpose LabVIEW accelerators, however. Not, at least, until we have a version of LabVIEW that cross-compiles for downloading to and execution on a DSP board. Currently, only the boards from National Instruments are fully supported by ready-to-use LabVIEW function libraries. The most useful board is probably the AT-DSP2200 for the PC which includes two 16-bit analog inputs and two 16-bit analog outputs for processing of dynamic signals. An older series of boards, the NB-DSP series for the Macintosh NuBus, is still available but not well supported because the compiler, a Texas Instruments product, is no longer available for the Macintosh. Boards by other manufacturers can certainly be used with LabVIEW, but you will be almost entirely on your own for software development.

DSP boards normally plug into your computer's bus and function as a second bus master or as a slave processor. They have their own onboard memory, their own unique instruction set, and most of them support direct connections to some form of I/O hardware. Data has to be transferred over your computer's bus to main memory for use by LabVIEW. This can be a limiting factor in the actual performance of a DSP board because the data transfer process (even using DMA) may take more time than the actual computations. You should be cautious when it comes to DSP performance specifications. Try to borrow a board or have someone give you a demonstration using data and algo-

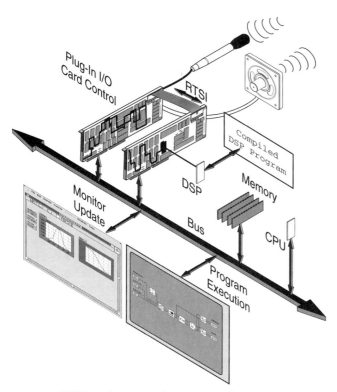

Figure 7.9 DSP boards can speed up some analysis processes. Note that all communications between the DSP board and the computer's CPU and memory (where LabVIEW runs) occur over the bus. This can limit performance.

rithms that are similar to your application before settling on the DSP solution.

To get the most out of a DSP board, you need to write programs in C or assembly language that execute on the board's CPU. If you can't do the programming yourself, there may be someone in your organization who can, and there are consultants who specialize in this type of work.

Looking to the future, **distributed LabVIEW** will be a solution to many of these real-time, processor-intensive applications. Conceptually, you will be able to write VIs that are part of your regular diagrams, yet they execute on other computers residing on plug-in boards, multiprocessor systems, or over a network. It will then be possible to off-load processing or I/O operations to other machines and improve overall system performance in a completely consistent manner and without resorting to lots of custom C programming. (For non-real-time situations, you can already exchange data with other processors using the network functions, but distributed LabVIEW will be light-years beyond that.) I can hardly wait!

Reducing the volume of data. Execution time for most algorithms is roughly proportional to the size of the data arrays. See if you can do something to reduce the size of your arrays, especially when they are to be processed by one of the slower functions. Here are some ideas.

Sample at the minimum rate consistent with the Nyquist criteria and input filtering for your signals. Many times, your data acquisition system will have to sample several channels that have widely different signal bandwidths. You may be able to rewrite the acquisition part of your program so that the low-bandwidth signals are sampled at a slower rate than the high-bandwidth signals. This may be more complex than using a single I/O function that reads all channels at once, but the reduction in array size may be worthwhile. See Chap. 6, "Using the DAQ Library," for techniques related to DAQ hardware and channels with widely different sampling rates.

Process only the meaningful part of the array. Try to develop a technique to locate the interesting part of a long data record and extract only that part by using the **Split Array** or **Array Subset** functions. Perhaps there is some timing information that points to the start of the important event. Or, you might be able to search for a critical level using **Search 1D Array**, **Peak Detector**, or a **Histogram** function. These techniques are particularly useful for sparse data, such as that received from a seismometer. In seismology, 99.9 percent of the data is just a noisy baseline containing no useful information. But every so often there is an interesting event that is detected, extracted, and subjected to extensive analysis. This implies a kind of triggering operation. In the DAQ library, there is a software triggering feature whereby data is transferred to the LabVIEW data space only if it passes some triggering criteria, including slope and level. This feature works for plug-in boards that don't have similar hardware triggering functionality.

Data **decimation** is another possible technique. *Decimation* is a process whereby the elements of an array are divided up into output arrays, like a dealer distributing cards. The **Decimate 1D Array** function can be sized to produce any number of output arrays. Or, you could write a program that averages every *n* incoming values into a smaller output array, as discussed in Chap. 5. Naturally, there is a performance price to pay with these techniques; they involve some amount of computation or memory management. Because the output array(s) is not the same size as the input array, new memory buffers must be allocated, and that takes time. But the payoff comes when you finally pass a smaller data array to those very time-consuming analysis VIs.

Improving display performance. All types of data displays—especially graphs and images—tend to bog down your system. Consider using smaller graphs and images, fewer displayed data points, and less-frequent updates when performance becomes a problem.

Figure 7.10 shows two ways of reducing the update rates of graphics, or anything else, be it an indicator or a computation. Figure 7.10*a* fixes the update rate of a graph in terms of a time interval by using the **Interval Timer** VI, described in Chap. 4 and included on the CD-ROM.

**platform\
timing\Interval
Timer.vi**

Figure 7.10*b* permits a graph to update every *n* cycles of a data acquisition loop by testing the remainder output of the **Quotient and Remainder** function. Yet another way to reduce display overhead is to add an *update display* button connected to the Case structure in lieu of these automatic update techniques.

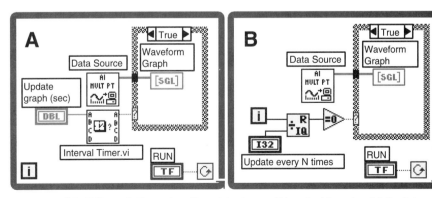

Figure 7.10 Limit the updating rates of graphics (or anything else) by using (*a*) the Interval Timer VI or (*b*) *modulo* arithmetic with the Quotient and Remainder function.

The displays could also appear in independent top-level VIs that receive data from the main acquisition loop via global variables. This is the client-server concept from Chap. 4, "Building an Application," and it works well here. You write the data (probably an array) to a global variable in the data acquisition loop (the server). Then, another VI containing graphs or other displays (the client) reads data from the global variable asynchronously. Analysis can be performed in either or both VIs. The advantage is that the client can be set to execute at lower priority than the server, as well as executing at a slower rate. Also, an arbitrary number of clients can run simultaneously. You could really get carried away and use another global that indicates that the display VI wants an update, thus creating a handshaking arrangement that avoids writing to the global on every acquisition. The disadvantage of the client-server scheme is that even more copies of the data are required, trading memory usage for speed.

Graphics accelerators are now fairly common. Most new PCs and Macs include graphics coprocessors that may significantly reduce the overhead associated with updating the display (by as much as a factor of 50 in some cases). LabVIEW still has to figure out where the text, lines, and boxes need to go, and that takes some main CPU time. But the graphics board will do most of the low-level pixel manipulation, which is certainly an improvement. The LabVIEW Preferences item, **Smooth Updates**, makes a difference in display performance and appearance as well. Smooth updates are created through a technique called *off-screen bitmaps* where graphics are drawn to a separate memory buffer and then quickly copied to the graphics display memory. The intent is to enhance performance while removing some jumpiness in graphics, but smooth updates may actually cause the update time to *increase,* at least on some systems. Experiment with this option, and see for yourself.

Sampling and Throughput

How much data do you need to acquire, analyze, display, and store in how much time? The answer to this question is a measure of system **throughput**. Every component of your data acquisition system—hardware and software—affects throughput. We've already looked at some analysis and display considerations. Next, we'll consider the input sampling requirements that determine the basic data generation rate.

Modern instrumentation can generate a veritable flood of data. There are digitizers that can sample at gigahertz rates, filling multimegabyte buffers in a fraction of a second. Even the ubiquitous, low-cost, plug-in data acquisition boards can saturate your computer's bus and disk drives when given a chance. But is that flood of data really useful? Sometimes; it depends on the signals you are sampling.

Signal bandwidth

As we saw in Chap. 2, "Inputs and Outputs," every signal has a minimum **bandwidth** and must be sampled at a rate at least two times this bandwidth, and preferably more, to avoid **aliasing**. Remember to include significant out-of-band signals in your determination of sampling rate.

If you can't adequately filter out high-frequency components of the signal or interference, then you will have to sample faster. A higher sampling rate may have an impact on throughput because of the larger amount of raw data that is collected. Evaluate every input to your system and determine what sampling rate is really needed to guarantee high signal fidelity.

Sometimes, you find yourself faced with an overwhelming aggregate sampling rate, such as 50 channels at 180 kHz. Then it's time to start asking simple questions like, "Is all this data really useful or necessary?" Quite often, there are channels that can be eliminated because of low priority or redundancy. Or, you may be able to significantly reduce the sampling rate for some channels by lowering the cutoff frequency of the analog lowpass filter in the signal conditioner. Just because *some* channels need to go fast doesn't mean that they *all* do.

Oversampling and digital filtering

Low-frequency analog signals give you some opportunities to further improve the quality of your acquired data. At first glance, that thermocouple signal with a sub-1-Hz bandwidth and little noise could be adequately sampled at 2 or 3 Hz. But by **oversampling**—sampling at a rate several times higher than the Nyquist frequency—you can enhance resolution and noise rejection. Noise is reduced in proportion to the square root of the number of samples that are averaged. For example, if you average 100 samples, the standard deviation of the average value will be reduced by a factor of 10 when compared to a single measurement. This topic is discussed in detail in "A Little Noise Can Be a Good Thing" in Chap. 2, "Inputs and Outputs." I use oversampling for nearly all my low-speed DAQ applications because it's easy to do, requires little extra execution time, and is very effective for noise reduction.

platform\ moving averagers

Once you have oversampled the incoming data, you can apply a digital lowpass filter to the raw data to remove high-frequency noise. There are a number of ways to do digital filtering in LabVIEW: by using the **Filter** functions in the analysis library, the **Moving Averager** VIs from the CD-ROM or by writing something of your own. Digital filter design is beyond the scope of this book, but at least we can look at a few ordinary examples that might be useful in a data acquisition system.

An excellent resource for filter design is National Instruments' **Digital Filter Design Toolkit** for LabVIEW and LabWindows/CVI. It is a stand-alone application for designing and testing all types of digital filters. You typically begin with a filter specification—requirements for the filter response in terms of attenuation versus frequency—and use the filter designer to compute the required coefficients that the LabVIEW VIs can use at runtime. The toolkit makes it easy by graphically displaying all results and allowing you to save specifications and coefficients in files for comparison and reuse. Displays include magnitude, phase, impulse, and step response, a z-plane plot, and the z-transform of the designed filter. Once you have designed a filter and saved its coefficients, an included LabVIEW VI can load those coefficients for use in real time.

FIR filters. If you are handling single-shot data, the built-in **Finite Impulse Response (FIR)** filter functions are ideal. The concept behind an FIR filter is a **convolution** (multiplication in the frequency domain) of a set of weighting coefficients with the incoming signal. In fact, if you look at the diagram of one of the FIR filters, you will usually see two VIs: one that calculates the filter coefficients based on your filter specifications, and the **Convolution** VI that does the actual computation. The response of an FIR filter depends only on the coefficients and the input signal and as a result the output quickly dies out when the signal is removed. That's why they call it *finite* impulse response. FIRs also require no initialization since there is no memory involved in the response.

For most filters, you just supply the sampling frequency (for calibration) and the desired filter characteristics, and the input array will be accurately filtered. You can also use highpass, bandpass, and bandstop filters, in addition to the usual lowpass, if you know the bandwidth of interest. Figure 7.11 shows a DAQ-based single-shot application where a noisy sine wave is the signal. I applied a sinusoidal input signal, and then added **Periodic Random Noise** to exercise our filter.

The **FIR Windowed Filter** VI is set up to perform a lowpass filter operation. The **sampling frequency (fs)** for the filter VI is the same one used by the DAQ VI and is measured in Hz. This calibrates the **low cutoff frequency** control in Hz, as well. Since the input signal was 10 Hz, I selected a cutoff of 50 Hz which is sufficiently high to avoid throwing away any significant part of the signal. The value for **taps** is really arbitrary on my part. A large number of taps makes the filter roll off more rapidly, but at the expense of greater computation time and greater delay. Examine the graph and note that the filtered waveform is delayed with respect to the raw data. This is where the Digital Filter Design Toolkit comes in handy. You can choose the minimum number of

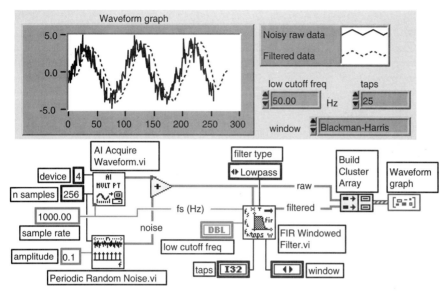

Figure 7.11 A practical application of FIR lowpass filtering applied to an array of single-shot data, a noisy sine wave. Bandpass filtering could also be used in this case, since we know the exact frequency of interest.

taps and the optimum cutoff frequency to yield the desired results. Filter design is always a compromise, so don't be disappointed if the final results are somehow less than perfect.

You can compensate for the delay in an FIR filter by routing the filtered signal through the **Array Subset** function and removing the required number of samples from the start of the waveform. That number is approximately equal to the number of taps; being the nonmathematical type, I usually test it out and see what the magic number is. Since the delay is invariant once you set the number of taps, FIR filters can effectively supply zero delay. (Technically, this is because they have *linear* phase distortion.) This is important when you need to maintain an absolute timing reference with respect to a trigger or another signal.

A **time window** generally should be applied to all signals prior to filtering or other frequency-domain processing. *Time windows* reduce **spectral leakage** and other **finite-sequence length** artifacts in spectral estimation calculations such as FFTs and power spectra. Spectral leakage occurs because an FFT has discrete frequency bins. If the signal does not happen to precisely land in one of these bins, the FFT smears the signal energy into adjacent bands. The other problem, due to the finite data record length, shows up as extra energy spread out all over the spectrum. If you think about it, an arbitrary buffer of data probably does not start and end at zero. The instantaneous step from zero to the initial value of the data represents a transient, and transients have energy at all frequencies.

The job of the time window is to gradually force the start and end of your data to zero. It does so by multiplying the data array by some function, typically a cosine raised to some power, which by definition is zero at both ends. This cleans up much of the spectral leakage and finite-sequence length problems, or at least makes them more predictable. One side effect is a change in absolute amplitude in the results. If you use the **Scaled Time Domain Window** VI from the Analysis>>Measurements palette, the gain for each type of window is properly compensated. The FIR Windowed Filter VI is also properly compensated. There are quite a few window functions available and each was designed to meet certain needs. You should definitely experiment with various time windows and observe the effects on actual data.

IIR filters. **Infinite Impulse Response (IIR)** filters are generally a closer approximation to their analog kin than FIR filters. The output of an IIR filter depends not only on the *input* signal and a set of **forward coefficients**, but also on the *output* of the filter and an additional set of **reverse coefficients**—a kind of feedback. The resulting response takes (theoretically) an infinite amount of time to arrive at its final value—an asymptotic response just like the exponential behavior of analog filters. The advantage of an IIR filter, compared to an FIR filter, is that the feedback permits more rapid cutoff transitions with fewer coefficients and hence fewer computations. However, they have *nonlinear phase distortion,* making them unsuitable for some phase-sensitive applications. Also, you can choose a set of coefficients that make an IIR filter *unstable,* an unavoidable fact with any feedback system.

IIR filters are best suited to continuous data, but with attention to initialization they are also usable with single-shot data. In the filter palette, you will find most of the classic analog filter responses in ready-to-use VIs: Butterworth, Chebyshev, Inverse Chebyshev, Elliptical, and Bessel. If you are at all familiar with RC or active analog filters, you'll be right at home with these implementations. In addition, you can specify arbitrary responses not available using analog techniques. Of course, this gets a bit tricky, and you will probably want the Digital Filter Design Toolkit or some other mathematical tool to obtain valid coefficients.

Figure 7.12 shows the **AI Continuous Scan** VI acquiring seamless buffers of data from a single channel containing a 5-Hz sine wave. For interest, I added noise, just like the previous FIR example. The IIR filter VI, **Butterworth Filter**, behaves in this application similarly to its analog counterpart, but I didn't need a soldering iron to build it. Note the Boolean input that is set to False when the While Loop begins. This

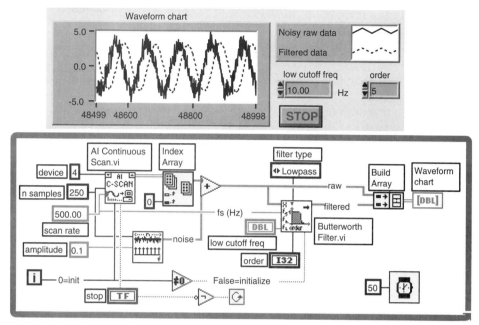

Figure 7.12   A continuous acquisition process with a Butterworth IIR filter. Once initialized, this digital filter works just like an analog filter.

initializes the filter's internal state, and then tells the filter to remember previous conditions on subsequent calls. The result is that part of the very first buffer of data contains some transient error due to initialization, but all subsequent buffers are accurately processed. If you want to experiment with this behavior, try the analysis example, **Online Filtering Example**.

For classical filters such as this Butterworth, controls are quite similar to the design parameters for corresponding analog filters. In particular, you choose the **filter type** (highpass, lowpass, etc.), and then choose the **order**. Order, in the analog world, translates to the number of inductors and capacitors in the filter implementation. Higher order results in a sharper response, but as you might expect, the implementation requires additional computations. Sampling frequency and high- and low-cutoff frequencies are calibrated in Hz as with the FIR filters.

Median filters.   If your data contains **outliers**—also known as *spikes* or *fliers*—consider the **Median Filter** VI. The median filter is based on a statistical, or nonlinear, algorithm. Its only tuning parameter is called **rank**, which determines the number of values in the incoming data that the filter acts upon at one time. For each location i in the incoming array, the filter sorts the values in the range $(i - rank)$ to $(i + rank)$ and then selects the median (middle) value, which then becomes the output value. The algorithm slides along through the entire data set in this manner. The beauty of the median filter is that it neatly removes outliers while adding no phase distortion. In contrast, regular IIR and FIR filters are nowhere near as effective at removing outliers, even with very high orders. The price you pay is speed: the median filter algorithm tends to be quite slow, especially for higher rank. To see how the median filter works, try out the Median Filtering example VI.

platform\ moving averagers\moving avg array

Moving averagers.   **Moving Averagers** are another appropriate filter for continuous data. The one demonstrated in Fig. 7.13, **Moving Avg Array**, operates on data from a typical multichannel data acquisition system. An array containing samples from each channel is the input, and the same array, but lowpass-filtered, is the output. Any number of samples can be included in the moving average, and the averaging can be turned on and off while running. This is a particular kind of FIR fil-

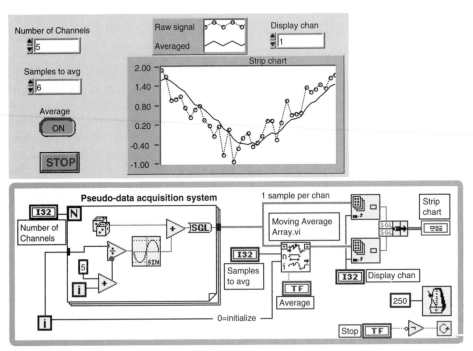

Figure 7.13 Demonstration of the Moving Avg Array function, which applies a lowpass filter to an array of independent channels. The For Loop creates several channels of data, like a data acquisition system. Each channel is filtered, then the selected channel is displayed in both raw and filtered form.

ter where all the coefficients are equal to one; it is also known as a *box-car* filter.

Other moving averagers are primarily for use with block-mode continuous data. They use local memory to maintain continuity between adjacent data buffers to faithfully process block-mode data as if it were a true, continuous stream. There are several versions included in the Moving Averagers directory on the CD-ROM.

After lowpass filtering, you can safely decimate data arrays to reduce the total amount of data. Decimation is in effect a **resampling** of the data at a lower frequency. Therefore, the resultant sampling rate must be at least twice the cutoff frequency of your digital lowpass filter or aliasing will occur. For instance, say that you have applied a 1-kHz lowpass filter to your data. To avoid aliasing, the time interval for each sample must be shorter than 0.5 ms. If the original data was sampled at 100 kHz (0.01 ms per sample), you could safely decimate it by a factor as large as 0.5/0.01, or 50 to 1. Whatever you do, don't decimate without knowledge of the power spectrum of your incoming signal. You can end up with exactly the same result as sampling too slowly in the first place.

Timing techniques

Using software to control the sampling rate for a data acquisition system can be a bit tricky. Because you are running LabVIEW on a general-purpose computer with lots of graphics, plus all that operating system activity going on in the background, there is bound to be some uncertainty in the timing of events, just as we discussed with regards to timestamps. Somewhere between 1 and 1000 Hz, your system will become an unreliable interval timer. For slower applications, however, a While Loop with a **Wait Until Next ms Multiple** function inside works just fine for timing a data acquisition operation.

The *best* way to pace any sampling operation is with a hardware timer. Most plug-in boards, scanning voltmeters, digitizers, oscilloscopes, and many other instruments have sampling clocks with excellent stability. Use them whenever possible. Your data acquisition program will be simpler and your timing more robust.

Your worst timing nightmare occurs when you have to sample one channel at a time—and *fast*—from a "dumb" I/O system that has no ability to scan multiple channels, no local memory, and no sampling clock. I ran into this with some old CAMAC A/D modules. They are very fast, but very dumb. Without a smart controller built into the CAMAC crate, it is simply impossible to get decent throughput to a LabVIEW system. Remember that a single I/O call to the NI-DAQ or NI-GPIB driver typically takes milliseconds to execute, thus limiting loop cycle time to perhaps 100 Hz. Other drivers, typically those based on peek and poke or other low-level operations including some DLL or CIN calls, can be much faster, on the order of microseconds per call. In that case, you at least have a fighting chance of making millisecond loops.

If the aggregate sampling rate (total channels per second) is pressing your system's reliable timing limit, be sure to do plenty of testing and/ or try to back off on the rate. Otherwise, you may end up with unevenly sampled signals that can be difficult or impossible to analyze. Better to choose the right I/O system in the first place—one that solves the fast sampling problem for you.

Configuration Management

You could write a data acquisition program with no configuration management features, but do so only after considering the consequences. The only thing that's constant in a laboratory environment is *change*, so it's silly to have to edit your LabVIEW diagram each time someone wants to change a channel assignment or scale factor. Make your program more flexible by including configuration management VIs that accommodate such routine changes with a convenient user interface.

What to configure

Even the simplest data acquisition systems have channel names that need to be associated with their respective physical I/O channels. As the I/O hardware becomes more complex, additional setup information is required. Also, information about the experiment itself may need to be inseparably tied to the acquired data. For instance, you certainly need to know some fundamental parameters such as channel names and sample intervals before you can possibly analyze the data. On the other hand, knowing the serial number of a transducer, while useful, is not mandatory for basic analysis. Table 7.3 is a list of configuration-related items you might want to consider for your system.

In a sense, all of this information comprises a **configuration database**, and any technique that applies to a database could be applied here: inserting and deleting records, sorting, searching, and of course storing and fetching database images from disk. These are tasks for a configuration **editor**. Additionally, you need a kind of **compiler** or translator program that reads this user-supplied information, validates it, then transmits it in suitable form to the I/O hardware and the acquisition program. (See Fig. 7.14.)

The level of sophistication of such an editor or compiler is limited only by your skill as a programmer and your creative use of other applications on your computer. The simplest editor is just a cluster

TABLE 7.3   Items to Include in Configuration

I/O hardware-related
Port number, such as GPIB board or serial port selection
Device address
Slot number, where multiple I/O modules or boards are used
Module or board type
Channel number
Channel name
Channel gain, scale factor, or linearization formula
Sampling rate; may be on a per-module or per-channel basis
Filtering specifications
Triggering parameters—slope, level, AC/DC coupling

Experiment-related
Experiment identifier; short ID numbers make good foundations for data file names
Purpose or description of the experiment
Operator's name
Start date and time
Data file path(s)
Transducer type or description for each channel
Transducer calibration information and serial number

array that you type values into. The most complex editor I've heard of uses a commercial database program which writes out a configuration file for LabVIEW to read and process. You can use the **SQL Toolkit** (available from National Instruments) to load the information into LabVIEW by issuing SQL commands to the database file. When the

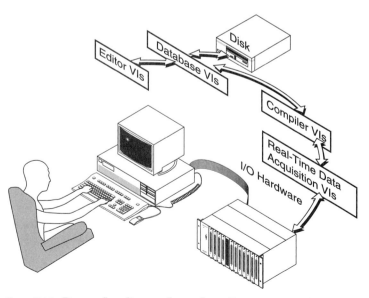

Figure 7.14   Process flow diagram for configuration management.

experiment is done, you might be able to pipe the data—or at least a summary of the results—back to the database. Feel adventurous?

Assuming that you're using the DAQ library, much of this configuration information is addressed by the **NI-DAQ Channel Wizard**. The Wizard is a convenient and feature-rich graphical user interface that you use to maintain a proprietary configuration file. The configuration file is then loaded by the NI-DAQ driver at runtime. From within Lab-VIEW, about all you need to do is let the user pick from a list of channel names defined in the configuration. All the other information about each channel—scale factors, hardware assignments, and so forth—are already defined in the file, so your LabVIEW program doesn't need to keep track of it. Supplementary information, such as experimental descriptions, will of course be maintained by programs that you write.

Configuration editors

By all means, use the NI-DAQ Channel Wizard if you can. But it can't address every imaginable need, so you should know something about the alternatives. Aside from that rather elaborate application of a commercial database, there are some reasonable ways for you to program LabVIEW as a configuration editor. There are two basic editor types: **interactive editors** and **static editors**. An *interactive editor* is a LabVIEW VI that runs while you enter configuration information, supplying you with immediate feedback as to the validity of your entries. A *static editor* is generally simpler, consisting of a VI that you run after entering information into all of its control fields. If an error occurs, you receive a dialog box and try again. With either editor, once the entries are validated, the information is passed on to a configuration compiler (which may actually be part of the editor program). If the configuration is loaded from an external file, it may pass through an editor for user updates or directly to the compiler for immediate use.

Static editors for starters.   Ordinary LabVIEW controls are just fine for entering configuration information, be it numeric, string, or Boolean format. Since a typical data acquisition system has many channels, it makes sense to create a configuration entry device that is a **cluster array**. The cluster contains all the items that define a channel. Making an array of these clusters provides a compact way of defining an arbitrary number of channels (Fig. 7.15).

One problem with this simple method is that it's a bit inconvenient to insert or delete items in an array control using the data selection items in the array control pop up. A solution is to include an **On Scan** switch, as I did in this example. Only when a channel is *on scan* is its configuration information passed along to the I/O driver. When a chan-

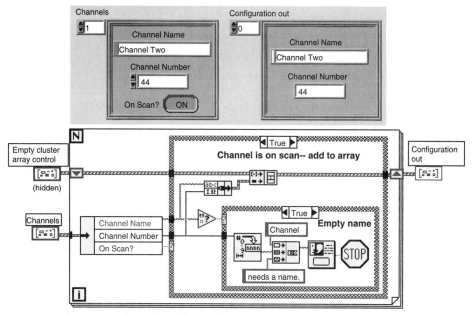

Figure 7.15   A static configuration editor using a cluster array. It checks to see that a channel name has been entered and appends *on scan* channels to the output configuration array.

nel is *off scan,* the ADC or digitizer may safely ignore that channel, thus saving some I/O operations. I usually make the switch turn red when a channel is off scan to make sure that the user doesn't accidentally leave a channel turned off.

The diagram for this editor checks to see that the channel name is not empty (you could also check for invalid characters, name too long, etc.). If the name is empty, a dialog pops up telling the user, "Channel 17 needs a name." If the name is OK, and the channel is on scan, then the name and channel number are appended to the output cluster array for use later on. You can also use the empty channel name as a switch to take the channel off scan.

Obviously, you can add as many items as you need to the channel description cluster, but the amount of error checking and cross-verification you could do will become extensive. Error checking is part of making your program robust. Even this simple example needs more checking: what if the user assigns the same channel number to two or more channels? What if two channels have the same name?

For more complex I/O systems, a nested structure of cluster arrays inside of cluster arrays may be required. Figure 7.16 configures Opto-22 analog input modules. The outer array selects a multiplexer (MUX) number. Each multiplexer has up to 16 channels that are configured by

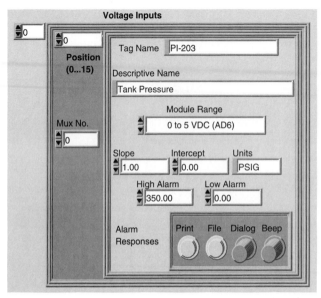

Figure 7.16 Configuration for a more complicated I/O system (Opto-22 *Optomux*) requires nested cluster arrays with lots of controls.

the inner cluster array. Since there were four possible alarm responses, I grouped them inside yet another cluster, way down inside. As you can see, the data structure becomes quite complex and might be unmanageable for a casual user. I've found that array controls are hopelessly confusing to some operators. This is a clear case of making the user interface convenient for the *programmer* rather than the *user*. Such a structure might, however, be used as the output of a more user-friendly interactive editor.

The LabVIEW **Table control** can also be used for configuration entries, and it's more likely that your users will understand it. Like a spreadsheet, columns can be assigned to each setup parameter with one row per channel. Tables have an advantage over cluster arrays because they have high information density; many channel definitions will fit in a small screen area. But tables have one glaring disadvantage: data validation is mandatory on each and every cell. Because a table is just a 2D string array, the user is free to type any characters into any cell. What happens when you are hoping for a numeric entry, but receive something nonnumeric?

Any time you write a loop to process a Table control, you will encounter the nefarious empty row problem. It occurs when the user types something into a cell, and then deletes everything. Even though the cell is empty, the 2D array now has another element that contains an empty string. If you pass this 2D array to a loop for processing, it will attempt to process the empty strings. You can test for empty strings later or use the VI in Fig. 7.17, **Remove Empty Table Elements**.

**platform\
control\
rampsoak.llb\
Remove empty
table elements**

It removes any number of trailing empty rows. Size the Table control so that it displays only the proper number of columns then hide the horizontal scroll bars to keep the user from entering too many columns of data.

Figure 7.18 is a static editor that interprets the data in a Table control. It does no error checking, but that could be added right after each of the Index Array functions. As a minimum, you would have to verify that all numbers are in range and that the channel name is acceptable. Cross-checking for more complex data inconsistency gets really interesting. For instance, you might have to verify that the right number of channels are assigned dependent upon the multiplexer type. Perhaps a future version of LabVIEW will include a more powerful table control that has many of these data filter features, such as numeric validation.

Interactive editors.   Interactive configuration editors are more versatile and more user-friendly than static editors because they provide instant feedback to the user. You can add pop-up windows, status displays, or even turn LabVIEW into a menu-driven system. Plan to do some extra programming if you want these extra features. Elaborate interactive editor projects are among the most challenging programming tasks I've ever tackled. The NI-DAQ Channel Wizard is evidence of what's possible in LabVIEW, assuming that you're *really good*.

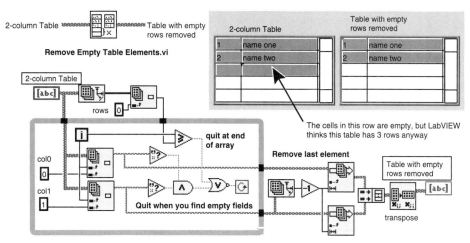

Figure 7.17   This VI gets rid of empty table rows. Erasing a cell completely does not remove that row of the 2D array. This VI does, though.

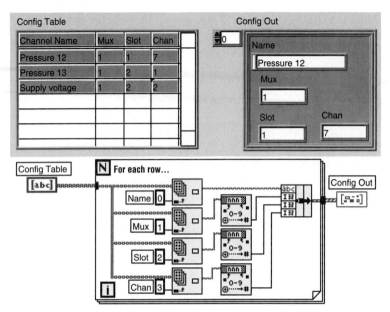

Figure 7.18   This is a simple configuration editor that interprets the contents of a Table control and converts the data into a cluster array.

Pop-up editors. Say you have several different kinds of I/O modules, and they all have significantly different configuration needs. If you try to accommodate them all with one big cluster array, various controls would be invalid depending on which module was selected. You really need separate input panels for each module type if you want to keep the program simple.

One solution is to put several buttons on the panel of the main configuration VI that open customized configuration editor subVIs (Fig. 7.19). Each button has its mechanical action set to **Latch When Released**, and each editor subVI is set to **Show front panel when called**. The editor subVIs do the real configuration work. Note that they don't really have to be any fancier than the static editors we already have discussed. When you create one of these pop-up subVIs, remember to disable **Allow user to close window** in the Window Options of the VI Setup dialog. Otherwise, the user may accidentally close the window of the VI while it's running and the calling VI will not be able to continue.

platform\ utility\Which Button.vi

I threw in a handy utility VI, called **Which Button** (Fig. 7.20), that makes these button-driven programs a little easier to write. To use it, build a Boolean array on your diagram containing all your buttons as shown in the previous example. The output of Which Button is zero when nothing is pressed, one for the first button, two for the second,

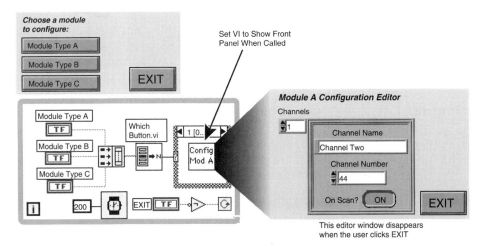

Figure 7.19 This configuration editor model uses subVIs that appear when an appropriate button is pressed. The subVI is the actual user interface (in this case, a configuration editor) and may do other processing as well. The Which Button function (shown in the next figure) chooses the right editing subVI.

and so on. I use Which Button in any application that has several Boolean choices.

Information may be returned by each editor subVI for further processing, or each editor can function as a stand-alone program, doing all the necessary I/O initialization, writing of global variables, and so forth. A worthy goal is for each editor to return a standard data structure (such as a cluster array), regardless of the type of I/O module that it supports. This may simplify the data acquisition and analysis processes (see the section entitled "Configuration Compilers" which follows).

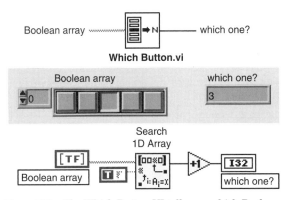

Figure 7.20 The Which Button VI tells you which Boolean in an array was set to True. Returns zero if none are True, one if the first one is True, etc.

Another way you can accommodate modules with different configuration needs is to use **Attribute nodes** to selectively hide controls when they don't apply. When the user selects module type *A,* the special controls for module *B* are hidden, and so forth. Note that you can selectively hide controls that are part of a cluster, but there's a trick. You must go to the front panel, pop up on the particular control you wish to hide, and select **Create>>Attribute Node**. This is not possible from the diagram because a cluster only has one terminal. There's another way to attack this problem: stack the clusters for each module on top of each other, with Attribute nodes making only one visible at a time, and have a **Module Select** ring that shows the cluster for the selected module.

Here is a model for an interactive editor hierarchy that I originally built to support SCXI analog input modules. It turned out to be quite versatile, and I've used it for many other kinds of instruments. Figure 7.21 shows the window that appears when the user clicks a button on the top-level configuration manager VI. The figure also shows a simplified version of the diagram. On the CD-ROM, you'll find the complete version of this VI, **SCXI Analog Config Dialog**, as well as a SCXI/DAQ-based acquisition VI, **Analog Input Scanner**, that uses the configurations produced by this nice user interface.

 platform\ scxi config\ scxi_io.llb
This program relies on a global variable, Inst Config Globals, to pass the configuration cluster array along to other parts of the data acquisition system. The configuration data is loaded from the global at startup, then circulates in a shift register until the user clicks the Exit button. Two subVIs act on the configuration data: **Read/Write SCXI Config** and **Edit SCXI Config**. The Read/Write Config VI can either load or store an image of the cluster array to a binary file. The file path is chosen by another subVI, **Change Config File**, which opens like a dialog box when called. It permits the user to pick an existing file or create a new one. The real work of editing the configuration occurs inside Edit SCXI Config.

Indeed, the tough part of this interactive editor is the Edit SCXI Config VI. Figure 7.22 shows the front panel, which I designed purely for user comfort and efficiency with no thought whatsoever for the complexity of the underlying program. So, where's the diagram? It's *way* too complicated to show here. It's based on a state machine that looks at the present control settings, then modifies the display accordingly. For instance, if the user changes the **Module #** control, all the other controls are updated to reflect the present setting of channel one of that module. This is accomplished by reading the settings from the configuration cluster array and loading them into the controls with Local variables. Also, the **Module Gain** and channel **Gain** controls are selectively disabled (dimmed) by Attribute Nodes. For instance, if the user picks an SCXI-

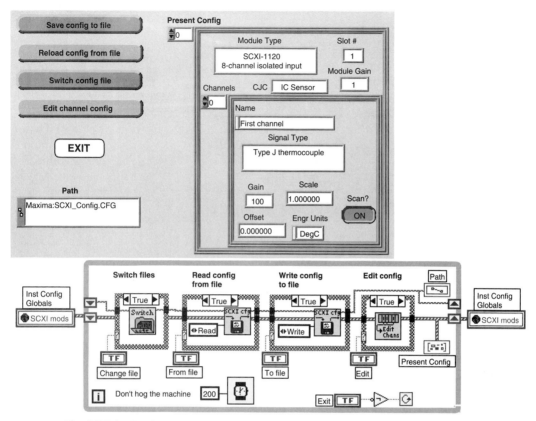

Figure 7.21 The SCXI Analog Config Dialog VI helps the user manage SCXI analog input modules. The configuration is stored in a global variable for use elsewhere in the data acquisition program, and it can be loaded from and saved to files. (False frames of all the Case structures simply pass each input to its respective output.)

1120 module, each channel has its own gain setting, so the **Gain** control is enabled while the **Module Gain** control is disabled.

This is the fanciest configuration editor that I could design in LabVIEW and it uses just about every feature of the language. The reason that this editor is so nice is that unlike the static editor with its cluster array, all of the controls update instantly without any clumsy array navigation problems. However, the programming is very involved—as it would be in any language. What I would suggest you do is stick to the simpler static editors and use some of the ideas described here until you're really confident about your programming skills. Then design a nice user interface, or start with my example VI, and have at it. If you design the overall configuration program in a modular fashion, you can replace the simple editor with the fancy editor when it's complete.

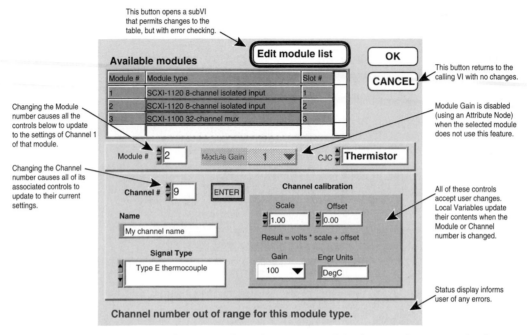

This button opens a subVI
that permits changes to the
table, but with error checking.

Available modules

Edit module list

OK

This button returns to the
calling VI with no changes.

CANCEL

Module #	Module type	Slot #
1	SCXI-1120 8-channel isolated input	1
2	SCXI-1120 8-channel isolated input	2
3	SCXI-1100 32-channel mux	3

Changing the Module
number causes all the
controls below to update
to the settings of Channel 1
of that module.

Module Gain is disabled
(using an Attribute Node)
when the selected module
does not use this feature.

Module # 2   Module Gain   1 ▼   CJC **Thermistor**

Changing the Channel
number causes all of its
associated controls to
update to their current
settings.

Channel # 9   ENTER

Channel calibration

Scale   Offset
1.00   0.00

Result = volts * scale + offset

All of these controls
accept user changes.
Local Variables update
their contents when the
Module or Channel
number is changed.

Name

My channel name

Signal Type

Type E thermocouple

Gain   Engr Units
100 ▼   DegC

Status display informs
user of any errors.

Channel number out of range for this module type.

Figure 7.22   Panel of my SCXI configuration editor, showing some of the features that you can implement if you spend lots of time programming.

Only you can decide if great expenditures of effort are necessary. If you only have one or two users, or they only have to deal with configuration management once a month, then it's probably not worth the effort. On the other hand, you may be able to develop an elaborate editor VI that can serve as a template for other purposes, thus leveraging your development efforts. When I wrote the SCXI configuration manager, I spent some time designing it with the intent that much of the code would be reused for other types of I/O hardware in my application. That's why the VI in Fig. 7.21 has such a clean design.

Status displays.   Since an interactive editor is a program that runs all the time, it can do such things as entry validation even as the user changes settings. You can give the user feedback by adding a status display that describes any errors or inconsistencies among the various settings. In Fig. 7.23, for instance, you have a choice of several I/O modules, each having a certain limited range of channels. Any disagreement between module type and channel quantity needs to be rectified. A Ring Indicator contains predefined status messages. Item zero is *OK to continue,* while item one is the error message shown. The status has to be zero to permit the *Exit* button to terminate the While Loop.

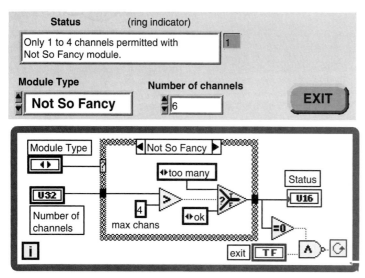

Figure 7.23   How to use a Ring Indicator as a status display. The While Loop runs all the time, so the user's settings are always being evaluated. The Ring contains predefined messages—in this case, item zero is *OK to continue*. Any real work for this configuration editor would be done inside the While Loop.

You can also use a string indicator to display status messages, feeding it various strings contained in constants on the diagram. The string indicator can also display error messages returned from I/O operations or from an error handler VI. You would probably use Local variables to write status messages from various places on your diagram or keep the status message in a shift register if you base your solution on a state machine. That's what I did with the SCXI configuration editor. Some configuration situations require constant interaction with the I/O hardware to confirm the validity of the setup. For instance, if you want to configure a set of VXI modules, you might need to verify that the chosen module is installed. If the module is not found, it's nice to receive an informative message telling you about the problem right away. Such I/O checks would be placed inside the overall While Loop.

A good status message is intended to convey information, not admonish the user. You should report not only what is wrong, but how to correct the problem. "ERROR IN SETUP" is definitely *not* helpful, though that is exactly what you get from many commercial software packages. **Dialogs** can also be used for status messages, but you should reserve them for really important events, such as confirming the overwriting of a file. It's annoying to have dialog boxes popping up all the time.

Menu-driven systems.   When PCs only ran DOS, and all the world was in darkness, menu-driven systems were the standard. They really are the easiest user interfaces to write when you have minimal graphics support. The classic menu interface looks like this:

```
Choose a function:
    1:     Initialize hardware
    2:     Set up files
    3:     Collect data
Enter a number >_
```

In turn, the user's choice will generate yet another menu of selections. The good thing about these menu-driven prompting systems is that the user can be a total idiot and still run your system. On the other hand, an experienced user gets frustrated by the inability to navigate through the various submenus in an expedient manner. Also, it's hard to figure out where you are in the hierarchy of menus. Therefore, I introduce menus as a LabVIEW technique with some reluctance. It's up to you to decide where this concept is appropriate, and how far to carry it.

The keys to a successful menu-driven system are aids to navigation and the ability to back up a step (or bail out completely, returning to step one) at any time. Using subVIs that open when called allows you to use any kind of controls, prompting, status, and data entry devices that might be required.

A LabVIEW menu could be made from buttons, ring controls, or sliders. If you use anything besides buttons, there would also have to be a *do it* button. Programming would be much like the first pop-up editor example, earlier in this section. To make nested menus, each subVI that opens when called would in turn offer selections that would open yet another set of subVIs.

If you lay out the windows carefully, the hierarchy can be visible on the screen. The highest-level menu VI would be located toward the upper-left corner of the screen. Lower-level menus would appear offset a bit lower and to the right, as shown in Fig. 7.24. This helps the user navigate through nested menus. LabVIEW remembers the exact size and location of a window when you save the VI. Don't forget that other people who use your VIs may have smaller screens.

Configuration compilers

A **configuration compiler** translates the user's settings obtained from a configuration editor into data that is used to set up or access hardware. It may also be responsible for storing and recalling old configuration records for reuse. The compiler program may or may not be

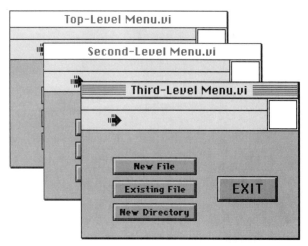

Figure 7.24 Layout for hierarchical menu subVIs that helps users navigate. The *Exit* button returns you to the previous menu. You might use the VI Setup dialog to customize the window presentation; the Run arrow is not needed.

an integral part of an editor VI. A good point of reference is the NI-DAQ Channel Wizard. It collects user input through a dynamic user interface and then compiles it into a binary database format that the NI-DAQ driver can efficiently load and use at runtime for the I/O operations.

The control layout on a configuration editor's panel should be optimized for efficient user interaction. But those controls may not be very efficient when it comes time to send information to a real-time data acquisition driver or file storage VI. It would be very inefficient, for example, to have the driver interpret and sort arrays of strings that describe channel assignments every time the driver is called. Rather, you should write a compiler that interprets the strings at configuration time and creates a numeric array that lists the channel numbers to be scanned. Your objective is to write a program that does as little as possible during data acquisition and analysis phases, thus enhancing throughput.

The next three figures illustrate a simple compiler that supports some digitizer modules. Each module has four channels with independent setups. Figure 7.25 is a cluster array into which the user has entered the desired setup information, perhaps by using an interactive editor VI. Channel setup information is in the form of four clusters, which makes it easy for the user to see all of the setups at once. However, this is not an efficient way to package the information for use by an acquisition VI. Figure 7.26 shows a more desirable structure, where each channel is an element of an array. The compiler must make this translation.

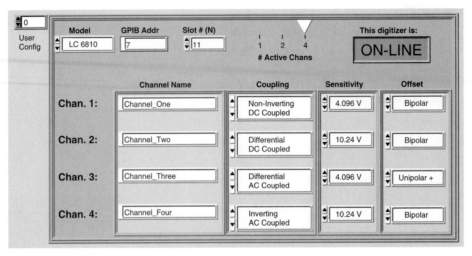

Figure 7.25   The input to this configuration compiler for digitizers is a cluster array that a user has filled in. The four clusters (channel names, coupling, sensitivity, and offset) need to be checked for consistency and converted to arrays for use by the acquisition VIs.

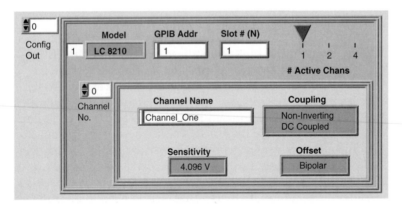

Figure 7.26   The compiler's output is a cluster array. Note that it carries all of the same information as the input cluster array, but in a more compact form.

Here are the steps to be taken by this configuration compiler, whose diagram appears in Fig. 7.27:

1. Convert the individual channel clusters into an array.

2. If the module is online, build the output configuration cluster and append it to the output array.

3. Check the settings for consistency (e.g., there may be limitations on sensitivity for certain coupling modes).

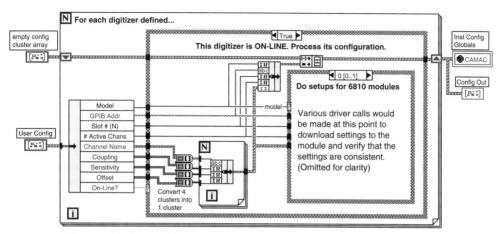

Figure 7.27 Diagram for the simple compiler. Data types are converted by the inner For Loop. Settings are checked for consistency and digitizers are initialized by the inner Case structure. If a digitizer is online, its configuration is added to the output array, which is passed to the acquisition VIs by a global variable.

4. Initialize each module and download the settings.

5. Write the output configuration cluster array to a global variable which will be read by the acquisition VI.

I left out the gory details of how the settings are validated and downloaded since that involves particular knowledge of the modules and their driver VIs. Even so, much of the diagram is taken up by bundlers and unbundlers and other conversion functions that are required to reformat the incoming data. This is typical of these compilers, and it sometimes gets rather messy because of the number of items and special conditions that you have to deal with. Where possible, encapsulate related parts of the compiler in subVIs to make the diagram easier to understand and more compact. I would probably put all the driver functions for a given type of digitizer module in a subVI because they are logically related.

Somewhere in the edit or compile phase you should try to communicate with each I/O device to see if it responds, and report an error if it doesn't. It would be uncouth to permit the user to get all the way to the data acquisition phase before announcing that an important instrument is DOA.

Saving and recalling configurations

Another useful function that the compiler can perform is the creation of a permanent record of the configuration. The record might be a spreadsheet-format text file suitable for printing, a special format for use by a data analysis program, or a LabVIEW datalog or binary file that you can read back into the configuration program for later reuse (that's how the NI-DAQ Channel Wizard does it). It makes sense to put this functionality in with the editors and compilers because all of the necessary information is readily available there. The SCXI configuration VI described above includes such functionality, and you can look at the VIs on the CD-ROM to see how I did it there.

Printable records (spreadsheet format). Many systems I've worked on needed a hardcopy record of the experiment's configuration for the lab notebook. The direct approach is to generate a text file that you can load and print with something like a spreadsheet or word processor. Add tab characters between fields and carriage returns where appropriate to clean up the layout. Titles are a big help, too. Figure 7.28 is a diagram that interprets the configuration cluster array of Fig. 7.26 into tab-delimited text. There is a great deal of string building to do, so don't be surprised if the diagram gets a little ugly.

Here is what this text converter VI produces, as interpreted by a word processor with suitable tab stops. As you can see, most of the settings are written in numeric form. You could add Case structures for Coupling, Sensitivity, and Offset to decode the numbers into something more descriptive.

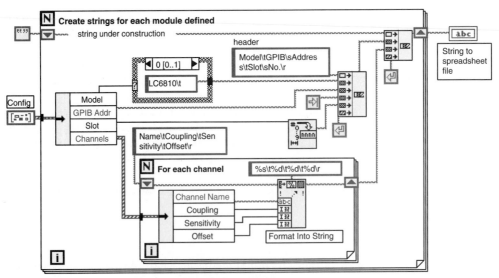

Figure 7.28   A routine that converts the configuration cluster of Fig. 7.27 into a tab-delimited text file for documentation purposes. As you can see, there's lots of string building to do.

```
Model           GPIB Address    Slot No.
LC6810          1               7
Name            Coupling        Sensitivity    Offset
Channel One     7               2              0
Channel Two     1               4              2
Channel Three   0               3              1
Channel Four    4               5              1
```

Another way to print a configuration record is to lay out a suitable LabVIEW front panel and print that. You can use all the usual indicators as well as formatted strings displayed in string indicators, if that helps you get more information crammed onto one screen. The obvious way to print the panel is to use the Print command in the File menu, but you can also print **programmatically**. Here's how. First, create a subVI with the displays you want to print. If there are extra inputs that you don't want to print, pop up on those items on the diagram and choose **Hide Control**. Second, turn on the **Print At Completion** option in the Operate menu to make the VI print automatically each time it finishes execution. All the print options in the VI Setup dialog will apply, as will the Page Setup settings. When you call this carefully formatted subVI, its panel need not be displayed in order to print.

Manual save and recall. Your configuration manager should be able to recall previous setups for reuse. Otherwise, the user would have to type in all that information each time. You can use the **Data Logging** functions in the Operate menu (see "Writing Datalog Files" in Chap. 3). The Data Logging functions make it easy to retrieve setups at a later time. Each record has a time- and date stamp so you can see when the setup was created. Thus, your operator can manually save the current front panel setup and sift through old setups at any time.

The crude way to save setups is by entering values into controls and then choosing **Make Current Values Default** from the Operate menu. However, this option is not available when the VI is running, so it's more of a system manager configuration item rather than something your operators would use. But these default values are appropriate for items that the operator doesn't need to change, and this is the easiest and most reliable way of saving setup data.

Automatic save and recall. I prefer to build the configuration editor with binary file support as previously described for the Read/Write SCXI Config VI. This solution is very convenient for the user. Previous settings can be automatically loaded from a standard file each time the

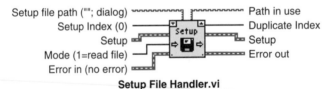

platform
setup file
handler.llb

configuration editor is called, then the file is updated when an editing session is complete.

To make this easy, you can use the **Setup File Handler** VI that I wrote for this purpose (Johnson 1995). It's also a handy way to manage front panel setups where you want to save user entries on various controls between LabVIEW sessions. For example, it's nice to have the last settings on runtime controls return to their previous states when you reload the VI. The Setup File Handler is an integrated subVI which stores a cluster containing all of the setup data in a shift register for quick access in real time and in a binary file for nonvolatile storage. Multiple setups can be managed by this VI. For instance, you might have several identical instruments running simultaneously, each with a private collection of settings.

As you can see from the panel in Fig. 7.29, the setup data is a cluster. Internally, setup clusters are maintained in an array. The element of the array to be accessed is determined by the Setup Index control. The **Setup** cluster is a typedef that you should edit with the Control Editor, and probably rename, for your application. I usually end up with a very large outer cluster containing several smaller clusters, one for each subVI that needs setup management.

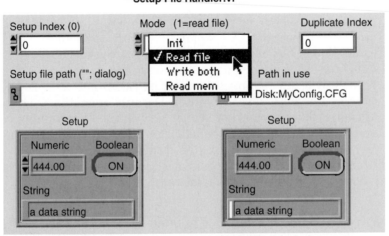

Figure 7.29 The Setup File Handler VI stores and retrieves setup clusters from disk. It's very useful for configuration management and for recalling runtime control settings at a later time. Get it from the CD-ROM.

platform\ setup file handler.llb

To see how this all works, look at the **Setup Handler Example** VI on the CD-ROM. It begins by calling the Setup File Handler VI with Mode=Init to create or open a setup file. If the file doesn't exist, the settings in a default setup cluster are used for all setups. In most applications, all subsequent calls to Setup File Handler would be performed in subVIs. In the example subVI, shown in Fig. 7.30, the Setup File Handler is the source for control initialization data. Local variables initialize controls for the user interface, or the data might be passed to a configuration subVI. After the main part of the program finishes execution, the new control settings or configuration data are bundled back into the setup cluster, and the Setup File Handler updates the memory and disk images. Bundle and Unbundle by Name are very handy functions, as you can see. Try to keep the item names short in the setup cluster to avoid huge Bundlers.

Where should the setup file be saved? I prefer to use the LabVIEW file constant, **This VI's Path**, to supply a guaranteed-valid location. This technique avoids a familiar configuration problem where you have a hand-entered master path name that's wrong every time you move the VI to a new computer. In your top-level VI, insert the little piece of code shown in Fig. 7.31 to create a setup file path. If the current VI is in a LabVIEW library, call the **Strip Path** function twice as shown. If the VI is in a regular directory, call Strip Path once. This technique even works for compiled, stand-alone executables created by the LabVIEW Application Builder.

Another way to obtain a guaranteed-valid (and locatable) path is with the Get System Directory VIs written by Jeff Parker and published in *LTR* (Parker 1994). He used CINs to locate standard directories, such as System:Preferences on the Macintosh or c:\windows on the PC. (You *could* simply assume that the drive and directory names are always the same but sooner or later, someone will rename them behind your back!)

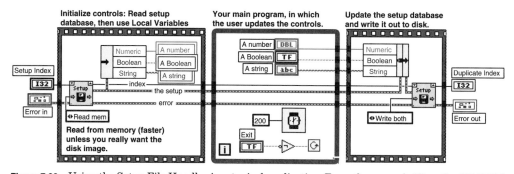

Figure 7.30 Using the Setup File Handler in a typical application. From the example VI on the CD-ROM.

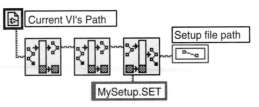

Figure 7.31 Use the path manipulation functions, Strip Path and Build Path, to create a guaranteed-valid path for your setup files. If the current VI is in a LabVIEW library, call Strip Path twice, as shown. Otherwise, only call it once.

A Low-Speed Data Acquisition Example

Life is unfair. You spend all this time reading about high-powered methods of building a data acquisition system, only to find out you need a system up and running *now*—not next week, not next month. What to do? As I've stated before, your best bet is to program by plagiarizing. Sift through the examples that come with LabVIEW and see if there's something that might do at least 50 percent of the job. Or, refer to some of the other resources listed in Chap. 1, "Roots," and tap into the works of others. Eventually, you will build a personal library of VIs that you can call on to quickly assemble working applications. Following is an example that qualifies as a real solution to everyday data acquisition needs.

Here is a low-speed data acquisition VI that I've used over and over, both as a training aid and as a quick solution in many real emergencies. I call it the **Simple Data Acq System** VI.

platform\ simple das\ Simple Data Acq System

It's flexible enough to be the foundation of a somewhat larger application. It is intended for situations where you need to acquire, display, and store data from a few dozen analog channels at speeds up to perhaps 10 samples per second—a very common set of requirements. The panel in Fig. 7.32 has only the most rudimentary controls and indicators. Remember that this is just a starting point and you can add features as required. On the left are configuration controls that determine the input channel assignments and sampling parameters. This example assumes the use of a DAQ board and the DAQ library, but you could easily convert it to some other kind of input device with an appropriate driver VI. There are three controls for timing. **Sample Interval** determines how often the inputs are sampled. **Display Interval** controls the update speed of any indicators, such as the strip chart. **Storage Interval** determines how often data is appended to the data file, which is in tab-delimited text format.

The configuration controls at the left could be scrolled off the screen if you don't want the user to see them. **Device** and **Channels** are the

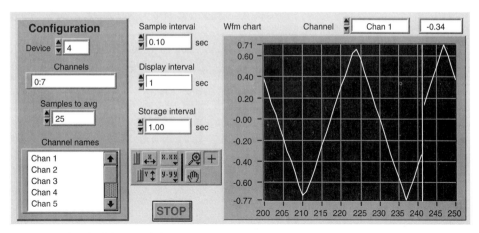

Figure 7.32 Panel of the simple low-speed data acquisition VI. It's useful for a few dozen channels at sampling rates up to about 10 Hz. This is a simple, but useful, example to which you can add features as required. Get it from the CD-ROM.

usual DAQ setup items. **Samples to avg** determines how many scans will be taken for averaging. You would probably change all of these items if you used a different kind of I/O interface. **Channel names** contains a list of names for each channel separated by carriage returns (it has to contain the same number of lines that the **Channels** control defines). Names from this list are used as the file header and are automatically copied into the **Channel** ring control above the Waveform Chart.

The diagram is shown in Fig. 7.33. To the left of the While Loop are initialization operations. The **String List Converter** VI converts the **Channel names** list into a tab-delimited string with a following carriage return and to an array of strings. The tab-delimited string is used for the file header. A text file is created by a subVI, **New File with Header**, which generates a file dialog, creates a file, and then writes the header string. It returns a file refnum and leaves the file open for writing inside the While Loop. The string array is written to the *Strings[]* item of an Attribute Node for the **Channels** ring control.

I used the Easy I/O VI, **AI Waveform Scan**, to acquire data because it is simple yet versatile and meets the requirement of taking many scans. You could also use a more elaborate set of VIs or a driver for some other type of hardware. Note that AI Waveform Scan is called twice: once during initialization and again inside the While Loop. I did this to show that it uses state memory (uninitialized shift registers) to keep track of most of the initialization parameters. What this means is that you could move all of the initialization operations, including AI Waveform Scan, to a subVI, thus cleaning up the main diagram even

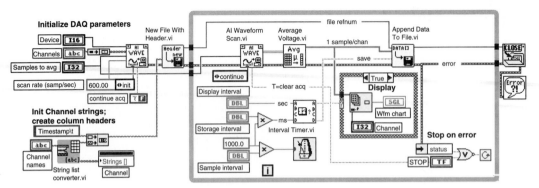

Figure 7.33   Diagram for the low-speed data acquisition system. It's made from simple utility VIs.

more. Inside the loop, AI Waveform Scan is called periodically at a rate determined by **Sample Interval** until the user clicks the **Stop** button, which clears the acquisition.

AI Waveform Scan returns a 2D array (scaled to voltage), which is then averaged on a channel-by-channel basis by the **Average Voltage** subVI, detailed in Chap. 6, "Using the DAQ Library." Average Voltage also has provisions for the deletion of some of the data at the start of a scan, in case your acquisition hardware has problems with settling time. Another subVI, called **Avg & Scale Voltage**, is included in the library with the main VI. Its terminals and operation are similar to that of the Average Voltage VI, but it includes a cluster array input containing scale and offset factors for each channel. This is useful for scaling raw voltage to engineering units.

Note that some VIs like Average Voltage perform many computations and do a good deal of memory reshuffling because of all the array accesses. This is an obvious performance penalty that may become a limiting factor in high-speed applications. If you run into problems with marginal performance (where you *almost* meet your throughput requirements), you may want to study alternatives to such array processing. For instance, you may have to go back to taking single scans of data without averaging and live with the higher noise level.

Reducing the frequency at which indicators are updated helps improve performance. For that reason, the strip chart (and any other indicators you might add) are placed inside a Case structure that is controlled by the **Interval Timer** VI. Similarly, data storage is also triggered by the Interval Timer. A subVI, **Append Data To File**, converts the data array to tab-delimited text, and prepends a timestamp in decimal hours to the string before it is written to the file. If you want to do more elaborate data formatting or file management, just edit the Append Data To File subVI. The straightforward, modular approach taken in this LabVIEW example makes the program easy to understand and easy to modify.

The one drawback to the Interval Timer method is that it induces some variability in the cycle rate of the main loop. Here's why: on several iterations, you don't update the displays, and the loop can cycle at top speed. But along comes the occasional iteration where the displays *are* updated, and that cycle runs a bit long. Your average throughput has been increased, but with a penalty of having added jitter to your sampling interval. Is this a problem? In many cases it's not. If you're just recording routine 1-Hz data where having a high-precision timebase is irrelevant to the data analysis, then the perceived improvement in the response time (*feel*) of your system is well worth it. Hardware-timed I/O may be another solution because it closely regulates loop cycle time (see Chap. 6, "Using the DAQ Library"). But ultimately, once your machine runs out of real-time computing power you have to back off on the graphics demands.

Most of the functions in the main diagram to the left of the While Loop could be placed in an initialization subVI. You could also add many features such as engineering units scaling and a nicer way for the user to enter channel setups. I did put in one bit of configuration help, the **String List Converter** VI. It permits the user to enter channel names in a list, separated by carriage returns. The outputs are a tab-delimited string for the data file header and a string array to initialize the Ring control.

I tested this example on my Quadra 950 with an NB-MIO-16X board and eight channels defined. With the settings shown, I could sample, display, and store data as fast as 10 Hz. It takes 50 ms to acquire 25 samples at 40 kHz, and there is about 50 ms of overhead in this program due to graphics and data conversion. To improve performance, you have several options.

First, lower the file system overhead: don't use the open/write/close features of a simple file I/O VI such as **Write To Spreadsheet File** inside the While Loop because it forces the file system to access the disk each time. Instead, create and open the file before entering the loop then use the Write File function inside the loop to append data. That's how I did it in this example. The Append Data To File VI contains only some string formatting and Write File. I should mention that there is one advantage to opening and closing the file for each record that you write: reliability. If a system failure should occur during your experiment, there is a good chance that all the data up to that point will be safely flushed to disk. If the file is left open, some data may reside in a memory-based disk cache that was never written to disk prior to the failure.

Second, for even better performance, save the data in binary format, either as LabVIEW datalogs or as a custom binary format of your choice. The Interval Timer becomes a limiting factor, however, because of uncertainty in its timing precision.

A third improvement you can make is to reduce the number of samples to average, which reduces the amount of time that it takes to acquire the raw data. Remember, the trade-off is an increase in apparent noise in your measurements. Finally, you can switch to buffered, continuous acquisition by using the intermediate DAQ VIs. The Easy I/O functions require you to wait for an entire buffer of data at each call, whereas a buffered system acquires all of the data asynchronously.

As you can see, this example is simple yet functional and is easily adapted and enhanced for other applications. By using the available utility VIs, such as the Interval Timer, file support, and Easy I/O, you avoid any serious programming problems. Keep this one in your hip pocket; that should be easy because it's on the CD-ROM in the Simple DAS directory.

Buy from the Pros!

So you've looked through the DAQ example VIs and tried out the Stream To Disk example, but found that it left much to be desired—no configuration management or other creature comforts. Then you tried my Simple Data Acquisition System and found that it was too . . . simple, not to mention too slow. Meanwhile, your chief scientist is wondering when the data acquisition system will be ready. What to do? Order a turnkey solution from a LabVIEW developer. Since the first edition of this book, several commercial packages have appeared on the market. I've had the chance to look at a couple of them, and the developers have indeed put in a lot of hours on the products I'm about to describe. You should also check the National Instruments *Solutions* guide before deciding what to buy; there are always new products coming out.

The DAQ Toolkit

The **DAQ Toolkit** from Advanced Measurements builds on the DAQ library to provide disk-based recording, real-time display, and postrun data retrieval. The toolkit can be used as a true turnkey system without LabVIEW programming or as a basis for your own applications. The author, Brad Hedstrom, apparently enjoyed the first edition of this book, because the basic concepts discussed in this chapter are fully implemented in the DAQ Toolkit.

Configuration management is nicely done, with an interactive user interface that gives you immediate feedback when a setup error occurs (Fig. 7.34). It also lets you test each defined channel to make sure it's working. You can enter channel names, scale factors, units, comments, and more for each channel, and setups are easily stored and retrieved.

Configurations are compiled for efficient use by the acquisition VI (DAQ Acquire and View) which in turn calls continuous acquisition VIs from the DAQ library. A memory-based circular buffer maintains a recent history of acquired data from each channel for real-time graphing. Data is stored in binary files for speed and compactness. Running the DAQ Acquire and View VI on a 166-MHz Pentium, acquiring eight channels, scaling and graphing two channels, the system can run at eight kHz per channel, or at a 64-kHz aggregate rate.

For top performance and minimum memory usage, there is also a simple stream-to-disk VI that does not use the configuration editor, but does write data in standard DAQ Toolkit binary format. Testing on the fast Pentium produced a top speed of 16 channels at 16 kHz/channel, or a 360-kHz aggregate throughput to disk.

When the run is over, you run the DAQ Data Display VI to load and graph selected channels. Decimation is implemented to reduce the amount of data displayed at one time, which enhances graphics performance. You can quickly scroll through the data file with convenient

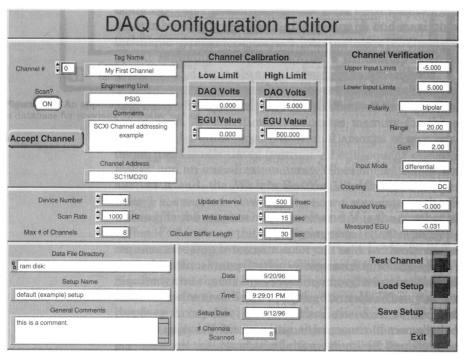

Figure 7.34 The configuration screen from the DAQ Toolkit handles all the basic setup information for your system and lets you test each channel to make sure it's working properly.

VCR-style buttons. This display and analysis VI alone make the DAQ Toolkit worthwhile.

The DAQ Toolkit is an open system that includes all the LabVIEW diagrams and all VIs are fully documented. It's not overly complex, so mere mortals can modify the code. You can hack away at it to fit your needs or just use the ready-to-run version.

The Little General

The **Little General** is a comprehensive data acquisition application from VI Engineering. It features engineering unit scaling, extensive configuration management, real-time displays, postrun analysis, and report generation. VI Engineering supplies the Little General package with all diagrams, so you can customize it easily. Or, you can hire them on a consulting basis to configure a custom application (Windows only).

TestVIEW 2000

Among the most sophisticated measurement and control packages is **TestVIEW 2000** from Sverdrup Technology. It's an elaborate application based on about 1000 VIs that works in conjunction with a collection of Microsoft Excel macros. More than just a data acquisition package, it also manages control (such as PID algorithms with setpoint profiling), automated testing, and data analysis. The application opens with a top-level menu that leads the user through configuration, diagnostics, procedures, execution of tests, and analysis. Hardware support includes DAQ boards and SCXI, programmable logic controllers (PLCs), single-loop controllers (SLCs), and various other I/O scanners. You can write your own user interface VIs or have Sverdrup do the customizing for you. A demonstration version is available (Windows only).

Bibliography

Johnson, Gary W., "LabVIEW Datalog Files," *LabVIEW Technical Resource,* vol. 2, no. 3, summer 1994. (Back issues available from LTR Publishing.)

Johnson, Gary W., "Managing Front-Panel Setup Data," *LabVIEW Technical Resource,* vol. 3, no. 1, winter 1995. (Back issues available from LTR Publishing.)

Parker, Jeff, "Put config files in their place!" *LabVIEW Technical Resource,* vol. 2, no. 3, summer 1994. (Back issues available from LTR Publishing.)

Press, William H., et al. *Numerical Recipes in C,* Cambridge Press, New York, 1990.

8

Process Control Applications

Industrial process control has its roots in the big process industries, sometimes called the Four Ps: paper, petrochemicals, paint, and pharmaceuticals. These plants are characterized by having *thousands* of instruments measuring such variables as pressure, temperature, flow, and level, plus hundreds of control elements such as valves, pumps, and heaters. They use a great deal of automatic control, including feedback, sequencing, interlocking, and recipe-driven schemes. Modern control systems for these plants are, as you might imagine, very complex and very expensive. Most large process control systems are designed and installed through cooperative efforts between manufacturers, system integrators, and the customer's control engineering staff. These are the *Big Guns* of process control.

Chances are that you are probably faced with a smaller production system, laboratory-scale system, or pilot plant that needs to be monitored and controlled. Also, your system may need to be much more flexible if it's experimental in nature. Even though your needs are different, many of the concepts and control principles you will use are the same as those used in the largest plants, making it worth your while to study their techniques.

Large process control systems generally rely on networked minicomputers with a variety of smart I/O subsystems, all using proprietary software. Until recently, most software for these larger systems was not *open,* meaning that the end user could not add custom I/O interfaces or special software routines nor interconnect the system with other computers. Even the smaller process control packages—most of which run on PCs—have some of these lingering limitations. You, however, have an advantage—the power and flexibility of LabVIEW. It's not *just* a process control package. You can begin with a clean slate and few fundamental limitations.

Since you're a LabVIEW user, you may also want to consider **Bridge-VIEW**, a software product from National Instruments designed specifically for process control and manufacturing applications. At its core, it is still 100 percent LabVIEW, but additional features—including a great deal of programming—have been added that address the particular needs of small-scale process control systems. Take everything that I talk about in this chapter, do all the programming, add device servers (drivers) for popular industrial I/O, roll it all into a package that's firmly wedded to LabVIEW's G language, and you have the essence of Bridge-VIEW. And if the basic BridgeVIEW package doesn't quite meet your needs, you can still do regular G programming and customize it to suit. How's *that* for flexibility? I'm really excited about BridgeVIEW because it's something I can learn quickly, and it immediately solves most of my process control applications. For now, though, LabVIEW is our topic of choice, so I'll just mention BridgeVIEW from time to time in this chapter to give you an idea how its enhancements might work to your advantage.

Process Control Basics

In this chapter, we'll cover the important concepts of process control and then design the pieces of a small process control system, using good LabVIEW practices. First, a plug for the ISA: the U.S.-based **International Society for Measurement and Control (ISA)** sets many of the standards and practices for industrial process control. I joined the ISA some years ago while working on the control system for a large experimental facility, and I've found my membership to be quite helpful. It offers a catalog of books, publications, standards documents, and practical training courses that can make your plant and your work practices safer and more efficient. Concepts and terminology presented in this chapter are straight out of the ISA publications, in an effort to keep us all speaking a common language. For information about membership or publications, contact the ISA at its Raleigh, North Carolina, headquarters at (919) 549-8411.

Industrial standards

Standards set by the ISA and other organizations address both the physical plant—including instruments, tanks, valves, piping, wiring, and so forth—as well as the **man-machine interface (MMI)** and any associated software and documentation. The classic MMI was a silk-screened control panel filled with controllers and sequencers, digital and analog display devices, chart recorders, and plenty of knobs and switches. Nowadays, we can use software-based virtual instruments to mimic these classic MMI functions. And what better way is there to create virtual instruments than LabVIEW?

Engineers communicate primarily through drawings, a simple but often overlooked fact. In process control, drawing standards have been in place long enough that it is possible to design and build a large process plant with just a few basic types of drawings, all of which are thoroughly specified by ISA standards. By the way, ISA standards are also registered as ANSI (American National Standards Institute) standards. Some of these drawings are of particular interest to you, the control engineer. (See? I've already promoted you to a new position and you're only on the third page. Now read on, or *you're fired.*)

Piping and instrument diagrams and symbols. The single most important drawing for your plant is the **piping and instrument diagram (P&ID)**. It shows the interconnections of all the vessels, pipes, valves, pumps, transducers, transmitters, and control loops. A simple P&ID is shown in Fig. 8.1. From such a drawing, you should be able to understand all of the fluid flows and the purpose of every major item in the plant. Furthermore, the identifiers, or **tag names**, of every instrument

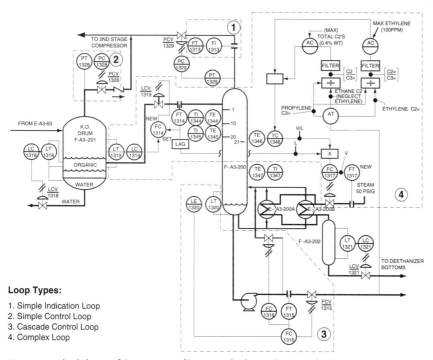

Loop Types:

1. Simple Indication Loop
2. Simple Control Loop
3. Cascade Control Loop
4. Complex Loop

Figure 8.1 A piping and instrument diagram, the basis for a good process plant design.

are shown and are consistent throughout all drawings and specifications for the plant. The P&ID is the key to a coherent plant design and it's a place to start when you create graphical displays in LabVIEW.

Tag names should follow ISA standard S5.1, a summary of which is shown in Table 8.1. The beauty of this naming system is that it is both meaningful and concise. With just a few characters, you can determine what the instrument controls or measures (e.g., P for pressure, T for temperature), as well as its function (e.g., C for controller, V for valve, T for transmitter). A numeric suffix is appended as a hierarchical serial number. Most plants use a scheme where the first digit is the zone or area, the second is the major vessel, and so forth. Tag names appear everywhere: on the P&ID, instrument data sheets, loop diagram, in your control system database, and, of course, on a little metal tag riveted to the instrument. Since this is the only national standard of its type, most process engineers are familiar with this naming scheme—a good reason to consider its use.

TABLE 8.1   Abbreviated List for the Generation of ISA Standard Instrument Tags

	First letter measured or initiating variable	Second letter readout or output function	Succeeding letters (if required)
A	Analysis	Alarm	Alarm
B	Burner, combustion	User's choice	User's choice
C	Conductivity	Controller	Controller
D	Density/damper	Differential	
E	Voltage (elect)	Primary element	
F	Flow	Ratio/bias	Ratio/bias
G	Gauging (dimensional)	Glass (viewing device)	
H	Hand (manual)		High
I	Current (electrical)	Indicate	Indicate
J	Power	Scanner	
K	Time	Control station	
L	Level	Light	Low
M	Moisture/mass		Middle/intermediate
N	User's choice	User's choice	User's choice
O	User's choice	Orifice, restriction	
P	Pressure	Point (test) connection	
Q	Quantity	Totalize/quantity	
R	Radiation	Record	Record
S	Speed/frequency	Safety/switch	Switch
T	Temperature	Transmitter	Transmitter
U	Multipoint/variable	Multifunction	Multifunction
V	Vibration	Valve, damper, louver	Valve, damper, louver
W	Weight	Well	
X	Special	Special	Special
Y	Interlock or state	Relay/compute	Relay/compute
Z	Position, dimension	Damper or louver drive	

SOURCE: From S5.1, *Instrumentation Symbols and Identification.* Copyright 1984 by Instrument Society of America. Reprinted by permission.

When I write a LabVIEW program for process control, I use tag names everywhere. On the diagram, you can label wires, cluster elements, and frames of Case and Sequence structures that are dedicated to processing a certain channel. On the panel, tag names make a convenient, traceable, and unambiguous way to name various objects.

Here are some examples of common tag names with explanations:

PI-203   Pressure Indicator—a mechanical pressure gauge

LT-203   Level Transmitter—electronic instrument with 4–20-mA output

TIC-203   Temperature Indicating Controller—a temperature controller with readout

PSV-203   Pressure Safety Valve—a relief valve

FCV-203   Flow Control Valve—valve to adjust flow rate

ZSL-203   Position Switch, Low-Level—switch that closes when a valve is closed

The little balloons all over the P&ID contain tag names for each instrument. Some balloons have lines through or boxes around them that convey information about the instrument's location and the method by which a readout may be obtained. Figure 8.2 shows some of the more common symbols. The intent is to differentiate between a field-mounted instrument (such as a valve or mechanical gauge) and various remotely mounted electronic or computer displays.

Every pipe, connection, valve, actuator, transducer, and function in the plant has an appropriate symbol, and these are also covered by ISA standard S5.1. Figure 8.3 shows some examples that you would be likely to see on the P&ID for any major industrial plant. Your system may use specialized instruments that are not explicitly covered by the

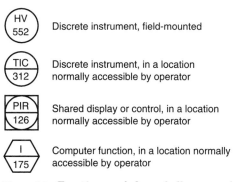

Figure 8.2 Function symbols, or *balloons,* used to identify instruments on the P&ID.

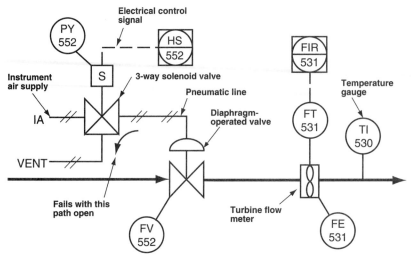

Figure 8.3 Some instrument symbols, showing valves, transmitters, and associated connections. These are right out of the standards documents; your situation may require some improvising.

standard. In that case, you are free to improvise while keeping with the spirit of the standard. None of this is *law,* you know; it's just there to help. You can also use replicas of these symbols on some of your Lab-VIEW or BridgeVIEW screens to make it more understandable to the technicians who build and operate the facility.

Other drawing and design standards.   Another of my favorite ISA standards, S5.4, addresses **instrument loop diagrams**, which are the control engineer's electrical wiring diagram. An example appears in Fig. 8.4. The reasons for the format of a loop diagram become clear once you have worked in a large plant environment where a signal may pass through several junction boxes or terminal panels before finally arriving at the computer or controller input. When a field technician must install or troubleshoot such a system, having one (or only a few) channels per page in a consistent format is most appreciated.

Notice that the tag name appears prominently in the title strip, among other places. This is how the drawings are indexed, because the tag name is *the* universal identifier. The loop diagram also tells you where each item is located, which cables the signal runs through, instrument specifications, calibration values (electrical as well as engineering units), and computer database or controller setting information. I've found this concise drawing format to be useful in many laboratory installations as well. It is easy to follow and easy to maintain. There are commercial instrument database programs available

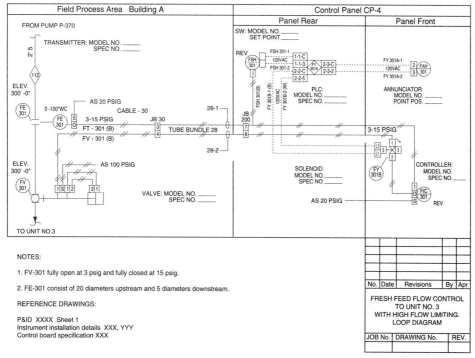

Figure 8.4 An instrument loop diagram, the control engineer's guide to wiring. (*Reprinted by permission. Copyright ©1991 by the Instrument Society of America. From S5.4*—Instrument Loop Diagrams.)

that contain built-in forms, drawing tools, and cross-referencing capability that make management of large process control projects much easier. Ask ISA for a catalog of process control products if you're interested.

Here are a few other ISA standards that can be valuable to you:

S5.5   *Graphic Symbols for Process Displays*

S51.1   *Process Instrumentation Terminology*

S50.1   *Compatibility of Analog Signals for Electronic Industrial Process Equipment*

If you are involved with the design of a major facility, many other national standards will come into play, such as the *National Electrical Code* and the *Uniform Mechanical Code*. That's why plants are designed by multidisciplinary teams with many engineers and designers who are well-versed in their respective areas of expertise. With these standards in hand and a few process control reference books, you might well move beyond the level of the mere LabVIEW hacker and into the realm of the registered professional control engineer.

Control = manipulating outputs

Controlling a process implies a need for some kind of output signal from the control system. (At last! Something that uses all those analog and digital output modules that somebody sold you!) The simplest control mode, **manual control**, relies on the operator to turn a knob or throw a switch to manipulate the process through some actuator. Programming a manual control system is about as simple as things get. The other control mode, **automatic control**, requires a hardware or software machine to make the adjustments. What both modes have in common (besides output hardware) is the use of **feedback**. In manual control, the operators see that the temperature is too high, and they turn down the heater. In automatic control, the controller makes a measurement (the **process variable**), compares it with the desired value, or **setpoint**, and adjusts the output, or **manipulated variable**, accordingly.

The output of the controller may be either digital or analog in nature. Digital-output controllers are also known as **on-off controllers** or **bang-bang controllers**. An example is the thermostat on your home's furnace. On-off controllers are generally the simplest and cheapest control technique, but they may be a bit imprecise—the process variable tends to cycle above and below the setpoint. Analog controllers, on the other hand, are proportional in nature, adjusting the output in infinitesimally small steps to minimize the error. They are powerful and versatile, but generally more complex and expensive than on-off controllers.

The most common types of automatic controllers in use today rely on the well-known **proportional-integral-derivative (PID)** family of algorithms. The simplest form of the algorithm is a pure **proportional (P)** controller (Fig. 8.5a). An **error** signal is derived by subtracting the process variable from the setpoint. Error is then multiplied by a proportional gain factor, and the result drives the output, or **manipulated variable**. If the process reacts by "going in the right direction," the process variable will tend toward the setpoint—the result of **negative feedback**. If the process goes the wrong direction, **positive feedback** results, followed by undesirable oscillation or saturation. By raising the proportional gain, the manipulated variable is more strongly driven, thus reducing the error more quickly. There is a practical limit to gain, however, due to delay (**lag**) in the process that will eventually cause a destabilizing phase shift in the control loop—the loop ends up responding to old information. Therefore, some residual error is always present with a proportional controller, but the error magnitude may be sufficiently small for your requirements that a simple proportional controller is adequate.

One way to eliminate this error is to mathematically **integrate** or **reset** the error over time. Combining these two control techniques

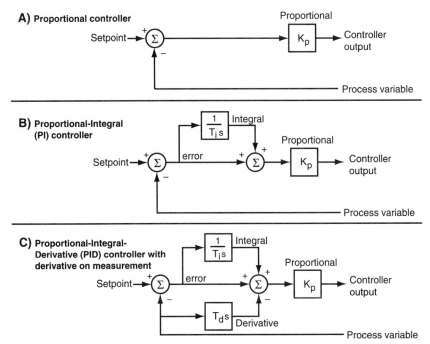

Figure 8.5 Signal flow diagrams for proportional, integral, and derivative algorithms—the basis for much of today's practical feedback control. These are just a few examples of P/PI/PID configuration; there are many more in actual use.

results in the **proportional-integral (PI)** controller (Fig. 8.5*b*). With the PI algorithm, the integral reduces the error by spreading the process reaction over time, thus giving it time to respond to controller commands. Like any control algorithm, too much of a good thing may result in substandard or unstable performance. Also, the integral can **wind up** (where the value of the integral grows to a very large value) when the process is sufficiently out of control for a long period of time or when the controlled device does not respond as expected. This can result in very long recovery times, so most controllers include an **antireset windup** feature to limit integral action. PI controllers are the most widely used in general applications.

When a process is subject to sudden upsets or large changes in setpoint, the controller may not respond quickly enough. In such cases, a **derivative**, or **rate**, term may be added (Fig. 8.5*c*). Taking the derivative of the error (a common technique) effectively increases the controller's gain during periods when the process variable is changing, forcing a quick correcting response. Unfortunately, the derivative is a kind of highpass filter that emphasizes the controller's response to noise. Therefore, the full PID algorithm can only be used when the signal has little noise or where suitable filtering or limiting has been applied.

National Instruments offers a set of PID algorithms available in the **PID Control Toolkit**. You can use them to build all kinds of control schemes; usage will be discussed later in this chapter. PID control can also be accomplished through the use of external "smart" controllers and modules. Greg Shinskey's excellent *Process Control Systems* (1988) discusses the application, design, and tuning of industrial controllers from a practical point of view. He's my kinda guy.

There are many alternatives to the common PID algorithm so often used in industrial control. For instance, there are algorithms based on *state variable analysis* which rely on a fairly accurate model of the process to obtain an optimal control algorithm. *Adaptive* controllers, which may or may not be based on a PID algorithm, modify the actions of the controller in response to changes in the characteristics of the process. *Predictive* controllers attempt to predict the trajectory of a process to minimize overshoot in controller response. Modern *fuzzy logic* controllers are also available in LabVIEW from **Bloomy Controls**, with its **Fuzzy Tools** development package. Fuzzy Tools includes a membership function editor, a rule base editor, and an inference engine that you can incorporate into your system. If you have experience in control theory, there are few limitations to what you can accomplish in the graphical programming environment. I encourage you to develop advanced control VIs and make them available to the rest of us. You might even make some money!

So far, we have been looking at **continuous control** concepts that apply to steady-state processes where feedback is applicable. There are other situations. **Sequential control** applies where discrete, ordered events occur over a period of time. Valves that open in a certain order, parts pickers, robots, and conveyors are processes that are sequential in nature. **Batch processes** may be sequential at startup and shutdown, but operate in steady-state throughout the middle of an operation. The difficulty with batch operations is that the continuous control algorithms need to be modified or compromised in some way to handle the transient conditions during startup, shutdown, and process upsets. A special form of batch process, called a **recipe operation**, uses some form of specification entry to determine the sequence of events and steady-state setpoints for each batch. Typical recipe processes are paint and fuel formulation (and making cookies!), where special blends of ingredients and processing conditions are required, depending on the final product.

Early sequential control systems used relay logic, where electromechanical switching devices were combined in such a way as to implement Boolean logic circuits. Other elements such as timers and stepper switches were added to facilitate time-dependent operations. System inputs were switch contacts (manual or machine-actuated), and outputs would drive a variety of power control devices such as contactors.

Most modern sequential control systems are based on **programmable logic controllers (PLCs)** which are specialized industrial computers with versatile and nearly bullet-proof I/O interface hardware. Millions of PLCs are in service in all industries, worldwide, and for good reasons: they are compact, cost-effective, reliable, and easy to program. It's much easier to modify a PLC's program than it is to rip out dozens of hardwired relays mounted in a rack. PLCs can be networked, and both LabVIEW and BridgeVIEW turn out to be fine man-machine interfaces.

Process signals

The signals you will encounter in most process control situations are low-frequency or DC analog signals and digital on-off signals, both inputs and outputs. Table 8.2 lists some of the more common ones. In a laboratory situation, this list would be augmented with lots of special analytical instruments, making your control system heavy on data acquisition needs. Actually, most control systems end up that way because it takes lots of information to accurately control a process.

Industry likes to differentiate between **transducers** and **transmitters**. In process control jargon, the simple transducer (like a thermocouple) is called a **primary element**. The signal conditioner that connects to a primary element is called a *transmitter*.

In the United States, the most common analog transmitter and controller signals are 4–20-mA current loops, followed by a variety of voltage signals including 1–5, 0–5, and 0–10 V. Current loops are preferred because they are resistant to ground referencing problems and voltage drops. Most transmitters have a maximum bandwidth of a few hertz, and some offer an adjustable time constant which you can use to optimize high-frequency noise rejection. To interface 4–20-mA signals to an ordinary voltage-sensing input, you will generally add a 250-Ω precision resistor in parallel with the analog input. (If you're using

TABLE 8.2 Typical Process Control Signals and Their Usage

Analog inputs	Digital inputs	Analog outputs	Digital outputs
Pressure	Pressure switch	Valve positioner	Valve open/close
Temperature	Temperature switch	Motor speed	Motor on/off
Flow rate	Flow switch	Controller setpoint	Indicator lamps
Level	Level switch	Heater power	
Power or energy	Position switch		

National Instruments signal conditioning—particularly SCXI—order its 250-Ω terminating resistor kits.) The resulting voltage is then 1–5 V. When you write your data acquisition program, remember to subtract out the 1-V offset before scaling to engineering units.

On-off signals are generally 24 VDC, 24 VAC, or 120 VAC. I prefer to use low-voltage signals because they are safer for personnel. In areas where potentially flammable dust or vapors may be present, the National Electrical Code requires you to eliminate sources of ignition. Low-voltage signals can help you meet these requirements, as well.

The world of process control is going through a major change with emerging digital **fieldbus** standards. These busses are designed to replace the 4–20-mA analog signal connections that have historically connected the field device to the distributed control systems with a digital bus that interconnects several field devices. In addition to using multidrop digital communications networks, these busses use very intelligent field devices. They are designed for device interoperability which means that any device can understand data supplied by any other device. Control applications are distributed across devices, each with function blocks that execute a given control algorithm. For instance, one control algorithm can orchestrate a pressure transmitter, a dedicated feedback controller, and a valve actuator in a field-based control loop.

The first of the digital communication protocols, **HART**, was created by Rosemount and is now supported by hundreds of manufacturers. It adds a high-frequency carrier (such as that used with 1200-baud modems) which rides on top of the usual 4–20-mA current loop signal. Up to 16 transmitters and/or controllers can reside on one HART bus, which is simply a twisted pair of wires. HART allows you to exchange messages with smart field devices, including data such as calibration information and the values of multiple outputs—things that are quite impossible with ordinary analog signals. It's easy for LabVIEW to talk to these instruments. **HartVIEW**, from CARDIAC of Norway, can access up to 64 HART transmitters via commercially available HART modems.

Perhaps the most important new, emerging standard is **Foundation Fieldbus** (from the Fieldbus Foundation, naturally), which has international industry backing. The ISA is also developing a new standard, **SP-50**, which will ultimately align with Foundation Fieldbus and other standards. Because the field devices on these fieldbus networks are so intelligent, and because the variables shared by devices are completely defined, the systems integration effort is greatly reduced. It is thus much more practical to implement a supervisory system with LabVIEW and one or more physical connections to the fieldbus network. You no longer need drivers for each specific field device. Instead, you can use drivers for *classes* of field devices (such as pressure transmitters or valves). National Instruments is an active player in the Foundation Fieldbus development process, offering an ISA bus plug-in board and NI-FBUS host software. At this writing, the standard is well established and has been demonstrated under actual plant conditions. As development continues, look for extensive LabVIEW and BridgeVIEW support for Foundation Fieldbus—it's in the National Instruments catalog.

Control system architectures

Hopefully, you will be designing your LabVIEW process control application along with the plant you wish to control. Choices of transducers and actuators, as well as the overall process topology, drastically affect the possibilities for adequate control. The process control engineer is responsible for evaluating the chemistry and physics of the plant with an eye toward controllability. The best software in the world can't overcome the actions of improperly specified valves, can't correct unusable data from the wrong type of flowmeter, nor can it control wildly unstable chemical reactions. You and your design team need to be on top of these issues during all phases of the project.

You will need to choose an appropriate control system architecture. There are many variables and many personal and corporate biases that point in different directions. Industrial control journals are filled with case histories and design methodologies that represent the cumulative knowledge of thousands of plant designs. For the novice, these journals are a source of inspiration, as are consultants and, of course, the major engineering firms. At the end of this section, I'll list some possible design parameters you might use to develop a checklist that leads to the right system.

Distributed control system (DCS). For the largest installations, distributed control systems have held the market for decades, though that position is being eroded by the improved capability of smaller, more open systems including PCs. Important characteristics of a DCS are as follows (see Fig. 8.6):

- A hierarchical set of intelligent nodes, or controllers, ranging from smart I/O scanners and controllers to man-machine interface stations, on up to corporate-level management information systems

- Loop controllers physically close to the process being controlled

- Heavy reliance on local area networks (usually redundant, for reliability)

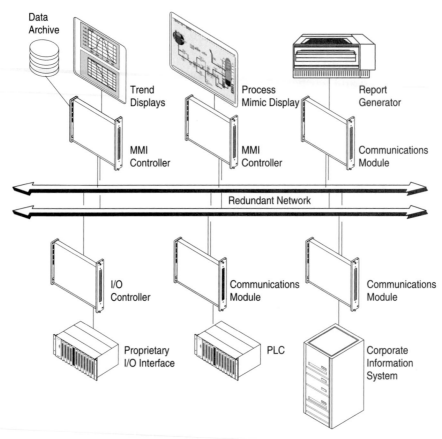

Figure 8.6 A distributed control system, or DCS, encompasses many nodes communicating over networks and many I/O points.

- A globally shared, real-time database scheme where all nodes can freely share information
- Multiple levels of access security through passwords and communications restrictions
- Integration of several different kinds of computers and I/O hardware
- Dozens, and sometimes hundreds, of nodes
- Many thousands of I/O points
- Very high cost, often in the millions of dollars

Older DCSs used proprietary operating systems and custom hardware, but new designs are moving more toward *open,* or public, standards in I/O hardware and operating systems such as Windows NT and UNIX. All DCS vendors work closely with the customer because the system specification, configuration, and startup phases are quite complex. *Turnkey* systems (where the system vendor does the lion's share of the work) are the rule rather than the exception.

A DCS may incorporate many kinds of computers and I/O subsystems, integrated into one (hopefully) harmonious package. In principle, a DCS could be designed with multiple systems running LabVIEW, but that may be stretching things a bit. At this time, it just isn't very well suited to this kind of massive application. Some major control system manufacturers are using LabVIEW at this time, but only in certain subsystems as part of an overall proprietary DCS. But given a few years, LabVIEW—and particularly BridgeVIEW—may well penetrate these high-end applications.

SCADA in the middle.   The middle ground in process control is handled by a broad range of systems collectively known as **Supervisory Control and Data Acquisition (SCADA)** systems (Boyer 1993). The name pretty well describes what they do. At the bottom of the architecture are the data acquisition features—measurements for the purpose of feedback and operator information. Next up the line are the control features, including manual commands and continuous and sequential automatic algorithms. At the top level are the supervisory aspects—the user interface, trending, report generation, and so forth. A key feature of SCADA is distributed I/O, including remote sensing and a heavy reliance on communications or networking with *remote terminal units*.

In contrast to a large DCS, SCADA systems are chosen for simpler systems where the total number of I/O points is unlikely to exceed a thousand, but with wide distribution. An example would be an oil or gas pipeline. You probably would not find control engineers at a large pulp plant who claim that their facility is run by a SCADA system. A small municipal waterworks is a more likely location. But the defining bounds of SCADA are becoming ever more fuzzy, thanks to the power and popularity of the personal computer and modern software.

Enter the personal computer.   At the other end of the scale from a mega-DCS is the personal computer, which has made an incredible impact on plant automation. The DCS world has provided us with software and hardware integration techniques that have successfully migrated to desktop machines. A host of manufacturers now offer ready-to-run PC-based process control and SCADA packages with most of the features of their larger cousins, but with a much lower price tag and a level of complexity that's almost . . . *human* in scale. LabVIEW and BridgeVIEW fit into this category.

A wide range of control problems can be solved by these cost-effective small systems. In the simplest cases, all you need is your PC running

LabVIEW with plug-in I/O boards or maybe some outboard I/O interface hardware. You can implement all the classical control schemes—continuous, sequential, batch, and recipe—with the functions built into LabVIEW and have a good user interface on top of it all. Such a system is easy to maintain because there is only one programming language, and only rarely would you need the services of a consultant or systems house to complete your project. The information in this chapter can lead you to a realistic solution for these applications.

There are some limitations with any stand-alone PC-based process control system. Because one machine is responsible for servicing real-time control algorithms as well as the user interface with all its graphics, there can be problems with real-time response. If you need millisecond response, consider using outboard smart controllers (see the following section). The I/O point count is another factor to consider. Piling on 3000 analog channels is likely to bring your machine to its knees; you must consider some kind of distributed processing scheme.

LabVIEW, like the specialized process control packages, permits you to connect several PCs in a network, much like a DCS. You can configure your system in such a way that the real-time tasks are assumed by dedicated PCs that serve as I/O control processors, while other PCs serve as the man-machine interfaces, data recorders, and so forth. All the machines run LabVIEW and communicate via a local area network using supported protocols such as NetDDE or TCP/IP. The result is an expandable system with the distributed power of a DCS, but at a scale that you (and perhaps a small staff) can create and manage yourself. The problem is programming. Dedicated process control packages have all the networking ready to run, but we don't have all those turnkey features in LabVIEW (yet).

PCs with smart controllers.   Another way to accommodate medium and small-scale plants is to use your PCs with *smart* external controllers, such as PLCs and single-loop PID controllers, to off-load critical real-time tasks. This approach has some advantages. Dedicated, special-purpose controllers are famous for their reliability, more so than the general-purpose computer on which you run LabVIEW. They use embedded microprocessors with small, efficient executive programs (like miniature operating systems) that run your control programs at very high speeds with no interference from file systems, graphics, and other overhead.

PLCs can be programmed to perform almost any kind of continuous or sequential control, and larger models can be configured to handle thousands of I/O points and control loops, especially when networked. However, the PLC lacks a user interface and a file system, among other amenities—just the kinds of things that your LabVIEW program can provide. LabVIEW makes an ideal man-machine interface, data recorder, alarm annunciator, and so forth. It's a really synergistic match. About the only disadvantage of this approach is that you have two programming environments to worry about: LabVIEW plus the PLC's programming package.

Single-loop controllers (SLCs) do an admirable job of PID, on-off, or fuzzy-logic control for industrial applications. They are generally easy to configure, very reliable, and many offer advanced features such as recipe generation and automatic tuning. Like PLCs, however, they lack the ability to record data, and it may not be feasible to locate the SLC close to the operator's preferred working location. By using a communications link (usually RS-232), LabVIEW can integrate SLCs into a distributed process control system.

Choose your system.   In summary, here are some important control system design parameters that might lead you to a first-cut decision as to whether LabVIEW or BridgeVIEW is a practical choice for your application.

Number of I/O points and number of network nodes.   What is the overall scale of your system? Up to a few hundred I/O points, even a stand-alone PC running LabVIEW has a good chance of doing the job. With somewhat higher point counts, high speed requirements, or a need to have the I/O distributed over a wider area, PLCs offer lots of advantages, and LabVIEW makes a nice MMI. If you are tackling an entire plant, then LabVIEW might be suited to some local control applications, but a DCS or a large, integrated SCADA package may be a better choice. BridgeVIEW, for example, is probably suitable for installations up to 1000 points.

Planned expansion.   Continuing with the first topic, remember to include any plans for future expansion. A lab-scale pilot plant is ideal for LabVIEW, but its plant-scale implementation may be a whole 'nother story. A poorly chosen control system may result from underestimation of the overall needs. Beware.

Integration with other systems.   Needs for corporate-level computing will influence your choice of control computers and networks. For instance, if you live in a UNIX/XWindows world, then a SPARCstation running LabVIEW might be a good platform.

Requirements for handling unique, nonstandard instruments.   LabVIEW has tremendous advantages over commercial process control software products when it comes to handling unusual instrument interfaces. Because you can easily write your own drivers in G, these special situations are a nonproblem. Similarly, BridgeVIEW permits you to add ordinary LabVIEW drivers, running in parallel with the native BridgeVIEW server-based drivers.

Ease of configuration and modification.   What plans do you have for modifying your process control system? Some system architectures and software products are rather inflexible, requiring many hours of reconfiguration for seemingly simple changes. Adding a new instrument interface to a large DCS may seemingly require an act of Congress, as many users have discovered. Meanwhile, LabVIEW remains a flexible solution, so long as you design your application with some forethought.

Overall reliability.   It's hard to compare computers, operating systems, and software when it comes to reliability. Suffice it to say that simple is better, and that's why many process engineers prefer PLCs and SLCs: they are simple and robust. The MMI software is, in a sense, of secondary importance in these systems because the process can continue to operate (if desired) even while the MMI is off-line. I've found that the system architecture is often more important than brand of computer or software. Using **redundant** hardware is the ultimate solution where reliability is paramount. Many PLC and DCS vendors offer redundancy. Additionally, you should consider adding fail-safe mechanisms, such as watchdog timers, to insure safety and prevent major hazards and losses when things go awry. Software bugs, hardware failures, and system crashes can be very costly in process control.

Existing company standards and personal biases.   Everyone from the CEO to the janitor will have opinions regarding your choice of hardware and software. For the small, experimental systems that I work on, LabVIEW has many advantages over other products. As such, it has become very popular—a definite positive bias—and with good reason. However, I would *not* use it to control a new hundred-million-dollar facility, no matter how biased I (we) might be.

Cost.   The bottom line is always cost. One cost factor is the need for system integration services and consultants, which is minimal with LabVIEW, but mandatory with a DCS. Another factor is the number of computers or smart controllers that you might need: a stand-alone PC is probably cheaper than a PC plus a PLC. Also, consider the long-term costs such as operator training, software upgrades and modifications, and maintenance. Plan to evaluate several process control packages—as well as LabVIEW and BridgeVIEW—before committing your resources.

Working with Smart Controllers

Adding smart controllers to your process control system is smart engineering. PLCs, SLCs, and other programmable devices are practical solutions to your real-world control problems. They are completely optimized to perform real-time continuous or sequential control with the utmost in reliability while managing to be flexible enough to adapt to many different situations. Take advantage of them whenever possible.

Programmable logic controllers (PLCs)

A *programmable logic controller (PLC)* is an industrial computer with a CPU, nonvolatile program memory, and dedicated I/O interface hardware (Bryan 1988). Conceived by General Motors Corporation in 1968 as a replacement for hardwired relay logic, PLCs have grown dramatically in their software and hardware capabilities and now offer incredible power and flexibility to the control engineer. Major features of a modern PLC are as follows:

- Modular construction
- Very high reliability (redundancy available for many models)
- Versatile and robust I/O interface hardware
- Wide range of control features included, such as logic, timing, and analog control algorithms
- Fast, deterministic execution of programs—a true real-time system
- Communications supported with host computers and other PLCs
- Many programming packages available
- Low cost

You can buy PLCs with a wide range of I/O capacity, program storage capacity, and CPU speed to suit your particular project. The simplest PLCs, also called *microcontrollers,* replace a modest number of relays and timers, do only discrete (on-off, or Boolean) logic operations, and support up to about 32 I/O points. Midrange PLCs add analog I/O and communications features and support up to about 1024 I/O points. The largest PLCs support several thousand I/O points and use the latest microprocessors for very high performance (with a proportionally high cost, as you might expect).

You usually program a PLC with an IBM PC compatible running a special-purpose application. **Ladder logic** (Fig. 8.7) is the most common language for programming in the United States, though a different concept, called **GRAFCET**, is more commonly used in Europe. Some programming applications also support BASIC, Pascal, or C, either intermixed with ladder logic or as a pure high-level language just as you would use with any computer system.

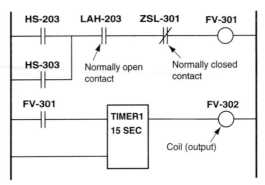

Figure 8.7 Ladder logic, a language for PLCs. Each item in the diagram corresponds to an emulated piece of hardware—contacts (switches), timers, relay coils, and so forth.

There are about 100 PLC manufacturers in the world today. Some of the major brands are currently supported by BridgeVIEW and Lab-VIEW drivers. Here's a brief list of driver sources. Others are sure to follow; check the National Instruments **Solutions** guide for new releases.

Allen Bradley	HighwayVIEW from SEG
Modicon	BusVIEW from SEG; ModBus View from Saphir
Siemens/TI	SinecVIEW from CIT (Fig. 8.8)
Telemechanique	UniTelVIEW from Saphir
Omron	InnerVIEW from Dateppli

The ISA offers some PLC-related training you may be interested in. Course number T420, Fundamentals of Programmable Controllers, gives you a good overview of the concepts required to use PLCs. The textbook for the class, *Programmable Controllers: Theory and Implementation* (Bryan 1988) is very good even if you can't attend the class. Another course, T425, Programmable Controller Applications, gets into practical aspects of system design, hardware selection, and programming in real situations.

Advantages of PLCs.   Programmable controllers have become a favorite tool in the control industry because of their simplicity, low cost, rugged hardware, and reliable real-time performance. These are clear-cut advantages that will make them candidates for your project, as well.

Interfacing couldn't be easier. Input and output modules are available for direct connection to 240-VAC and lower AC and DC voltages and a wide range of analog signals. Compare this with most interface

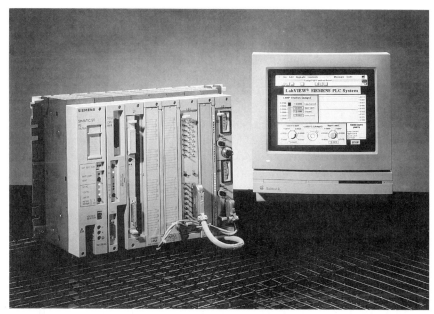

Figure 8.8   PLCs like this Siemens model are popular in process control. SinecVIEW is a LabVIEW driver package that communicates with Siemens PLCs via a serial interface. *(Photo courtesy of National Instruments and CITvzw Belgium.)*

systems which require extra isolation devices or adapters, especially for high voltages and currents.

Reliability may be the main reason for choosing a PLC over other solutions. Both the hardware and the operating software in a PLC are simple in nature, making it easier to prove correctness of design and simultaneously lowering the number of possible failure points. Contrast this with a general-purpose, desktop computer. How often does *your* computer hang up or crash? If your process demands predictable performance, day in and day out, better consider using a PLC.

PLC communications and register access.   Manufacturers of PLCs have devised many communications techniques and pseudostandard protocols. For instance, Modicon has its proprietary *Modbus* protocol, while Allen-Bradley has its *Data Highway Plus*—and the two are completely incompatible. The good news is, through an adapter module, any computer with RS-232 capability can communicate with these various data highways, assuming that you have the right driver software. All midrange and high-end PLCs have the ability to communicate peer-to-peer, that is, between individual PLCs without host intervention. A variety of schemes exist for host computers as well, serving as masters or slaves on the network.

Once a PLC has been programmed, your LabVIEW program is free to read data from and write data to the PLC's registers. A register may represent a Boolean (either zero or one), a set of Booleans (perhaps 8 or 16 in one register), an ASCII character, or an integer or floating point number. Register access is performed at a surprisingly low level on most PLCs. Instead of sending a message like you would with a GPIB instrument ("start sequence 1"), you poke a value into a register that your ladder logic program interprets as a command. For instance, the ladder logic might be written such that a *1* in register number 10035 is interpreted as a closed contact in an interlock string that triggers a sequential operation.

There are a few things to watch out for when you program your PLC and team it with LabVIEW or any other host computer. First, watch out for conflicts when writing to registers. If the ladder logic *and* your LabVIEW program both write to a register, you have an obvious conflict. Instead, all registers should be one-way, that is, either the PLC writes to them or your LabVIEW program does. Second, you may want to implement a **watchdog program** on the PLC that responds to failures of the host computer. This is especially important when a host failure might leave the process in a dangerous condition. A watchdog is a timer that the host must *hit*, or reset, periodically. If the timer runs to its limit, the PLC takes a preprogrammed action. For instance, the PLC may close important valves or reset the host computer in an attempt to reawaken it from a locked-up state.

PLC communications is another area where BridgeVIEW has some advantages over the much-simpler LabVIEW driver model. In BridgeVIEW, you define tag names that map to the PLC registers. The real-time database automatically scans each tag, so you don't have to write your own I/O polling loops. Instead, you simply enter the desired tag names into string controls or constants, and then call an appropriate BridgeVIEW VI that exchanges data with the database.

PLC driver example: HighwayVIEW. Of the PLC driver packages currently available, HighwayVIEW, from SEG, was the first. It supports Allen-Bradley models PLC-2, PLC-3, and PLC-5 and accepts all data types for both inputs and outputs. Communications are handled by a program that is installed in your computer's operating system (a Control Panel device on the Macintosh; a DLL under Windows). This communications handler is particularly robust, offering automatic retries if an error occurs. Figure 8.9 shows a simple example of HighwayVIEW in action as a simple on-off limit controller application. An array of floating point values is read by the PLC-5 Read Float VI. If the tank

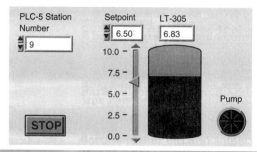

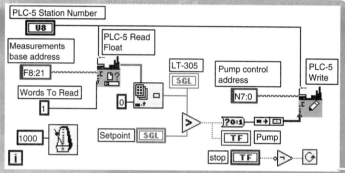

Figure 8.9 A simple example using HighwayVIEW. An array of floating point values is read from the PLC, and one is compared with a setpoint. If the tank level is too high, a pump is turned on by setting a bit within a PLC register to *1*.

level is greater than the setpoint, a drain pump is turned on by setting a bit with the PLC-5 Write VI.

Single-loop controllers (SLCs)

Single-loop controllers are an old favorite of process engineers. Years ago, they were pneumatically operated, using springs, levers, bellows, and orifices to implement an accurate PID algorithm. To this day, there are still many installations that are entirely pneumatic, mostly where an intrinsically safe control system is required. Modern SLCs are compact, microprocessor-based units that mount in a control panel. Some models can control more than one loop. They are compatible with common input signals including thermocouples, RTDs, currents, and voltages, with various ranges. The output may be an analog voltage or current or an on-off digital signal controlled by a relay or triac. Other features are alarms with contact closure outputs and ramp-and-soak recipe operation. (See Fig. 8.10.)

The front panel of a typical SLC consists of an array of buttons and one or more digital displays. They are fairly easy to understand and

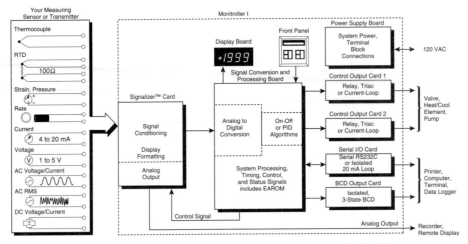

Figure 8.10 Block diagram of a typical single-loop controller. *(Courtesy Analogic.)*

use, though some operators are frustrated by the VCR programming syndrome where there are too many obscure functions and too many menu choices. This is where LabVIEW can enhance the usefulness of an SLC by simplifying the presentation of controls and indicators. Low-level setup information can be hidden from the user while being properly maintained by your program.

All of the more sophisticated controllers offer communications options. Most use RS-232 or RS-422/485 serial, but at least one features GPIB (Research, Incorporated, with its Micristar controller). The communications protocols all vary widely, generally following no standard at all. One exception is a line of controllers from Anafaze that use the Allen-Bradley Data Highway protocol, the same one used by Allen-Bradley PLCs. Anafaze controllers are supported by AnaVIEW from SEG. As a bonus, some Anafaze models can handle up to 16 PID loops in one compact controller; they are more appropriately named **multiple-loop controllers**. A few other SLCs have LabVIEW drivers, such as the Eurotherm 808/847, the driver which was dissected in Chap. 5, "Instrument Drivers." With a data highway, GPIB, or RS-422 party line, a multidrop network of controllers is feasible, permitting many stations to communicate with your LabVIEW system while consuming only one communications port.

The easiest way to control an SLC is with a good driver. A few controllers are in the instrument library (e.g., Eurotherm and Micristar), and a few are supported by commercial software vendors, as in the case of Anafaze. Consider the availability of drivers when choosing a controller; otherwise, you will have to write your own. A good driver package will permit you to read and write most any function in the controller.

Back in Chap. 4, "Building an Application," I talked about the Vacuum Brazing Laboratory project, where several Eurotherm SLCs controlled furnace temperatures. LabVIEW simplified the operator's life by performing the following functions:

- Recipe entry through a table, with a graph showing time versus temperature
- Programmable limiting of controller outputs to prevent heater burnout
- Automatic system startup and shutdown based on time of day or other events
- Trending of setpoints and measured temperature
- Audible and visual alarms

These are typical functions that you might consider implementing. Another thing you might want to add is configuration management. The Eurotherm controllers have about 40 setup items that have to be set and verified at installation. A LabVIEW program could easily upload and download such settings to files, saving the operator a lot of button pushing with its attendant errors. Figure 8.11 shows a simple example with the Eurotherm driver VI.

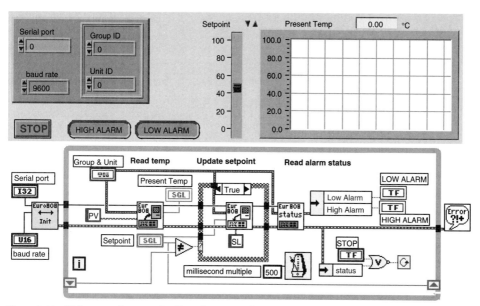

Figure 8.11 This example uses the Eurotherm 808/847 single-loop controller driver to update the setpoint and read the process variable and alarm status.

In my application, LabVIEW generated the ramp-and-soak profiles by calculating and transmitting a new setpoint every second. This was easier for the user than using the controller's built-in ramp functions because the profile could then be interrupted or modified on the fly. However, the programming is rather complex.

I really recommend SLCs when you have a modest number of control loops. Their high reliability and simplicity, combined with the power and flexibility of a LabVIEW MMI, makes a fine process control system.

Other smart I/O subsystems

There are many other ways to distribute the intelligence in your process control system besides PLCs and SLCs. All you really need is a remote or distributed I/O subsystem with local intelligence and communications that can execute either sequential or continuous control algorithms.

Multifunction scanners, such as the HP3852A, are more often used as simple data acquisition units, but they contain a surprising amount of control functionality as well. You can download programs to do scanning and units conversion, limit checking, and some kinds of feedback control. You have many options with the many types of interface modules available for these scanners. Check for availability of LabVIEW drivers before deciding on a particular model.

Another example is the Azonix μMAC series of controllers (formerly made by Analog Devices), particularly the μMAC-6000, for which a LabVIEW driver has been available for years. This controller is driven by an embedded microprocessor with a resident BASIC interpreter. It supports a variety of analog and digital I/O modules and communicates via RS-485 in a multidrop configuration. The driver permits you to download BASIC code (in text format) to perform scanning, conversion, and control algorithms of all kinds. It's easy to program, and the board runs autonomously much like a PLC. However, you should be aware that the interpreted BASIC runs quite slowly; don't expect millisecond response times from a μMAC-6000.

An often overlooked option is to use LabVIEW-based slave systems with little or no MMI functionality. The slave nodes communicate with the main MMI node, exchanging data in some LabVIEW formats that you decide upon. Slaves handle all the real-time data acquisition and control activity without the performance penalties of a busy graphical display or lots of user intervention. This technique is advantageous when you need sophisticated algorithms that a PLC or other simple processor can't handle. Also, since everything is written in LabVIEW, it's easier to maintain. Networking techniques are discussed later in this chapter.

One downside to using LabVIEW in the loop *may* be in the area of reliability, depending upon how critical your tasks are. Where I work, it is a policy never to use a general-purpose computer for safety interlocks. PLCs, on the other hand, are considered acceptable. The differences are in the ruggedness of the hardware and in the simplicity of the PLC software, which simply doesn't crash and which also has a very deterministic response time. The same cannot be said of a typical LabVIEW system running on top of a complex operating system. You will have to be the judge on this matter of safety and reliability.

Man-Machine Interfaces

When it comes to graphical man-machine interfaces, LabVIEW is among the very best products you can choose. The library of standard and customizable controls is extensive, but more than that, the function of each control is determined by you, the crafty programmer. In the process control world, there are several commonly used displays that you will probably want to implement in one form or another (Fig. 8.12).

- **Process mimic displays** are based on simplified P&ID diagrams. Various elements of the display are animated, tying measurements

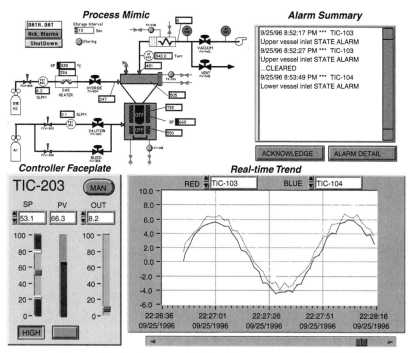

Figure 8.12 Some of the basic process displays that you can make in LabVIEW.

and status information directly to physical elements in the plant. Operators really like this kind of display. You can draw a representation of the system and import the picture into LabVIEW, then overlay it with various controls and indicators. Valves, heaters, and alarm indicators are usually Booleans, while various numeric controls and indicators are placed near their respective instruments. BridgeVIEW provides a library of process control symbols that speed the creation of your displays.

- **Trending displays** (graphs or strip charts), of which there are two types: historical trends and real-time trends. A real-time trend displays up-to-the-minute data, but may not go very far back in time. It relies primarily on data stored in memory. Historical trends usually read and display data from large disk files. Trending is discussed later in this chapter.

- **Controller faceplate displays** look and act much like the front panels of SLCs. They permit the operator to observe and control all the settings of PID and other types of analog controllers. Digital I/O or alarm status can also be presented in the form of Boolean indicators, like the example in Fig. 8.13.

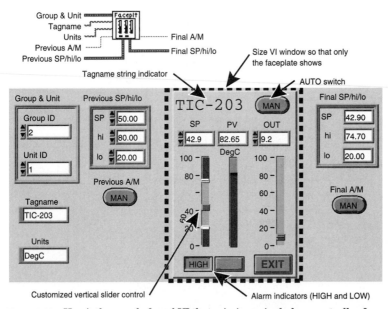

Figure 8.13 Here's the panel of a subVI that mimics a single-loop controller faceplate. You can call it from other VIs to operate many controllers since everything is programmable.

■ **Alarm summary displays** give the operator a concise overview of important status information, particularly I/O points that are out of specification in some way. You can use scrolling string indicators to list recent messages or Boolean indicators as a kind of status panel.

As an example, I decided to create a nice controller faceplate display that uses some of LabVIEW's more advanced features. This one mimics some of the commercial SLC front panels and is typical of the faceplates I've seen displayed on commercial DCS screens. (On a DCS, they usually put 8 or 10 faceplates on one screen, and the faceplate is a standard indicator element.) Figure 8.13 shows the panel of the controller subVI. You would normally size the VI window such that only the faceplate part of the panel is visible; the other items are just parameters for the calling VI. This subVI is programmable in the sense that the tag name, units, and other parameters are passed from the caller. This fact permits you to use one subVI to operate many control loops. The VI must be set to *Show front panel when called.*

The SP (setpoint) slider control is customized via the various pop-up options and the **Control Editor**. I first added two extra sliders by popping up on the control and selecting *Add Slider.* They serve as high and low alarm limits. I set the Fill Options for each of these alarm sliders to *Fill to Maximum* (upper one) and *Fill to Minimum* (lower one). In the Control Editor, I effectively erased the digital indicators for the two alarm limits by setting their vertical and horizontal sizes to the smallest possible values.

The diagram in Fig. 8.14 is fairly complex, so I'll go through it step-by-step. It illustrates the use of Local variables for control initialization. The I/O hardware in this example is, again, the Eurotherm 808 SLC. This VI relies on the controller to perform the PID algorithm, though you could write a set of subVIs that perform the same task with the PID Control Toolkit in LabVIEW, in conjunction with any type of I/O.

1. **Tagname** and **Units** are copied from incoming parameters to indicators on the faceplate. This gives the faceplate a custom look—as if it was written just for the particular channel in use.

2. Previous settings for **Auto?** (the auto/manual switch) and **SP** (the setpoint slider) are written to the user controls on the faceplate by using local variables. This step, like step 1, must be completed before the While Loop begins, so they are contained in a Sequence structure with a wire from one of the items to the border of the While Loop.

3. The process variable (current temperature) is read from the controller, checked against the alarm limits, and displayed.

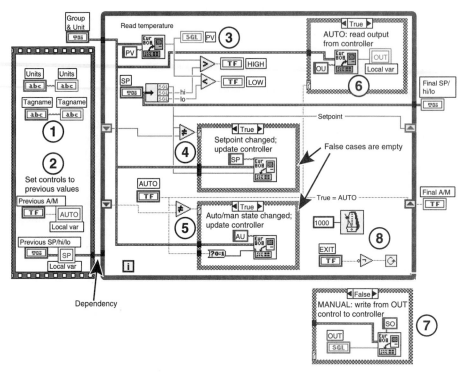

Figure 8.14   Diagram for the faceplate controller.

4. The current value for the setpoint is compared against the previous value in a Shift Register. If the value has changed, the setpoint is sent to the controller. This saves time by avoiding retransmission of the same value over and over.

5. In a similar fashion, the **Auto?** switch is checked for change-of-state. If it has changed, the new setting is sent to the controller.

6. If the mode is automatic, the **Out** (output) control is updated by using a Local variable. The value is read from the controller.

7. If the mode is manual, **Out** supplies a value that is sent to the controller. These two steps illustrate an acceptable use of read-write controls that avoids race conditions or other aberrant behavior.

8. The loop runs every second until the user clicks **Exit**, after which the final values for **Auto?** and **SP/hi/lo** are returned to the calling VI for use next time this VI is called.

Figure 8.15 shows how this subVI might be used in an application to support multiple controllers. The panel contains a configuration array that identifies each controller, a set of buttons to call the *desired con-*

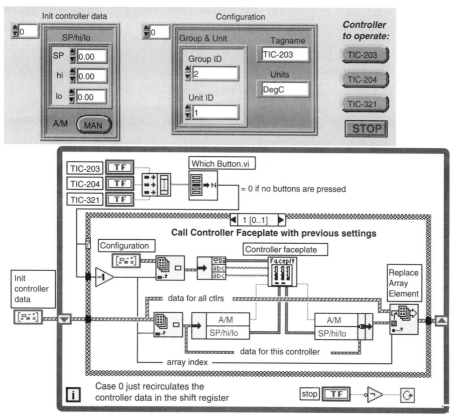

Figure 8.15   An application that uses the Faceplate Controller subVI. The Shift Register acts as a database for previous controller values.

troller, and an initialization array. When one of the buttons is pressed, our old friend, the **Which Button** VI, returns a nonzero value and Case 1 is executed (Case 0 just recirculates data in the Shift Register, waiting for a button to be pressed).

Inside the Case, the **Configuration** cluster array is indexed to extract the setup information for the selected controller, which is then passed to the Controller Faceplate subVI, which opens when called. Similarly, the controller data array, circulating in the Shift Register, is indexed and unbundled. When the Controller Faceplate subVI finishes, the data it returns is bundled and the current element in the data array is replaced. The next time this controller is called, data from the previous call will be available from the Shift Register. Note the use of **Bundle by Name** and **Unbundle by Name**. These functions show the signal names so you can keep them straight.

This overall procedure of indexing, unbundling, bundling, and replacing an array element is a versatile database management concept that you can use in configuration management. Sometimes the data structures are very complex (arrays of clusters of arrays, etc.), but the procedure is the same, and the diagram is very symmetrical when properly laid out. Little memory management is required, so the operations are reasonably fast. One final note regarding the use of global memory of this type. All database updates must be controlled by one VI to serialize the operations. If you access a global variable from many locations, sooner or later you will encounter a race condition where two callers attempt to write data at the same time. There is no way of knowing who will get there first. Each caller got an original copy of the data at the same time, but the last one to write the data wins. This is true for both the built-in LabVIEW globals and the one based on Shift Registers that you build yourself.

If you want to save yourself lots of effort, check out the BridgeVIEW **MMI G Wizard**. It lets you interactively create your MMI from a library of standard display elements such as trends, faceplates, and alarms. What's amazing is that you don't have to do any G programming at all, if you don't want to.

Display hierarchy

Naturally, you can mix elements from each of the various types of displays freely because LabVIEW has no particular restrictions. Many commercial software packages have preformatted displays that make setups easy, but somewhat less versatile. You could put several of these fundamental types of displays on one panel, or better, you may want to segregate them into individual panels that include only one type of display per panel. A possible hierarchy of displays is shown in Fig. 8.16.

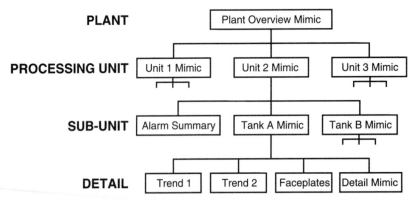

Figure 8.16 Hierarchical process displays allow the operator to see any level of detail without having overcrowded screens.

Such a hierarchy relies heavily on global variables for access to information about every I/O point and on pop-up windows (VIs that open when called).

Your displays need to be organized in a manner that is easily understood by the operator and one that is easy to navigate. A problem that is common to large, integrated control systems is that it takes too long to find the desired information, especially when an emergency arises. Therefore, you must work with the operators so that the display hierarchy and navigation process make sense. The organization in Fig. 8.16 is closely aligned with that of the plant that it controls. Each subdisplay gives a greater level of detail about, or a different view of, a particular subsystem. This method is generally accepted by operators and is a good starting point.

The VI hierarchy can be mapped one-for-one with the display hierarchy by using pop-up windows (subVIs set to **Show front panel when called**). Each VI contains a **dispatcher** loop similar to the one shown later in this chapter (in Fig. 8.28). Buttons on the panel select which display to bring up. A Case structure contains a separate display subVI in each frame. The utility VI, **Which Button**, multiplexes all the buttons into a number that selects the appropriate case. The dispatcher loop runs in parallel with other loops in the calling VI.

Each subVI in turn is structured the same way as the top-level VI, with a dispatcher loop calling other subVIs as desired. When it's time to exit a subVI and return to a higher level, an exit button is pressed,

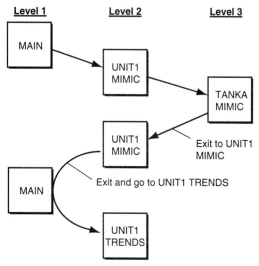

Figure 8.17 Traversing the display hierarchy. When you click an exit button on a subdisplay VI, it returns a value that tells the calling VI where to go next.

terminating the subVI execution, closing its panel, and returning control to the caller. An extension of this exit action is to have more than one button with which to exit the subVI. A value is returned by the subVI indicating where the user wants to go next (Fig. 8.17). The caller's dispatcher is then responsible for figuring out which subVI to call next.

Making the actual buttons is the fun part. The simplest ones are the built-in labeled buttons: **TREND**. Or, you can paste in a picture that is a little more descriptive. Another method is to use a transparent Boolean control on top of a graphic item on a mimic display, such as a tank or reactor. Then, all the operator has to do is click on the tank and a predefined display pops up. This is a good way to jump quickly to an associated trend, alarm, or other detail display. Remember that the operator has to *know* that the buttons are there because he or she can't *see* them. Therefore, you must be consistent in your use of such buttons or the operators will get confused. To make a transparent Boolean, select a simple Boolean control such as the Flat Square Button, and use the Coloring tool to make both the foreground and background transparent (T).

Power Windows: VI Control VIs.   You can do some really interesting display tricks (and a lot more) with the **VI Control VIs**, which you find in the **Advanced>>VI Control** function menu. They provide methods to manipulate VIs that go way beyond the regular VI Setup items, such as *Show front panel when called*. All of them use a call-by-name approach, where you supply a string containing the exact name of the VI. That should spark some new ideas. . . . Consider the fact that you can now let the *user* decide which subVIs will be loaded and run simply by selecting from a list. Let's see what else you can do with the VI Controllers.

You gain the ability to dynamically load VIs from disk with the **Call Instrument VI** and **Run Instrument VI**. These are particularly useful when you need to change modes in a significant way and you would prefer not to have all the required VIs in memory at all times. For instance, when the user clicks the Configure button, you can load the configuration manager from disk, rather than having it memory-resident at all times. The Run Instrument VI actually loads and runs the VI, and then returns immediately, leaving the newly loaded VI running in parallel. This effectively "spawns another task," as they call it in the world of operating systems. The Call Instrument VI operates in a manner similar to calling the designated subVI directly from the diagram, right down to passing parameters to controls and receiving results back from indicators on the subVI. The important difference is that the subVI is dynamically loaded and unloaded, and *which* subVI is loaded is determined by the path name you supply.

Passing parameters to a subVI through Call Instrument requires some care. The LabVIEW developers decided to make the connection through clusters, one for the controls and one for the indicators on the subVI (Fig. 8.18). You first convert the information about each control into a string by calling the **Flatten To String** function. Then, build a cluster containing the exact name of the control, the type descriptor, and the flattened data. The name is case-sensitive, and the type descriptor must match that of the control in the subVI you're calling. You can call any, all, or none of the controls on the subVI. Assemble all the clusters into an array and pass the cluster array to the **input** terminal of the Call Instrument VI. When it actually calls the subVI, Call Instrument now has enough information to figure out which value goes to which control. This is exactly the same as wiring to the subVI, only you must manually construct all the data type information. Wiring is much easier and clearer, wouldn't you say? For that reason alone, it makes sense *not* to use Call Instrument unless there is no other dataflow alternative.

For outputs (indicators coming from the subVI), you supply data type information in exactly the same way as you do for controls. You index the output array, unbundle the flattened data, and call the **Unflatten From String** function to obtain the actual data for each indicator.

The VI Control VIs offer additional opportunities for navigation among display VIs. An example is the **Open Panel** VI. To speed the apparent response time of your user interface when changing from one MMI window to another, consider leaving several of the VIs running with panels open at all times, but have only the currently active one visible. When the user clicks a button to activate another window, call

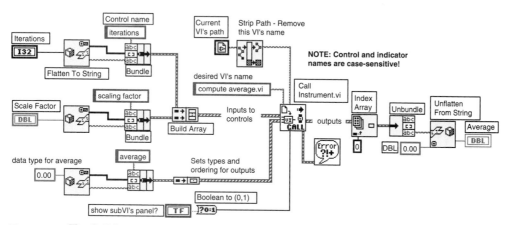

Figure 8.18 The Call Instrument VI loads a VI from disk and exchanges parameters with it as if the subVI were wired directly into the diagram. This can save memory since the subVI is loaded only when required, but as you can see, there's a bit of diagram work to do.

Open Panel with the name of the desired VI. Its window will pop to the front as fast as your computer can redraw the screen. A similar trick can prevent users from getting lost in a sea of windows. If your display hierarchy is complex and you allow more than one active window at a time, it's possible for the user to accidentally hide one behind the other. It's very confusing and requires excessive training to keep the user out of trouble. Instead, try to simplify your display navigation scheme, or use a combination of Open Panel and **Close Panel** to assist the user.

You can display special information, such as a miniature alarm summary panel or a custom help window, by creating a dedicated VI that opens when called. The **Resize Panel** VI might be useful here. It allows you to set the size and location of a panel, whether the panel is presently displayed or not. This gives you the flexibility of using a single display VI but having it appear in a specific location depending upon the needs of the calling VI. To keep the user from resizing the VI, you can disable resizing and scroll bars through the VI Setup dialog.

Other interesting display techniques

You can customize controls and indicators by replacing the built-in pictures with custom ones from a drawing package. A useful example, submitted by Corrie Karlsen of LLNL, is shown in Fig. 8.19. The system being controlled has a carousel with 10 sample bottles and a liquid sampling valve. When the operator moves the valve icon, a stepper motor moves the carousel to the appropriate bottle. The operator presses a **fill** button (not shown), and the valve is cycled open for a predetermined period of time and then closed. This LabVIEW indicator then responds by updating the full/empty status of the sample bottles, which are Boolean indicators.

Figure 8.19   The sample valve is a horizontal slider control with the valve picture pasted in as the handle. The control has no axis labels and the housing is colored transparent. The bottles are Boolean indicators and the pipes are static pictures.

You can create Boolean controls that look like valves with different open and closed states by pasting in a pair of pictures. If the operator prefers feedback regarding the status of a valve that has limit switches, you can place a **Pict Ring** indicator for status on top of a transparent Boolean control for manual actuation. For a valve with high and low limit switches, the ring indicator would show open, transit, closed, and an illegal value where both limit switches are activated.

You can animate pipes, pumps, heaters, and a host of other process equipment by using picture Booleans or Pict Rings. To simulate motion, create a picture such as a paddle wheel in a drawing program, then duplicate it and modify each duplicate in some way, such as rotating the wheel. Then, paste the pictures into the Pict Ring in sequence. Connect the ring indicator to a number that cycles through the appropriate range of values on a periodic basis. This is the LabVIEW equivalent of those novelty movies that are drawn in the margins of books.

Perhaps the most impressive and useful display is a process mimic based on a pictorial representation of your process. A simple line drawing such as a P&ID showing important valves and instruments is easy to create and remarkably effective. If your plant is better represented as a photograph or other artwork, by all means use that. You can import CAD drawings, scanned images, or images from a video frame grabber to enhance a process display.

Attribute nodes allow you to dynamically change the size, position, color, and visibility of controls and indicators. This adds a kind of animation capability to LabVIEW. The Blinking attribute is especially useful for alarm indicators. You can choose the on-off state colors and the blink rate through the LabVIEW Preferences.

Handling all those front panel items

Process control panels tend to be loaded with many controls and indicators. This can make your diagram very busy and hard to understand. What you need to do is bundle related controls into arrays or clusters and pass them to subVIs for processing. Similarly, indicators are unbundled for display after being returned from source VIs (Fig. 8.20). A Sequence structure helps to conserve screen space. It doesn't impair the visual flow of the program too much because only a single item is passed from one frame to the next.

One hazard in this array-based scheme is that all the controls and indicators are order-dependent; that is, element three of the control array is always PV-401. Any wiring or indexing errors anywhere in your program will send the wrong value. An alternative is to use clusters and the Bundle by Name and Unbundle by Name functions. There is still a limitation with named clusters, however; you can't arbitrarily

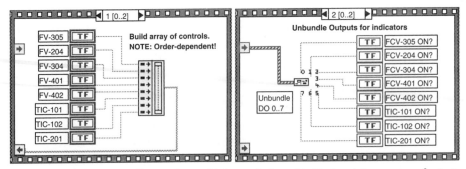

Figure 8.20   Clean up your diagram by combining controls and indicators into arrays or clusters. Other frames in this sequence are the sources and sinks for data. The unbundler subVI on the right extracts Boolean values from an array or cluster. You could also use Unbundle By Name.

configure channels (insert or delete them) during execution with a configuration manager. Channels that you access must always exist, and editing of one or more diagrams will always be necessary to change the overall configuration. The way out of this quandary is a *real-time database,* a topic we cover later in this chapter.

Experts in human factors tell us that having too much information on one screen leads to information overload. Operators can't find what they're looking for, and the important values get lost in a sea of colored lights. If you find that your MMI display VI has a ridiculous number of controls and/or indicators, it's time to break it into multiple panels. It will then be easier for operators to use, and easier for the programmer to design and maintain. This is just one more reason for using hierarchical displays.

Data Distribution

If you think about MMI display hierarchies, one thing you may wonder about is how the many subVIs exchange current data. This is a data distribution problem, and it can be a big one. A complex process control system may have many I/O subsystems of different types, some of which are accessed over a network. If you don't use a coherent plan of attack, performance (and perhaps reliability) is sure to suffer. In homemade LabVIEW applications, global variables generally solve the problem, if used with some caution.

Most commercial process control systems, including BridgeVIEW, use a **real-time database** to make data globally accessible in real time. You can emulate this in your LabVIEW program at any level of sophistication. The general concept is to use centralized, asynchronous **I/O handler tasks** to perform the actual I/O operations (translation: standalone VIs that talk to the I/O hardware through the use of LabVIEW drivers). Data is exchanged with the I/O handlers via one or more global

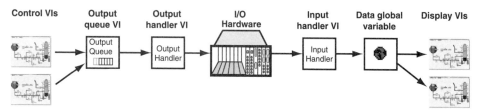

Figure 8.21 Data distribution in a simple LabVIEW process control system. Control VIs write new settings to an output queue, from which values are written to the hardware by an output handler VI. An input handler VI reads data and stores it in a global variable for use by multiple display VIs.

variables or queues (Fig. 8.21). User interface VIs and control VIs all operate in parallel with the I/O handlers.

Input scanners as servers

The **client-server** model is very effective for the input data in process control systems. An input handler task, a server VI which I like to call a **scanner**, periodically polls all the defined input channels, applies scale factors, and writes the results to global variables. The scanner is also a logical place to check any alarm limits. Depending on your application's complexity, the scanner VI may also be responsible for some aspects of trending or data archiving.

Figure 8.22 is a simplified scanner VI. It is called by a top-level VI and runs periodically (in parallel with the top-level VI) until a Boolean

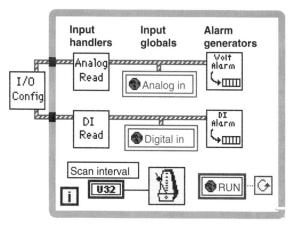

Figure 8.22 A scanner VI that handles analog and digital inputs. The I/O configuration subVI, at left, passes information to the input handlers. Data from the input handlers is written to other global variables for use by client VIs. Alarm limits are also checked and the results are written to alarm message queues.

global variable called *RUN* is set to false. Two input handler VIs—one for analog inputs and the other for digital—acquire raw data, filter it, and scale it to engineering units. Handler outputs are cluster arrays containing each channel's value, its name, and any other information that client tasks might need. This information is written to global variables and passed to alarm generator VIs that test each channel for alarm limit violations. Alarm flags or messages are stored in a queue (see the section entitled "Using an Alarm Handler," which follows).

As you might expect, process control has many of the same configuration needs as a data acquisition system. Each input handler requires information about its associated input hardware, channel assignments, and so forth. This information comes from an I/O configuration VI, which supplies the configurations in cluster arrays. If configuration information is needed elsewhere in the hierarchy, it can be passed directly in global variables, or it can be included in the data cluster arrays produced by the input handlers.

Here's an important tip regarding performance. Where possible, avoid frequent access of string data, particularly in global variables. Strings require extra memory management, and the associated overhead yields relatively poor performance when compared to all other data types. Not that you should *never* use strings, but try to use them sparingly and only for infrequent access. For instance, when you open an operator display panel, read channel names and units from the configuration database and display them just once, not every cycle of a loop.

Handling output data

For efficiency, it may be better to update an output only when its value changes because some devices have a fair amount of overhead associated with communications. Like the input model we've been discussing, you can use an output handler and an output global variable that contains the values for each output channel. The global variable carries an array with each element of the array corresponding to an output channel. Any control VI can update values in the output global. The output handler checks for changes in any of the output channels and updates the specific channels that have changed. You can combine the handler and its associated global variable into an output scanner, as in Fig. 8.23, which works like an input scanner in reverse.

To test for changes of state on an array of output values, use a program similar to the one in Fig. 8.24. A Shift Register contains the values of all channels from the last time the handler was called. Each channel's new value is compared with its previous value, and if a change has occurred, the output is written. Another Shift Register is used to force all outputs to update when the VI is loaded. You could also

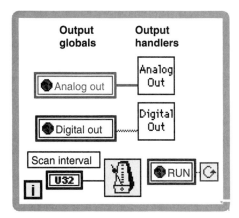

Figure 8.23 An output scanner, which is quite similar to an input scanner.

add a **force update** or **initialize** Boolean control to do the same thing. Depending upon the complexity of your system, channel configuration information may be required to perform the output write operation. If so, you can read the configuration global variable and pass that information along to the subVI that writes the data.

Because the Analog Output global variable contains an *array* of values, control VIs have to *update* that array, not overwrite it. Updates are easy to do. Just read the array from the global, use **Replace Array Element** to surgically change the value of a single channel, then write the array back to the global. Please note that there is again a great probability of a race condition arising. If the global variable is accessed

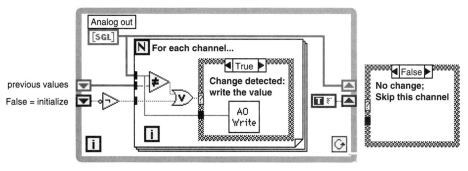

Figure 8.24 An output handler that only writes to an output channel when a change of value is detected. The upper Shift Register stores the previous values for comparison, while the lower Shift Register is used for initialization. Its value is false when the VI is loaded, forcing all outputs to update. Additional initialization features may be required if the program is stopped then restarted.

by multiple callers, they will clash over who writes last. The solution is to encapsulate all *write* operations for a global variable inside a subVI, effectively serializing access. There is, of course, no limit to the number of VIs that can simultaneously read the global data.

Another way to avoid race conditions is to use an output **queue**. A queue is a first-in, first-out, or FIFO, construct that works like people standing in line. When a high-level VI needs to update an output, it calls an intermediate VI that adds the request to an output queue (Fig. 8.25). Later, the output handler VI reads and empties the queue and updates each specified output. A working model of this scheme is included on the CD-ROM in the SCXI I/O driver examples. It includes VIs for both analog and digital I/O. Though it's written for DAQ hardware, you could modify the output handler VIs for other kinds of hardware.

**platform\
scxi config\
scxi_io.llb**

Display VIs as clients

By now you should be getting the idea that global variables are key elements when designing a versatile process control system. VIs that display data are very easy to write because global variables solve the data distribution problem. The input scanner supplies up-to-date values for all inputs, while the configuration part of your system supplies such things as channel names, units, and other general information, all available through globals. The next two figures show how I wrote a typical display/control VI using the methods we've discussed.

Since this display example (Fig. 8.26) is part of a hierarchical suite, there are buttons marked *Display Select* near the top. Clicking one of them causes this VI to terminate and returns an appropriate value in **Goto Screen** (which would normally be positioned off-screen so the user doesn't see it). The rest of the panel is a collection of numeric controls and indicators, grouped by function, with the help of some decorations. A fancy process mimic graphic could also be placed underneath the controls.

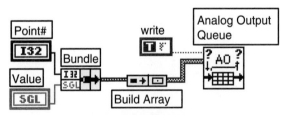

Figure 8.25 An output queue prevents race conditions and simplifies access. Just supply the channel number and value. An output handler VI reads the queue and does the actual hardware output commands.

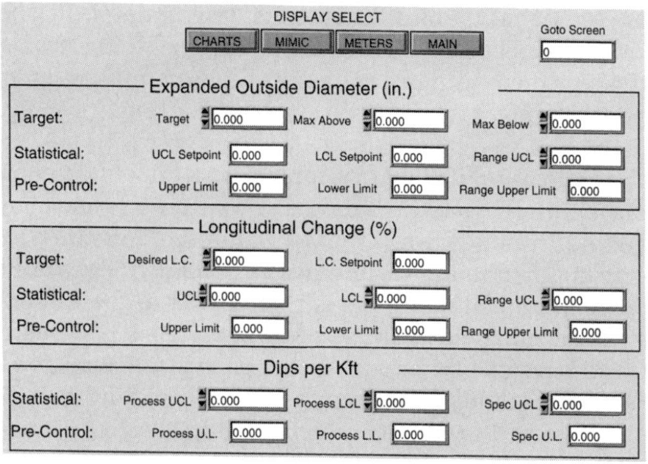

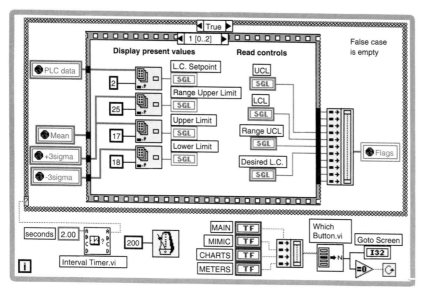

Figure 8.26 Front panel of a display and control VI that is used to monitor and set operating specifications.

In the associated diagram in Fig. 8.27, you can see that the **Which Button** VI determines whether the VI will continue to run, based on the state of all the Display Select buttons. The While Loop runs at a fairly fast rate, on the order of every 200 ms or so, to provide rapid response to the buttons. It would be wasteful, however, to update all

Figure 8.27 Diagram for the display/control VI. The Case structure and interval timer limit how often the displays and controls are updated. A Sequence logically groups the controls and indicators, eliminating clutter. The VI loops until the user clicks a button to jump to another display.

the display items at that rate, since the data is only updated by the scanners every couple of seconds. The **Interval Timer VI** controls a Case structure that contains all the real activity. Every two seconds, the Case is True; otherwise, the False case, which contains nothing, executes.

Input data comes from several global variables containing data from a PLC and some computed statistics which are written by the input scanner VI. Output data from controls on the panel are built into an array and written to another global variable called *Flags,* which is used elsewhere to indicate system status. This is the only VI in the hierarchy that writes to Flags global variable, so there is no reason to create a queue or other protective device for that global variable. For clarity, I used a Sequence structure to logically group the front panel items.

If the display needs to call lower-level displays, add a second, independent While Loop as a **dispatcher**, as shown in Fig. 8.28, just like the top-level VIs have. Some buttons will then activate the lower-level displays. Other buttons that cause a return to higher-level displays are wired as shown in Fig. 8.27. This dispatcher concept is flexible and easy to program.

Initializing controls.   All controls present on your display panel have to be initialized when the VI is called. Otherwise, they will revert to their default values which will then be accepted as if those were user inputs—probably not a great idea. The simplest way to initialize controls is to supply initial values from the calling VI through the connector pane. Every control will have to be wired to the connector pane, and that may be a problem: you have only 20 terminals, one of which is

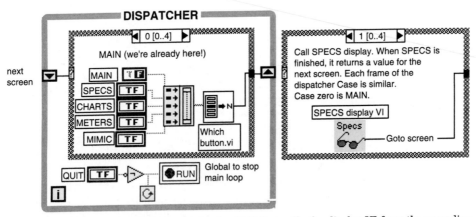

Figure 8.28   The dispatcher loop in a higher-level VI that calls the display VI from the preceding figures.

probably the Goto Display output. If you have more than 19 controls to initialize, some will have to be colocated in clusters. Think about your panel layout and figure out which controls might be logically grouped in this way. You can effectively hide the border of a cluster by coloring it transparent so that it disappears behind the other graphical elements of your display.

You can also initialize controls with local variables from within the display VI. For the present example, initial values for the manual flag controls are easy to obtain because each control's previous value was written to the Flags global variable. After indexing each value out of the Flags array, use local variables to set each control's value, then start the main While Loop.

 **platform\ setup file handler.llb**   Alternatively, you could use the Setup File Handler utility VI described in Chap. 7, "Writing a Data Acquisition System." That utility lets you store and retrieve large sets of values in a convenient manner, then use local variables to initialize controls. It's just the ticket for this class of problem.

Using network connections

To create a distributed control system (even a very small one), you will need to use a network. The most versatile network connections use Ethernet and TCP/IP, which is directly supported by LabVIEW through VIs in the Networking function palette. **IP (Internet Protocol)** performs the low-level packaging of data into *datagrams* and determines a network path by which messages can reach their destination. However, it offers no handshaking and doesn't even guarantee delivery. **TCP (Transmission Control Protocol)** adds handshaking and guarantees that messages arrive in the right order, making it quite reliable. **UDP (Universal Datagram Protocol)** is similar to TCP, but does no handshaking, making it somewhat faster and also offering the possibility of broadcasting a message to many recipients. You establish sessions between each LabVIEW system on the network, then exchange binary data in formats of your choosing. There are several examples of TCP/IP clients and servers included in the networking examples. These example VIs could be modified to run in the background with local communications via global variables. A *Data Server* VI would then act as a tunnel for data that reappears in a *Data Client* elsewhere on the network. You can have as many connections, or *ports,* open simultaneously as you need. An excellent article on this subject appeared in *LTR* (Hedstrom 1995), written by Brad Hedstrom of Advanced Measurements.

On the Macintosh, you can use the lowest level of **AppleEvents**, called **Program to Program (PPC) Communication**. PPC is a high-performance, low-overhead means of transferring blocks of data between applications anywhere on a network or on the same machine. As with TCP, you must choose the data format and use Type Casting or other data conversion operations to encode and decode the data. The networking examples contain some reasonably simple examples that test the speed of PPC transmission; the examples can be modified for use in a real program. Some applications support PPC, but it requires a lot of study and detailed knowledge of the data formats to successfully exchange data between LabVIEW and these other programs. You can also use AppleEvents to remotely launch applications or VIs; run, abort, or inquire about the status of a VI; or send high-level AppleEvent messages to other applications on any Macintosh on the network.

Dynamic Data Exchange (DDE) is a text-based message-passing scheme for Windows that is supported by many applications. It's slower than TCP/IP or PPC for transferring large quantities of data, but it is standardized to a fair extent, making it easier to use. DDE will work over a network (NetDDE) if you are running Windows 3.1 for Workgroups or a later version such as Windows NT or 95 that includes networking. NetDDE works fine with the standard LabVIEW package. Applications such as spreadsheets accept DDE commands and are fairly easy to use. The example VIs show how to set up a real-time exchange with Microsoft Excel, and there are more examples in Chap. 11, "Automated Test Applications."

As you can see, these networking techniques are still, to a great degree, an advanced topic. Because of the lack of overall standardization of data formatting and high-level protocols, it's still somewhat difficult to just drop in a networking VI and have it act as a magic data tunnel. Many developers are hard at work trying to make life easier for you. Keep watching for improved example VIs and third-party networking packages.

Files as mailboxes.   An old reliable way to exchange data between VIs over the network is to use files as mailboxes that any node can remotely fetch and read or write. This assumes that you have a means by which files can be transmitted under the control of LabVIEW. On the Macintosh, file sharing is built in to System 7 and is totally transparent because every Macintosh can act like a server. You simply specify the file path and open it in the usual manner, no matter where the volume resides. Windows 95 is similarly easy to use. For Windows 3.1, there are numerous third-party networking options that permit you to mount a volume over the network such as Novell NetWare. Windows NT is similar to the UNIX platforms where you can use the Network File System (NFS).

For one-way transmission, files are easy to use. Just write data to a file in some predetermined format on a periodic basis, then the remote node can fetch it asynchronously, read, and decode the information. Things get tricky when you need synchronized, bidirectional communications because you must create a system of file access permission limits using flags or some other technique.

Real-time process control databases

If you buy a commercial DCS or PC-based industrial process control package, you will find that the entire software environment is **database-driven**. For user interaction, there is invariably a program called the Database Builder that edits and compiles all of the configuration information. The run-time programs are then centered around this database: I/O handlers pass values in and out to hardware, alarm handlers compare measurements with limit values, and trenders display values on the screen. LabVIEW, however, is not in itself a database-driven package. In fact, it would be much less flexible if it were centered around a predefined database structure.

A particular requirement for a database used in process control is that it must be a *real-time* database, which implies that it is memory-resident and available for thousands of transactions per second. For added versatility, the database may also be distributed among various nodes in the system. This permits any node to efficiently exchange information with any other node on the network through a consistent message-passing scheme. A global, real-time, database requires a sophisticated client-server or peer-to-peer relationship among all nodes on the network. Another attribute of a good database is access by name. That is, you supply the tag name and attribute (such as Setpoint or Alarm High) that you wish to access, and the database looks up the name and accesses the correct items. This eliminates the headaches we've all experienced trying to keep track of array index values when data is carried in arrays. Such programming is possible in LabVIEW, but is beyond the scope of this book and beyond the abilities of all but the most experienced programmers.

This is one of the areas where you may want to turn to BridgeVIEW or another SCADA product. In its initial release, BridgeVIEW implements a simple but effective real-time database built from VI-based global variables. The developers were careful to avoid the use of strings, that old performance killer, and as a result, you can access the database some thousands of times per second. National Instruments will also be integrating the historical database, **Citadel**, from its SCADA product, **Lookout**, into BridgeVIEW. The Lookout database is full-featured, high-performance, and definitely not programmed as LabVIEW diagrams! Some third-party developers have also successfully built real-time databases as we'll see at the end of this chapter.

Simulation for validation

An effective way of testing or validating your process control system is by simulating real I/O. The obvious way is to replace each physical input with an appropriate control or calculated data source and replace each physical output with an appropriate indicator. If you've designed your application with the client-server model discussed here, simulation turns out to be quite easy. When I wrote my first well-designed client-server-based system, I didn't have any hardware for testing, so it was imperative that the software have a built-in test mode. Since the inputs all came from a PLC, the core of the input scanner VI consisted of a series of PLC input operations, and all values were collected in a single array for use by the clients. I created a Boolean control that selected either *normal* or *simulation* mode and used that to control a Case structure. The *normal* frame of the Case structure contained the PLC programming, while the *simulation* frame contained a set of mathematical expressions in a big Formula Node. There was one expression for each signal, and all results were collected into an array, just like the real data. To keep things interesting, the formulas contained sine functions and random number generators.

The status of almost all output signals in a process control system are probably displayed by indicators on various panels. For simulation, then, all you must do is disable the VIs that talk to the hardware. If your outputs are handled by output servers, encapsulate the hardware output VIs in a Case structure tied to a mode control, just like I did for those simulated inputs.

If your system has closed-loop controls, where inputs respond to outputs, consider writing output data to global variables that can be read by the input simulation code. Then add some scale factors or perhaps some time-dependent response to this feedback data. The PID Control Toolkit contains a simple plant simulator that does such a trick.

There are great payoffs to built-in simulation. Most importantly, you can do a thorough job of testing your application off-line. That means you can work anywhere you like and you don't have to wait for time on the real equipment. There is a much lower risk of sending the real process out of control, losing data, or encountering some other unforeseen condition or bug. As a bonus, the simulation mode is handy for demonstration purposes, like showing the boss how crafty you are.

Sequential Control

Every process has some need for sequential control in the form of interlocking or time-ordered events. I usually include manual inputs in this area—virtual switches and buttons that open valves, start motors, and the like. This is the great bastion of PLCs, but you can do an admirable job in LabVIEW without too much work. We've already discussed methods by which you read, write, and distribute data. The examples that follow fit between the input and output handlers.

Interlocking with logic and tables

G's Boolean logic functions make ordinary interlocking simple (Fig. 8.29). Boolean conditions can be derived from a variety of sources such as front panel switches, digital inputs, or comparison functions acting on analog signals. **Ladder logic**, as shown in the figure, is the most common language for PLC programming. It comes from the days of electromechanical switching and remains a useful documentation technique for logical systems.

One way to add versatility to your logical operations is to use a **Boolean table** as shown in Fig. 8.30. A table is a two-dimensional array where the columns are the mode or step number, and the ele-

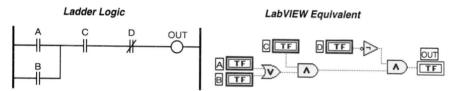

Figure 8.29 Simple interlock logic, comparing a ladder logic network with its LabVIEW equivalent.

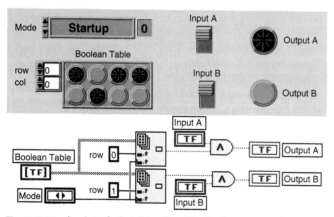

Figure 8.30 An interlock table. The 2D Boolean array (a table) is sliced by an array indexer to deliver an interlock permissive vector, which then is ANDed with a series of inputs.

ments in each row represent some state of the system, such as a permissive interlock. The **Mode** control selects the column through the use of a 2D **Index Array** function. The output of the Index Array function is a 1D array of Booleans—a column slice from the incoming table. Another set of Index Array functions selects the individual interlock permissives. If one of the input switches is True *and* its corresponding permissive (from the table) is True, then the output is True. You can add whatever kind of logic is required and expand the table as necessary.

The **Mode** control could be a Ring control that selects between system modes such as *Startup, Run,* and *Maintenance.* This is an effective way to change the action of a large number of interlock chains without a great deal of wiring. Another use for the **Mode** control is to tie it to an internally generated value in your program. For instance, the mode might change in response to the time of day or the temperature in a reactor.

Tables are an efficient way to store interlock information, and they are very fast. The only bad thing about tables is that they can be hard to debug. When a table is very large and your program changes modes very often, it's not always obvious what is going on. Directly wired logic is generally easier to understand and debug and should be used preferentially.

State machines

The **state machine** architecture is about the most powerful LabVIEW solution for sequential control problems. Introduced in Chap. 4, "Building an Application," it consists of a Case structure inside of a While Loop with the Case selector carried in a Shift Register. Each frame of the state machine's Case structure has the ability to transfer control to any other frame on the next iteration or to cause immediate termination of the While Loop. This allows you to perform operations in any order depending on any number of conditions—the very essence of sequential control.

Figure 8.31 is an example of a tank-filling operation. The objective is to fill the tank, stopping when an upper level is reached or when a certain time has passed. In the first frame, *Start,* you would open a valve (presumably by writing to an output device) that starts filling the tank. The starting time is saved in a Shift Register. The program then proceeds to the second frame, *Fill,* where the elapsed time and present tank level are checked. The tank level is obtained from an analog input or from a global variable, which in turn is written by an analog input handler. If the elapsed time exceeds the specified dura-

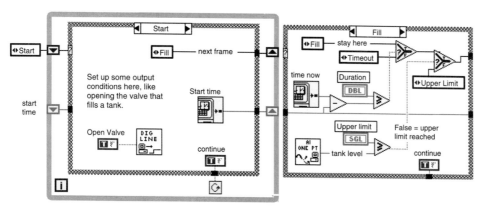

Figure 8.31 This state machine implements an operation that terminates when the tank is full or when a time limit has passed. The *Timeout* of the Case (not shown) takes action if a time-out occurs. The *Upper Limit* frame (also not shown) is activated when the upper limit for tank level is exceeded.

tion, the program goes to the *Timeout* frame. If the upper limit is exceeded, jump to the *Upper Limit* frame. Otherwise, keep looping on the *Fill* frame. The *Timeout* and *Upper Limit* frames may then take appropriate action to close the valve, or whatever; other operations may follow.

More activity can be managed in this same structure by looping over several frames rather than just one. The sequence could be: 1-2-3-1-2-3, and so forth, with the termination conditions causing a jump to the fourth or fifth frame. Very complex looping is possible, though, like any scheme, it can be hard to debug if you're not careful. I usually put an indicator on the panel that shows which state it's in at the moment. Single stepping then shows the execution order. If the process has to run fast, you can accumulate a history of all the states by building an array on the boundary of the While Loop for later review.

Multiple state machines can run in parallel with each managing a different task. You could have several on one diagram with a global Boolean that requests all the loops to stop. This would permit you to break your control problem down into logical, related pieces that are easier to design and debug.

Initialization problems

Initialization is important in all control situations and particularly so in batch processes that spend much of their time in the startup phase. When you first load your LabVIEW program, or when you restart for some reason, the program needs to know the state of each input and output to prevent a jarring process upset. For instance, the default values for all your front panel controls may or may not be the right values to send to the output devices. A good deal of thought is necessary with regards to this initialization problem.

When your program starts, a predictable startup sequence is necessary to avoid output transients. Begin by scanning all the inputs. It's certainly a safe operation, and you probably need some input data in order to set any outputs. Then, compute and initialize any output values. If the values are stored in global variables, the problem is somewhat easier because a special initialization VI may be able to write the desired settings without going through all of the control algorithms. Finally, call the output handler VI(s) to transfer the settings to the output devices. Also remember to initialize front panel controls as discussed earlier.

Control algorithms may need initialization as well. If you use any uninitialized Shift Registers to store state information, add initialization. The method in Fig. 8.32 qualifies as another Canonical VI. The technique relies on the fact that an uninitialized Boolean Shift Register contains False when the VI is freshly loaded or compiled. (Remember that once the VI has been run, this is no longer the case.) The Shift Register is tested, and if it's False, some initialization logic inside the Case structure is executed. A Boolean control called *Initialize* is included to permit programmatic initialization at any time, such as during restarts.

You could also send flags to your control algorithms via dedicated controls or global variables. Such a flag might cause the clearing of intermediate calculations, generation of empty arrays for data storage, or cause the outputs to go to a desired state. All of these items are worth considering. Be sure to test your control system thoroughly by stopping and then restarting in various states. Startup is the time where most process disasters occur. Of course, bad things never happen on *my* projects.

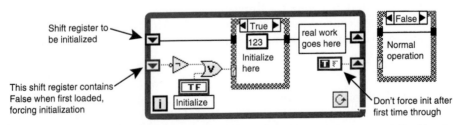

Figure 8.32   The upper Shift Register, perhaps used for a control algorithm, is initialized by the lower Shift Register at startup or by setting the Initialize control to True.

GrafcetVIEW—A graphical process control package

There is an international standard for process control programming called **GRAFCET**. It's more popular in Europe, having originated in France, but is found occasionally in the United States and other countries. You usually need a special GRAFCET programming package, much like you need a ladder logic package to program a target machine, which is usually a PLC. The language is the forerunner of **sequential function charts (SFCs)** (IEC standard 848), which are similar to flowcharts, but optimized for process control, and PLCs, in particular (Fig. 8.33). Emmanuel Geveaux and Francis Cottet at LISI/ENSMA, in conjunction with Saphir (all in France) have developed a LabVIEW package called GrafcetVIEW that allows you to do GRAFCET programming on LabVIEW diagrams. It's a natural match because of the graphical nature of both languages.

One enhancement to LabVIEW that the authors had to make was additional synchronization through the use of **semaphores**, a classic software handshaking technique. In many control schemes, you may have parallel tasks that execute continuously and independently, but which occasionally need to force one another to pause to guarantee sequential timing during certain operations. The GrafcetVIEW solution is a set of subVIs that manages semaphores; it may also be possible to implement the solution via Occurrences, but their semaphore trick seems to be immune to some of the difficult starting and ending occurrence-generation situations.

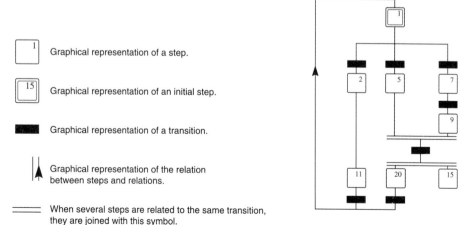

1	Graphical representation of a step.
15	Graphical representation of an initial step.
▬	Graphical representation of a transition.
⬆	Graphical representation of the relation between steps and relations.
═══	When several steps are related to the same transition, they are joined with this symbol.

Figure 8.33 The GRAFCET language, a kind of sequential function chart. Once you understand the symbols, it's a reasonably clear way to describe a sequential operation. *(Courtesy Emmanuel Geveaux, LISI / ENSMA.)*

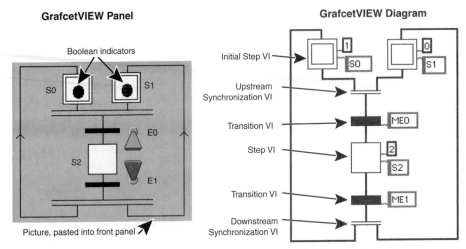

Figure 8.34 This is one of the GrafcetVIEW demonstration VIs. The panel graphic was pasted in, and Boolean controls and indicators were placed on top. Compare the LabVIEW diagram with actual GRAFCET programming in the previous figure.

GrafcetVIEW requires only a few subVIs to mimic the GRAFCET language, and they are wired together in a manner that matches the drawings. Figure 8.34 shows the panel and diagram of one of the GrafcetVIEW example programs. The most remarkable feature of this diagram is that it apparently implements **cycles**, or closed loops, in LabVIEW. As you may know, cycles of any type are illegal; just try wiring the output of a function or VI to its input. That's why G is properly called an **acyclic dataflow** programming language. So how did they do it? If you inspect the GrafcetVIEW subVI terminals, the wiring really does flow from inputs to outputs in the usual, legal manner, but the routing makes it *seem* cyclic. Amazing!

Once your GRAFCET logic diagram has been built into a subVI, you combine it with some run-time VIs that initialize the digital I/O hardware and others that actually execute the logic with appropriate synchronization. GrafcetVIEW uses a series of global variables to pass information about the logic to the run-time engine VIs. The final diagrams are very concise. The package also makes it easy to simulate the behavior of an application by replacing actual I/O points with Boolean controls and indicators. Such a validation technique is valuable in any control implementation.

Even if you're not planning to run your system with GrafcetVIEW, it makes a good learning and demonstration tool for the language. For more information on GRAFCET, see the Web page http://www.lurpa.ens-cachan.fr/grafcet.html. To obtain GrafcetVIEW, contact the National Instruments France office (see App. B).

Continuous Control

Continuous control generally implies that a steady-state condition is reached in a process and that feedback stabilizes the operation over some prolonged period of time. Single-loop controllers, PLCs, and other programmable devices are well suited to continuous control tasks, or you can program LabVIEW to perform the low-level feedback algorithms and have it orchestrate the overall control scheme. LabVIEW has some advantages, particularly in experimental systems, because it's so easy to reconfigure. Also, you can handle tricky linearizations and complex situations that are quite difficult with dedicated controllers. Not to mention the free user interface.

Most processes use some form of the PID algorithm as the basis for feedback control. I wrote the original PID VIs in the LabVIEW **PID Control Toolkit** with the goal that they should be easy to apply and easy to modify. Every control engineer has personal preferences as to which flavor of PID algorithm should be used in any particular situation. You can easily rewrite the supplied PID functions to incorporate your favorite algorithm. Just because I programmed this particular set (which I personally trust) doesn't mean it's always the best for every application. The three algorithms in the package came right out of Shinskey's book (1988). They are

- **PID**. An interacting positional PID algorithm with derivative action on the process variable only.

- **PID-Error Squared**.   Similar to the PID, but with a nonlinear proportional response. May exhibit superior performance with some nonlinear processes.

- **PID-External Reset Fdbk**.   Similar to the PID, but with external access to the input to the reset (integral) term. For use in control schemes where a controller might be switched off-line, resulting in reset windup or saturation.

There is also a **Lead/Lag** VI that is useful for more advanced control strategies, such as feedforward control. **Lead** refers to the phase shift associated with a single-pole highpass filter or differentiator, while **lag** refers to a lowpass filter or integrator. The Lead/Lag VI is also useful in simulations where you need to emulate the time-domain response of a first-order system. I won't elaborate on the contents of the whole package here. Just order the toolkit from National Instruments and read the manual.

You can use the math and logic functions in LabVIEW to implement almost any other continuous control technique. For instance, on-off or bang-bang control operates much like the thermostat in your refrigerator. To program a simple on-off control scheme, all you need to do is compare the setpoint with the process variable, and drive the output accordingly. A comparison function does the trick, though you might want to add hysteresis to prevent short-cycling of the output, as I did in the **Hysteresis OnOff Controller** VI in Fig. 8.35. This control algorithm is similar to the ones in the PID Control Toolkit in that it uses an uninitialized shift register to remember the previous state of the output.

platform\ control\Hysteresis OnOff Controller.vi

Designing a control strategy

The first step in designing a continuous control strategy is to sketch a flowchart of your process showing control elements (i.e., valves) and measurements. Then, add feedback controllers and any other required computations, as textbooks on the subject of process control recommend. The finished product will probably look like some kind of a P&ID diagram. Your goal is to translate this diagram into a working LabVIEW system. The question is whether to have LabVIEW do the real-time feedback control loop calculations or to have an external smart controller do the job. As we've already discussed, the choice depends on performance and reliability requirements, as well as personal preference.

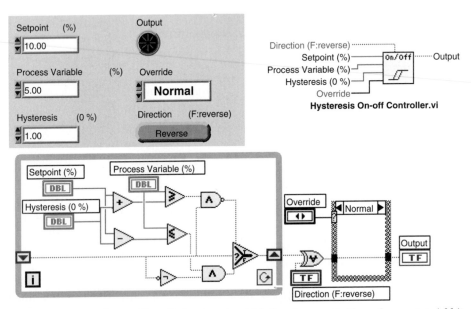

Figure 8.35 An on-off controller with hysteresis, which functions much like a thermostat. Add it to your process control library.

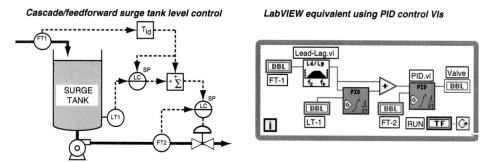

Figure 8.36 With the PID functions, you can map a control strategy from a textbook diagram to a LabVIEW diagram.

If you decide to have LabVIEW do the processing, translate the flow-chart into a LabVIEW block diagram using the PID control VIs with the math and logic functions of LabVIEW. An example of a translated control scheme is shown in Fig. 8.36. The only elements missing from this simplified program are the loop tuning parameters and auto/manual switching.

If you use an external controller, the program is even simpler. All you will have to do is write settings such as setpoints and tuning parameters and read the status of various measurements from the controller. You can supplement the functionality of the external controllers with math and logic in your LabVIEW program. In all cases, there will be the usual requirements for interlocking and initialization.

Your choice of control topology must complement the process, or the resulting performance may suffer from instability, overshoot, or long-term error, and it may be very difficult to tune or optimize. This is where training in process control strategies, books, and practical experience come into play. It's better to choose the right approach, if possible, rather than force-fitting a generic controller into a difficult process situation. Here is one very common example, taken from an exchange I had with someone on the info-labview mailgroup.

> *Question:* I am using the PID algorithm to control temperature. I would like to make a step change in controlled temperature as sharp as possible without overshoot and ripples.

Seems like a reasonable request, doesn't it? Well, it turns out that control engineers have been struggling with this exact problem for the last 60 years with mixed results and a very wide range of possible solutions, depending upon the exact character of the process, the available control equipment, and the sophistication of the engineer. I can list a few solutions that you might want to look into.

1. Use **feedforward** control techniques. Basically, this is where you characterize your process (temperature versus controller output, both static and dynamic response) and force the output to move in the right direction with the proper dynamics to compensate for the response of the process. Feedforward is quite safe as far as instability is concerned. The Lead/Lag VI was included in the PID Control Toolkit for such control schemes. You can read about it in several books (Corripio 1990; McMillan 1995; Shinskey 1988). I would use this technique as my first choice. Note that it's not available in single-loop controllers, but LabVIEW can do it.

2. Create a **PID tuning schedule**. Your process gain and temporal response vary with absolute temperature, which implies that your PID tuning must be different at every temperature. Process gain is the temperature change divided by the controller output change. Typically, the process gain is much lower at high temperatures, leading to sluggish response. Ideally, you create a mathematical model of your process either theoretically or by gathering empirical data. The model is then loaded into a simulation package (such as Matlab's SimuLink), and you derive optimal control parameters from that. For simpletons like me, I generally perform an open-loop step response measurement at several temperatures as described in the Toolkit manual and create a table of tuning parameters. Then I use a cluster array containing those PID parameters and index the array based on process temperature as shown in Fig. 8.37. In some processes, you can get away with constant values for the integral and derivative terms while varying only the proportional gain.

3. Another technique related to tuning schedules is sometimes called **approach control gain adjustment** or *startup management* and is included with some single-loop controllers. Basically, you reduce the controller's gain as the error (setpoint minus process variable) decreases. This can reduce overshoots (sometimes). It generally fails with processes that have a long dead time.

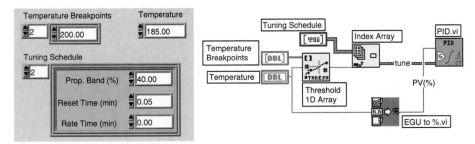

Figure 8.37 This is one way to implement a PID tuning schedule. Properly tuned, it yields good control performance over a wide range of operating conditions.

4. Ramp the setpoint. Many controllers will nicely track a ramped setpoint without the severe upset normally seen with large step changes in setpoint. You can add a profile to the ramp to further improve the response. Typically, the ramp's rate of change can be larger at the outset, decreasing as it nears the final value.

5. If you want to use a simple PID algorithm, use as much proportional gain as the process can stand without oscillation. The proportional term is your friend. Also, be sure to use derivative, which is a stabilizing feedback term. In fact, you can make a PD controller, thus avoiding the reset (integral) term which encourages overshoot. The trouble is, there will be some long-term error, which you can cancel by adding a DC bias to the controller output. The bias is determined experimentally. For one experiment, I generated lots of small steps in temperature, recording the process response, then determined a bias schedule, which can be a piecewise-linear fit. Resulting error is pretty low for an invariant process. An alternative is a control scheme that switches modes, from PD at startup to PID at steady-state. Again, a tuning schedule can perform this trick. Look up **batch controllers** in Shinskey (1988). Batch systems cannot tolerate overshoot.

6. Consider **fuzzy logic**, **predictive**, or **model-based** controllers. These are advanced control schemes beyond the scope of this book, but exceptional performance is possible, with enough effort.

Automatic parameter tuning is available from VI Engineering. Its Automatic PID Tuner can help you select optimum tuning parameters using a variety of well-known analysis techniques. Note that these tools are not for continuous, online use, so they won't automatically solve your *dynamic* problems.

Scaling input and output values.   All the functions in the PID Control Toolkit use inputs and outputs that are scaled by percentages, which is a convention in the process control world. This makes control calculations and subVI interconnections simpler because fewer intermediate scaling calculations are required. However, you must be sure to properly scale your physical measurements and outputs between engineering units (*EGU* is my abbreviation) and percent. The **EGU to %** and **% to EGU** VIs can help you with these conversions. (This is another place where BridgeVIEW simplifies life: it does all the scaling for you, automatically. I like that.)

Here is an example. You can use an MIO-16 channel to acquire a 4–20-mA signal with a 250-Ω current sampling resistor, giving a voltage of 1 to 5 V. Assuming that the returned value has been scaled to volts, you need to subtract 1.0 then multiply by 25 to scale the signal to percentage.

When calculating controller gain (proportional band), you can easily scale your physical measurement to percentage of span. The *span* is defined as the difference between the maximum and minimum measurements.

For example, consider a temperature transmitter scaled from −100 to +1200°C. Its span is 1300°C. A controller proportional band of 10 percent means that an input error of 130°C relative to the setpoint is just enough to drive the controller output to saturation, if you have also scaled your setpoint control in a similar manner.

Timing and performance limitations.   Always be wary of timing limitations and system performance when you are doing continuous control. DCS manufacturers rate their I/O controllers in terms of *loops per second,* referring to how many PID calculations can be performed in one second under average conditions. If the system software is well written, adding more loops will cause a gradual degradation of performance rather than an outright failure of any kind. It's much better to have a loop running 20 percent slow than not at all. Also, there should be no way to accidentally upset the steady operation of a continuous control algorithm. Real processes have plenty of unpredictable features without help from cantankerous software controls.

According to control theory, a sampled control system needs to run about 10 times faster than the fastest time constant in the plant under control. For instance, a temperature control loop is probably quite slow—a time constant of 60 s is common in a small system. In this case, a cycle time of about 6 s is sufficient. Faster cycling offers little or no improvement in performance. In fact, running all your control VIs too fast degrades the overall response time of your LabVIEW application. If you use the timing functions available in LabVIEW to regulate execution of a feedback algorithm, be aware of the actual precision available on your computer—typically 1 ms. Therefore, the fastest practical loop cycle times are on the order of 10 ms (100 Hz) for most LabVIEW systems. To go faster, you must obtain better timing information (from a hardware timer) or run the algorithm on a DSP board or use another external device with suitable performance. By the way, most industrial single-loop controllers cycle no faster than about 5 Hz (200 ms).

Here is an example of how timing accuracy can affect a control algorithm. A PID algorithm has two time-dependent terms, the *integral* and *derivative* responses. When the algorithm is called, the amount of time since the last execution, $\Delta t,$ is used in the calculation. If Δt is in error, then the response of the algorithm may also be in error. The error magnitude depends on the tuning parameters of the PID as well as the state of the process. If the process is in steady-state, then the time-dependent terms are zero anyway, and the timing error does not matter. But during a process upset, the response to timing errors can be very hard to predict. For best results, you had better make sure that your control loops run with a steady rhythm and at a sufficiently high speed.

The PID Control Toolkit supports either *internal* or *external* timing. Internal timing uses LabVIEW timing functions with the resolution limits previously mentioned. The advantage of this method is that the PID functions keep track of the elapsed time between each execution. External timing requires you to supply the actual cycle time (in seconds) to the PID function VI. If you are using the DAQ library, the actual scan period for an acquisition operation is returned by the **Waveform Scan** VI, for instance, and the value is very precise. Each PID VI has an input called **Cycle Time**. If **Cycle Time** is set to a value less than or equal to zero seconds (the default), internal timing is used. Positive values are taken as gospel by the PID algorithm.

The DAQ analog I/O example, **Analog IO Control Loop (hw timed)**, is an example of a data acquisition operation where you can place a PID loop on one of the input channels driving an analog output. The trick is to wire **actual scan rate** (in scans per second) from the DAQ VI, **AI Start**, through a reciprocal function to the PID VI. This provides the PID algorithm with an accurate time interval calibration. The data acquisition board precisely times each data scan so you can be assured that the While Loop runs at the specified rate. This example should run reliably and accurately at nearly 1 kHz, including the display.

Trending

The process control industry calls graphs and charts **trend displays**. They are further broken down into **real-time trends** and **historical trends**, depending on the timeliness of the data displayed. Exactly where the transition occurs, nobody agrees. Typically, a historical trend displays data quite a long time into the past for a process that runs continuously. A real-time trend is updated frequently and only displays a fairly recent time history. Naturally, you can blur this distinction to any degree through crafty programming. Historical trending also implies archival storage of data on disk for later review while real-time trending may not use disk files.

Real-time trends

The obvious way to display a real-time trend is to use a **Waveform Chart** indicator. The first problem you will encounter with chart indicators is that historical data is displayed only if the panel containing the chart is showing at all times. As soon as the panel is closed, the old data is gone. If the chart is updating slowly, it could take quite a long time before the operator sees a reasonable historical record. A solution is to write a program that stores the historical data in arrays, and then write the historical data to the chart with the **Chart History** item in an Attribute node. A second shortcoming of the chart indicator is that its *x* axis only counts samples and not actual elapsed time. Unless you know that the data is acquired at perfect, even intervals, the time axis is likely to be in error. Nevertheless, you should take advantage of strip charts whenever possible because they are simple, efficient, and require no programming on your part.

Consider using an **XY Graph** as a real-time trend display for extra versatility. You maintain arrays that contain some number of recent measurements and another array containing accurate timestamps. Then, it's a simple matter of graphing the data versus the timestamps whenever a real-time trend needs to be displayed. If the arrays are stored in global variables, any VI can read and display data from any channel at any time.

An important concern with this technique is memory management. If you just keep appending samples to your trending arrays, you will ultimately run out of memory. Also, the graphs will gradually become sluggish because of the large numbers of plot points. Some kind of length-limited array or a data compression technique is required for long-term operation.

A sophisticated method of trend data management uses a **circular buffer**. A *circular buffer* is an array that you program to act as if it is a continuous ring of data in memory rather than a straight line of finite length. Because the array never has to change size or be relocated, no real-time memory management is required and the performance is very good. The amount of data you can store is limited only by available memory. Unfortunately, the programming is rather complex: you must keep track of where the oldest and newest data are in the buffer and figure out a way to map the (physical) linear array into a (virtual) circular one.

platform\ cirbuff.llb

No problem! I did it for you, and it's included on the CD-ROM. The **Circular Buffer VI** has some interesting features that make it more useful than the regular strip charts. First, you preallocate all the required memory by setting the desired number of channels and samples per channel. Next, you periodically call the VI, supplying an array that contains the measurements for each channel. These are written to the next location in the circular buffer. At the same time, timestamps are recorded in a separate buffer. The timestamps are in epoch seconds, where zero is 1-Jan-1904. They are internally managed so you don't even have to supply a time measurement.

The interesting part comes when you want to read the data. The VI returns an array of data for any one channel and an array of timestamps suitable for *xy* plotting. The number of samples is adjustable, as is the start time of the returned array. That way, you can scroll back through time, looking at a window of data rather than trying to zoom in by using the graph controls. It's much faster, too, because the graph only has to display a limited number of points. If the buffer is sized for 10,000 samples, you would be hesitant to attempt to display them all at once.

Figure 8.38 shows the panel and diagram of an example VI that uses the Circular Buffer VI for real-time trending. Two independent While Loops store and retrieve data. Because the Circular Buffer VI is a kind of global variable, you can call it in read or write mode any place, any time. The data written here is a set of sine waves, one for each of the 10 channels defined. The buffer is initialized to contain 1000 samples per channel in this example. Every two seconds, a fresh set of values for all 10 channels is written.

The **Data Scroll** slider allows you to display a range of data from the past without disturbing the data recording operation. The **Points in Graph Window** control lets you display a selected number of data points on the graph. To properly display time, I used the graph's X Scale Formatting menu to set the scale to time/date. On the diagram, an Attribute node sets the *x*-axis minimum and maximum values. This technique guarantees correct interpretation of timing regardless of actual sampling intervals because a timestamp is stored with each sample, and data is always plotted versus timestamps.

Memory usage and performance are very good. There is a noticeably long delay when you call Circular Buffer with its initialization Boolean set to True. At that time, it allocates memory for the entire buffer, which can be quite large. The actual amount of memory used for the buffer itself is calculated from

$$\text{bytes} = (N + 1) \times M \times 8$$

where N is the number of channels and M is the number of samples per buffer. For instance, 10 channels and 10,000 samples per channel requires 880,000 bytes of memory. (The 1 in the formula accounts for the hidden timestamp buffer.) Only one duplication of the data array is required, and that is also static memory usage, so the actual memory usage is twice the result from the formula. When you write data, the **Replace Array Element** function is used, so no reallocation of memory is required. When reading, the amount of memory required is proportional to the number of data points to be displayed, a number significantly smaller than the size of the buffer for practical usage.

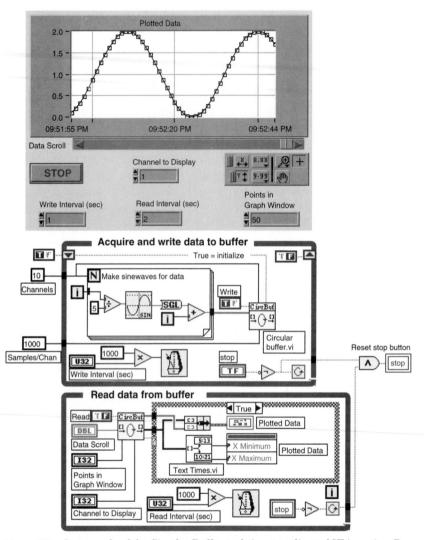

Figure 8.38 An example of the Circular Buffer real-time trending subVI in action. Parallel While Loops are used, one to write sinusoidal data for 10 channels, and the other to read a specified range from a channel for display. Note that the graphed data can be scrolled back in time.

Thanks go to Marty Vasey for his original work on this memory-based circular buffer concept. He designed it out of necessity: a customer was threatening bodily harm if they couldn't scroll back through their real-time data and do it *fast*. This program does the trick.

Historical trends

Memory-resident data is fine for real-time trending where speed is your major objective. But long-term historical data needs to reside on disk both because you want a permanent record and because disks generally have more room. You should begin by making an estimate of the space required for historical data in your application. Consider the number of channels, recording rates, and how far back in time the records need to extend. Also, the data format and content will make a big difference in volume. Finally, you need to decide what means will be used to access the data. Let's look at some of your options.

All of the basic file formats discussed in Chap. 3, "LabVIEW Programming Techniques" (datalogs, ASCII text, and proprietary binary formats), are generally applicable to historical trending. ASCII text has a distinct speed *disadvantage*, however, and is probably not suited to high-performance trending where you want to read large blocks of data from files for periodic redisplay. Surprisingly, many commercial PC-based process control applications do exactly that, and their plotting speed suffers accordingly. Do you want to wait several minutes to read a few thousand data points? Then don't use text files. On the other hand, it's nice being able to directly open a historical trending file with your favorite spreadsheet, so text files are certainly worth considering when performance is not too demanding.

LabVIEW datalog files are a better choice for random-access historical trending applications because they are fast, compact, and easy to program. However, you must remember that only LabVIEW can read such a format unless you write custom code for the foreign application or a LabVIEW translator program that writes a more common file format for export purposes.

The HIST package.   A custom binary file format is the optimum solution for historical trending. By using a more sophisticated storage algorithm such as a circular buffer or linked list on disk, you can directly access data from any single channel over any time range. I wrote such a package, called **HIST**, which I sell commercially.

The HIST package actually includes two versions: Fast HIST and Standard HIST. Fast HIST is based on the real-time circular buffer that we've just discussed, but adds the ability to record data to disk in either binary or tab-delimited text format. This approach works well for many data acquisition and process control packages. Based on a single, integrated subVI, Fast HIST has very low overhead and is capable of recording 100 channels at about 80 Hz to both the memory-based circular buffer and to disk. Utility VIs are included for reading data, which is particularly important for the higher-performance binary format files.

Standard HIST is based on a suite of VIs that set up the files, store data, and read data using circular buffers *on disk* rather than in memory. At startup time, you determine how many channels are to be trended and how many samples are to be saved in the circular buffers on disk. Sampling rates are variable on a per-channel basis. The use of circular buffers permits infinite record lengths without worry of overflowing your disk. However, this also means that old data will eventually be overwritten. Through judicious choice of buffer length and sampling parameters and periodic dumping of data to other files, you can effectively trend forever. (See Fig. 8.39.)

Data compression is another novel feature of Standard HIST. There are two compression parameters: **fencepost** and **deadband** for each channel (Fig. 8.40). *Fencepost* is a guaranteed maximum update time. *Deadband* is the amount by which a channel's value must change before it is updated on disk. The combination of these two parameters is very flexible. If deadband is zero, then the channel will be updated each time the **Store HIST Data VI** is called (as fast as once per second). If deadband is a very large number, then the channel will be updated every time the fencepost period passes. If you choose a moderate deadband value, then transients will be stored with high fidelity while steady-state conditions will be trended with a minimum frequency to preserve buffer space. Each time you store data, you update each channel's fencepost and deadband (data compression parameters), giving real-time control over which channels are being trended at what rates. Similar data compression techniques are found in BridgeVIEW and in many other process control packages.

Standard HIST includes all the necessary file services, such as file creation, and in addition, it allows you to restart historical trending with an existing set of files, picking up right where you left off. This is

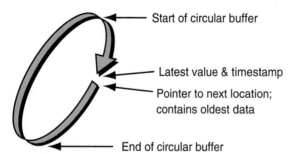

Figure 8.39 Representation of a circular buffer on disc. This buffer contains the values and timestamps from a single channel. Other channels would be located before and after this one. The program must keep track of pointers to the start, end, and next locations in the file.

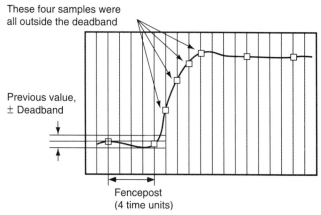

These four samples were
all outside the deadband

Previous value,
± Deadband

Fencepost
(4 time units)

Figure 8.40 Illustration of the action of deadband-fencepost data compression. Values are stored at guaranteed intervals determined by the fencepost setting, which is four time units in this example. Also, a value is stored when it deviates from the last-stored value by greater than ±deadband (measured in engineering units).

possible because the indexing information in the circular buffer data file is kept in a separate file. Also, you can run up to four separate HIST file sets simultaneously. That permits you to break up your data as you see fit. The data files are in a special binary format which makes reading the data in other programs impossible without writing special programs. For this reason, a VI called **HIST Data to Text File** is included to do a translation to tab-delimited text within LabVIEW. You could also write your own translation VIs since the data from every channel is readily available in ordinary LabVIEW arrays.

The Data Historian package. The **Data Historian** package was written by Lewis Drake of Process Automation Corporation specifically for long-term trending in process control applications. It uses a polynomial data compression technique to drastically reduce the volume of data, typically by a factor between 10 and 40 to 1 (BridgeVIEW uses a similar approach). It's available separately and is also included in the SCADA Toolkit, described at the end of this chapter.

Each tag, or channel, can be configured for automatic historical data storage at regular intervals by the Store Tag History VI, which saves data in a short-term RAM buffer. Data saved in the short-term buffer will eventually be compressed and saved to disk. The Compress History Data VI runs continuously as a parallel task. Periodically, it compresses data in the short-term buffer, using a quadratic polynomial curve fit. Each compressed block of value/time data is represented by four double-precision numbers and stored to disk. Typically, you can expect to achieve data compression ratios of between 10 and 40. Data is stored in binary files, with one file per tag per day, and all files are managed by the Write Compressed Data To Disk VI. To retrieve data, you use the Get Tag History VI. It reads data for a single Tag over a range specified by start time, end time, number of points, or sample time. Value/time data can be retrieved at any specified time resolution greater than one second. Data can also be retrieved in time blocks over which the data is averaged. For example, twelve 5-minute averages can be retrieved for a time span of one hour. This feature is useful for tabular reporting.

Statistical process control (SPC)

What do you do with tons of data you've collected from monitoring your process or test system? In manufacturing situations, **statistical process control** (*SPC,* also known as **statistical quality control**, or *SQC*) techniques are commonly used to emphasize the range over which the process is in control and what the process is capable of producing. Once a process is in control it can be improved. Statistical techniques are used to monitor the mean and variability of a process. There is always some random variability in a process, but there may also be other nonrandom causes (i.e., systematic errors) present which must be identified and corrected.

SPC techniques aid in identifying whether or not special causes are present so that the process is corrected only when necessary. A process parameter is usually plotted against *control limits*. If the process parameter exceeds these control limits, there is a very high probability that the process is not in control which means that there is some special cause present in the process. This special cause could be a new piece of equipment, a new untrained operator, or sundry other problems. Once a process is in control, SPC techniques can predict the yield or defect rate (in parts per million for example) of the process. There are also techniques for designing experiments in order to improve the process capability. SPC techniques are pretty popular these days with everybody trying to meet ISO 9000 quality criteria. Some good references for applying SPC techniques are listed at the end of this chapter (Montgomery 1992; Wheeler 1992).

The **Statistical Process Control Toolkit**, available from National Instruments, makes a great starting point for any SPC application (Fig. 8.41). It comes with a comprehensive set of VIs and examples and a thorough manual. Common presentation techniques for SPC are *control charts, Pareto analysis, histograms,* and other statistical calculations. To make your life easier, the toolkit includes a set of graph and

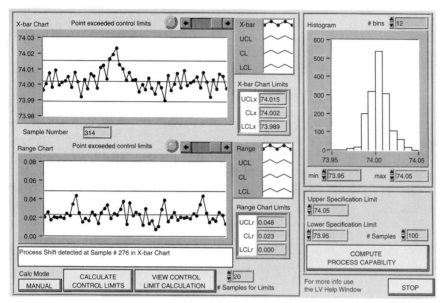

Figure 8.41   The SPC Toolkit demo VI displays several of the built-in chart types and statistical analysis techniques included in the package.

table controls that are customized for these standard presentations. Special VIs compute process statistics and prepare data for display. Most of the VIs expect arrays of data for processing, so you can either load historical data from disk or maintain recent data in memory, perhaps in a circular buffer. Application is straightforward, but be warned that the world of SPC can be daunting to the newcomer. Don't expect magical improvements in your process unless you study the references or get clear instructions from an expert.

Alarms

A vital function of any process control system is to alert the operator when important parameters have deviated outside specified limits. Any signal can be a source of an **alarm** condition, whether it's a measurement from a transducer, a calculated value such as an SQC control limit, or the status of an output. Alarms are generally classified by severity, such as *informative, caution,* or *warning,* and there are a variety of audiovisual alarm presentation methods available.

You should start by listing the signals and conditions in your process that require some form of alarm response and determining the appropriate responses. For analog signals and computed values, use the **comparison** functions (Fig. 8.42, top) to generate Boolean alarm flags.

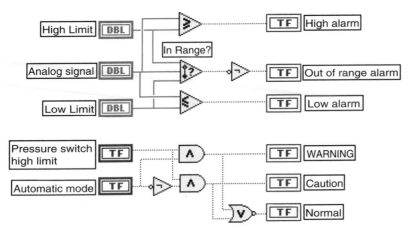

Figure 8.42 Using comparison functions to detect alarm conditions on analog signals (*top*). Digital signals are combined with Boolean logic to generate alarm states (*bottom*).

Digital signals, such as contact closure inputs, are combined with the logic functions such as AND, OR, and NOT to generate flags (Fig. 8.42, *bottom*). Naturally, you can combine these techniques as required.

Change-of-state detection is another important function that you may need for alarm generation. This enables you to react to a signal that is generally constant but occasionally undergoes a sudden deviation. To detect a change of state, the VI must remember the previous state of the signal, which implies the use of a Shift Register as shown in Fig. 8.43.

Whenever the input changes state, the appropriate Boolean indicators will be set to true. Because the logic functions are polymorphic, you can change all of the Boolean controls and indicators to arrays of

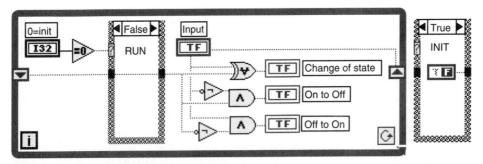

Figure 8.43 A change-of-state can be detected by comparing a Boolean's present value with its previous value stored in a Shift Register. Three different comparisons are shown here. This would make a reasonable subVI for general use.

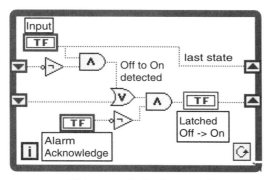

Figure 8.44 This example latches an alarm state until the Alarm Acknowledge input is set to True.

Booleans without rewiring these last two VIs (Figs. 8.42 and 8.43). This allows you to process several channels at once. If you *do* modify this example to use arrays, the initial array inside the Case must contain the desired number of elements.

An extension of this technique employs **latching**, used when you need the Boolean indicator to remain in the alarm state until a separate reset signal clears the alarm. The reset function is called **alarm acknowledge** in process control terminology. In Fig. 8.44, the upper Shift Register detects an off-to-on change of state as in the previous example. The lower Shift Register is set to True when a change of state occurs, and stays that way until **Alarm Acknowledge** is True. Again, the inputs and outputs could be arrays.

Using an alarm handler

Detecting alarms is the easy part. But there is a potential data distribution problem just like we encountered with input and output signals. If your system is fairly complex, alarms may be generated by several VIs with a need for display elsewhere. An **alarm handler** adds a great deal of versatility to your process control system much as the I/O handlers do for analog and digital signals. It acts as a centralized clearinghouse for alarm messages and status information.

Global Alarm Queue VI   One way to handle distributed alarm generation is to store alarm messages in a **global queue**. The approach is similar to the one we used with an output handler VI. Multiple VIs can deposit alarm messages in the queue for later retrieval by the alarm handler. A queue guarantees that the oldest messages are handled first and that there is no chance that a message will be missed because of a timing error. The alarm message queue in Fig. 8.45 was lifted directly

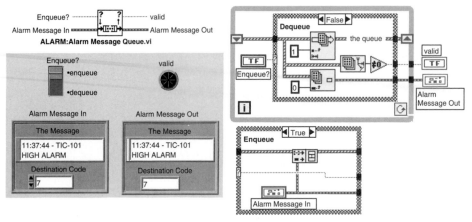

Figure 8.45 A global queue stores alarm messages. A message consists of a cluster containing a string and a numeric. In Enqueue mode, elements are appended to the array carried in the Shift Register. In Dequeue mode, elements are removed one at a time.

from the Global Queue utility VI that was supplied with older versions of LabVIEW. All I did is change the original numeric inputs and outputs to clusters. The clusters contain a message string and a numeric that tells the alarm handler what to do with the message. You could add other items as necessary. This is an unbounded queue which grows without limits.

Alarms can be generated anywhere in your VI hierarchy, but the I/O handlers may be the best places to do so because they have full access to most of the signals that you would want to alarm. You can combine the output of an alarm detector with information from your configuration database to produce a suitable alarm message based on the alarm condition. For instance, one channel may only need a high-limit alarm while another needs both high- and low-limit alarms. And the contents of the message will probably be different for each case. All of these dependencies can be carried along in the configuration. Once you have formatted the message, deposit it in the global alarm queue.

platform\control\alarms.llb\Alarm Handler.vi

Alarm Handler VI.   Once the alarm messages are queued up, an alarm handler can dequeue them asynchronously and then report or distribute them as required. The alarm handler in Fig. 8.46 performs two such actions: (1) it reports each alarm by one of four means as determined by the bits set in the **Destination Code** number that's part of the message cluster; and (2) it appends message strings to a string indicator, **Current Messages**, for direct display. This alarm handler would be called periodically by a high-level VI that contains the alarm message display.

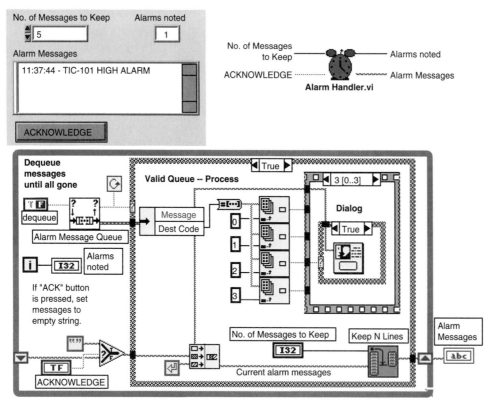

Figure 8.46   An alarm handler VI. It reads messages from the global alarm queue and reports them according to the bits set in the *Destination code*. Messages are appended to the *Current Messages* string. The subVI, Keep N Lines, keeps several of the latest messages and throws away the older ones to conserve space in the indicator for current messages.

There are other operations that an alarm handler might perform. If many other VIs need to display alarm messages or status information, you could have the alarm handler copy messages to a global variable for reading and display elsewhere. The handler could also call subVIs or set special global flags that cause some control operations to occur.

Another way to manage alarms is to use a global database as a repository for all your data. Each I/O point is represented by a cluster of information, and part of that information is a set of flags that represents alarm limits and alarm status flags. Alarm generators (probably part of the I/O handlers) set the alarm status flags based on the current value and the desired limits. Since the database is globally accessible, any VI can read the status of any alarm and take appropriate action. All of this is limited by the real-time performance of the database, so you should approach with caution.

Techniques for operator notification

The fun part of this whole alarm business is notifying the operator. You can use all kinds of LabVIEW indicators, log messages to files, make sounds, or use external annunciator hardware. Human factors specialists report that a consistent and well-thought-out approach to alarm presentation is vital to the safe operation of modern control systems. Everything from the choice of color to the wording of messages to the physical location of the alarm readouts deserve your attention early in the design phase. When automatic controls fail to respond properly, it's up to the operator to take over, and he or she needs to be alerted in a reliable fashion.

Boolean indicators are simple and effective alarm annunciators. Besides the built-in versions, you can paste in graphics for the true and/or false cases for any of the Boolean indicators. Attention-getting colors or shapes, icons, and descriptive text are all valuable ideas for alarm presentation.

You can log alarm messages to a file to provide a permanent record. Each time an alarm is generated, the alarm handler can call a subVI that adds the time and date to the message then appends that string to a preexisting text file. Useful information to include in the message includes the tag name, the present value, the nature of the alarm, and whether the alarm has just occurred or has been cleared. This same file can also be used to log other operational data and important system events, such as cycle start/stop times, mode changes, and so forth. BridgeVIEW stores alarms and other events in an event log file. SubVIs are available to access and display information stored in the event log.

The same information that goes to a file can also be sent directly to a printer. This is a really good use for all those old dot matrix serial printers you have lying around. Since the printer is just a serial instrument, it's a simple matter to use the **Serial Port Write** VI to send it an ASCII string. If you want to get fancy, look in your printer's manual and find out about the special escape codes that control the style of the output. You could write a driver VI that formats each line to emphasize certain parts of the message. As a bonus, dot matrix printers also serve as an audible alarm annunciator if located near the operator's station. When the control room printer starts making lots of noise, you know you're in for some excitement.

Audible alarms can be helpful or an outright nuisance. Traditional control rooms and DCSs had a snotty-sounding buzzer for some alarms, and maybe a big bell or Klaxon for real emergencies. If the system engineer programs too many alarms to trigger the buzzer, it quickly becomes a sore point with the operators. However, sound does have its place, especially in situations where the operator can't see the display.

You could hook up a buzzer or something to a digital output device or make use of the more advanced sound recording and playback capabilities of your computer (see Chap. 10, "Data Visualization, Image Processing, and Sound"). LabVIEW has a utility VI, **Beep**, that works on all platforms and serves as a simple annunciator.

Commercial **alarm annunciator panels** are popular in industry because they are easy to understand and use and are modestly priced. You can configure these units with a variety of colored indicators that include highly visible labels. They are rugged and meant for use on the factory floor. Hathaway/Beta Corporation makes several models, ranging from a simple collection of lamps to digitally programmed units.

That covers sight and sound; what about our other senses? Use your imagination. LabVIEW has the ability to control most any actuator. Maybe you could spray some odoriferous compound into the air or dribble something interesting into the supervisor's coffee.

Commercial Packages

Lewis Drake of Process Automation Corporation wrote an elaborate package called the Supervisory Control and Data Acquisition (SCADA) Toolkit. It provides a basic platform on which to build a custom process control application. The SCADA Toolkit consists of several libraries of VIs that implement key SCADA functions such as a real-time database, a data historian with data compression, alarm handling, report generation, and many other useful functions. To build a SCADA system, you must write drivers for the I/O devices being used and then combine them with Toolkit programs (standard drivers for DAQ boards, SCXI, and various PLCs are available). This approach can cut total system development time tremendously.

Like any real process control system, the SCADA Toolkit is based on a real-time database (Fig. 8.47). In this case, it's some big data structures stored in global variables which are accessible to all of the various tasks. The following functions are configurable for each Tag, or I/O point (tags can be physical I/O points or calculated values): conversion from source units (e.g., voltage) to engineering units, alarm scanning and message generation, filtering (lowpass, moving average, and median), and trending. All database configuration information is stored in a tab-delimited text file that can be read and modified by a spreadsheet. Typically, the Toolkit can handle a maximum of between 200 and 500 Tags, depending on your CPU. I found that the performance of the demonstration package was completely satisfactory, even on my older Macintosh. A quick check with the LabVIEW Profiler indicates that the database is quite

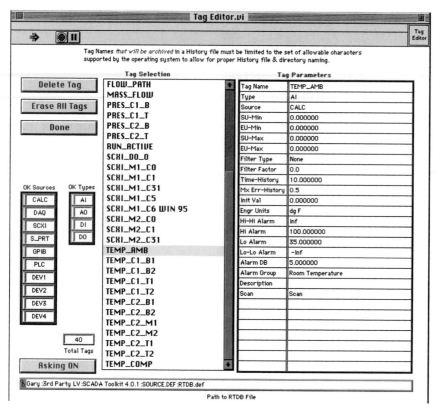

Figure 8.47 This is how you edit the real-time database in the SCADA Toolkit. Tags can be added, deleted, or modified on the fly.

busy, but Lewis did a nice job of allocating execution time so it doesn't get overloaded.

Trending is handled by the Data Historian, another Process Automation Corporation product that was described earlier in this chapter. It's nicely integrated with the database. The example application also includes an *Automatic Tag Report Generator*. It steps the user through the process of specifying a report header, selecting Tags for the report, selecting the report start and end times, and selecting the size of the time blocks used for averaging data for the report. Report data is retrieved from the Data Historian and formatted as specified into a text file for your permanent records. It's a nice way to summarize system performance over a standard period of a time.

The user's manual explains how to write device drivers and how to configure and use the included VIs. The SCADA Toolkit contains example device drivers for SCXI and DAQ boards, as well as a complete example SCADA system. Process Automation Corporation can provide driver development support if needed.

Bibliography

Boyer, S. A., *SCADA: Supervisory Control and Data Acquisition,* ISA Press, Raleigh, North Carolina, 1993. (ISBN 1-55617-210-9.)

Bryan, Luis A. and E. A. Bryan, *Programmable Controllers: Theory and Implementation.* C Industrial Text Company, 1988. (ISBN 0-944107-30-3.)

Corripio, Armondo B., *Tuning of Industrial Control Systems.* ISA Press, Raleigh, North Carolina, 1990. (ISBN 1-55617-233-8.)

Hedstrom, Brad, "LabVIEW to LabVIEW: TCP/IP Networking in LabVIEW," *LTR,* vol. 3, no. 3, summer 1995. (Back issues available from LTR Publishing.)

Hughes, Thomas A., *Measurement and Control Basics,* ISA Press, Raleigh, North Carolina, 1988. (ISBN 1-55617-098-1.)

McMillan, Gregory K., *Advanced Temperature Control,* ISA Press, Raleigh, North Carolina, 1995. (ISBN 1-55617-540-X.)

Montgomery, Douglas C., *Introduction to Statistical Quality Control,* John Wiley and Sons, New York, 1992.

Shinskey, F. G. *Process Control Systems,* McGraw-Hill, New York, 1988. (ISBN 0-07-056903-7.)

Wheeler, Donald J. and D. S. Chambers, *Understanding Statistical Process Control,* SPC Press, 2nd ed., 1992.

Physics Applications

Physics is Phun, they told me in Physics 101 and, by golly, they were right! Once I got started at LLNL, where there are plenty of physics experiments going on, I found out how interesting the business of instrumenting such an experiment can be. One problem I discovered is just how little material is available in the way of instructional guides for the budding diagnostic engineer. Unfortunately, there isn't enough space for me to do a complete brain dump in this chapter. What I will pass along are a few references: Bologna and Vincelli 1983; and Mass and Brueckner 1965. Particularly, I've gotten a lot of good tips and application notes from the makers of specialized instruments (LeCroy Corporation 1997). Like National Instruments, they're all in the business of selling equipment, and the more they educate their customers, the more equipment they are likely to sell. So, start by collecting catalogs and look for goodies like sample applications inside. Then, get to know your local sales representatives, and ask them how to use their products. Having an experienced experimental physicist or engineer on your project is a big help, too.

I'm going to treat the subject of physics in its broadest sense for the purpose of discussing LabVIEW programming techniques. The common threads among these unusual applications are that they use unconventional sensors, signal conditioning, and data acquisition equipment, and often involve very large data sets. Even if you're not involved in physics research, you are sure to find some interesting ideas in this chapter.

Remember that the whole reason for investing in automated data acquisition and control is to improve the quality of the experiment. You can do this by improving the quality and accuracy of the recorded data and by improving the operating conditions of the experiment. Calibrating transducers, instruments, and recording devices, as well as monitoring and stabilizing the physical parameters of the experiment all lead to better results. Having a flexible tool such as LabVIEW makes these goals much easier to achieve than in the past. Twenty years ago, we had computers, but they were so cumbersome to configure that the researcher needed a large staff just to support simple data acquisition. That meant less money and time available for improving the experiment, examining the data, and doing physics.

Special Hardware

In stark contrast to ordinary industrial situations, physics experiments are by their nature involved with exotic measurement techniques and apparatus. I feel lucky to come across a plain, old low-frequency pressure transducer or thermocouple. More often, I'm asked to measure microamps of current at high frequencies, riding on a 35-kV DC potential. Needless to say, some fairly exotic signal conditioning is required. Also, some specialized data acquisition hardware, much of which is rarely seen outside of the physics lab, must become part of the researcher's repertoire. Thankfully, LabVIEW is flexible enough to accommodate these unusual instrumentation needs.

Signal conditioning

High-voltage, high-current, and high-frequency measurements require specialized signal conditioning and acquisition equipment. The sources of the signals, though wide and varied, are important only as far as their electrical characteristics are concerned. Interfacing the instrument to the data acquisition equipment is a critical design step. Special amplifiers, attenuators, delay generators, matching networks, and overload protection are important parts of the physics diagnostician's arsenal.

High-voltage measurements. To measure high-voltage signals, you will need to reduce the magnitude of the signal to something that your ADC can safely and accurately accommodate. For most signals, resistive voltage dividers are the easiest to use. You can buy commercial high-voltage probes of several types. Those intended for routine AC and DC voltmeters, such as those made by Fluke-Phillips, are sufficient for frequencies up to about 60 Hz. Special high-voltage oscilloscope probes such as the Tektronix P6015 are available with divider ratios of 10, 100, and 1000 to 1 and are useful up to 20 kVDC, at frequencies up to 75 MHz, and with input impedances of 10 to 100 MΩ. All you have to do is match the output impedance (and capacitance, for high frequencies) to that of your data acquisition equipment, perhaps by using a suitable amplifier. A 'scope probe with a 1-MΩ resistor for termination works fine with a plug-in data acquisition board.

For measurements up to hundreds of kilovolts, you can buy high-voltage probes from Ross Engineering and others. These probes are compact (considering their voltage ratings) and are intended for permanent installation. As with 'scope probes, you have to match the output impedance for highest accuracy (Fig. 9.1).

Pulsed high voltages can be challenging because of their extra high frequency content. Resistive probes incorporate frequency compensation capacitors to flatten frequency response (as always, proper matching at the output is paramount). Capacitive dividers and custom-made pulse transformers may be optimum in certain cases.

If the measurement you are making is part of a floating system (that is, it is not referenced to ground), you will also need an **isolation amplifier**. Most commercial isolation amplifiers operate only at lower voltages, so they must be inserted after a voltage divider. Sometimes, you can float an entire measurement system at high voltage. This requires an isolated power supply for the electronics and typically incorporates a fiber-optic link for communications. Many accelerator experiments have been constructed around such systems.

Safety is your number-one concern in high-voltage system design. First, protect the personnel, then protect the equipment, then protect the data. Floating systems are probably the most dangerous because they tempt you to reach in and turn a knob—a sure way to an early grave. Cover all high-voltage conductors with adequate insulation and mark all enclosures with warning labels. Enclosures should be interlocked with safety devices that shut down and *crowbar* (short-circuit)

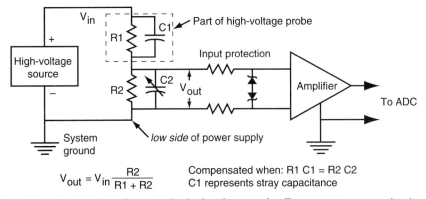

$$V_{out} = V_{in} \frac{R2}{R1 + R2}$$

Compensated when: R1 C1 = R2 C2
C1 represents stray capacitance

Figure 9.1 General application of a high-voltage probe. Frequency compensation is only needed for AC measurements. Always make sure that your amplifier doesn't load down the voltage divider.

the source of high voltage. Cables emerging from high-voltage equipment must be properly grounded to prevent accidental energization. At the input to your signal conditioning equipment, add over-voltage protection devices such as current-limiting resistors, zener diodes, Transorbs, metal-oxide varistors (MOVs), and so forth. Protect *all* inputs, because improper connections and transients have a way of creeping in and zapping your expensive equipment . . . and it always happens two minutes before a scheduled experiment.

Current measurements.   It seems that I spend more time measuring electrical currents than almost anything else in the physics lab. Whether it's high or low current, AC or DC, the measurement is always more complex than expected.

AC and pulse currents are often the easiest to measure because you can use a **current transformer**. Simple, robust devices, current transformers rely on a dynamic magnetic field to couple a fraction of the measured current in the primary winding into the secondary winding. Pearson Electronics makes a wide variety of solenoidal current transformers, usable up to tens of thousands of amps and 20 MHz. The output has an impedance of 50 Ω, so it matches well to wideband amplifiers and digitizer inputs. There are two limitations to current transformers. First, DC current tends to prematurely saturate the core, resulting in distortion and other amplitude errors. Second, these transformers are naturally AC-coupled, so you have to be aware of the low-frequency response limit of your transformer. Specifically, DC and low-frequency AC information will be lost. On the other hand, there is no concern about contact with high DC voltages unless the transformer insulation breaks down. Note that the output of a current transformer is an image of the current waveform, not an equivalent rms or average value. Therefore, you must record *waveforms,* not low-speed DC signals.

Hall Effect devices are used to make clamp-on DC-coupled current probes. These solid-state devices respond to the instantaneous magnetic field intensity surrounding a conductor, producing a proportional output. One commercial Hall Effect current probe is the Tektronix AM503S. With it, you can measure AC or DC currents from milliamps to 500 A at frequencies up to 50 MHz, and to do this you merely clamp the probe around the conductor. Though expensive, they are real problem solvers.

Current shunts, also known as **current viewing resistors**, are the simplest, and often cheapest, current transducers, consisting of a resistor that is placed in series with the source of current. The resulting voltage drop follows Ohm's Law, where the voltage is equal to the current multiplied by the resistance. You can make your own shunt for

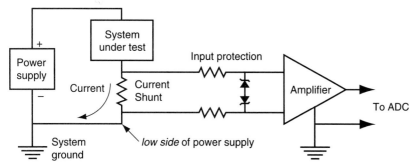

Figure 9.2 Signal conditioning for a current shunt installed on the preferred side of the system under test.

low currents by inserting a low-value resistor in the circuit. For high currents, up to thousands of amps, there are commercially made shunts available. Standard outputs are usually 50 or 100 mV at full current, so you may need an amplifier if your ADC system can't handle low-level signals. Try to connect the shunt on the *low side,* or ground return, of the power source to eliminate the common-mode voltage (Fig. 9.2). Note that this method is only feasible if the system under test or the power supply can be isolated from ground. If you must wire the shunt in series with the *high side* of the power source, you need an isolation amplifier (Fig. 9.3). Unfortunately, isolation amplifiers are expensive and they generally don't have very wide bandwidths.

High-frequency measurements. Many experiments involve the detection of pulsed phenomena, such as nuclear particle interactions, lasers, and explosions. The detector may sense ion currents or some electrical

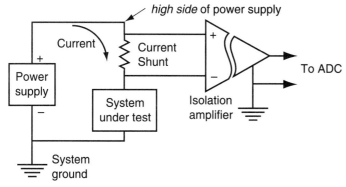

Figure 9.3 This example shows an isolation amplifier with a *high side* current shunt. The common-mode voltage is that which appears across the system under test and may exceed the capability of nonisolated amplifiers.

event in a direct manner, or it may use a multistep process, such as the conversion of particle energy to light, then light to an electrical signal through the use of a photomultiplier or photodiode. Making quantitative measurements on fast, dynamic phenomena is quite challenging, even with the latest equipment, because there are so many second-order effects that you must consider. High-frequency losses due to stray capacitance, cable dispersion, and reflections from improperly matched transmission lines can severely distort a critical waveform. It's a rather complex subject. If you're not well versed in the area of pulsed diagnostics, your best bet is to find someone who is.

There are a number of instruments and ancillary devices that you will often see in high-frequency systems. For data acquisition, you have a choice of acquiring the entire waveform or just measuring some particular characteristic in real time. Waveform acquisition implies the use of a fast **transient digitizer** or digitizing oscilloscope, for which you can no doubt find a LabVIEW driver to upload the data. Later in this chapter, we'll look at waveform acquisition in detail. Some experiments, such as those involving particle drift chambers, depend only on time interval or pulse coincidence measurements. Then, you can use a time interval meter, or **time-to-digital converter** (**TDC**), a device that directly measures the time between events. Another specialized instrument is the **boxcar averager**, or **gated integrator**. This is an analog instrument that averages the signal over a short gate interval and then optionally averages the measurements from many gates. For periodic signals, you can use a boxcar averager with a low-speed ADC to reconstruct very high frequency waveforms.

CAMAC

CAMAC (*Computer Automated Measurement and Control*) is an old, reliable, and somewhat outdated standard for data acquisition in the world of high-energy physics research. Way back in 1964, the European Standard of Nuclear Electronics (ESONE) committees decided that a genuine data acquisition standard was necessary. It's fortunate that nuclear physics researchers have traditionally cooperated on a worldwide basis: CAMAC was established as both a European standard (IEC 516) in 1975 and as a U.S. standard (IEEE 583) in 1967. These standards guarantee interoperability between the many brands of controllers and modules. Though the standard is quite old, it remains a very important player in research labs all over the world. LabVIEW has instrument drivers available for use with a variety of CAMAC instruments and controllers. To my knowledge, there are no other references available on the CAMAC driver library, so I've kept this book up-to-date. (See Fig. 9.4.)

Figure 9.4 CAMAC equipment in action with a LabVIEW system. *(Courtesy NASA.)*

CAMAC basics. Modules in a CAMAC system plug into a CAMAC crate which contains a power supply and a passive backplane, or dataway, with up to 25 slots. Slot 25 is reserved for the crate controller which is responsible for initiating and timing all command and data transfers over the dataway. The dataway consists of 24 read-write data (R) lines, 24 station address (N) lines, 5 function code (F) lines, 4 subaddress (A) lines, and 9 control and timing lines. One of the control lines is called the Look-at-Me (LAM) line and serves as a method by which a module can asynchronously request service from the crate controller (i.e., an interrupt). LAMs are frequently used to indicate that an operation is complete. The 32 available function codes are generally allocated to read, write, control, and test classes. Subaddress codes are used to access different channels or memory areas in a module or as a kind of subfunction code. A dataway operation takes exactly 1 μs which implies a maximum 1-MHz command or data rate. In each cycle, 8-, 16-, or 24-bit transfers may occur.

There are several types of crate controllers available. *Parallel* crate controllers connect directly to your host computer via a ribbon cable and plug-in adapter board. These offer the highest performance. An example is the Kinetic Systems 3922 with either the 2926 bus adapter for the PC or the 2932 bus adapter for the Macintosh NuBus (a LabVIEW driver is available from Kinetic Systems). This is an excellent controller with a 100-m range over a differential twisted-pair cable.

Serial crate controllers permit remote operation of a CAMAC crate over coaxial or fiber-optic links. (To my knowledge, nobody has written a LabVIEW driver for a serial crate controller.) Both parallel and serial controllers support multiple crates. *GPIB* crate controllers are the easiest way to connect CAMAC to LabVIEW-based systems, and that is what I'll discuss here. In all cases, the crate controller accepts simple commands to address the desired module (N-A-F codes), then proceeds to read or write data as requested. When a LAM occurs, serial or parallel controllers cause an interrupt on the host computer, while GPIB controllers can generate a service request (SRQ).

Another type of crate controller uses an embedded processor. Traditionally, LSI11 microprocessors were the standard for this application, but 80X86 controllers are available as well—an example is the Kinetic Systems 3966. This offers the advantage of local intelligence tightly coupled to the I/O subsystem, off-loading much real-time work from your host system and the communications link. The end result is much like a VXI system with an embedded controller. With sufficient processing power, it is very reasonable to set up a Windows-based LabVIEW system, right in the crate.

If you want to learn more about CAMAC, contact any of the manufacturers and request one of their introductory guides. You could also get a copy of the IEEE standard, but it's not what you would call user friendly.

Here's a bit of history. Back in 1987, when LabVIEW version 1.2 was around, Jack MacCrisken, one of the LabVIEW inventors, came to LLNL to ask us what instruments LabVIEW needed to support. I said, "CAMAC." Jack said, "What's that?" So, I sent them a CAMAC crate, a GPIB crate controller, and some modules for which to write drivers. And so the CAMAC library was born. Then, in late 1989, a beta copy of LabVIEW 2.0 appeared on my desk. I was desperate to replace our old LSI11/CAMAC-based data acquisition system, and the new features in 2.0 (particularly the fact that it was compiled) made LabVIEW the logical choice. So, Hank Andreski and I set about writing a general-purpose package, which was eventually christened **MacDALE** (Macintosh Data Acquisition for Laboratory Environments). MacDALE provided all the services you would expect—configuration management, support for lots of instruments (even non-CAMAC stuff), logging of user comments, file management, and so forth. I even went through the pain and suffering of a formal software release, so it's available (for a price) to anyone who wants a copy. Unfortunately, it's written in LabVIEW 2.1 for the Macintosh (with CINs), so it's impractical to port it to later versions of LabVIEW. Such is the fate of some very early LabVIEW applications which predated many of our modern programming practices!

Limitations and performance of CAMAC.   Though popular, CAMAC has a number of limitations that you should understand. First, its transfer rate is only 1 MHz, which translates to 2 megabytes per second for 16-bit transfers. If you are using a GPIB crate controller, this is of little concern because GPIB is limited to about 800 kilobytes per second. Parallel controllers and embedded processors run at the full speed of CAMAC. Second, it has a rather small (24-bit) address space, which limits your options regarding large memory modules. Third, the standard is rather old and sometimes perceived as obsolete. But judging by the number of new modules entering the market, CAMAC has a long life ahead.

Another limitation that is not unique to CAMAC is its extensive dependency on the host computer. Most CAMAC modules and crate controllers are *really dumb*. Many of the older ADC modules, for instance, can't even scan a list of channels or do multiple acquisitions. Instead, you have to send a command to read each and every sample, resulting in enormous overhead. Because LabVIEW runs on top of rather complex operating systems, each I/O operation is rather expensive in terms of execution time. On a fast Mac or PC using a GPIB crate controller, for instance, you can perform about 200 CAMAC writes or 100 reads per second. That's all. The good news is that each read or write operation can transfer a very large buffer of data using DMA, so the situation is not so bad for such modules as transient digitizers with large memories. What you need to avoid is the situation where you need to do lots of single-channel operations in a short period of time. That was acceptable on the old LSI11 systems, but must be avoided now.

When you read data from digitizers with large memories, throughput will rarely be limited by the performance of CAMAC, GPIB, or the overhead I/O calls because a single block read operation, with DMA support, is used. Limitations are more likely to come from your use of graphics and disk performance.

Manufacturers and modules.   There are still quite a few manufacturers of CAMAC equipment in the world today making hundreds of modules, and releasing new ones all the time. Some of the major players are Kinetic Systems Corporation (KSC), LeCroy, DSP Technology, AEON, and Joerger Enterprises.

The general functions that are available are ADCs, DACs, transient digitizers, time-to-digital converters, trigger generators, clock generators, delays, and signal conditioners. Modules are available with state-of-the-art gigasample per second digitizing rates. Consult the current instrument library listing to see what modules are supported with LabVIEW drivers. Also look at the info-labview FTP site, ftp.pica.army.mil, where you will find drivers for additional instruments and controllers.

In particular, there is a driver for the DSP Technology CC-488 GPIB crate controller, written by Tom Coradeschi, manager of the info-labview mailgroup.

My favorite crate controller is the Kinetic Systems 3988-G3A GPIB Crate Controller, with the LeCroy 8901A GPIB Crate Controller coming in second. The 3988 is the easiest to program if you have to write a driver, and it supports all of the CAMAC data transfer modes.

CAMAC drivers. The instrument library contains many CAMAC instrument drivers, most of which are based on the two most popular GPIB crate controllers, the KSC 3988 and the LeCroy 8901A. If you are lucky enough to be using a module that's already supported, it should pretty much be plug-and-go. If you need to write your own driver or add a function that is not already supported, study the 3988 or 8901A support libraries for tips and techniques. National Instruments has done its best to keep the driver libraries up-to-date and portable. Considering the fact that many of the drivers were written in LabVIEW 1.2 almost 10 years ago, and the fact that it does not own any of the instruments, it's amazing that there aren't more problems. I occasionally hear of trouble with LAM handling or GPIB timing problems, especially when a new version of LabVIEW or NI-GPIB ships. This is not surprising considering the complexity of the binary message protocols and the critical timing employed by most CAMAC controllers and modules. If you have trouble, post a note to the info-labview mailgroup where many CAMAC users hang out.

All of the driver VIs have a common method of addressing modules, using N-A-F codes. N is the slot number (1–25), F is the function code (0–31), and A is the subaddress (0–15). Consult the manual for your module to see what F and A codes are required for each operation. You can read or write data in 8-, 16-, or 24-bit words; be sure to use the right word length, because some modules return garbage in the unused bits. There are several data transfer modes to choose from. Single-word transfers are the simplest and do just what you would expect. Block-mode transfers are very efficient when you need to move a large buffer of data to or from a module's memory. Only one subVI call is required for a block-mode transfer. A simple driver for a DAC is shown in Fig. 9.5. It uses the 3988 crate controller driver in address scan mode, which writes an array of values to the eight outputs on a Kinetic Systems 3112 DAC.

Here are some tricks I've learned by suffering through the development of some big CAMAC drivers.

- Like many driver development efforts, it's easiest to start by sending simple commands. You could write a test VI that writes a command and then reads a response, much like the serial and GPIB test VIs. Start out by talking to a simple module, such as a digital output reg-

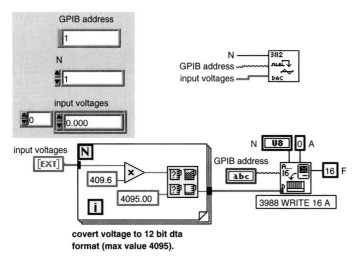

Figure 9.5 A simple driver, for the Kinetic Systems 3112 DAC using its 3988 GPIB crate controller. A driver using the LeCroy 8901A controller is also included in the library.

ister, that doesn't require complex programming to get some results. Also, you should spend plenty of time looking over drivers for similar modules to get an idea of how things should be done.

- Command ordering is important. Various registers need to be set in the right order, and LAMs must be enabled and disabled at the right time. Owing to the "dumbness" of some modules, failure to get the ordering right will result in a locked-up module. The LeCroy 6810 digitizer is such a module. When I wrote that driver, it took me two weeks to get the command ordering right; even LeCroy wasn't aware of some of the pitfalls!

- LAMs within one crate are hard to sort out. The problem is that, unlike the SRQ function in GPIB where each instrument has one address, a CAMAC crate gives you just one LAM for any module that needs attention. You have to send a special command to the crate controller to find out which module raised the LAM.

- Data byte ordering is selectable on the LeCroy 8901A and is sometimes other than what you expect on many modules. If you typecast a binary string from a digitizer into, say, an I16 array, don't be surprised if you have to swap bytes or words first. Misordered bytes make no sense when typecast.

- If you can't establish communications at all, begin by verifying that your GPIB interface is working by testing it with another GPIB instrument. Be sure that **readdressing** is enabled in your NI-GPIB driver. Check the crate controller GPIB address setting. And if all else fails, post a message to the info-labview mailgroup and see if anyone has any advice.

- A dataway display module is handy for debugging. It has indicator lights for each line on the CAMAC bus to indicate status.

Controller subVIs for the Kinetic Systems 3988. For the Kinetic Systems 3988, there are 12 read and 12 write VIs, divided into 8-, 16-, and 24-bit groups. Each group contains 4 read and 4 write operations which support the single, address scan, Q-stop scan, and Q-repeat transfer modes. Each subVI requires N, A, F, and the GPIB address. The read VIs have an additional binary input which selects between signed and unsigned data formats. The connector pane is standardized for all the read VIs.

Controller subVIs for the LeCroy 8901A. For the LeCroy 8901A, there are six read and one write VI. Read operations are divided into 8-, bit, 16-, and 24-bit groups, each containing two read operations which support the single- or block-mode transfers. The write VI writes a single word, up to 24 bits. There is no block-mode transfer for write operations. Each subVI requires N, A, F, and the GPIB address. The read VIs have an additional binary input which selects between signed and unsigned data formats. The connector pane is standardized for all the read VIs.

Other I/O hardware

Though CAMAC is still popular, there are some other I/O and signal conditioning standards that you may run into in the world of physics research. And, of course, there really is no limit on what you can use; it's just that there are some specialized functions that have been implemented over the years that aren't always commonly available.

FASTBUS. FASTBUS (ANSI/IEEE 960-1986) represents the fastest, highest-density data acquisition hardware available today. It is a modular standard featuring a 32-bit address and data bus, an asynchronous ECL backplane capable of 80 MHz (now that's *fast*), and the ability to use multiple masters or controllers. It's in fairly wide use in high-energy physics at such institutions as CERN in Switzerland. It's a sophisticated I/O system, but it's not for the casual user or those with miniature budgets. But if you get involved with the right laboratory, you may well see FASTBUS equipment. Currently, you can interface it to a LabVIEW system by using CAMAC as an intermediary or with a PC bus interface, either of which is perfectly acceptable.

VME. The VME bus is a high-performance, general-purpose computing platform. It's an open standard with modules available from hundreds of manufacturers offering state-of-the-art CPUs and peripherals, as well as a wide variety of I/O hardware. Interfaces for everything from analog I/O to image processing hardware to exotic military test equipment is available in VME format. You can use LabVIEW on VME-based CPUs that run a suitable operating system, such as Windows. Or, you can use an MXI interface to connect a desktop machine to a VME backplane. An example is the National Instruments VME-PCI8000, which connects a PCI-bus computer to a B-size VME system, making your computer appear as if it were plugged into the VME backplane. Your computer can directly access the VME address space, and VME bus masters can directly access the computer's memory and resources. Up to eight MXI-based devices, such as VXI crates, can be daisy-chained into such a system. To access devices on the VME bus, you use NI-VXI/VISA drivers. VISA and VXI drivers are discussed in detail in Chap. 5, "Instrument Drivers."

VXI. VXI is taking over the title of workhorse data acquisition interface for physics applications, particularly when high-performance transient digitizers are required. It's a new standard, well-planned, supported by dozens of major manufacturers, and offers many of the basic functions you need. And, of course, there is excellent LabVIEW support. Drivers are available for many instruments and PCs can be installed right in the crate. An application written by Los Alamos National Laboratory, described later in this chapter, makes extensive use of VXI equipment.

NIM. Another older standard still in use in the physics community is the **NIM (Nuclear Instrumentation Manufacturers)** module format, originally established in 1964. It's not an I/O subsystem like CAMAC or VXI; instead, it's a modular signal conditioning standard. Modules are either full- or half-height and plug into a powered NIM bin with limited backplane interconnections. Because the CAMAC format was derived from the earlier NIM standard, NIM modules can plug into a CAMAC crate with the use of a simple adapter.

Many modern instruments are still based on NIM modules, particularly nuclear particle detectors, pulse height analyzers, and boxcar averagers such as the Stanford Research SR250. I still use them in the lab because there are so many nice functions available in this compact format, such as amplifiers, trigger discriminators, trigger fanouts, and clock generators.

Field and Plasma Diagnostics

Among the many low-speed applications of LabVIEW in physics are those that deal with **field mapping** and **DC plasma diagnostics**.

These applications combine data acquisition with motion control for field mapping, and the generation of ramped potentials for plasma diagnostics. There are many variations on these experiments, so I'll just cover a few simple applications that might give you some insight as to how LabVIEW might help out in your lab.

Step-and-measure experiments

When you have a system that generates a static field or a steady-state beam, you probably will want to map its intensity in one, two, or three dimensions, and maybe over time as well. I call these step-and-measure experiments because they generally involve a cyclic procedure that moves a sensor to a known position, makes a measurement, moves, measures, and so forth, until the region of interest is entirely mapped. Some type of **motion control** hardware is required, along with a suitable probe or sensor to detect the phenomenon of interest.

Motion control systems.   There are many actuators that you can use to move things around under computer control—the actuators that make robotics and numerically controlled machines possible.

For simple two-position operations, a pneumatic cylinder can be controlled by a solenoid valve that you turn on and off from a digital output port. Its piston moves at a velocity determined by the driving air pressure and the load. Electromagnetic solenoids can also move small objects back and forth through a limited range.

But more important for your step-and-measure experiments is the ability to move from one location to another with high precision. Two kinds of motors are commonly used in these applications, **stepper motors** and **servo motors**. Think of a stepper motor as a kind of digital motor. It uses an array of permanent magnets and coils arranged in such a way that the armature (the part that moves) tends to snap from one location to the other in response to changes in the polarity of the DC current that is applied to each coil. Stepper motors are available with anywhere from 4 to 200 steps per revolution. Linear stepper motors are also available. Steppers have the advantage of simplicity and reasonable precision. Their main disadvantages are that you can't position them with infinite resolution and their speed is somewhat limited, typically 1000 to 2000 steps per second. There is one option for increasing resolution, called **microstepping**. With microstepping, the effective steps per revolution can be increased 10 times, and sometimes more. This requires special control hardware and sometimes compromises the performance of the motor with regard to torque.

Servo motors are similar to ordinary motors except that they are intended for variable speed operation, down to and including stalled, for indefinite periods. Both AC and DC servo motors are in wide use. A servo system also includes a positional or velocity feedback device, such as a shaft encoder or tachometer, to precisely control the motion of the shaft. (Such feedback may also be used with stepper motors.) With the use of feedback, servo motor systems offer extremely high precision and the ability to run at high speed. Their disadvantage is the requirement for somewhat complex control circuitry.

The next item you need to select is a motion controller (Fig. 9.6). It may take the form of a packaged system with RS-232 or GPIB communications from companies such as nuLogic, Parker Compumotor, or Klinger, or as plug-in boards for the PC and Mac from companies such as nuLogic and Parker Compumotor. Motor controllers are also available in various modular formats such as CAMAC, VME, and VXI. Lab-VIEW drivers are available for many of these devices; we'll discuss some of them later.

With any motor, you also need a power supply—also known as an *amplifier*—which is a power electronics package to drive the coils of the motor in an appropriate fashion. The amplifier supplies current to the motor, provides signal conditioning for encoders or tachometers, and isolates the sensitive I/O ports of the motion controller from the harsh external world.

For basic control of stepper motors or servo motors, several products from **nuLogic** are available. For many years, it has supplied plug-in boards for the PC (pcControl and pcStep) and for the Macintosh (nuControl and nuStep). The nuControl and pcControl series of boards are four-axis DC servo motor controllers that support quadrature encoders for position and velocity feedback. The nuStep and pcStep boards are four-axis stepper motor controllers. A unique feature of the

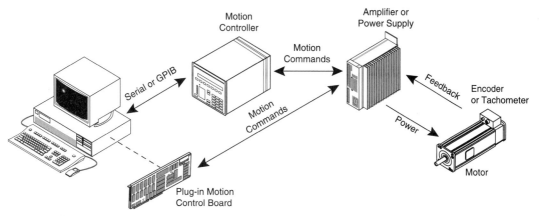

Figure 9.6 A typical motion control system consists of a computer, a controller (internal or external), an amplifier or power supply, and a motor, perhaps with an encoder or tachometer for feedback.

stepper control boards is the ability to tailor the acceleration profile to match the torque versus speed characteristics of your stepper motor. This minimizes the time spent in acceleration and deceleration phases of a point-to-point move. All of these boards have onboard intelligence, supporting indexing, velocity profiling, limit switches, and home switches. You can program the boards with a low-level communications packet protocol (if you are masochistic), or you can just use nuLogic's **Motion VIs** with LabVIEW. The Motion VI libraries are broadly divided into support for servos and steppers, and demonstration VIs are included to help you get started. The nuControl servo support includes interactive PID control tuning and Bode (gain and phase) analysis, trajectory control (acceleration and velocity), and limit switch functions. The nuStep library is similar, except that stepper motors don't necessarily require the extensive feedback control features.

For more sophisticated motion control, consider a fully programmable controller in the form of an external box or plug-in board. These systems permit you to preprogram very complex motion control procedures and applications that require no intervention from the host computer. This alleviates all kinds of timing problems since the motion controller includes a real-time operating system and computer. You can, of course, send individual low-level commands if desired.

A comprehensive motion control product line comes from **Parker Compumotor**. It makes a full range of stepper and servo motors, amplifiers, indexers, motion controllers, and software products. Of particular interest to the LabVIEW user are the 6000-series controllers, for which the **Motion Toolbox** provides extensive programmability. Within the 6000 series, you can choose from stepper or servo controllers in the form of either plug-in boards (ISA bus) or as external units with RS-232 communications. Either two or four axes with encoder feedback are available in a single controller, and they also include 48 digital I/O lines and four analog inputs.

Written by Dan Snider of **Snider Integration**, Motion Toolbox supports all features of the 6000-series controllers. You can wire up sequences of motion commands on a LabVIEW diagram, or for better real-time performance, download complete program files. To develop a program, you can use one of Compumotor's proprietary Windows-based applications (Motion Architect or CompuCAM), either of which can save multiple, complex programs in a text file. Motion Toolbox can then download those files, after which LabVIEW acts as a supervisory system (Fig. 9.7).

nuLogic FlexMotion boards bring extensive programmability to PCs (ISA or PCI bus) or Macintoshes (PCI bus). Each board can handle up to 10 axes of servo or stepper motors in any combination, with optional encoders, plus general-purpose analog, digital, and counter-

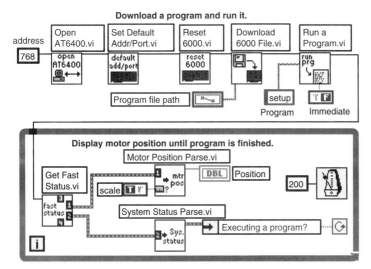

Figure 9.7   Motion Toolbox for Compumotor 6000-series boards allows you the option of downloading and executing programs with LabVIEW in a supervisory role.

timer I/O. (The general-purpose functionality rivals that of an MIO-16 DAQ board.) Programming is facilitated by Windows DLLs and drivers for many popular languages including LabVIEW. nuLogic also offers all the necessary interface hardware including cables and amplifiers compatible with a wide range of motors and encoders.

Figure 9.8 shows an example of a FlexMotion application. Like any programmable motion controller, you can load a sequence of commands into a buffer on the FlexMotion board, and then have it execute that sequence autonomously. The first VI in the upper left-hand corner (begin_store) tells the board that all subsequent commands are to be stored, not executed immediately. Several trajectory commands are sent next, including acceleration, deceleration, velocity, and so forth. Finally the end_store VI tells the board to terminate command storage. The sequence can now be initiated through software by calling the run_prog VI, or you can configure the board to run the program when a hardware trigger occurs.

A few other motion control systems are also supported by LabVIEW drivers. In the driver library, you'll find VIs for several models from **Aerotech Unidex** and **Newport Corporation**. For other products, check with your favorite manufacturer or at the info-labview FTP site, ftp.pica.army.mil for freeware solutions.

Reading encoders.   A recurring theme in the world of motion control is reading an **encoder**. Encoders can be of the **incremental** or **absolute**

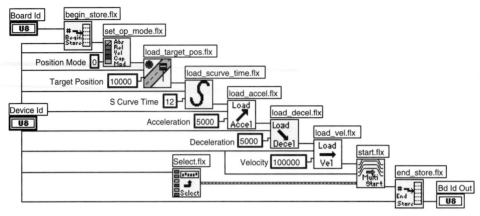

Figure 9.8   The Motion VIs from nuLogic control its FlexMotion board. This example stores a motion sequence for later execution.

type. Incremental encoders produce a continuous train of pulses when moved while absolute encoders have a parallel output that directly tells you the absolute position of a shaft or linear actuator. Incremental encoders typically have two outputs that are 90 degrees out of phase, in which case they are called *quadrature* encoders. The phase shift permits determination of direction, assuming that you have the proper readout logic.

To read an encoder with LabVIEW you have several choices. First, you can use any of the motion control products described previously. Second, you can buy a special-purpose board or module. Third, you can use a general-purpose digital I/O board.

One external module that's easy to use is part of the ControlNet system from Group3 Technology (its general product line was described in Chap. 2, "Inputs and Outputs"). It makes an encoder board that accepts four sets of quadrature pulse trains and it has LabVIEW drivers available.

For plug-in DAQ boards, you can use the onboard counter-timers and a driver library from National Instruments called Encoder.llb, which you can find on ftp.natinst.com. The driver uses two cascaded counters and keeps track of the absolute count with proper attention to direction. The only thing it doesn't do is *resolution enhancement,* or *rate multiplication,* which requires more elaborate (and dedicated) logic available only in specialized hardware.

Motion application: An ion beam intensity mapper.   One lab that I worked in had a commercially made ion beam gun that we used to test the sputter rate of various materials. We had evidence that the beam had a nonuniform intensity cross section (the *xy* plane), and that the beam diverged (along the z axis) in some unpredictable fashion. In order to obtain quality data from our specimens, we needed to characterize the beam intensity in x, y, and z. One way to do this is to place sample coupons (thin sheets of metal or glass) at various locations in the beam and weigh them before and after a timed exposure to obtain relative beam intensity values. However, this is a tedious and time-consuming process that yields only low-resolution spatial data. Preliminary tests indicated that the beam was steady and repeatable, so high-speed motion and data acquisition was not a requirement.

Our solution was to use a plate covered with 61 electrically isolated metal targets (Fig. 9.9). The plate moves along the z axis, powered by a stepper motor that drives a fine-pitch lead screw. The stepper motor is powered by a Kinetic Systems 3361 Stepper Motor Controller CAMAC module. Since the targets are arranged in an xy grid, we can obtain the desired xyz mapping by moving the plate and taking data at each location. Each target is connected to a negative bias supply through a 100-Ω current-sensing resistor, so the voltage across each resistor is 100 mV/mA of beam current. Current flows because the tar-

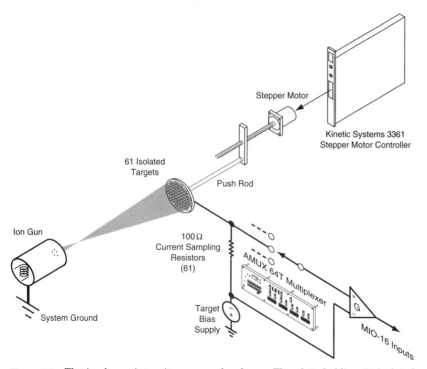

Figure 9.9 The ion beam intensity mapper hardware. The plate holding 61 isolated probes moves along the axis of the ion beam. Current at each probe is measured at various positions to reconstruct a 3D picture of the beam intensity.

gets are at a potential that is negative with respect to the (positive) ion gun, which is grounded. A National Instruments AMUX-64T samples and multiplexes the resulting voltages into an NB-MIO-16 multifunction board. The bias voltage was limited to less than 10 V because that's the common-mode voltage limit of the board. We would have liked to increase that to perhaps 30–50 V to collect more ions, but that would mean buying 61 isolation amplifiers.

platform\ ionprobe.llb\ Ion Probe Experiment

The front panel for this experiment is shown in Fig. 9.10. Two modes of scanning are supported: unidirectional or bidirectional (out-and-back), selectable by a Boolean control (**Scan Mode**) with pictures pasted in that represent these motions. A horizontal fill indicator shows the probe position as the scan progresses to cover the desired limits.

Examine the diagram of the main VI in Fig. 9.11. An overall While Loop keeps track of the probe location in a shift register, which starts at zero, increases to a limit set by **Total Range**, then steps back to zero if a bidirectional scan is selected. The VI stops when the scan is finished, then returns the probe to its starting location. Arithmetic in the upper half of the loop generates this stepped ramp.

The Sequence structure inside the main loop has three frames. Frame zero commands the motor controller to move to the new position. Frame one polls the motor controller, awaiting the *done* flag, which indicates that the move is complete. If the VI encounters a limit switch, it tells the user with a dialog box and execution is aborted.

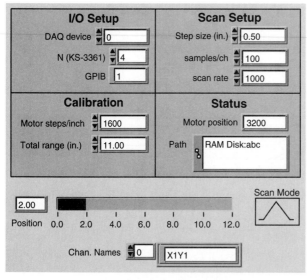

Figure 9.10 Front panel of the ion beam intensity scan VI. The user runs the VI after setting all the parameters of the scan. A horizontal fill indicator shows the probe position.

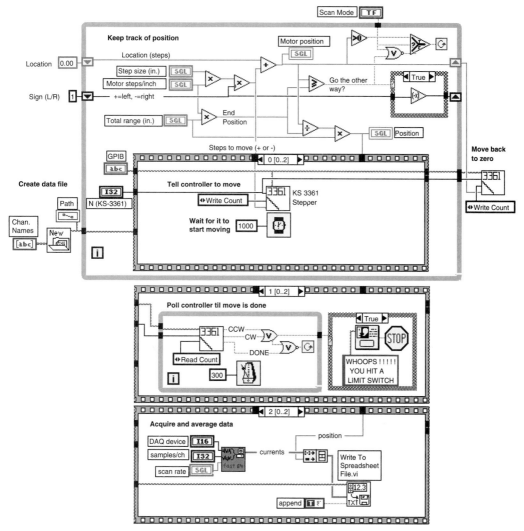

Figure 9.11 Diagram of the ion beam intensity scan VI. The While Loop executes once for each step of the positional ramp. The sequence moves the probe and acquires data.

Frame two acquires data by calling a subVI that scans the 64 input channels at high speed and averages the number of scans determined by a front panel control. Finally, the position and the data are appended to a data file in tab-delimited text format for later analysis. As always, the format of the data was determined beforehand to assure compatibility with the analysis software.

Preliminary plotting of the data was performed in another Macintosh application, Delta Graph, because it has 3D graphics capability and is very easy to use. Serious analysis and model simulations were performed on mainframe computers. This application was actually written several years ago, before Metric Systems created **Surface-View**, a LabVIEW add-on package that permits live 3D plotting. SurfaceView could easily be integrated into this program, giving the experimenter a progressive real-time picture of the beam's intensity. SurfaceView is discussed in Chap. 10, "Data Visualization, Imaging, and Sound."

For your convenience, I've placed a copy of the ion beam probe experiment on this book's CD-ROM. I included a dummy version of the KS3361 motor driver, so you can run the VI without that specialized module. You could easily replace the KS3361 subVI with VIs from one of the motion control packages we've already discussed.

Plasma potential experiments

The plasma we're talking about here doesn't flow in your veins. This plasma is the so-called fourth state of matter, where most all of the atoms are ionized. Plasma is formed by depositing sufficient energy into a substance (usually a gas) to rip away one or more electrons from the atoms, leaving them positively charged. The ionizing energy may come from an electrical discharge (an electron bombardment) or some form of ionizing radiation, such as light, gamma rays, or nuclear particles. The ions and electrons in a plasma love to recombine and react with other materials, so most plasma experiments are performed in a vacuum chamber with a controlled atmosphere containing only the desired gaseous species.

Some parameters that we like to determine in experiments are the plasma space potential, electron temperature, floating potential, and ion and electron densities. A very simple plasma diagnostic technique, the **Langmuir probe**, makes most of these measurements simple. The method involves the measurement of ion and/or electron current flowing in a small metal probe that is positioned in contact with the plasma. By varying the voltage (potential) applied to the probe and measuring the current, a curve called the *probe characteristic* is acquired. All you need is a variable voltage source, a sensitive current monitor, and a recording mechanism (anyone for LabVIEW?). Figure 9.12 shows how a simple Langmuir probe experiment might be connected.

Electrically, the most important piece of equipment is the voltage source that drives the probe. Depending on the experiment, you may need a source that can produce anywhere from ± 10 V at 10 mA up to ± 50V at 100 mA, or greater. Ordinary DACs, such as those built into a typical plug-in board, can only reach ± 10 V and a few mA, which may be sufficient for some laboratory experiments. For low-speed DC exper-

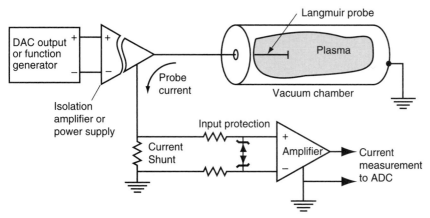

Figure 9.12 Basic electrical connections for a Langmuir probe experiment. The probe voltage is supplied by an isolation amplifier, programmable power supply, or function generator with a large output voltage swing.

iments, I like to use a laboratory power supply with an external analog input driven by a DAC. The output of such a supply is isolated from ground and is nearly bullet-proof. For experiments where you need a high-speed ramp waveform or pulse, you may need a function generator and a high-performance amplifier. As for the current-sensing function, pick a shunt resistor that only drops a fraction of a volt at the expected probe current ($R = V/I$), and follow it with the usual differential amplifier on your DAQ board or signal conditioner. Input protection is a good idea because the plasma source generally has a high-voltage source. Accidental contact with any high-voltage elements (or arcing) will likely destroy the amplifier.

To obtain the Langmuir probe characteristic, your LabVIEW program will have to generate a ramp waveform. Steady-state plasma experiments can be performed at low speeds over a period of seconds or minutes, so it's practical for your program to calculate the desired voltage and drive an output device. Figure 9.13 shows a simple V-I scan experiment that uses a precalculated array of values representing a ramp waveform that is sent to a DAC repeatedly. You can use any conceivable waveform to initialize the data array. Nested For Loops step through the values. After each step, a measurement is taken from the system (for instance, the current from a Langmuir probe). Inside the inner For Loop the new voltage is written to the output, then the resulting probe current is measured. Error I/O links the DAC Out and Read Probe sub-VIs so that they execute in the proper order. If extra settling time is required before the measurement, add a suitable delay between the DAC Out and Read Probe VIs.

The XY Graph (**current versus voltage**) acts like a real-time *xy* recorder. Since LabVIEW doesn't have a built-in *xy* strip chart, you can

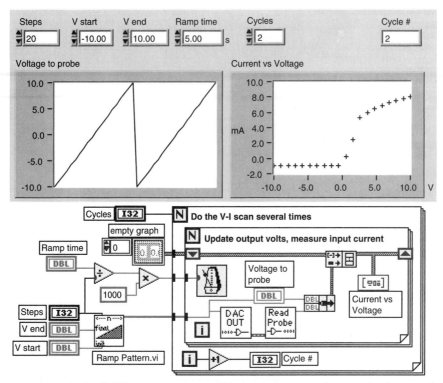

Figure 9.13 A simple V-I scan experiment. This is another way of generating low-speed, recurrent ramps, using a precalculated array of output voltages. Values are sent to a DAC repeatedly, and the response of the system under test is measured and recorded after each output update. The current versus voltage graph acts like a real-time *xy* chart recorder.

simulate one by updating the graph each time the inner For Loop executes. A shift register carries the accumulated array of clusters, where the cluster contains *x* (voltage) and *y* (current) data. An empty graph constant initializes the shift register. If you don't care to see the graph update for every sample point, put it outside the inner For Loop and let the cluster array build itself on the border of the loop. This is much faster and more efficient, too.

The Read Probe subVI acquires and scales the current measurement. If you want to store the data on disk, that subVI would be a logical place to write the data to a file. Outside the For Loops, you would open a suitable file and probably write some kind of header information. Remember to close the file when the VI is through.

In faster experiments, LabVIEW may not have enough time to directly control the stimulus and response sequence. In that case, you can use a couple of different approaches, based on plug-in data acquisition boards or external, programmable equipment.

The data acquisition library supports buffered waveform generation as well as buffered waveform acquisition on plug-in boards with DMA. Essentially, you create an array of data representing the waveform, then tell the DMA controller to write the array to the DAC, one sample at a time, at a predetermined rate. Meanwhile, you can run a data acquisition operation also using DMA that is synchronized with the waveform generation. Synchronization of the input and output operations can be determined three possible ways.

- The DAC update clock is externally wired to an input (SCANCLK) which triggers a scan of the ADC. Each time a new step value in the ramp is generated, the ADC collects one value from each defined input channel (i.e., one scan).
- The ADC scans continuously, and its clock output triggers the DAC updates.
- An external input is supplied to both the ADC and DAC clocks. The signal can be derived from an onboard counter-timer set up as a pulse generator or from an external pulse generator.

 **platform\ daq\Synchronized AI_AO.llb**

The VI in Fig. 9.14 uses the first method where DAC updates trigger ADC scans. The controls allow you to specify the ramp waveform's start and stop voltages, number of points, and the DAC update rate. Multiple cycles can be generated, and each cycle is plotted independently. For the analog inputs, you can acquire data from one or more channels with adjustable scan rate and adjustable number of points to acquire. Only one channel is plotted in this example, but data from all scanned channels is available on the diagram.

This example makes effective use of the intermediate-level data acquisition functions. Two tasks are defined, one for input and one for output. Error I/O controls the execution sequence and, of course, handles errors. Synchronization of the input and output operations is determined by the DAC update clock which is externally wired to an input which clocks each scan of the ADC. Each time a new step value in the ramp is generated, the ADC collects one value from each defined input channel (i.e., one scan). Referring to the diagram, here are the details of the program's steps:

1. The **Ramp Pattern** VI (from the Signal Generation VIs in the Analysis library) creates an array of values corresponding to a ramp waveform. You could use other functions if you needed a different waveform.

2. **AI Config** sets up the analog input hardware on the board for the desired number of channels and allocates a data acquisition buffer that's sized for the number of scans to be acquired.

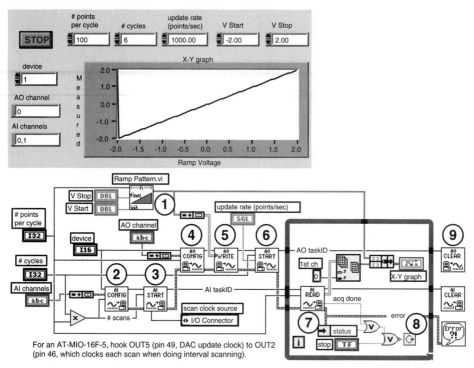

Figure 9.14 Using the Data Acquisition library and an AT-MIO-16F-5 board, this VI simultaneously generates a ramp waveform and acquires data from one or more analog inputs. Only one external jumper connection is required; note that the pin number and signal name vary slightly between models of DAQ boards.

3. **AI Start** begins the buffered acquisition process that was defined by AI Config. The Trigger Type is set to *2* (I/O connector) which tells the board to use an external scan clock.

4. **AO Config** sets up the analog output hardware on the board and allocates a data buffer sized for the number of points to generate.

5. **AO Write** loads the ramp waveform into the output buffer in preparation for waveform generation.

6. **AO Start** starts the buffer waveform generation process that was defined by AO Config. The number of buffer iterations is set by the **Number of Cycles** control, meaning that the waveform will be produced several times.

7. **AI Read** fetches the acquired data from the buffer and makes it available to the XY Graph, where the measured voltage is plotted versus the calculated scan ramp. AI Read makes an estimate (based on the number of points to acquire and the sample rate) of how long

to wait for data before timing out, so your program won't get stuck if there is a hardware failure.

8. The While Loop will continue executing the AI Read until an error occurs or the user clicks the **Stop** button.

9. Always clean up your mess. **AI Clear** and **AO Clear** terminate any I/O in progress and release their respective memory buffers. No error checking is done here because these functions can do no harm, even if no AI or AO operations are in progress. The **Simple Error Handler** checks for and reports any data acquisition errors.

In this example, where the analog output is updated first, there is a very short time delay before the ADC acquires a sample. Your experiment may not have time to settle, resulting in an unpredictable error. An alternative is to acquire a new reading from the ADC, and then update the DAC output. This maximizes settling time and is probably a better overall solution.

Two other examples are included on the CD-ROM to accommodate some other DAQ boards. For older MIO boards, such as the AT- and NB-MIO-16, the **Synchronize AI AO for MIO-16** VI is a possible solution. The lack of external clock signals makes the task more difficult for these older boards, and the DAQ Application Engineers had to work pretty hard to create the VI, using advanced-level DAQ VIs. Essentially, it uses a pulse generator that triggers DAC updates and ADC single-sample acquisitions. It is limited to a single analog input and a single analog output.

For the E-series boards, a multitude of internal soft connections are possible, thanks to some elaborate onboard switching. This makes it easier to configure an E-series board for flexible scanning, like our synchronization problem. The **Synchronize AI AO for E-Series Boards** VI obtains the ADC scan clock from the DAC update clock in a manner similar to the example in Fig. 9.14. Multiple AI and AO channels are supported.

Another way to solve this problem is to use a function generator for the stimulus waveform and a plug-in board or external digitizing instrument for the measurement. A great way to synchronize the stimulus and measurement operations is to use a timebase clock. If you can get your hands on a modern **arbitrary waveform generator**, you will find that it has a clock output. Each time the instrument updates its DAC output, a pulse is delivered to the clock output. This clock can then be applied to the external clock input of your data acquisition board or digitizer. If the signal generator is programmed to produce 1024 clocks in one cycle of the waveform, your digitizer is guaranteed to acquire exactly 1024 ADC samples. Nice and neat, and always in-phase. To see how to program your DAQ board, look at the

DAQ example VIs, **Acquire N Scans-ExtChanClk** and **Acquire N Scans-ExtScanClk**.

If you can't use a clock, then there may be some way to use a trigger signal. Even simple analog function generators have a trigger output that occurs when the waveform starts. Use that to start a data acquisition operation or trigger a digital oscilloscope (see the section on **triggering** which follows). All you have to do is make sure that the period of the waveform is a little longer than the DAQ operation. Also, as with any external signal generation, you may want to dedicate a second ADC channel to monitoring the stimulus waveform, just to be sure that the amplitude is what you think it is.

Handling Fast Pulses

Pulse and transient phenomena abound in the world of physics research. As I mentioned before, there is a host of specialized instrumentation to accompany the various detectors that produce transient waveforms. In this section, we'll look at some of those instruments, the LabVIEW programs that support them, and some of the programming tricks that may be of general use.

Transient digitizers

A whole class of instruments, called **transient digitizers**, have been developed over the years to accommodate pulsed signals. They are essentially high-speed ADCs with memory and triggering subsystems and are often sold in modular form, such as CAMAC and VXI. Transient digitizers are like digital oscilloscopes without the display, saving you money when you need more than just a few channels. In fact, the digital oscilloscope as we know it today is somewhat of a latecomer. There were modular digitizers, supported by computers and with analog CRTs for displays, back in the 1960s. Before that, we used analog oscilloscopes with Polaroid cameras, and digitizing tablets to convert the image to ones and zeros. Anyone pine for the "good ol' days"? The fact is, digitizers make lots of sense today because we have virtual instruments, courtesy of LabVIEW. The digitizer is just so much hardware, but VIs make it into an oscilloscope, or a spectrum analyzer, or the world's fastest strip-chart recorder.

Table 9.1 lists some of the modular transient digitizers that are currently supported by LabVIEW. The driver for a typical digitizer consists of some setup VIs to set sampling rates, scale factors, and so forth, VIs to arm and trigger the digitizer, and a VI to read the data. The data is generally returned as a floating-point array scaled to voltage. Figure 9.15 shows the panel and connector pane for a typical transient recorder, the LeCroy 6810.

TABLE 9.1   Representative Transient Recorders for Which There Are LabVIEW Drivers*

Manufacturer	Model	Channels per module	Speed sample/sec	Bits	Memory samples	Format
Tektronix	VX4250	2	100 M	8	16 K	VXI
Tektronix	VX4240	1	10 M	12	1 M	VXI
Tektronix	RTD720A	4	2 G	8	4 M	Rackmount
DSP	2012	1	20 M	12	8 K	CAMAC
LeCroy	6810	4	5 M	12	8 M	CAMAC

* Digitizing oscilloscopes are also useful in these applications.

If you can't find a transient recorder that meets your requirements, check out the digital oscilloscopes available from the major manufacturers. They've got amazing specifications, capability, and excellent value these days. You might also consider plug-in oscilloscope boards which have the basic functionality of a 'scope but without the user interface. National Instruments recently introduced its **DAQScope** family. Its first models, the 5102 series, feature two 20 megasample/sec, 8-bit ADCs, full analog triggering capability, and 330 Ksamples of memory per channel. The boards come in several bus formats, including ISA, PCI, and PCMCIA, and they're programmed through NI-DAQ, just like any DAQ board. Look for a steady stream of new products in the DAQScope line.

There are several other major manufacturers of oscilloscope boards that supply LabVIEW drivers. **Gage Applied Sciences** offers a very wide range of models, in ISA and PCI bus format for Windows machines. For Mac users, **Information Systems Technology** offers

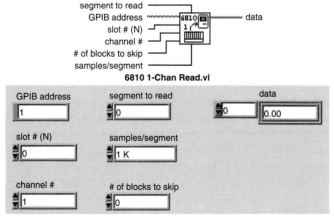

Figure 9.15   The front panel and connector pane for a typical transient digitizer, the LeCroy 6810. This one lets you read data in small chunks (using the blocks to skip control), which really helps when you have a full 8 megasamples of memory!

the **MacQuire** NuBus board, running at 100 Msamples/sec with 4 MB
of memory.

Input characteristics. High-speed digitizers, including fast oscilloscopes, generally have a 50-Ω input impedance. Low-speed models may
be high-impedance, and many offer switchable input impedance. AC or
DC coupling is also available on most models, but you can always add
your own coupling capacitor if the input is DC-coupled only. Another
useful feature is an input offset adjustment. Because many of the high-
speed digitizers only have 8-bit resolution,* you should offset the
actual range of the ADC to match that of your signal, thus optimizing
the dynamic range. All modern digitizers have input amplifiers and/or
attenuators to adjust the scale factor. Old CAMAC digitizers were fixed
at one range, such as 2 V. You have to supply your own wideband amplifiers and attenuators with those.

Triggering.   Most digitizers rely on a TTL or ECL-level external trigger
to start or stop acquisition. Most models have some form of internal,
level- or edge-sensitive triggering, much like an oscilloscope. Through
software commands, you begin acquisition by arming the digitizer after
which you either poll the digitizer to see if it has received a trigger
event, or, in the case of most GPIB instruments, wait for an SRQ telling
you that it's time to read the data.

   Like digital oscilloscopes, you can store **pretrigger** and/or **posttrigger** data. Once the digitizer is armed, its ADC samples at the desired
rate and stores data in high-speed memory, which is arranged as a circular buffer. When the trigger occurs, the current memory location is
saved, and sampling continues until the desired number of posttrigger
samples are acquired. Because data was being stored before the trigger, you can retrieve pretrigger data, as well. This is very useful
because there may well be important information that arrives before
the trigger event in many experiments. The DAQ library does a similar
trick with plug-in boards of all types.

Data storage and sampling.   An important choice you have to make when
picking a transient recorder is how much memory you will need, and
how that memory should be organized. Single-shot transient events
with a well-characterized waveshape are pretty easy to handle. Just
multiply the expected recording time by the required number of sam-

---

* High-speed digitizer systems have another specification, *effective bits*. At high sampling rates, resolution decreases due to the sample-and-hold aperture time which averages the signal over a small time interval. Don't expect maximum resolution at
maximum speed!

ples per second. With any luck, someone makes a digitizer with enough memory to do the job. Another option is streaming data to your computer's memory, which is possible with plug-in oscilloscope boards. For instance, a good PCI bus board can theoretically move about 60 million 1-byte samples per second to memory, assuming uninterrupted DMA transfers. Similarly, VXI systems can be configured with gigabytes of shared memory tightly coupled to digitizer modules. It appears that the possibilities with these systems are limited only by your budget.

Far more interesting than simple transient events is the observation of a long tail pulse, such as atomic fluorescence decay. In this case, the intensity appears very suddenly, perhaps in tens of nanoseconds, decays rapidly for a few microseconds, then settles into a quasi-exponential decay that tails out for the best part of a second. If you want to see the detail of the initial pulse, you need to sample at many megahertz. But maintaining this rate over a full second implies the storage of millions of samples, with much greater temporal resolution than is really necessary. For this reason, hardware designers have come up with digitizers that offer **multiple timebases**. While taking data, the digitizer can vary the sampling rate according to a programmed schedule. For instance, you could use a LeCroy 6810 (which has dual timebases) to sample at 5 MHz for 100 µs, then have it switch to 50 kHz for the remainder of the data record. This conserves memory and disk space and speeds analysis.

Another common experiment involves the recording of many rapid-fire pulses. For instance, the shot-to-shot variation in the output of a pulsed laser might tell you something significant about the stability of the laser's power supplies, flash lamps, and so forth. If the pulse rate is too high, you probably won't have time to upload the data to your computer and recycle the digitizer between pulses. Instead, you can use a digitizer that has **segmented memory**. The Tektronix RTD720A is such a beast. It can store up to 1024 events separated by as little as 5 µs, limited only by the amount of memory installed. After this rapid-fire sequence, you can upload the data at your leisure via GPIB. Other instruments with segmented memory capability are various HP, Tektronix, and LeCroy digital oscilloscopes, and the LeCroy 6810. Figure 9.16 shows how it's done with a 6810. The instrument returns the waveform from any memory segment you choose. In this example, sequential segments are returned in a 2D array.

This is a perfect example of letting specialized hardware do the work where it is most appropriate. I get lots of calls asking me why Lab-VIEW can't deliver this type of machine-gun performance on waveform acquisition. Sorry, but general-purpose computers with plug-in boards just don't offer that kind of speed (yet); such a problem is best solved with hardware, not software, at least until we have computers with

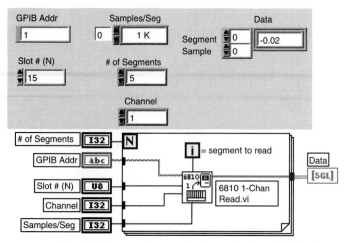

Figure 9.16 Reading segmented memories from a LeCroy 6810 digitizer. It's easy; the driver does all the work.

gigahertz clock speeds. Conceptually, PC-based virtual instruments can replace real instruments, but that is true only to a point, limited by practical matters such as size, heat, and cost effectiveness. VIs can control and augment high-performance, special-purpose instruments, but not replace them.

Calibration.   As a practical precaution, I never trust a digitizer when it comes to amplitude calibration. While the timebases are generally quite accurate, the same cannot be said for high-speed ADC scale factors. I like to warm up the rack of digitizers, then apply known calibration signals, such as a series of precision DC voltages, and store the measured values. For greater accuracy at high frequencies, you should apply a pulse waveform of known amplitude that simulates the actual signal as closely as possible. If you want to get fancy, add an input switching system that directs all the input channels to a calibration source. Then, LabVIEW can do an automatic calibration before and after each experiment. You can either store the calibration data and apply it to the data later or apply the prerun calibration corrections on the fly. One precaution: if you have several digitizers with 50-Ω inputs, make sure they don't overload the output of your calibrator. It's an embarrassing, but common, mistake.

Digital storage oscilloscopes (DSOs)

As far as the physics researcher is concerned, the **digital storage oscilloscope (DSO)** has several uses—for troubleshooting and initial setup of experimental apparatus, for convenient display of live waveforms during an experiment, and as a transient digitizer when combined with a LabVIEW system. Most DSOs have a GPIB interface and a LabVIEW driver. Therefore, you can use them to make permanent records of transient events while simultaneously gaining a convenient real-time waveform display. The only limitation I've seen is in some really old models that were incredibly slow at accepting commands and transferring data.

As a utility instrument, the oscilloscope (either analog or digital) is unsurpassed. As much as I would like to think that a digitizer and a LabVIEW display can duplicate an oscilloscope, it never really pans out in the practical world. The reasons are partly aesthetic, partly portability, but mostly . . . I like *real knobs*. Some of the digital 'scopes aren't very good in this respect, either. All covered with buttons and nary a knob in sight. For general-purpose tests and measurements, I'll take a real 'scope any day.

For real-time waveform display, LabVIEW sometimes approaches the common DSO in terms of display update speed. If you have a modest record length such as 512 samples, and a fast computer, a GPIB or VXI digitizer can do a credible job of mimicking a real-time display. You can also throw lots of traces on one screen, which is something that most DSOs can't do. Nevertheless, every lab I've ever worked in has had every available oscilloscope fired up, displaying the live waveforms.

Timing and triggering

The key to your success in pulsed experiments is setting up timing and triggering of all the diagnostic instruments and recording equipment. Just having a rack full of digitizers that all go off at the same time may, or may not, solve your problems. All of your pulsed diagnostics must trigger at the proper time, and you have to know exactly when that trigger occurred.

What's all this triggering stuff, anyhow? The experiment itself may be the source of the main trigger event, or the trigger may be externally generated. As an example of an externally triggered experiment, you might trigger a high-voltage pulse generator to produce a plasma. Experiments that run on an internally generated timebase and experiments that produce random events, such as nuclear decay, generally are the source of the trigger event. The instruments must be armed and ready to acquire the data when the next event occurs. All of these situations generate what we might classify as a first-level, or primary, trigger (Bologna and Vincelli 1983).

First-level triggers are distributed to all of your pulsed diagnostic instruments to promote accurate synchronization. Some utility hardware has been devised over the years to make the job easier. First, you probably need a **trigger fanout**, which has a single input and multiple outputs to distribute a single trigger pulse to several instruments, such as a bank of digitizers. A fanout module may offer selectable gating (enabling) and inverting of each output. A commercial trigger fanout CAMAC module is the LeCroy 4418 with 16 channels. Second, you often need **trigger delays**. Many times, you need to generate a rapid sequence of events to accomplish an experiment. Modern digital delays are very easy to use. Just supply a TTL or ECL-level trigger pulse, and after a programmed delay, an output pulse of programmable width and polarity occurs. Examples of commercial trigger delays are the Stanford Research Systems DG535 and the LeCroy 4222. Third, you may need a **trigger discriminator** to clean up the raw trigger pulse from your experimental apparatus. It works much like the trigger controls on an oscilloscope, permitting you to select a desired slope and level on the incoming waveform.

A fine point regarding triggering is timing uncertainty, variously known as trigger **skew** or **jitter**. Sometimes you need to be certain as to the exact timing relationship between the trigger event and the sampling clock of the ADC. A situation where this is important is waveform averaging. If the captured waveforms shift excessively in time, then the averaged result will not accurately represent the true waveshape. Most transient digitizers have a sampling clock that runs all the time. When an external trigger occurs, the current sample number is remembered by the digitizer's hardware. Note that the trigger event could fall somewhere in between the actual sampling events that are driven by the clock. One way to force synchronization is to use a master clock for your experiment that drives all the digitizers. Then, derive the trigger signal from the clock so that triggering always occurs at the same time relative to the clock. Unfortunately, this trick can't be used when the trigger event is random or uncontrollable in nature. In those cases, you must make sure that the trigger generator is stable and repeatable and that the sampling rate is high enough that a timing offset of plus or minus one sample will do no harm.

Figure 9.17 illustrates an application using several of these trigger processing devices with a pulsed laser as the source of the primary trigger event. In this case, the laser excites some plasma phenomenon in a target chamber. A photodiode samples the laser beam to provide a primary trigger pulse. Then, a high-voltage pulse generator is triggered to collect ions in the plasma. Finally, the digitizers are triggered to observe the ion current. The delay helps adjust the zero time for the digitizers to center the recorded data with respect to the physical event. Note that a delay generator cannot produce an output that occurs *before* the input. (I can't count the number of times I needed

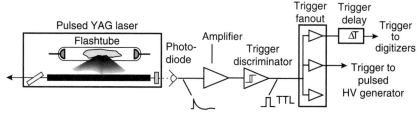

Figure 9.17 Typical application of a trigger discriminator, fanout, and delays used in a pulsed laser experiment.

such a device!) If you want a physical event to occur before the trigger, you have to delay everything else in the experiment.

Second-level triggers are another useful tool in physics diagnostics. Some experiments require a bit more intelligence to decide when to trigger the data acquisition hardware. For instance, the coincidence of two pulses or digital words (a logical operation) is commonly used to detect high-energy particles. Coincidence detection helps to filter out undesired, anomalous events. In such cases, you can use commercial triggering logic systems, such as those made by LeCroy. Or, if it's a simple problem, just put together some analog and/or digital logic yourself.

Third-level triggers represent an even higher level of sophistication in trigger event detection. In many experiments, there may be enough noise or other false events that the first-level and even the second-level triggers cause you to record many nonevents. If this occurs very often, you end up with a disk full of empty baselines and just a few records of good data. That's okay, except for experiments where each event consists of 85 megabytes of data. The poor person analyzing the data (you?) is stuck plowing through all this useless information.

The solution is to use a hardware- or software-based second-level trigger that examines some part of the data before storage. For instance, if you have 150 digitizers, it might make sense to write a subVI that loads the data from one or two of them and checks for the presence of some critical feature—perhaps a critical voltage level or pulse shape can be detected. Then, you can decide whether to load and store all the data or just clear the digitizer memories and rearm.

If there is sufficient time between events, the operator might be able to accept or reject the data through visual inspection. By all means, try to automate the process. However, often there is barely time to do any checking at all. The evaluation plus recycle time may cause you to miss the actual event. If there is insufficient time for a software pattern recognition program to work, you can either store all the data (good and bad), or come up with a hardware solution, or perhaps a solution that uses fast, dedicated microprocessors to do the pattern recognition.

The LeCroy 9300-series digital oscilloscopes (and some models by HP and Tektronix, as well) have a *trigger exclusion* feature that may be of value in physics experiments. You define the shape of a good pulse in terms of amplitude and time, typically with some tolerance on each parameter. After arming, the 'scope samples incoming waveforms and stores any out-of-tolerance pulses. This is good for experiments where most of the data is highly repetitive and nearly identical, but an occasional different event of some significance occurs.

Managing trigger setups.   Traditionally, triggering equipment consists of rack after rack of timing and delay modules, fanouts, buffers, and patch panels. If that's your system, you manage triggering by keeping careful track of which signal goes where and what all the knobs are set to. No shortcuts there. But, if you have moved into the New Age of data acquisition and control, you can use programmable modules to do much of this work. In that case, a good LabVIEW program can simplify the setup and management of your experiment's timing and triggering.

Here is a good example. The radio frequency (RF) Controls and Signal Processing section of the RF Technology group at Los Alamos National Laboratory (LANL) designed, built, and delivered a low-level RF control system for the University of Twente's Free Electron Laser in Holland (Accelerator Technology Division AT-5 1993). The purpose of the RF system in such a particle accelerator is to create a controlled high-power RF field in the accelerator cavity which enables the bunching and acceleration of a charged-particle beam. The purpose of the low-level RF control system is to maintain the amplitude and phase of the cavity's RF field within specifications. Measurement and control of amplitude, phase, and timing is crucial, and because the system is quite complex, automatic controls are a must.

LANL engineers decided to use a VXI-based LabVIEW control system to meet these requirements. The controller is a National Instruments VXIpc30, which is an embedded Macintosh SE-30, with an MXIbus interface to support two VXI chassis. A total of 14 modules were used, and many of them were custom-designed for the experiment. The LabVIEW program monitors and controls the RF equipment, maintains resonance conditions in an RF cavity through PID feedback control, and displays alarm and status conditions.

A particular subVI of interest, shown in Fig. 9.18, supports a custom timing distribution module with programmable delays and pulse widths. The graph displays a nice timing diagram which makes the timing relationships among the many channels very clear. You could easily adapt this type of display to your own timing control system.

Each of the waveforms is constructed through the use of a Build Array function. High and low *y*-axis values for a given waveform are

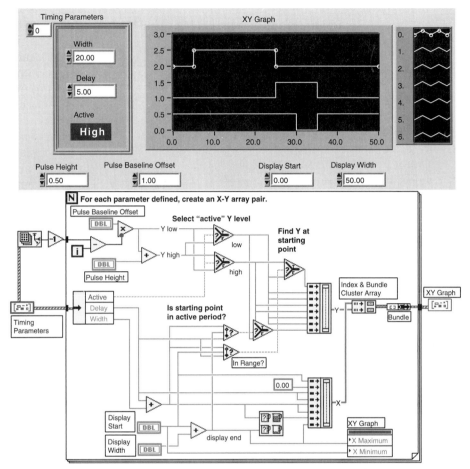

Figure 9.18 Timing setup display from the LANL low-level RF control package. This is a really intuitive way of displaying timing and triggering information. The diagram is complex; I did the best I could to label important parts.

selected based on the For Loop's index and the polarity of the waveform (active *high* means a more positive level occurs after the delay time). The user can adjust the height and spacing of the displayed waveforms through the **Pulse Height** and **Pulse Baseline Offset** controls. **Width** and **delay** parameters determine which of these (high or low) values are to be placed at which location on the graph. An *x*-axis array has to be built for each waveform because each waveform has different transition points. To show where the transitions occur, I made the upper trace in the graph display points as little circles.

The user can adjust the time scale of the graph by changing **Display Start** and **Display Width**. Those values affect the generation of points to be displayed and are also applied to an Attribute Node for the graph to set the *x*-axis minimum and maximum. That's easier than forcing the user to manually scale the graph.

Credit where credit is due: Lynda Gruggett of G Systems (Dallas, Texas) did much of the programming on this project, which amounted to about 150 VIs. And thanks to Amy Regan of LANL for supplying the VIs and the technical description of the project.

Capturing many pulses

Many pulsed experiments produce rapid streams of pulses that you need to grab without missing any events. Assuming that you have all the right detectors and wideband amplifiers, you need to select the right acquisition hardware.

There are two ways to treat multipulse data: capture each pulse individually, or average the pulses as they occur. Averaging has the distinct advantage of improving the signal-to-noise ratio on the order of $\sqrt{n}$, where n is the number of pulses averaged. Of course, if you are able to capture and store all of the pulses, you can always average them afterward. Figure 9.19 is a VI that uses a digitizer with segmented memories to acquire many waveforms. Note that the digitizer must be accurately

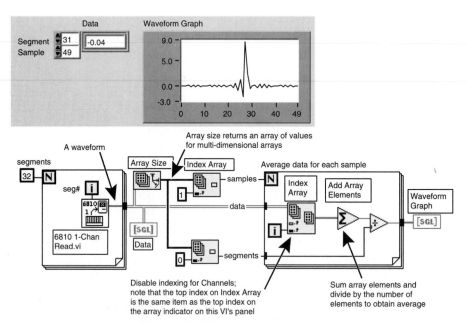

Figure 9.19 Averaging waveforms acquired from a digitizer that has segmented memories. Be really careful with array indexing; this example shows that LabVIEW has a consistent pattern with regards to indexes. The first index is always on top, both on the panel and on the diagram.

triggered and in-phase with every pulse to avoid statistical errors. Additionally, all the pulses must be similar. The diagram shows some of the array indexing tricks required to average the waveforms.

This VI is memory-intensive because it assembles multiple waveforms (1D arrays) into a large 2D array. At first, it may seem that there is no other solution because you need to have all of the waveforms available before averaging can be performed. There is another solution: use an **ensemble averager** subVI like the one in Fig. 9.20. Each time this VI is called, it sums the incoming data with the previous data on a sample-by-sample basis. When called with **Average** set to True, the sum is divided by the number of samples. The **Iteration** control initializes the two uninitialized shift registers. At initialization time, the incoming waveform determines the length of the array.

Now you can rewrite the data averaging VI in a way that saves memory. The improved version is shown in Fig. 9.21, and it produces the same result but with much less memory usage. To further improve performance, averaging is turned off until the last iteration of the For Loop. This step saves many floating point division operations. If you want to see the averaging operation evolve in real-time, you could move the Waveform Graph inside the For Loop and turn averaging on all the time. Each time a new segment of data is read, the graph will be updated with a newly computed average.

Individual pulses need to be stored when the information contained in each pulse is significant. The big issues (as far as LabVIEW is concerned) are how often the pulses occur and how fast your data transfer

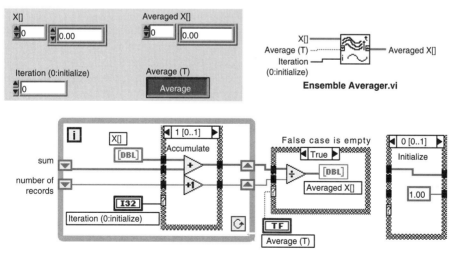

platform\ Moving Averagers\Ensemble Averager.vi

Figure 9.20   This shows an ensemble averager VI. It accumulates (sums) the data from multiple waveforms, then calculates the average on command. It uses uninitialized shift registers to store the data between calls.

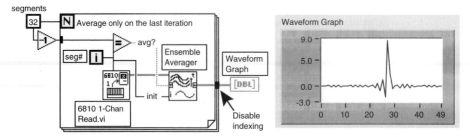

Figure 9.21   Using the ensemble averager drastically simplifies the diagram and cuts memory usage while yielding the same results as before.

rate and throughput are. If the pulses only occur every second or so, there is no problem. Any simple acquisition loop that you write with a good external digitizer will probably work. But sometimes you will want to capture pulses at much higher rates, perhaps tens or hundreds of pulses per seconds. That calls for digitizers with segmented memories, as previously mentioned. For intermediate rates, it's *possible* to do the acquisition in LabVIEW, but you had better do some testing to verify performance. Remember to optimize your program (described later in this chapter), primarily by minimizing graphics and memory usage.

If the running average value of many pulses is interesting, then you can use some other instruments. Most DSOs offer built-in signal averaging. Assuming that you can trigger the DSO reliably, this is a really easy way to obtain averaged waveforms over GPIB. For a more modular approach, DSP Technology makes a line of averaging memories for use with its CAMAC digitizers. It uses high-speed memory and an adder to accumulate data from synchronized waveforms. After the desired number of events (N), you read out the memory and divide the data by N. Some advanced VXI modules may support this kind of waveform acquisition and processing, as well.

You can also use a **boxcar averager** to acquire averaged pulse waveforms. The basic timing diagram for a boxcar averager is shown in Fig. 9.22. The gate interval is a short period of time during which the analog signal voltage is sampled and its amplitude stored as charge on a capacitor. The output of the boxcar is the average of many such gate events over a selected period of time. If the gate is fixed at one location in time, relative to the recurrent analog waveform, then the boxcar output represents the average value of the waveform at that time—just like putting cursors on the graph of the waveform. Now we can vary the gate delay with an analog voltage, thus scanning the sampling location over the entire period of the pulse. By scanning slowly, the boxcar output accurately reconstructs the analog waveform. With this technique, a simple *xy* chart recorder or slow data acquisition system can record the shape of *nanosecond* waveforms.

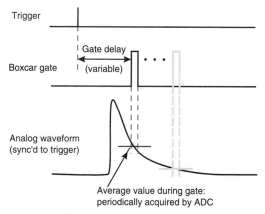

Figure 9.22 Basic timing diagram for a boxcar averager. The output of the boxcar is the average of
many measurements that are acquired during
many gate events. By slowly varying the gate delay,
the boxcar output reconstructs the shape of the analog waveform.

One boxcar system, the Stanford Research Systems SR250, offers a
GPIB interface module (for which we have a LabVIEW driver) that
directly supports gate scanning and also measures the boxcar output.
Even without this special support, you can use a ramp generator VI
like the one described in Plasma Potential Experiments to scan the
gate and make the output measurements. On the SR250, the gate
delay signal is a 0–10-V input (drive it directly from your MIO-16 output), and the gate delay ranges from 1 ns to 10 ms, so you can cover a
very wide range of pulse widths. It also offers a high-speed sampling
module that shrinks the gate time to about 10 ps. The boxcar output
ranges up to ±2 V and is well filtered, making accurate measurements
a snap.

Equivalent time sampling (**ETS**) is a trick used by high-speed digitizers, DSOs, and the E-series DAQ boards from National Instruments. Realize that very fast ADCs are expensive and often lack high
resolution. But sample-and-hold amplifiers can be designed with very
short aperture (sampling) times—on the order of picoseconds—at a
more reasonable cost. This allows the hardware designer to use a
scheme similar to that of the boxcar averager. They delay the triggering of the sample-and-hold and ADC by a variable amount, just like the
boxcar's gate, thus scanning the sampling point across the period of a
recurrent waveform. Once the sample-and-hold has acquired a voltage,
a low-speed ADC can read that voltage at a relatively leisurely rate
and with good resolution. The trigger delay can be chosen randomly or
it may proceed in a monotonic fashion like the boxcar. Thus, the waveform is reconstructed in memory for readout and display.

ETS, like the boxcar, is a specialized *hardware* solution that solves a particular problem: acquiring fast, recurrent waveforms. Physics diagnostic problems often require esoteric hardware like that, and you should try to learn about special instruments to enhance your arsenal of solutions. LabVIEW alone can't replace every kind of system, but it can sure make the job easier, once you've got the right front-end hardware.

Recovering signals from synchronous experiments

Say that you have a beam of light chopped at 10 kHz that is partially absorbed in an experiment. The remaining light strikes a photodiode, producing a small-amplitude square wave, and you want to measure the amplitude. To complicate things, assume the likely scenario where there is a great deal of 60-Hz noise and some nasty impulse noise from other apparatus. If you digitize this signal and display it, there's a good chance you won't even *find* the 10-kHz waveform, let alone measure its amplitude. You must do some signal processing first.

**platform\\
lock-in.llb\\
Signal Recovery
by BP Filter**

One solution is to apply a narrow-bandwidth digital bandpass filter, tuned to the desired center frequency. The concept is also known as a **frequency-selective voltmeter**. It's simple and often adequate because much out-of-band noise is rejected. All it takes is a DAQ waveform acquisition VI, followed by one of the IIR filter VIs. To determine the amplitude, you might use the **AC & DC Estimator** VI from the Measurement function palette in the Analysis library. Its AC amplitude estimate is obtained from the mean and variance of the time-domain signal after passing the signal through a Hann time window. On the CD-ROM you'll find a VI called **Signal Recovery by BP Filter** in the lock-in library. It acquires data from one channel of a DAQ board, applies a lowpass filter, and displays the AC estimate (Fig. 9.23).

There are some shortcomings to this filter-based technique. Impulses and other transient signals often contain energy that falls within the passband of the filter, making that polluting energy inseparable from your signal. Also, filters with narrow passbands (high Q) are prone to ringing when excited by impulse or step waveforms. If the incoming signal is sufficiently noisy, you may not be able to recover your signal reliably. To see how bad the problem can be, try the Pulse Demo VI from the Analysis examples. Turn the noise way up, and watch the pulse disappear from view. Note that the addition of some signal conditioning filters and amplifiers, plus proper grounding and shielding, may remove some of the interference from your signal and is always a worthwhile investment.

In experiments that operate with a constant carrier or chopping frequency, the signal amplitude can be recovered with **lock-in amplifiers**, which are also called **synchronous amplifiers** or **phase-sensitive**

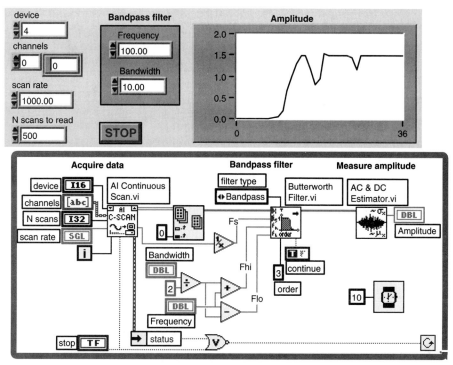

Figure 9.23 The Signal Recovery by BP Filter VI demonstrates a way of measuring amplitude in a selected frequency band. For this screen shot, I swept the input frequency around the 100-Hz region while running the VI.

detectors (PSDs). The basic principle revolves around the fact that you need only observe (demodulate) the range of frequencies within a narrow band around the carrier frequency. To do this, the lock-in requires a reference signal—a continuous sine or square wave that is perfectly synchronized with the excitation frequency for the experiment. The lock-in mixes (multiplies) the signal with the reference, resulting in an output containing the sum and difference frequencies. Since the two frequencies are equal, the difference is zero, or DC. By lowpass-filtering the mixer output, you can reject all out-of-band signals. The bandwidth, and hence the response time, of the lock-in is determined by the bandwidth of the lowpass filter. For instance, a 1-Hz lowpass filter applied to our example with the 10-kHz signal results in (approximately) a 1-Hz bandpass centered at 10 kHz. That's a very sharp filter, indeed, and the resulting signal-to-noise ratio can be shown to be superior to any filter (Meade 1983).

platform\ lock-in.llb   Lock-ins can be implemented by analog or digital (DSP) techniques. It's easiest to use a commercial lock-in with a LabVIEW driver, available from Stanford Research or EG&G Princeton Applied Research. If you want to see a fairly complete implementation of a lock-in in LabVIEW, check out the example on the CD-ROM in the lock-in library. For a simple no-hardware demonstration, I created a two-phase lock-in with an internal sinusoidal reference generator. This example VI, **Two-phase Lock-in Demo**, simulates a noisy 8-kHz sine wave, and you can change the noise level to see the effect on the resulting signal-to-noise ratio.

The **DAQ 2-Phase Lock-in VI** is a real, working, two-phase DSP lock-in where the signal and reference are acquired by a plug-in board. The reference signal can be a sine or square wave, and the amplitude is unimportant. SubVIs clean up the reference signal and return a quadrature pair of constant-amplitude sinewaves. To generate these quadrature sine waves, I had to implement a phase-locked loop (PLL) in LabVIEW. I used a calibrated IIR lowpass filter as a phase shift element. When the filter's cutoff frequency is properly adjusted, the input and output of the filter are exactly 90 degrees out of phase. This condition is monitored by a phase comparator, which feeds an error signal back to the lowpass filter to keep the loop in lock.

I did some testing with my NB-MIO-16X board and Quadra 950. I found that it's possible to obtain a stable amplitude and phase measurement for a 200-Hz sine-wave signal even when the rms amplitude of that signal is on the order of 1 LSB on the ADC! My biggest limitation is CPU speed. These DSP applications require many floating point operations, and I could only sample at about 2 kHz before overflowing the DAQ buffer. If you're interested in DSP lock-in applications, give these VIs a try, and let me know if you come up with improvements.

Handling Huge Data Sets

Experiments have a way of getting out of hand with respect to the quantity of data generated. At the NASA Ames Research Center's Hypervelocity Free-Flight Aerodynamic Facility (HFFAF) (Bogdanoff et al. 1992), they use about 124 channels of transient digitizers with anywhere from 8 to 256K samples per channel—about 16 megabytes per shot, typical. (The good news is, they can only do a couple of shots per week). In another common situation, seismology, they need to digitize and record data at hundreds of samples per second from many channels . . . forever. *Forever* implies a *really big* disk drive. Obviously, there must be some practical solutions to memory and disk limitations, and that's what we'll look at next.

Reducing the amount of data

The concept of third-level triggers can certainly reduce the amount of data to be handled. Or, you can do some kind of preliminary data reduction to compact the raw data before storing it on disk.

In seismology, an algorithm called a *P-picker* continuously processes the incoming data stream, searching for features that indicate the presence of a P wave (a high-frequency, perpendicular shock wave) which indicates that an interesting seismic event has occurred. If a P wave is detected, then a specified range of recent and future data is streamed to disk for later, more detailed, analysis. Saving all of the raw data would be impractical, though they sometimes set up large circular buffer schemes just in case a really important event (*The Big One*) occurs. That permits a moderate time history to remain in memory and/or on disk for immediate access. But in the long run, the P-picker is key.

If your data is of a contiguous but sparse nature, like that of a seismic data recording system, consider writing a continuous algorithm to detect and keep interesting events. Because the detection algorithm may require significant execution time, it probably needs to run asynchronously with the data acquisition task. If you are using a plug-in board, you can use buffered DMA (see Chap. 6, "Using the DAQ Library," for examples). Some kinds of smart data acquisition units also support buffering of data, such as the HP3852. Either way, the hardware continues collecting and storing data to a new buffer even while the computer is busy analyzing the previous buffer.

If you can't afford to throw away any of your data, then data reduction on-the-fly might help reduce the amount of disk space required. It will also save time in the post-experiment data reduction phase. Is your data of a simple, statistical nature? Then maybe all you really need to save are those few statistical values, rather than the entire data arrays. Maybe there are other characteristics—pulse parameters, amplitude at a specific frequency, or whatever—that you can save in lieu of raw data. Can many buffers of data be averaged? That reduces the stored volume in proportion to the number averaged. If nothing else, you might get away with storing the reduced data for every waveform, plus the raw data for every Nth waveform. Decimation is another alternative if you can pick a decimation algorithm that keeps the critical information, such as the min/max values over a time period. (See Chap. 7, "Writing a Data Acquisition System," for information on decimation.) As you can see, it's worth putting some thought into real-time analysis. Again, there may be performance limitations that put some constrains on how much real-time work you can do. Be sure to test and benchmark before committing yourself to a certain processing scheme.

Optimizing VIs for memory usage

Large data sets tend to consume vast quantities of memory. Some experiments require the use of digitizers that can internally store millions of samples because there simply isn't time during the run to stream the data to your computer. When the run is over, it's time to upload, analyze, and save all those samples. If your computer has only, say, 16 MB of RAM, then it's unlikely that you will be able to load more than a few hundred thousand samples of data in one chunk. You have two choices: buy more memory or write a smarter program.

Expanding the memory capacity of your machine is certainly worthwhile. LabVIEW is a big memory user, no doubt about it. And modern operating systems aren't getting any smaller. Even **virtual memory (VM)**, available on all of LabVIEW's platforms, may not save you because there are significant real-time performance penalties due to the disk swapping that VM causes. For best performance and simplicity in programming, nothing beats having extra memory. Of course it costs money, but memory is cheap compared to the aggravation of poor system performance.

So, you find yourself a little short on memory, a little short on cash, and a little down in the mouth because LabVIEW dies every time you try to load those megasamples of data. It's time to optimize, and perhaps rewrite, your program. By the way, I guarantee that you will see an increase in the *performance* of your program when you optimize memory usage. Anything you do to reduce the activity of our old friend the memory manager will speed things up considerably. Here are the basic memory optimization techniques that everyone should know.

Begin by RTFMing (reading the fine manual), this time concentrating on the chapter in the LabVIEW user manual called "Performance Issues." The LabVIEW team is fully aware of the importance of explaining how LabVIEW allocates memory, and they continue to improve and expand the available documentation. Also check the current technical notes. LabVIEW Technical Note TN020, "Minimizing the Number of Data Buffers," is relevant to the current problem: handling large quantities of data.

Tip 1: Use cyclic processing rather than trying to load all channels at once. Once you see this concept, it becomes obvious. As an example, here is a trivial example of the way you can restructure a data acquisition program. In Fig. 9.24*a,* 10 waveforms are acquired in a For Loop, which builds a 10-by-N 2D numeric array. After collection, the 2D array is passed to a subVI for storage on disk. The 2D array is likely to be a memory burner. Figure 9.24*b* shows a simple, but effective, change. By putting the data storage subVI in the loop, only one 1D array of data needs to be created, and its data space in memory is reused by each waveform. It's an instant factor of 10 reduction in memory usage.

Of course, you can't always use cyclic processing. If you need to perform an operation on two or more of the waveforms, they have to be

A. All the data is loaded at once into a huge 2D array. Not memory efficient!

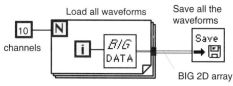

B. One waveform at a time is loaded and written to a file. Much more memory-efficient.

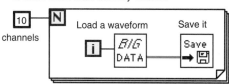

Figure 9.24 Use cyclic processing of data (*b*) to avoid storing all of your data in memory at the same time, as in *a*.

concurrently memory-resident. But keep trying: if you only need to have *two* waveforms in memory, then just keep *two*, and not the whole bunch. Perhaps you can use shift registers for temporary storage and some logic to decide which waveforms to keep temporarily.

Tip 2: Break the data into smaller chunks.   Just because the data source contains a zillion bytes of data, you don't necessarily have to load it all at once. Many instruments permit you to read selected portions of memory, so you can sequence through it in smaller chunks that are easier to handle. The LeCroy 6810 CAMAC digitizer and most digital oscilloscopes have such a feature, which is supported by the LabVIEW driver. If you're using a plug-in board, the DAQ VI, **AI Read**, permits you to read any number of samples from any location in the acquisition buffer. Regardless of the data source, it's relatively simple to write a looping program that loads these subdivided buffers and appends them to a binary file one at a time. Similarly, you can stream data to disk and then read it back in for analysis in manageable chunks. The **DAQ Toolkit** from Advanced Measurements has this feature. Read about it in Chap. 7, "Writing a Data Acquisition System."

Tip 3: Use the smallest practical numeric types.   Remember that LabVIEW supports many numeric types, from a single-byte integer on up to a 16-byte extended-precision (EXT) float. The minimum amount of memory that your data will consume is the number of samples multiplied by the size of the numeric type, in bytes. Lots of digitizers have 8-bit resolution, which fits perfectly into a single-byte integer, either signed (I8) or unsigned (U8). That's a case of maximum efficiency. Many times, however, you will want to scale the raw binary data to engineering units which require a floating point representation. For most cases, try to use the single-precision float (SGL), which is 4 bytes long and offers seven significant figures of precision. In the rare case that greater precision is required, use double-precision (DBL) which occupies 8 bytes. The latter type is also required by all VIs in the analysis library. If you use any of those VIs, you may as well keep all of your data in DBL format. Why? That's the next tip.

Tip 4: Avoid coercion and conversion when handling arrays.   Minimizing data space requires constant vigilance. Begin by looking at your data sources, such as driver VIs. Make sure that the data is born in the smallest practical type. Drivers that were created way back in version 1.2 of LabVIEW are notorious for supplying all data in EXT format (the only numeric type then available). Figure 9.25 shows one such example, an old CAMAC driver VI. You might even create your own versions of driver VIs, optimized for your memory-intensive application.

Most of the analysis functions in the LabVIEW library are not polymorphic and handle only DBL-format floating point data. Using one of these functions on your more compact SGL data results in a doubling of memory usage. There are several things you can do if you need to conserve memory. First, call National Instruments and complain that you want polymorphic analysis VIs. Second, if it's not too complex, try writing your own equivalent function subVI in LabVIEW, one which uses only your chosen (smaller) data type. Realize that your routine may run a bit slower than the optimized, CIN-based analysis VI. The **G Math Toolkit** contains a plethora of analysis VIs that use no CINs, and that can be the basis for your custom, memory-optimized analysis. Third, you can perform the analysis at a time when less data is resident in memory—perhaps after the data acquisition phase is complete.

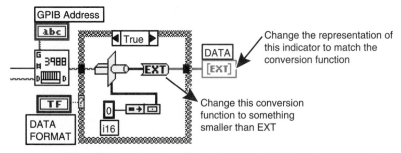

Figure 9.25   This old driver (from the Kinetic Systems 3988 library) converts 16-bit binary data to EXT floating point, which wastes much memory. Change the indicated conversion function to something smaller, such as SGL. Save big! And get the Ginsu Knife!

Keep a sharp eye open for **coercion dots** at terminals that handle large arrays. Anywhere you see one, the data type is being changed and that means that reallocation of memory is required. This takes time and, especially if the new data type is larger, results in the consumption of even more memory. If the coercion dot appears on a subVI, open the subVI and try to change all of the related controls, indicators, and functions to the same data type as your source. Eliminate as many coercion dots as you can. Sometimes this is impossible, as with the analysis library, or with any VI that contains a CIN. By the way, *never* change the data type that feeds data into a CIN! A crash will surely ensue because the CIN expects a certain data type; it has to be recompiled to change the data type. Maybe one day we'll have polymorphic CINs, too. Finally, don't convert between data types unnecessarily. For instance, changing a numeric array to a string for display purposes is costly in terms of memory and performance. If you must display data, try to use an indicator in the native format of that data.

Tip 5: Avoid data duplication. LabVIEW technical note TN020, "Minimizing the Number of Data Buffers," goes into some detail on the subject of efficient use of memory. In general, the G compiler tries very hard to avoid data duplication by reusing memory buffers. You can help by choosing the best combination of functions and structures to promote reuse. Here are some of the most important rules to keep in mind.

- *An output of a function reuses an input buffer if the output and the input have the same data type, representation, and—for arrays, strings, and clusters—the same structure and number of elements.* This category includes all of the Trig & Log functions; most of the Arithmetic functions, including those that operate on Boolean data; a few string functions such as *To Upper Case;* the Transpose Array function; and the Bundle function to the extent that the cluster input and output can use the same buffer. Most other functions do not meet this criteria; among them are the Build Array and Concatenate String functions.

- *In general, only one destination can use the buffer of the data source.* More specifically, where the source of a data path branches to two or more destinations that *change* the input data, the source buffer can be used by only one. A way to conserve memory is to do processing in a serial fashion—one subVI after another—rather than wiring the subVIs in parallel.

- *If there are multiple destinations that read data but do not change it, they may use the same source buffer.* For example, Array Size doesn't duplicate the buffer since it doesn't change it. Also, under certain circumstances, when a node that alters data and one or more nodes that merely read data have the same source, LabVIEW can determine that the readers execute before the node that changes the data so that the source buffer can be reused. (For this to occur, all nodes involved must be synchronous.)

- *If the source is a terminal of a control that is not assigned to a connector terminal or receives no data from the calling VI, the source data is stored in a separate buffer.* Without an external source to supply data when the subVI executes, the data is locally supplied. This means you can save memory by not trying to display it. You can also use the VI Setup dialog to change the priority to **Subroutine**. Subroutine priority eliminates all extra buffers associated with indicators and slightly reduces subVI calling overhead. Note that it also prevents you from running the VI interactively!

- *If a buffer can be reused by an input and output of a structure or subVI, the buffer can be used by other nodes wired to that node.* Thus, in a hierarchical program, a buffer can be reused from the top-level VI to the lowest subVI and back up to the top. Don't be afraid to use subVIs, so long as they contain no additional array duplications internally.

- *Data allocated to a top-level VI cannot be deallocated during execution.* On the other hand, data allocated in a subVI can be deallocated.

You have some control over the LabVIEW memory manger through the Preferences dialog, in the **Performance and Disk** items. The first option is *Deallocate memory as soon as possible*. When a subVI finishes execution, this option determines whether or not its local buffers will be deallocated immediately. If they are deallocated, you gain some free memory, but performance may suffer because the memory will have to be *reallocated* the next time the subVI is called. On the Macintosh, there is an option called *Compact memory during execution*. When enabled, LabVIEW tells the Macintosh memory manager to defragment memory every 30 seconds. Defragmented memory enhances speed when allocating new buffers. However, this compacting operation usually induces a lull in performance every 30 seconds which may be objectionable in real-time applications.

If your application uses much more memory than you think it should, it's probably because of array duplication. Try to sift through these rules (study the technical note for more) and figure out where you might modify your program to conserve memory.

Tip 6: Use memory diagnostics. There are some ways to find out how much memory your VIs are actually using. Please note that these techniques are not absolutely accurate. The reasons for the inaccuracy are generally related to the intrusiveness of the diagnostic code and the complexity of the memory management system. But as a relative measure, they are quite valuable.

Begin by using the **Show VI Info** dialog in the Windows menu to find out how much memory is allocated to your VI's panel, diagram, code, and data segments. Of primary interest is the data segment, because that's where your buffers appear. Immediately after compiling a VI, the data segment is at its minimum. Run your VI, and open the VI Info dialog again to see how much data is now allocated. You can try some simple tests to see how this works. Using an array control, empty the array and check the data size. Next, set the array index to a large number (such as 10,000), enter a value, and check the data size again. You should see it grow by 10,000 times the number of bytes in the data type.

The most extensive memory statistics are available through the **Profiling** feature of LabVIEW. Select **Show Profile Window** from the Project menu, and start profiling with the **Enable Memory Profiling** and **Memory usage** items selected (Fig. 9.26). Run your VIs, take a snapshot at some critical time, and examine the memory-related columns. If you click on a column header, the entire spreadsheet will be sorted in descending order by that column. Important statistics include minimum, maximum, and average bytes used, in addition to timing information. Find out which VIs use the most memory and try to optimize them first. The Profiler is a quantitative tool for this effort. Sometimes, the least-expected VI is the biggest memory hog!

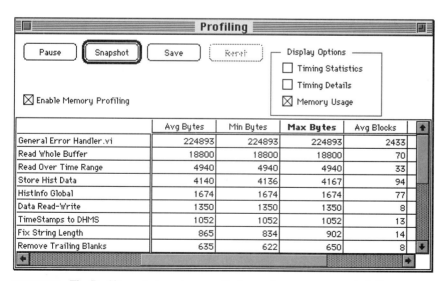

Figure 9.26 The Profiling window gives you timing and memory usage statistics on your application. The first VI in the list is the biggest memory user; that's the place to concentrate your efforts.

Bibliography

Accelerator Technology Division AT-5, *Low-Level RF LabVIEW Control Software User's Manual,* Los Alamos National Laboratory, LA-12409-M, 1992. (Available from National Technical Information Service, Springfield, Virginia.)

Bogdanoff, D. W., et al., "Reactivation and Upgrade of the NASA Ames 16 Inch Shock Tunnel: Status Report," *American Inst. of Aeronautics and Astronautics* 92-0327.

Bologna, G., and M. I. Vincelli, eds., "Data Acquisition in High-Energy Physics," *Proc. International School of Physics.* Amsterdam: North Holland, 1983. (ISBN 0-444-86520-9.)

Mass, H. S. W., and Keith A. Brueckner, ed., *Plasma Diagnostic Techniques,* Academic Press, New York, 1965.

Meade, M. L., *Lock-in Amplifiers: Principles and Applications,* Peter Peregrinus, LTD, England, 1983. (ISBN 0906048-94-X, out of print.)

1997 LeCroy Research Instrumentation Catalog. LeCroy Corporation, New York, 1997. (Call (914) 578-5984.)

10

Data Visualization, Imaging, and Sound

Today's sophisticated computer systems make it possible for you to collect and observe information in ways that used to be impractical or impossible. Once the bastion of the High Priests of Graphic Arts, the ability to produce multidimensional color plots, acquire and manipulate images, and even make movies of your data is directly available (live!) through LabVIEW. All you need to do is configure your system appropriately and, for some features, buy some third-party LabVIEW applications that offer these advanced capabilities. This chapter tells you how.

We humans have a marvelous ability to absorb visual information, but only when it is presented in optimum form. A well-designed graph or image conveys a great deal of information and gives us unexpected insight into hidden relationships buried in our data. You have to invest some programming effort, time, money, and thought to create the right visualization instrument, but the results are both valuable and impressive.

Keep in mind the fact that **imaging** is just another data acquisition and analysis technique. That's a fact that is overlooked when you haven't seen it in action. Images can be born of cameras and live scenes—the usual pictures—or they can arise from other forms of numerical data. Images are more than pretty pictures; they can be quantitative as well, spatially and in intensity. Further, you can make those images into movies and even combine them with sound by using the new concepts embodied in **multimedia**. LabVIEW does all of these things with the help of some add-on products.

There are dozens—perhaps hundreds—of data visualization (graphing, imaging, and presentation) programs available on various computer platforms these days. But LabVIEW has one big advantage over most of them: it can tie in data visualization with other operations in your real-world laboratory. For example, you can direct a robot arm, measure temperatures, control an electron beam welder, acquire images of the weld, process and display those images, store data on disk . . . and do it *all in real time, right there in LabVIEW.* This is an exceptional capability! Only a few years ago, you had to use several different programs (probably not simultaneously, either) or write a zillion lines of custom code to perform all of these tasks. Sometimes, the processing you wish to perform isn't practical in LabVIEW. In that case, you can still exchange data files with other specialized programs on various computers.

This chapter covers graphing of data, image acquisition and processing, and the recording and production of sound. LabVIEW has built-in graphs that are adequate for both real-time and posttest data presentation of ordinary two-dimensional data. It also has the capability to display images in color or grayscale. With the addition of third-party products discussed here, you can also acquire and analyze video images, make multidimensional plots, QuickTime movies, and other advanced displays. Sound I/O requires suitable hardware and some additional VIs.

Graphing

The simplest way to display lots of data is in the form of a graph. We've been drawing graphs for about 200 years with pens and paper, but LabVIEW makes graphs faster and more accurate. Most important, they become an integral part of your data acquisition and analysis system.

Part of your responsibility as a programmer and data analyst is remembering that a well-designed graph is intuitive in its meaning and concise in its presentation. In his book, *The Visual Display of Quantitative Information* (1983), Edward Tufte explains the fundamentals of graphical excellence and integrity and preaches the avoidance of graphical excess that tends to hide the data. Personally, I've been appalled by the way modern presentation packages push glitzy graphics for their own sake. Have you ever looked at one of those 256-color three-dimensional vibrating charts and tried to *actually see the information?*

Here are your major objectives in plotting data in graphical format:

- Induce the viewer to think about the substance rather than the methodology, graphic design, the technology of graphic production, or something else.

- Avoid distorting what the data have to say (for instance, by truncating the scales, or plotting linear data on logarithmic scales).

- Try to present many numbers in a small space, as opposed to diffusing just a few data points over a vast area. This makes trends in the data stand out.

- Make large data sets more understandable by preprocessing.

- Encourage the eye to compare different pieces of data.

- Reveal the data at several levels of detail, from a broad overview to the fine structure. You can do this by making more than one plot with different scales or by allowing the user to rescale a graph—a standard LabVIEW feature.

- Design the graph in such a way that it serves a clear purpose with respect to the data—for description, exploration, or tabulation.

- The graph should be closely integrated with other descriptions of the data. For example, a graph should be synergistic with numeric displays of statistics derived from the same data.

- Note that some data is better displayed in a format other than a graph, such as a table.

- Above all, make sure that the graph *shows the data*.

The worst thing you can do is overdecorate a graph with what Tufte calls *chartjunk*. Chartjunk is graphical elements that may catch the eye but tend to hide the data. You don't want to end up with a graphical puzzle. Simply stated, *less is more* (Fig. 10.1). Though this is more of a problem in presentation applications, there are some things to avoid when you set up LabVIEW graphs:

- High-density grid lines—they cause excessive clutter.

- Oversized symbols for data points, particularly when the symbols tend to overlap.

- Colors for lines and symbols that contrast poorly with the background.

- Color combinations that a color-blind user can't interpret (know thy users!)

- Too many curves on one graph.

- Insufficient numeric resolution on axis scales. Sometimes scientific or engineering notation helps (but sometimes it hinders—the number 10 is easier to read than 1.0E1).

- Remove or hide extra bounding boxes, borders, and outrageous colors. Use the coloring tool, the transparent (T) color, and the control editor to simplify your graphs.

Default graph

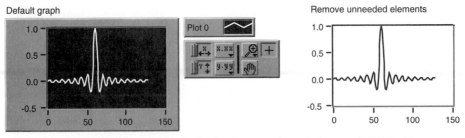

Remove unneeded elements

...but maybe all you really need is the data itself. Axis values are only required for quantitative graphing.
Controls and legends should not be displayed unless needed.

Figure 10.1   Sometimes, *less is more* when presenting data in graphs. Use the coloring tool, the control editor, and the various pop-up menus to customize your displays.

Displaying waveform and cartesian data

Most data that you'll acquire is a function of time or some other variable and is described by $y = f(x)$, where x is the independent variable (e.g., time) and y is the dependent variable (e.g., voltage). This is generalized **cartesian** (xy) data. The x values are most often based on time. Time-series, or **waveform**, data is effectively displayed as an ordinary graph or in the case of real-time data, as a strip chart. Graphs and charts are standard LabVIEW indicators with many programmable features. Read through the graphing chapter of the LabVIEW user manual to see how all those features are used. In particular, Attribute Nodes are worthy of much study because graphs have a large number of variant features.

Figure 10.2 shows the simplest way to use the **Waveform Graph**. Like many LabVIEW indicators, it's polymorphic, so you can wire several data types directly to it. Numeric arrays (any numeric representation) can be wired directly and are displayed with the x axis scaled with values beginning with zero $(x_0 = 0)$ and increasing by one $(\Delta x = 1)$ for each data point in the array. You can also control x_0 and Δx by bundling your data into a cluster as shown in Fig. 10.2. Any time your data has evenly spaced x values, use the Waveform Graph. Compared with an XY Graph, it takes less memory, is faster, and is certainly the easiest to set up.

Polymorphism makes the Waveform Graph more versatile because the graph directly accepts several data types. In the previous example, you saw that a single variable could be plotted with or without x-axis

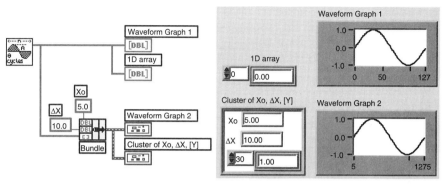

Figure 10.2   The Waveform Graph is polymorphic. This example shows the two basic data types that it accepts for the making of single-variable plots.

scaling. Figure 10.3 shows how to make a multiplot graph where each signal has the same number of points. You scale the x axis in a manner consistent with the previous example.

What if the signals don't have the same number of points? Two-dimensional arrays require that each row of data has the same number of points, so that approach won't work. Your first guess might be to make an array of arrays. Sorry, can't do that in LabVIEW. Instead, make an array that contains a cluster with an array inside it (Fig. 10.4). There are two ways to build this data structure, one using a **Bundle** function for each array followed by **Build Array**. The other way uses the **Build Cluster Array** function, which saves some wiring. The index of the outer array is the plot number and the index of the inner array is the sample number.

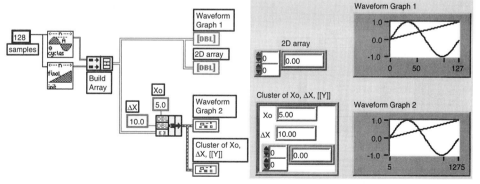

Figure 10.3   Two ways of making multiple plots with a Waveform Graph when the number of data points in each plot is equal. Note that the Build Array function can have any number of inputs. Also, the 2D array could be created by nested loops.

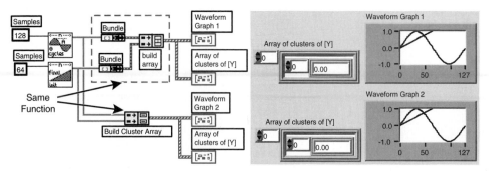

Figure 10.4 Making multiple plots where each plot has a different number of samples. Build Cluster Array performs the same function as the combination in the dashed rectangle.

A slightly different approach, shown in Fig. 10.5, is required if you want to make multiple plots with different numbers of points *and* you want to scale the *x* axis. For this example, I plotted a sine wave and a line representing its mean value (which might be useful for a control chart in statistical process control). The mean value is used as both elements of a two-element array, which is the *y*-axis data for the second plot. The trick is to use some math to force those two data points to come out at the left and right edges of the plot.

So far, we've been looking at graphs with simple, linear *x* axes which are nice for most time-based applications, but not acceptable for **para-**

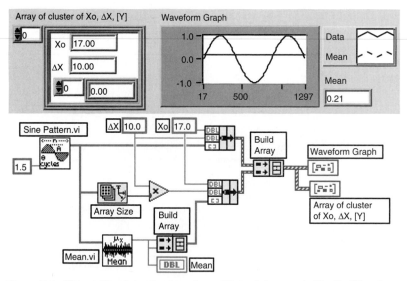

Figure 10.5 Yet another data structure for multiple plots accepted by the Waveform Graph. In this example, the sine wave is plotted with a line representing the mean value. This second plot has only two data points.

metric plots where one variable is plotted as a function of another. For that, use the **XY Graph**. Figure 10.6 shows a way of building one of the data structures that defines a multiplot *xy* graph. A plot is defined as an array of clusters that contains *x* and *y* data-point pairs. In this example, I turned on all the display options on the graph: the Legend, Palette, and Cursor Display. These are also available on the Waveform Graph.

Figure 10.7 shows how to use the other available data structure for an *xy* graph. Here, a plot is defined as a cluster of *x* and *y* data arrays. Why would you use this format in place of the previous one? That depends on how your data is acquired or created. If you collect single data-point pairs, for instance with a low-speed data recorder, then the previous format is probably best. For data that arrives in complete arrays for each plot, use the format in Fig. 10.7.

A **real-time xy strip chart** can be constructed as shown in Fig. 10.8. The trick is to add a new *xy* data pair to an ever-growing array that resides in a Shift Register. For each iteration of the While Loop, the acquired data is stored in the array, and all data is displayed in

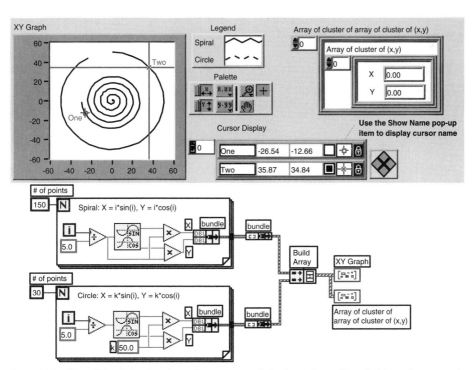

Figure 10.6 One of the data structures for an *xy* graph is shown here. It probably makes sense to use this structure when you gather (*x,y*) data-point pairs one at a time. This is the way it had to be done in LabVIEW 2.

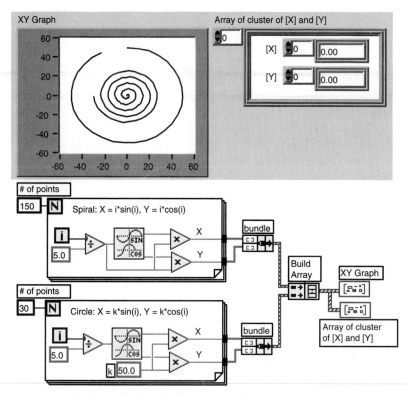

Figure 10.7 Similar to the last XY Graph example (Fig. 10.6), but using the other available data structure. This one is convenient when you have complete arrays of *x* and *y* data.

an *xy* graph. The biggest limitation is that performance decreases as time goes on because the amount of data to be displayed keeps growing. You also risk running out of memory. As an alternative, consider using the **Circular Buffer** VI, described in Chap. 8, "Process Control Applications."

Bivariate data

Beyond the ordinary cartesian data we are so familiar with, there is also **bivariate** data, which is described by a function of two variables, such as $z = f(x,y)$. Here are some examples of bivariate data that you might encounter:

■ A photographic image is an example of bivariate data because the intensity (z) changes as you move about the (x,y) area of the picture.

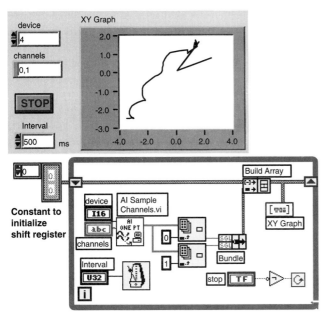

Figure 10.8 An XY Graph makes a handy real-time *xy* chart recorder. Keep appending data to an array stored in a shift register. *Caution:* You may run out of memory after extensive operation.

- Topographic data of a surface, such as the Earth, contains elevations (z) that are a function of latitude and longitude (x,y).

- A series of waveforms can be treated as bivariate data. For instance, the z axis can be amplitude, the x axis time, and y the sequence number. This is also called a **waterfall plot**.

Bivariate data may be displayed in many formats. **Surface plots** have a three-dimensional (3D) look to them and are the most computationally intensive displays to generate. Surface plots may be solid models (sometimes including shading) or wireframes with or without hidden lines removed. These plots can be very dramatic and give the reader insight into the general nature of the data, if properly displayed. The disadvantage of surface plots is that it is often difficult to use them quantitatively. Even with calibrated axes and the application of color, it's still hard to read out the value of a particular point as you would do on a simple *xy* graph. We'll look at a practical way of obtaining three-dimensional plots in LabVIEW in the next section.

Adding color to a surface plot effectively adds another dimension to the display, though it can be more confusing than helpful unless the data is well behaved. An example of effective use of color would be to display the topography of a mountain range and color the surface according to the temperature at each location. In general, temperature decreases with elevation, so a smooth progression of colors (or grays) will result. On the other hand, if you used color to encode wind speed at each location, you would probably end up with every pixel being a different color because of the rather uncorrelated and chaotic nature of wind-speed variations over large areas. Don't be afraid to try coloring your plots—just be sure that it adds *information* not just glitz.

Bivariate data can also be displayed as an image. The **Intensity Graph** is a LabVIEW indicator that displays the value at each (x,y) location as an appropriate color. You choose the mapping of values to colors through a Color Array control, which is part of the Intensity Graph. This type of display is very effective for data such as temperatures measured over an area and, of course, for actual images. Use of the Intensity Graph is covered later in this chapter.

Yet another way to display bivariate data is to use a **contour plot**. A contour plot consists of a series of isometric lines that represent constant values in the data set. Familiar examples are topographical maps, maps of the ocean's depth, and isobars on a weather chart showing constant barometric pressure. LabVIEW does not offer a contour plotting capability at this time, but **Metric Systems** offers **ContourView**, which may do the trick for your data. Many other data analysis and graphing packages already offer contour plotting, so you might plan on exporting your data. I might mention that contour plots are not as easy to generate as it might seem. The big problem is interpolation of the raw data. For instance, even though your measurements are acquired on a nice xy grid, how should the program interpolate between actual data points? Is it linear, logarithmic, or something else? Is it the same in all directions? Worse yet, how do you handle missing data points or measurement locations that are not on an even grid? I watched an analyst friend of mine struggle for *years* on such a problem in atmospheric dispersion. Every change to the interpolation algorithm produced drastically different displays. You generally need some other display or analysis techniques to validate any contour plot.

platform \ waterfall graph \ waterfall.llb

Waterfall plots are useful for observing a series of waveforms that change with time. For instance, you may want to observe the behavior of a power spectrum display while changing the system under observation. On the CD-ROM, I've included a simple and efficient waterfall graphing VI that originally shipped with the LabVIEW 2 examples. It accepts a 1D array of data and does hidden-line removal (Fig. 10.9).

Multivariate data

Beyond bivariate data is the world of **multivariate data**. Statisticians often work in a veritable sea of data that is challenging to present

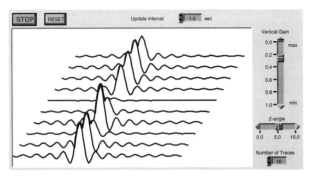

Figure 10.9 Example VI from the waterfall library on the CD-ROM. It's a simple and efficient way to display waveforms that change with time.

because they can rarely separate just one or two variables for display. For instance, a simple demographic study may have several variables: *location, age, marital status,* and *alcohol usage.* All of the variables are important, yet it is very difficult to display them all at once in an effective manner.

The first thing you should try to do with multivariate data is analyze your data before attempting a formal graphical presentation. In the demographic study example, maybe the *location* variable turns out to be irrelevant; it can be discarded without loss of information (though you would certainly want to tell the reader that *location* was evaluated). Ordinary *xy* graphs can help you in the analysis process, perhaps by making quick plots of one or two variables at a time to find the important relationships.

Some interesting multivariate display techniques have been devised (Wang 1978). One method that you see all the time is a **map**. Maps can be colored, shaded, distorted, and annotated to show the distribution of almost anything over an area. Can you draw a map in LabVIEW? If you have a map digitized as *xy* coordinates, then the map is just an *xy* plot. Or, you can paste a predrawn map into your LabVIEW panel and overlay it with a graph as I did in Fig. 10.10. In this example, I created a cluster array containing the names and locations of three cities in California with coordinates that corresponded to the map. When the VI runs, the horizontal and vertical coordinates create a scatter plot. This might be useful for indicating some specific activity in a city (like an earthquake). Or, you could add cursors to read out locations, then write a program the searches through the array to find the nearest city. Note that a map need not represent the Earth; it could just as well represent the layout of a sensor array or the surface of a specimen. The hardest part of this example was aligning the graph with the map. The map that I pasted into LabVIEW was already scaled to a reasonable size. I placed the *xy* graph on top of it and carefully sized the graph so that the axes were nicely aligned with the edges of the map. Through trial and error, I typed horizontal and vertical coordinates into the cluster, running the VI after each change to observe the actual city location.

City names are displayed on the graph with **cursor names**. On the diagram, you can see an Attribute Node for the graph with many elements—all cursor-related—displayed. You can programmatically set the cursor names, as well as setting the cursor positions, marker styles, colors, and so forth. This trick is very useful for displaying strings on graphs; there is currently no other way.

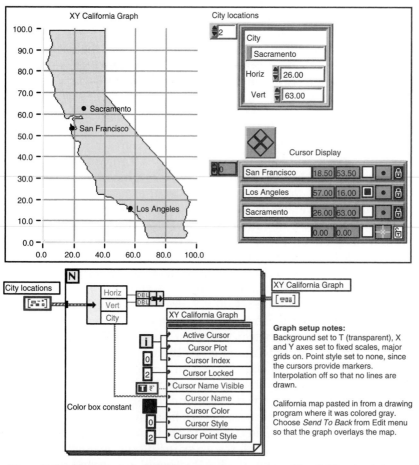

Figure 10.10 Mapping in LabVIEW. I pasted in a picture (the California state map) from a drawing program, then overlaid it with an *xy* graph to display city locations. Cursor names annotate each city location.

The Picture Control Toolkit. The **Picture Control Toolkit** is a Lab-VIEW option that you can purchase separately from National Instruments. It adds a new indicator, called a **Picture**, into which you can programmatically draw all types of geometric figures, bitmaps, and text. The toolkit includes many examples, most of them for the creation of specialized graphs with features that exceed those of the standard LabVIEW types. Figure 10.11 shows a few samples. The basic concept behind the Picture Control Toolkit is that you start with an empty picture, then chain the various drawing VIs together, adding objects at each step. Each object requires specifications, such as position, size, and color. Let's take a look at an interesting example using this toolkit.

The most interesting multivariate data display technique I've heard of is the **Chernoff Face** (Wang 1978). The technique was invented by Herman Chernoff at Stanford University in 1971 for the purpose of simultaneously displaying up to 18 variables in the form of a simplified human face. His idea works because we are quite sensitive to subtle changes in facial expressions. Some applications where the Chernoff face has been successful are showing relative living quality in various

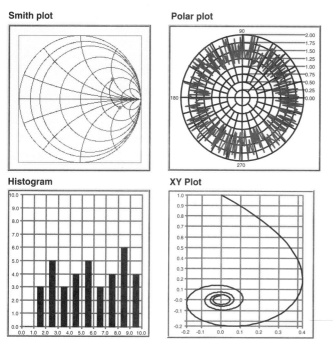

Figure 10.11   Here are some of the specialized plots that you can draw with the Picture Control Toolkit. These are included in the examples.

metropolitan areas, displaying psychological profiles, and my favorite, showing the state of Soviet foreign policy over the years. The trick is to map your variables into the proper elements of the face with appropriate sensitivity, and of course, to draw the face in a controllable manner. I spent some time with the VIs in the Picture Control Toolkit, and managed to build a crude face (Fig. 10.12) with three variables: face width, eye width, and mouth shape.

Because the Picture functions are all very low-level operations, you will generally have to write your own subVIs that perform a practical operation. In this example, I wrote one that draws a centered oval (for the face outline and the eyes) and another that draws a simple mouth (see Fig. 10.13). All of the Picture functions use *Picture in–Picture out* to support dataflow programming, so the diagram doesn't need any sequence structures. Each VI draws additional items into the incoming picture—much like string concatenation. Don't be surprised if your higher-level subVIs become very complicated. Drawing arbitrary objects

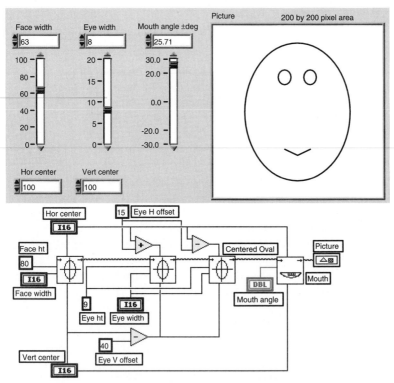

Figure 10.12   A simplified Chernoff Face VI, with only three variables: face width, eye width, and mouth angle. This VI calls two subVIs that I wrote to draw some simple objects using the Picture Control Toolkit.

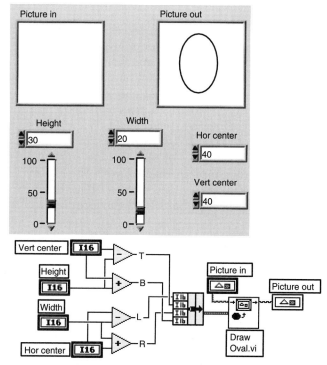

Figure 10.13   This Draw Centered Oval VI does some simple calculations to locate an oval on a desired center point, then calls
the Draw Oval picture VI. Note the consistent use of Picture
in–Picture out to maintain dataflow.

is not simple. In fact, this exercise took me back to the bad old days when
computer graphics (on a mainframe) were performed at this level, using
Fortran, no less. The first time I saw a Macintosh in action, my jaw
dropped because I knew what those programmers had gone through at
the lowest levels to create such wonderful graphics.

You could proceed with this train of development and implement a
good portion of the actual Chernoff Face specification, or you could take
a different tack. Using the flexibility of the Picture VIs, you could create some other objects, such as polygons, and vary their morphologies,
positions, colors, or quantities in response to your multivariate data
parameters. Be creative, and have some fun.

Special Graphing and Display Products

Besides the Intensity Graph and Picture Control VIs that are part of
LabVIEW, there are some third-party packages that you can use to create sophisticated data displays from within your LabVIEW programs.

SurfaceView

SurfaceView is a package of VIs for plotting bivariate data as a 3D wireframe surface. It was written by Jeff Parker of **Metric Systems**—you can order it directly from them. Jeff was a member of the first LabVIEW development team way back in 1985, and he's among the most capable programmers I've ever met. He's just the kind of guy who would write a 3D plotting package, which is a really challenging programming project. Figure 10.14 shows a typical SurfaceView plot.

SurfaceView uses the concept of a **CIN window**: a window that is not a regular LabVIEW panel or control. The CIN window concept was invented some years ago to provide programmers with the ability to create arbitrary displays (including interactive ones) without having to ask National Instruments to customize LabVIEW. SurfaceView's CIN window behaves the same as any other window on your computer, but its contents and actions are controlled by CINs inside VIs that you call from a diagram.

The package contains many VIs arranged in layers of increasing complexity. You can start off with one of the demonstration VIs which illustrates how to integrate SurfaceView into your application by call-

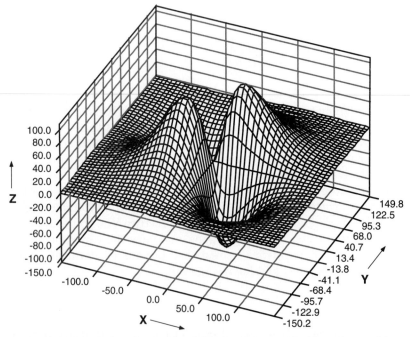

Figure 10.14 Output from SurfaceView. Note the inclusion of grids and axis calibration. Plotted data changes color as a function of its z axis (vertical) value. You should see it in color!

ing some of the low-level functions. I prefer to work at this level—keeps the old brain from boiling over. At the next level are dialog panels that open when called to present a nice palette of choices to manipulate the plot characteristics. For instance, you can easily change axis scaling, colors, and styles from these VIs. Next, there are some utility VIs that provide services such as data conversion. At the lowest level are the SurfaceView primitives, most of which are implemented as CINs. These primitives act directly on the surface plot in the CIN window. By working with the primitive functions, you can create highly customized SurfaceView applications.

How SurfaceView manages windows. It is instructive to explore how SurfaceView stores the information associated with a plot window in a data structure in memory, because many other LabVIEW third-party packages (and LabVIEW itself) use these same techniques. A VI called **SurfaceView New** allocates a block of memory and assigns a reference number (refnum) to it, much the way the LabVIEW file system uses refnums to keep track of files. This refnum is actually a **handle** to the window.

Figure 10.15 explains the concept of a handle, a mechanism used by the memory manager scheme in LabVIEW and many operating systems. Essentially, a handle is a pointer to a pointer, which gives you the

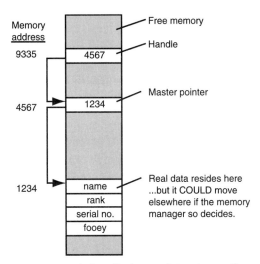

Figure 10.15 A *handle* is a pointer to another pointer that points to the data you are trying to access. If that seems confusing, just be glad you're using LabVIEW and not C, where you have to deal with it all the time. The scheme was designed for the convenience of the Memory Manager, not you.

location in memory at which your data (in this case, a SurfaceView plot) resides. Handles are a means by which our modern computer systems dynamically manage memory. Every time LabVIEW or any other program needs to store information, it calls the Memory Manager and requests some space. If there isn't enough contiguous space, other pieces of data need to be moved. This *double-dereferencing* scheme, as it is sometimes known, permits the Memory Manager to keep track of thousands of different blocks of memory. You really don't need to know much about handles unless you are writing CINs or other programs outside of LabVIEW, where they are very important.

Once SurfaceView New creates a new window and its associated refnum, you pass the refnum along to the other SurfaceView functions to manipulate the contents of that window. Note that you can have more than one window active at a time and that SurfaceView New is the only way to create a new window. When you are finished with the window, you should call SurfaceView Dispose to destroy the window and release the memory used by its data structures. Failure to do so will keep the memory unavailable for other uses until you quit and restart LabVIEW.

Other window operations are **SurfaceView Open** and **Surface-View Close** which show or hide an existing window, **SurfaceView Open?** which checks to see if the window is visible, and **SurfaceView Update** which redraws the window. The Update VI saves time because you can call many SurfaceView functions that change the plot without actually drawing any graphics, then call Update to redraw.

Formatting data.   SurfaceView requires that the $z = f(x,y)$ data lie on a grid where there is one and only one z value for each (x,y) location. Depending on your source of data, you may need to use one of the SurfaceView utility VIs, and perhaps some ingenuity, to format the data properly. Figure 10.16 shows two conversion routes and the required cluster containing x, y, and z arrays. The SurfaceView utility that makes the vital conversion is the **Convert Data** (**Mins&Deltas**) VI. Once the data cluster is ready, you need only create a new SurfaceView window and pass the data to one of the display functions.

Here is an example I put together that handles the kind of data you might collect with a two-axis motion control system that collects measurements over an even grid. Assume that the data from your program is stored in a spreadsheet-format text file. Here's the sample data:

```
0.152 0.258 0.261 0.294 0.180
0.370 0.671 0.976 0.735 0.333
0.526 1.305 2.104 1.292 0.247
0.328 0.912 1.892 0.829 0.303
0.256 0.381 0.214 0.261 0.108
```

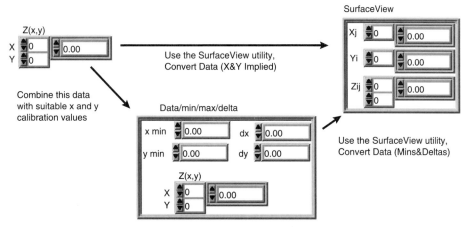

Figure 10.16 Starting with a two-dimensional array of data where $z = f(x,y)$, you can use one of two SurfaceView utilities to convert the array into the proper format.

The program in Fig. 10.17 loads this file, displays it in an intensity graph, converts it to SurfaceView format, and displays it as a 3D wireframe. Never work too hard when loading spreadsheet data. The utility VI, **Read From Spreadsheet File**, makes it easy. It has lots of options, but I only needed to access two of them to achieve the desired results: set the **number of rows** to a large number to assure that all the data is read, and set the **transpose** Boolean to True so that the rows and columns map correctly.

An array indicator displays the loaded data numerically and the intensity graph displays it as a coarse, gray-scale image. I had to use the *color array* option on the intensity graph to adjust the range of colors. Next, the 2D array is passed to **Convert Data** (**Mins&Deltas**) with suitable scale factors. I set *xMin* and *yMin* to zero and the incremental values to one. To display the data, call **SurfaceView New** and pass the refnum to the **Update Data, Title, Scales** VI, which is one of the high-level SurfaceView functions that serves to plot the data and name the window (Fig. 10.18). Just like the file utilities, I prefer to use the highest-level functions I can to save programming. If the utility VI doesn't do exactly what I want, I modify it and save it with a different name. After this VI runs, the user clicks *Quit,* the plot window disappears, and its memory is released by **SurfaceView Dispose**.

FastDraw

FastDraw is another third-party product that uses the CIN window to provide special graphing capability for the Macintosh. FastDraw is produced by **Aster** of France, a company that specializes in signal analy-

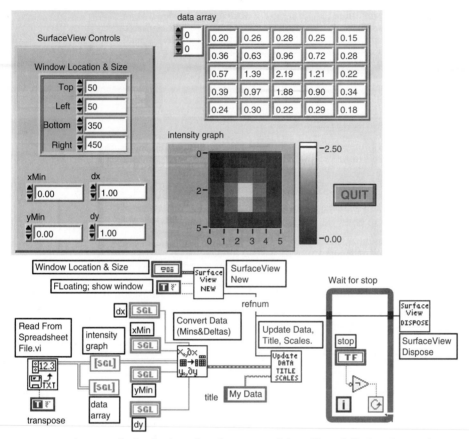

Figure 10.17 An example that loads xy data from a spreadsheet file and displays it as an intensity graph and as a SurfaceView wireframe.

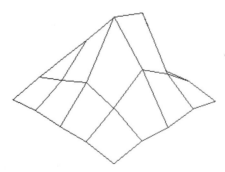

Figure 10.18 Screen shot of the SurfaceView plot produced by the previous example. Yeah, I know it's not very dramatic, but this was a simple data set and I didn't call any of the fancy formatting VIs in the package.

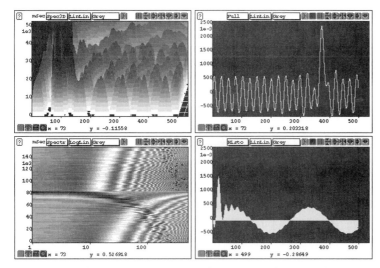

Figure 10.19   Plots that you can make with FastDraw. (*Clockwise from upper left*) 3D spectrogram, waveform plot, histogram, and flat spectrogram.

sis and real-time systems. It plots 1D data as line plots, histograms, 3D flat spectrograms, 3D sonograms, and 3D spectrograms, at very high speeds (Fig. 10.19). The window has a set of controls to scroll, zoom, and scale the plot, plus cursors. One of the cursor options that I really like is called a *harmonic* cursor. You place the cursor at a location corresponding to a fundamental frequency in a spectrogram, and several other cursors automatically appear at the related harmonics.

FastDraw uses just one VI to access all of its many programmable features. You feed it a numeric array which it then analyzes by performing a spectrogram or histogram operation, and then displays. Currently, FastDraw is only available for the Macintosh.

LabQD

Another Aster product is **LabQD** for the Macintosh. A specialized graphics product, it is effectively a LabVIEW implementation of many of the Mac's QuickDraw functions. Again using a CIN window, you create a new window and draw arbitrary objects into it using an array of high- and low-level drawing VIs. The high-level VIs include useful functions such as 2D and 3D graphs, spectrograms, image displays, and QuickTime movie manipulation. You can also import and export PICT and scrapbook files. The windows are interactive; that is, you can monitor and respond to mouse and keyboard events for features such as cursors and region selections. LabQD is like the Picture Control Toolkit on steroids—it's got much more capability.

QuickTime movies

Apple Computer invented **QuickTime** to fill a perceived need in multi-media—the need to conveniently and efficiently display movies with synchronized sound in *any* computer document. It turned out to be an enabling technology for data visualization as well because you can now *play* your data as a live, fluid entity, rather than just a stack of plots or pictures. Subtle interframe differences otherwise missed are readily apparent.

The first time I saw the use for movies in data analysis was when a physicist I worked with at LLNL, Ed Ng, pasted a series of plots into a HyperCard stack, one at a time. The plots represented a recurrent pulsed waveform that varied little from frame to frame. But when played in a movie . . . obvious differences appeared. We immediately observed mutations in the pulse shape and gained a qualitative insight into the magnitude of the changes. This kind of observation points us in unexpected directions—exactly the reason we use data visualization. Movies are also useful as an information source, like an animated **help** window. For instance, in an automated test application, you could show the operator what to do in a complicated operation.

Originated on the Macintosh, **QuickTime** is now available for Windows and the Sun as well. There are many multimedia applications available that you can use to manually load images or graphics files into QuickTime movies, and some data analysis packages can directly generate a QuickTime movie containing sequences of plots. Or, you can take advantage of one of the LabVIEW QuickTime extensions.

FastDraw and LabQD can also create QuickTime movies. Each time the window is updated with fresh data, another movie frame is generated. You can start and stop the recording of a movie programmatically or through a button in the plot window.

Metric Systems offers **MovieView** for recording and playback of QuickTime movies. The movie plays in an external window, with full programmatic control over speed, direction, timing, and volume. Alternatively, MovieView can convert the movie data to Picture control format for direct display on a LabVIEW panel with the Picture Control Toolkit.

Sophisticated QuickTime support comes with the **Py/QT** VIs from **Pyxis**. In addition to recording and playback with full programmatic control, you can also superimpose geometric grid shapes in the QuickTime playback window and detect mouse clicks. This enables an interactive movie, at least to a minimal extent. The synchronized audio track can also be separately recorded and extracted for analysis (Fig. 10.20). Some of the VIs are reentrant, allowing multiple movies to play simultaneously. Individual frames of the movie can also be copied to the clipboard for export or sent to a printer, all under programmatic control.

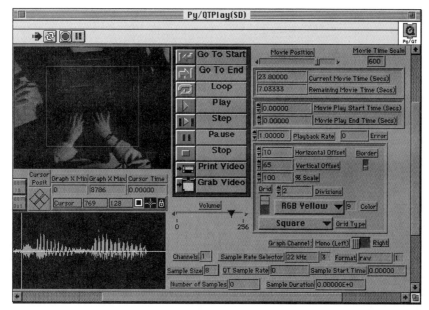

Figure 10.20 The Pyxis Py/QT VIs allow you to record, playback, and interact with QuickTime movies from within LabVIEW. This example displays a graph of the audio waveform.

The Intensity Chart

Another interesting indicator, the **Intensity Chart**, adds a third dimension to the ordinary strip chart. It accepts a 2D array of numbers, where the first dimension represents points along the y axis, and the second dimension represents points along the x axis, like a block-mode strip chart. Each value in the array is mapped to a color or intensity level. The biggest trick is setting the color or gray-scale range to accommodate your data. Fortunately, there is an option in the Intensity Chart pop up for the z-scale called *AutoScale Z*. That gets you into the ballpark, afterwhich you can set the overall range and the breakpoints along the scale by editing the values on the color ramp. The colors can also be determined by an attribute node. This is discussed in the Lab-VIEW user's manual.

In Fig. 10.21, the Intensity Chart gives you another way to look at a rather conventional display, a power spectrum. In this example, you can see how the power spectrum has changed over a period of time. The horizontal axis is time, the vertical axis is frequency (corresponding to the same frequency range as the Spectrum Plot), and the gray-scale value corresponds to the amplitude of the signal. I adjusted the gray-scale values to correspond to the interesting –20- to –100-dB range of the spectrum.

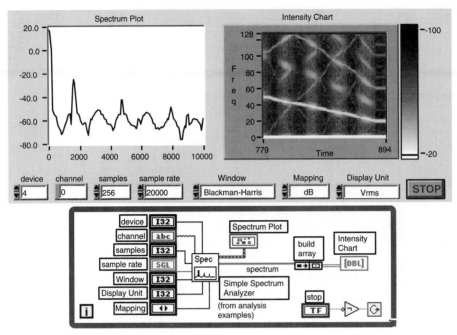

Figure 10.21   The Intensity Chart in action displaying a power spectrum. White regions on the chart represent high amplitudes. Frequency of a triangle wave was swept from 4 to 2 kHz while this VI was running. The chart scrolls to the left in real time.

Image Acquisition and Processing

Your LabVIEW system can be a powerful imaging tool if you add the right combination of hardware and software products. You will likely need hardware, in the form of a frame grabber and perhaps some video output devices, and software, in the form of image acquisition and processing VIs. The important thing to remember is that images are just another kind of data, and once you're working in LabVIEW, that data is going to be easy to handle. In fact, it's no harder to acquire, analyze, and display images than it is to acquire, analyze, and display analog waveforms. Good news, indeed.

The basic data format for an image is a two-dimensional (2D) matrix, where the value of each element (a **pixel**) is the intensity at a physical location. **Image acquisition** involves the use of a frame grabber for live video signals or the use of mathematical transforms applied to other forms of data to convert it into a suitable 2D format. Standard image processing algorithms operate only on this normally formatted image data. **Image processing** algorithms can be broadly grouped into five areas:

- **Image enhancement**: Processing an image so that the result is of greater value than the original image for some specific purpose.

Examples: adjusting contrast and brightness, removing noise, and applying false color.

- **Image restoration**: A process in which you attempt to reconstruct or recover a corrupted image (which is obviously easier when you know what messed up the image in the first place). Examples: deblurring, removal of interference patterns, and correcting geometric distortion. The Hubbell Space Telescope benefited from these techniques during its initial operation.

- **Image segmentation**: Dividing an image into relevant parts, objects, or particles. These algorithms allow a machine to extract important features from an image for further processing in order to recognize or otherwise measure those features.

- **Object representation and description**: Once an image has been segmented, the objects need to be described in some coherent and standardized fashion. Examples of these descriptive parameters are size, coordinates, shape factors, shape equivalents, and intensity distribution.

- **Image encoding**: Processing of images to reduce the amount of data needed to represent them. In other words, data compression and decompression algorithms. These methods are very important when images must be transmitted or stored.

Like signal processing, image processing is at once enticing and foreboding: there are so many nifty algorithms to choose from, but which ones are really needed for your particular application? When I first decided to tackle an imaging problem, I ran across the hall to visit a fellow EE and asked for a book. What I came back with was, *Digital Image Processing* by Gonzales and Wintz (1987), which is the favorite of many short courses in image processing. It's also *my* favorite. What you really need to do is study a textbook such as that one and get to know the world of image processing—the theory and applications—before you stumble blindly into a VI library of algorithms. Also, having example programs, and perhaps a mentor, are of great value to the beginner.

The most important imaging software for LabVIEW is **IMAQ Vision** from National Instruments. Years ago, **Graftek** developed **Concept V.i**, a highly modular package of CIN-based VIs that supports image acquisition and processing with interactive displays, file I/O, and a generally free exchange of data with the rest of LabVIEW. In 1996, National Instruments decided that imaging technology had reached the point where images could be acquired and manipulated just like data from a DAQ board. It reached an agreement with Graftek, purchased Concept V.i, and renamed it IMAQ Vision. You can now develop a flexible imaging application with LabVIEW and IMAQ as easily as you would write a data acquisition program with the DAQ library. Hence the name, IMaging ACquisition.

IMAQ has two family members offering different levels of image processing capability. The base package includes fundamental functions for image acquisition and file management, display and sizing utilities, histogram computation, and image-to-array conversions. The advanced package includes image processing and analysis functions such as lookup table transformations and spatial filters to allow for contrast and brightness adjustment, extraction of continuous and directional edges, noise removal, detail attenuation, texture enhancement, and so forth. It also includes frequency processing operations, arithmetic and logic operators, and object manipulations such as thresholding, erosion, dilation, opening, closing, labeling, hole filling, particle detection, and so forth.

Graftek will continue to support IMAQ Vision (as well as older versions of Concept V.i). Its specialty will be drivers for third-party frame grabbers, advanced and specialized algorithms, and custom application development. If you need special assistance with a custom imaging application, contact Graftek or its primary U.S. representative, GTFS.

System requirements for imaging

Basic graphing and simple image processing tasks are handled easily by any of the common LabVIEW-compatible computers, even the older, lower-performance Macs and PCs. But serious, real-time display and analysis call for more CPU power, more memory, and more disk space. Audio and video I/O adds requirements for specialized interface hardware that may not be included with your average computer, though the newer multimedia-ready machines sometimes have decent configurations. Let's see what kinds of hardware you might consider above and beyond your generic data acquisition system.

Computer configuration.   When it comes to computer configuration, don't worry yourself too much if your data is presented in the form of simple *xy* graphs because the LabVIEW charts and graphs are fast and efficient. Problems may arise, however, if you routinely plot tens of thousands of data points at a shot. Some quick benchmarking in LabVIEW will tell you if an older, low-power PC is up to the task. If not, plan on reducing the amount of data displayed or upgrading your system.

If it's images you're dealing with, then it's time to get serious about hardware. Image processing and display are positively the most CPU- and memory-intensive tasks you can run on your computer. Images contain enormous quantities of data. Many algorithms perform millions of calculations, even for apparently simple operations. And storing high-resolution images requires a disk drive with endless capacity. You can never afford the ideal computer that's really fast enough, or has enough memory, or big enough disks. But practical cost-performance trade-offs can lead you to a reasonable choice of hardware.

For real-time image processing (typically 30 frames per second), you will probably have to add specialized DSP hardware, often in conjunction with a frame grabber board. The fastest general-purpose computers available today come *close* to handling full-speed video, but be really cautious of manufacturers' claims. If you run custom-written applications with direct access to the I/O hardware, real-time video is possible on these faster machines. But if you expect LabVIEW to do lots of other things at the same time—such as running an experiment—there will be performance problems. As with high-speed data acquisition, buy and use specialized hardware to off-load these burdensome processing tasks and you will be much happier with the performance of your system.

Video I/O devices. Unless your computer already has built-in video support (and LabVIEW support for *that*), you will need to install a **frame grabber** in order to acquire images from cameras and other video sources. A *frame grabber* is a high-speed ADC with memory that is synchronized to an incoming video signal. Almost all frame grabbers have 8-bit resolution, which is adequate for most sources. It turns out that cameras aren't always the quietest signal sources, so any extra bits of ADC resolution may not be worth the extra cost. Preceding the ADC, you will generally find an amplifier with programmable gain (*contrast*) and offset (*brightness*). These adjustments help match the available dynamic range to that of the signal. For the North American NTSC standard (RS-170) video signal, 640 by 480 pixels of resolution is common. For the European PAL standard, up to 768 by 512 pixels may be available, if you buy the right grabber. Keep in mind that the resolution of the acquisition system (the frame grabber) may exceed that of the video source, especially if the source is *videotape*. Both color and monochrome frame grabbers are available. Color images are usually stored in separate red-green-blue (RGB) image planes, thus tripling the amount of memory required.

Frame grabbers have been around for many years, previously as large, expensive, outboard video digitizers, and more recently in the form of plug-in boards for desktop computers. With the birth of multimedia, frame grabbers have become cheaper and even more capable and are sometimes built into off-the-shelf computer bundles. The trick is to choose a board that LabVIEW can control through the use of suitable driver software or DLLs. Alternatively, you can use a separate software package to acquire images, write the data to a file, and then import the data into LabVIEW, but that defeats the purpose of building a real-time system.

In general, there are three classes of frame grabbers. First, there are the low-cost multimedia types, sometimes implemented as an external camera with a digitizer, such as the Connectix Quickcam. Also in this class are cheap plug-in boards and the built-in video capability in some Macintosh models. The primary limitations on these low-cost systems are that they include no hardware triggering so you can't synchronize image acquisition with an experiment, and they often contain an autogain feature. Like automatic gain control in a radio, this feature attempts to normalize the contrast, whether you like it or not. This can be a problem for quantitative applications, so beware!

The second class includes midrange plug-in boards, such as the Neotech Image Grabber, the BitFlow Video Raptor, the IMAQ PCI-1408, and Scion LG-3. These boards have triggering, hardware gain and offset control, and various synchronization options. They offer good value for scientific applications.

High-performance boards make up the third class. In addition to the features of the midrange boards, you can install large frame buffers on these boards to capture bursts of full-speed images for several seconds, regardless of your system's main memory availability or performance. Special video sources are also accommodated, such as line scan cameras, variable-rate scanning cameras, and digital cameras. Some DSP functionality is also available, including built-in frame averaging, differencing, and other mathematical operations, in addition to full programmability if you're a C or assembly language hacker. Examples are the BitFlow Data Raptor, Imaging Technology IC-PCI, the Scion AG5, and the Perceptics PixelTools series.

Following is a list of hardware products that definitely have LabVIEW drivers. The associated drivers or imaging packages are identified, and are discussed in detail later in this chapter.

Macintosh frame grabbers. Table 10.1 is a comprehensive list of frame grabbers for the Macintosh for which you can obtain LabVIEW drivers. Contact the software vendors for availability of drivers for other boards.

There are two other special video input options available for the Mac:

- The built-in video on the Macintosh AV-series machines and the Apple AV PCI board acquire 24-bit color images. It's supported by **Video VI** from Stellar Solutions (described later in this chapter).

- The Connectix Color Quickcam system is a very low-cost color CCD camera with a digitizer that plugs into the serial port. While not a scientific-grade instrument, it is adequate for casual use. Christophe Salzmann of EPFL has written some CIN-based VIs for the Connec-

TABLE 10.1   Frame Grabbers for Macintosh

Manufacturer/model	Bus	Color	Bits	Software support
Scion LG3	NuBus	N	8	IMAQ, Video VI
Scion LG3	PCI	N	8	IMAQ, Video VI
Scion AG5	PCI	N	8	Video VI
Scion AG5	NuBus	N	8	Video VI
Neotech Image Grabber	PCI	Y	8, 24	IMAQ
Neotech Image Grabber	NuBus	Y	8, 24	IMAQ
Precision Digital PDI Select	PCI	N	8	IMAQ
Macintosh AV hardware	PCI	Y	8	Video VI
National Instruments IMAQ PCI-1408	PCI	N	8	IMAQ

tix Quickcam. The Web page with links to the software is http://iawww.epfl.ch/Software/IA_Software.html.

Windows frame grabbers.   Many frame grabbers are available for the PC (Table 10.2). If you don't see your favorite board in this list, ask the vendor if it supplies a DLL driver with the board. If so, you can probably call the DLL with a LabVIEW Call Library node. Alternatively, you can contact Graftek and see if it has what you need; you might also check the info-labview mailgroup.

Real-time image processors.   Acquiring, processing, and storing live video requires gobs of processor power and bus bandwidth—capability that your computer may not have. One workaround is to record the video on tape and play it back frame by frame later, though this is not an option for real-time situations. Instead, you will have to consider buying an image grabber system that includes a large image memory and maybe a DSP processor. Extra memory adds the ability to store rapid bursts of frames, or perhaps the chance to devise an exotic buffering scheme to overlap acquisition and disk storage. Adding DSP support opens the door to *real* real-time image processing. Remember, though, that you

TABLE 10.2   Frame Grabbers for Windows

Manufacturer/model	Bus	Color	Software support
National Instruments IMAQ PCI-1408	PCI	N	IMAQ
BitFlow Video Raptor	PCI	N	IMAQ
BitFlow Data Raptor	PCI	N	IMAQ
Imaging Technology IC-PCI w/ AMVS	PCI	N	IMAQ
Imaging Technology IC-PCI w/ AMDIG	PCI	N	IMAQ
Imaging Technology IC-PCI w/ AMCLR	PCI	Y	IMAQ
Imaging Technology IC-PCI w/ AMFA	PCI	Y	IMAQ
NeoTech Image Grabber PCI	PCI	Y	IMAQ
ViewPoint SnapShot	ISA	N	ViewPoint SnapShot

generally must write your own special programs using the DSP manufacturer's C compiler or assembly language.

There are a couple of practical solutions I'm aware of. Perceptics offers two products for the Macintosh NuBus that qualify in the real-time realm. To acquire and store many frames in a short period of time, you can add its PixelStore board with up to 16 megabytes of video RAM. This hardware solution eliminates the disk throughput limitations of live video capture. An extension of the PixelStore, the Smart-Store, adds an onboard DSP processor, a TMS320C30 running at 32 MHz, and up to 32 megabytes of video RAM. The C language support includes an image processing library, which might make the programming job . . . bearable.

The Scion LG/3, available in NuBus or PCI bus formats, is another solution. It has space for memory expansion that permits storage of up to 128 frames of real-time video (that's 4.27 s at 30 frames per second). To keep cost low, it uses ordinary dynamic RAM SIMMs. If you only need to handle a few seconds of full-speed images, this is the way to go.

Now that you've got an image, how are you going to show it to someone? For live display you can use your computer's monitor from within LabVIEW or another application, or you might be able to use an external monitor. Hardcopy or desktop-published documents are always in demand.

One catch in the business of video output from your computer is the fact that high-resolution computer displays use a signal format (RGB component video) that is much different than the regular baseband NTSC or PAL standard format required by VCRs. There are several solutions (again, multimedia demands easy and cheap solutions, so expect to see some better ways of doing this). First, you can buy special converter boxes that accept various RGB video signals and convert them to NTSC. An example is **TelevEyes** from Digital Vision Corporation, which converts the signals from many 640-by-480 pixel resolution RGB color displays to NTSC or S-video (the still-video standard).

Another solution is to use a frame grabber board with video output capability (most boards have this feature). You write processed images to the output buffer and the data passes through a DAC to create a standard video signal. You can also use computer display boards that generate NTSC outputs. On the newer Macintosh models, for instance, the built-in video circuits support NTSC video, as do many third-party boards. This scheme is really tidy because all you're doing is plugging in a second monitor.

Using IMAQ Vision

IMAQ Vision is very well designed and the included example programs make it pretty clear how you put together an image acquisition and processing application. Also, the manual is quite thorough. You can also buy **Imaging Sandbox**, an IMAQ starter application developed by **GTFS** and distributed as an imaging tutorial tool. It includes all the diagrams and makes it easy to try out various features of IMAQ. What I'll show you here are a few basic concepts and a real-world application. The first thing you need to understand is how images are managed.

Image handles.   IMAQ carries information about an image (name, size, resolution, data, and so forth) in a data structure that is accessible by each function in the IMAQ library but hidden from LabVIEW. To indicate which image you are working with, you use a cluster called an **image handle** which is a kind of refnum. Image handles are normally created by **Cvi Create** and marked for destruction by **Cvi Dispose**. You must never fiddle with the value of an image handle, or the program will cease to function (or *worse*). A new image handle must be created for every independent image. Like all data in LabVIEW, images (and their handles) are no longer accessible once the calling VI finishes execution.

One advantage to this image handle scheme is that you have explicit control of image creation and destruction, unlike the situation with LabVIEW's data types. If you create an image handle, load an image, then submit the handle to 10 different image processing functions from the IMAQ library, rest assured that there will be no duplication of the data array (image). In contrast, a LabVIEW array, if passed in parallel fashion to several different DSP subVIs, may require many duplicates. You might be able to chain some functions in series, if you're careful, thus eliminating much duplication.

Managing the image window.   Images are displayed in a CIN window (as in SurfaceView) that is separate from your LabVIEW front panel. It is a normal, well-behaved, interactive window over which you and your program have full control. Figure 10.22 shows the diagram for a simple IMAQ application that acquires an image from a plug-in frame grabber board and then displays it.

Notice that the diagram begins at the left with an image handle that is created by Cvi Create. Next, the **IMAQ_Snap** VI initializes the frame grabber, acquires an image, and stores it in memory at the location spec-

Figure 10.22   A simple IMAQ application that grabs an image from a plug-in frame grabber and displays it.

ified by the image handle. Finally, **Cvi WindDraw** creates and positions the window, draws the image, and sets the window's title. There are many other window control options available through the window management functions.

Windows can be interactive. If the user clicks and/or drags in the image window, and one of the drawing options have been enabled, the selected object, such as a rectangle, is drawn in the window and the coordinates of the new object are returned in an array. This allows you to interactively select a **region of interest (ROI)** for later processing (not to mention playing *Etch-A-Sketch*). The concept of a ROI (sometimes pronounced "roy") is widely used in image processing to refer to an area in which an interesting feature resides or to a line crossing such a feature.

Here are some other interesting tools for drawing: **Cvi InsertText** allows you to annotate an image by drawing a string of any font, style, or size at any position, in black or white. **Cvi Draw** programmatically draws lines, ovals, rectangles, rounded rectangles, and arcs, with optional fill patterns. Lines, rectangles, and ovals can also be drawn interactively with **Cvi WindToolsSetup**. With these and other IMAQ tools, you can build a fully interactive image display in LabVIEW. Refer to the example VIs for more interesting demonstrations.

Acquiring an image.   High-level IMAQ VIs allow you to easily perform such operations as acquiring images in single-shot (**snap**) or continuous (**grab**) mode without advanced knowledge of the IMAQ low-level function calls and image acquisition details. As we saw in the previous example, the easy-level IMAQ Snap VI made it easy to grab an image from a National Instruments frame grabber. For other, third-party boards, you will have to contact Graftek and obtain a suitable driver VI. My experience with those drivers is that they are nearly as easy to use as the IMAQ drivers, though you give up RTSI bus synchronization.

The **IMAQ grab** functions perform a continuous buffered image acquisition, much like the buffered DAQ acquisition VIs for analog signals. Basically, you configure an internal software buffer, then start the acquisition process. Acquisition can be triggered, either by RTSI signals or by an external trigger applied directly to the frame grabber board. The buffer fills asynchronously, allowing you to process and store images in parallel with the acquisition process. When you're done acquiring images, you stop the process and free up the buffer memory.

Transforming data.   An important feature of IMAQ is the ability to convert images to and from LabVIEW 2D arrays. This opens a world of possibilities in data transformations and computations because you aren't stuck with just the functions that come with the package. Figure 10.23 is a simple example VI that demonstrates several useful

Read image from file. Display in Intensity Graph.

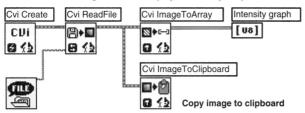

Figure 10.23 This example demonstrates reading a file, image to array conversion, and copying the image to the clipboard.

functions. First, **Cvi ReadFile** loads data from an image file. The VI can convert several image file formats including TIFF and PICT. The **Cvi ImageToArray** VI fetches the image identified by the incoming image handle and returns it as a 2D array of U8, I16, or SGL values. After some processing, you could call the complementary function, **Cvi ArrayToImage**, to convert the array back to the regular IMAQ domain. In this example, I wired the 2D array to an Intensity Graph indicator—an easy way to put the image right on the LabVIEW panel, rather than having it float around in the external window. I also sent the image to the **Cvi ImageToClipboard** VI, which leaves you with a copy of the image on your system's clipboard. That's a handy way to export an image. You can also read an image from the clipboard.

When performance is critical, you should remember that **IMAQ ImageToArray** has to create a new (large) array to store the converted image. This will cost you some time in memory management, especially the first time the VI is called. The function remains useful; any time that you create data mathematically or transform data from other sources into a 2D array, you can display it as an image and use the advanced processing features of IMAQ.

One thing to remember is that in some cases you have to limit all values to a range of zero (typically black) to 255 (typically white). Values outside this range are folded back in with unexpected results. For instance, converting the integer –1 to a U8 (unsigned byte) format results in a value of 255—a real surprise when you expected –1 to be very *black* and it comes out very *white*. Fortunately, the IMAQ library supports several numeric types, including I8, U16, and single-precision floating point. This eliminates many disconcerting underflow and overflow problems.

Video VI

Surely, this isn't a one-product imaging market! While IMAQ is the most comprehensive imaging package for LabVIEW, there are alternatives. One product that Macintosh users might consider, especially on a budget, is **Video VI** by **Stellar Solutions** (it's also distributed by GTFS). Video VI supports several frame grabber boards including the built-in Apple AV features, reads and writes TIFF files, performs rudimentary analysis, and manages its display window. All data is returned as LabVIEW 2D arrays, so you can easily write your own VIs for image processing. It's also a bargain.

In contrast to the CIN Window approach used by IMAQ and other specialized imaging packages, Video VI relies on a separate application, Video Companion, to handle all the I/O and display interaction (Fig. 10.24). Video Companion is a basic image acquisition and display application to which the Stellar Solutions developers will continue to add features. Video VI communicates with Video Companion via AppleEvents. A modest number of VIs handle all the interaction, including window and image attributes, drawing graphical items into the window, and reading user mouse activity (including drawing) from the window.

Image files.   To export and import data, you need to write an image out to disk and/or read it back in again with predictable results. IMAQ and Video VI include functions to read and write standard image-format files, notably **TIFF** (Tagged Image File Format). TIFF is one of the most useful formats because many other applications, such as image processing, desktop publishing, and drawing programs can all read it. The format supports various resolutions and pixel depths (from 8 to 32

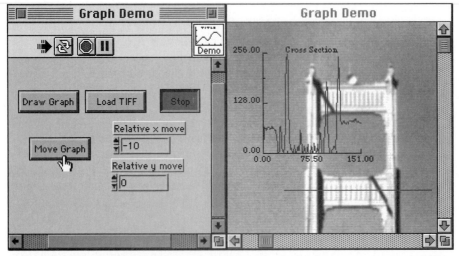

Figure 10.24   Video VI controls another application, Video Companion (right window) through AppleEvents.

bits per pixel), as well as color. It is portable between all of LabVIEW's platforms. IMAQ can also import **PICT** images.

Windows **BMP** (bitmap) format is another candidate for image storage. To my knowledge, the only support for BMP images is the LVBMPS library written by Brian Paquette of Metric Systems and available from ftp.pica.army.mil. Sadly, the VIs only *read* BMP files, and they're pretty slow. Perhaps Brian or someone else will continue to work on BMP and other image file I/O. Keep watching the info-labview mailgroup.

You can also write the data to files of your own format. For instance, you can convert the image to a 2D array, then pass it to the **Write File** function, which writes the data as straight binary or as LabVIEW datalogs. These binary formats are fast and efficient, especially if you're just trying to read the data back into LabVIEW at a later time. Some applications such as Adobe Photoshop can read raw binary files if the format is simple (such as 8-bit gray scale), but you have to manually tell the application how many rows and columns the image contains. That's why TIFF is generally a better solution.

The Intensity Graph for built-in image display.   Regardless of where you obtain your images, LabVIEW has a means by which you can display them right on the front panel: the **Intensity Graph**. The Intensity Graph accepts several data types, among them a 2D array corresponding to an image. I wrote a simple VI (Fig. 10.25) to load a raw binary image from a file and format the data for display in an Intensity Graph. Because a raw binary file contains no header to describe the dimensions of the image, the user has to supply that information. The control called **Rows** supplies this key information. If you enter the wrong number, the image is hopelessly scrambled.

Looking at the diagram, the file is read as a string which is then converted to an array of U8 using the **String to Byte Array** conversion function. A For Loop breaks the long array of values into rows, which are then placed in a 2D array for display. An **Attribute Node** for the Intensity Graph sets the y- and x-axis scales to fit the actual number of rows and columns in the image. Note that the y axis has zero at the top, rather than its usual place at the bottom. That makes the image come out right-side up. You also have to select **Transpose Array** from the pop-up menu on the Intensity Graph to swap the x- and y-axis data.

An important tweak that you can make is to match the number of displayed pixels to the data. Ideally, one array element maps to one pixel, or at least there is an integral ratio between the two. This reduces aliasing in the image. In this example, I made this adjustment by setting the Plot Area Size (x and y values) with the Attribute Node.

The Ramp control (part of the Intensity Graph) sets the data range to 0–200, corresponding to a pleasing gray scale ranging from black to

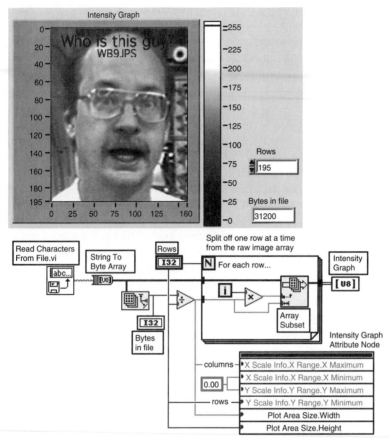

Figure 10.25   The Intensity Graph displaying an image from a binary file. The user has to know the size of the image—particularly the number of rows. The raw data string is converted to an array, which is then transformed into a 2D array suitable for display.

white. You can adjust the gray scale or color gradations by editing the numeric markers on the Ramp. Pop up on the Ramp control and set the marker spacing to *Arbitrary*. Pop up again to add or delete markers. You can then change the value of each marker and slide it up and down the ramp to create breakpoints in the (normally linear) mapping of intensity values to display brightness or color. For fun, you can pick various colors or put in palette breakpoints by adding elements to the Color Table, another item available through the Attribute Node. This is a means of generating a kind of color lookup table (CLUT).

Colors are stored as unsigned long integers (U32) with the following representation. The least-significant byte is the value of blue, the next byte is green, the next is red, and the most-significant byte is unused, but is normally set to zero. (In some applications, this extra byte is called the **alpha channel** and represents transparency.) For instance, 100 percent red (255 in the red byte) plus 50 percent green produces orange. This is also known as **32-bit color**. To select a color, you have several options. On the diagram, you can place a Color Box Constant (from the Additional Numeric Constants palette), then pop up on it to choose a color from those available in LabVIEW. A corresponding control on the panel is the Color Box constant from the Numerics palette. A related control, the Color Ramp, allows you to map an arbitrary number to an arbitrary color. All of these controls and constants use a visual, rather than numeric, representation of color. Remember that the actual color on your monitor is limited to the palette permitted by LabVIEW, which in turn is limited by your monitor setting.

For arbitrary colors, you must generate an appropriate U32 number. Figure 10.26 shows two of the possible ways to combine values for red, green, and blue into a composite RGB value. The data conversion functions (**Type Cast** and **Join Numbers**) come from the Advanced>>Data Manipulation palette. You might use this technique for combining separate RGB color image planes into a single, displayable color image. The complementary operation is also feasible, using the **Split Numbers** function to break a color into its RGB components.

Imaging example: Counting objects

Image processing is a bit like digital signal processing: the computer is only as smart as the programmer. The mathematical algorithms are beyond the scope of this book, but you'll find that there are quite a few operations that you can use successfully with an intuitive approach. Let's take a common example, counting objects, which is formally known as **image segmentation**. Our first question is what, exactly, is an

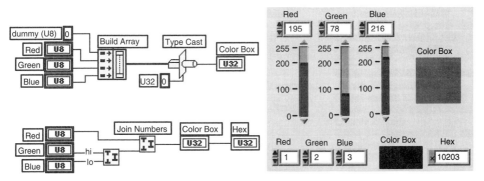

Figure 10.26 Colors can be generated programmatically, but it requires some data-manipulation tricks.

object? In image processing, 2D objects are usually referred to as **parti-cles**. A particle can have many attributes, such as area, circumference, one or more holes, and *x*- and *y*-axis projection lengths. These attributes can collectively be called the **morphological** parameters of a particle. By measuring or modifying the morphology of a desired particle, you may be able to separate it from other undesired particles.

Figure 10.27 is an example where we're trying to count the number of nuts and bolts in an image. For a human, the exercise is trivial. For a computer, the reliability of the algorithm depends on the programmer's approach. The first trick is separating the possible objects of interest from their background. Next, you must discriminate between objects—the nuts, the bolts, and any noise objects. Finally, you can count the valid objects. In this example VI, the user must help the IMAQ program by entering some key parameters.

In Fig. 10.28, the diagram for the main VI shows the framework for the application. It's a one-shot VI where an image file is loaded from disk, processed, and displayed. Examining the diagram from left to right, it starts with the creation of two images, one for the original image (named *Live*), and a second one containing the processed image (named *Binary*). Actual images are displayed along with the front panel in Fig. 10.27. A histogram is computed and graphed, from which the user must choose a threshold value. **Thresholding** is a simple way

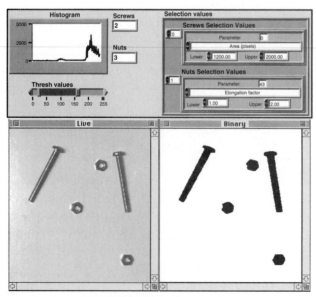

Figure 10.27 Front panel and images for a nut and bolt counter. The user must enter some object selection parameters.

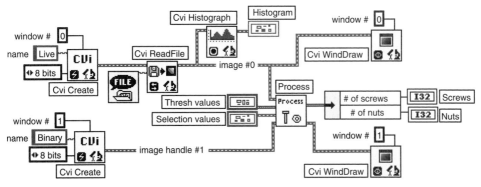

Figure 10.28 Diagram for the nut and bolt counter main VI. This VI is responsible for loading and displaying the image.

to separate objects from a contrasting background. All you have to do is choose the right intensity level. The level can be chosen automatically by the **Cvi Auto-Threshold** VI, which includes a choice of five different thresholding algorithms. But thresholding is not always necessary as long as the images are fairly consistent. Next, the Process subVI is called, where the image segmentation occurs. The results are displayed by separate calls to Cvi WindDraw.

Looking inside the Process subVI (Fig. 10.29), you can see the straightforward block diagram approach for which LabVIEW is so famous. First, the **Cvi Threshold** VI turns the original image into a binary one (black and white only). Such images are much easier to analyze. Next, the **Cvi Morphology** VI closes any open paths in the image. This versatile VI can do many other operations that modify object morphology, such as dilation, opening, eroding, and thinning. The third function, **Cvi FillHole**, fills in the holes in the nuts and eliminates any pinholes or single-pixel flaws. The image is now ready for particle

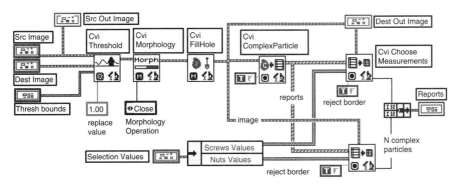

Figure 10.29 The Process subVI separates valid objects (nuts from bolts) from the background.

analysis by the **Cvi ComplexParticle** VI. It's a very powerful function for object identification, returning a cluster array of reports for each object in the image. The cluster in the report contains 20 basic morphological parameters. The report array is then passed to the **Cvi Choose Measurements** VI, which segregates objects according to a set of **selection values**, or parameters. There are about 50 different parameters to choose from, and each parameter has an upper and lower value. For the nuts and bolts, *area* and *elongation factor* are selected. Clearly, a bolt has a larger area than a nut, and it's a much longer object (the ratio of its x and y projections is much different than 1.0). Each copy of the Cvi Choose Measurements VI returns a particle count, which is the number of nuts or bolts.

If I was really smart, I might be able to automate parameter selection to a greater degree. Perhaps a trainable program using an **artificial neural network (ANN)** would be a good approach. Graftek offers such a product, if you're interested.

Sound I/O

Recording and reproducing sound can be useful for scientific analysis, operator notification, or as a novelty. The whole idea is to convert acoustic vibrations into an electrical signal (probably with a microphone), digitize that signal, and then reverse the process. In most cases, we use the human audible range of 20 Hz to 20 kHz to define sound, but the spectrum may be extended in both directions for applications such as sonar and ultrasonic work. Depending upon the critical specifications of your application, you may use your computer's built-in sound hardware, a plug-in board (DAQ or something more specialized), or external ADC or DAC hardware. As usual, a key element is having a LabVIEW driver or other means to exchange data with the hardware.

The one and only sound function that's included with LabVIEW is the **Beep** VI, found in the Advanced function palette. On all platforms, it plays the system alert sound through the built-in sound hardware.

DAQ for sound I/O

An ordinary DAQ board is quite capable of recording and reproducing sound up to its Nyquist sampling limit. The only technical shortcomings of such a board may be in the areas of harmonic and intermodulation distortion, the lack of built-in antialiasing filters, and perhaps a dynamic range limitation with 12-bit boards. For those reasons, National Instruments developed its dynamic signal acquisition boards, such as the A2100 and A2150 series, featuring antialiased 16-bit inputs and outputs and very low distortion. In any case, all you need is the standard DAQ library to do the recording and playback in LabVIEW.

The maximum frequency that your system can process continuously is probably limited by CPU performance. The keyword is *process:* do you want to do real-time filtering, FFTs, and display of signals with a 40-kHz bandwidth? You won't make it, at least with today's general-purpose CPUs and LabVIEW. Perhaps a DSP board can take care of the numerical processing; check out the DSP products from National Instruments, but remember that extra programming—usually in C—is required. At lower frequencies, though, you can certainly build a usable real-time system. Be sure to run some benchmarks before committing to a real-time DAQ approach.

The good news about DAQ for sound applications is that it's easy to use. Review the analog I/O part of Chap. 5, "Using the DAQ Library," for details on single-shot and continuous waveform acquisition and generation. For wide-bandwidth signals, disk streaming is usually the answer, and again, the solutions are built into the DAQ and file I/O libraries.

A recurring issue with sound I/O is that of file formats and standards. On each platform, there are certain file formats that the operating system can conveniently record and play back through standard hardware. Therefore, it's desirable to use those formats for your own, DAQ-based sound I/O. In the sections that follow, we'll look at some options for handling those formats.

Macintosh sound options

Every Macintosh has built-in sound hardware, though the earliest models did not have inputs. Beginning with the AV (audio-visual) models and continuing through the latest Power Macs, 16-bit audio I/O is standard, and many models offer stereo as well as monaural ports. The operating system includes a Sound Manager with extensive capabilities, and that is the means by which LabVIEW can access the built-in hardware. A CIN is required to make calls to the Sound Manager, so unless you're a good C programmer, you'll have to rely on third parties for LabVIEW sound drivers.

mac\ sound\sound.sea Many moons ago, I put together a little package for 68K Macs that allows you to record and play 8-bit monaural audio from the sound port, and play 8-bit data from any source as long as the sample rate is about 22 kHz. In addition, VIs for playing system sound (SND) resources were contributed by O. Le Dortz ledortz@lpnaxp.in2p3.fr. These VIs are included on the CD-ROM. There are two main limitations to note. First, they only work on 68K Macs, though perhaps some enterprising users will convert them to the PowerPC one day (search ftp.pica.army.mil to find updates). Second, they are all *synchronous* VIs. That is, your LabVIEW program (and your Macintosh) can do nothing else while a sound is being recorded or played.

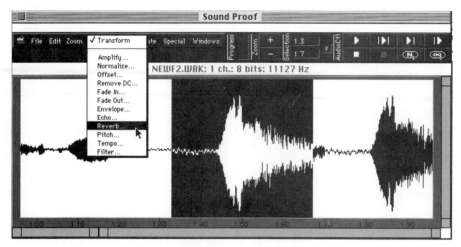

Figure 10.30 SoundProof handles all aspects of audio signal acquisition, analysis, display, and storage on the Macintosh.

A very elaborate sound package, **SoundProof**, is available from **Aster** of France (Fig. 10.30). It's a framework for recording, playing back, editing, and processing sounds and other signals with LabVIEW for Macintosh (both 68K and PowerMacs). SoundProof provides *fully asynchronous* Sound Manager–compatible recording and playback to and from files in the Apple-standard audio interchange file format (AIFF). Several other common file formats, including WAV, AU, SoundEdit Pro, and SD I and II files, can be imported for analysis and display.

The package offers extensive display and editing (copy, paste, and so forth) of signals with no limitations on the maximum amount of data. SoundProof uses RAM disk techniques for improving performances when plotting, reading, and writing big chunks of data under LabVIEW. Some examples of sound effects and processing are included (Reverb, Echo, Filter, Shift Pitch, Tempo, Mix Tracks, and FFT analysis) and are implemented as simple LabVIEW diagrams. Performance is very good because of extensive use of CINs for display manipulation.

Pyxis offers its **Sound VI** package for recording and playing back sound at all sampling rates between 5.5 and 64 kHz on Macs with the latest sound I/O hardware. Data can be stored to and retrieved from AIFF files. For real-time applications, you can simultaneously record and play back. This might be useful for measurement of system response.

Speak to me. Apple has released some interesting system extensions that permit your Mac to speak. Apple's speech technology includes text-to-speech conversion with a variety of voice synthesizers that mimic various ages and genders. No special hardware is required. The **Speech VIs** from **Pyxis** give you full control over these features, making it easy to vocalize text from within LabVIEW. Some interesting applications come to mind. Important events, such as alarms and error conditions, can be announced with specific information that is programmatically generated. Or, a machine operator could be prompted to perform a specific task, or results could be announced. Data results could even be tape-recorded or transmitted over radio links.

Pyxis has also developed speech recognition capability for LabVIEW (Power Macintosh only). Included with the Speech VI package are some amazing **Speech Recognition VIs** that decode speech input from the built-in microphone port. The VIs can be instructed to recognize a predefined list of commands sufficient for operating front panel controls of a LabVIEW application to allow PPC Mac LabVIEW users to utilize speech input for user control of LabVIEW front panel controls. By augmenting the normal point-and-click approach to Boolean or numeric control manipulation, Speech Recognition VIs allow operators of computer-controlled heavy machinery, automated hazardous environment control systems, or remotely located automation systems to command and control LabVIEW-based applications using the human voice.

Windows sound options

The Creative Labs **SoundBlaster** board has become a de facto standard for sound I/O on Windows machines. It features 16-bit stereo I/O and generally plugs-and-plays in most systems. There are plenty of compatible clones available, too. The Windows multimedia features make it fairly easy to access the features of these boards, though the necessary VIs are not included with LabVIEW.

To record data from a SoundBlaster (and *much more*), there is a useful collection of VIs written by Thijs Bolhuis at the University of Twente (t.bolhuis@el.utwente.nl). The library is called sndblexm.llb (SoundBlaster Examples) and is available from ftp.pica.army.mil. He implemented a general-purpose multimedia control interface (the **MciSendString** VI) by using a Call Library function that sends text commands to the Windows 95 multimedia system. With this VI you can use numerous multimedia functions such as playing and recording sounds, **MIDI (Musical Instrument Digital Interface)** files, playing Microsoft **AVI (Audio Visual Interface)** movie files (forward and reverse, slow and fast, all programmatically), or controlling the CD player. The only trick is that you have to know the string commands.

You can find these commands in the Windows System Developer Kit from Microsoft or from the Web page at http://www.macromedia.com/text/support/technotes/general/.

A similar, but more comprehensive package is available from Greg Burlingame (gregb@ultranet.com). Again using the Windows multimedia interface, you can select from sampling rates supported by the individual sound card, as well as bit resolution, and the number of channels. The data can be played from and/or recorded to memory, as well as being played from and/or recorded to disk. Depending upon the features of your sound card, you may be able to simultaneously play and record. Some cards cards even support synchronized simultaneous playback and record which is necessary for situations where accurate absolute phase information is required.

Greg's SoundBlaster library includes an example that shows how you can use the **MciSendString** VI and the **Read Wav** VI together to make an audio data acquisition program for the SoundBlaster. The example is limited to 8-bit resolution and 11.025 kHz.

In the LabVIEW DLL examples, there is a VI called **Play Sound** that allows you to play any standard Windows sound file. Such files normally have a .wav extension and contain binary data in a standard format. The VI contains a Call Library function that calls the sndPlaySound function that is exported from the Windows multimedia system DLL. There is also a VI to abort the playing of a sound.

Since the .wav files have a standard format, it's possible to extract the binary waveform data for general use. If you're interested in details on the format, see the Web site at http://www.cwi.nl/ftp/audio/RIFF-format. For your convenience, Frederic Villeneuve, an application engineer at National Instruments France, wrote a **Read Wavefile** VI that can read 8- or 16-bit mono or stereo wav files and play them on the analog output of a DAQ board. The VI library is available from ftp.pica.army.mil.

 win95-nt\ sound\ wavefile.llb

Another set of VIs for accessing .wav files were written by Jason Dunham of New Visions Engineering. In his **wavfile** library are VIs to read and write .wav format, graph the waveforms, and play the sound using the Play Sound example VI. They're on the CD-ROM.

Bibliography

Cleveland, William S., *The Elements of Graphing Data,* Wadsworth, Monterey, California, 1985. (ISBN 0-534-03729-1.)

Gonzalez, Rafael C., and Paul Wintz, *Digital Image Processing.* Addison-Wesley, Reading, Massachusetts, 1987. (ISBN 0-201-11026-1.)

Tufte, Edward R., *The Visual Display of Quantitative Information.* Graphics Press, Cheshire, Connecticut, 1983.

Wang, Peter C. C., *Graphical Representation of Multivariate Data,* Academic Press, New York, 1978. (ISBN 0-12-734750-X.)

Automated Test Applications

Automated testing generally applies to manufacturing and production test applications. Automated testing removes the *human factor* from the testing process, thus increasing data consistency and enhancing throughput—the number of items tested in a period of time. Most **automated test equipment (ATE)** setups are intended for use by semiskilled operators. Therefore, the equipment and software must be simple, robust, and very easy to use. The more automation and built-in intelligence, the better. Finally, a general goal of ATE system design is to maintain a high degree of flexibility so that one system can be easily reconfigured to test different products.

A major development leading to more frequent use of LabVIEW in the ATE world is VXI, which has its roots in the automated test systems used by the United States military. Military testing applications have always placed a high premium on modular, reliable automated test systems. The military branches each developed separate specifications for their own standardized modular test systems and even their own ATE languages. A key goal of these standards was to compact the large racks of instrumentation and standardize the test software. These standardization activities, in conjunction with instrument manufacturers' efforts to meet military needs and to produce high-speed, small-footprint test systems, led to the creation of the VXI Consortium and ultimately the VXI specification.

VXI instruments have no front panels, so you need a computer for the user interface. Enter LabVIEW, whose combination of graphical front panels and programming paradigm makes it an obvious match with VXI. And, because in its initial phase VXI was used primarily in ATE applications, LabVIEW has become popular in modern ATE.*

LabVIEW is a natural tool for bridging the testing requirements of design and production. The methods you use for developing test VIs are pretty much the same in the lab as in automated production tests. In fact, a big bonus in using LabVIEW in production tests is that you can use the VIs you developed in the design phase. The many examples in this book about developing VIs, especially those involving instrument drivers, are all applicable to automated testing.

Unlike laboratory research, where the developer and operator of an experiment are often the same person, an ATE system requires a very clear distinction between capabilities available to the *developer* of test programs and capabilities available to the *operator* of test programs. Developers can simulate tests and devices, interactively control instruments from front panels, and generally see improved programming efficiency from LabVIEW's block diagram programming. The test operator, however, is not a LabVIEW developer. In fact, operators have no reason to know or care how a test was developed. They have no knowledge of block diagrams, instrument drivers, VXI, or any of the myriad details that concern test developers. Operators do exactly what the title implies—they operate a test program.

This distinction between developer and operator distinguishes ATE from the laboratory. There are numerous ways to use LabVIEW to satisfy the different requirements for the developer and the operator. This chapter focuses primarily on using LabVIEW as a centralized platform for automated testing. A number of third parties also use LabVIEW for automated testing by invoking LabVIEW VIs from an external application. This external application implements the operator environment. These types of applications are also discussed in this chapter. Note that this chapter does not discuss specific types of testing, such as analog or digital testing, or types of measurements.

Here are a few ATE-specific terms that we'll be using. A device being tested is called the **unit under test (UUT)**. The term **test** refers to a routine or procedure that determines a specific characteristic of a UUT. In LabVIEW terms, the software module that performs the operations of a test is a *VI*. A test may consist of any operation that you can create a VI to perform, including instrument configuration, measurements, and numeric calculations. A **test program** is a collection of tests that, taken as a whole, verifies all of the characteristics of the UUT needed

---

* If you remember the story in Chap. 1, "Roots," the initial purpose in creating LabVIEW was to replace Basic in ATE applications. But unlike specialized ATE packages, the flexibility of LabVIEW has led it far beyond ATE today.

to determine that the UUT performs acceptably. A UUT **passes** if it meets all of the parameters characterized by a test program and **fails** if it does not meet those requirements. (See Fig. 11.1.)

Before proceeding with specific LabVIEW programming details, let's consider some of the standard approaches used in ATE. In many cases, the test is called **Go/No-Go**. In Go/No-Go testing, the operator runs a test program simply to see if the UUT passes or fails. If the UUT passes, it's placed in the *good pile,* and if it fails, it's placed in the *functionally challenged pile.* In Go/No-Go testing, the operator does not try to figure out why the UUT failed. He or she simply moves on to the next UUT. The test program produces a test report that documents the reason that the UUT failed. This report may be used later to repair the UUT. In Go/No-Go testing, you can generally use the LabVIEW Run-time System or generate a stand-alone application using the LabVIEW Application Builder because the operator needs no low-level access to your VI suite.

In some test systems, the operator may actually be expected to diagnose the UUT failure or make some adjustment, such as a manual calibration. In order to perform diagnostics, the operator must have some flexibility beyond simply running a test program from start to finish. The operator may need to execute individual tests, change input param-

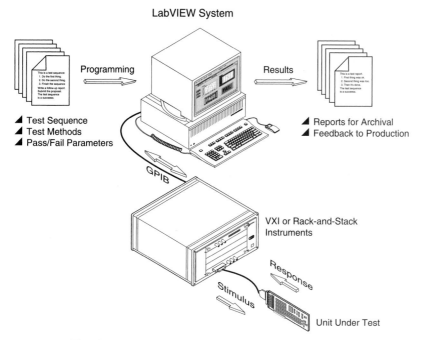

Figure 11.1 The elements of a typical ATE system include a computer, some I/O hardware, and the unit under test.

eters to a given test, or even write a new test to measure a characteristic of the UUT in a different way. The operator may need to view the front panels of individual VIs and run interactively. In such cases, a development copy of LabVIEW is needed, and this skilled operator—who is really a technician or engineer at this level—will of course need extra training.

Test Executive

The most distinguishing feature of the automated test environment is the **test executive**. The test executive is an application that sequences the execution of tests, so it's also called a **test sequencer**. While this definition sounds simple, there are many possible ways to implement a test executive, and the development process can be quite lengthy. A test executive performs the following basic operations:

- Schedules tests based upon pass/fail status
- Interfaces the operator to the testing process
- Organizes and logs test results

You don't have to write your own test executive from scratch (though we will go through the basic design concepts you will need to know). Instead, you can order the **LabVIEW Test Executive** from National Instruments or one of the third-party packages listed in the *Solutions* guide, also available from National Instruments. Most of this chapter describes the concepts behind the Test Executive because it represents a full-featured system with a rational foundation. However, I'm not going to duplicate that application's user manual, on which the National Instruments team did a fine job. You can read that when you start your own ATE development.

Execution control

The most fundamental job of the test executive is to run a set of test subVIs in a prescribed order. If you have a fixed number of test subVIs, you can create a simple test sequencer by dropping the VIs in a Sequence structure. Or better yet, you can use a common thread such as error I/O to link your test subVIs in order across the diagram. If your application always runs from start to finish, waiting until the last test finishes before determining if the UUT passed, such a linear, sequential approach may be sufficient. In most cases, however, you will want more flexibility in defining the order in which test subVIs run.

An automatic **sequencer** engine is at the core of most ATE applications. The order of execution is determined not by the order of the VIs placed on the diagram, but by a user-programmed list. Furthermore, conditional execution and other forms of sequence flow control are usually permitted. Flow control options may include repeating a failed test or skipping over certain steps based on the results of a previous test (such as a case statement or if-then-else structure) or looping. With this user-programmable flow control capability, the sequencer engine becomes a powerful tool for ATE and other automatic control tasks.

Returning test data—a common thread

Before you can develop a test executive, you must decide how you will return the results from each test. (Imagine that! Doing some design work before writing your program. . . .) The simplest approach is for each test subVI to contain a Boolean indicator on its front panel and connector pane. This Boolean indicator serves as the Pass/Fail flag for the test. The subVI performs the complete test, determines if the test passes and sets the Pass/Fail flag to true if the test passed and false if it failed. The test executive block diagram, in which the test subVIs reside, inspects this Boolean value to see if the test passed. This approach places the burden of determining the test result on the subVI itself. The drawback here is that you must write the test subVI for a specific test scenario. Suppose you have a common type of test, such as output power of an amplifier, that differs from UUT to UUT only in the desired measured value that is considered passing. You could expand upon the Boolean flag approach and make your test subVI more generic by passing in the comparison limit as a control for the subVI. This approach still places the logic for making the pass/fail comparison inside the subVI.

Consider an approach in which the subVI does not actually make the comparison itself, but merely returns results. The cluster shown in Fig. 11.2 contains several pieces of information and functions much like the familiar error I/O cluster. The results may be returned as either a Boolean **Pass/Fail flag** or as a measured value, which might be a numeric, a string, or something else. In the general case, the test subVI is simply a measurement routine that returns its measured value using one of the measurement indicators. The test executive determines if the test passed by comparing the measurement with limits specified elsewhere. If the measurement for a test requires more than one value, you can still perform the comparison in the subVI itself and set the Pass/Fail flag. Alternatively, you could include an array as a standard output. In either case, a separate test program specification tells the test executive how to determine if the test passed. This arrangement achieves a separation between the test executive and test subVIs, which helps you reuse test subVIs. A later section discusses the data logging responsibility of the test executive. A common data output

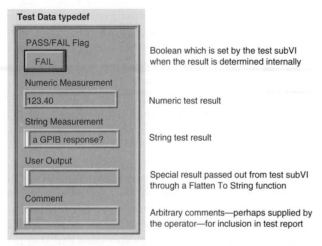

Test Data typedef

PASS/FAIL Flag

FAIL — Boolean which is set by the test subVI when the result is determined internally

Numeric Measurement

123.40 — Numeric test result

String Measurement

a GPIB response? — String test result

User Output — Special result passed out from test subVI through a Flatten To String function

Comment — Arbitrary comments—perhaps supplied by the operator—for inclusion in test report

Figure 11.2   A standard data type for test results, as used in the LabVIEW Test Executive. Test VIs return either a numeric or string measurement or the Boolean Pass/Fail Flag indicating pass/fail status.

for all VIs provides a standard mechanism for test subVIs to pass their measurement data to the test executive. Figure 11.2 shows the actual test data typedef from the LabVIEW Test Executive.

An architecture for test sequencing

Once you have a mechanism for returning the result of a test, you can decide on the sequencing capabilities you require and how best to implement them in LabVIEW. Clearly, a Sequence structure for sequencing test programs is quite limiting because it doesn't support flexible flow control. How about Case structures? Figure 11.3 shows

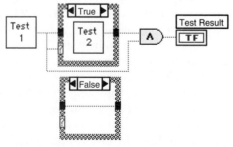

Figure 11.3   The Case structure permits skipping Test 2 if Test 1 has failed, thus saving some time. This technique quickly becomes cumbersome and inflexible for complex sequences.

how the diagram might look if you wanted the Test 2 VI to execute only if the Test 1 VI passed. It's apparent that extending this approach for many tests will quickly become unmanageable, with many Case structures. And suppose you wish to execute only one test or even execute the tests in a different order than they are originally placed? Either of these alternatives requires that you modify the block diagram to get the desired behavior. These simple Sequence and Case structure combinations are most appropriate for a short, fixed sequence of VIs that always execute from start to finish.

A more flexible sequencing method is shown in Fig. 11.4. This approach places all of the test subVIs in a Case structure, one VI per case. The **Multiple Selection ListBox** control is an ideal way to list which cases to execute. Alternatively, you could use an array of numbers, perhaps stored in a file, to prescribe tests. Using autoindexing, the For Loop executes once for each element in the array of test numbers. For each iteration, the test number selects the VI to execute. This block diagram replicates the functionality of the simple Sequence structure but allows you to specify any order of VI execution by changing the specification in the test list. Results from each test are accumulated in a Boolean array. A logical AND operation is performed on all of the results by the **AND Array Elements** function. The final result is true only if all of the individual results are true.

If you want to stop the tests when any one fails, use a While Loop as shown in Fig. 11.5. A While Loop lets you break out of a test sequence. In this example, front panel controls specify the list of case numbers and whether or not to stop on a failure. You must also include the logic to stop the loop when all of the tests are done.

The architecture illustrated in Fig. 11.5 forms the basis for a test executive with many capabilities. This architecture is used by many third-party test executives as well as by the LabVIEW Test Executive. An important feature of this approach is that, for a given set of VIs, you can create different sequences of tests without modifying the block diagram of the test executive. Even adding a new VI is a simple matter of adding one case to the Case structure. You can encapsulate the Case

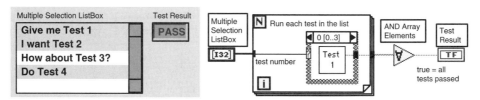

Figure 11.4   This For Loop sequencer is more versatile than the previous examples. Numbers in the array returned by the Multiple Selection List Box correspond to frame numbers in the Case structure.

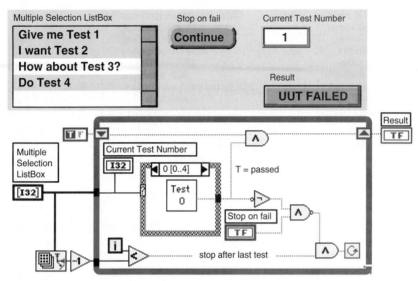

Figure 11.5   A canonical VI for a test executive. This sequencer steps through tests in an arbitrary order and can stop after any test fails.

structure itself in a subVI (called a **test container**). A person writing test subVIs could thus add them to the test executive in a well-defined location (the test container) without having to modify (and possibly mess up) the block diagram of the test executive itself. Alternatively, the test subVIs can be dynamically loaded by name and executed without any editing of the diagram. This is the approach actually used by the LabVIEW Test Executive. Dynamic loading is handled by the VI Control VIs, which are discussed in Chap. 8, "Process Control Applications."

Another possible architecture for test executives should be mentioned: **state machines**. As we've discovered through many examples in this book, a state machine permits you to jump from one test to another depending on the results encountered at each step. This can be of great value in situations where a subsequence of tests must be repeated because of a failure or readjustment that was performed at an earlier time. However, the state machine requires a much greater degree of programming skill and care during configuration; it is unlikely that the casual user would be very successful in rewiring such a complex VI. Therefore, you should consider state machines only for applications where

- The state machine is embedded in a test subVI that nobody will need to modify.
- Your test executive will be maintained only by expert programmers.
- There is no other alternative to the state machine architecture.

Operator interface

The second major task of the test executive is to present an effective user interface for the testing process. When creating the user interface, you must keep in mind the skills of the operator, which may be far different from your own. The complexity of the front panel depends upon the capabilities you wish to give to the operator. In many applications, the test executive's user interface consists of a single front panel that contains every control and indicator of interest to the operator. The simplest front panel may have a single button labeled GO. The operator presses this button to run a given test. After the testing is completed, a message tells the operator to move on to the next UUT and press GO when ready. For a versatile test executive, you will probably have a front panel that's not quite this simple-minded. If you want the operator to be able to run an individual test, for example, you'll need a mechanism for selecting individual tests. And, if you want the same test executive to work for both simple and sophisticated operators, you'll want to selectively hide or display options based on a password or flag of some kind.

Figure 11.6 shows the front panel for a test executive that allows the operator to test the entire UUT or just run specific tests; it's similar to the one found in the LabVIEW Test Executive. At startup, the particular tests are disabled through the use of an Attribute Node for the ListBox, which is visible at the left side of the diagram, shown in Fig. 11.7. The **Set Operating Mode** button opens a dialog box asking for a password. If the password is correct, the other test items are enabled, allowing the operator to select an arbitrary set of tests. A test report, summarizing the results of each test, is displayed in a string indicator. Adding a new test requires that you add a new item to the ListBox control as well as a new test subVI to the diagram. That's not too much work.

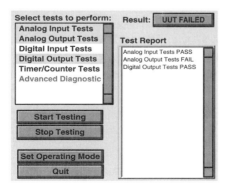

Figure 11.6 This panel for a typical test executive is simple yet effective.

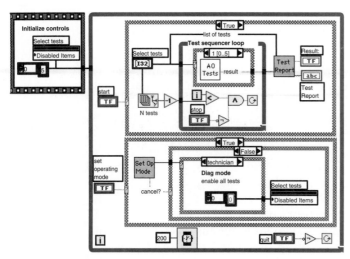

Figure 11.7 Diagram for the simple test executive. Initialization occurs in the Sequence structure, followed by continuous execution of the While Loop. The upper Case contains the real testing work, and the lower Case manages mode changes.

The diagram for this test executive has several major zones: control initialization in a Sequence structure and two major Case structures inside the main While Loop. At startup, items for test selection are enabled and disabled with an Attribute Node. All initialization items are grouped inside a Sequence structure with one wire tunneling out to the While Loop, thus guaranteeing that initialization occurs first.

After initialization, the loop runs until the user presses the Quit button. When the user presses the Start Testing button, the upper Case structure starts the test sequencer loop—a loop similar to the kind we've already seen. Each test subVI returns a Boolean value to indicate if the test passed. The Boolean values from each test are accumulated into an array. After testing completes, the array of test results and the original sequence array are passed to the **Create Test Report** VI, which formats the test report for display on the front panel.

The lower Case structure allows the operator to change operating modes from *Operator* (the default) to an arbitrary selection of tests (*Technician* mode). The **Set Operating Mode** VI opens when called and requests the password. If the password is correct, the innermost Case structure sends values to an Attribute Node to enable and disable the appropriate tests.

The Set Operating Mode VI is shown in Fig. 11.8. The VI clears the **Password** control using a Local Variable and sets the Key Focus on the Password control using an Attribute Node, then waits for the operator to select **OK** or **Cancel**. Set Operating Mode uses a single password for changing the operating mode of the test executive. If the operator enters the word *please,* then the VI returns *technician* in the enum indicator for the mode of operation. The VI also returns a Boolean to indicate if the operator selected **Cancel**. Note that the indicator for **mode** and **canceled** would not normally be visible on the front panel; you should scroll them off to the side and resize the VI's window to hide them. You should also edit the VI Setup options to make such a VI look like a real dialog box. This is obviously not a sophisticated password mechanism, but does illustrate how you can use attribute nodes and local variables to selectively enable or disable front panel controls.

Figure 11.9 shows the main panel from the LabVIEW Test Executive. This test executive uses a state machine architecture where the state is determined by a set of buttons (Login, Load, Edit, Run, etc.). It allows you to store and recall multiple test sequences from disk, generate reports, and edit test sequences. The sequencer is very powerful, permitting loops, conditional testing, branching, and other useful constructs. (I wish the complete diagram were available; it must be among the most sophisticated pieces of LabVIEW programming around!) Test VIs are not inserted into any diagram. Rather, they are dynamically loaded and run *by name* through the use of the **VI Control** VIs (see Chap. 8, "Process Control Applications," for information on VI Control VIs). Call-by-name is a powerful technique because the sequence editor is all you need to build an arbitrarily complex test sequence. The only diagrammatic programming required is in the test subVIs themselves. Of course, you are free to customize most aspects of the Test Executive, particularly the operator interface VIs. Some of the most important and complex VIs, such as the Sequence Editor VI, do not have dia-

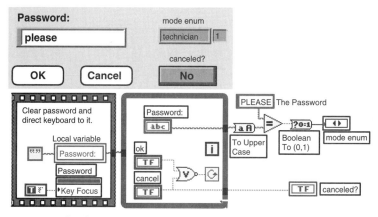

Figure 11.8 Set Operating mode is password dialog VI. You would normally scroll the panel such that the *mode* and *canceled?* buttons are not visible, then use VI Setup to configure the window like a dialog box.

grams. This is because National Instruments wants to be able to upgrade your Test Executive without too much difficulty. Also, the programming on some of these elaborate VIs is beyond the skill of most programmers, making diagrams downright dangerous. If you want to learn all the details, by all means order the whole package. It's a large, comprehensive, flexible framework with a nice user manual.

There are lots of interesting features in this test executive application. I plan to steal lots of them for my next project. Let's look at a few (refer to Fig. 11.9). The table labeled **Sequence Display** shows the status of each test in the sequence. When a test is running, the word *RUNNING* appears next to the name of the test. After the test executes, the word *PASS* appears if the test passed, *FAIL* if the test failed, and *SKIP* if the test executive did not execute the test. The same control is also used to select single tests for selective execution. How did they do all that in one control? It starts life as a **Single Selection ListBox** control. Using an Attribute Node, the item names (a string array) can be updated at any time—for instance, when a new sequence is loaded or when the status needs updating. Since it's also a control, the user can select any item in the list, just like we discussed earlier.

By now you can see how LabVIEW allows you to control the user interface and tune it for the particular operator who will be executing tests. These examples show only a few of the capabilities available using attribute nodes, local variables, and VI Setup options.

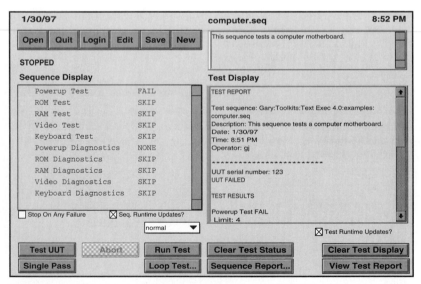

Figure 11.9 A serious test executive panel from the LabVIEW Test Executive. This is the default panel; you're free to customize it as desired to enhance operator efficiency.

Data organization and report generation

The third major responsibility of a test executive is to organize and log test data and to generate test reports. While the test sequencing mechanisms and user interfaces tend to be quite common across many ATE applications, test data logging and reporting formats vary greatly. The best datalog or test report format depends on how you intend to use the data. If it's to be printed and stored in file cabinets, then the main concern is requirements for formatting of the test report. Many companies have quality guidelines and standard forms that dictate how to present the test data. Military and government applications have very specific documentation standards. You may wish to use another application, such as a spreadsheet or word processor, to actually prepare the document. In this case, you can write the data to a file or use an interapplication communication mechanism to send the report directly to the other application.

If you plan to process the data further, then you have to consider what form of data storage is most appropriate for the recipient data processing application. (This topic was discussed at length in Chap. 7, "Writing a Data Acquisition System," where data formatting is a major concern.) You may want to write the data to the corporate database. There may be strict rules for time stamping data and ensuring the integrity and security of the data. Most of these issues may be handled by the recipient application, so your LabVIEW application only has to present the data in the correct data format (proper location of tab characters, new-line characters, numeric formatting, etc.).

Earlier in this chapter, we discussed the use of a common data structure (a cluster) for passing data from a test subVI to the test executive. The data structure you've chosen goes a long way toward defining the best structure in LabVIEW for accumulating the results of multiple tests for a UUT. Figure 11.10 shows a data structure that you could use for accumulating test results for multiple UUTs.

The basic data structure is an array of clusters. The cluster in the outer array contains the serial number and the test data for one UUT. The **Test Data** array contains the results of each test for the UUT. Each element of the **Test Data** array is a cluster containing the name of the test, the results (PASS or FAIL), the measured value, and the type of comparison made to determine if the test passed. Use of this four-element cluster assumes that your test executive has a way to specify whether pass/fail determination for a specific test is done by looking at the Boolean Pass/Fail flag or by comparing the numeric measurement to some limits. The **Comparison** Boolean indicates whether the comparison was Boolean or numeric, thus determining if the value in **Measurement** is relevant for this test. You may also wish to include the actual test limits in the **Test Results** array.

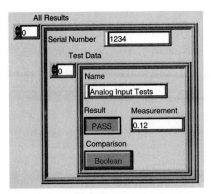

Figure 11.10 Likely data structure for returning results from a sequence of tests on many UUTs.

Figure 11.11 shows a test executive engine VI that creates the data structure previously shown. The input to the VI (**Sequence**) is an array of clusters containing a list of tests to run, comparison types, and acceptance limits. This VI references tests by names, as in our earlier examples. After creating the test array, the outer While Loop runs once for each UUT to be tested. The first thing that happens in the loop is a prompt for the UUT serial number, performed by the **UUT S/N Prompt** VI. This VI is configured, via its VI Setup options, to pop up like a dialog box. When testing is complete, the operator clicks the *Stop* button on the panel of UUT S/N Prompt, which causes the main VI to stop.

The For Loop cycles through each requested test in order. The test result along with the name and comparison type of the test and the measurement value from the test are bundled together into a cluster. These clusters are accumulated into an array using autoindexing on the For Loop. After the test sequence completes, the UUT serial number and array of results clusters are bundled into a cluster. This cluster is appended to the array of results contained in the shift register of the outer While Loop. When the user decides to stop testing, the True case of the Case structure executes. That case simply recycles data in the shift register. If you chose instead to accumulate results by autoindexing on the border of the While Loop, the final cycle of the While Loop would produce an empty array element that you would have to remove. The one problem with accumulating data in an ever growing array is that memory is gradually used up and often becomes badly fragmented. This is not good for performance. Instead, consider storing results in a file (perhaps a temporary one) as you go.

LabVIEW datalog file. If you plan to process the data in LabVIEW, perhaps using the analysis library or Statistical Process Control (SPC)

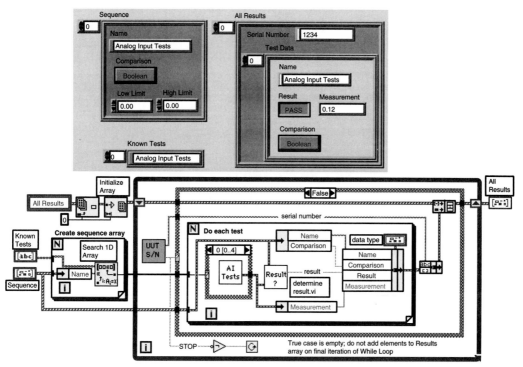

Figure 11.11   An *ATE engine* that cycles through a set of tests specified by the *Sequence* cluster array. Results are accumulated into the *All Results* cluster array for later reporting.

Toolkit, you will want to maintain the data in a native LabVIEW format in a datalog file. You can perform automatic data logging directly from the front panel of your test VIs by enabling data logging for the VIs when you place them in your test executive. The input and output data for each VI is logged automatically after the VI executes. A drawback to this approach is that you cannot easily disable data logging for all test VIs from the test executive. If you are interactively running tests, you may not want all of the intermediate data going into your datalog file. To turn off data logging, you must open each VI's front panel and turn off data logging.

A solution that gives you more flexibility for data logging is to log the combined test results accumulated into the cluster array previously shown in Fig. 11.10. You can write the test results to a datalog file by placing that cluster array on the front panel of a VI, making the array an input on the VI's connector pane, and executing the VI. This VI does not need any diagram because you simply want to execute it to force data logging. To enable or disable data logging, you only need to access this one VI.

You could alternatively write a VI that saves the data programmatically, as shown in Fig. 11.12. The block diagram method gives you the ability to change the name of the target datalog file without having to open the front panel of the datalog VI and setting the file name manually. This example creates a new datalog file, writes an image of the **All Results** cluster array to it, then closes the file. You could change the **New File** function to **Open File**, which would permit appending of results to an ever growing datalog. For more information on datalog files, see the section on files in Chap. 3, "Programming Techniques."

ASCII test report. If you wish to save test results for importing into other applications, such as a database or spreadsheet, you'll probably want to save the data in ASCII text format. Once you've accumulated your test results into a structure as shown in Fig. 11.10, it's easy to develop a VI that formats the data into an ASCII string. The VI shown in Fig. 11.13 does the trick.

The report contains the serial and test results for each UUT. This VI first creates a test report header with the date and time of testing. The outer For Loop executes once for each UUT tested (the outer array in the **All Results** cluster array), creating a header for each UUT. The inner For Loop processes each element in the inner cluster array of **All**

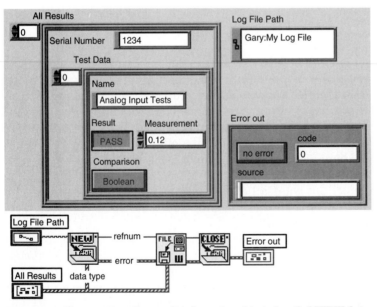

Figure 11.12   You can store the results of a series of tests in a LabVIEW datalog file with a simple VI like this. It creates a new file each time it's called; you could change New File to Open File, thus appending results to an existing file.

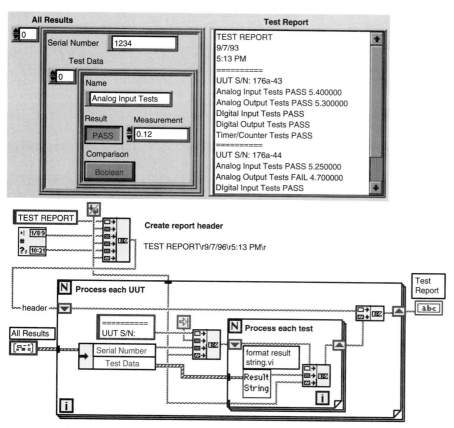

Figure 11.13 Lots of string handling is required when you format your results as ASCII text. The *Test Report* string would probably be written to a file for use in another application.

Results, corresponding to each test performed on the UUT. A subVI, **Format Result String**, creates one line in the string for each test, with an end-of-line character separating lines. Figure 11.14 shows the front panel and block diagram of Format Result String. Note how the **All Results** data structure maps nicely into this report generation VI. Results were collected by a test executive that had a similar loop-within-a-loop construct. This demonstrates the close coupling between algorithms and data structures.

The Format Result String VI produces each line in the test report with the following format:

<test name><TAB><result><TAB><measurement>

Notice that if the comparison type is Boolean, the ASCII test report does not include the measurement. The calling VI appends an appropriate

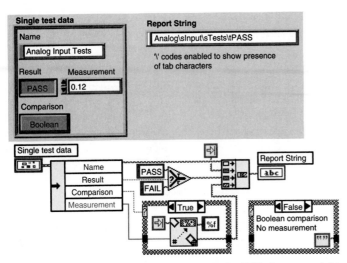

Figure 11.14 Format Result String is typical of subVIs that you might write to translate a cluster of information into one line of a text-format report.

end-of-line character. Under Windows, you should use carriage return/ line feed. For the Macintosh, use a carriage return. For UNIX, use a line feed. To simplify this portability problem, you can use the constant **End of Line** that automatically inserts the proper character(s).

This VI formats the test report into an ASCII string, which gives you some options. Within the test executive, you can use this string to display the test results to the operator using a front panel string indicator. You can also write the string to a file so that other applications can load the test results for generating reports. This format, using end-of-line characters to separate lines and tabs to separate fields on a single line, can be imported by many applications, including spreadsheets, databases, and word processors.

Generating formatted reports. Ordinary text files are OK except that there's no formatting of the data—no font styles, ruling lines, illustrations, or other niceties—things that might make a report more useful. One way to create such a document is through a word processing application, such as Microsoft Word, that has *print merge* features (designed for junk mail!). You begin by creating a template document in Word, containing all sorts of preformatted text, graphics, and so forth. Then, you insert uniquely named keywords in the text. You then enter these keywords into a print merge table. Finally, you create a data document, containing the variable text for insertion at the location flagged by the various keywords.

It's possible to create suitable data documents from LabVIEW. **Rich Text Format (RTF)** is the trick that makes it possible. RTF documents are plain text, but with extra flag characters that tell the word processing application how to format the text when loaded. To get you started, there are **printing utility** VIs in a library called FormUtil.llb that are available from ftp.natinst.com. The VIs use extensive string search and replace operations to surgically insert variable data into your data document. The example included in the library inserts text into a Word data document that you can merge with a template document. All the example documents are supplied, and there's a helpful writeup that explains the whole process.

Using interapplication communication for report generation. LabVIEW has many functions for passing data directly to another application without writing the data to a file. For example, you can use **Dynamic Data Exchange (DDE)** on Microsoft Windows to send the ASCII test report to Microsoft Excel. On the Macintosh, you can use **AppleEvents**. All of these **interapplication communication (IAC)** techniques are included with LabVIEW under the Communication function menu and are documented in the *LabVIEW Communications VI Reference Manual*. You should also check out the DDE examples—most of them work with Excel, and they're easy to modify. Be aware that you need detailed knowledge of the data formats required by other applications. I might mention that, as of this writing, software manufacturers rarely publish much information about their IAC interfaces. You may have to make some phone calls and request additional information, and be sure to have the latest version of the application.

DDE is a popular, text-based protocol that is easy to use, so let's study how test results may be sent from LabVIEW to an Excel spreadsheet using DDE. It's a true client-server protocol (as opposed to the internal data distribution model using global variables that we've used throughout this book) where LabVIEW and other applications exchange data and commands. To use DDE, both applications must be running and both must register with Windows—an operation that is normally performed automatically when you launch an application. Next, the client (in this case, LabVIEW) establishes a **conversation** with a server, referred to as the **service**. Associated with each service is a **topic**, which normally refers to the current file. If you have an application like Excel running, you could have more than one topic active by having more than one spreadsheet open.

Once a conversation is established using the **DDE Open Conversation** VI, you can send data with the **DDE Poke** VI, send commands with the **DDE Execute** VI, or obtain data with the **DDE Request** VI.

All of these operations transmit single messages. For a bit less overhead, you can use the **DDE Advise Start** VI to establish an ongoing link with the server. The server will send LabVIEW a message each time new data is available. Your VI has to periodically call the **DDE Advise Check** VI to see if new data is ready. If so, it is returned as a string.

The VI shown in Fig. 11.15 uses DDE to send an ASCII test report to an Excel spreadsheet. On the diagram, **service** identifies the server application—Excel. The **topic** identifies the server's data container, which is a worksheet file in Excel called *Sheet1*. The DDE Open Conversation VI accepts strings for the **service** and **topic** with which you wish to communicate and returns a refnum for use with other DDE functions.

Before sending the report to Excel, the VI determines the number of lines in the report by counting the number of line feeds. You need to know the length of the report because Excel requires you to specify the range of cells in which to place the data. The VI assumes that the first cell is *r1c1*, the cell in the upper left-hand corner of the spreadsheet, and that the report is no more than 10 cells wide. Using the Format & Append string function, the VI creates the range specification. The DDE Poke VI sends the data to Excel. You must specify the **item** that is to receive the test report. This item is the range of cells in the worksheet. After sending the test report, the VI executes DDE Close Conversation to disconnect from Excel. Notice that the DDE VIs in LabVIEW use error I/O, greatly simplifying the diagram of the VI.

Figure 11.16 shows how the test report shown on the front panel in Fig. 11.13 appears in the Excel spreadsheet. It's possible to send formatting information to Excel via DDE, as well. In an *LTR* article

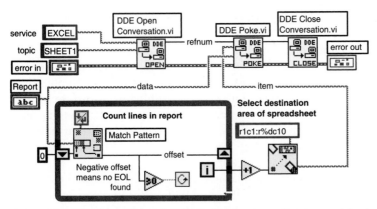

Figure 11.15 This VI sends a tab-delimited string to an Excel spreadsheet using DDE.

(Gruggett 1995), Rande Johnson of Stress Engineering uses DDE commands and Excel macros to autoformat a report spreadsheet. That saves work on the part of the user.

Controlling LabVIEW via DDE

In some automated test applications, the test executive is not actually a LabVIEW application. Some other application presents the high-level operator interface and list of tests to run and sends messages to LabVIEW via an interapplication communication mechanism. The basic structure of the LabVIEW portion of this application is the same as described for the test executive built entirely in LabVIEW, namely a test executive engine built around a Case structure or state machine. The main difference is that the list of tests to execute now resides outside of LabVIEW and the Case selection for choosing the test to run is passed into the test executive engine via an interapplication communication mechanism.

Figure 11.17 shows a VI that implements a simple DDE server in LabVIEW. This VI does not have any front panel controls because all input comes from a DDE connection and all results are returned by the same path. Unlike in the previous example, where Excel was the server, this VI creates a server to which other applications can connect. The server is created by calling the **DDE Srv Register Service** VI. This VI registers a DDE service and topic with the Windows operating system. This server has a name of *LVServer* and a topic named

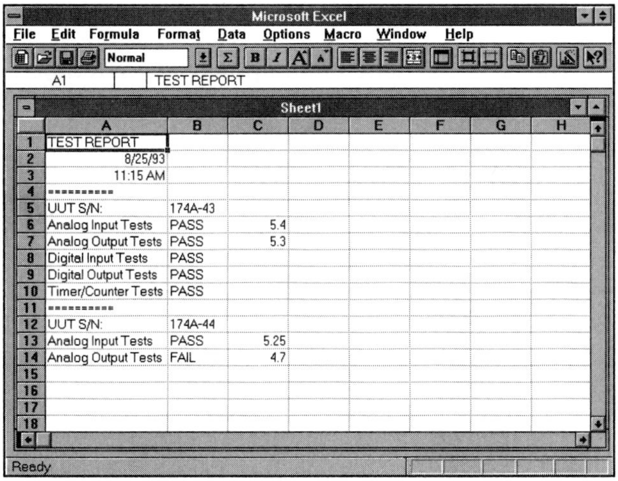

Figure 11.16 The spreadsheet, filled with data from the Lab-VIEW VI previously described.

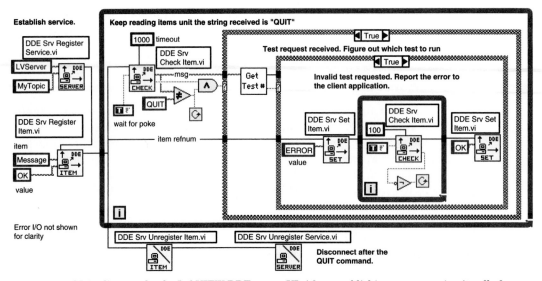

Figure 11.17   Main diagram for the LabVIEW DDE server VI. After establishing a new service, it polls for messages from a client, expecting a string that specifies which test to run. Results of the test are reported back to the client.

MyTopic. The **DDE Srv Register Item** VI adds an item to the server registered by DDE Srv Register Server. This server has just one item, named *Message,* associated with the topic named *MyTopic.* After creating the item, the VI enters a loop that continuously monitors the topic for incoming messages using the **DDE Srv Check Item** VI. It has a Boolean output that is set to True if a client has written data to the topic it is monitoring. If no message arrives within the time-out period (1 s), the loop cycles again.

If the server receives the message *QUIT,* it stops looping and unregisters the topic, item, and service by executing the **DDE Srv Unregister Item** VI and the **DDE Srv Unregister Service** VI, located below the While Loop on the diagram. If the message is not *QUIT,* the message is passed to a subVI, **Get Test Number**. This example accepts the name of a test to run and uses a list of known names to determine the correct case number to execute. If the name is not recognized, Get Test Number sets its error indicator to True; otherwise, the error indicator is set to False and the test number is passed into the inner Case structure. In Fig. 11.17, the inner Case shows the state where an invalid test was requested. The following steps take place:

1. Set *Message* to *ERROR.*

2. Wait for the client to acknowledge the error by writing any value back to *Message.*

3. Set *Message* to *OK* and wait for another command.

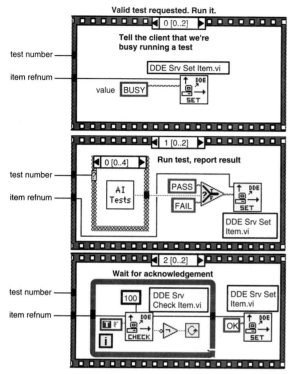

Figure 11.18 Contents of the inner Case structure, executed when a valid test is requested.

If the Boolean error output from the Get Test Number VI is False, indicating no error, the following steps take place. Figure 11.18 shows the contents of the Sequence structure that resides in the False frame of the inner Case structure.

1. Set *Message* to *BUSY,* so the client knows that you've accepted the command.

2. Execute the test in the case number passed out from *Get Test Number.*

3. Set *Message* to either *PASS* or *FAIL,* depending on the output from the test. The client application knows the test is done when *Message* changes from *BUSY* to *PASS* or *FAIL.*

4. Wait for the client to acknowledge receipt of the test result by writing any value back to *Message.*

5. Set *Message* to *OK* and wait for another command.

DDE is a simple and reliable protocol with some limitations. First, it works only under Windows, so you may have a portability issue. Second, it's limited to 32K per message—a problem for large data sets. Third, it's a bit slow. Expect to transmit perhaps 20 messages per second, depending on the target application.

Some Closing Words

Appropriately, we end where we began: with LabVIEW assisting in the automation of a measurement process. I hope that this chapter, like the others, has been enjoyable, enlightening, and relevant to your particular situation. In the years that I've worked on this book, I've talked to a lot of people just like you, studying their problems, asking and answering questions, and learning more with every encounter. So my advice to you is, take a class, join a user group, hang out on the e-mail circuit, talk to your neighbor—and *learn*.

Bibliography

Gruggett, Lynda, "LabVIEW 'Excels' at Auto-Formatting," *LabVIEW Technical Resource,* vol. 3, no. 3, summer 1995. (Back issues available from LTR Publishing.)

Index to the Accompanying CD-ROM

This is an index to the VIs and other information on the CD-ROM that accompanies this book. It's a multiplatform disk, readable on Macintosh, Windows (3.1/95/NT), and all UNIX computers. You can run everything right off the CD-ROM because no file compression or installers were used. The basic directory structure and file names are the same on all platforms except for Mac and UNIX where shortened file names are required due to limitations of the multiplatform CD-ROM format. Windows users can run the **setup.exe** application to copy all VIs from the CD-ROM to their hard disk. That application assures that all the files are not read-only.

VIs on the CD-ROM are flagged in the book with this icon and a path name: **platform/ directory/ file_name.vi**.

To locate a particular VI in the book, look up its name in the index.

Many documents are in Portable Document Format (PDF). In order to view PDF files, you must obtain the Adobe Acrobat Reader for your operating system. Installers for Adobe Acrobat Reader are located on the CD-ROM in the top-level directory. They are also available on the National Instruments FTP site ftp.natinst.com for the following platforms and operating systems:

Adobe Acrobat Reader 2.1 for Windows 3.1, 95, and NT
Location: /pub/acrobat-readers/windows/

Adobe Acrobat Reader 2.1 for Macintosh (68K and PowerMacintosh)
Location: /pub/acrobat-readers/mac/

Adobe Acrobat Reader 1.0 for SunOS 4.1.3 and Solaris 2.3 and 2.4 on Sun SPARCstations.
Location: /pub/acrobat-readers/sun/

CD-ROM Contents

appnotes   All of the available National Instruments application notes and technical notes in PDF format. Includes LabVIEW, DAQ, GPIB, and VXI. A complete index is in the appnotes directory.

benchmark (*Chapter 1*)   LabVIEW benchmark program, written by National Instruments, including a comparison engine to see how fast your LabVIEW system is.

circbuff.llb (*Chapter 8*)   Circular buffer VIs store data from many channels in a memory-based buffer in real time, then allow you to selectively read back and display data over any period of time.

control\alarms (*Chapter 9*)   An alarm handler VI.

control\rampsoak.llb (*Chapter 9*)   A ramp-and-soak controller, including a table-driven programmer and runtime engine. Uses a dummy single-loop controller, similar to a Eurotherm 808/847.

daq (*Chapters 5 and 6*)   Useful DAQ programs including analog output streaming, synchronized inputs and outputs, and a stepper motor driver.

datalog file handler.llb (*Chapter 7*)   An all-in-one VI that makes it easy to read and write LabVIEW datalog format files.

decimate (*Chapter 6*)   Data decimation VIs for reducing the quantity of data your program has to handle. Includes DAQ examples.

drivers\comm test VIs (*Chapter 6*)   Test VIs for developing drivers with GPIB, serial, and VXI interfaces.

drivers\driver utilities (*Chapter 6*)   Handy utility VIs for driver development.

drivers\eurotherm 808 (*Chapter 6*)   Complete driver for the Eurotherm 808/847 single-loop controllers, in both VISA and traditional serial versions. Includes document.

ionprobe.llb (*Chapter 9*)   An experiment described in Chap. 9, including motion control and data acquisition.

lock-in.llb (*Chapter 9*)   Includes signal recovery by bandpass filtering, phase-locked loops, and a LabVIEW DSP implementation of a two-phase lock-in amplifier.

moving averagers (*Chapter 7*)   Several moving average VIs for filtering data in real time.

scxi config (*Chapter 7*)   My best shot at a SCXI-based DAQ configuration utility. Includes a demonstration with a nice interactive user interface and a runtime engine for analog and digital inputs and outputs.

setup file handler.llb (*Chapter 7*)   Another all-in-one VI designed for storing and recalling front panel setup data.

simple das (*Chapter 7*)   Use this for getting started with analog data acquisition. Acquires, displays, and stores data using DAQ hardware.

sound (*Chapter 10*)   Windows and Macintosh sound support VIs. Not fancy, but better than nothing! (Not included in the UNIX platform directories.)

style guide (*Chapter 4*)   The LabVIEW style guide and a helper document for creating your own LabVIEW documentation.

timing (*Chapters 3 and 4*)   Utility VIs for keeping track of time.

utility   General-purpose VIs, including the famous Which Button function.

vi_hist.llb (*Chapter 4*)   A National Instruments utility that reads information from VI history and saves it in a text file.

vi_list.llb (*Chapter 4*)   A National Instruments utility that reads the Get Info text from VIs on disk and saves it in a text file.

waterfall graph (*Chapter 10*)   A simple way of displaying a cascade of waveforms in 3D fashion.

Absolute Time Corporation
800 Charcot Ave., Suite 110
San Jose, CA 95131
(408) 383-1515
Fax: (408) 383-0706

GPS receivers and precision timing
sources with serial interfaces

Advanced Logic Integration
(214) 243-8700
Fax: (214) 243-4280
http://www.advlogicint.com
E-mail: sales@advlogicint.com

Serial interfaces

Advanced Measurements, Inc.
2-5510 3rd Street SE
Calgary, Alberta, Canada, T2H 1J9
(403) 571-7273
Fax: (403) 571-7279
http://vvv.com/advmeas/
E-mail: hedstrom@pinc.com

DAQ Toolkit; consulting

Action Instruments, Inc.
8601 Aero Drive
San Diego, CA 92123
(619) 279-5726 or (800) 767-5726
Fax: (619) 279-6290

Industrial signal conditioning
modules

Allen-Bradley Co.
1201 South Second St.
Milwaukee, WI 53204
(414) 382-2000
Fax: (414) 382-2400

Programmable logic controllers

Anafaze
314 Westridge Dr.
Watsonville, CA 95076
(408) 714-3800
Fax: (408) 724-0320

Single-loop controllers

Analog Devices, Inc.   Signal conditioning modules
One Technology Way
P.O. Box 9106
Norwood, MA 02062
(617) 329-4700 or (800) 4ANALOG

ASTER   Acoustic signal analysis
U.S. distributor: *See* Pyxis, Inc.
European distributor: *See* Saphir

Azonix Corporation   μMAC scanners
900 Middlesex Turnpike, Bldg. 6
Billerica, MA 01821
(508) 670-6300
Fax: (508) 670-8855

Bancomm-Timing   Plug-in precision timing boards; GPS
  (division of Datum, Inc.)
781 Del Oro
San Jose, CA 95119
(800) 537-0277 or (408) 578-4161
Fax: (408) 578-4165

Biopac Systems, Inc   Electrophysiological instrumentation
275 South Orange Ave.
Santa Barbara, CA 93117
(805) 685-0066
Fax: (805) 685-0067
http://www.biopac.com
E-mail: info@biopac.com

Black Box Corporation   Communications interface equipment
P.O. Box 12800
Pittsburgh, PA 15241
(412) 746-5500
Fax: (412) 746-0746

Bloomy Controls, Inc.   Fuzzy Tools fuzzy logic control toolkit
14 Timber Trail or P.O. Box 1158
South Windsor, CT 06074
(860) 291-9971
Fax: (860) 291-8596
E-mail: 75240,117@compuserve.com

CARDIAC, Inc.   HartVIEW; drivers; consulting
Fossegrenda 30b
P.O. Box 4290
N-7002 Trondheim
Norway
(+47) 7396 5950
Fax: (+47) 7396 8288
E-mail: cardiac@cardiac.no

Cimetrics Technology
55 Temple Place
Boston, MA 02111-1300
(617) 350-7550
Fax: (617) 350-7552

9-Bit Solution uLAN serial network

CIT
Kleinhoefstraat 4
B2440 Geel
Belgium
32 14 58 55 88
Fax: 32 14 58 10 65

SinecVIEW; 4D Open

Creative Solutions, Inc.
7509 Connelley Dr., Ste. D
Hanover, MD 21076
(800) 367-8465 or (410) 766-4080
Fax: (410) 766-4087

Serial interfaces for Macintosh

Dateppli
3333 East Patrick Rd.
Midland, MI 48642
(517) 839-1040
Fax: (517) 839-1042
E-mail: niteam@dateppli.com

InnerVIEW PLC driver

Digital Vision, Inc.
270 Bridge St.
Dedham, MA 02026
(617) 329-5400
Fax: (617) 329-6286

Video converters

DSP Technology
48500 Kato Dr.
Fremont, CA 94538
(510) 657-7555
Fax: (510) 657-7576

CAMAC, instrumentation

Ectron Corporation
8159 Engineer Rd.
San Diego, CA 92111-1980
(619) 278-0600 or (800) 732-8159
Fax: (714) 278-0372

Instrumentation amplifier systems

EG&G Princeton Applied Research
P.O. Box 2565
Princeton, NJ 08540
(609) 530-1000
Fax: (609) 883-7259
 or
375 Phillips Blvd.
Trenton, NJ 08618

Instrumentation

Ellipsis Products, Inc.   DatabaseVIEW
412 Columbus Ave
Boston, MA 02116
(800) MEDIUM6
Fax: (617) 236-0141
http://www.ellipsisproducts.com
E-mail: dmoschella@ellipsisproducts.com

FAST-DAQ   FAST-DAQ DAQ toolkit; consulting
P.O. Box 940095
Maitland, FL 32794
(800) 732-7832 (contact Geoff Rowe)

Frequency Devices, Inc.   Antialiasing filters
25 Locust St.
Haverhill, MA 01830
(508) 374-0761 or (800) 252-7074
Fax: (508) 521-1839

Gage Applied Sciences   Oscilloscope boards
1233 Shelburne Road, Suite 400
South Burlington, VT 05403
(800) 567-4243
Fax: (800) 780-8411
  or
5610 Bois Franc
Montreal, PQ H4S 1A9 Canada
http://www.gage-applied.com
E-mail: prodinfo@gage-applied.com

GMW Associates   ControlNet I/O fiber-optic systems
955 Industrial Road
San Carlos, CA 94070
(415) 802-8292 or (800) 991-1338
Fax: (415) 802-8298

Group3, Inc.
See GMW Associates

GTFS   Imaging products and services
2455 Bennett Valley Rd., Suite 100C
Santa Rosa, CA 95404
(707) 579-1733
Fax: (707) 578-3195

Guide Technology, Inc.   Time interval analyzer boards
1630 Zanker Rd.
San Jose, CA 95112
(408) 453-8511
Fax: (408) 453-8515

Hathaway Process Instrumentation   Alarm annunciators
1840 Hutton Dr., Ste 200
Carrollton, TX 75006
(800) 537-2181
Fax: (214) 241-6752

Imaging Technology   Frame grabbers
55 Middlesex Turnpike
Bedford, MA 01730-1421
(617) 275-2700
Fax: (617) 938-1757

IOTech   GPIB equipment
25971 Cannon Road
Cleveland, OH 44146
(216) 439-4091
Fax: (216) 439-4093

Joerger Enterprises   CAMAC; VXI
166 Laurel Rd
East Northport, NY 11731
(516) 757-6200
Fax: (516) 757-6201

Keyspan   Serial interfaces for Macintosh
3095 Richmond Parkway, #207
Richmond, CA 94806
(510) 222-0131
Fax: (510) 222-0323
E-mail: info@keyspan.com
http://www.keyspan.com

LeCroy USA   Oscilloscopes; CAMAC;
700 Chestnut Ridge Rd.   instrumentation
Chestnut Ridge, NY 10977
(914) 578-6020
Fax: (914) 578-5985

Leybold Inficon, Inc   Transpector residual gas analyzer
Two Technology Place
East Syracuse, NY 13057-9714
(315) 434-1157
Fax: (315) 434-9908

LTR Publishing   *LabVIEW Technical Resource*
6060 N. Central Expressway,
  Suite 502
Dallas, TX 75206
(214) 827-9931
Fax: (214) 827-9932
http://www.natinst.com/ltr.ltr.htm

MegaWolf, Inc.   Serial interfaces
1771 Grasso Blvd.
New Haven, CT 06511
Voice/fax: (203) 562-1243
http://www.megawolf.com
E-mail: ward@megawolf.com

Metric Systems   SurfaceView; MovieView
16418 Chitina Court
Cedar Park, TX 78613
(512) 259-5583
Fax: (512) 259-7552

Moore Industries   Industrial signal conditioning
16650 Schoenborn St.   modules
Sepulveda, CA 91343
(818) 894-7111 or (800) 999-2900
Fax: (818) 891-2816

Mutech (formerly Scentech)   Frame grabbers
85 Rangeway Road
North Billerica, MA 01862
(508) 663-2400
http://www.mutech.com

National Instruments Corporation   LabVIEW; DAQ; GPIB
Corporate office: software and hardware
6504 Bridgepoint Parkway
Austin, TX 78730-5039
(800) 433-3488 or (512) 794-0100
http://www.natinst.com
E-mail: info@natinst.com

NuLogic Corporation   Motion control
475 Hillside Ave
Needham, MA 02194
(888) NULOGIC or (617) 444-7680
Fax: (617) 444-2803
http://www.nulogic.com
E-mail: sales@nulogic.com

Ohio Semitronics, Inc.   AC power, voltage, current
4242 Reynolds Drive   transducers
Hilliard, OH 43026
(614) 777-1005
Fax: (614) 777-4511

Opto 22, Inc.   Distributed I/O systems
43044 Business Park Drive
Temecula, CA 92590-3614
(800) 321-6786 or (909) 695-3000
Fax: (909) 695-2712 or
  (909) 695-9299

Parker Compumotor   Motion control
5500 Business Park Drive
Rohnert Park, CA 94928
(707) 584-7558
Fax: (707) 584-2446
E-mail: tech_help@cmotor.com

Pearson Electronics, Inc.   Current transformers
1860 Embarcadero Rd.
Palo Alto, CA 94303
(415) 494-6444
Fax: (415) 494-6716

Perceptics Corporation   Frame grabbers
725 Pellissippi Parkway
Knoxville, TN 37932-3350
(423) 966-9200
Fax: (423) 966-9330

Precision Filters, Inc.   Filters and amplifiers
240 Cherry St.
Ithaca, NY 14850-5099
(607) 277-3550
Fax: (607) 277-4466

Preston Scientific   Instrumentation amplifier systems
1180 North Blue Gum St.
Anaheim, CA 92806
(714) 632-3700
Fax: (714) 632-7355

Process Automation Corporation   SCADA Toolkit; Data Historian
P.O. Box 492
Belle Mead, NJ 08502
(908) 359-1011
Fax: (908) 359-1599
E-mail: 75031.2513@compuserve.com

Pyxis Corporation   Multimedia VIs; networking; utilities
3104 E. Camelback Rd., Suite 624
Phoenix, AZ 85016-4595
Phone/fax: (602) 451-8985
E-mail: pyxis1@pyxis.com

Research, Inc.   Micristar controllers
P.O. Box 24064
Minneapolis, MN 55424
(612) 941-3000
Fax: (612) 941-3628

Ross Engineering   High-voltage probes and equipment
540 Westchester Dr.
Campbell, CA 95008
(408) 377-4621 or (800) 654-3205
Fax: (408) 377-5182

Saphir L'Epinette F38 530 Chapareillan France +33 76 45 21 21 Fax: +33 76 45 20 78	PLC drivers; imaging products
Scion Corporation 82 Wormans Mill Court, Ste. H Frederick, MD 21701 (301) 695-7870 Fax: (301) 695-0035	Frame grabbers
Silicon Valley Bus Company 475 Brown Road San Juan Bautista, CA 95045 (800) 775-0555 or (408) 623-2300 Fax: (408) 623-4440 http://www.svbus.com E-mail: info@svbus.com	Serial interfaces
Software Engineering Group (SEG) 126A Main St.—Second Floor Watertown, MA 02172 (617) 924-6664 Fax: (617) 924-3402	HighwayVIEW; BusVIEW; AnaVIEW
Sony Electronics Computer Peripherals Products Company 3300 Zanker Road San Jose, CA 95134-1940 (800) 352-7669	Video equipment
Stanford Research Systems, Inc. 1290 D Reamwood Ave. Sunnyvale, CA 94089-2233 (408) 744-9040 Fax: (408) 744-9049 http://www.srsys.com/srsys/ E-mail info@srsys.com	Instrumentation
Stellar Solutions 735 Hickey Blvd, Suite 301 Pacifica, CA 94044-1214 Voice/fax: (415) 738-1139	Video VI
Sverdrup Technology, Inc. 600 William Northern Blvd. Tullahoma, TN 37388 (800) 251-3540 or (615) 455-6400 Fax: (615) 393-6211 E-mail:testview@edge.net	TestVIEW 2000

Tektronix
(Sales offices in all major cities
  worldwide)

Oscilloscopes; instrumentation

Trimble Navigation
645 North Mary Ave.
PO Box 3642
Sunnyvale, CA 94088-3642
(408) 481-8000

GPS equipment including a PCMCIA
board

TrueTime Corporation
3243 Santa Rosa Ave.
Santa Rosa, CA 95407
(707) 528-1230
Fax: (707) 527-6640

Plug-in IRIG timing boards

TTE, Inc.
2251 Barry Ave.
Los Angeles, CA 90064
(310) 478-8224
Fax: (310) 445-2791

Filters (modular and card modular)

VI Engineering
37800 Hills Tech Dr.
Farmington Hills, MI 48331
(810) 489-1200
Fax: (810) 489-1904
E-mail:vieng@ic.NET

Automatic PID Tuner; Little General
DAQ

Viewpoint Software Solutions
2320 Brighton Townline Rd.
Rochester, NY 14623
(716) 475-9555
Fax: (716) 475-9645
http://www.ViewpointUSA.com
E-mail:info@ViewpointUSA.com

Serial interfaces; Peek/Poke VIs

ABOUT THE AUTHOR

Gary W. Johnson is an instrumentation engineer in the
Chemical and Materials Science Department at the
Lawrence Livermore National Laboratory in Livermore,
California. He has a BS degree in electrical engineering/
bioengineering from the University of Illinois and holds
commercial radiotelephone and amateur radio licenses.
His professional interests include physics diagnostics,
material characterization, measurement and control
systems, transducers, analog circuit design, and, of course,
LabVIEW programming. In his spare time, he enjoys
woodworking, bicycling, and audio. He and his wife,
Katharine, a scientific illustrator, live in Livermore.

Index

SOFTWARE AND INFORMATION LICENSE

The software and information on this diskette (collectively referred to as the "Product") are the property of The McGraw-Hill Companies, Inc. ("McGraw-Hill") and are protected by both United States copyright law and international copyright treaty provision. You must treat this Product just like a book, except that you may copy it into a computer to be used and you may make archival copies of the Products for the sole purpose of backing up our software and protecting your investment from loss.

By saying "just like a book," McGraw-Hill means, for example, that the Product may be used by any number of people and may be freely moved from one computer location to another, so long as there is no possibility of the Product (or any part of the Product) being used at one location or on one computer while it is being used at another. Just as a book cannot be read by two different people in two different places at the same time, neither can the Product be used by two different people in two different places at the same time (unless, of course, McGraw-Hill's rights are being violated).

McGraw-Hill reserves the right to alter or modify the contents of the Product at any time.

This agreement is effective until terminated. The Agreement will terminate automatically without notice if you fail to comply with any provisions of this Agreement. In the event of termination by reason of your breach, you will destroy or erase all copies of the Product installed on any computer system or made for backup purposes and shall expunge the Product from your data storage facilities.

LIMITED WARRANTY

McGraw-Hill warrants the physical diskette(s) enclosed herein to be free of defects in materials and workmanship for a period of sixty days from the purchase date. If McGraw-Hill receives written notification within the warranty period of defects in materials or workmanship, and such notification is determined by McGraw-Hill to be correct, McGraw-Hill will replace the defective diskette(s). Send request to:

Customer Service
McGraw-Hill
Gahanna Industrial Park
860 Taylor Station Road
Blacklick, OH 43004-9615

The entire and exclusive liability and remedy for breach of this Limited Warranty shall be limited to replacement of defective diskette(s) and shall not include or extend to any claim for or right to cover any other damages, including but not limited to, loss of profit, data, or use of the software, or special, incidental, or consequential damages or other similar claims, even if McGraw-Hill has been specifically advised as to the possibility of such damages. In no event will McGraw-Hill's liability for any damages to you or any other person ever exceed the lower of suggested list price or actual price paid for the license to use the Product, regardless of any form of the claim.

THE McGRAW-HILL COMPANIES, INC. SPECIFICALLY DISCLAIMS ALL OTHER WARRANTIES, EXPRESS OR IMPLIED, INCLUDING BUT NOT LIMITED TO, ANY IMPLIED WARRANTY OF MERCHANTABILITY OR FITNESS FOR A PARTICULAR PURPOSE. Specifically, McGraw-Hill makes no representation or warranty that the Product is fit for any particular purpose and any implied warranty of merchantability is limited to the sixty day duration of the Limited Warranty covering the physical diskette(s) only (and not the software or in-formation) and is otherwise expressly and specifically disclaimed.

This Limited Warranty gives you specific legal rights; you may have others which may vary from state to state. Some states do not allow the exclusion of incidental or consequential damages, or the limitation on how long an implied warranty lasts, so some of the above may not apply to you.

This Agreement constitutes the entire agreement between the parties relating to use of the Product. The terms of any purchase order shall have no effect on the terms of this Agreement. Failure of McGraw-Hill to insist at any time on strict compliance with this Agreement shall not constitute a waiver of any rights under this Agreement. This Agreement shall be construed and governed in accordance with the laws of New York. If any provision of this Agreement is held to be contrary to law, that provision will be enforced to the maximum extent permissible and the remaining provisions will remain in force and effect.